around my french table

around my french table

more than 300 recipes from my home to yours

Dorie Greenspan

PHOTOGRAPHS BY ALAN RICHARDSON

HOUGHTON MIFFLIN HARCOURT

BOSTON   NEW YORK   2010

Library of Congress Cataloging-in-
Publication Data
Greenspan, Dorie.
Around my French table : more than
300 recipes from my home to yours /
Dorie Greenspan ; photographs by Alan
Richardson.
p. cm.
Includes index.
ISBN 978-0-618-87553-5
1. Cookery, French. I. Title.
TX719.G758 2010
641.5944—dc22
2010014232

Book design by George Restrepo
Food styling by Karen Tack
Prop styling by Deb Donahue

Printed in China
SCP 10 9 8 7 6 5 4 3 2 1

For Michael, who made my dream of a French
life come true, and with whom I am so lucky to
share the joys of that life.

For Joshua, who makes life even sweeter.

For my French friends, who have shared their
lives and their tables with me.

And in memory of my mother, Helen Burg, who
visited Paris just once, but who cherished the
pleasures of that city for the rest of her life.

acknowledgments

THIS BOOK IS SPECIAL TO ME in every way. Special because I got to write about the food I love in France, a country that means so much to me, and *very* special because I got to work with an extraordinary group of people, many of whom I've been fortunate enough to work with for years.

From the day I met my agent, David Black, he told me that this was a book I had to do. Now that it's written, I know he was right, but I also know that it would not have been the book it is without his constant encouragement, his wise eye, and his warm heart.

Anyone who knows me is probably tired of hearing me say this, but I was so very lucky to have Rux Martin as my editor. As she did with *Baking: From My Home to Yours,* Rux, with her sharp intelligence; profound appreciation of food, writing, and writers; and ever-ready blue pencil made this a better book than it was when it arrived on her doorstep. She also made me laugh, and when you're racing a tight deadline for a big book, the benefits of laughter can't be overestimated.

At Houghton Mifflin Harcourt, I got to work with the A-team. Many thanks to George Restrepo, for his beautiful book design; Eugenie Delaney, for carrying it out; Teresa Elsey, who saw the book through production; Jacinta Monniere, who once again "translated" scribbles into type; and Rux's ever helpful and always patient assistant, Tim Mudie.

When photographer Alan Richardson, food stylist Karen Tack, and prop stylist Deb Donahue signed on to work on this book, I was so happy that I actually burst into tears. It had been my dream that we could work together again — this is the team that made *Baking* so gorgeous — but I hadn't dared to imagine that it would happen. As an author, you trust your food to those who will illustrate it — never has there been a more trustworthy crew.

This book, my tenth, marks the twentieth anniversary of my working with the best cookbook copyeditor ever, Judith Sutton. We've worked together on all my books, and I hope we always will. Thanks also to proofreaders Jessica Sherman and Susan Dickinson, whose sharp eyes made this book better.

I am grateful to Jennifer King, a founder of Liddabit Sweets, for testing — and retesting — my recipes. Jen has all the qualities you want in a tester: skillfulness, meticulousness, a love of food, and an appetite for learning.

Barbara Fairchild, the editor in chief of *Bon Appétit,* has encouraged me for years, and with each year, I appreciate her support more and more. I'm also deeply appreciative for the enthusiasm and support of Janice Kaplan, who was my editor at *Parade.*

More so than any other book I've written, this one depended on and was made infinitely richer by the generosity of friends. In America, I had great help from Eric Render, Beth and Michael Vogel, Laura Shapiro, and Stephanie Lyness. While I was in France, among the friends who were at my side or with me around my table or theirs were Martine and Bernard Collet, Hélène Samuel, Juan Sanchez, Drew Harré, Christian Holthausen, Simon Maurel, David Lebovitz, Alec Lobrano, Paule Caillat, Patricia and Walter Wells, and my friend and mentor in all things sweet, Pierre Hermé, and his wife, Barbara.

Many people shared their wonderful recipes with me, among them: Bertrand Auboyneau; Marie-Hélène Brunet-Lhoste; Yves Camdeborde; Béatrix Collet; Marie-Claude Delaveau; Jacques Drouot; Danielle Easton; Sonia Ezgulian; Didier Frayssou; Laëtitia Ghipponi; Sophie-Charlotte Guitter; Rosa Jackson; Pierre Jancou; Gérard Jeannin and his wife, Sylvie Rougetet; Anne Leblanc; Nick Malgieri; Françoise Maloberti; Sonia Maman; Claudine Martina; Olivier Martina; Marie Naël; Anne Noblet; Marie-Cécile Noblet; Braden Perkins; Betty Rosbottom; Kerrin Rousset; Kim Sunée; Yannis Théodore; Alice Vasseur; Christine Vasseur; and Meg Zimbeck.

Merci mille fois and a thousand times more to France for being the country of my heart and the land where food, wine, friendship, and home cooking flourish.

And, as always and forever, my love and thanks to the men in my life, Michael, my husband, and Joshua, our son.

contents

introduction

I WAS RECENTLY MARRIED, JUST OUT OF college, and working at my first grown-up job when Michael, my husband, came into a bit of money, a few hundred dollars that seemed to fall from the sky. He took one look at the check and thought, "Car payments!" I, ever the romantic, saw it and almost screamed, "Paris!"

Whoever said screaming will get you nothing was wrong. A month later, we landed in France.

Somewhere there's a picture of me from that trip. I'm an impossibly skinny young woman with a huge grin. I'm spinning around with arms out wide, and I look like I'm about to grab Paris and hold on to her forever. Which I did.

There were a million reasons I took Paris into my heart. Everything about the city entranced me, from the way the women walked on towering stiletto heels over bumpy cobblestoned streets to how old-fashioned neighborhood restaurants still had cubbyholes where regulars could keep their napkin rings. I loved the rhythm of Parisian life, the sound of the language, the way people sat in cafés for hours.

I fell in love with the city because it fit all my girlish ideas of what it was supposed to be, but I stayed in love with all of France because of its food and its people.

I'm convinced my fate turned on a strawberry tartlet. We were walking up the very chic rue Saint-Honoré, pressing our noses against the windows of the fashionable stores and admiring everything we couldn't afford, when the tartlet, a treat within our means, called out to me. It was the first morsel I had on French soil, and more than thirty years later, I still think it was the best tartlet of my life, a life that became rich in tartlets.

This one was a *barquette,* a boat-shaped tartlet so teensy that all it could hold was a lick of pastry cream and three little strawberries, but everything about it excited me. The crust was so beautifully baked and flaky that when I took the first bite, small shards of it flew across my scarf. It was butter that gave the crust its texture, remarkable flavor, and deep golden color, and a little more butter and pure vanilla that made the pastry cream so memorable. And those strawberries. They were *fraises des bois* — tiny wild strawberries — but I had no idea of that then. What I did know was that they tasted like real strawberries, whose flavor I must have subconsciously tucked away in my memory.

That evening, after searching for a restaurant that would keep us within the budget set by *Europe on $5 a Day,* we settled into a *crêperie* near our hotel. It was startling to see a big menu offering nothing but crepes, and not a single one famous in America! Everything we tasted was a novelty: the buckwheat crepe was lacy and chewy, and the sunny-side-up egg that accompanied it had a yolk the color of marigolds and the true taste of eggs.

I returned home to New York City, assured my mother that I loved her even though she'd made the mistake of having me in Brooklyn instead of Paris, and proceeded to devote the rest of my life to remedying her lapse in judgment.

I took French lessons, learned to tie a scarf the French way, and in anticipation of spending more time in cafés, I practiced making an espresso last long enough to get through a chapter of Sartre.

And I cooked. I made the food I'd loved in France, the food you'll find in this book — simple, delicious, everyday food, like beef stews made with rough country wine and carrots that I could have sworn were candied but weren't (I've got a similar dish on page 244); salads dressed with vinaigrettes that had enough sharp mustard in them to make your eyes pop open (see page 484); and hand-formed tarts with uneven edges that charred a bit when they caught the oven's heat (just as the one on page 458 does).

I returned to Paris as often as I could and traveled through France as much as I could. On each trip, I'd buy cookbooks, collect recipes from anyone who'd share them (and almost everyone I asked, from farmers in the markets to chefs, was happy to share), and take cooking and baking classes everywhere they were offered. Then I'd come back and spend days at a stretch trying to perfect what I'd learned or to teach myself something new.

When Marie-Cécile Noblet, a Frenchwoman from a hotel-restaurant family in Brittany, came to live with us as an au pair for Joshua, our infant son, I was working on a doctoral thesis in gerontology but thinking I wanted to make a change in my life. Within weeks of her arrival, I was spending more time in the kitchen with her than in school with my advisors.

Marie-Cécile was a born cook. When she made something particularly wonderful and I asked a question, she'd give me a perfect Gallic shrug, put her index finger to the tip of her nose, and claim that she'd made it *au pif,* or just by instinct. And she had. She could feel her way around almost any recipe — as I'd later see so many good French cooks do — and she taught me to trust my own instincts and to always have one tool at my side: a spoon to taste with.

IT WOULD TAKE ME A DECADE TO make my passion my work, but shortly after Marie-Cécile arrived, I put aside my dissertation, left my job in a research center, and got a position as a pastry cook in a restaurant. A couple of years later, I landed some assignments as a food writer: I became the editor of the James Beard Foundation publications and was hired to write for *Elle* magazine. Best of all, I got to work with the greatest French chefs both here and in France.

It was the late 1980s; some of *les grands,* as the top chefs were called, were shaking up haute French cuisine and I had a front-row seat at the revolution. I worked in Jean-Georges Vongerichten's first American kitchen when he banished butter from his sauces and did away with long-cooked stocks in favor of light pan *jus,* vegetable purees, and his then-radical flavored oils. I tagged along with Gilbert Le Coze, the chef-owner of Le Bernardin, a new breed of seafood restaurant in New York City, as he strode through the Fulton Fish Market picking the best of the catch and teaching other city chefs how to get the most out of fish, like monkfish and skate, they'd once ignored. And I was lucky enough to spend some time with Alain Ducasse learning how he worked the sunny ingredients and the easygoing style of the Mediterranean into his personal take on rigorous French cuisine.

These amazingly talented chefs and others like them were adding flavors from all parts of the world to their cooking and, in the process, not only loosening up French cooking, but making it more understandable to us Americans — more like the melting-pot cooking that's the hallmark of our own tradition.

I was dazzled by their brilliance, but I was fascinated by something else: the unbroken connection to the cooking of their childhoods. After making a startlingly original ginger sauce for his famous molten chocolate cake, Jean-Georges urged me to taste a cup of thick lentil soup, because it was made exactly as his mother would have made it (my version is on page 90). Having prepared a meal that included a kingly amount of precious black truffles, Daniel Boulud told me he couldn't wait to have hachis Parmentier, a humble shepherd's pie (see page 258). And Pierre Hermé, France's most famous pastry chef, after making a chocolate dessert that was masterly, revealed that its haunting flavor came from a jar of Nutella (just as it does in his tartine on page 415).

FOR YEARS I CONTINUED TO TRAVEL BACK and forth between New York City and France. Then, thirteen years ago, I became truly bicontinental: Michael and I moved into an apartment in Paris's 6th arrondissement, and I got the French life I couldn't ever have really imagined but had always longed for. Finally I could be a regular in the small shops of my neighborhood and at the vendors' stalls at the market, and nicest of all, I could cook for my French friends, and they for me.

Now I can chart the changing seasons by what my friends and I are cooking. When asparagus arrives, dinner at Martine Collet's starts with pounds of them, perfectly peeled to their tips, steamed just until a knife slips through them (see page 128), piled on a platter, and flanked by two bowls of her lemony mayonnaise. In early fall, when the days are warm but the nights are a little cooler, Hélène Samuel makes her all-white salad (page 108), a mix of mushrooms, apples, celery, and cabbage dressed with a tangy yogurt vinaigrette. When the cold weather is with us for real, Paule Caillat can be counted upon to serve Parisian gnocchi (page 374), a recipe passed down to her by her Tante Léo. And throughout the year, we lift the lids of Dutch ovens to reveal tagines, the beloved spice-scented Moroccan stews (try the one for lamb with apricots on page 284), or slowly braised *boeuf à la mode* (page 252) with a sauce gently seasoned with anchovies, or chicken braised in Armagnac (page 204), or an all-vegetable pot-au-feu (page 376).

What's being cooked in French homes today is wonderful partly because it's so unexpected. One week you might have a creamy cheese and potato gratin (see page 360) just like the one a cook's great-grandmother used to make, and the next week you'll be treated to a simply cooked fish with a ginger-spiked salsa (page 489) taking the place of the butter sauce that would once have been standard.

I love this mix of old and new, traditional and exotic, store-bought and homemade, simple and complex, and you'll find it in this book. These are the recipes gathered over my years of traveling and living in France. They're recipes from friends I love, bistros I cherish, and my own Paris kitchen. Some are steeped in history or tied to a story, and others are as fresh as the ingredients that go into them; some are time-honored, and many others are created on the spur of the moment from a basket full of food from the day's market.

This is elbows-on-the-table food, dishes you don't need a Grand Diplôme from Le Cordon Bleu to make. It's the food I would cook for you if you came to visit me in Paris — or in New York City, where all of these recipes were tested. The ingredients are readily available in the United States; almost everything can be bought at your neighborhood supermarket, and the techniques are straightforward and practical, as they must be — French home cooks are as busy as we are.

Holding this book of recipes, a record of my time in France, I have the sense of something meant to be: the reason that Michael and I ended up with plane tickets and a strawberry tartlet all those years ago.

about the recipes

❧ All the recipes in this book were made with large eggs, unsalted butter, and whole milk unless otherwise specified.

❧ Just about every time you cook or bake, you've got to make a judgment call — it's the nature of the craft. I tested these recipes over and over and wrote them as carefully and precisely as I could, but there's no way I could take into account all the individual variables that will turn up in your kitchen. I couldn't know exactly how powerful "medium heat" is on your stovetop, how constant your oven temperature is, how cool your steak is when you slide it into the pan, how full your skillet is when you're sautéing, and a million other little things that affect the outcome of what you're making. And so, I've given you as many clues as I can for you to decide when something is done, and I've often given you a range of cooking or baking times, but the success of any cooking — whether from this book or any other — depends on using your judgment. Don't cook something for 15 minutes just because I tell you to — check it a little before the 15-minute mark, and then keep checking until it's just right. I always feel that when I send a recipe out into the world, I'm asking you to be my partner in making it, and I love this about cookbookery. I trust your judgment, and you should too.

nibbles and hors d'oeuvres

PROVENÇAL OLIVE FOUGASSE (PAGE 48), HERBED OLIVES (PAGE 16), AND MUSTARD BÂTONS (PAGE 15)

nibbles and hors d'oeuvres

gougères

SERVING
Gougères are good straight
from the oven and at room
temperature. I like them
both ways, but I think you
can appreciate them best
when they're still warm.
Serve with kir, white wine,
or Champagne.

STORING
The best way to store
gougères is to shape the
dough, freeze the mounds
on a baking sheet, and
then, when they're solid,
lift them off the sheet
and pack them airtight in
plastic bags. Bake them
straight from the freezer —
no need to defrost — just
give them a minute or two
more in the oven. Leftover
puffs can be kept at room
temperature overnight and
reheated in a 350-degree-F
oven, or they can be
frozen and reheated before
serving.

WHEN YOU'RE AN AMERICAN IN PARIS, there's nothing more flattering than to have French people ask you to share your recipe for one of their national treasures. Of all the things I make for my French friends, this is the one that gets the most requests.

The easiest way to describe gougères is to call them cheese puffs. Their dough, *pâte à choux*, is the same one you'd use for sweet cream puffs or profiteroles (page 502), but when the *pâte à choux* is destined to become gougères, you fold in a fair amount of grated cheese. In France, I use Gruyère, Comté, Emmenthal, or, just for fun and a spot of color, Mimolette, Gouda's French cousin; in America, I reach for extra-sharp cheddar, and sometimes I add a little smoked cheese to the mix.

Gougères are made everywhere in France (and can be bought frozen in many stores), but their home is Burgundy, where they are the first thing you get when you sit down in almost any restaurant. In Burgundy, gougères are often served with the local aperitif, kir (see box, page 6); chez Greenspan, while I serve them no matter what I'm pouring as a welcoming glass, my favorite sip-along is Champagne. I love the way Champagne's toastiness and gougères' egginess play together.

Although you must spoon out the puffs as soon as the dough is made, the little puffs can be frozen and then baked straight from the freezer, putting them in the realm of the doable even on the spur of the moment.

½ cup whole milk	1 cup all-purpose flour
½ cup water	5 large eggs, at room temperature
8 tablespoons (1 stick) unsalted butter, cut into 4 pieces	1½ cups coarsely grated cheese, such as Gruyère or cheddar
½ teaspoon salt	(about 6 ounces; see above)

Position the racks to divide the oven into thirds and preheat the oven to 425 degrees F. Line two baking sheets with silicone baking mats or parchment paper.

Bring the milk, water, butter, and salt to a rapid boil in a heavy-bottomed medium saucepan over high heat. Add the flour all at once, lower the heat to medium-low, and immediately start stirring energetically with a wooden spoon or heavy whisk. The dough will come together and a light crust will form on the bottom of the pan. Keep stirring — with vigor — for another minute or two to dry the dough. The dough should now be very smooth.

Turn the dough into the bowl of a mixer fitted with the paddle attachment or into a bowl that you can use for mixing with a hand mixer or a wooden spoon and elbow grease. Let the dough sit for a minute, then add the eggs one by one and beat, beat, beat until the dough is thick and shiny. Make sure that each egg is completely incorporated before you add the next, and don't be concerned if the dough separates — by the time the last egg goes in, the dough will come

together again. Beat in the grated cheese. Once the dough is made, it should be spooned out immediately.

Using about 1 tablespoon of dough for each gougère, drop the dough from a spoon onto the lined baking sheets, leaving about 2 inches of puff space between the mounds.

Slide the baking sheets into the oven and immediately turn the oven temperature down to 375 degrees F. Bake for 12 minutes, then rotate the pans from front to back and top to bottom. Continue baking until the gougères are golden, firm, and, yes, puffed, another 12 to 15 minutes or so. Serve warm, or transfer the pans to racks to cool.

dijon's famous aperitif

Arguably the best-known aperitif of France, kir is named for Canon Félix Kir, who was a priest, a World War II hero, and the mayor of Dijon. It was he who popularized the drink, a cocktail of crème de cassis (black currant liqueur) and white wine, by serving it at town gatherings. Today's kir is usually made in the ratio of one part crème de cassis to four or five parts (or more, to taste) white wine. Earlier kirs are said to have been one-third crème de cassis and two-thirds wine, producing a very sweet and quickly intoxicating aperitif, since crème de cassis is quite alcoholic. To get the best and prettiest mix, first pour the cassis into the glass — a white-wine glass or Champagne flute — and then pour in the chilled white wine. In Burgundy, the traditional wine for kir is Aligoté, a somewhat acidic white wine of no prestige in the region. Of course, you can use whatever wine you wish: use red wine, and you'll have a kir communard or cardinale; use Champagne, and it'll be a kir royale.

goat-cheese mini puffs

I T'S HARD TO IMAGINE A TIME when cream puffs wouldn't be a hit, but there's something particularly appealing and surprising about them when they're savory. The puffs themselves, which look like something precious plucked from a pâtisserie, are made from basic *pâte à choux,* or cream puff dough, and the filling is a mix of herbed goat cheese, cream cheese (I use Neufchâtel in France), and a little heavy cream. They're much richer than popcorn — classier too — but they're no less serially munchable.

MAKES ABOUT
40 CHEESE PUFFS

1 recipe Cream Puff Dough
  (page 502), ready to bake
1 egg, for glaze (optional)
6 ounces herbed fresh goat
  cheese, at room
  temperature
6 ounces cream cheese, at room
  temperature
6 tablespoons heavy cream
  Salt and freshly ground pepper

Position the racks to divide the oven into thirds and preheat the oven to 425 degrees F. Line two baking sheets with silicone baking mats or parchment paper.

Using about ½ tablespoon of dough for each puff, drop the dough from a spoon onto the lined baking sheets, leaving about 2 inches of space between the mounds.

If you'd like to glaze the puffs, lightly beat the egg with a splash of cold water and, using a pastry brush, coat just the top of the puffs with a little glaze. Try not to let the glaze dribble down the sides of the dough, or the drips will hamper the puffs' rise.

Slide the baking sheets into the oven and immediately turn the oven temperature down to 375 degrees F. Bake for 12 minutes, then rotate the pans from front to back and top to bottom. Continue baking until the puffs are golden, firm, and, yes, puffed, another 12 to 15 minutes or so. Place the baking sheets on cooling racks and let the puffs cool to room temperature.

TO MAKE THE FILLING: Using a flexible rubber spatula or an electric mixer, beat the goat cheese, cream cheese, and heavy cream together in a bowl until smooth. Taste for seasoning and add salt and pepper as needed.

If you'd like to fill the puffs without cutting them, fit a pastry bag with a small plain decorating tip and spoon the filling into the bag. Use the tip to poke a hole in the side of each puff and squeeze the filling into the puffs. Alternatively, you can cut off the top third or so of each puff, spoon in some filling, and replace the caps.

Serve warm, at room temperature, or slightly chilled.

SERVING
The puffs are good slightly warm, at room temperature, or even ever so slightly chilled. They're great with white wine, particularly a white from the Loire Valley (consider a Sancerre), which is as well known for its goat cheese as it is for its wine.

STORING
Although you must spoon out the puffs as soon as the dough is made, the mini puffs can be frozen and then baked straight from the freezer. Unfilled puffs can be kept lightly covered at room temperature overnight. You can reheat them in a 350-degree-F oven for a few minutes to refresh them before filling. Cover any leftover filled puffs and keep them in the refrigerator; let them stand at room temperature for about 20 minutes before serving.

saint-germain-des-prés onion biscuits

MAKES ABOUT
32 BISCUITS

SERVING
Biscuits are always best right out of the oven while still warm. However, these are also good at room temperature — the onion flavor is interesting enough to compensate for whatever fluffiness is lost when the biscuits cool.

STORING
Unbaked biscuits can be frozen for up to 2 months and baked straight from the freezer — just add a couple of minutes to the baking time. Once the biscuits are baked, they're best eaten quickly.

WHILE I'M A REGULAR BISCUIT BAKER in New York, it had never occurred to me to make the little quick breads in France until one New Year's Eve, more than ten years ago, when my friend Jim Ferguson told me he was bringing a good ole Carolina country ham to our very Parisian party and asked me to have biscuits at the ready. Who knew they'd be such a hit!

I made traditional plain biscuits for the country ham, but when I saw how much my French friends appreciated them, I created these onion biscuits, named them after our neighborhood, Saint-Germain-des-Prés, and made them a house special.

I make the dough, pat it out, and cut it into small rounds — I use a piece of PVC pipe, about 1½ inches in diameter, that the plumber left after doing some kitchen repairs — then freeze the quick breads. Right before friends are due to arrive, I pop the frozen biscuits into the oven.

I think you'll be as surprised as I was to discover how good this simple Southern staple is with fine French Champagne.

6½ tablespoons cold unsalted butter	1 tablespoon baking powder
1 small onion, finely chopped (about ½ cup)	2 teaspoons sugar
	½ teaspoon salt
2 cups all-purpose flour	¾ cup cold whole milk

Center a rack in the oven and preheat the oven to 425 degrees F. Line a baking sheet with a silicone baking mat or parchment paper. Have a biscuit cutter or tall cookie cutter, one that's between 1 and 2 inches in diameter, at hand.

Put ½ tablespoon of the butter in a small skillet or saucepan and cut the remaining butter into 12 pieces.

Set the pan over low heat, melt the butter, and add the onion. Cook, stirring, just until it softens, about 3 minutes. Pull the pan from the heat.

Put the flour, baking powder, sugar, and salt in a bowl and whisk to combine. Drop the butter pieces into the bowl and, using your fingers, rub the butter into the flour mixture until you've got a bowl full of flour-covered pieces, some small and flaky, some the size of peas. Scatter the cooked onion over the mixture, then pour over the cold milk and, using a fork, toss and turn everything together until you've got a soft dough. If there are some dry bits at the bottom of the bowl, reach in and knead the dough gently a couple of times.

Lightly dust a work surface with flour, turn the dough out, and dust the top of the dough very lightly with flour. Pat the dough down gently with your hands (or roll it out with a pin) until it is about ½ inch thick. It doesn't have to be an even square or round; just do the best you can, and do it quickly.

Dip the biscuit cutter into the flour bin, then cut out as many biscuits as you can — cutting the biscuits as close to one another as possible — and transfer them to the baking sheet, leaving a little space between them. Gather the scraps of dough together, pat them down, and cut out as many more biscuits as you can; put these on the lined baking sheet too. Alternatively (and perhaps more economically), you can pat or roll out the dough into a rectangle or square, then, using a long knife, cut square biscuits, about 1 to 1½ inches on a side. (*You can make the biscuits to this point and freeze them on the baking sheet; when they're solid, pack them airtight and freeze them for up to 2 months.*)

Bake the biscuits for 15 to 18 minutes, or until they are puffed and lightly browned. They're ready to eat now or to use to make cocktail sandwiches.

cheez-it-ish crackers

MAKES ABOUT
50 CRACKERS

SERVING
Just pile these into a basket and serve them with aperitifs, or keep them handy for snacking.

STORING
Packed in an airtight tin, the crackers will keep for at least 4 days. While you can freeze them, I find it's better to freeze the dough instead. To make things really simple, roll the dough out, leave it between the sheets of plastic or wax paper, and put it in the freezer. When the dough is frozen solid, peel off the plastic or paper and rewrap it airtight. To use, let the dough soften just enough so that you can cut out the rounds, then bake as directed; the crackers might need another minute or two in the oven if the dough is still frozen when you start to bake.

BONNE IDÉE
Slice-and-Bake Crackers.
You can make this simple recipe even simpler by dividing the dough into thirds and shaping each piece into a log. (The diameter is up to you.) Wrap the logs in plastic and chill for at least 3 hours — or freeze them — then slice them into rounds that are a scant ¼ inch thick. Bake just as you do the cutouts.

I LOVE WHITE WINE WITH CHEESE, and I love to serve something cheesy as a nibble with before-dinner drinks (see the recipe for Gougères on page 4). So, since it's just not done to serve a hunk of cheese with aperitifs in France — hunks, rounds, and wedges are served after the main course, before dessert — and since the preferred nibble with that first *coupe de Champagne* or glass of wine is something small and often crunchy, I created these little crackers, which are so much chicer than pretzels. The dough is easily made in a food processor (although you could do it by hand), and it can be either rolled out or shaped into logs, chilled, and then sliced and baked (see Bonne Idée). While I make these most often with Gruyère, Comté, or Emmenthal, they're awfully good with cheddar, a cheese I'm convinced the French would love if only it could be made on their *terroir*.

8 tablespoons (1 stick) cold unsalted butter, cut into 16 pieces	⅛ teaspoon freshly ground white pepper
¼ pound Gruyère, Comté, or Emmenthal, grated (about 1 cup)	Pinch of Aleppo pepper (see Sources) or cayenne (optional)
½ teaspoon salt	1 cup plus 2 tablespoons all-purpose flour

Put the butter, cheese, salt, white pepper, and Aleppo pepper or cayenne, if you're using it, in a food processor and pulse until the butter is broken up into uneven bits and the mixture forms small curds. Add the flour and pulse until the dough forms moist curds again — these will be larger. There are times, though, when you pulse and pulse and never get curds — in that case, just process for a minute, so that everything is as moist as possible.

Turn the dough out onto a work surface and knead it gently until it comes together. Divide the dough in half, pat each half into a disk, and wrap the disks in plastic. Chill for at least an hour, or for up to 3 days.

Center a rack in the oven and preheat the oven to 350 degrees F. Line a baking sheet with a silicone baking mat or parchment paper.

Working with 1 disk at a time, roll the dough out between sheets of plastic wrap or wax paper to a scant ¼ inch thick. Using a small cookie cutter — I use a cutter with a diameter of about 1¼ inches — cut the dough into crackers. Gather the scraps together, so you can combine them with the scraps from the second disk, chill, and roll them out to make more crackers. Place the rounds on the baking sheet, leaving a scant inch between the rounds.

Bake for 14 to 17 minutes, or until the crackers are lightly golden and firm to the touch; transfer the crackers to a rack to cool. Repeat with the second disk of dough (and the scraps), making certain that your baking sheet is cool. You can serve these while they're still a little warm, or you can wait until they reach room temperature.

pierre hermé's olive sablés

**MAKES ABOUT
60 COOKIES**

SERVING
Great with white wine and Champagne, these are also perfect with cocktails.

STORING
The logs of dough can be frozen for up to 2 months; there's no need to defrost before slicing and baking.

Y OU CAN LOOK AT THIS COCKTAIL nibble as either a sweet cookie with a spot of savoriness or a savory cookie with a touch of sweetness, but either way you'll have something beyond the borders of the expected and deep within the realm of the irresistible. The sablés (French shortbreads) are undeniably sweet — in fact, that's the first taste you get — but then, just as you're about to shake your head in wonder, up come the salty olives, followed by the base flavor of olive oil. The only thing that's not surprising about these remarkable cookies is that the recipe was given to me by Pierre Hermé, France's most famous pastry chef and the *roi* of remarkable.

The dough for these slice-and-bake sablés includes the grated yolk of a hard-boiled egg, an ingredient not uncommon in Austrian baking, a tradition Pierre knows well. Combined with the recipe's potato starch and confectioners' sugar, it creates a cookie of supernatural tenderness.

I use oil-cured black olives, plain or herb-flecked, for these. You want a meaty, chewy olive with a lot of flavor, so stay away from canned black olives (they won't work in these at all) or the kinds of olives that fall apart or turn mushy when chopped.

BE PREPARED: The dough should chill for at least several hours, or, preferably, overnight. This rest not only firms the logs enough so that you can work with them easily but gives the olives time to fully flavor the dough.

1	large hard-boiled egg, white discarded	15	tablespoons (1 stick plus 7 tablespoons) unsalted butter, at room temperature
2¼	cups all-purpose flour	⅓	cup olive oil (a fruity oil is best)
6	tablespoons potato starch (available at health food stores and in the kosher section of supermarkets)	1	cup confectioners' sugar, sifted
		2½	ounces (about ½ cup) pitted black olives, preferably oil-cured, chopped

Grate the hard-boiled yolk onto a piece of wax paper. Put the flour and potato starch in a strainer set over a large bowl and sift into the bowl; whisk to thoroughly blend.

Working with a stand mixer, preferably fitted with a paddle attachment, or with a hand mixer in a large bowl, beat the butter on medium speed until it's soft and creamy. Beat in the olive oil, followed by the grated yolk. Blend in the confectioners' sugar, reduce the speed to low, and add the dry ingredients. Mix until the dough just comes together — there's no reason to beat this dough, and you shouldn't — then stir in the chopped olives. You'll have a very soft, very pliable dough. (If you prefer, you can make the dough by hand, using a rubber spatula to blend the butter, oil, yolk, and sugar and to fold in the dry ingredients and olives.)

Turn the dough out onto a work surface, divide it into thirds, and shape each piece into a log about 1½ inches in diameter. Wrap the dough in plastic and chill for at least several hours, or, better yet, overnight. If you're in a hurry, you can freeze the logs for an hour or so.

When you're ready to bake the sablés, center a rack in the oven and preheat the oven to 325 degrees F. Line a baking sheet with a silicone baking mat or parchment paper.

Working with 1 log at a time, slice the cookies ¼ inch thick and arrange them on the baking sheet — you want to bake these one sheet at a time.

Bake the sablés for 15 to 18 minutes, rotating the baking sheet at the midway mark, or until the cookies are firm but not colored. They may turn golden around the edges, but you don't want them to brown. Transfer the cookies to a rack to cool, and repeat with the remaining logs of dough, making sure to use a cool baking sheet each time.

david's seaweed sablés

MAKES ABOUT
70 COOKIES

SERVING
These can be served with red wine, but they're particularly good with white and sparkling wines that are not very dry.

STORING
The logs of dough can be kept tightly wrapped in the refrigerator for up to 5 days or frozen for up to 2 months. You can slice and bake the sablés straight from the freezer — there's no need to defrost the logs — but you might need to bake the cookies an extra minute. Seaweed sablés are best the day they are made, but they can be stored overnight in an airtight container.

THESE BUTTER COOKIES ARE AS SURPRISING as you'd guess they'd be from their name. They're truly sablés, sweet, buttery slice-and-bake cookies; truly salty, as salty as pretzels; and truly a Paris trend. Pâtisseries all over the city offer some version of classic sablés with unclassic add-ins like olives (see Pierre Hermé's recipe on page 12), cheese (see page 10), bacon, cracked spices, or seasoned salt. The salty cookies are playful, chic, and attention-getting; in other words, the perfect cocktail-party tidbit.

The recipe for these treats was given to me by cookbook author, pastry chef, blogger, American-in-Paris, and friend David Lebovitz. Originally David made these with French seaweed fleur de sel, but since it is not that easy to come by, I use plain fleur de sel and stir finely chopped toasted nori into the dough.

BE PREPARED: The dough should chill for at least 1 hour.

6 tablespoons (¾ stick) unsalted butter, at room temperature	1 large egg yolk
3 tablespoons finely chopped toasted nori	1½ tablespoons olive oil
2 teaspoons fleur de sel or 1½ teaspoons fine sea salt	1 cup plus 2 tablespoons all-purpose flour
½ cup plus 1 tablespoon confectioners' sugar	Flaky sea salt, for sprinkling (optional)

You can make the dough with a mixer, but if your butter is really soft, the dough is easy to make by hand with a sturdy rubber spatula. Beat the butter, nori, and salt together in a bowl until smooth and creamy. Beat in the sugar, then the egg yolk. Stir in the olive oil, then mix in the flour. When the dough is smooth, stop; you don't want to overwork it.

Divide the dough in half and roll each half into a slender log about 8 inches long. Wrap the logs tightly in plastic wrap and chill them for at least 1 hour, or for up to 5 days.

When you're ready to bake the sablés, center a rack in the oven and preheat the oven to 350 degrees F. Line a baking sheet with a silicone baking mat or parchment paper.

Working with 1 log at a time, slice the cookies on the scant side of ¼ inch (as David says) and arrange them on the baking sheet — you want to bake these one sheet at a time. If you'd like, sprinkle a couple of grains of salt over the top of each cookie.

Bake the cookies for 12 to 14 minutes, or until they are slightly firm but not colored. Transfer the cookies to a rack to cool, and repeat with the second log.

mustard bâtons

LIKE ANNE LEBLANC'S STARTLINGLY SIMPLE AVOCADO with pistachio oil (page 106), mustard bâtons are proof that it doesn't take much to make something great tasting, and good looking too. I'm embarrassed to admit that I resisted this recipe for years. No fewer than three friends told me I had to try it, but looking at the ingredient list — puff pastry, Dijon mustard, and an egg for the glaze — I just couldn't drum up the enthusiasm to bake a batch. It wasn't until I was at a party in Paris and tasted the slender strips that I ran home and made them myself. They're a terrific hors d'oeuvre and they're make-aheadable. The only caveat is to make sure your mustard packs some punch — these are best when the mustard is strong. The photo is on page 2.

MAKES ABOUT
40 BÂTONS

SERVING
These are especially good with white wine or kir (see box, page 6), the official aperitif of Dijon.

STORING
Unbaked bâtons can be kept in the freezer for up to 2 months and baked while still frozen. Brush them with the egg wash and sprinkle them with the poppy seeds, if using them, just before baking.

2 sheets frozen puff pastry (each about 8½ ounces), thawed
All-purpose flour, for rolling

½ cup Dijon mustard
1 large egg
Poppy seeds, for topping (optional)

Position the racks to divide the oven into thirds and preheat the oven to 400 degrees F. Line two baking sheets with silicone baking mats or parchment paper. Have a ruler and a pizza cutter (or sharp knife) at hand.

Working with 1 sheet of pastry at a time, roll the dough out on a lightly floured surface until you have a rectangle that's about 12 x 16 inches. If necessary, turn the dough so that a short side of the rectangle is closest to you. Measure the length so that you can find the middle, and spread ¼ cup of the mustard over the lower half of the dough, stopping about ⅛ inch from the side and bottom edges. Fold the top portion of the dough over the bottom and, using the pizza cutter (or knife), with your ruler as a guide, cut the pastry from top to bottom into strips about 1 inch wide (I actually use the width of the ruler itself as my guide), then cut the strips crosswise in half. (If you prefer, you can leave the strips long.)

Carefully transfer the bâtons to one of the baking sheets and chill or freeze them while you work on the second batch. (You can make all the strips to this point and freeze them on the baking sheets, then pack them airtight and keep them frozen for up to 2 months.)

Lightly beat the egg with a splash of cold water and brush just the tops of the strips with this glaze. If you'd like, sprinkle them with poppy seeds.

Bake the bâtons for 8 minutes. Rotate the sheets from front to back and top to bottom and bake for another 7 to 8 minutes, or until the strips are puffed and golden brown. Remove the baking sheets from the oven and let the bâtons rest for a couple of minutes before serving.

BONNE IDÉE
Tapenade Bâtons. Spreading the puff pastry with tapenade, homemade (page 487) or store-bought, makes savory strips that are great on a summer's evening with an iced rosé. Before folding over the puff pastry, I like to sprinkle the tapenade with grated lemon zest and/or grated Parmesan; other good add-ins are teensy slivers of roasted peppers or sun-dried tomatoes, paper-thin slices of onion, and toasted sliced almonds.

herbed olives

**MAKES ABOUT
2 CUPS**

SERVING
Olives like these are
the perfect nibble with
cocktails, but they're also
good to take along on a
picnic. While I like them
just as they are, if you want
to, you can warm them
slightly, either in a small
saucepan over very gentle
heat or in 5-second spurts
in a microwave, before
serving at home.

STORING
Stored in a covered
container in the
refrigerator, the olives will
keep for about 2 months.
When the olives are gone,
use the oil to dress salads,
toss with pasta, or drizzle
over chicken.

N O MATTER THE SIZE of a French outdoor market, you can be sure that among the vegetable sellers and butchers, the cheese makers and fishmongers, you'll find a stand where the specialty is olives. Well, olives, along with nuts and spices, dried fruit, *citrons confits* (preserved lemons), and often a few savory snackables, like stuffed cherry peppers or rice-filled grape leaves, hints that the vendors have their roots in regions around the Mediterranean. Their selections of olives are wide, ranging from small, shiny black Niçoise olives to shriveled oil-cured olives and green olives the size of Ping-Pong balls; some glisten with olive oil, and others are speckled with herbs and strips of lemon zest. I prefer to buy the plainest olives in the bunch, bring them home, and flavor them myself.

Although it's rare that I season the olives the same way twice — the tweaks are usually a result of what herbs are on hand or what zest I can grab — I do keep the basic proportion of olives to oil pretty consistent. So here's a base recipe that you can play with and make your own. And as to the olives themselves: just use ones you like. In fact, if you've got different olives on hand, some left over from one party and some from another, put them together and flavor them — it will give them a delicious second life. The photo is on page 2.

BE PREPARED: Although you can serve these as soon as they've cooled, it's best to let them stand for at least 8 hours, and they'll be so, so much better if you allow them to flavor for a week or two.

2	cups olives (see above)	4	garlic cloves, split, germ removed, and halved again
3	rosemary sprigs	2	bay leaves, cut lengthwise in half
3	thyme sprigs		
¼	teaspoon coriander seeds	1	dried red chile, split, or ¼ teaspoon red pepper flakes
¼	teaspoon black peppercorns		
⅛	teaspoon fennel seeds (optional)	2	strips orange or lemon zest, white pith removed
½	cup extra-virgin olive oil		Salt to taste

Spoon the olives into a clean 1-quart jar (I like a canning jar here), another heatproof sealable container, or a bowl. Remove the leaves from 2 rosemary sprigs and 2 thyme sprigs (discard the stems), and chop the leaves.

Put a heavy skillet over medium heat, and when it's hot, toss in the coriander seeds, peppercorns, and fennel seeds, if you're using them. Swirl them around in the pan just until you catch a whiff of their fragrance, then scrape them out of the pan into a small bowl.

Let the pan cool down for a couple of minutes, then put it over very low heat. Pour in ¼ cup of the olive oil and add all the remaining ingredients, including the spices, herb leaves, and the intact rosemary and thyme sprigs. Heat the mixture just until it's warm and fragrant, about 2 minutes.

Pour the herbed oil over the olives and add as much of the remaining oil as needed to cover them. Mix everything around once or twice, and let the jar stand until the ingredients reach room temperature. You can serve the olives now, but they'll be much tastier if you seal the jar or cover the bowl and let them macerate in the refrigerator for at least 8 hours or for up to a week or two.

buttered radishes

At first mention, butter and radishes seem an odd couple, but they're a classic French combination that, given how great American radishes are, should be adopted across our land. Like most right-minded people, the French prefer their radishes young, mild, and lacking a serious hit of heat (something all radishes develop with age), but no matter the kind of radish,

Gallic taste decrees that the force of the radish needs a mellowing counterbalance, and butter does the trick (just as it does when you have buttered bread with briny oysters or salty Roquefort).

If you want to serve radishes in the French style, wash them well, and if they came with stems and leaves, trim their topknots, leaving just enough greenery to

serve as handles. Drop the radishes into a bowl of ice water and keep them there until serving. (You can even serve them on ice.) Serve the radishes whole accompanied by very soft butter for spreading on the radishes and a bowl of sea salt, preferably fleur de sel, for dipping; small rounds of dark bread or baguette are optional.

sweet and spicy cocktail nuts

MAKES 2 CUPS

SERVING
These are good with everything from cider and beer to Champagne.

STORING
Covered and in a dry place, the nuts will keep for about 5 days at room temperature.

BONNE IDÉE
You can swap the spices at whim. For a change, omit the chili powder and go for Chinese five-spice powder (you can keep the cinnamon if you like), curry powder (use just a smidgen of cinnamon with the curry), or even cardamom (in which case, cut the cinnamon). You can also make herb-flavored nuts using finely chopped fresh herbs or dried herbs (just make sure your dried herbs are bright colored and still fragrant). Try mixing the nuts with fresh rosemary or thyme or dried herbes de Provence; keep the sugar and salt, and drop the chili powder and cinnamon.

IF A SURVEY WERE TAKEN to find out the most popular nibble offered with drinks in France, nuts would take first place, followed by olives. You get peanuts at many cafés when you order an aperitif; pistachios and salted almonds at friends' homes; and cashews chez us, because they're Michael and my son, Joshua's, favorite. But as good as fresh nuts are in their natural state, they're better when they've been personalized a bit. In fact, flavored nuts are the kind of thing that can quickly become a *spécialité de la maison,* something friends look forward to having when they're at your house.

I like to make the nuts with a mix of chili powder (I bring it from New York to Paris, where the closest thing to chili powder I can find is a mixture suggested for cooking things *à la Mexicaine*), cinnamon, salt, and sugar, but you can play with the flavors as well as with the nuts. This is a recipe meant to be tinkered with, so that it can be yours, truly.

½ cup sugar
1½ teaspoons salt
1½ teaspoons chili powder
½ teaspoon ground cinnamon
Pinch of cayenne
1 large egg white

2 cups nuts (whole or halves, but not small pieces), such as almonds, cashews, peanuts, or pecans (hard to find in France — and expensive), or a mix

Center a rack in the oven and preheat the oven to 300 degrees F. Spray a nonstick baking sheet with cooking spray or line a baking sheet with a silicone baking mat or parchment paper.

Mix the sugar, salt, and spices together in a small bowl. Beat the egg white lightly with a fork in a larger bowl, just breaking up the white so that it's runny. Toss in the nuts and stir to coat them with the egg white, then add the sugar and spice mixture and continue to stir so that the nuts are evenly coated.

Using your fingers, lift the nuts one by one from the bowl, letting the excess egg white drip back into the bowl (you can run the dipped nuts against the side of the bowl to get rid of the last bit of egg white), and transfer them to the baking sheet, separating them as best you can.

Bake for 30 to 35 minutes, or until the nuts are browned and the coating is dry. Cool for 5 minutes, then transfer the nuts to another baking sheet, a cutting board, or a piece of parchment paper, breaking them apart as necessary, and let cool completely.

hummus

THE SAME WAY THAT IMPORTS like tzatziki (page 24) and guacamole (page 22) have captured the culinary imagination of the French, so hummus has wiggled its way into the Gallic repertoire: supermarkets large and small stock the Middle Eastern dip in a dizzying number of varieties. At heart, hummus is a simple, basic, satisfying blend of chickpeas, tahini, and lemon juice, and, although it can be paired with many foods — it's particularly good with grilled chicken — it's most often served as a dip with triangles of pita or lavash doing dipper duty.

Making hummus at home is easy and very quick, and once you've got a bowl of it, it's an inspiration: you can make your own "house hummus" by adding chopped roasted peppers, sun-dried tomatoes, caramelized onions, garlic (raw or roasted), spices, herbs, or the same vegetables, chopped, that you might want to use as scoops.

MAKES ABOUT 2 CUPS OR 8 TO 10 SERVINGS

SERVING
The hummus can be served, as is, with pita, lavash, crackers, or thin slices of baguette or an assortment of crunchy vegetables (like carrots, cucumbers, celery, and radishes) as dippers. You can fold a generous amount of chopped parsley into the hummus before serving, or drizzle over some olive oil and dot the top of the hummus with whole chickpeas.

STORING
The hummus can be refrigerated for up to 3 days. If you are making it ahead and want to add parsley, add it at the last minute so it doesn't blacken.

1 can (about 16 ounces) chickpeas, drained (reserve the liquid), rinsed, and patted dry	⅓ cup well-stirred tahini
	2 tablespoons fresh lemon juice, or to taste
2 garlic cloves, split, germ removed, and chopped	About ½ teaspoon ground cumin (optional)
	Salt and freshly ground pepper

Put the chickpeas, garlic, tahini, and lemon juice in a food processor and whir until smooth. With the machine running, add some of the reserved chickpea liquid a little at a time until the hummus is a nice thick, scoopable texture — you'll probably need about 4 tablespoons of liquid. Add the cumin, if you'd like, tasting to get the amount you want, then season with salt and pepper and more lemon juice, if you think it needs it.

Scoop the hummus into a bowl or refrigerator container, press a piece of plastic wrap against the surface, and chill until serving time. *(The hummus can be refrigerated for up to 3 days.)*

When you're ready to serve, taste again for salt, pepper, and lemon juice.

lyonnaise garlic and
herb cheese *(aka boursin's mama)*

MAKES ABOUT
2 CUPS OR
4 TO 6 SERVINGS

SERVING
The cheese can be served
as a dip with lots of raw
vegetables or as a spread
with crackers or hunks
of warm toasted country
bread.

STORING
Covered well, the cheese
will keep in the refrigerator
for up to 2 days; stir gently
before serving.

BONNE IDÉE
Cheese-Stuffed Tomatoes.
**Choose 4 medium
tomatoes that are ripe but
still firm, and blanch them
for 15 seconds so that you
can peel them (see page
120). Cut the top third off
each tomato (reserve it)
and, using a small spoon or
your fingers, pull the pulp
and seeds from the tomato,
leaving a sturdy wall. Turn
the tomatoes over onto a
paper towel and drain for
about 30 minutes. To serve,
fill each tomato with some
herb cheese and cap with
the reserved tops. I like to
drizzle a little Basil Pesto
(page 488) or Basil Coulis
(see Bonne Idée, page 488)
around the tomatoes.**

AUTHENTICALLY CALLED *CERVELLE DE CANUT*, or, literally, "the silk-weaver's brains," this luscious mix, part dip, part spread, part salad dressing, strikes everyone, me included, as the inspiration for Boursin, the soft herb cheese that's as much a supermarket favorite in the United States as it is in France. Created at a time when Lyon was the center of a thriving silk industry, the dish is traditionally made with fromage blanc, which is sometimes mixed with cream. And it is always mixed with a little vinegar or white wine, a little oil, and lots of herbs, usually parsley, chives, and chervil, the licoricey herb that is beloved and easily available in France but less known and much less gettable in America — where tarragon makes a fine stand-in.

While fromage blanc is also difficult to find here and, when found, quite expensive, ricotta, if spooned into a strainer and left to drain for a few hours, works perfectly — it has precisely the right mild flavor and soft, thick, airy texture for this dish.

If you want to serve the herb cheese for an hors d'oeuvre, just put it out with a selection of raw vegetables — it's particularly good with radishes — or crackers or bread. Should you want to use it as a dressing, thin it with a lick of milk or cream and use it over greens of any kind, especially bitter greens. To fancy it up a bit, use it as a stuffing for hollowed-out tomatoes (see Bonne Idée), piquillo peppers, or store-bought cherry peppers. Or, to make it part of a cheese platter, just shape it into quenelles or present it in a bowl with a spoon, so guests can scoop their own.

BE PREPARED: No matter how you serve it, you'll want it to be cold, so plan ahead. (Plan even further ahead if you're using ricotta.)

2 cups fromage blanc or ricotta (can be part-skim)	About 1 tablespoon minced fresh parsley
½ shallot, minced, rinsed, and patted dry	About 1 teaspoon minced fresh tarragon
1 garlic clove (or a little more, if you'd like), split, germ removed, and minced	2 teaspoons red wine vinegar
About 2 tablespoons snipped fresh chives	2 tablespoons extra-virgin olive oil Salt and freshly ground white pepper to taste

If you're using fromage blanc, put it in a medium bowl. If you're using ricotta, you'll need to drain it for a few hours to thicken its texture a bit. Spoon the ricotta into a fine-mesh strainer, put the strainer over a bowl, and cover the setup with a large plate or plastic wrap. Refrigerate for at least 2 hours, or overnight, if that's more convenient. When you're ready to use it, spoon the ricotta into a medium bowl and discard whatever liquid has drained from it.

Add the remaining ingredients to the bowl and mix everything together lightly with a rubber spatula. (You don't want to beat the cheese and risk thinning it.) Taste and adjust the seasonings as you wish, adding a little more garlic, herbs, and/or vinegar. Cover and refrigerate for at least 3 hours.

Taste the cheese and season again if needed before serving.

guacamole with tomatoes and bell peppers

MAKES ABOUT
1½ CUPS OR
4 SERVINGS

SERVING
If you've made the guacamole in a mortar, use it as your serving bowl. No matter how you've made it, serve it with your favorite chips.

STORING
The guacamole is at its best freshly made, but if you have to hold it for a little while, press a piece of plastic wrap directly against the surface to create an airtight seal and keep it in the refrigerator.

GUACAMOLE HAS BECOME A STANDARD IN FRANCE, particularly in Paris, where, as often as it's served with chips, that's how often it turns up in unexpected roles. At Cuisine de Bar, the chic sandwich restaurant next to the famous Poilâne boulangerie (see page 42), guacamole is turned into a tartine (see box, page 41), dotted with small shrimp. At fancier restaurants, I've seen it used as the base of a salmon tartare, or as part of a layered crab salad served in a glass, or spooned into pretty quenelles to become a garnish for gazpacho.

While the French tend to buy their guacamole rather than prepare it themselves, I like to make my own, even in Paris, where one of the ingredients I consider essential is rarely available: jalapeño peppers. I keep dried jalapeño powder in my cupboard and cans of jalapeño too — both brought from the United States — and usually add whatever hot pepper I can find at the market.

I make this guacamole two ways: chunky and smooth. For chunky, I mix the ingredients in a bowl with a fork; for smooth, I reach for my mortar and pestle. It's good both ways, so I leave it to you to decide on the method.

1 lime	2 ripe Hass avocados, halved, pitted, and peeled
Leaves from 4–6 cilantro sprigs, plus chopped fresh cilantro to taste	Freshly ground pepper
2 slices red onion, chopped	Hot sauce
½ jalapeño, or more to taste, finely chopped	About 6 grape tomatoes, quartered
Salt	About ¼ red bell pepper, finely chopped

TO MAKE A SMOOTH GUACAMOLE: Grate the lime zest into a mortar. Toss in the cilantro leaves, onion, jalapeño, and a good pinch of salt and go to work with the pestle, pressing on the ingredients and moving the pestle around in a circular motion. You'll crush the cilantro but only just bruise the onion and jalapeño, and that's fine. Add the avocado, squeeze in all the juice from the lime, and use the pestle to break up the avocado and blend it with the other ingredients. Taste for salt, add pepper and hot sauce as you like, and then stir in the tomatoes, bell pepper, and chopped cilantro.

TO MAKE A CHUNKIER GUACAMOLE: Grate the lime zest into a bowl. Finely chop the cilantro leaves and add them, along with the onion, jalapeño, and a good pinch of salt, and toss with a fork. Chop the avocado and put the pieces in the bowl, along with the tomatoes and bell pepper. Squeeze all the juice from the lime over the ingredients and stir everything together gently. Taste for salt, add pepper and hot sauce as you like, and sprinkle with the chopped cilantro.

eggplant caviar

DESPITE ITS FANCY NAME, EGGPLANT CAVIAR IS a humble dish, one you find as a starter in student restaurants, a take-out item in just about any specialty shop, and a staple in the ready-mades section of most supermarkets. But, made with care and seasoned with generosity, the dish — half dip, half spread, and closely related to Middle Eastern baba ghanoush — can live up to its moniker. In my version, there's lemon juice for brightness, onion for sharpness, tomato for sweetness, and fresh herbs for complexity, all of which give the classic new life.

I like to serve the caviar the day it's made, so if I'm serving 4 people or fewer, I halve the recipe to avoid having leftovers.

MAKES 3½ TO 4 CUPS OR 8 TO 10 SERVINGS

2   firm eggplants, each about 1½ pounds

2   garlic cloves, split, germ removed, and minced

2   tablespoons extra-virgin olive oil

Grated zest and juice of 1 lemon

1   small onion, finely chopped, rinsed, and patted dry

1–2 tablespoons finely shredded fresh basil

1–2 tablespoons finely chopped fresh cilantro

1   teaspoon finely chopped fresh thyme

Pinch of piment d'Espelette (see Sources) or cayenne

Salt and freshly ground pepper

2   medium tomatoes, peeled (optional), seeded, and finely chopped

Center a rack in the oven and preheat the oven to 400 degrees F. Line a baking sheet with foil.

Rinse and dry the eggplants and prick them all over with a fork, or stab them in a few places with the point of a small knife. Put the eggplants on the foil-lined baking sheet and roast them for 45 minutes to an hour, until they're soft and shriveled. Remove them from the oven and leave them on the baking sheet until they're cool enough to handle (or until they reach room temperature).

Slit the eggplants open and scrape the soft flesh into a bowl; discard the skin. Add the garlic and olive oil. Using a fork, stir and press the eggplant until you have a chunky puree. If you like smooth eggplant caviar, you can work the puree a little more; my preference is for one that's got an uneven texture. Add the zest, most of the lemon juice, the onion, and the herbs, and season with the piment d'Espelette or cayenne and salt and pepper. Then taste and see if you want to add more of anything or everything. (At this point, you can press a piece of plastic against the surface of the eggplant caviar and chill it for a few hours. Right before serving, taste and re-season if necessary.)

Fold in the chopped tomatoes, if you like, and transfer to a serving bowl.

SERVING
My favorite way to enjoy eggplant caviar is to spread it on wedges of toasted country bread, but it's good on pita or scooped up with crackers, and it makes a great addition to sandwiches — try it with chicken, beef, or grilled vegetables (it's especially delicious with Roasted Peppers, page 112).

STORING
You can keep the eggplant caviar tightly covered in the refrigerator overnight — make sure to stir any liquid that accumulates back into the puree — but it's really best the day it's made.

BONNE IDÉE
Remove the germ from another 1 or 2 garlic cloves and slice them paper-thin. Using a sharp paring knife, poke about 10 slender slashes into each eggplant and work the garlic slivers into them before roasting.

tzatziki

MAKES ABOUT
3 CUPS OR
6 TO 8 SERVINGS

SERVING
Tzatziki should be served cold and simply. While it's often served as a dip for raw vegetables, it's good with crackers, spread on thick toasted country bread, added to a sandwich, spooned over a hamburger, or, dare I suggest it, scooped up with potato chips.

STORING
Covered and refrigerated, tzatziki will keep for about 2 days. Stir before serving.

PARIS'S 5TH ARRONDISSEMENT, PART OF WHICH is the Latin Quarter, is home to the Sorbonne, the Panthéon, the student bookstores along the boulevard Saint-Michel, and a surprising number of shops offering Greek specialties. But, in fact, Greek pastries, olives, stuffed grape leaves, tuna-filled peppers (page 174), tarama (or taramasalata), and this fresh cucumber-yogurt mix can be found in most of the outdoor markets in the city, something that surprised me when I first started shopping in Paris.

A yogurt-based blend (thick Greek yogurt is best here) of cucumbers, fresh herbs, lemon juice, garlic, and a little olive oil, tzatziki is a recipe that tastes rich but is actually very low in calories — not that the French would favor it for this reason. Creamy and versatile, it can be used as a dip for crudités, a first layer for tartines (top with thinly sliced radishes and sprinkle with fleur de sel), or a dressing for a tomato salad.

BE PREPARED: If you're not using Greek yogurt, you'll need to drain the yogurt for about 4 hours.

2 cups yogurt, preferably Greek (it can be nonfat)	1 tablespoon extra-virgin olive oil
1 cup finely cubed seedless cucumber	2–3 garlic cloves, split, germ removed, and minced
Salt	2 tablespoons minced fresh dill
2 tablespoons fresh lemon juice	2 tablespoons minced fresh mint
	Freshly ground white pepper to taste

If you're using Greek yogurt, you're good to start mixing; if you're using regular yogurt, you'll need to drain it in order to make it thicker. Line a strainer with a layer of damp cheesecloth, put the strainer over a bowl, spoon in the yogurt, and cover the whole setup with a plate or plastic wrap. Chill for about 4 hours, or for as long as overnight, then gather up the edges of the cheesecloth and squeeze gently to get the last bit of liquid out (discard the liquid that's accumulated in the bowl).

Toss the cucumber into a bowl, sprinkle with about ½ teaspoon salt, stir, and let sit for 30 minutes.

Drain off the liquid in the bowl, put the cucumber in a clean dish towel, and dry it by twisting the cloth and squeezing. Return the cucumber to the bowl and stir in all the remaining ingredients, including the yogurt. Taste for salt and white pepper, and, if you've got the time, chill for a few hours before serving.

sardine rillettes

TIME WAS, NOT SO LONG AGO, that if you said "rillettes," it was understood that you were talking about a rich, salty spread made from pork, goose, or duck slowly cooked in its own fat. Nowadays rillettes is just as likely to be piscine as porcine and more than likely to be lighter and less rich. While salmon rillettes (page 26) is the one you find most often at restaurants and cocktail parties, sardine rillettes is giving it a run for first place.

This rillettes, made in under 10 minutes, is a combination of canned sardines, shallots, herbs, and cream cheese (low-fat, if you'd like). You can use skinless, boneless fillets, but I think you get more flavor if you buy sardines in olive oil, bone them yourself (it takes a second per fish), and leave the skin in place. Obviously the cream cheese is an American stand-in, but it's a very good one. In France you'd use *fromage frais,* a soft, smooth, mild cheese that is as common as yogurt and found right next to the yogurt in every supermarket in the country. If you can get it, of course you can use it, but there's no need to go out of your way for it; cream cheese is more than fine.

Rillettes is usually served with small toasts or crackers (it's perfect on Triscuits), and it also lends itself to being used as a filling.

BE PREPARED: The rillettes should be refrigerated for at least 2 hours before serving.

MAKES 1 CUP OR
ABOUT 6 SERVINGS

SERVING
Offer the rillettes in a bowl surrounded by toasted country bread, crackers, or Pringles, if you dare, or use it as a stuffing for cherry tomatoes, hard-boiled eggs, or piquillo or Peppadew peppers.

STORING
Wrapped airtight, the rillettes will keep for up to 2 days; stir well before serving.

BONNE IDÉE
At the avant-garde Parisian bistro Itinéraires, sardine rillettes is served in a martini glass topped with a baby scoop of cornichon sorbet. Pairing the creamy, smooth rillettes with vinegary pickles is both surprising and exciting, and while cornichon sorbet is not very practical at home, adding just a few thin slices of cornichons to the mixture is. In the same spirit, a spoonful or two of capers is an equally lively addition.

2 3¾-ounce cans sardines packed in olive oil (see above), drained	Juice of 2 limes or 1 lemon, or to taste
2½ ounces cream cheese or Neufchâtel cheese	2–3 tablespoons minced fresh herbs, such as chives, cilantro, parsley, and/or dill
2 shallots or 1 small onion, minced, rinsed, and patted dry	Pinch of piment d'Espelette (see Sources) or cayenne
1–2 scallions, white and light green parts only, halved lengthwise and thinly sliced	Salt and freshly ground pepper to taste

If you've chosen sardines that have not been boned, use a paring knife to cut them open down the belly and back and separate the fish into 2 fillets. Lift away the bones and, if there is a little bit of tail still attached to the fish, cut it off.

Put the cream cheese in a medium bowl and, using a rubber spatula, work it until it is smooth. Add everything else except the sardines — holding back some of the lime or lemon juice until the rillettes are blended — and mix with the spatula. Add the sardines to the bowl, switch to a fork, and mash and stir the sardines into the mixture. Taste for seasoning, adding more juice, salt, and/or pepper, if you'd like.

Scrape the rillettes into a bowl and cover, pressing a piece of plastic wrap against the surface. Chill for at least 2 hours, or for as long as overnight.

salmon rillettes

SERVING
Rillettes is served as a
spread, so have lots of
bread, crackers, or toast
available. If you'd like to
dress it up, serve it on
warm blini (page 172) or
spread it on small rounds
of toasted brioche (think
canapés) and top with
salmon roe.

STORING
Packed airtight, the rillettes
will keep in the refrigerator
for up to 2 days.

THIS SPREAD IS AS HAPPY sharing a table with the fixings for an American brunch as it is on the buffet of a chic Parisian cocktail party. A mix of quickly poached fresh salmon and bits of smoked salmon, mashed with a fork and seasoned with a little hot pepper and a lot of lemon juice, it can be served pressed into a canning jar (the way you'd serve the most traditional pork rillettes), with a knife and hunks of bread, or spooned onto toast points or blini. Either way, I'd suggest you make more than you think you'll need. While you can certainly cut this recipe in half, do that, and you'll regret it the following day — when, if you're like me, you'll crave the rillettes as a snack.

BE PREPARED: The rillettes must be refrigerated for at least 2 hours so it firms up.

1 lemon	Salt
1 small red chile pepper	½ pound salmon fillet, cut into
½ cup dry white wine or white	small (about ½-inch) cubes
vermouth	4–6 ounces smoked salmon, cut
½ cup water	into small (about ¼-inch) dice
1 bay leaf	Freshly ground white pepper
5 white peppercorns	3 tablespoons unsalted butter,
5 coriander seeds	at room temperature
2 small spring onions, trimmed	About ¼ teaspoon pink
and finely chopped, long	peppercorns, crushed
green tops reserved, or	
1 shallot, finely chopped,	Bread, crackers, or toast,
rinsed, and patted dry	for serving

Using a vegetable peeler, remove a strip of zest from the lemon and toss it into a medium saucepan. Finely grate the rest of the zest, and set it and the lemon aside. With a small knife, cut away a sliver of the chile pepper; discard the seeds, and toss the sliver into the saucepan. Seed and finely chop the remainder of the chile pepper.

Pour the wine or vermouth and the water into the pan, add the bay leaf, white peppercorns, coriander, onion tops if you're using spring onions, and ½ teaspoon salt, and bring to a boil over medium heat. Lower the heat, cover, and simmer gently for 5 minutes.

Drop the cubes of fresh salmon into the pan, cover, and poach for just 1 minute. Turn everything into a strainer, drain, and transfer the cubes of salmon to a bowl. Discard herbs, spices, and vegetables.

With the back of a fork, lightly mash the poached salmon. Toss the smoked salmon, grated lemon zest, chile pepper, and chopped onions or shallot into the bowl, season with salt and white pepper, and give everything a good stir. Add the butter and use the fork to stir and mash it into the mixture until it's well incorporated and you have a thick spread. Squeeze about half of the lemon's

juice into the bowl, stir it in, and season the rillettes again with salt and white pepper. Taste and add more lemon juice (it's nice when it's lemony) if you'd like, then stir in the pink peppercorns.

Pack the rillettes into a jar (a canning jar is traditional) or bowl, press a piece of plastic wrap against the surface, and chill for at least 2 hours — you want it to be firm.

Serve the rillettes with bread, crackers, or toast.

tuna rillettes

MAKES 1 CUP OR
ABOUT 6 SERVINGS

SERVING
I like to offer rillettes
as a nibble with drinks.
Surround the rillettes with
whole-grain crackers and/
or slices of tart, crisp
apples and make sure to
provide a small knife —
this is a spread, not a dip.

STORING
Covered tightly, tuna
rillettes will keep in the
fridge for up to 3 days.

THIS RECIPE WAS GIVEN TO ME by my friend Olivier Martina, and from the moment I got it, I've been making it and surprising French and Americans alike. The French do a double take because of the curry powder in the mix, and the Americans keep imagining how good the rillettes would be as a stand-in for regular tuna salad in the classic tuna, lettuce, and tomato on toast. (The answer to "how good?" is "very good.") As with other rillettes — like salmon, page 26, and sardine, page 25 — this is soft, spreadable, and just a tad rich, and it's also quickly made. However, once it's mixed together (a process that takes less than 10 minutes), I urge you to forget about it for an hour or so — left in the fridge, the flavors blend and the curry powder, as well as that dash of quatre-épices (a mix of ginger, nutmeg, cloves, and allspice), comes to the fore.

Because tuna varies in flavor and moistness, I've given you only a guideline for the quantities of spices and cream. Taste and see for yourself what you'd like.

BE PREPARED: The rillettes should chill for at least 1 hour before serving.

2 5- to 6-ounce cans chunk light tuna packed in oil, drained (albacore tuna is too firm and dry)	About 3 tablespoons crème fraîche or 3–5 tablespoons heavy cream
1 shallot, thinly sliced, rinsed, and dried	¼ teaspoon salt, or to taste
½–1 teaspoon curry powder	Freshly ground pepper
Up to ¼ teaspoon quatre-épices (see Sources) or a very small pinch of ground allspice	Fresh lemon or lime juice to taste (optional)

Put the tuna, shallot, ½ teaspoon curry powder, a pinch of quatre-épices or allspice, 3 tablespoons crème fraîche or heavy cream, the salt, and pepper to taste into a food processor (a mini processor is just right for this job). Whir until the tuna becomes a nice just-right-on-a-cracker paste, then taste it and add more curry, quatre-épices, salt, pepper, and/or cream. Although the flavors will intensify and the texture thicken slightly as the rillettes chills, you'll be able to get a good idea of the balance now. Adjust the seasonings and give the rillettes a squeeze of lemon or lime juice, if you think it needs it — you can always add juice or more of anything else right before serving.

Pack the rillettes into a container, cover with plastic wrap, and chill for at least 1 hour before serving.

arman's caviar in aspic

ONCE YOU'VE SEEN A SCULPTURE by the late French artist Arman, you'll recognize his work immediately ever after. Arman's signature piece is a musical instrument, most famously a violin or saxophone, sliced, deconstructed, cast (or not), and mounted. Walk around Paris, and every once in a while, you'll turn and there'll be an Arman to delight you. (There's one in the outdoor sculpture garden along the Seine, another at the entrance to the Palais de Justice.) You'll also find them in several grand restaurants all over the country. Arman was a great friend to great chefs and a very good cook himself.

I got a glimpse of Arman's culinary side in 1988 when we worked together on some of his recipes for a dinner party. While the main course was an earthy, rustic osso buco (page 270), the passed hors d'oeuvre was pure city-chic: clear wiggly-jiggly cubes of lightly flavored aspic, their bellies scooped out and the resulting indentation filled with caviar. Like Arman's art, these are beautiful, surprising, and fun. They're also delicious.

BE PREPARED: You'll need about 3 hours for the aspic to set (if it's easier for you, leave it overnight).

MAKES 6 SERVINGS

SERVING
For the most strikingly artistic presentation, put the aspic squares on a black, white, or clear glass plate. Champagne or vodka is the drink of choice here, but white wine would be very right as well.

STORING
You can make the aspic up to 1 day ahead, but once you've crafted the cubes, you need to serve them immediately.

2 cups cold water	3 ounces caviar (paddlefish roe, salmon roe, or lumpfish roe)
2 packages unflavored gelatin	
½ fish bouillon cube, crumbled	

Have a 9-x-5-inch metal loaf pan at hand. You can use a Pyrex pan, but it will be a little more difficult to unmold the gelatin and the edges won't be as square.

Set a medium heatproof bowl over a saucepan of simmering water, pour in the water, and stir in the gelatin. Reduce the heat to medium and cook gently until the water is hot and the gelatin has completely dissolved. Stir in the crumbled bouillon cube, but don't worry about dissolving it now.

Remove the bowl from the saucepan, pour out the water in the pan, and pour the gelatin mixture into it. Put the pan over medium heat, bring the mixture to a boil, and boil for about 3 minutes, or until the bouillon is completely dissolved. Pour the liquid into the loaf pan and set it aside to cool.

Skim any foam off the top of the bouillon mixture and refrigerate until the aspic is set, about 3 hours. (Once the aspic is cold, you can cover the pan and leave it in the fridge overnight.)

Right before serving, carefully run a thin sharp knife around the sides of the pan. Dip the bottom of the pan into hot water, wipe it dry, and unmold the aspic onto a cutting board. Using a ruler as a guide and the thin sharp knife, cut the aspic into 1-inch cubes. Now — this is the tricky part, because the aspic is jiggly — use the knife to cut a square indentation in each cube, stopping before you cut through the bottom. Don't fret if it's not perfect — there's nothing caviar can't cover. Alternatively, you can use the tip of a grapefruit spoon or a teensy melon baller to scoop out a circle of aspic.

Fill each little indentation with caviar, and serve immediately.

dilled gravlax
with mustard sauce

MAKES 8 SERVINGS

SERVING
To serve DIY-style, arrange the salmon on a large serving platter, spoon the sauce into a sauceboat or a small bowl with a ladle, and pile the bread attractively on a plate. Alternatively, you can arrange a platter of ready-made gravlax toasts, putting a small slice of gravlax on each piece of bread or toast and topping the salmon with a bit of sauce. If you'd like, finish each slice with a sprig of dill.

STORING
Once you've rinsed off the cure and patted the salmon dry, you can cover it and refrigerate for up to 2 more days before serving.

GRAVLAX, SUGAR-AND-SPICE-CURED SALMON with a honey mustard sauce, could be the poster dish for party food. Not only does it go with just about every aperitif from vodka, its original companion in its Scandinavian homeland, to Champagne, its most common companion in France, it's a dish that has to be made ahead, so it can get checked off the to-do list very early.

You can find gravlax, the thin slices of salmon tinged dark at the edges from the spice rub, displayed in almost every *traiteur,* or specialty prepared-foods shop, in Paris, but I prefer to make it myself and to have control over what goes into the cure and the sauce. I also love being able to make something chez moi that looks and tastes as if the pros produced it.

Gravlax is a standard at our New Year's Eve dinner, and when the party is large — we were once twenty-six for dinner! — I make a whole side of salmon. If, like me, you don't have a pan large enough for a side of salmon (or enough refrigerator space — Paris fridges are pint-sized), cut the fish crosswise in half and rub all the surfaces with the spice mix, then lay one half in the pan, flesh side up, spread with dill, and top with the other half, flesh side down.

BE PREPARED: Start the dish at least 2 days ahead.

FOR THE SALMON
1 teaspoon white peppercorns
1 teaspoon black peppercorns
1 teaspoon coriander seeds
2 tablespoons sea salt or kosher salt
2 teaspoons sugar
1 1- to 1½-pound skin-on center-cut salmon fillet
1 cup chopped fresh dill

FOR THE SAUCE
2 tablespoons honey mustard, preferably Dijon
1 tablespoon distilled white vinegar
3 tablespoons mild oil, such as grapeseed or canola
¼ teaspoon salt
2 tablespoons chopped fresh dill
Freshly ground pepper (optional)

Small thin slices rye bread or toasted brioche, for serving
Small dill sprigs, for garnish (optional)

TO MAKE THE SALMON: Put the peppercorns and coriander seeds in a small skillet and warm the spices over medium heat until they are fragrant and so hot they jump in the pan, about 2 minutes. Spill the spices into a mortar and crush them with a pestle, or turn them onto a cutting board, cover with a clean kitchen towel, and crush with the bottom of a heavy pan or the heel of a knife.

Scrape the spices into a bowl, add the salt and sugar, and mix.

Poke a dozen small holes in the skin of the salmon with a sharp paring knife. Put the salmon skin side up in an 8-inch square baking dish (Pyrex is perfect for this) and pat about one-third of the spice mixture over the skin. Cover the skin with one-third of the dill and flip the fish over. Rub the salmon flesh with the remaining spices and cover with the remaining dill. Press a piece of plastic wrap over the salmon and weight the salmon evenly — two large cans of tomatoes make good weights. Refrigerate for 48 to 72 hours.

TO MAKE THE SAUCE: Put the mustard, vinegar, and oil in a small jar, cover, and shake to blend (or whisk in a small bowl). Add the salt, dill, and pepper, if you'd like, shake again, and refrigerate until needed. *(The sauce can be refrigerated for up to 4 days.)*

Scrape the spices and dill off both sides of the salmon and rinse the salmon quickly under cold water; dry thoroughly. Using a knife with a long, thin sharp blade and cutting on the diagonal, thinly slice the salmon, leaving the skin behind. Serve with the sauce and bread or toasts, garnished with dill, if you like.

mme. maman's chopped liver

MAKES **8** HORS
D'OEUVRE
SERVINGS OR **6**
STARTER SERVINGS

SERVING
Serve the chopped liver
surrounded by crackers or
thin slices of baguette. If
you're not serving this as
an hors d'oeuvre, you can
use it as a sandwich filling,
in which case I'd follow my
husband's lead and slather
the bread with mayonnaise,
then add lettuce and
tomato.

STORING
Tightly covered, the chicken
liver will keep in the
refrigerator for up to 3 days.

ALTHOUGH SONIA MAMAN IS FRENCH, her chopped liver is hardly the refined pâté or mousse of chicken livers you find in restaurants or specialty shops. It's a rough, savory mix of well-browned onions and chicken livers, cooked in oil and then chopped, so that you get a spread with plenty of texture.

Sonia cooks her onions in lots of oil and then drains them, the better to get them really, really brown; she cooks the livers only until they're still rosy at the center, the better to keep them moist and flavorful; and then she's done. But there are times when I keep going, adding a pinch of allspice or quatre-épices, the French blend of spices that's traditional in pâtés, and/or folding in some chopped hard-boiled eggs.

BE PREPARED: The liver needs to chill for a few hours before serving.

½ cup peanut oil (or other high-heat oil, like grapeseed)
2 large onions, chopped
Salt and freshly ground pepper
1 pound chicken livers, veins and any fat or green spots re-moved, halved and patted dry

¼–½ teaspoon quatre-épices (see Sources) or ¼ teaspoon ground allspice (optional)
1–2 hard-boiled eggs, finely chopped (optional)
Chicken fat or mayonnaise, for finishing (optional)

Pour the oil into a large skillet and put the skillet over medium-high heat. When the oil is hot, add the onions and cook, stirring, until they're well browned. Season with salt and pepper, stir again, and take the skillet off the heat. Using a slotted spoon, transfer the onions to a strainer set over a heatproof bowl, leaving whatever oil drips through the slots behind in the skillet.

Return the oil that's drained from the onions to the skillet and put the skillet back over medium-high heat. When the oil is hot, add the chicken livers and cook, nudging them occasionally to make sure they're not sticking to the skillet, until browned, about 2 minutes. Season with salt and pepper and turn the livers over to cook until brown on the other side, 1 to 2 minutes more, just until rosy in the middle. With a slotted spoon, transfer the livers to a cutting board; reserve the oil.

Let the livers cool for about 5 minutes. Either coarsely chop them or cut them into small pieces.

Scrape the onions into a bowl, add the chopped liver, and stir with a fork to mix. Taste for salt and pepper — the liver should be generously seasoned. Add the quatre-épices or allspice, if you're using it, and, if you'd like, the hard-boiled eggs. If the mixture seems dry, you can add a little more oil from the skillet, some chicken fat, if you've got it, or a tad of mayonnaise, which is what my husband likes in his chopped liver.

Pack the chopped liver into a container or a small terrine, cover well, and chill for a few hours before serving.

back-of-the-card cheese and olive bread

NOT QUITE A BACK-OF-THE-BOX RECIPE, but close. . . . Originally this recipe was printed on a card produced by the Comté cheese makers' organization and distributed to *fromageries* all over France. My friend the cookbook author and teacher Patricia Wells and I each picked up a card when we were shopping near her home in Provence and when we got into our kitchens, each of us tweaked the recipe to make it our own.

Now it's your turn. My loaf has cheese (Comté, Gruyère, Swiss, or even cheddar), olives, and tapenade, but it doesn't have to be like that. Keep the basic proportions and play around with the additions, and you can have your own house loaf. Add diced ham and subtract the tapenade, and you'll come close to the original recipe.

1⅔ cups all-purpose flour	6 ounces Comté, Gruyère, Swiss, or cheddar, coarsely grated (about 1½ cups)
2¾ teaspoons baking powder	
¾ teaspoon salt	
4 large eggs, at room temperature	⅔ cup pitted oil-cured black olives, halved or coarsely chopped
½ cup whole milk	Grated zest of 1 lemon or ½ orange (optional)
6½ tablespoons extra-virgin olive oil	
1½ tablespoons tapenade, homemade (page 487) or store-bought	

Center a rack in the oven and preheat the oven to 400 degrees F. Oil or butter an 8½-x-4½-inch loaf pan (nonstick is nice here).

Whisk the flour, baking powder, and salt together in a medium bowl.

In another bowl or a large measuring cup, lightly beat the eggs, then whisk in the milk, olive oil, and tapenade. Pour the liquid ingredients over the flour mixture and stir gently to blend. Switch to a rubber spatula and fold in the cheese, olives, and grated zest, if you're using it. Scrape the batter into the pan.

Bake the loaf for 10 minutes. Turn the oven down to 375 degrees F and continue to bake the loaf for another 35 minutes or so, until it's puffed and beautifully golden and a slender knife inserted deep into the center comes out clean. Transfer the pan to a cooling rack and let it rest for about 5 minutes, then turn it out. Turn the loaf right side up and let cool completely on the rack.

SERVING
In true French fashion, this loaf is meant to be served as a predinner nibble with a glass of Champagne or white wine. Cut the loaf into slices about ½ inch thick, then cut the slices in half the long way, for easy eating. While it's not the French custom to serve this bread with a meal, it's awfully good with salads.

STORING
Wrapped well, the bread will keep for up to 3 days at room temperature or for up to 2 months in the freezer (thaw in the wrapper).

BONNE IDÉE
There's a lot you can do to vary this loaf; an easy change is to swap the tapenade for pesto (homemade, page 488, or store-bought) and to replace the olives with bits of sun-dried tomatoes (or go half olives, half tomatoes). If you use pesto, you might want to add some toasted pine nuts to the mix. No matter what you use, you can top the loaf with some grated cheese before it goes into the oven, but watch it carefully: if it browns too quickly, cover the top loosely with a foil tent.

savory cheese and chive bread

MAKES 1 LOAF OR
ABOUT 8 SERVINGS

SERVING
The bread can be served when it is still slightly warm, but I think it tastes better when it has cooled completely. If the bread is keeping company with drinks, cut it into 8 slices, about ½ inch thick, and cut the slices into strips or cubes.

STORING
Well wrapped, the loaf will keep for about 2 days at room temperature or for up to 2 months in the freezer (thaw in the wrapper). This is not a very moist loaf — it's not meant to be — so it may seem a little dry after a couple of days. At that point, it's good to toast the slices.

BONNE IDÉE
You can use whatever hard cheese you like most or whatever combination of cheeses you have on hand. You can vary the herbs just about any way you wish — I really like this with basil or a mix of herbs that includes basil — or you can skip the herbs. And you can have a field day with add-ins; for example, you can mix in diced ham, bacon bits, toasted chopped nuts, olives, sun-dried tomatoes, minced shallots, or small pieces of cooked vegetables.

I KNOW THIS LOOKS LIKE A GOOD OLD American quick bread, but it's got a French soul, since I was inspired to make it after having had so many versions in so many places across France, particularly in the Champagne region. There the savory cake (just about anything baked in a loaf pan is called a *cake* in France) is often served with aperitifs, but it's also perfect for brunch, really good with salads, and so satisfying when lightly toasted and buttered.

The *cake salé,* as it's known (*salé* means salty or savory), is about as simple a recipe as you can find in the baker's repertoire. In many ways, it's like a muffin, and it's prepared in much the same manner: you whisk all the dry ingredients together in one bowl, all the wet in another, and then gently combine the two. It takes less than 10 minutes to put together and requires no special equipment.

In France, the basic loaf usually has some cheese — generally Gruyère, Emmenthal, or Comté, sometimes Parmesan, and often a combination (it's a great way to use those odd-sized pieces of cheese that seem to collect in the fridge) — and can have more add-ins. For this version, I've kept it simple, using just cheese and lots of snipped chives. In the United States, my preference is for cheddar and some chives from the garden. But this is a recipe that begs for variation (see Bonne Idée) and something to sip along with it. While you're cooling the bread, cool some wine too.

1¾ cups all-purpose flour	⅓ cup extra-virgin olive oil
1 tablespoon baking powder	1 generous cup coarsely grated
½–1 teaspoon salt (depending	Gruyère, Comté, Emmenthal,
on what cheese and add-ins	or cheddar (about 4 ounces)
you're using)	2 ounces Gruyère, Comté,
¼ teaspoon freshly ground	Emmenthal, or cheddar, cut
white pepper (or more to	into very small cubes
taste; you could even add a	(½–⅔ cup)
pinch of cayenne)	½ cup minced fresh chives or
3 large eggs, at room	other herbs (or thinly sliced
temperature	scallions)
⅓ cup whole milk, at room	⅓ cup toasted walnuts, chopped
temperature	(optional)

Center a rack in the oven and preheat the oven to 350 degrees F. Generously butter an 8-x-4½-x-2¾-inch loaf pan — a Pyrex pan is perfect here. If your pan is slightly larger, go ahead and use it, but your loaf will be lower and you'll have to check it for doneness a little earlier.

Whisk the flour, baking powder, salt, and white pepper together in a large bowl.

Put the eggs in a medium bowl and whisk for about 1 minute, until they're foamy and blended. Whisk in the milk and olive oil.

Bacon, Cheese, and Dried Pear Bread. For this bread, you'll need 5 strips of bacon, cooked until crisp, patted dry, and chopped into thick bits, 1 cup finely chopped moist dried pears (about 3½ ounces), and 1 tablespoon minced fresh sage instead of the chives, stirred in just before the dough goes into the pan. I think the toasted walnuts are a must in this one. If you really want to change things up, instead of adding cubes of Gruyère or other hard cheese, fold in a blue cheese, like Roquefort, Fourme d'Ambert, or Gorgonzola.

Pour the wet ingredients over the dry ingredients and, using a sturdy rubber spatula or a wooden spoon, gently mix until the dough comes together. There's no need to be energetic — in fact, beating the dough toughens it — nor do you need to be very thorough: just stir until all the dry ingredients are moistened. Stir in the cheese, grated and cubed, the herbs, and the walnuts, if you're using them. You'll have a thick dough. Turn the dough into the buttered pan and even the top with the back of the spatula or spoon.

Bake for 35 to 45 minutes, or until the bread is golden and a slender knife inserted into the center comes out clean. Transfer the pan to a cooling rack and wait for about 3 minutes, then run a knife around the sides of the pan and turn the loaf over onto the rack; invert and cool right side up.

complaining, the french way

Shortly after we'd moved into our first Paris apartment, I went shopping in one of the city's most esteemed cheese shops. It's very narrow, with barely enough room for the salespeople and a couple of customers to maneuver. It's not an easy place for a beginner because the lines are long and when it's your turn, it's not just the person behind you, but the salesperson as well, who wants you to be snappy about making your choices.

One day, I was having six people for dinner and needed some help choosing an assortment for my cheese platter. I asked for *quelques conseils* (some advice) and made it as clear as I could that I wanted everything to be absolutely perfect, meaning the cheese had to be at its prime, no leaving it under a dome for a day or two or microwaving it to "age" it.

It turned out to be my lucky day: the saleswoman was patient, and after discussing each cheese and giving me a taste of those I didn't know, she handed me my purchases and wished me *une très bonne soirée.* And the evening really was very good and the cheese was terrific — everything except the Brie, which was just shy of ready and probably would have benefited from a quick spin in the microwave, if only I'd had the nerve.

The next day, with four more friends expected for dinner, I was back in line for cheese, and, as it happened, I ended up with the same saleswoman. She greeted me warmly — show up twice to the same store and you're almost a regular — and asked how my dinner had gone. I told her everything was great and then I sheepishly mentioned that the Brie wasn't as creamy as I thought it should have been: it was white at its heart. You'd have thought I'd told her she was responsible for the collapse of the Eiffel Tower. Such regret. Such desolation. Such profound sadness. (The French can be charmingly overdramatic.)

This was a little overwhelming, since I'm the person who thinks that when I get home from the market and find that the milk's sour, it's my fault. But it seems that diffidently mumbled disappointment conformed to the rules and, after all the apologies, the saleswoman helped me choose a new assortment, then declared, "Tonight's cheese will be *impeccable.*" And it was.

Having caused a fuss, I thought it was only right to return to compliment her on her choices. So, there I was, in line for the third time in as many days. When I hit the front of the queue, it was a gentleman salesperson who started to offer his services. However, after seeing me, he stopped his standard, how-may-I-help-you greeting and said, "Ah, you're the American who is Janine's customer. *Un instant,* I'll get her."

Now, after three days, I wasn't just a regular, I was someone with my own personal cheese coach. And why? Because I'd complained. Months later, I checked with Janine to make sure I had it right.

Yes, it was because I'd complained — nicely. By doing this, I scored a point for Americans, assured myself a steady supply of the finest cheeses, and learned something important about cultural differences: in America, if you complain, you're a crank; in France you're a connoisseur.

dieter's tartine

MAKES 1 SERVING

STORING
If you're using a mix
of cottage cheese and
sour cream, you can get
the blend together the
night before and keep it
covered in the refrigerator.
Otherwise, as with salads
of any kind, this is meant to
be put together and eaten
within minutes.

YOU CAN FIND TARTINES IN MOST every café, certainly in Paris, but it's rare anywhere to find a place like Cuisine de Bar, a casual restaurant that devotes itself entirely to tartines. Rare but inspired — it's next door to the famous Poilâne boulangerie (see page 42) and is owned by the same family. Who better to make great tartines than the bakery that makes the most perfect tartineable bread in the country?

At Cuisine de Bar, there is, in fact, a bar at the front of the restaurant and it's there that the cooking — if you can call it cooking — is done. The ingredients for the tartines are on or under the wood bar, and to the back of the bar are the ovens: a battery of toaster ovens, ideal for grilling the large slices of bread.

This *tartine régime*, or diet tartine, is extremely popular among ladies-who-lunch in Paris, since it is filling but not fattening, pretty but not precious, and fine for any season. In Paris it is made with nonfat fromage blanc, a creamy cheese slightly more fluid than our sour cream. You can find it in many American markets, or you can make a mix of cottage cheese and sour cream, both nonfat, of course. The tartine is finished with cubes of cucumbers and tomatoes, but, depending on the season and what's in your vegetable bin, you can scatter any combination of diced vegetables and herbs over it. (I like it with paper-thin slices of radishes and some scallions.) You can drizzle the finished tartine with some fruity olive oil — it will make it a little less dietetic and a little more flavorful.

Obviously pain Poilâne is the bread of choice here, but a hearty farm bread, sourdough or not, makes fine tartines, as does a baguette, sliced the long way, rye bread, or thick-sliced firm white bread. This is a casual dish, so go with what you've got. It's what the French do daily.

1	large slice country bread, about ⅓ inch thick		Salt and freshly ground white pepper
½	cup nonfat fromage blanc or nonfat cottage cheese thinned with nonfat sour cream (about 6 tablespoons cottage cheese to 2 table-spoons sour cream)	⅓	seedless cucumber, peeled and diced
		1	small tomato, preferably peeled and seeded, diced
			Chopped fresh chives
			Herbes de Provence (optional)

Lightly grill one side of the bread or toast it on one side in a toaster oven. Place the bread toasted side up on a large plate, spread with the fromage blanc, and season with salt and white pepper. Or whisk the cottage cheese and sour cream together vigorously (or, if you'd like a smoother blend, pulse them a few times in a mini processor or with a handheld blender), spread on the bread, and season. Toss the cucumber and tomato cubes with salt and white pepper and spoon them over the tartine, paying no attention to what spills over onto the plate. Sprinkle with chives and a tiny pinch of herbes de Provence, if you're using them. Leave the slice of bread whole or cut it in half; serve immediately.

the luckiest guy on the plane
a black truffle sandwich to go

The last thing I said to my husband one winter morning in Paris when he was leaving for the airport was, "I put a little snack in your computer bag." The first thing he said to me when he called from New York was, "I wish you could have seen the faces on all the French passengers when I opened my snack! The second I removed the plastic, everyone turned in my direction, and the flight attendant came over to my seat almost immediately — she was so envious that I gave her a bite." The snack that caused the fuss was a black truffle sandwich. It's not that everyone could see it — they didn't have to: the smell of truffles is so powerful and so distinctive that it's immediately recognizable to those who know and love them, a group that includes almost everyone in France.

Black truffles are rare and expensive, and it's not often that I've got them. But one winter (the season for truffles runs from about November to March, with the holidays being prime time), I went in with a couple of friends on a truffle buy and ended up with two beautiful truffles, each fresh, fragrant, and the size of a small walnut. I hoarded my supply, using the fungi judiciously to make the pleasure last.

Since the less you do with truffles, the better — you don't want to really cook them, but you do want to warm them to bring out their aroma (which is a major part of their draw) — I used a few slices in coddled eggs (page 194), a few with sautéed potatoes, and a few (well, more than a few) raw, with aged Comté (a truly sublime combination). And I stashed some away so that I could make Michael's surprise snack.

Michael's sandwich was my version of one almost synonymous with Michel Rostang, the Michelin-starred chef. In Rostang's mythic creation, two slices of country bread (such as pain Poilâne; see page 42) are spread with salted butter and thickly sliced fresh black truffles — an entire ounce of them! The sandwich is wrapped in plastic and refrigerated for two days so that the bread and butter are thoroughly infused with truffleness. Right before the sandwich is served, it's heated. Chez Rostang, it's run under the broiler, but it could be warmed in a buttered skillet.

So Michael's snack was a shadow of Rostang's. His didn't have an ounce of truffles, and it wasn't warmed, but it was still the best sandwich he'd ever had — and the only one he still talks about.

tartine de viande des grisons

MAKES 1 SERVING

F OR TEN YEARS, I LIVED DOWN the street from the Chai de l'Abbaye and it was *my* café — also, at times, my living room and office. It was the place I went to meet friends, do work, and have meetings. And often it was the place I went for lunch. If I walked in at lunchtime, Rabat, my favorite waiter, would hold the menu out and say, "Do you need this, or are you having *une tartine de viande des Grisons?*"

Viande des Grisons is air-dried beef that comes from Grisons, in Switzerland. It's like Italian bresaola, and it's a popular component of winter meals and snacks in the French Alps, where it's often served with melted cheese and potatoes or on its own with drinks. At the Chai de l'Abbaye, it finds its way into salads that include hunks of Gruyère and walnuts as well as into my tartine. If you can't find air-dried beef, try making this tartine with prosciutto or another thinly sliced dry ham.

SERVING
At the Chai de l'Abbaye, the tartine is served just as is, although you can order the snack portion, which is a half slice of bread and a small handful of green salad. Whichever you decide on, a glass of red wine is a good idea.

STORING
This is a make-and-munch treat.

1 very large slice country bread, about ⅓ inch thick, or 2 smaller slices heavy tight-grained bread (rye works)
Butter

Enough slices of viande des Grisons or bresaola or other air-dried beef to completely cover the bread
Walnut oil or olive oil
Walnut halves (about 10)

Lightly grill one side of the bread or toast it on one side in a toaster oven. As soon as it's toasted, slather that side with butter. Cover the bread with the beef — the pieces should overlap only slightly — and, using a long heavy knife, cut the bread crosswise into strips about 1 inch wide. Drizzle with a tiny bit of oil and strew with nuts.

tartines

Although the word sounds as if it should describe teensy tarts, what *tartines* really signals is a huge range of open-faced sandwiches, the French equivalent of Italian bruschetta. The verb *tartiner* means to spread, and a tartine is a slice of bread spread (although in many cases it's more rightly topped) with something or several somethings.

Tartines can be light or substantial, simple or elaborate; they can even be sweet (see page 415). Tartines are concept more

than recipe, a kind of crafts project that encourages you to use your imagination — and your leftovers. Because, unlike American sandwiches (open-faced or closed), tartines are slender, carrying just a thin layer or two of ingredients, you can use up that lone slice of ham, the one tomato left in the basket, the few spoonfuls of soft cheese, or the odd olives to construct a good-looking and very tasty tartine.

You can build your sandwich on any kind of bread. In France, most

tartines are constructed on thinnish slices of country bread that's been grilled more often than toasted, and usually on just one side. (The tartine bread Parisians love is pain Poilâne; see page 42.) But you can use a piece of baguette — sliced into rounds or cut lengthwise — or, if you're using delicate ingredients, you can base the tartine on a slice of brioche (see Bonne Idée, page 497), challah, or white or whole wheat bread.

two tartines
from la croix rouge

LA CROIX ROUGE IS ONE OF the busiest cafés in our neighborhood. It's also one of the best places to get an idea of what's in fashion, since it's around the corner from designer boutiques like Sonia Rykiel, Prada, and Yves Saint Laurent, and everyone who works in the shops crams in at lunch time — or waits outside in the hopes of cramming in. And *cramming* is really the operative word: there isn't a millimeter of space between tables! But the staff is friendly, the location unbeatable, and the best-selling Saint-Germain roast beef and Norvégienne smoked salmon tartines as stylish and thin as the café's clientele.

pain poilâne

While the baguette remains the symbol of France and the daily or thrice-daily bread of the land, there are dozens of other loaves that are made by bakers of every region. But one bread and one name that stands above all others is the *miche* from Poilâne. The *miche* is not just a bread you can sink your teeth into, it's one you can wrap your arms around: it boasts a diameter of 12 inches and tips the scale at over 4 pounds. Its crust is dark and crackly but chewy; its crumb, or *mie,* moist, tight, and the color of café au lait; and its taste is wholesome, wheaty, and just a bit sour, the signature tang of *levain,* a natural leavening akin to a sourdough starter.

The Poilâne *miche* is remarkable for its beauty as well as its substance

— you get the sense that this is a bread that could sustain you for days. For sure, it sustains thousands of Parisians each day, some of whom buy it directly from the boulangerie, where it is baked in an ancient wood-burning oven, some of whom find it in their local supermarkets, and many of whom pay an extra euro at neighborhood cafés to have their tartines made on pain Poilâne. Walk around the city, and you'll see cafés with signs saying "Ici Pain Poilâne," and where you find the signs, you'll find people having plate-sized slices of Poilâne bread, grilled and buttered for breakfast or covered with anything from roast beef to sardines for lunch. In fact, while any bread can be used to make a tartine (see page

41), the quintessential slice for the French open-faced sandwich is cut from the center of a *miche* and then cut crosswise in half, giving you a generous amount of real estate on which to build a tasty sandwich and allowing you the option of cutting the halves into strips dainty enough for tea. These days, all across America, artisan bakers are producing loaves reminiscent of Poilâne's *miche.* If you can find one, grab it; if not, make your tartines on slices of hearty rye bread or any other large close-grained loaf available. And then, when you're in Paris, do what so many food-loving visitors do: make a pilgrimage to Poilâne and taste the loaf that bread bakers around the world hold up as the standard to which they aspire.

tartine norvégienne

Whenever you see the word *norvégienne*, meaning Norwegian, in France, you can be sure smoked salmon is in the picture.

1 very large slice country bread, about ⅓ inch thick, or 2 smaller slices heavy tight-grained bread (rye works)
Butter

Enough paper-thin slices smoked salmon to cover the bread in a single layer
Capers
Freshly ground pepper
Lemon wedges

MAKES 1 SERVING

SERVING
White wine's the drink of choice here.

Lightly grill one side of the bread or toast it on one side in a toaster oven. As soon as it's toasted, spread that side with butter. Cover the bread with the salmon and, using a long heavy knife, cut the bread crosswise into strips about 1 inch wide. Scatter the capers over the salmon, sprinkle with pepper, and put a couple of lemon wedges on the side of the plate.

tartine saint-germain

1 very large slice country bread, about ⅓ inch thick, or 2 smaller slices heavy tight-grained bread (rye works)
Mayonnaise

Cornichons or gherkin
2 paper-thin slices rarest-possible roast beef
Salt and freshly ground pepper

MAKES 1 SERVING

SERVING
At La Croix Rouge, this sandwich is served with a knife and fork, but the best way to eat it is to treat it as finger food. A glass of red wine is perfect with this.

Lightly grill one side of the bread or toast it on one side in a toaster oven. As soon as it's toasted, slather that side with mayonnaise. Thinly slice a cornichon or two (or part of a gherkin) and scatter over the bread, then cover the whole surface of the bread with the beef. Season with salt and pepper and, using a long heavy knife, cut the bread crosswise into strips about 1 inch wide.

goat cheese and strawberry tartine

MAKES 4 SERVINGS

SERVING
I like this tartine with a chilled white wine, preferably one from the Loire Valley, where chenin blanc is the reigning grape and goat the *roi* of cheeses. But if you end up using cherries or dried fruits, you might want to pour red wine. In fact, topped with dried fruit, these tartines would make a nice addition to a cheese platter served before dessert.

STORING
These should be made as close to serving time as possible.

THIS TARTINE ALMOST CREATED ITSELF ONE Sunday morning on my return from the boulevard Raspail market. When I set my flimsy market bag on the counter, it toppled over — it was the baguette's fault — and out tipped the soft goat cheese from Philippe Grégoire's stand and a brown paper bag of strawberries so ripe their aroma had made me dizzy all the way home. The bread, cheese, and berries looked so beautiful strewn across my counter that I put them together immediately. And the combination was so good that I used it at dinner the following night, topping the tartine with a few drops of syrupy aged balsamic — truly unnecessary and truly good.

While most tartines are made on large slices of country bread, I think this one is best on a slice of baguette about 1/3 inch thick (think crostini). And while other tartines make good afternoon snacks, I think this one is best served later in the day with a glass of wine.

I've given instructions for making 12 cocktail-sized tartines, but since this is more an idea than a formal recipe, feel free to use more or less cheese or strawberries, to change the bread — thinly sliced pumpernickel would be great, but it's not a bread that's easily available in Paris — to use or not use the balsamic, or even to swap the berries for cherries or figs, fresh or dried, depending on the season.

12 slices baguette, about 1/3 inch thick
About 3/4 cup soft, spreadable goat cheese
About 16 ripe strawberries, hulled and cut in half

Coarsely ground or crushed black pepper
Balsamic vinegar (optional)

The day I first made this tartine, I just cut slices off the baguette and used them fresh, and you can do the same, or you can treat the baguette as you do breads for other tartines and grill or toast just one side of it. If you warm the bread, let it cool a bit so that the heat won't melt the cheese. Spread the goat cheese over the bread and top each tartine with a few berry halves. Sprinkle with black pepper and finish with a couple of drops of balsamic vinegar, if you'd like.

pissaladière

THIS RECIPE COMES FROM MY FRIEND Rosa Jackson, who teaches cooking in Nice, her hometown, and Paris, her former hometown. It's what Rosa calls "a treasured Niçoise street food, sold in every boulangerie of Vieux Nice [the old city] and at several stands specializing in quick eats." Not that it's so quick to make, since the base is a simple yeast dough that needs about an hour to puff, and the onion topping, the hallmark of a proper pissaladière, needs almost as much time in a skillet to become golden, slightly caramelized, and full of flavor. However, both the dough and the onions can be made ahead, so that with a little planning, you can get your pissaladière into the oven in a flash.

The name *pissaladière* can make you think of pizza, but it derives from the anchovy paste, *pissala*, that is sometimes stirred into the onions to intensify their flavor. Indeed, anchovies are frequently part of a pissaladière's decoration — you often see them placed on top of the onions in a crosshatch pattern — as are black olives, preferably the small black, shiny olives native to the Niçoise area, which are strewn over the pissaladière.

Pissaladière can be a starter, a snack, or, paired with a salad, a light meal. If you fall in love with the pissaladière but find yourself short on time, you can substitute puff pastry for the dough — it's not truly Niçoise, but it's often done, and often by chefs. (See Fresh Tuna, Mozzarella, and Basil Pizza, page 166, for inspiration.)

MAKES **6** SERVINGS

SERVING
Use a pizza wheel to cut the pissaladière into serving pieces and eat them out of hand or on a plate with fork and knife. If I'm serving this as a lunch, I usually make one pissaladière for 4 people and top it with a lightly dressed arugula salad.

STORING
The onions can be made up to 1 day ahead and refrigerated, as can the dough; just punch it down and cover it well. When you're ready to use the dough, bring it to room temperature. Once made, the pissaladière can be kept at room temperature for a few hours.

FOR THE DOUGH
- 1¼ cups bread flour or all-purpose flour
- 1 teaspoon salt
- 1 teaspoon sugar
- 1 packet active dry yeast (you can use rapid-rise)
- ⅓ cup warm water
- 2 tablespoons olive oil
- 1 large egg, at room temperature

FOR THE ONION TOPPING
- 2 tablespoons olive oil
- 6 medium onions, halved and thinly sliced
- 1 thyme sprig
- 1 bay leaf
- About 12 good-quality anchovies packed in oil
- Sea salt and freshly ground pepper
- About 12 Niçoise olives, pitted or not

TO MAKE THE DOUGH: Whisk the flour, salt, and sugar together in a large bowl.

Stir the yeast into the warm water and, when it's dissolved, whisk in the olive oil and egg (make sure the egg is not cold). Using your hand, a sturdy rubber spatula, or a wooden spoon, make a little well in the center of the flour, then pour in the yeast mixture and mix until you have a rough dough, a matter of minutes.

Turn the dough out onto a lightly floured work surface and knead for about 5 minutes, or until it is smooth. Rinse out the bowl, rub it lightly with oil, and turn the dough around in it until it glistens with oil. Cover the bowl, set it

aside in a warm place, and let the dough rise for at least an hour, or until it has doubled in size.

WHILE THE DOUGH IS RISING, MAKE THE ONION TOPPING: Pour the olive oil into a large skillet (nonstick is nice here) and warm it over low heat. Toss in the onions, thyme, and bay leaf, stirring to coat everything with oil, then cook, stirring often, until the onions are translucent, soft, and golden, about 45 minutes, maybe more — this isn't a job you should rush.

While the onions are cooking, chop 6 of the anchovies. When the onions are cooked, pull the pan from the heat, stir in the chopped anchovies, which will dissolve into the onions, and season lightly with sea salt and generously with pepper. Set aside until needed. (*You can keep the onions covered at room temperature for a few hours or refrigerate them for up to 1 day.*)

Center a rack in the oven and preheat the oven to 425 degrees F. Line a large baking sheet with a silicone baking mat or parchment paper.

Press down on the dough to deflate it, turn it out onto a lightly floured work surface, cover it with a kitchen towel, and let it rest for 5 to 10 minutes.

Roll the dough out on a floured surface until it is about 10 x 14 inches. The exact size of the rectangle isn't really important — what you're going for is thinness. Transfer the dough to the baking sheet and top it with the onion mixture, leaving a scant inch of dough around the edges bare.

Bake the pissaladière for about 20 minutes, or until the dough is golden. Pull the pan from the oven, decorate the top with the olives and the remaining anchovies, and bake the pissaladière for 5 minutes more, just to warm the new additions. Serve hot, warm, or at room temperature.

provençal olive fougasse

MAKES 2
FLATBREADS,
EACH SERVING 6

SERVING

Fougasse should be eaten warm or at room temperature. While it's good with cubes of cheese and delicious dipped in olive oil, it's really best just on its own with a glass of wine. For me, the very best way to eat fougasse is on a picnic, one with lots of savory nibbles at hand and plenty of chilled rosé.

STORING

You can keep the dough in the refrigerator for up to 3 days, but once baked, the bread should be eaten the same day.

EVERY ONCE IN A WHILE, YOU'LL come across a fougasse in a Parisian boulangerie, and as beautiful as it might be, it somehow looks a little lost. For sure, it's far from home. Considered a cousin of the Italian focaccia, it is a bread rooted in Provence, where olive oil trumps butter and rusticity reigns over prim, precise, and formal. A yeast-raised bread, this one scented with olive oil and rosemary and studded with olives, it's a fancifully shaped loaf that's meant to be served whole, the better to admire its form, then tugged and torn into pieces to be nibbled with wine and maybe a few slices of a nice garlicky *saucisson*.

The fougasse is not a solid loaf of bread — once it's rolled out and shaped, it's slashed so that it will have an open pattern. Most often, a fougasse is shaped into a leaf, but a ladder shape is popular too — roll the dough into a long rectangle, make 3 or 4 horizontal slashes in it, and then nudge the slashes open to form rungs. However, unless you plan to set up shop in Provence, you're free to shape the bread any way you please. When I want to go nonstandard, I roll the dough into a large circle, slash a few spokes in the dough, and make a cut in the center of the wheel. These odd-shaped breads are often called *pains fantaisies* (fantasy breads), a name I love almost as much as I love the act of making bread in fantastical shapes.

BE PREPARED: The dough needs to rise for an hour or two and chill for as long as overnight before you can shape and bake it.

1⅔	cups plus 2 teaspoons warm-to-the-touch water
1¾	teaspoons active dry yeast
1	teaspoon sugar
5½	tablespoons extra-virgin olive oil
4	cups all-purpose flour
1¼	teaspoons salt

1	cup oil-cured black olives, pitted and coarsely chopped
1	tablespoon minced fresh rosemary
	Grated zest of 1 lemon or ½ orange
	Kosher salt or other coarse salt, for sprinkling

Pour ⅔ cup of the water into a measuring cup and sprinkle over the yeast and sugar. Stir with a wooden spoon or rubber spatula, and let the yeast dissolve for about 5 minutes. When the mixture bubbles and looks creamy, add 1 more cup of the water, along with 4½ tablespoons of the olive oil.

Put the flour and salt in a mixer bowl and stir to combine. Pour in the yeast mixture, attach the dough hook, and beat at medium-low speed for 2 to 3 minutes, or until the flour is moistened. Turn the speed up to medium and beat for 10 minutes more, or until the dough cleans the sides of the bowl. The dough will be very soft and sticky, almost like a batter, and it will pool at the bottom of the bowl, but that's fine. (You can mix this dough by hand using a wooden

spoon, but you'll need time and a lot of energy, since the dough is so very soft and stretchy.)

Mix the olives, rosemary, and lemon or orange zest together, add them to the mixer, and beat for another minute or so. The olives won't blend into the dough completely, so finish the job with a sturdy rubber spatula or a wooden spoon.

Lightly oil a large bowl and scrape the dough into it. Lightly oil the top of the dough, then oil a piece of plastic wrap. Cover the bowl with the plastic, oiled side down, and put it in a warm place until the dough doubles in volume, 1 to 2 hours, depending upon the warmth of your room.

Stir the dough, cover it again, and refrigerate it for at least 6 hours, or for as long as 3 days. (I prefer to let the dough rest overnight.) If you're keeping it in the fridge for a while, it will probably rise to the top of the bowl again, in which case you can stir it down, or not — it's not crucial.

Remove the dough from the refrigerator, stir it down, and divide it in half. Turn 1 piece of dough out onto a floured surface and flour the top of the dough. Roll the dough into a rectangle that's about 12 inches long and 7 to 9 inches wide. Precision isn't important here. As you're working, lift the dough and flour the counter again if the dough is sticking. Transfer the dough to a large nonstick baking sheet or one lined with a silicone baking mat or parchment paper.

Using a pizza cutter, a single-edged razor blade, or an X-Acto knife, cut about 4 slashes, about 2 inches long, at an angle down each long side of the rectangle, rather like the veins on a leaf. If you'd like, make another 2-inch vertical slash near the top of the rectangle. Again, don't worry about precision. With your fingers, gently push and pull the slashes open, tugging the dough a little as you go. Try to get the holes to open to about an inch wide. As you cajole the dough, you might want to tug a little more at the base than at the top, so you end up with a bread that's flat at the bottom and tapers toward the top, like a leaf.

Repeat with the second piece of dough on a second baking sheet (or cover that portion and return it to the refrigerator to bake later).

Cover the dough with a kitchen towel and let it rest for 15 minutes.

Position the racks to divide the oven into thirds and preheat the oven to 450 degrees F. (If you're baking just 1 bread, bake it on the lower or middle rack.)

Mix the remaining tablespoon of olive oil with the remaining 2 teaspoons water in a small cup. Prick the dough all over with a fork and, with a pastry brush, lightly coat the fougasse with the oil and water mixture. Sprinkle the bread all over with kosher or other coarse salt.

Slide the baking sheets into the oven and bake for 10 minutes. Rotate the sheets from top to bottom and front to back and bake for another 8 to 10 minutes, or until the bread is golden — it won't get too dark. Transfer the fougasse to a cooling rack and let rest for at least 10 to 15 minutes before serving.

socca from vieux nice

I F YOU'VE BEEN TO THE MARKET in Old Nice, you probably remember seeing people strolling around snacking on pieces of steaming-hot socca, a large pancake made from chickpea flour. Or maybe you remember seeing the socca guys zipping around on their motorbikes with pans of socca on their fenders — like pizza guys in New York City. Socca came to Nice from Liguria, Italy, just across the border, where it's best known as *farinata* (and is sometimes made with chestnut flour). This socca came to me from Rosa Jackson, a culinary teacher and tour guide who lives in the old part of town near the market.

Socca is a snack, but it makes a great nibble with drinks, and it's a terrific icebreaker, since the best way to eat the pizza-sized pancake is with your fingers. There's nothing knife-and-fork about it.

Traditionally socca, which is meant to be peppered generously after it's baked, is seasoned with just salt and pepper, but Rosa likes to add some chopped rosemary to the batter, and I'm with her on this. I've also seen recipes in which a little chopped onion is added to the batter, and that's nice too.

BE PREPARED: Like crepe batters in general, the socca batter improves if you let it rest for a few hours, or overnight. And you've really got to preheat both the oven and the pan (a big pizza pan or a couple of smaller cake pans) before you bake your socca, so take that into account as well.

MAKES 4 TO 6 SERVINGS

SERVING
Cut the socca into pieces — Rosa says "rough pieces" — and encourage everyone to season the socca with plenty of freshly ground pepper.

STORING
Socca's not meant to be kept — eat and enjoy.

1	cup chickpea (garbanzo) flour (found in health food markets and supermarkets like Whole Foods, or see Sources)	3½ tablespoons olive oil
		½–¾ teaspoon salt (to taste)
		2 teaspoons finely chopped fresh rosemary
1	cup cool water	Freshly ground pepper

Put the flour, water, 1½ tablespoons of the oil, the salt, and the rosemary in a bowl and whisk until the batter is smooth — it will be the consistency of light cream. Cover the bowl and set aside at room temperature for 2 hours, or pour the batter into a covered container and refrigerate it for as long as overnight.

Have a 12- or 13-inch-diameter pizza pan at hand, or two 8- or 9-inch cake pans. About 20 minutes before you're ready to bake the socca, position a rack in the upper third of the oven if your oven has a top broiler; if not, put the rack in the lower third or center. Put the pizza pan or cake pans on the rack and preheat the oven to 500 degrees F.

Carefully remove the pan(s) from the oven, pour 2 tablespoons oil into the pizza pan, or 1 tablespoon into each of the cake pans, and tilt the pan(s) to coat with oil. Heat the pan(s) for another 5 minutes.

Pour the batter into the pan(s), trying as best you can to get an even layer, and bake the socca for 5 minutes. Turn on the broiler and run the socca under it for 3 to 4 minutes, or until it starts to burn. If it burns here and there, it will look authentically Niçoise. Serve hot, sprinkled generously with pepper.

soups

CHEESE-TOPPED
ONION SOUP (PAGE 56)

soups

cheese-topped onion soup

MAKES **6** SERVINGS

SERVING

The best accompaniment to onion soup is a warning about its heat. And the most helpful accompaniment is a saucer under the bowl — this is not a soup meant to be eaten daintily, and some of it is bound to slip over the sides of the bowl when you're negotiating the bread-and-cheese crust.

STORING

The soup, minus the bread and cheese, can be made up to 3 days ahead and kept covered in the refrigerator. Alternatively, it can be packed airtight and kept in the freezer for up to 3 months. To reheat, bring the soup to a boil, lower the heat, and simmer for 10 minutes or so before topping it with bread and cheese — you want to make sure the soup is super-hot.

BY THE TIME I GOT TO PARIS, the wreckers had dismantled much of Les Halles, the legendary food market in the heart of the city. Some of the building's graceful cast-ironwork remained, some panels still had glass, and in a couple of places, it was still possible to peer inside to get an idea of the market's immensity and, with a vivid imagination, produce a dreamscape of what it might have been like when Émile Zola called it "the belly of Paris." I longed to have been there when the market was in action, but I'd missed the moment. I was never going to hear the raucous sounds of commerce or rub shoulders with the market's characters, who, by all accounts, might have come straight from central casting. There was only one ritual left from the days of Les Halles that could still be practiced, and Michael and I did it: we ate onion soup in one of the brasseries that surround the market's remains.

In novels by Zola and Hemingway, it always seemed to be four in the morning, and ladies in evening gowns and fur shrugs, butchers in bloodstained white jackets, and rich men in tuxedos sat elbow-to-elbow on the brasseries' red-leather banquettes. But if the crowd wasn't the same, the fare was — cheese-topped onion soup served in heavy crockery bowls.

Some say that, technically, it's the bubbling melted cheese that makes onion soup Parisian, although there are plenty of cooks in Lyon who might argue. Regardless of where in France the soup is made, the cheese is traditionally Gruyère or Comté, both Alpine cow's-milk cheeses that are firm, grateable, very nutty in flavor, and supremely meltable. (You can also use Swiss cheese, but you'll get a stretchier and sweetish rather than nutty topping.)

There's nothing tricky about making perfect onion soup, but it does take time and patience to coax every little bit of caramelized flavor and color from the onions. Cook the onions until they are almost the color of mahogany, and everything after that will be perfect.

Just one more thing: If you want the soup to live up to Les Halles standards, you must serve it *brûlante,* or burning hot. All the old recipes I've seen insist on this. My guess is that at 4 a.m., when the market was closing down, workers and revelers alike needed every bit of warmth they could get, and with steaming onion soup, they got that and something filling, comforting, and delicious as well. The photo is on page 54.

4–5	large Spanish onions (about 4 pounds)	1	cup dry white wine
2	tablespoons olive oil	8	cups chicken broth
1	tablespoon unsalted butter		Freshly ground white pepper
3	garlic cloves, split, germ removed, and minced	6	slices country bread
	Salt		About 2 tablespoons Cognac or other brandy
1	tablespoon all-purpose flour	1½	cups coarsely grated Gruyère, Comté, or Emmenthal (6 ounces)

Using a long chef's knife, cut 1 onion in half from top to bottom. Lay it cut side down on the cutting board, cut it lengthwise in half again, leaving it intact at the root end, and then thinly slice crosswise (discard the root end). Repeat with the remaining onions.

Put the olive oil and butter in a large Dutch oven or soup pot and put the pot over low heat. (I use an enameled cast-iron Dutch oven.) When the butter is melted, add the onions and garlic, season with salt, and stir with a wooden spoon. Reduce the heat to the lowest setting and cook the onions, stirring frequently, until they are a deep caramel color. Have patience: depending on the heat and the onions, this may take an hour or more. And don't be tempted to try to speed things up, because if you burn the onions, your soup will have a bitter taste. On the other hand, if you don't get the onions really brown, your soup will be pale in both taste and looks.

Sprinkle the flour over the onions and stir for a minute or so to cook away the flour's raw taste. Pour in ⅓ cup of the wine and, stirring to pick up any browned bits sticking to the bottom of the pot, let the wine cook away, a matter of a minute or two. Pour in the chicken broth and the remaining ⅔ cup wine, season with salt, and bring to a boil. Reduce the heat so that the liquid just simmers, partially cover the pot, and cook for 30 minutes. Check the soup for seasoning, adding white pepper and more salt if needed. (*You can set the soup aside for up to 2 hours, until serving time, or refrigerate it for up to 3 days; bring to a boil and simmer for about 10 minutes before continuing.*)

Preheat the broiler. Line a baking sheet with aluminum foil or parchment paper, and have six deep ovenproof soup bowls at the ready.

If necessary, cut the slices of bread so that they fit into your soup bowls. It's up to you whether you want the bread to almost cover the surface of the soup or to float in the soup like a large crouton. (For true *soupe à l'oignon gratinée* Paris-style, you want the bread to cover the entire surface, and you hope that the cheese will melt and bubble so exuberantly that some of it will stick to the sides of the bowls.) Place the bread on the lined baking sheet and broil just until the slices are toasted; flip over and color the other side.

Remove the bread, and put the soup bowls on the baking sheet. Pour about 1 teaspoon Cognac (use more or less according to your taste) into each bowl. Ladle in the soup, top each with a slice of bread, and cover the bread with the grated cheese. Run the soup under the broiler just until the cheese is melted and bubbling. Serve immediately, while the soup is *brûlante*.

BONNE IDÉE
To make the soup substantial enough to serve as lunch or even supper with salad and a cheese course, add some meat to it. Shredded beef from a daube (page 244) or other braised dish, or even small cubes of leftover chicken, are good, if very untraditional. Just put them in the bottom of the bowls along with the Cognac, then ladle in the soup.

asparagus soup

MAKES 6 SERVINGS

SERVING
Whether the soup is hot or cold, I often serve it in smaller-than-usual portions because I think it adds to the soup's sophistication. I use small bowls, the kind normally used for rice, for the cold soup and demitasse cups for the hot. Of course, if you use smaller bowls, you'll get more than 6 servings.

STORING
The soup can be kept tightly covered in the refrigerator overnight. If you're serving the soup hot, reheat it gently in an uncovered pot; if you're serving it cold, make sure to shake the sealed container or stir the soup well.

I COULD HAVE CALLED THIS SOUP *"ENFIN!* It's spring." Even though it's delicate and the color of the first little leaves on a sapling, the definitive flavor of asparagus shines through.

2½ pounds asparagus	1 large shallot, sliced
Kosher salt or other coarse salt	1 garlic clove, split, germ removed, and sliced
1 tablespoon extra-virgin olive oil	Salt and freshly ground white pepper
1 tablespoon unsalted butter	
2 medium leeks, white and light green parts only, split lengthwise, washed, and sliced	Crème fraîche, if serving the soup hot
	Unsweetened whipped cream, if serving the soup cold
1 large white onion, thinly sliced	Snipped fresh chives, for garnish (optional)

Using a vegetable peeler, peel the asparagus from about an inch below their tips to the ends of their stalks; reserve the trimmings. Cut the bottoms of the stalks off at the point at which they become woody, and keep these trimmings too. Cut the spears in half. Bundle up the trimmings in a piece of cheesecloth and tie it like a hobo's sack with some kitchen twine.

Bring a large pot of water to a boil, adding 1 teaspoon of kosher or other coarse salt for every quart of water. Have a colander and at least a dozen ice cubes at the ready.

Toss the asparagus and the bundle of trimmings into the boiling water and cook for 4 minutes. Scoop the asparagus out of the pot and into the colander (don't discard the cooking liquid), run the asparagus under cold water for a minute to cool them down, and then cover them with the ice cubes; set aside in the sink or a bowl. Discard the trimmings; reserve 6 cups of the cooking liquid.

Dry the pot, add the oil and butter, and warm over low heat. Toss in the leeks, onion, shallot, and garlic, season with salt and white pepper, and stir everything around until it glistens. Cover the pot and cook gently for about 15 minutes, until the onion and its companions are very soft but not colored.

Pour in the reserved cooking liquid and bring the mixture to a boil, then reduce the heat so that it simmers, cover, and cook for 10 minutes. Remove the cover, toss in the asparagus, and simmer, uncovered, for 5 minutes.

Working in batches, puree the soup in a blender or food processor; or use an immersion blender. For a finer, even more elegant soup, run the soup through a strainer. Taste the soup for salt and pepper, reheat it very, very gently if you're serving it hot, or chill it to serve cold.

At serving time, top with a spoonful of crème fraîche if the soup is hot, or whipped cream if it's cold. If you'd like, sprinkle the cream with chives.

cheating-on-winter pea soup

PEAS, ALONG WITH ASPARAGUS, ANNOUNCE SPRING with more veracity than the first robin redbreast. As soon as the pods appear, pea soups, pea purees, and peas with onions show up on restaurant menus all across France. But I have a sneaking suspicion that, with the exception of the Michelin-starred places with phalanxes of *commis* to de-pod and even sometimes peel the peas, most places do what French home cooks do year-round: they buy ready-to-cook frozen peas. Peas are one of those vegetables that freeze really well (in fact, many cooks believe that only just-picked peas deliver better taste), and having a sack of them on hand gives you the chance to quickly add color, texture, and another flavor to many dishes (see page 221) and to make this cheery soup in the dead of winter.

The soup, made in about 15 minutes, is the liquid version of a classic French dish, peas with lettuce and onions. It's a gorgeous spring green color and looks a bit dressy served in small bowls or cups with a dollop of cream in the center. The bonus: when the weather warms up, the soup is just as flavorful chilled, and even more beautiful poured into clear glasses.

MAKES **6** TO **8** SERVINGS

SERVING

The soup can be served either hot or chilled. No matter the temperature, it's nice with a dollop of cream. You can use crème fraîche, sour cream, or heavy cream, and you can either put a spoonful in the center of each bowl or swirl it into the soup before you ladle it out. For a little something extra, scatter some crumbled bacon over the cream or on top of the soup.

STORING

The soup can be kept covered in the refrigerator (where it's possible that oxidation will darken its color a little) for up to 2 days. Reheat it, or serve it cold.

1 tablespoon unsalted butter	1 medium head romaine lettuce, trimmed and sliced
1 medium onion, coarsely chopped	
Salt and freshly ground pepper	Crème fraîche, sour cream, or heavy cream, for serving (optional)
6 cups vegetable broth, chicken broth, or water	Crumbled bacon, for serving (optional)
1 pound frozen peas	

Melt the butter in a medium Dutch oven or soup pot. Toss in the onion and cook, stirring, just until it softens, about 3 minutes. Season with salt and pepper, pour in the broth or water, and bring to a boil. Stir in the peas (it's okay if they're still frozen) and lettuce. Lower the heat to a simmer and allow the soup to gently bubble away, uncovered, for 10 minutes.

Working in batches, puree the soup in a blender or food processor or use an immersion blender until it's as smooth as you can get it; a blender will give you the smoothest soup, but even a blender can't perfectly puree pea skins. If you want a smoother soup, push it through a strainer.

Taste the soup for salt and pepper, and, if it needs to be hotter, return it to the pot and warm it over very low heat. Or chill it to serve cold. If desired, garnish each serving with a dollop of cream and/or a sprinkling of bacon.

corn soup

MAKES 4 SERVINGS

SERVING
Divide the garnish among the soup bowls if you're using it, ladle the soup over the garnish, and top each bowl with a spoonful of crème fraîche, if desired.

STORING
The soup can be kept covered in the refrigerator for up to 3 days, or it can be packed airtight and frozen for up to 2 months.

AFTER THE VEGETABLE VENDOR AT the boulevard Raspail market kept everyone in line waiting for ten minutes while she told a customer how to roast corn (see page 336), I had corn on my brain. But when I finally bought some, instead of roasting it, I made this soup, which I think of as something the French would have created had sweet corn been one of their native crops.

The soup is not thick, but it is quite substantial, very corny, and softly and naturally sweet. It can stand on its own, but its flavor is so compatible with so many other ingredients that I like to put a spoonful of something surprising in the center of the bowls before I ladle in the soup. I've included instructions for a simple garnish of fresh corn kernels, scallions, bacon, and a touch of chile pepper, but for special occasions, I urge you to try crème fraîche and caviar and/or very thin slices of scallops or shrimp (see Bonne Idée).

FOR THE SOUP

3 ears corn (preferably yellow corn for its color), husked
3 cups whole milk
2 tablespoons unsalted butter
1 large onion, preferably Spanish, finely chopped
Fine sea salt
1 celery stalk, trimmed and thinly sliced
1 carrot, trimmed, peeled, and thinly sliced
1 garlic clove, split, germ removed, and finely chopped
2 cups water
2 thyme sprigs
2 rosemary sprigs
1 bay leaf
Freshly ground white pepper

FOR THE GARNISH
(OPTIONAL BUT VERY GOOD)
Kernels from ½ ear of corn
1 scallion, white and light green parts only, thinly sliced
½ small chile pepper, halved, seeded, and thinly sliced, or a pinch of piment d'Espelette (see Sources) or cayenne
2 strips bacon, cooked and finely chopped

¼ cup crème fraîche, for serving (optional)

TO MAKE THE SOUP: You need to strip the corn kernels from the cobs — a messy job that's best done by standing each cob upright in a large bowl, grabbing a sturdy chef's knife, and cutting straight down the cob through the base of the kernels. Turn the cob and cut, and continue turning and cutting until all the kernels have been released; reserve the cob. Set the kernels aside and cut each cob into 3 pieces.

Put the cobs in a saucepan, pour in the milk, and bring to a boil. Turn off the heat, cover the pot, and let the milk steep while you work on the rest of the soup.

Melt the butter in a large Dutch oven or soup pot. Add the onion and a pinch of sea salt and cook over low heat, stirring occasionally, for about 5 minutes, or until the onion softens and glistens with butter — it shouldn't take on any color. Toss in the celery, carrot, garlic, and corn kernels, season with a pinch of salt, and cook, stirring now and then, until the vegetables are soft, about 10 minutes.

Add the water, milk, and corncobs to the pot, along with the herbs and 1 teaspoon salt. Bring to a boil, then immediately lower the heat, partially cover the pot, and cook the soup at a gentle simmer for 20 minutes.

MEANWHILE, TO MAKE THE GARNISH, IF USING: Mix all the ingredients together in a small bowl.

Taste the soup and season with salt and white pepper as needed. Remove and discard the cobs, bay leaf, and whatever herb sprigs you can fish out easily from the soup. Working in batches, puree the soup in a blender or food processor; or use an immersion blender. If you'd like the soup to be smoother, push it through a strainer, pressing down on the solids to squeeze out every last bit of flavor. Taste again for salt and pepper and, if the soup has cooled considerably, reheat it — this soup is at its best really hot.

Serve immediately, with or without the garnish, topping each bowl with a dollop of crème fraîche, if you like.

BONNE IDÉE
Because the soup is sweet, it takes well to salty additions, of which the simplest and most elegant is a spoonful of crème fraîche (or unsweetened whipped cream) and some caviar. Many of the less expensive roes, particularly Avruga, smoked herring roe (available in specialty stores), are wonderful here. If you want to go all out, place a few thin slices of raw shrimp or sea scallops (my favorite), a couple of raw bay scallops, or some very thin slices of raw or lightly cooked lobster in the bottom of each soup plate, and use the crème fraîche and caviar to top the soup. If you'd like, you can use just the seafood, seasoned with a little fleur de sel and piment d'Espelette or cayenne.

crème fraîche

While its name translates as "fresh cream," crème fraîche is almost the opposite of that: it's heavy cream that's been cultured or fermented, rendering it *not* fresh, but alluringly tangy. Crème fraîche's closest American relative is sour cream, but crème fraîche is thicker (the best crème fraîche pulls from the tub like taffy), denser, silkier, and slightly sweeter. It can also do two things that sour cream can't: it can handle heat without curdling, making it a terrific sauce thickener, and it can be whipped. In cooking, heavy cream is the best substitute for crème fraîche — you won't get crème fraîche's tang, but you won't have any separation anxiety either. In baking, the best substitute is heavy cream, although sour cream will work in some recipes. But when you want the texture and slight sourness, crème fraîche is the choice. While it's expensive and not always easy to find here, you can easily make a faux crème fraîche at home; you just have to plan ahead (page 491).

christine's simple party soups
cream-topped asparagus, red pepper, and broccoli

MAKES 4 STARTER
SERVINGS OR 8
HORS D'OEUVRE
SERVINGS

SERVING
Pour the soup — or soups — into bowls or glasses and top with the cream. If you've whipped the cream with a beater, you can form the cream into quenelles or dollops; if you've used a siphon, the cream will be very soft, and when you spoon it over the soup, it will spread on its own. No matter what you do, it's going to be stunning.

STORING
Well covered, the soups can be kept in the refrigerator for up to 3 days. Serve them cold or warm them over gentle heat before serving.

MY FRIEND CHRISTINE VASSEUR IS the kind of Parisian who can grab one of her kid's mufflers, tie it around her neck, and have it look as if she got it at Dior. And what she does with fashion, she can do with food. As proof, I offer you recipes for three of her soups, each of which has vibrant color, full flavor, a fanciful crown of spiced whipped cream, and an ingredient list so short it can be printed on a Post-it.

These three soups are nothing more than the star vegetable (plus a zucchini for color when you're making the green soups) and some broth. And, yes, Christine makes the broth from bouillon cubes. Everything's cooked for about 15 minutes, whirred in a blender, and served hot or cold. Either way, the soups get topped with spiced whipped cream: cardamom for the asparagus, curry for the broccoli, and piment d'Espelette or crushed pink peppercorns for the red pepper.

The colors are stunning, and you can play them up easily if you serve them à la Christine, in glasses: lowballs or snifters if you're serving one soup, tall shot glasses if you're offering all three. Fill the glasses just halfway, then top with the cream. For even more drama, use a siphon (a whipper with a carbon dioxide charger), and you'll have a topping so airy it just about bubbles and pops on your spoon.

FOR THE ASPARAGUS SOUP
- 4 cups water
- 2 bouillon cubes, vegetable or chicken (or 4 cups broth to replace the water and cubes)
- 1 pound asparagus, trimmed and peeled
- ½ pound zucchini, trimmed
  Salt and freshly ground pepper

FOR THE BROCCOLI SOUP
- 4 cups water
- 2 bouillon cubes, vegetable or chicken (or 4 cups broth to replace the water and cubes)
- ¾ pound broccoli florets (from 1 large bunch)
- ½ pound zucchini, trimmed
  Salt and freshly ground pepper

FOR THE RED PEPPER SOUP
- 4 cups water
- 2 bouillon cubes, vegetable or chicken (or 4 cups broth to replace the water and cubes)
- 1 pound red bell peppers, cored and seeded
  Salt and freshly ground pepper

FOR THE CREAM TOPPING
- 1 cup cold heavy cream (for each soup)
  Salt
  Ground cardamom, curry powder, piment d'Espelette (see Sources), or crushed pink peppercorns, depending on the soup(s) you're making (see above)

BONNE IDÉE
Chilled Red Pepper–Raspberry Soup. This is a terrific combination — the berries intensify the color of the soup and add both acidity and mystery to the flavor. Once the red pepper soup is chilled, puree about 2 cups fresh raspberries and push the pureed berries through a strainer to remove the seeds. Whisk the puree into the soup (taste as you go, so you get just the balance of berries to pepper you like). Serve, or chill for another hour or so. This soup is good with the piment d'Espelette or pink peppercorns you'd use with the plain red pepper soup, but it's also good with crushed black pepper or herbs like rosemary, thyme, or lemon verbena. If you'd like, scatter a few berries over the cream.

TO MAKE THE SOUPS: Each soup should be made separately, but the techniques, such as they are, are essentially the same. Bring the water and bouillon cubes (or the broth) to a boil in a medium saucepan. Cut the vegetables into smallish chunks, drop into the pot, and season with salt and pepper. (Bouillon cubes are usually saltier than broth, so season accordingly.) Lower the heat so that the liquid simmers, partially cover the pan, and cook until the vegetables can be pierced easily with the tip of a knife, about 10 minutes for the asparagus, 15 for the broccoli, and 15 to 20 for the peppers.

Puree the soup in a blender or food processor; or use an immersion blender. The asparagus and broccoli soups puree very smoothly, but because of the skins on the peppers, the red pepper soup needs a push through a strainer after it's been pureed.

If you're serving the soup warm, rinse out the saucepan, pour in the soup, and keep it warm over the gentlest heat while you whip the cream. If cold soup is on the menu, pour the soup into a pitcher and chill.

TO MAKE THE CREAM TOPPING: In a medium bowl, with an electric mixer (use the whisk attachment for a stand mixer), beat the cream on medium-high speed until it holds soft peaks. Add a pinch of salt and some of your chosen spice. Start with ½ teaspoon spice, taste, and then add more until you get the intensity you're after, whipping just until the cream holds firm peaks.

Alternatively, you can use a siphon to whip the cream. Season the cream, pour it into the siphon, and keep it chilled until serving time. (If you're seasoning the cream with pink peppercorns, it's best to salt the cream, whip it in the siphon, and then sprinkle the cream with the peppercorns before serving.) When you're ready to serve, follow the manufacturer's directions for inserting the charger and whipping the cream.

Ladle or pour the soup into bowls or glasses and top with the cream.

celery-celery soup

Pairing celery root and stalk celery gives you a soup that is both sweet (that's from the root) and bright (that's the work of the stalks). I love that two vegetables from the same family can deliver the same underlying flavor in such different packages and with such different high notes. I've had double-celery soups all over France, but the one I remember as a standout is the one from the Paris bistro Les Papilles (whose mushroom soup is also memorable; see page 72), where a little sauté of curried apples is spooned into the bowl before the soup is ladled in. It's a sweet surprise and a nice flavor tie-in, since the soup has apples too. If you'd like another surprise, top the soup with tiny croutons, which can also be curried. (See Bonne Idées for more on both the apples and the croutons.)

MAKES 8 TO 10 SERVINGS

2 tablespoons unsalted butter

3 celery stalks with leaves, trimmed and sliced

2 large onions, coarsely chopped

2 sweet apples, such as McIntosh or Fuji, peeled, cored, and cut into 1- to 2-inch cubes

Salt and freshly ground pepper

1 pound celery root, trimmed, peeled, and cut into 1- to 2-inch cubes

1 bay leaf

1 thyme sprig

6 cups chicken broth

Crème fraîche, heavy cream, or sour cream, for serving (optional)

Melt the butter in a large Dutch oven or soup pot over low heat. Toss in the sliced celery, onions, and apples, season with salt and pepper, and cook, stirring often, for about 5 minutes, or until the vegetables are soft. Add the celery root cubes and turn them around in the butter. Toss the herbs into the pot, add the broth, and bring to a boil. Lower the heat and cook at a gentle simmer for about 30 minutes, or until the celery root is soft enough to mash with the back of a spoon. If you can, pull out the bay leaf and what's left of the thyme.

Working in small batches, puree the soup in a blender or food processor until it is very smooth; or use an immersion blender. (If you're using a processor or immersion blender, you probably won't get a super-smooth soup. If you'd like, you can push the pureed soup through a strainer, but it's really not necessary.) Reheat if needed and season to taste with salt and pepper.

Ladle into bowls, and garnish with cream, if you like.

SERVING
For a little richness, you can swirl crème fraîche, heavy cream, or sour cream into the soup at serving time.

STORING
This can be kept covered in the refrigerator for a few days; in fact, I think it's best the day after it's made. You can also freeze it, packed airtight, for up to 2 months.

BONNE IDÉES
Curried Apples. Peel, core, and cut 2 apples (tart or sweet) into spoonable cubes. Melt 1 tablespoon unsalted butter in a large skillet and stir in ¼ teaspoon curry powder. Add the apples and sauté over medium heat just until crisp-tender, about 2 minutes. Taste and stir in a pinch more curry, if you'd like. Spoon some apples into the bottom of each bowl before pouring in the soup.

Curried Croutons. Cut enough crustless stale bread — white, country, or baguette — into small cubes to measure about 2 cups. Melt 1 tablespoon unsalted butter in a large skillet and stir in ¼ teaspoon curry powder. Toss in the bread and cook, stirring and turning, over medium-high heat just until the croutons are browned. Season with salt and pepper and perhaps a pinch more curry powder. Sprinkle croutons over soup.

leek and potato soup, smooth or chunky, hot or cold

MAKES 6 SERVINGS

SERVING
Serve the soup plain, or top each bowl with minced herbs, snipped chives, a sprinkling of cheese, a few croutons, or the teensiest drizzle of truffle oil.

STORING
The soup can be kept covered in the refrigerator for up to 4 days or, packed airtight, in the freezer for up to 2 months.

BONNE IDÉE
Vichyssoise. Reduce the liquid to 6 cups and use all chicken broth. Puree the soup and chill for at least several hours, or, preferably, overnight. When you're ready to serve, stir in 1 cup heavy cream. Taste again for salt — saltiness diminishes on chilling. Ladle into chilled bowls or cups and, if you'd like, top with snipped fresh chives or chopped fresh parsley.

SOUPS DON'T GET SIMPLER OR MORE French than leek and potato. One of the most elemental versions, called *soupe Parmentier* in honor of Antoine-Auguste Parmentier, who championed potatoes as a food to feed the poor in the eighteenth century, is nothing more than leeks and potatoes cooked in water and then mashed, pureed, or left chunky. Often bolstered with cream or butter, it's proof that Parmentier was on to something when he opened soup kitchens throughout Paris and nourished the masses with his *potage*.

As good as the plain soup is, it's tastier made with chicken broth and better yet with a mix of chicken broth and milk. Then there's no need to add cream or butter — you've built what the French would call the enrichment into the soup at the start.

I like this soup chunky, but you can certainly puree it. And, if you'd like, chill it and turn it into that Franco-American classic, vichyssoise, which was invented in 1917 by the French chef Louis Diat, who ran the kitchens at the Ritz-Carlton Hotel in New York City. Not surprisingly, the soup can be the base for lots of add-ins, among them spinach, watercress, fennel (one of my favorites), and, if you're willing to throw tradition completely to the winds, corn, which is bound to put you in mind of New England chowder (see Bonne Idées).

2 tablespoons unsalted butter

1 large onion, preferably Spanish, chopped (or 1–2 more leeks)

2 garlic cloves, split, germ removed, and thinly sliced
Salt and freshly ground white pepper

3 leeks, white and light green parts only, split lengthwise, washed, and thinly sliced

1 large Idaho (russet) potato, peeled and cubed

6 thyme sprigs

2 fresh sage leaves (optional)

4 cups chicken broth (or water)

3 cups whole milk (or water)

OPTIONAL TOPPINGS
Minced fresh parsley, sage, tarragon, or marjoram, or a combination
Snipped fresh chives
Grated Parmesan or Gruyère
Croutons
Truffle oil

Melt the butter in a Dutch oven or soup pot over low heat. Add the onion and garlic and stir until they glisten with butter, then season with salt and white pepper, cover, and cook for about 10 minutes, until the onion is soft but not colored.

Add the remaining ingredients, along with a little more salt, increase the heat, and bring to a boil. As soon as the soup bubbles, turn the heat to low, mostly cover the pot, and simmer gently for 30 to 40 minutes, or until all the vegetables are mashably soft. Taste the soup and season generously with salt and white pepper.

You've got many choices now: you can ladle the soup into warmed bowls and serve as is, mash the vegetables lightly with the back of a spoon, or puree the soup through a food mill (my first choice — you'll get a more interesting texture) or with a blender — regular or immersion — or food processor. If desired, garnish with the topping of your choice.

ANOTHER BONNE IDÉE
Leek and Potato Soup with Spinach, Watercress, or Corn. Five minutes or so before the soup is done, add a generous handful of washed and shredded spinach, washed and stemmed watercress, or about 1 cup corn kernels. While a soup with spinach or watercress can be pureed or not, the corn soup is best served in its naturally chunky state.

ONE MORE BONNE IDÉE
Leek and Potato Soup with Fennel. Trim a medium fennel bulb, cut it lengthwise in half, and cut away any tough parts near the base. Slice the fennel into short thin strips and add them to the pot either when you're sautéing the onion and garlic or when you toss in the leeks and potatoes. Like the original, this soup is good pureed or chunky.

croutons

Croutons are small cubes of stale bread that are either tossed with melted butter or olive oil and roasted in the oven (easy) or sautéed in oil or butter (a little messier, but so nice). I don't know when croutons became more popular in Caesar salad than in soup in America, but in France, the country that named the bits of toasted bread, soup is still the crouton's primary residence. *Croûton* comes from the word for crust, and while croutons are not made from bread crusts (indeed, the crust is often eliminated), by the time they find their way into a dish, their outer edges are pretty crusty.

Croutons are a way to make something delicious out of something you'd otherwise discard, and a few croutons scattered over a smooth soup add a touch of richness and some good crunch. You can make croutons from any kind of bread, from a rich brioche or a plain baguette to a hearty, wheaty country loaf. You can also give your croutons a little personality by flavoring the butter or oil with chopped fresh herbs, a pinch of spice, or some seasoned salt.

If you want to super-size the croutons, cut little rafts from the bread, toast them, cover them with grated cheese, then melt the cheese under the broiler. This is the classic topping for French onion soup (page 56), but there's no reason not to use the technique with other cheese-friendly soups.

creamy cauliflower soup
sans cream

MAKES **8** SERVINGS

SERVING
Because it is elegant, this
soup seems more suited to
shallow soup plates than
big bowls, but nothing
about the crockery is going
to change the enjoyment it
delivers. If you'd like, top
the soup with a drizzle of
oil (olive or walnut), some
grated cheese, toasted
nuts, crème fraîche (or
sour cream), caviar, or
truffles.

STORING
The soup can be kept
covered in the refrigerator
for 3 days or, packed
airtight, in the freezer for
up to 2 months.

CAULIFLOWER HAS AN ENTHUSIASTIC FOLLOWING IN France, where it is one of the staples of the winter market, its big, nubbled, snowy white heads standing out among the season's mostly brown vegetables. The hefty heads, the majority of which come from Brittany and are beautiful enough to be centerpieces, often serve as the base for rich sauces and cheesy toppings. Cauliflower's earthiness does lend itself well to cream and cheese (try it in a wonderful gratin, page 362), but the vegetable also has an elegant side, the one that shines in this light, smooth, pale soup, which has the look and texture of a *velouté* (cream soup) but not a drop of cream (there isn't even a potato in it to thicken it). This is the soup I served to American friends in Paris in the hopes of making cauliflower converts of them — and it worked.

I served it generously peppered and plain, but it's a soup that welcomes embellishments, simple or lavish. For simple, consider drizzling the soup with a little walnut oil or dusting it with grated Parmesan or Comté. If you want to go lavish, top the soup with crème fraîche or, better still, crème fraîche and caviar — the slight saltiness of caviar is perfection with cauliflower. Or, if you're lucky enough to have a truffle, shave it over the soup; cauliflower and black truffles are an inspired combination. To get every bit of pleasure out of the combo, you should bring the hot soup to the table and shave the truffle over each person's bowl individually so that everyone can enjoy the fragrance that's released when the truffle is cut and further intensified when it's warmed by the soup.

For another elegant version of this soup, one that pairs it with a sister treasure from coastal Brittany, mussels, see Bonne Idée.

1 tablespoon olive oil

1 tablespoon unsalted butter

2 Vidalia, Spanish, or large
  yellow onions (about
  ¾ pound), coarsely chopped

2 garlic cloves, split, germ
  removed, and thinly sliced

3 celery stalks, trimmed and
  thinly sliced

2 thyme sprigs, leaves only
  Salt and freshly ground white
  pepper

1 head cauliflower, leaves
  removed, broken into
  florets (discard the tough
  core)

6 cups chicken or vegetable broth

OPTIONAL TOPPINGS
Extra-virgin olive oil or
  walnut oil
Grated cheese
Crushed toasted walnuts
Crème fraîche or sour cream
Caviar
Shaved truffles

Put the olive oil and butter in a large Dutch oven or soup pot and warm over low heat. When the butter is melted, add the onions, garlic, celery, thyme, ½ teaspoon salt, and a few grinds of white pepper. Stir until all the ingredients glisten with oil and butter, then cover the pot and cook slowly, stirring often, for 20 minutes.

Toss the cauliflower into the pot and pour in the broth. Bring to a boil, reduce the heat so that the broth simmers gently, and cook, uncovered, for another 20 minutes, or until the cauliflower is very soft.

Puree the soup in batches in a blender or food processor; or use an immersion blender. This soup is best when it is very smooth, so if you think it needs it, push it through a strainer. (If you've used a standard blender, this shouldn't be necessary.) Taste for salt and pepper; I like to pepper the soup generously.

Serve plain or garnished with the topping of your choice.

BONNE IDÉE
Cauliflower-Mussel Soup. This isn't a Breton tradition, but since Brittany produces both cauliflower and mussels, it could be. Warm 1 tablespoon olive oil in a Dutch oven or soup pot, toss in a bay leaf, 1 small onion, cut into eighths, and a pinch of salt, and stir the ingredients around in the oil until they glisten. Stir in 1½ to 2 pounds mussels, scrubbed and debearded, and ½ cup dry white wine, cover the pot, and cook just until the mussels open, about 4 minutes. Shell the mussels and set them aside in a covered bowl. Discard the shells and strain the broth; discard the solids. Measure the mussel broth and use it in place of an equal quantity of the chicken or vegetable broth. At serving time, divide the mussels among the bowls and spoon the hot soup over them.

côte d'azur cure-all soup

MAKES **6** SERVINGS

SERVING
Ladle the soup into warm bowls or mugs — mugs are untraditional, but it seems to me that they're perfect for cure-alls — and drizzle about a teaspoon of olive oil over each serving.

STORING
Because of the egg yolks, the soup is not meant to be kept, but if you refrigerate any leftovers, you'll find that the cold soup is pretty good the next day.

THE SOUTH OF FRANCE EQUIVALENT OF chicken soup, this is the go-to cure for everything from the common cold to the just-as-common hangover. Known as *aigo bouido*, or boiled garlic, in Provençal dialect, it's a very old and very traditional recipe that relies on garlic, and a lot of it, to give it flavor, fragrance, and healing powers. The recipe was given to me by my friend the baker and cookbook author Nick Malgieri, who worked on the Côte d'Azur when he was starting out in pastry and who collected recipes from his fellow cooks as well as from the family with whom he lived.

It is usual to make this soup with water, but if you'd like a richer soup, you can use chicken broth. What's important is to use lots of plump, fresh, unblemished garlic. You need a fat head so that when you slice it, you end up with about ¾ cup slivers, which is a lot of garlic in anyone's book. Just in case you're wondering, after simmering, the garlic retains its flavor but loses its boldness.

A note on the egg yolks: Nick suggests 6 for the soup, 1 per person, but I buck tradition and use just 3. I'd suggest you start there and then decide if you want to add more (the yolks are considered a medicinal part of the brew). Because they are added at the end, the number can be a last-minute decision.

1	large unblemished garlic head (with at least 10 cloves)		Salt
6	fresh sage leaves	3–6	large egg yolks
2	bay leaves	1	cup freshly grated Parmesan
2	large thyme sprigs		Freshly ground pepper
6	cups water or 3 cups water plus 3 cups chicken broth or vegetable broth		Extra-virgin olive oil, for serving

Separate the garlic into cloves and peel them. Split each clove and remove the little germ at the center, then thinly slice the garlic. (If you've got one of those mini mandolines or garlic slicers, now's a good time to use it.) Toss the slivers into a Dutch oven or soup pot.

Tie the sage, bay leaves, and thyme together with kitchen twine, or bundle them into a piece of cheesecloth and close with twine, and put this bouquet garni into the pot. Pour in the water or water and broth, add 1 teaspoon salt, and bring to a boil. Lower the heat and let the soup simmer gently for 30 minutes.

Pull out the bouquet garni (discard it), taste the soup, and decide whether or not you want to puree it. Nick points out that it's more traditional not to, but the choice is yours (I'm a non-puree-er). If you puree it, use a blender or food processor (or an immersion blender), then return the soup to the pot.

Bring the soup back to a boil, then lower the heat to a simmer. Whisk 3 yolks and the Parmesan together in a medium bowl and, whisking constantly, add a few ladlefuls of the soup. Now, whisking the soup, gradually add the yolks and cheese in a steady stream. Whisk for a minute and decide whether or not you want to add more yolks. If you do, whisk the additional yolk(s) in a bowl with a little soup before adding them. The yolks will thicken the soup somewhat, but not much. Remove the pot from the heat — if you keep it over heat too long, especially if you're not whisking, you risk curdling the yolks — and whisk for 1 minute more. Taste the soup for salt, season with pepper, and serve immediately, with a drizzle of olive oil over each portion.

taking garlic down a notch

As I was making pesto one day, a friend did a double take when he saw me removing the germ from the center of each clove of garlic. He'd never seen anyone do that, but I'd been doing it for so long that I no longer thought about it.

Removing the germ (some people call it the sprout), the slender teardrop-shaped central piece, is a trick I learned working in French kitchens. It's unnecessary with new garlic in the spring — when the cloves are soft and the germ is minuscule — but taking it out of older cloves can make the garlic taste less bitter. Just slice the clove in half lengthwise and use the tip of a paring knife to scoop out the germ.

Blanching is another way to tone down garlic's bite, and it's something I do when I'm using garlic raw but want it to be a tad mellower. Just pop the cloves into a pot of boiling water for a minute or two, drain, and carry on.

I'm not sure if these tricks make garlic more digestible — lots of people claim it's so — but they rid it of its harshest, sharpest, and most bitter flavors. I like to think they allow garlic to be its best — kinder, gentler — self.

I often give garlic's cousins, shallots and onions, a little pre-treatment to make them gentler too: after I slice, dice, or chop them, I rinse them in cold water. The rinse rids them of that bitter liquid that seeps out when you're cutting them, leaving just their basic sweet and sharp flavors. In fact, if I'm going to use onions raw in a salad, I'll do one more thing — after I've rinsed them, I'll dunk them in a bowl of ice water and leave them there for a few minutes. This little dip makes them crisper, and crisp is always welcome in a salad.

paris mushroom soup

MAKES **6** SERVINGS

SERVING
Arrange the salad in the bowls, and ladle the soup over the salad — if you're looking for a little drama, do this at the table. If you'd like, finish the soup with a spoonful of crème fraîche.

STORING
The soup can be covered and refrigerated for up to 3 days or packed airtight and frozen for up to 2 months.

THIS SMOOTH SOUP IS A TRUE Parisian creation: it's made with *champignons de Paris*, or what we know as plain white or button mushrooms, and it's inspired by a soup I had in one of my favorite Paris bistros, Les Papilles (whose name means taste buds). At the little restaurant, the soup comes to the table in a big tureen, and you're encouraged to dip the ladle into it as often as you like. I love that way of serving — it's so welcoming and so generous.

When we had the soup at Les Papilles, our shallow soup plates were brought to the table sans soup but with a small mushroom "salad": thin slices of raw mushrooms seasoned with salt, pepper, chopped chives, and parsley and topped with a tiny bit of crème fraîche. When the hot soup was poured over the salad, the mushrooms cooked just slightly. You can easily adopt the practice at home, or you can be a little more casual about it and just float the seasoned mushroom slices on top of the soup. Either way, you'll get to enjoy that nice contrast between the cooked soup and the raw vegetable.

Just so you know, the name *champignons de Paris* is more honorific than correct these days. While the mushrooms did get their start near Paris — Louis XIV had them in the gardens at Versailles — and while they were found growing in the catacombs beneath Paris when construction for the metro began, today the mushrooms are more likely to come from the Loire Valley.

FOR THE SOUP
- 2 tablespoons unsalted butter
- 1½ large onions, coarsely chopped
- 3 large garlic cloves, split, germ removed, and coarsely chopped
  Salt and freshly ground white pepper
- 1½ pounds white mushrooms, wiped clean, trimmed, and sliced
- ⅓ cup dry white wine
- 2 parsley sprigs
- 1 rosemary sprig
- 6 cups chicken broth or water (if you're using water, you can add 2 large or 4 regular-sized chicken bouillon cubes)

FOR THE SALAD
- 6 large white mushrooms, wiped clean and trimmed
- 2 scallions, white and light green parts only, thinly sliced (optional)
- 2 tablespoons minced fresh parsley
- 1 tablespoon minced fresh chives
  Salt and freshly ground white pepper

  Crème fraîche, for serving (optional)

TO MAKE THE SOUP: Melt 1 tablespoon of the butter in a large Dutch oven or soup pot over low heat. Toss in the onions and garlic, season with salt and white pepper, and cook, stirring often, for about 5 minutes, until the vegetables are

soft. Add the mushrooms and the remaining tablespoon of butter, raise the heat to medium, and cook, continuing to stir, for another 3 minutes or so, until the mushrooms release their liquid. Increase the heat to high and cook until almost all of the liquid evaporates. Pour in the wine and let it boil until it, too, almost evaporates.

Toss the herbs into the pot, add the broth or water (and the bouillon cubes, if you're using them), and bring to a boil. Lower the heat, cover the pot almost completely, and cook at a gentle simmer for 20 minutes. If you can, pull out the rosemary sprig (it will have lost its leaves).

Working in small batches in a blender or food processor, puree the soup until it is very smooth; or use an immersion blender. If you're using a processor or an immersion blender, you probably won't get a super-smooth soup. If you'd like, you can push the pureed soup through a strainer, but it's really not necessary. Taste for salt and white pepper. Pour the soup back into the pot and heat it gently — it shouldn't boil, but it should be very hot.

TO MAKE THE SALAD AND SERVE: Divide the mushrooms, scallions (if using), parsley, and chives among six soup plates; season lightly with salt and white pepper. Ladle the soup into the bowls, and top each with a dollop of crème fraîche, if desired.

spur-of-the moment vegetable soup,

aka stone soup (the carrot version)

MAKES **8** SERVINGS

SERVING

If you'd like, top the
pureed soup with a dollop
of crème fraîche or sour
cream or a spoonful of
unsweetened whipped
cream and a sprinkling of
chopped fresh rosemary
or thyme. The soup is also
good with a swirl of Basil
Pesto (page 488) or a
drizzle of olive or nut oil.

STORING

The soup can be covered
and refrigerated for up to
3 days or packed airtight
and kept in the freezer for
up to 3 months. Bring the
soup to a boil, then lower
the heat and simmer for
10 minutes or so before
serving.

WHENEVER IT LOOKS LIKE THERE'S NOTHING in the house to eat, I declare that I'll make stone soup. The reference is to a children's story about a beggar who comes to a house and offers to make soup from a stone in exchange for being invited in. His host and hostess are intrigued by the idea, welcome him, and the tale begins. First the man places a stone in a tall soup pot. He adds water and suggests that the soup would taste really good with a little onion. When the onion is added, he suggests some carrots. And, so it goes, until he's got a thick, savory soup packed with vegetables simmering on the stove.

My "stone" is a couple of always-in-the-kitchen ingredients plus one star vegetable, and the soup is built on the traditional French formula for a soup made with ingredients from the market or *potager,* the kitchen garden. The base of the soup is slowly cooked aromatics: onions, for sure; garlic, if you'd like; and celery, if you have it. The liquid can be water — in a French home, it would likely be water flavored with a few bouillon cubes or maybe a bit of whatever cooking juices remain from a roast or a chicken — or it can be canned chicken broth (an ingredient that's hard to come by in French supermarkets) or soup from a dried mix (an often-used French shortcut). The thickener is optional, but the standard is one smallish potato. Or, if there's rice left over from dinner the night before, the potato will be spared, and the rice will get tossed in.

The main event is the vegetable, and it can be just about anything or even a couple of anythings: I use carrots routinely, but the featured ingredient can be broccoli, celery (root or stalk), potatoes (in which case, leeks would be good too), parsnips, beets, or cabbage (and bacon). After that, the rest depends on whim and what's around. Herbs are a good addition, ditto spices. A little ginger is good with carrots, more garlic is fine with broccoli, a scrape of nutmeg is nice with cabbage, and dill can be right with beets. The soup can be left chunky or pureed into velvety smoothness, and if there's a spoonful of crème fraîche or a bit of heavy cream in the house, it can be added for a drop of luxe.

As you can see, it's more an idea for a recipe than a real recipe, and it's meant to be kept in mind when you're in the market and at your wits' end wondering what to cook.

2 tablespoons unsalted butter or olive oil, or a combination

1 pound carrots, trimmed, peeled, and thinly sliced

1 big onion (I like to use a Spanish onion), coarsely chopped

2 celery stalks, trimmed and thinly sliced

1–2 garlic cloves, split, germ removed, and thinly sliced (optional)

1 1-inch piece fresh ginger, peeled and coarsely chopped (optional)

1 rosemary sprig (optional)

1 thyme sprig (optional)

Salt

6 cups chicken broth (plus perhaps 1 cup more, for thinning)

1 small potato, peeled and cut into 1-inch cubes

Freshly ground pepper

Put a large Dutch oven or soup pot over medium heat and add the butter and/or oil. When the butter is melted, or the oil is hot, toss in the carrots, onion, celery, and, if you're using them, the garlic, ginger, rosemary, and/or thyme. Season with salt, reduce the heat to low, and give the ingredients a couple of turns to coat them with butter or oil. Cover the pot and cook for 15 to 20 minutes, stirring a few times, until the vegetables are very soft but not colored.

Remove the lid, pour in the chicken broth, turn up the heat, and bring to a boil. Toss in the potato cubes and adjust the heat so that the soup is at a simmer. Partially cover the pot and let the soup simmer gently for another 20 minutes, or until the potato can be mashed easily with a spoon.

Now you must decide if you'd like to serve the soup just as it is or if you'd like to puree it — I usually opt for the puree. In either case, do the best you can to fish out the rosemary and thyme sprigs, if you used them. If you're serving the soup in its chunky state, taste it and season as needed with salt and pepper. Or puree the soup in a blender (which will give you the silkiest texture) or food processor, or use a food mill or an immersion blender. Taste it for salt and pepper and reheat it before serving. If you find the soup a little too thick for your taste, when you're reheating it, pour in enough additional chicken broth (or water) to get the texture you like.

jerusalem artichoke soup with parsley coulis

MAKES **8** SERVINGS

SERVING
Ladle the soup into soup plates or bowls. Put a spoonful of cream in the center of each bowl and drizzle a circlet of parsley coulis around the cream — leave it to your guests to swirl everything together.

STORING
The soup will keep covered for up to 3 days in the refrigerator or, packed airtight, for up to 2 months in the freezer. The coulis can be kept for up to 3 days in the fridge.

BONNE IDÉE
You can replace the parsley coulis with a drizzle of truffle oil. If you've got truffles, you can't do better than to top each serving with a few thin rounds. The soup also takes to a topping of coarsely grated Parmesan or a side order of country bread, toasted and topped with butter or truffle butter.

JERUSALEM ARTICHOKES, SOMETIMES CALLED SUNCHOKES, have a place as deeply etched in the memories of many French people as potatoes are engraved in the minds of the Irish, and for exactly the same reason: they were the food of survival. A gnarly tuber that tastes like an artichoke (a mild artichoke, to my mind) but looks like a mix of sweet potato (its color ranges from beige to rusty red), ginger (it's got that knobbiness), and water chestnut (its texture is similar), the Jerusalem artichoke was one of the few vegetables in the markets during World War II and for some years after.

And while there are older French people who won't touch the vegetable — "I ate enough of them to last a lifetime," one elderly woman told me — young chefs, for whom the tuber is memory-free, have taken to it, turning it into soups and purees; pairing it with herbs, mushrooms, and potatoes; and finding that, like the globe artichoke, it's great with truffles.

When I started cooking in Paris, I knew nothing about the Jerusalem artichoke's history or the sentiment surrounding it, and so I happily made this thick, deeply flavored soup and blithely served it to my French friends — all of whom loved it and many of whom were surprised to find themselves enjoying it, since they'd never been fed the vegetable, just the wartime stories.

Jerusalem artichokes in France are about the size of a medium potato and usually have a reddish color; in America, they're smaller and beiger. No matter what they look like, they need to be washed — scrubbed, really — before using. You can peel them, but it's not necessary. Sometimes I take a vegetable peeler and give each knob a quick once-over, getting off most of the peel but not fussing with whatever is deep in the crannies. If you do peel the chokes, drop them into a bowl of water with a squirt of lemon juice to keep them from darkening.

FOR THE SOUP
- 3 tablespoons unsalted butter
- 2 large onions, halved lengthwise and thinly sliced
- 2 celery stalks, trimmed and thinly sliced
- 1 leek, white and light green parts only, split lengthwise, washed, and sliced
- 2 garlic cloves, split, germ removed, and sliced
  Salt and freshly ground white pepper

- 1¾–2 pounds Jerusalem artichokes (sunchokes), scrubbed and cut into 1-inch cubes
- 6 cups chicken broth

FOR THE PARSLEY COULIS
- 1 packed cup fresh parsley leaves
- 2½ tablespoons extra-virgin olive oil
  Salt and freshly ground white pepper

  About ½ cup crème fraîche or heavy cream, for serving

TO MAKE THE SOUP: Melt the butter in a large Dutch oven or soup pot over low heat. Toss in the onions, celery, leek, and garlic and stir until they're glistening with butter. Season with salt and white pepper and cook, stirring now and then, until the vegetables are soft, about 10 minutes. Add the Jerusalem artichokes, season again with salt and white pepper, and cook, stirring occasionally, for about 15 minutes more — you want the vegetables to be soft but not colored. Pour in the broth and bring it to a boil, then lower the heat and cook, partially covered, for 45 minutes, or until the artichokes fall apart when pierced with a fork.

MEANWHILE, MAKE THE PARSLEY COULIS: Put a saucepan of salted water on to boil; fill a bowl with ice water. Toss the parsley into the boiling water and blanch for 30 seconds, then drain and drop into the ice water (this will set the color). Remove the parsley and dry well between paper towels, then, using a mini food processor (my favorite tool for this), regular processor, or blender, puree the leaves with the olive oil. Season with salt and white pepper, and set aside.

When the soup is done, remove the pot from the heat and puree it using a blender or food processor; or use an immersion blender. This soup is best when it's smoothest, so puree it well, and if you think it needs it, push it through a strainer after it's been blended. Taste for salt and pepper.

Reheat the soup if necessary, then ladle into plates or bowls and garnish with the cream and parsley coulis.

swirl-ins

The French are very fond of soups they call *velouté,* or velvety, those beautifully smooth purees that, were no one around to scold you, you would slurp. Because the ingredients have been pureed — and often pushed through a strainer après blending to ensure their impeccable velvetiness — every spoonful is as smooth as the last was and the next will be. I, for one, enjoy this textural uniformity and find, in fact, that the soup gets more interesting with each spoonful even though the consistency never changes.

Be that as it may, it's fun to add a little surprise to these smoothies, and the French often do this by swirling in another flavor, color, or texture. The most common swirl-in is the ever-at-hand and always delicious crème fraîche, but a few drops of olive oil, balsamic vinegar, or soy sauce drizzled over a soup will do the trick as well. I'm partial to spooning a little pesto or other herb coulis into soups.

To make the coulis, I puree fresh herbs with salt, pepper, and enough olive oil to make the mix swirlable. (Do this in a food processor, mini or regular; a blender; or mortar and pestle; or use an immersion blender.) And, depending on the soup, I might mix in some grated citrus zest too — zest is a great picker-upper for winter vegetable soups.

But not all swirl-ins have to go on top of the soup. These days, lots of stylish bistros bring soup plates to the table devoid of the soup but sporting a spare still life of crunchies. In the bottom of the bowl, there might be some tiny croutons, a fluff of chopped herbs, teensy cubes of onions or peppers or mushrooms, slivers of garlic, or pieces of nuts — little additions that will be covered when the soup is ladled into the bowl and will emerge when you swirl it around. It's surprising, delicious, and another way to add even more flavor and panache to comforting soups.

béatrix's red kuri soup

MAKES **6** SERVINGS

SERVING
If you're using the apples and nuts, spoon some into the bottom of each soup bowl and ladle over the hot soup; top each with a little cream.

STORING
The soup can be kept covered in the refrigerator for up to 3 days (it will thicken as it stands, so you might want to thin it when you reheat it) and for up to 2 months packed airtight in the freezer.

BONNE IDÉE
Butternut Squash and Chestnut Soup. If you're intrigued by the flavor combination of squash and chestnuts, the pair that come packed together in Red Kuri squash, but you can't find the squash, you can use butternut squash. Choose one that's about 3 pounds, peel and seed it, and cut into small cubes; and add 7 ounces shelled chestnuts to the mix. You can use jarred or vacuum-packed chestnuts. Look for packs of chestnut pieces — they're perfect for pureeing and less expensive than intact nuts.

THERE ARE SOME FOODS THAT INVARIABLY produce a sigh of delight and a smile when you mention them to the French. It's easy to imagine this being the case with chocolate or fresh-from-the-farm crème fraîche, oysters, truffles, or even simple dishes like rice pudding and roast chicken. But when a squash gets a swoon, you know you've hit on something. The squash of sighs is the Red Kuri, or what the French call *potimarron*, a name that probably describes the vegetable's genetic makeup and certainly gives you a heads-up on what it's going to taste like. The *poti* comes from the French word for pumpkin, *potiron*, and *marron* is the word for chestnut. The squash is remarkable, it's great tasting, it's beautiful, and it has a characteristic that neither pumpkins nor chestnuts have: it doesn't need to be peeled, always the most difficult task when you're dealing with hard-shelled squash. For reasons only botanists can fathom, the shell of the *potimarron* softens in cooking and becomes completely edible, a lovely culinary anomaly.

So, there I was at a French dinner party and I mentioned that I'd seen *potimarron* in the market that morning. "To me," I said, "it signals that fall is really here." "Ah, to me," said my friend Béatrix Collet, "it means I can make the first *potimarron* soup of the season." And, no sooner did she say that, than her husband, Jean-Paul, who was engaged in conversation but who must have caught the critical words *potimarron* and soup, turned, smiled, and asked if it would be that weekend. After everyone around the table sang the squash's praises, I asked Béatrix about her soup. "It's so simple, it's almost foolish to give you the recipe," she claimed, "but it's just so good, you must try it." That was on a Thursday night, and I made the soup on Friday night and have been making it ever since. It is easy in the extreme and as good as Béatrix claimed — thick, velvety, and a pretty pumpkin color, and it does, indeed, taste as though you cooked the squash with a pile of chestnuts.

Béatrix's soup has nothing in it but squash, leeks, milk, and water, and, as she said, that's *suffisant*, or sufficient. But because I'm an incorrigible tweaker, I routinely add nutmeg as a seasoning and apples and nuts as a garnish. See Bonne Idée for more ways to play around with this simple recipe, as well as how to make this soup when you can't find Red Kuri squash at the market.

FOR THE SOUP
1 Red Kuri squash (about 3 pounds)
3 slender or 1½ larger leeks, white parts only, split lengthwise, washed, and cut into 1-inch-long pieces
3 cups whole milk, or as needed
3 cups water, or as needed

Salt and freshly ground pepper
Freshly grated nutmeg

OPTIONAL GARNISH
1 tart apple, peeled, cored, and cut into tiny dice
About ⅓ cup chopped toasted hazelnuts or walnuts
About ½ cup crème fraîche or heavy cream

TO MAKE THE SOUP: Scrub the squash under running water, using a brush if necessary to scrape off any dirt. With a sharp chef's knife, cut off the pointy tip of the squash, then cut the squash in half from top to bottom. Scoop out the seeds and the strings that bind them, then cut the squash into 1- to 2-inch chunks, skin and all. Toss the squash into a large Dutch oven or soup pot.

Add the leeks to the pot, then add the milk and water, salt generously, and bring to a boil. Lower the heat to a simmer and cook for 25 to 35 minutes, or until the squash is soft enough to mash when pressed lightly with the back of spoon.

Using a blender or a food processor, puree the soup, in batches if necessary, until it is very smooth; or use an immersion blender. Depending on how much liquid boiled away, you may have a thick soup and a decision to make: leave it thick (I do) or thin it to whatever consistency pleases you with more milk or more water. Taste for salt and season with pepper and nutmeg. Heat the soup if it cooled in the blender or processor or if you thinned it — this soup is at its best truly hot.

Spoon the apple and nuts into the soup bowls, if using, ladle in the soup, and garnish with the cream, if you like.

ANOTHER
BONNE IDÉE
You can top the soup with olive-oil-sautéed bread cubes — toss some shredded sage into the skillet along with the bread. Or top with toasted thin slices of baguette that have been sprinkled with grated cheese and run under the broiler — use a nutty cheese, like Gruyère or Emmenthal, or a blue cheese, like Gorgonzola or Roquefort. Or sauté some cooked chopped chestnuts (you can use bottled chestnuts) in a little butter or oil, season with salt and pepper and chopped fresh thyme or sage, and spoon a little over the soup or, better yet, over the crème fraîche.

spiced squash, fennel, and pear soup

MAKES **6** TO **8** SERVINGS

SERVING
Either squeeze a little fresh lemon juice into each bowl or put a wedge of lemon next to each bowl so guests can squeeze for themselves. Finish the soup with cream and/or pumpkin seeds, or serve as is.

STORING
The soup can be kept covered in the refrigerator for up to 3 days or packed airtight and stored in the freezer for up to 2 months. As it chills, it will thicken, so you might want to thin it with a little broth or water when you reheat it.

A FEW SUMMERS AGO, A VENDOR at my farmers' market in Connecticut started selling Long Island Cheese, a pale orange, pumpkinish squash that's big, fat, and as swirly as a Bundt pan. The instant I saw the hefty wedges arranged along the table, I smiled — they looked just like the squashes that turn up in French markets when the chestnuts start falling. I was ready to exclaim about their resemblance when Michael, the farmer, who grew up in Paris, beat me to the punch: "They're just like the ones in France, aren't they?" he asked with some pride. Indeed, and they're as good for soup as their Gallic cousins.

Whichever side of the ocean I'm on, I roast the squash before I cook it in the soup. Roasting not only boosts the vegetable's flavor, it also makes it so much easier to peel.

The soup I like to make with squash (or pumpkin) is sweet, because I add pears; lightly vegetal, because of the fennel and celery; and just a little exotic, because it's seasoned with ginger, nutmeg, and cumin. I cook it with a couple of strips of orange peel, which mellow as they simmer, and give it a squirt of fresh lemon juice right before serving.

About 3 pounds squash, such as Long Island Cheese Pumpkin, acorn, or butternut (if you are using peeled squash, count on 1½ pounds)

About 3 tablespoons olive oil
Salt

1 large Spanish onion, coarsely chopped

1 spring onion, trimmed and coarsely chopped, or 1 large shallot, coarsely chopped

1 medium fennel bulb, trimmed, tough core removed, and sliced

2 celery stalks, trimmed and thinly sliced

1 large garlic clove, split, germ removed, and sliced

1½ teaspoons ground ginger
½ teaspoon ground cumin
¼ teaspoon freshly grated nutmeg
Freshly ground pepper

5–6 cups chicken broth or vegetable broth

2 ripe pears, peeled, cored, and coarsely chopped

2 strips orange or tangerine peel, pith removed

1–2 lemons

Crème fraîche or heavy cream, for serving (optional)

Toasted salted pumpkin seeds, for serving (optional)

Preheat the oven to 425 degrees F. Line a baking sheet with foil.

If you're using a whole squash, cut it in half, scoop out the innards, and rub the exposed flesh with a little olive oil. If you're using peeled and cut squash, just toss it with a little oil. Sprinkle the squash with a pinch of salt, put it on the baking sheet, and slide it into the oven. Whole squash will need to roast for 60 to 75 minutes, cut squash for about 45 minutes. With either, trust your knife, not the clock: when you can pierce the flesh easily with the tip of the knife, it's ready to come out of the oven. As soon as the squash is cool enough to handle, peel it and cut it into cubes, about 2 inches on a side.

Warm 2 tablespoons of the olive oil in a Dutch oven or soup pot over low heat, then stir in the onions, Spanish and spring (or shallot). Season lightly with salt and cook for 5 minutes, or until the onions start to soften but not color. Add the fennel, celery, garlic, and a pinch more salt and cook, stirring often, for another 5 to 10 minutes, or until all the vegetables are soft but still pale. Stir in the ginger, cumin, nutmeg, ¼ teaspoon salt, and a few grinds of pepper, then add the roasted squash. Pour in 5 cups broth, increase the heat, and bring to a boil, then reduce the heat so that the soup simmers gently; add the pears and orange peel. Partially cover the pot and simmer for about 20 minutes, or until the pears and squash are soft enough to be mashed with the back of a spoon.

Puree the soup, in batches, in a blender or a food processor; or use an immersion blender. Taste for salt and pepper. If the soup is too thick for you, stir in up to 1 cup more broth and reheat until hot.

Ladle the soup into bowls and finish with a little lemon juice, or serve with lemon wedges. Garnish with the cream and pumpkin seeds, if you like.

chestnut-pear soup

MAKES 6 SERVINGS

SERVING
I like to serve this soup in shallow soup plates with nothing more than a circle of cream in the center. If you want, you can put a little mound of shredded pear or a small spoonful of chopped chestnuts on top of the cream.

STORING
The soup can be refrigerated, covered, for up to 3 days or packed airtight and frozen for up to 2 months. Reheat over low heat before serving.

I WAS INSPIRED TO CREATE THIS SOUP by something Pierre Hermé, the wildly talented Parisian pastry chef, said to me years ago. We were working on a pear and chestnut tart, and he said, "Chestnuts have a very linear flavor," which I took as a very politic way of saying they can be bland. "And so," he continued, "they need something to give them a little sex appeal — pears!" It worked in the tart, and so, contemplating a jar of chestnuts and the winter wind rattling our kitchen windows in Paris, I figured the logic would hold for soup.

This soup, in the end, is smooth, soothing, elegant, and sexy, in a sophisticated way. Of course, you can make it with freshly roasted chestnuts, but peeled chestnuts that are dry-packed in a jar, vacuum-packed in a bag, or frozen work perfectly and help make easy work of the soup.

2 tablespoons unsalted butter
1 onion, thinly sliced
2 leeks, white and light green parts only, split lengthwise, washed, and thinly sliced (if you don't have leeks, add 3 more onions to the mix)
5 celery stalks, trimmed and thinly sliced
Salt and freshly ground pepper
2 ripe pears, peeled, cored, and cubed

2 thyme or rosemary sprigs
6 cups chicken broth or vegetable broth
1 jar (about 15 ounces) roasted or steamed chestnuts, to make about 2 cups (or use vacuum-packed or frozen chestnuts)

OPTIONAL GARNISH
Crème fraîche or heavy cream
Shredded pear and/or chopped chestnuts

Melt the butter in a Dutch oven or soup pot over low heat, then add the onion, leeks, and celery. Stir until the ingredients glisten with butter, season with salt and pepper, cover, and cook for about 10 minutes, until the onion is soft but not colored.

Toss in the pears and thyme or rosemary and stir to blend them with the vegetables. Pour in the broth, add the chestnuts, increase the heat, and bring to a boil. As soon as the soup bubbles, turn the heat to low, mostly cover the pot, and simmer gently for another 45 minutes or so, or until the chestnuts can be mashed easily with the back of a spoon.

Working in batches, puree the soup in a blender or food processor until it's truly smooth; or use an immersion blender. Taste the soup for salt and pepper. If it has cooled in the process of pureeing, pour it back into the pot and reheat it gently — like most soups, this one is best when it's really hot.

Ladle the soup into plates or bowls and garnish, if you like, with cream and the pear and/or chestnuts.

provençal vegetable soup

THIS CLASSIC DISH FROM THE SOUTH OF FRANCE is so typical of what we love in America that it's easy to imagine it coming from Napa Valley. It's technically a soup, but it's so jam-packed with vegetables that it could double as a stew and a whole summer meal. The only ingredient that must appear in it is the *pistou,* or French pesto. (In fact, the French call this *soupe au pistou.*) You can play around with the vegetables, although I'd suggest you keep the zucchini, green beans, garlic, tomato, potato, and beans. I use canned beans — chickpeas or cannellini — but dried flageolets or white or red beans are more traditional. If you're using dried beans, soak them in cold water for about an hour, then simmer until almost tender; drain before you add them to the soup.

In this version, I've used macaroni and every vegetable that I've ever had in a *soupe au pistou* plus one: corn, which I love for its color, crunch, and sweetness.

MAKES ABOUT
6 SERVINGS

SERVING
You can add the pesto to the soup in the pot, or you can ladle the soup into bowls and add a big spoonful to each serving. Either way, top each bowl with a few drops of olive oil and scatter over the fresh basil leaves. You can add some Parmesan or pass it at the table.

STORING
The soup can be kept covered in the refrigerator for up to 2 days, but after you reheat it, the pasta will be pretty mushy. If the soup thickens too much in the fridge, as it probably will, thin it with a little water or broth.

2 tablespoons extra-virgin olive oil

1 large onion, finely chopped

4 garlic cloves, split, germ removed, and finely chopped
Salt and freshly ground white pepper

6 cups vegetable broth, chicken broth, or water

3 parsley sprigs

2 thyme sprigs

1 rosemary sprig

1 bay leaf

2 slender carrots, trimmed, peeled, halved lengthwise, and cut into ¼-inch half-moons

1 small potato, peeled and cut into ½-inch cubes

⅓ cup small pasta (elbow, fusilli, or mini penne)

¼ pound green beans, trimmed and cut into 1½-inch lengths

1 cup rinsed canned chickpeas or cannellini beans (or ½ cup dried beans; see above)

1 medium zucchini, trimmed, halved lengthwise, and cut into ½-inch half-moons

2 medium tomatoes, peeled, seeded, and cut into small cubes, or a handful of cherry tomatoes, cut into cubes (no need to peel or seed)

1 ear fresh corn, husked and kernels sliced off

Basil Pesto (page 488), to finish
Extra-virgin olive oil, to finish

12 fresh basil leaves, torn or cut into shreds
Grated or shaved Parmesan, for serving

Pour the olive oil into a large casserole — a stockpot or a Dutch oven that holds at least 5 quarts — and warm it over medium heat. Add the onion and garlic, season fairly generously with salt (about ¾ teaspoon), and white pepper (about ¼ teaspoon), lower the heat, and cook, stirring, until the onion is soft, about 10 minutes. Add the broth or water and herbs and bring to a boil, then reduce the heat to low and simmer for 5 minutes.

Stir in the carrots and potato and cook for 10 minutes. Add the pasta and cook for 10 minutes, then stir in the beans (green and canned) and zucchini and cook for 10 minutes more. (This is not a soup in which any of the vegetables should be crunchy.) Finally, add the tomatoes and corn kernels and cook for 3 minutes.

Finish the soup with some pesto, drizzle with a little olive oil, and scatter the basil over the top. Top with Parmesan, or pass the cheese at the table.

garbure from the supermarket

SERVING
I serve the soup in the biggest bowls I've got, making sure that everyone gets some of every vegetable. If you've got hearty country bread and butter on the table and a salad for later, the soup is all you need for a filling and very satisfying supper.

STORING
You can make the soup up to 3 days ahead, keep it covered in the refrigerator, and reheat it as needed. The longer you keep the soup, the thicker the beans and potatoes will make it. To thin it or not is your call. You can freeze the soup for up to 2 months.

EVEN BEFORE I'D TASTED MY FIRST GARBURE, I fell in love with it. Once I heard that the bean, cabbage, and duck soup would traditionally sit on the back of the stove (wood-burning, of course) simmering gently until it was thick enough for a heavy spoon to stand upright in it, I fell for it. It was the whiff of rusticity that did it for me. When I finally tasted a *garbure* (in a not-so-rustic Paris restaurant), I wasn't disappointed, just surprised — there were no heavy spoons, no woodstove, just a big bowl filled with a long-simmered soup not unlike one my own non-French grandmother would have made. Essentially, it is a hearty vegetable soup made heartier with the addition of meat.

A true *garbure,* born in Southwest France, always has vegetables, chief among them white beans, cabbage, and potatoes, cooked in duck or goose fat. While there may be bacon or salt pork, cured ham, and/or garlic sausages, there is almost always duck confit.

Sadly, duck confit is not as easy to find or as reasonably priced in the United States as it is in France, where you can pick it up along with other household staples at the corner grocer. But since the soup is too good to pass up even if you can't lay your hands on confit, I've created this almost-*garbure,* which can be put together any day of the week with ingredients from a market in any part of America and is guaranteed to make everyone around the table happy.

For a more authentic recipe for *garbure,* see Bonne Idée.

1 cup dried navy or cannellini beans

2–3 pounds pork shoulder or 1 ham bone

1 tablespoon vegetable oil or bacon fat, if necessary

1 large Spanish onion, cut into 8 or 10 wedges

2 leeks, white and light green parts only, split lengthwise, washed, and cut into 1-inch-long pieces

2 shallots, thinly sliced

2 garlic cloves, split, germ removed, and crushed

10 cups chicken broth, vegetable broth, or water, or as needed

2 large or 3 medium carrots, trimmed, peeled, sliced lengthwise in half, and cut into 1-inch-long pieces

2 celery stalks, trimmed, peeled, and cut into 1-inch-long pieces

2 turnips, trimmed, peeled, and quartered

2 medium potatoes (Yukon Golds are good), peeled and cubed

1 small green cabbage, cored and tough outer leaves removed, shredded

1 duck leg (optional)
  Salt and freshly ground pepper
  Piment d'Espelette (see Sources) or red pepper flakes (optional)

1 garlic sausage, cut into ½-inch-thick slices (optional)

Rinse the beans, pick out any stones, dirt, or debris, and put them in a Dutch oven or soup pot. Cover with several inches of cold water, bring to a boil, and boil for 1 minute. Cover and set aside for 1 hour at room temperature. *(The beans can be prepared ahead to this point and refrigerated overnight.)*

Drain the beans and rinse out the pot. Set the pot over medium-high heat and brown the pork shoulder on all sides. (If you're using a ham bone, skip to the next step.) If the pork isn't producing enough of its own fat to brown nicely, add a little vegetable oil or bacon fat to the pot. When the meat is browned, transfer it to a plate, leaving the fat in the pot.

BONNE IDÉE
A More Authentic Garbure. Adding duck confit to this soup (alone or with the pork shoulder or ham bone and garlic sausage) and cooking the vegetables in duck fat will bring it closer to the original. (D'Artagnan makes an excellent duck confit; see Sources.) Figure ½ duck leg per person. Remove the fat that surrounds the legs and use some of it to cook the vegetables; save the rest for another use, like roasted potatoes. Add the duck confit, which is fully cooked, to the soup during the last hour of cooking. At serving time, remove the duck legs, slice or shred the meat, and divide it among the soup bowls, then ladle over the broth and vegetables. Finally, you might want to offer the soup the way it's often served in Southwest France: Separate the meats and vegetables from the broth and slice the meat. Serve the broth over hunks of toasted bread, and bring the vegetables and meats to the table on a platter. Have coarse salt, cracked pepper, and a mustard pot within easy reach, and let everyone dig in.

Reduce the heat to medium and toss in the onion, leeks, shallots, and garlic. Stir the vegetables around until they're coated with oil, then turn the heat to low, cover the pot, and cook, stirring frequently, until the vegetables are soft and translucent but not colored, about 10 minutes.

Pour the broth or water into the pot, add the carrots, celery, turnips, potatoes, and cabbage, as well as the reserved beans, the pork shoulder or ham bone, and the duck leg, if using it, and bring to a boil. Reduce the heat so that the soup simmers gently, partially cover, and cook for 1 hour, stirring now and then.

Season the soup with salt, pepper, and piment d'Espelette or pepper flakes, if using, and cook for another hour or so. If it looks as if the liquid is cooking away quickly — it shouldn't be — check that it's only simmering, not boiling, and add another cup or so of broth or water. You want the ingredients to be covered by liquid at all times.

Add the sausage, if using, to the pot. Continue to cook the soup for another hour — with or without the sausage.

Very carefully pull the pork shoulder out of the pot. If it's held its shape (a rare occurrence) and you can slice it, do it; if it hasn't, shred the meat, discarding the skin and any particularly fatty pieces. If you've used a ham bone or if you added a duck leg, shred that meat, discarding the skin and bones. Return the meat to the pot, and check for salt and pepper. Reheat, if necessary.

Ladle the soup into big bowls and serve.

good to the last drop

There's a wonderful French custom that's fun when you're sharing a hearty soup at home. It's called *faire chabrot* (*faire* means to make and *chabrot* is the act of mixing two liquids), and it's a delicious way of enjoying both the last of your wine and the last of your soup. When you've got just a few spoonfuls of soup left in your bowl and only a few sips left in your glass, pour your wine into your soup, swirl it around, and finish it off. This is a very old custom and one that's definitely country, not city — so country that the authentic way to drink the *faire chabrot* is to slurp it directly from the bowl.

vegetable barley soup
with the taste of little india

THERE'S NOTHING AUTHENTICALLY FRENCH OR INDIAN about this soup, but it's one that I started making in Paris after I'd bought a few little sachets of mixed spices in the city's small Indian neighborhood. Without the fresh ginger, turmeric, and garam masala (a mix of cardamom, cinnamon, mace, nutmeg, and other somewhat sweet spices), it would be a delicious but fairly conventional root vegetable and barley soup. With the spices, it's a surprising, satisfying, and very warming soup, one that's welcome on a cold winter's night.

MAKES 6 SERVINGS

SERVING
If you'd like, you can drizzle a little olive oil over each serving.

STORING
You can keep the soup covered in the refrigerator overnight, though the barley will drink up liquid as it sits and you'll have a very thick soup the next day. Just thin it with broth or water before you reheat it, and pay attention to the seasonings — adding more liquid may mean you'll need a little more spice.

1 tablespoon olive oil, plus (optional) extra for drizzling	Salt and freshly ground pepper
2–3 onions, chopped	Turmeric to taste (start with about ½ teaspoon)
3 big carrots, trimmed, peeled, and chopped	Garam masala (see Sources) to taste (start with about ¾ teaspoon)
1 parsnip, peeled, trimmed (cut out the core if it's woody), and chopped	Red pepper flakes to taste (optional)
3 garlic cloves, split, germ removed, and chopped	6 cups chicken broth, vegetable broth, or water
1 1-inch piece fresh ginger, peeled and chopped	½ cup pearl barley, rinsed

Warm the oil in a Dutch oven or soup pot. Add the onions, carrots, parsnip, garlic, and ginger and turn them around in the pot until they glisten with oil. Season with salt and pepper, cover, and cook for about 5 minutes over low heat. Stir in the turmeric, garam masala, and red pepper, if you're using it, cover, and continue to cook very gently, stirring often, until the vegetables are soft but not colored, about 15 minutes.

Add the broth or water and bring to a boil over medium-high heat, then stir in the barley. Reduce the heat — you want the broth to just simmer — cover, and cook until the barley is tender and considerably puffed (the kernels will blossom and open a little). Depending on the type of barley you have, this can take from 15 to 40 minutes. Taste and add more salt, pepper, and/or spices, as needed.

Ladle the soup into bowls and finish with a drizzle of olive oil, if you like.

orange-scented lentil soup

MAKES ABOUT
6 SERVINGS

SERVING
Ladle the very hot soup into wide soup plates, add a spoonful of yogurt to each, and sprinkle over the lardons or bacon bits, if you're using them.

STORING
The soup can be kept covered in the refrigerator for up to 3 days, but it will get thicker, probably thicker than you'd like it to be. If that's the case, add more broth or water to the soup as it heats — and make sure to adjust the seasoning when you do this.

LENTIL SOUP SEEMS TO HAVE A LOCK on French hearts, particularly the hearts of Gallic men, who, when asked about their favorite foods, usually immediately flash on their mothers' soups. And even though the best lentils in France come from Puy, in the center of the country, the love of lentil soup knows no regional boundaries. Lentil soup was the first recipe Jean-Georges Vongerichten, a native of Alsace, told me about when we talked about childhood favorites, just as it was top pick for a friend of mine from Gascony, clear across the country. Not that everyone's soup was the same — some had bacon, some had goose fat; some had a hunk of ham tossed in, some were completely vegetarian; and some were chunky, while others were smooth. Knowing that there were so many variations and that each had a happy following, I set to work making my own house lentil soup. (And, yes, I did secretly hope that, when asked, our son would one day name the soup among the favorites his *maman* cooked for him.)

Lentil soup chez Greenspan does or does not have bacon and it's best pureed. It's made with lentils du Puy, which I hope you'll search out (see Sources), and it's got a couple of surprises: a touch of ginger and, more prominently, the fragrance and taste of orange.

The orange is a more recent addition to my recipe, and like so many good things, it came about by chance. I had all the ingredients for the soup bubbling away in the pot when I walked into the kitchen to snack on a clementine. Just as I was about to toss the peel in the trash, I backed up and dropped it into the soup pot. I've been flavoring the soup with orange, tangerine, clementine, or mandarin peel ever since. It brightens and enlivens the mix and adds a bit of freshness to a winter soup you rely on when freshness is hard to come by. Serve the soup with a spoonful of yogurt, and you'll get an extra bit of tang, a nice go-along with the orange.

2 tablespoons olive oil or unsalted butter

2 yellow onions or 1 Spanish onion, thinly sliced

2 celery stalks, trimmed (save the leaves from 1 stalk) and thinly sliced

1 large carrot, trimmed, peeled, and thinly sliced

6 cups chicken broth or vegetable broth

1 cup lentils du Puy (French green lentils), rinsed and picked over

1 strip orange or tangerine peel, about 1 x 2 inches, white pith removed and cut into 3 pieces

6 black peppercorns

3 coriander seeds

1 clove

1 1-inch piece fresh ginger, peeled and coarsely chopped, or ½ teaspoon ground ginger

Salt and freshly ground pepper

Yogurt, for topping

Lardons (see box, opposite) or crumbled or chopped cooked bacon, for topping (optional)

Warm the oil or melt the butter in a large Dutch oven or soup pot over low heat. Toss in the onions, celery (including leaves), and carrot and stir the vegetables around until they glisten, then cover the pot and cook, stirring often, until they soften but don't color, about 10 minutes.

Add the broth, lentils, citrus peel, peppercorns, coriander, clove, and ginger, raise the heat, and bring to a boil. Lower the heat so that the broth just simmers, put the cover on the pot, and gently simmer until the lentils are so soft you can mash them with the back of a spoon, 60 to 90 minutes (the time will depend on the age of your lentils). After the soup has simmered for about 45 minutes, season it with salt (be generous — I usually add at least 1 teaspoon) and pepper.

Working in batches, puree the soup — spices, celery leaves, orange peel, and all — in a blender or food processor until smooth; or use an immersion blender. If you use an immersion blender, the soup may be a little chunky; if you'd like a smoother soup, just push it through a strainer. Wipe out the pot, pour the soup back into it, and reheat.

Ladle the soup into plates or bowls, garnish each with a dollop of yogurt, and sprinkle with lardons or bacon, if you like.

lardons

If you were stuck in the middle of nowhere in France with only a gas-station convenience store to shop in, you'd probably be able to find bacon and maybe even lardons (lahr-*dahn*), short strips of bacon that are about ¼ inch thick. French cooks often buy their bacon in large slabs, so that they can cut pieces of any thickness to match the dish they're making.

At home, I mostly use sliced bacon, but I cut lardons from slab bacon. Once they're cut, I blanch the lardons for a minute in boiling water, then drain and pat them dry and sauté them. Lardons make a good topping for soups and salads and are a prime ingredient in Quiche Lorraine (see Bonne Idée, page 157).

riviera fish soup

MAKES 4 SERVINGS

SERVING
Ladle the soup into soup plates or bowls. At the table, put a slice of the bread in the center of each bowl and top with some rouille or aïoli; let everyone add more rouille or aïoli as desired.

STORING
Ideally the soup should be served shortly after it is made; however, it can be made a few hours ahead and reheated. Or you can cool the soup, pack it airtight, and freeze it for up to a month.

THE FIRST TIME MICHAEL AND I went to Cannes, the playground of the stars, it was out of season, our hotel was out of fashion, and we were almost out of money. The conditions sound a lot less than ideal, but the reality was great. With the summer crowds gone, we had the beaches to ourselves; our hotel was adorable, and the hotelier even cuter (he must have liked us too, since he sent us home with a bottle of wine from his cellar); and our frugality turned up a find: an affordable restaurant (that we returned to three nights in a row) with a view of the beach and a fish soup that I dreamed about for years.

I'm guessing that it was made from the tiny little creatures that I'd see in the market every morning. Tucked into the corner of the fishmonger's display would be an assortment of very small fish and a large metal scoop. The fish were labeled something like "fish for soup," and you bought whatever came up in the scoop, no picking out the pink ones from the gray ones or the skinny ones from the chubs. Of course, these little rockfish were part of what made the soup a regional treasure, but there was more. There was the texture: thin but with enough fish bits that you felt you were eating the soup as much as sipping it; the mysterious base flavors: saffron and pastis (a licorice-flavored liquor); and the ritual that went with enjoying it: floating a raft of grilled bread, rubbed with garlic and doused with olive oil, in the soup; topping it with rouille, a peppery rust-colored mayonnaise (*rouille* means rust; you can use aïoli if you prefer); and figuring out how to get all three elements into every spoonful.

To make the soup in the United States, I had to give up on the idea of small fish by the scoop, but I discovered that I could get a lot of flavor from fish that were local to my fishmonger. Red snapper, a fish with Mediterranean relatives, is great for this soup, as are other lean white-fleshed fish like flounder and sole. More important are the saffron and pastis and a food mill (see below).

Here's the recipe that will get you the texture, the flavor, and the ritual — I leave it to you to add the beach view.

a plea for a food mill

A food mill is a very old-school, pre–food processor piece of kitchen gear that presses food through a strainer and, in one fell swoop, both purees the food and separates from it whatever peel, pith, skin, bones, and other culinary detritus might be attached to it. It's perfect for mashed potatoes, great for vegetables and sauces (it's a wonderful tool for making fresh tomato sauce), and indispensable for this recipe, where you cook a whole fish and then want to mash and strain the "meat" while avoiding all the skin and bones. You can do this in two steps with a food processor or blender and a strainer, but you'll get a smoother soup, and with this soup, what you gain in suavity, you lose in savor — it's much faster, and it's more satisfying to come across slender shreds of fish in every spoonful.

1 whole red snapper (about
    2 pounds), cleaned and
    scaled (head on, if possible)
3–4 tablespoons extra-virgin
    olive oil
2 medium onions, chopped
2 carrots (1 if it's very thick),
    trimmed, peeled, and
    chopped
4 garlic cloves, split, germ
    removed, and smashed
1 small fennel bulb, trimmed,
    tough core removed, and
    chopped
1 28-ounce can plum tomatoes
¼ cup tomato paste
3 pinches of saffron threads
2–4 tablespoons pastis (I use
    Pernod or Ricard)

1 wide strip orange zest, any
    white pith removed
A bouquet garni: 2 parsley
    sprigs, 2 thyme sprigs, and
    1 bay leaf, tied together or
    wrapped in cheesecloth
Salt and freshly ground pepper
Piment d'Espelette (see
    Sources) or cayenne

FOR THE ACCOMPANIMENTS

4 slices country bread
1 garlic clove, split and germ
    removed
Extra-virgin olive oil
Rouille (see Bonne Idée, page
    491) or Aïoli (page 490)

If your fishmonger is your friend (or if he's not busy), perhaps he'll chop up the snapper for you. If not, grab a heavy chef's knife or a Chinese cleaver and go to work, removing the head (save it) and then cutting the body of the fish into small pieces. The smaller the better here — 2 inches on a side is ideal but difficult, so just do the best you can.

Place a large Dutch oven or stockpot over medium-low heat and pour in 3 tablespoons oil. When the oil is warm, toss in the onions, carrots, garlic, and fennel and stir everything around so that it's glistening with oil, then cover the pot and cook slowly, stirring once or twice, for 10 minutes, to soften but not color the vegetables.

Add the fish chunks and head to the pot and stir well; if the mix looks a little dry, add another tablespoon of oil. Cover and cook for 5 minutes.

While the fish is cooking, drain the liquid from the tomatoes into a large measuring cup. Keep the tomatoes in the can and, using a pair of scissors (easier) or a long knife, cut the tomatoes into chunks (don't worry about getting everything even).

Turn the tomatoes into the pot, add the tomato paste and saffron, stir to incorporate, and cook for a minute or two. Add enough water to the tomato juice to make 6 cups of liquid and pour it into the pot, along with 1 tablespoon of the pastis. Toss in the zest and bouquet garni, season with salt, pepper, and piment d'Espelette or cayenne, and bring to a boil. Lower the heat so that the soup simmers gently but steadily and cook, uncovered, for 40 minutes.

If using a food mill, fit it with the medium disk and place the mill over a bowl. Ladle the soup (liquid and solids) into the food mill in small batches (discard the head and the bouquet garni when you come to them) and puree, scraping the solids that accumulate on the underside of the disk into the bowl and discarding the solids that build up in the mill; pour the soup into a clean pot. If using a food processor or blender, puree the soup in batches, discarding the head and bouquet garni, and then, if you'd like, press the soup through a strainer into a clean pot.

TO MAKE THE ACCOMPANIMENTS: Preheat the broiler. Give the slices of bread a rubdown on both sides with the cut sides of the garlic. Brush or drizzle a little olive oil over the bread and put the bread on a baking sheet. Run the bread under the broiler until it's lightly browned on one side, then flip the slices over and brown the other side. Put the warm bread on a plate and the rouille or aïoli in a bowl.

Meanwhile, reheat the soup over medium heat and taste it. Add more salt and pepper if needed (you'll probably need more salt) and 1 more tablespoon of pastis. For some, that will be just enough; for others, another tablespoon or even 2 should be right. (I usually add at least 3 tablespoons.)

Serve the soup with the toasts and sauce.

pastis

Licorice may be a love-it-or-loathe-it flavor in America, but in France it's a given, like chocolate and vanilla, and certainly it's beloved in the South of France, where pastis is the local drink. (It was even in the title of a Peter Mayle novel.) A liquor containing anise, licorice, and sugar, pastis may be what you think of when you're daydreaming about men in berets drinking in a small café or playing *pétanque,* but it's a relatively new addition to the culture, having been introduced in the 1930s, after absinthe was banned. While I love licorice and I love the ritual of pastis — you pour a little into a tall glass and then fill the glass with water and watch as the liquor turns milky — I've never drunk a glass of it. However, each one of my kitchens stocks a bottle of Ricard pastis: you never know when the urge to make a Riviera fish soup might strike, and without a splash of pastis, the soup just wouldn't pack any memory-evoking pow.

SIMPLEST BRETON FISH SOUP (PAGE 96)

simplest breton fish soup

MAKES 6 SERVINGS

SERVING

Most often, I cut the fish into spoon-eatable chunks, bring the kettle to the table (traditional with this dish), and ladle the soup into big bowls with a slice of toast in the bottom of each. You can also use fillets and serve the dish as a multi-plate dinner, as is often done in Brittany. Leave it up to each person to decide whether or not to drizzle a little vinaigrette over the fish. Lift the fish, mussels, and potatoes onto dinner plates, serve the soup in bowls over hunks of toasted country bread, and pass around the vinaigrette to drizzle over the fish and potatoes.

STORING

The soup really should be served the instant it's ready, but you can keep leftovers in the refrigerator overnight. If you do this, before serving, remove the mussels from their shells, cut the fish into chunks (if you haven't already), and ladle the gently reheated soup into large bowls.

THIS IS MY VERSION OF A *COTRIADE,* the stewish soup Breton fishermen made aboard their boats in the days when they could be out on the sea for weeks on end. It's an elemental soup, as it had to be, and one that's completely satisfying in much the same way as is New England clam chowder.

Given the literal catch-as-catch-can nature of this soup, the recipe leaves plenty of room for improvisation and substitution. To keep the spirit of the soup, you should have some mussels; a few oily fish, like mackerel or sardines (or both); some meaty, flaky fish, like cod; and plenty of potatoes, spuds being the principal vegetable in the mix. As with most French fish soups, this one is best with a mix of fish, but I've made it when I've had just mussels and only one kind of fish (like blackfish, a good stewing fish). The photo is on page 95.

FOR THE OPTIONAL
VINAIGRETTE

1 tablespoon Dijon mustard

2 tablespoons red or white wine vinegar

6 tablespoons extra-virgin olive oil
   Salt and freshly ground white pepper

1 shallot (not too big), minced

1 teaspoon chopped fresh parsley

FOR THE SOUP

2 tablespoons butter, salted (a Breton staple) or unsalted

2 large onions, chopped

2 shallots, chopped

2 garlic cloves, split, germ removed, and chopped

1 celery stalk, trimmed (reserve a few leaves), halved length-wise, and thinly sliced

1 leek, white and light green parts only (reserve a section of the green part to make the bouquet garni), quartered lengthwise, washed, and thinly sliced

Salt and freshly ground white pepper

6 cups fish broth (or, in a pinch, vegetable broth)
   A bouquet garni — 2 parsley sprigs, 2 thyme sprigs, the reserved celery leaves, and 1 bay leaf, tied together in a leek green

1 pound all-purpose potatoes (such as big round white pota-toes), peeled, quartered, and cut into ½-inch-thick slices
   About 2 pounds fish, in fillets or bone-in, cut into chunks — don't use more than ½ pound of oily fish, such as sardines, mackerel, or bluefish

2 pounds mussels, scrubbed and debearded

4 thick slices country bread, toasted, for serving

TO MAKE THE OPTIONAL VINAIGRETTE: Put the mustard, vinegar, and olive oil in a jar and shake to blend (or whisk together in a bowl). Season with salt and white pepper and stir in the shallot and parsley; set aside.

TO MAKE THE SOUP: Put a large Dutch oven or soup pot over medium heat and toss in the butter. When it has melted, stir in the onions, shallots, garlic, celery, and leek, season lightly with salt and white pepper, and cook, stirring frequently, until the vegetables are very soft but not colored, about 10 minutes.

Add the fish broth and bouquet garni and bring to a boil, then lower the heat and simmer gently for 5 minutes. Toss in the potatoes and cook for another 7 minutes. Add the fish and simmer for 7 to 10 minutes, or until almost cooked through — you'll need to poke around in the pot to get a sense of how the cooking is going. Stir in the mussels and cook for 2 to 4 minutes more, or until they've opened.

Discard any closed mussels, give everything one last stir to mix up the mussels and fish, and taste for salt and pepper, then head for the table, armed with the toasts and the vinaigrette, if serving.

BONNE IDÉE
There is absolutely no reason not to add more vegetables or even a touch of saffron to the soup — it's exactly what the fishermen and their wives would do when they had the luxury of more ingredients at hand. Carrots are a very good and colorful addition, as is a little fennel, some cubes of celery root, or even chunks of peeled and seeded tomatoes. As for the saffron, use a pinch of it, and just dissolve it in a little hot broth before stirring it into the pot.

spicy vietnamese chicken noodle soup

MAKES 4 SERVINGS

SERVING
Ladle the soup into four big bowls. If you like, set out bowls of basil and mint leaves, lime wedges, and bean sprouts. Put the hoisin sauce and chile oil on the table, and make the final seasoning of the soup a do-it-yourself affair.

STORING
Although you can refrigerate the soup base and the poached chicken overnight, it's best to serve the soup soon after the noodles and seasonings are added.

BONNE IDÉE
Curried Spicy Vietnamese Chicken Noodle Soup. To make a soup with the curry flavor that's more reminiscent of *la sa ga,* warm 2 tablespoons vegetable oil in the soup pot over low heat, then add 3 to 4 tablespoons (more or less to taste) curry powder. Cook, stirring, for about 30 seconds, then add some of the broth to stop the cooking, and proceed with the recipe. If you'd like, you can add about 2 tablespoons minced lemongrass to the soup — it's nice with the curry.

BECAUSE OF FRANCE'S LONG AND DEEP ties to Vietnam (a former colony), it's common to find Vietnamese restaurants in even the smallest French towns, a sprinkling of Vietnamese dishes in most French cooks' repertoires, and a few Vietnamese ingredients in many refrigerators. While it's usually only Vietnamese people who'll make authentic dishes from their native land at home, the bones of Vietnamese cooking, as well as its spices, condiments, and seasonings, turn up often. This soup is my mix of two traditional Vietnamese soups that I have as often as I can at Kim Lien, a restaurant near the rue des Carmes market in Paris's 5ᵗʰ arrondissement: *pho ga,* a clear chicken broth with noodles, and *la sa ga,* a curried coconut-milk soup. I've skipped the curry in this hybrid, but if you'd like to add it, see Bonne Idée.

Stems from 1 bunch cilantro
2 points star anise
1 teaspoon coriander seeds
1 teaspoon white peppercorns
1 small onion, chopped
3 garlic cloves, split, germ removed, and thinly sliced
1 1-inch piece fresh ginger, peeled and minced
2 dried red chiles
6 cups chicken broth
1 can (about 14 ounces) unsweetened coconut milk
About ¼ cup Asian fish sauce (such as nuoc mam), or to taste
1 teaspoon brown sugar (optional)
Salt
1 pound chicken breasts with skin and bones or about ¾ pound skinless, boneless chicken breasts

5 ounces Chinese egg noodles or rice vermicelli (found in the Asian section of the supermarket)
4–6 tablespoons fresh lime juice, or to taste
About ¼ cup chopped fresh cilantro

OPTIONAL GARNISHES
Fresh basil leaves (if you can find Thai basil, use it)
Fresh mint leaves
Lime wedges
Bean sprouts
Hoisin sauce
Asian chile oil

Put the cilantro stems, star anise, coriander seeds, and white peppercorns in a square of cheesecloth and tie the bundle together with a piece of kitchen twine; toss the packet into a Dutch oven or soup pot. Add the onion, garlic, ginger, and chiles, then pour in the chicken broth and coconut milk. Season the mixture with 2 tablespoons of the fish sauce, the brown sugar (if using), and a pinch

of salt and bring to a boil. (Don't be concerned if the coconut milk separates a little — it's only natural, and the soup will come together when you stir it.)

Lower the heat to a simmer, drop in the chicken, cover the pot, and poach the chicken gently for 15 to 20 minutes, or until cooked through. Transfer the chicken to a bowl to cool enough to handle; turn off the heat under the soup, but keep it covered. *(The soup can be made up to this point and refrigerated overnight; cover and refrigerate the chicken too.)*

While the chicken is cooling, cook the noodles following the package directions. (Usually, boiling them for 4 minutes in a large pot of salted water is all you've got to do.) Pour them into a colander, run them under cold water, and drain well.

Using your fingers, shred the chicken — minus the skin and bones, if there were any — into small pieces. Bring the soup back to a boil, lower the temperature so it just simmers, and stir in the chicken and noodles. When everything is hot, add more fish sauce to taste and as much lime juice as you'd like. Stir in the cilantro, taste, and add more salt if you think the soup needs it.

Ladle the soup into large bowls and serve with any or all of the optional garnishes.

cold melon-berry soup

MAKES 4 SERVINGS

WHEN MELONS ARE PLENTIFUL in the markets, they're common on the French table. During the season, just about every restaurant has melon somewhere on the menu. And just about every home cook is serving melon as well, usually as a starter and often in dishes as basic as slices of melon wrapped with ham, hunks drizzled with balsamic, or halves filled with port.

This soup is inspired by one I had at Alain Ducasse's former hilltop retreat, Ostapé, in the Pays Basque. It's a cross between a soup and a fruit salad and, in many ways, a cross between a fancy restaurant dish and one that's exceedingly fast and easily made at home. It's nothing more than pureed melon (the soup), topped with melon balls and strawberries (the salad). The only must-have is an absolutely ripe melon. In France, that would be a small Cavaillon; in America, it's a cantaloupe.

At Ostapé, the soup was served in glasses, and I'd suggest that you serve it that way too — it would be a shame to hide the soup's beautiful color.

BE PREPARED: You'll want to allow at least 2 hours for the soup to chill.

1	dead-ripe cantaloupe (about 2½ pounds)	¼	cup sweetish white wine, such as Muscat de Beaumes de Venise (optional)
1	teaspoon grated fresh ginger		About 20 small strawberries
1½–2	tablespoons fresh lime juice		
	Pinch of sea salt	4	mint sprigs

Cut the cantaloupe in half and scoop out the seeds. Using a melon baller or a small spoon, cut balls from one of the melon halves. Put them in a bowl, cover, and chill for at least 2 hours, or for up to 6 hours.

Meanwhile, peel the other half of the melon, cut it into chunks, and toss the chunks into a blender or food processor. Process, scraping down the container often, until the melon is reduced to a juice. Add the ginger, 1½ tablespoons lime juice, and the salt. Taste and, if you think it needs it, add the remaining ½ tablespoon of lime juice. Pour the soup into a pitcher and chill for at least 2 hours, or for up to 6 hours.

At serving time, divide the soup among four widemouthed glasses (or four small bowls) and top each portion with a tablespoon of wine, if you're using it. Spoon in the melon balls (depending on the size of your glass and the size of the melon balls, you may have some left over; you want the fruit to come about halfway up the sides of the glass, so you have room to spoon out the fruit and the soup), top with the berries, and finish each with a sprig of mint.

SERVING
Serve the soup well chilled. If you're serving it in glasses, you might want to serve it with long spoons of the iced-tea variety.

STORING
While the soup and melon balls should be well chilled at serving time, the soup is meant to be made and eaten the same day.

salads, starters,
and small plates

FRESH TUNA, MOZZARELLA, AND BASIL PIZZA (PAGE 166)

salads, starters, and small plates

anne leblanc's pistachio avocado

MAKES 4 SERVINGS

SERVING
If you'd like, serve the avocados with a wedge of lemon on the side of each plate. Or make the avocado and pistachio oil combo part of a heartier dish (see Bonne Idée).

BONNE IDÉE
I make this combination part of my Salmon Tartare (page 180), but you can also slice the avocado, drizzle it with the oil, and serve the slender wedges with crab salad (page 134), grilled shrimp tossed with vinaigrette, or chicken (it's great with Lemon-Grilled Chicken Breasts; see Bonne Idée, page 137).

AS SOON AS WE MOVED INTO our first apartment in Paris, I walked around the corner and stocked up on oils from Huilerie J. Leblanc, makers of some of the finest, fullest-flavored nut oils in the world. (You can find Leblanc oils at many specialty stores in the United States.) The shop was run by the late Anne Leblanc; it's her brother who makes the oils (and it was their father before him). That first day, Anne had me taste many of the oils, and when I fell in love with the pistachio oil — as many people do — she told me that the best way to eat it was with a perfectly ripe avocado.

Anne was so enthusiastic about the combination that I went directly to the fruit stand when I left her. That night, more than ten years ago, I served Anne's dish, and I've been serving it ever since. And everyone falls for it as quickly and as happily as I did.

Because this is hardly a recipe — more a list of ingredients — I was hesitant to include it, but it's just too good not to share.

2 perfectly ripe Hass avocados
Fresh lemon juice
Fleur de sel or other sea salt
Great-quality pistachio oil
  (see Sources)

Lemon wedges, for serving
  (optional)

Cut the avocados in half and slice off a sliver of skin from the bottom of each half to make a steady resting place for the fruit. Remove the pits and quickly sprinkle the flesh with lemon juice to keep it from blackening. Give the hollow in the center an extra squirt or two — you want about ⅛ teaspoon juice in the cavities. To make transporting the filled avocados easier, put them on plates or in small bowls now. Season with fleur de sel and fill the hollows almost to the top with pistachio oil. That's it.

Serve immediately, with lemon wedges, if desired.

café-style grated carrot salad

W HEN I FIRST WENT TO PARIS, *carottes râpées,* or grated carrot salad, was served at the least expensive student cafés and offered at the priciest take-out shops. Decades later, you can still find the salad just about everywhere, sometimes speckled with raisins, sometimes not; sometimes dressed with lemon juice and a splash of oil, sometimes with a vinaigrette that plays sweet against sharp (the version I like). You can even find grated and salad-ready carrots in every supermarket.

Carrot salad falls into the category the French call *crudités,* or raw salads. But since the French aren't all that crazy about uncooked vegetables in general, the fact that this salad has held on for so many years speaks to its goodness — and its versatility. While it's most often served as a starter, sometimes side by side with other salads, like vinaigrette-dressed beets (page 123) or pickled cucumbers (page 340), it's a good platemate for leftover chicken or beef and, not surprisingly, the perfect pack-along for a picnic.

1	pound carrots, trimmed and peeled		Salt and freshly ground pepper
2	tablespoons Dijon mustard		Moist, plump currants or raisins (optional)
1	tablespoon honey		Coarsely chopped walnuts (optional)
¼	cup cider vinegar		Chopped fresh parsley (optional)
½	cup mild oil, such as grapeseed or canola		

Grate the carrots by hand, using the large holes of a box grater, or by push-button, using the grating blade of a food processor. Either way, if the grating causes the carrots to weep, press them between your palms to rid them of excess liquid before you toss them into a serving bowl.

If you've used a processor, make the dressing in it; if not, use a small jar. Put the mustard, honey, vinegar, and oil in the processor or jar, season with salt and pepper, and whir or shake until blended — you'll have a thick, smooth vinaigrette. (Or whisk the dressing together in a small bowl.)

Toss the carrots with the currants or raisins and nuts, if you're using them. Just before serving, pour over the dressing, toss well, and adjust the salt and pepper if needed. If you're using the parsley, add it.

MAKES 4 SERVINGS

SERVING
Whether served as a solo starter, part of a crudités plate, or a side to a casual main, this is best at room temperature or just slightly chilled. And while I prefer it right after it's been dressed, when the carrots still have a teensy bit of crunch, the French fashion is for a softer salad, one that's been left to marinate for a while.

STORING
Although you can grate the carrots ahead and keep them covered and chilled, and you can make the vinaigrette up to 3 days ahead, the dressed salad should be eaten within a few hours.

hélène's all-white salad

MAKES 6 SERVINGS

SERVING

It almost goes without saying that at Délicabar, the salad was served on white plates. If you're not too strict about whiteness, you can use colorful plates — or even serve the salad on a bed of greens dressed with just a squirt of lemon juice, a little olive oil, and salt and white pepper.

STORING

The vinaigrette can be made a day ahead and kept in the fridge (press a piece of plastic wrap against the surface); whisk it before using. You can cut the vegetables, sprinkle them with lemon juice, and chill them for a few hours before assembling the salad.

WHEN MY FRIEND HÉLÈNE SAMUEL CREATED the now-gone but still talked-about café Délicabar Snack Chic in Paris's Le Bon Marché department store, she wanted the menu to have as much color as the room (which had tons), and so she came up with a bunch of salads named for their hues. Of course there was a green salad, but there were yellow, orange, red, and white ones too. And while each had its appeal, the white salad became my regular. Maybe it was the combination of crunchy apples and celery with Napa cabbage, or maybe it was the dressing, a yogurt vinaigrette made like a light mayonnaise. Whatever it was, I was happy when she gave me the recipe, which I make in both Paris and New York, since the ingredients are easily available pretty much everywhere.

FOR THE SALAD

- 6 celery stalks
- 3 Granny Smith apples
- Fresh lemon juice
- 10 ounces mushrooms (white, of course)
- 1 small Napa cabbage

FOR THE YOGURT VINAIGRETTE

- 1 large egg yolk
- Scant ½ cup (½ cup minus 1 tablespoon) Greek yogurt
- Fleur de sel or other sea salt and freshly ground white pepper (at Délicabar, it was Sarawak pepper; see Sources)
- ¾ cup olive oil (extra-virgin is nice but not necessary)
- Juice of ½ lemon

Sesame seeds, for serving

TO MAKE THE SALAD: Trim the celery stalks and peel them with a vegetable peeler to remove the tough, stringy outer layer (or at least the tough strings that the peeler catches). At Délicabar, the celery was cut into ribbons. If you want to do this, cut each stalk crosswise in half, then use the peeler to shave thin strips. To curl the ribbons and keep them until serving time, put them in a bowl filled with ice cubes and water and store them in the refrigerator. Alternatively, you can simply cut the celery crosswise into thin slices and toss them into a bowl.

Peel, halve, and core the apples. Cut them into ¼- to ½- inch cubes. Sprinkle and toss the apples with a little lemon juice to keep them from going brown, and add them to the celery.

Depending on how dirty your mushrooms are, brush them to remove any loose dirt or wipe them clean with a damp paper towel. If their feet are fat and spongy, snap them off and discard them (or pop them into the freezer to save for vegetable broth); if not, just trim them and leave them on. In either case, cut the mushrooms into thin slices. Sprinkle and toss the slices with a squirt of lemon juice and add them to the bowl.

Remove any tough outer leaves from the cabbage and quarter the cabbage

the long way. Cut away the tough core at the base, then cut the cabbage crosswise into thin (coleslaw-like) slices. Add to the bowl and give everything a good mix.

TO MAKE THE VINAIGRETTE: You can make this dressing, essentially a mayonnaise, in a food processor or blender, or you can do it by hand with a whisk (which is the way I do it, because it's fast and the cleanup is easy). Put the egg yolk in the processor, blender, or bowl, add 1 tablespoon of the yogurt, season with salt and white pepper, and pulse or whisk to blend. With the processor or blender running, or whisking constantly, add the olive oil drop by drop. When the mixture starts to look like mayonnaise, you can pour in the oil in a steady but gentle stream. When you've added about half of the oil, blend or whisk in most of the lemon juice, then return to the oil. Finally, add the remaining 6 tablespoons yogurt. Taste and add more lemon juice, salt, and/or white pepper, if you'd like. *(The vinaigrette can be made up to a day ahead and refrigerated; whisk before using.)*

To serve, drain the celery ribbons, if you made them, pat them dry, and mix them in with the rest of the vegetables in the bowl. Pour over the vinaigrette and give everything a good toss. Transfer to a serving bowl or salad plates and sprinkle over the sesame seeds.

leeks vinaigrette with mimosa

THIS CLASSIC DISH IS SERVED in the hippest places, including the wine bar/wine shop Le Verre Volé near the Canal Saint-Martin in Paris. The always-crowded restaurant doesn't have a real kitchen, and the owners depend on their chef friends to supply dishes that they can assemble or heat in their small countertop oven. However, there are a few dishes that are *fait maison,* or homemade, and leeks vinaigrette is one of them.

A plate of tender leeks (leeks are not meant to be crunchy — ever) generously bathed in vinaigrette, it's a model of simplicity and an age-old standard. But at Le Verre Volé, there's a little something that makes the dish different — the walnut oil in the vinaigrette. It's perfect with the leeks.

The most traditional way to serve this dish is *au mimosa,* or showered with sieved hard-boiled egg, the specks of which resemble mimosa flowers. It gives the simple dish a touch of style.

MAKES 4 SERVINGS

SERVING
I think the leeks are at their best served warm, shortly after they've come out of the pot; however, they are also excellent at room temperature. They can be served cold, but the chill lessens their distinctive flavor.

STORING
The leeks, mixed with the vinaigrette, can be kept covered in the refrigerator overnight. Held overnight, the grated hard-boiled egg won't fare as well.

16 young leeks, the youngest, thinnest you can find	1 tablespoon extra-virgin olive oil Salt and freshly ground pepper
½ teaspoon Dijon mustard	1 hard-boiled egg, chilled or at room temperature
1 tablespoon sherry vinegar	
2 tablespoons walnut oil	

You'll be using the white part of the leeks and just the palest green part, so trim your leeks accordingly and cut off the whiskers at the root end, taking care not to cut into the leeks. (You can save the dark green parts to add to vegetable soup; discard before serving.) If your leeks are very young and very tight, you can just run the cut part under cold water and drain. Older, fatter leeks need a more thorough cleaning, so split them down the center, stopping before you cut through the root end, and give them a good rinse, making sure to get rid of any dirt that has found its way between the leeks' outer layers.

Divide the leeks into 2 piles and tie each bundle together with kitchen twine. Bring a large pot of salted water to a boil and drop in the leeks. Lower the heat so that the water bubbles steadily but gently and cook the leeks for 10 to 20 minutes, or until they can be pierced easily with the tip of a knife. (How long the leeks need to be cooked will depend on their size and their age.)

MEANWHILE, MAKE THE VINAIGRETTE: Put the mustard, vinegar, and walnut and olive oils in a small covered jar and shake until the dressing is emulsified; or whisk together in a small bowl. Season with salt and pepper.

Lift the tender leeks out of the water, snip the twine, and pat the leeks dry in a clean dish towel or between layers of paper towels. If the leeks are thick, finish cutting them in half lengthwise. If you'd like, you can cut the leeks crosswise into 1- to 2-inch-long pieces.

Put the leeks on a serving platter, pour over the vinaigrette, and let them cool a little bit.

Grate the hard-boiled egg over the leeks and serve immediately.

roasted peppers

MAKES 4 SERVINGS

SERVING
If you haven't already done so, arrange the peppers on a platter, moistening each layer with some of the oil. Scatter over fresh herbs and serve with a peppermill and some plate-cleaning bread. The peppers are fine at room temperature and nice slightly chilled.

STORING
Covered well, the peppers will keep in the refrigerator for about 5 days. If you plan to keep them this long, you might think about packing them in a canning jar and making sure they're covered with oil.

BONNE IDÉE
Roasted Pepper Vinaigrette. If you've kept the peppers for a day or more, the oil you poured over them will be extremely flavorful and make a delicious vinaigrette. I make my vinaigrette in a mini processor using ½ roasted pepper, 1 tablespoon sherry vinegar (you can use Champagne vinegar), ¼ cup of the pepper oil, and salt and pepper to taste. If you'd like, you can make the vinaigrette without the roasted pepper — it will be more subtle.

BECAUSE ROASTED PEPPERS ARE SO ATTRACTIVE, it's easy to forget that they can be delicious and that they can stand on their own as a starter. At least I think it's easy for us Americans to forget — we never seem to use them for anything but color. Not so the French. In France, roasted red peppers, slicked with olive oil, sometimes scattered with garlic, and often speckled with herbs, are a time-honored bistro dish; they're served as a starter with a fork, a knife, and plenty of bread. They make an appetizer that couldn't be plainer, but we order them often at a favorite restaurant in Paris, Brasserie Fernand. It's also a dish that delights everyone when our friend Martine Collet makes it.

When Martine serves roasted peppers, she makes them look like jewels. She roasts lots and lots of them, arranges them in beautifully overlapping rows on a large platter, interlaces the rows with herbs, gives each row a gloss of olive oil, and finishes the platter with a scattering of small black Niçoise olives. It's a lesson in how to give something simple some dazzle.

While you can certainly prepare green peppers in this fashion, their flavor is a bit strong for the dish. The best peppers to use are the thick-fleshed boxy Holland peppers and, while red is the color you see most often in France, yellow, orange, and purple peppers roast nicely too.

This recipe can be multiplied, and multiplied, and multiplied.

5 large bell peppers, preferably not green (see above) Salt, preferably fleur de sel, and freshly ground pepper Fresh parsley, basil, rosemary, or thyme leaves, or a combination, plus extra for serving	1–2 garlic cloves, split, germ removed, and very thinly sliced (optional) About ½ cup extra-virgin olive oil

Center a rack in the oven and preheat the oven to 425 degrees F. Line a baking sheet with a silicone baking mat, parchment paper, or aluminum foil (this is a good job for nonstick foil).

Wash and dry the peppers, put them on the baking sheet, and roast them, turning them every 15 minutes, until some of the skin on every side of the peppers is blistered, 45 to 60 minutes. The peppers may collapse and some may seep some juice — that's fine. Transfer the peppers to a bowl (be careful — that juice is very hot), cover the bowl with foil, and let the peppers rest until they are cool enough to handle.

In the meantime, pull out a Pyrex loaf pan or, if you plan to serve the peppers soon, a large platter, preferably one with a slightly raised rim.

Working with 1 pepper at a time and working over the bowl, remove the stem, let the liquid drain from the pepper, and separate the peel from the flesh. You can usually do this with your fingers, but if a little peel sticks stubbornly, scrape

it away with a paring knife. Cut the pepper open along its natural separations — depending on the pepper, this will mean cutting it in half or thirds — and scrape away the seeds and ribs on the inside. Place the pepper pieces cut side down in the loaf pan (or on the platter), season with salt and pepper, strew with herb leaves and garlic slices, if you're using them, and pour over some olive oil. (If you're working on a platter, you can just brush the peppers with oil.) Continue until all the peppers are in the pan (or on the platter).

If you've got time, cover and chill before serving, garnished with fresh herbs.

vanilla vegetable salad

MAKES 4 SERVINGS

SERVING
You can present the salad
the way it was served at
Racines by putting the
carrot and squash ribbons
on top of the greens, or
you can toss the salad and
serve it on individual plates
or in one large bowl.

STORING
The vanilla vinaigrette can
be made up to a few hours
ahead, but it's best to toss
and dress this salad at the
last minute.

RACINES WAS THE KIND OF WINE BAR you thought existed only in romantic novels about Paris. Squeezed into an always-busy shopping arcade, it was owned by the devastatingly charming Pierre Jancou, who chose wines that were all natural, all from small producers, and many sure to be discoveries. The atmosphere was like a house party, and the food was simple but surprising.

On a typical day, there might be four starters, four main courses, and a couple of desserts, and Pierre would have a story about each dish. If there was pasta, as there often was, it was likely to be connected to the half of his family that's Italian. If there was charcuterie, a friend probably made it. And if vegetables were in the spotlight, then the chances were good that they were plucked from the garden of Michelin three-star chef Alain Passard, as they were the afternoon we had this salad of ribbon-cut carrots and summer squash tossed with mesclun and a light dressing with a flavor that stopped all of us mid-forkful: vanilla! It was so unexpected, yet it seemed perfect.

At Racines, Pierre added a pinch of vanilla bean pulp; at home, I've been making the vinaigrette with a very fragrant pure vanilla extract. You can do it either way, just as you can make the salad with whatever vegetables you have at hand. My instructions are for a salad similar to Pierre's, but feel free to use more or less of any vegetable or to change the vegetables completely; to make the salad with spinach or arugula instead of mesclun; or to toss in some herbs as well. Like so many simple dishes, this one relies less on a set recipe than on inspiration.

2	young sweet carrots, trimmed and scrubbed or peeled		About ¼ teaspoon pure vanilla extract
2	young yellow summer squash, trimmed		Salt, preferably fleur de sel, and freshly ground pepper
1½–2	tablespoons extra-virgin olive oil	4	handfuls mixed salad greens or mesclun
	About 1 tablespoon fresh lemon juice		

You can cut the vegetables into ribbons with a vegetable peeler, but if you've got a mandoline, a Benriner slicer, or a V-slicer, you might find it more efficient. Start slicing each carrot on one side, continuing until you reach the core. Turn the carrot and continue slicing, turning again when you reach the core — when you finish, you'll be left with a rectangular piece of carrot. Before you make ribbons from the summer squash, slice off a small piece from all four sides so that the first cut you make on each side produces a slice that has skin only on the edges; slice the squash until you see seeds, then turn to slice the next side, and continue around the squash.

Combine 1½ tablespoons olive oil, 1 tablespoon lemon juice, ¼ teaspoon vanilla extract, and a little salt and pepper in a jar and shake; or whisk together

in a bowl. Taste for balance, adjusting the amounts of oil, lemon, and vanilla if you think the vinaigrette needs it. What you're after is a light, lemony dressing, one in which the flavor of the vanilla is present but not very strong.

To serve the salad, put the greens into a bowl, season with salt and pepper, and toss with a little of the vinaigrette. Divide the greens among four plates. Put the carrot and squash ribbons in the bowl, season, and dress with vinaigrette to taste, then arrange them over the greens. If you'd like, give each plate a little toss before serving. Alternatively, you can make a single salad in a large bowl and toss and serve it at the table.

a fistful of salad

Just when I got the hang of asking the vendors at the market for stuff in metric quantities, I realized I was still clueless when it came to buying greens. Things that were sold by the head were easy. But what about the multicolored greens labeled mesclun — which, just to confuse things, is also called *salade* (the word defines both the raw ingredient and the dish you make with it) — the baby spinach, the tight little clusters of (always expensive) mâche, and the jagged-edged arugula with stems as long as beanpoles? I couldn't grasp whether 100 grams of the featherweight greens would be just enough for a white mouse or for a family of four, so I lurked around the stalls and listened to the way savvy shoppers bought their leaves, and I discovered just how easy and sensible it was.

Ask for *une poignée de roquette,* and you get a fistful of arugula; say *encore,* and you get another. I didn't even have to worry about one guy's handful being twice the size of another's because vendors always look up after grabbing the greens, turn their harvest toward you, and cock an eyebrow, the universal symbol for "Okay?"

And, by the way, 100 grams is too much for one mouse and not enough for four people. It's best to buy enough to tip the scale at about 250 grams.

orange and olive salad

A RIFF ON THE FAMOUS MOROCCAN ORANGE SALAD that's usually accented with cinnamon, this is an exceedingly simple first-course salad that's less sweet than the original and just as welcome as a side dish or chaser when the main event is a tagine or rich stew. Here, slices of orange are drizzled with olive oil and strewn with onion rings and small black olives. I'm most likely to make it to follow Osso Buco à l'Arman (page 270), which calls for the zest of 4 navel oranges and leaves the fruit begging to be used. True, the rules of menu-planning discourage using the same ingredient in more than one dish, but no one who's ever experienced the one-two of osso buco–orange salad has quibbled while cleaning his or her plate. If you'd like a salad that follows tradition a little more closely, take a look at the Bonne Idée or, if you'd like to play up the olive part of the salad, dress it with tapenade vinaigrette (page 485).

MAKES 4 SERVINGS

SERVING
The salad can be served as an appetizer or a side dish — it's nice with grilled fish — or after a rich main course.

STORING
You can chill the oranges for a couple of hours before serving, if you'd like. If there are leftovers, they can be refrigerated overnight, but don't expect the salad to have the same verve a day later.

1   small onion, red or yellow
4   navel, Temple, or other "meaty" oranges
    About 2 tablespoons extra-virgin olive oil

    Niçoise or other small black olives, pitted or not
    Salt, preferably fleur de sel, and freshly ground pepper

You can leave the onion whole or cut it in half. Thinly slice it, and separate the slices into rings or half rings. Rinse the slices and drop them into a bowl of ice water. If you've got the time, let them sit in their water bath for about 20 minutes — the rinse will wash away some of their bitterness, and the bath will make them crisp.

You may want to remove the zest and save it before peeling the oranges. (It's too precious to lose; see above.) You can remove it in wide strips, cut away the white pith on the underside, and freeze the strips; you can sliver or chop the zest; or you can grate it. (Slivered or grated zest won't freeze as well.)

Remove a thin slice from the top and bottom of each orange to give yourself flat surfaces, stand the orange up, and, working your knife around the contours of the orange, cut away the peel, the pith, and the tiniest bit of flesh. Once they are peeled, cut the oranges into rounds ⅓ to ½ inch thick, and arrange attractively on a large serving platter. If you'd like, you can cover the oranges and chill them before you finish and serve the salad.

Drain the onions and pat them dry. Drizzle the olive oil over the oranges, scatter over the onions, top with the olives, and season with salt and pepper.

BONNE IDÉE
A More Moroccanish Orange Salad. Instead of olive oil, drizzle the oranges with lemon juice and a few drops of orange flower water and then sprinkle the salad with a little confectioners' sugar, a pinch of cinnamon, and some salt. If you'd like, scatter over some nuts — almonds or walnuts — and finish with slivers of dates.

mozzarella, tomato, and strawberry salad

MAKES 4 SERVINGS

SERVING
The salad needs nothing more than a basket of baguette slices on the table so that the last little bit of juice can be sopped up and enjoyed.

STORING
This salad must be eaten as soon as it's assembled.

I CAN'T REMEMBER WHERE I FIRST SAW tomatoes and strawberries together — I want to say that the combination had something to do with the pastry chef Pierre Hermé — but I do remember that it made sense to me immediately. It wasn't just that they made a gorgeous pair, it was that they were both sweet, both a little acidic, and both sweet and acidic in complementary ways. It's irresistible to use the duo to riff on the classic tomato and mozzarella salad, which is as popular in France as it is in the United States.

The success of the salad depends entirely on the quality of your ingredients. You need sweet ripe tomatoes and strawberries — this is a summer salad. But, as ripe and sweet as they should be, the fruits should retain some of their characteristic acidity. If they're ripe and right, then you won't need even a micro splash of vinegar on the salad. If the berries and tomatoes are just a tad shy of acid, give the salad a tiny drizzle of raspberry vinegar or balsamic — but when I say tiny, I mean it.

I like to use grape or cherry tomatoes for the salad, so that when they're cut, they're about the same size as the sliced strawberries, but choose whatever tomatoes are at their prime in your market. And, while I've given quantities for the ingredients, like so many salad recipes, this is one you can play by ear.

½ pound fresh mozzarella, preferably mozzarella di bufala (burrata is delicious)	Salt, preferably fleur de sel, and freshly ground pepper
16 small sweet strawberries, hulled	Extra-virgin olive oil
	A few pink peppercorns
16 grape or cherry tomatoes or 2 regular tomatoes	4 fresh basil leaves, halved lengthwise and shredded
	Raspberry or balsamic vinegar (optional)

For the best flavor and texture, assemble this salad as close to serving time as possible.

Drain the mozzarella, if it's in water, and lightly pat it dry. Cut into 8 slices. If you're serving the salad family-style, put the slices on a platter; if you're arranging individual salads, put 2 slices on each plate.

Cut the strawberries in half the long way — if your strawberries are large, you might want to slice them into thirds — and put them in a bowl. Cut the grape or cherry tomatoes crosswise into thirds or, if you've got larger tomatoes, cut them into cubes about the size of the sliced berries, and put them in the bowl. Season lightly with salt and pepper and moisten — just moisten — with a few drops of olive oil. Turn the fruit around gently in the bowl and taste it for seasoning to decide whether or not you're going to want to add a dash of

vinegar (but don't add it yet). Arrange the berries and tomatoes alongside the mozzarella on the platter or salad plates.

Finish the salad by pouring a little olive oil over the mozzarella, then crushing the pink peppercorns between your fingertips and sprinkling the pieces over both the fruit and the cheese; scatter the shredded basil leaves over them. If you've decided on vinegar, drizzle it over the salad. Serve immediately — you don't want the salt and vinegar to diminish the juiciness of the fruit.

peeled tomatoes

There are two surefire ways to tell that you're in France. The first is that there are cafés on every corner and pâtisseries every few blocks. The second is that whether you order a sandwich at one of those cafés or an elaborate starter at a fancy restaurant, the dish's tomatoes will be peeled.

Tomatoes are peeled in France for the same reason that bell peppers are usually served cooked: they're more digestible that way. And, as a very young Parisian friend told me: they feel better in your mouth.

The practice is so widespread that even back-of-the-box recipes

that might take just five to ten minutes to make specify peeled tomatoes. And, no, unlike so many other nifty French products, you can't buy "ready-made" peeled tomatoes.

However, peeling tomatoes is easy. Bring a pot of water to a boil and have a strainer and a bowl at the ready. Using a paring knife, cut a small, very shallow X in the base of each tomato. Drop some of the tomatoes into the boiling water — you don't want to crowd the pot — and count to 20. Using the strainer, scoop the tomatoes out of the pot and into the bowl. Repeat with any remaining tomatoes.

When the tomatoes are cool enough to handle, you should be able to slip off their skins. If the skins are recalcitrant, return the tomatoes to the pot for another 10 seconds.

And, if you want to be really French, while you're peeling the tomatoes, seed them too. Halve them and use the tip of a small spoon or your fingers to scoop out the seeds and jelly-like pulp.

Why do it? Once again, digestibility (the French take their stomachs very seriously) and the pleasure of having something homogeneous in your mouth.

lime and honey beet salad

WHAT MAKES THIS SIMPLE SALAD so interesting is the play between the earthy, almost mineral flavor of the beets, the sweetness of the honey, and the punch you get from the dressing's lime and vinegar. I like to serve these cool beets alongside Salmon and Potatoes in a Jar (page 182) or grilled chicken or fish, particularly in summer, but they're a good addition to a main-course salad. Think of them when you're making a plated salad with poached or grilled shrimp, slices of chicken breast, or, best of all, smoked trout. And turn to them when you've got a lineup of salads for a starter — they go well with pickled cucumbers (page 340), grated carrot salad (page 107), and leeks vinaigrette (page 111).

For another, less pungent beet salad, try Chunky Beets and Icy Red Onions (page 123).

BE PREPARED: The beets need to be chilled for at least 2 hours.

MAKES 4 SERVINGS

SERVING
The salad is good chilled or at room temperature, served alongside a main dish, partnered with other salads as a starter, or given star treatment by setting it on a bed of lightly dressed greens (I like arugula) and topping it with a mini spoonful of crème fraîche or sour cream.

STORING
The salad can be kept covered in the refrigerator for up to 2 days.

2 teaspoons cider vinegar	2 teaspoons minced fresh chives
Grated zest and juice of ½ lime	Salt and freshly ground pepper
2 teaspoons honey	1 pound cooked beets (see page 332; I use red beets here, but goldens are good too), peeled
2–3 teaspoons extra-virgin olive oil	
2 teaspoons minced fresh dill	Minced fresh dill and chives, for garnish (optional)

Whisk together the vinegar, lime zest and juice, and honey in a medium bowl until smooth. Whisk in 2 teaspoons olive oil. Add the dill and chives, and season with salt and pepper.

Cut the beets into wedges (about ½ inch thick), add them to the bowl, and gently turn them around in the vinaigrette. Cover the bowl and chill the beets for at least 2 hours, or for as long as overnight.

At serving time, stir in another teaspoon of oil, if you think the salad needs it, and taste for salt and pepper. If you're using them, top with minced herbs.

chunky beets
and icy red onions

Here's my go-to beet salad, the one I like to serve alongside anything grilled or to pair with soft goat cheese. While I think of Lime and Honey Beet Salad (page 121) as a summer salad, this combination can take you through every season. It's most typical of the kind of dish you'd get if you ordered a salad plate as a starter in a simple bistro. Like its zestier cousin, the salad has a little honey, just enough to soften the edges of the sherry vinegar dressing.

BE PREPARED: The beets and dressing need to be refrigerated for about an hour before serving.

MAKES **4** SERVINGS

SERVING
The salad is good chilled and nicest when the herb and onion are added at the last minute.

STORING
The salad can be kept covered overnight in the refrigerator.

1 small red onion, quartered and very thinly sliced	Salt and freshly ground pepper
1 teaspoon Dijon mustard	1 pound cooked beets (see page 332), peeled and cut into ½-inch cubes
1 teaspoon honey	
1 tablespoon sherry vinegar	2 teaspoons minced fresh oregano (my first choice), marjoram, thyme, or parsley
2 tablespoons extra-virgin olive oil	

Put the sliced onion in a small bowl of cold water and slosh the slices around for a second to rinse and remove any bitterness. To give the onions crunch, pour off the water and refill the bowl with fresh cold water and ice cubes. Refrigerate until you're ready to serve.

Meanwhile, put the mustard, honey, vinegar, olive oil, and salt and pepper to taste in a small jar, cover, and shake until the dressing is emulsified; or whisk in a bowl. *(You can make the dressing up to 1 week ahead and keep it covered in the refrigerator.)*

Toss the cubed beets with the dressing in a bowl, and chill for about an hour.

At serving time, fold the fresh herb into the salad and taste for salt and pepper. Drain the onion slices, pat them dry, and sprinkle over the top of the salad.

BONNE IDÉE
Chunky Beets and Icy Red Onions with Goat Cheese and Arugula. Toss a handful of arugula with a little of the vinaigrette and spread the greens on a platter. Cut about 12 grape or cherry tomatoes in half and, at serving time, toss these with the beets and herb. Scatter the vegetables over the greens and top with 4 serving-sized pieces of goat cheese, either rounds cut from a log of soft fresh goat cheese or wedges cut from a disk of fresh cheese. Top with the icy onions. Alternatively, you can make this salad with crumbled firm goat cheese in place of the soft cheese, or you can make crumbled Roquefort the cheese topping. Do this, and you might want to omit the onions.

minted zucchini tagliatelle with cucumbers and lemon

MAKES 6 SERVINGS

SERVING
Just before you're ready to bring this dish to the table, toss it with the remaining mint — it gives it a jolt of freshness. Serve it alone or with other salads as a starter, or pair the tagliatelle with chicken or fish.

STORING
Although the tagliatelle should be chilled before serving, it really shouldn't be kept overnight.

MY FRIEND THE FABULOUS COOK Frédérick Grasser-Hermé made a version of this dish, in which zucchini is cut like tagliatelle, about fifteen years ago, when we were sharing a cottage on the Bassin d'Arcachon. At the time, the idea of making one food look like another was a novelty — today it's a trend, one that works really well here. The zucchini is cut into ribbons, crunchy cucumber is added for texture, and onion, mint, lemon, and pistachio oil are added for zip. This is a great summer dish and good for picnics.

BE PREPARED: The salad needs to be refrigerated for at least 1 hour before serving.

3 zucchini (about 1½ pounds total), trimmed

1 large cucumber, peeled, cut lengthwise in half, and seeded

1 cup finely diced Vidalia or other sweet onion (if you use a regular onion, rinse and dry the diced onion)

Grated zest of 1 lemon

1½ cups loosely packed fresh mint leaves (preferably not peppermint), coarsely chopped

¼ cup fresh lemon juice

2 tablespoons pistachio oil (see Sources)

Salt and freshly ground pepper

How you treat the zucchini skin is up to you. I don't like the taste of the skin but I do like the look of it, so I peel away strips and get half as much of it. If the skin doesn't bother you, leave it on; if it really bothers you, peel it off completely.

Working with a mandoline, a Benriner slicer, or the slicing blade of a box grater, cut each zucchini lengthwise into strips — tagliatelle — about ⅛ inch thick. Work on one side of the zucchini until you reach the seeds, then turn and cut the next side; continue to turn each time you reach the seeds. You'll be left with a seedy inner rectangle of zucchini; discard it. Toss the zucchini into a large bowl.

Cut each cucumber half lengthwise into 4 strips, then cut the strips into slices about ¼ inch thick; toss them into the bowl. Add the onion, lemon zest, and half of the chopped mint and toss everything together gently but thoroughly.

Combine the lemon juice, pistachio oil, and salt to taste in a small jar and shake until blended; or whisk together in a bowl. Pour over the salad, and toss well. Season generously with pepper (zucchini and pepper are a sublime match) and more salt if needed. Cover and chill for at least 1 hour, or for up to 3 hours.

Just before serving, toss the salad with the remaining mint.

salade niçoise

LIKE CAESAR SALAD, SALADE NIÇOISE (which gets its name from its hometown, Nice) has traveled the globe and, like the Caesar, lost a little of its authenticity and excitement along the way. But even as it teeters between classic and cliché, you can see why the salad has endured: it's got lots of different textures, so it's always interesting; it's colorful, so it's always beautiful; and, most important, it's tasty — it's hard to resist the allure of hard-boiled eggs, tomatoes, green beans, olives, shallots, anchovies, boiled baby potatoes, lettuce, and tuna, the salad's linchpin. The customary tuna for a salade Niçoise comes straight from the tin. In fact, when I told a French friend that I was writing this book, he said, "Please, please, please, don't go all modern and use fresh tuna!" I think he would be glad to hear that most of the time I stick to canned tuna. However, if I've got any leftovers from tuna confit (page 305), I make a salade Niçoise just for the chance to use them. Actually, I'm not so sure that using confit is all that modern. After all, what is canned tuna but tuna preserved in oil?

MAKES 4 SERVINGS

SERVING
The salad should be served as soon as it's arranged. It's truly a one-dish meal and needs nothing more than bread. A sliced baguette would be perfect, but you might consider a savory fougasse (page 48); it's from the same part of the country as the salad.

STORING
The potatoes and green beans can be cooked earlier in the day; just be sure to dry them well. Keep the potatoes at room temperature and chill the beans. The eggs can be hard-boiled as much as a day ahead and kept refrigerated.

8–12 small potatoes, such as fingerlings or baby Yukon Golds, scrubbed

¾ pound green beans, trimmed

4 hard-boiled eggs

4–6 handfuls Boston lettuce, mesclun, or other soft salad greens, rinsed and dried

1 shallot, finely chopped, rinsed, and patted dry

Salt and freshly ground pepper

Double recipe of Everyday Vinaigrette (page 484) or Tapenade Vinaigrette (page 485)

2 5- to 6-ounce cans tuna packed in oil, drained

4 tomatoes, cut into chunks, or about 20 grape tomatoes, halved

About 20 Niçoise olives, pitted or not

2 tablespoons capers, drained and patted dry

8 anchovies, rinsed and patted dry

Chopped fresh parsley, for garnish (optional)

Put the potatoes in a large pot of salted water and bring to a boil. Cook until the potatoes are tender enough to be pierced easily with the tip of a knife, 10 to 20 minutes (maybe even a little longer), depending on the size and age of your potatoes. Scoop the potatoes out of the pot with a slotted spoon and put them in a bowl to cool.

Toss the green beans into the pot and cook them until tender, or crisp-tender — start checking them after 4 minutes. Drain the beans and run them under cold water, or dunk them into a bowl of cold water and ice, to cool them and set their color. Drain, then pat dry.

When you're ready to serve, depending on their size, halve or quarter the

potatoes. Peel the eggs and cut them in half. Choose a large platter (or shallow serving bowl) and put the greens on it. Sprinkle over the chopped shallot, season with salt and pepper, and drizzle over a spoonful or so of the vinaigrette; toss.

You can now compose the salad any way you wish. I'm from the symmetrical school, so I lay the ingredients out in rows, but circles or a hither-and-thither approach is fine as well. Lay the potatoes, beans, eggs, tuna, and tomatoes over the greens. Scatter over the olives and capers, and either cut the anchovies in half and crisscross the eggs with them or arrange the anchovies attractively over the salad. Season the salad with salt and pepper and drizzle over a little more vinaigrette; pour the remainder of the vinaigrette into a small pitcher that can be brought to the table. Finish the salad with a flurry of parsley, if you like.

dressed greens

French salads are like French women — always stylishly dressed. Salads can be topped with mayonnaise or even tossed with heavy cream that's been infused with something delicious — say truffles — and boiled down until it thickens slightly. But the little black dress of salad dressings is the rightfully classic vinaigrette, a mix of vinegar and oil, salt and pepper, and a dab of Dijon mustard . . . or not.

The usual proportions for a vinaigrette are 1 part vinegar to 3 parts oil, but you can play around with the mix to match the kind of salad you're making and your own preference for acidity. My "house dressing" is more vinegary than the standard — 1 tablespoon vinegar to 2 tablespoons oil — and often more mustardy too. Mustard gives a vinaigrette a touch of sharpness, and it also serves to help emulsify the dressing. Use mustard, and your vinaigrette will be creamy; without it, it'll be thinner and it might separate — but that's fine.

You've got plenty of leeway with a vinaigrette. Instead of vinegar (red, white, or fruity), you can use fresh lemon juice, which is less acidic. If you use the juice, you might want to use less oil. As for the oil, extra-virgin olive oil is always the first choice, but if you're adding a lot of spices or garlic or making a dressing that's really mustardy, you might want to use something a little less flavorful or not flavorful at all, like grapeseed oil. For the most distinctively flavored vinaigrette, replace a little of the olive oil with a nut oil and pair it with aged sherry vinegar.

I know this borders on the heretical, but if I've got a mix of absolutely gorgeous greens that are especially tasty, maybe a mix that has mustard greens, mizuna, arugula, and other kinds of bold leaves, I'll season them with salt (usually fleur de sel), freshly ground pepper, and terrific olive oil — just olive oil, no vinegar to cut their natural flavor.

And no matter what I use on a salad, I use it sparingly. Whether we're talking fashion or food, dressing with restraint is always in style.

BONNE IDÉE
Fried Garlic Petals. The salade Niçoise at Le Comptoir in Paris includes a scattering of fried garlic, a small touch that makes the dish a standout. (Le Comptoir's salad also goes against form and, instead of soft lettuces, uses crisp sucrine, a kind of baby romaine with the crunch of iceberg.) To make the petals, slice a large garlic clove (or two) lengthwise paper-thin, avoiding the germ. If you have a mini mandoline (there are some made specifically for garlic) or a Benriner slicer, this is a job for it. Heat a little mild oil, such as grapeseed or canola, in a small saucepan, and when it's hot, start frying the garlic. Drop in a few slices and let them cook until they're golden, then lift them out of the oil with a small slotted spoon and transfer them to a plate lined with a double thickness of paper towels; pat off the excess oil. Repeat with the remaining slices. You can keep the garlic covered in a cool, dry place overnight. Make the garlic the last thing you add to the salade Niçoise.

asparagus

In France fresh asparagus that is grown within the country (often in the Loire Valley) and rushed to market is considered a delicacy, as prized as caviar or truffles and given the same star treatment. In fact, as soon as the stalks start crowding the vendors' stands, they top the menus of restaurants and family dinners too. I take it as a given that when I'm invited to a friend's home for dinner during the season, asparagus is what I'll be having as a first course.

There are two kinds of French asparagus that are rarely seen in our markets: wild and white. The wild spears look like something meant for decoration only. They're fern green and about six inches long. Their stems are as thin as reeds, and their tops look like miniature sheaves of wheat. They can be steamed and used as a garnish, but very often they're quickly sautéed and tucked into an omelet. Their presence in the market is truly fleeting, so just seeing them is a treat.

As for the white asparagus, many consider them the ultimate incarnation of the vegetable, although there is nothing genetically different between them and the green variety: their paleness comes from their never having seen the light of day. To achieve their ivory color, earth is mounded around the stalks so that they aren't exposed to sunlight and therefore can't develop chlorophyll, which would turn them green.

People say that white and green asparagus taste alike. I've never done a blind tasting, but I think the white is milder and the texture is more tender — though I'm willing to concede that I might be swayed by the stereotypes of fragility associated with whiteness.

In general, especially if the asparagus is white, it's likely to turn up as a starter. It may be part of a salad, but in all probability, it will be served in abundance, hot or at room temperature, without much more than a dipping sauce, perhaps hollandaise, mayonnaise, or a vinaigrette, and it may be topped off with a poached or soft-boiled egg. In fact, more and more, the egg has become the fashionable finisher, and with good reason: asparagus and eggs have a profound affinity for each other.

I love the drama of a pile of asparagus in the center of the table and the fun of being able to eat them with your fingers. While the French almost never use their fingers, asparagus is a full-contact food. Even if you were eating asparagus with the president in the Elysée Palace, you'd be doing the right thing by picking up the spears, dipping them into the sauce, and munching them from the tip down.

Asparagus can be boiled, steamed, or roasted, but no matter how you cook them, if you're using any kind of asparagus other than those that are pencil-thin, I think they should be peeled, even if they're young, fresh, and local. It takes just a few minutes, but since the peel can be stringy, peeling makes a huge difference in the eating. Start peeling the asparagus from about an inch or so beneath the tip and go all the way to the base, then snap the asparagus at what seems to be its natural breaking point or cut all the asparagus in your batch to the same size. (You can save the peels and woody bases for a vegetable broth.) If you choose asparagus of a similar thickness and trim them evenly, they should all be properly cooked at the same time. The way to test for doneness, regardless of the cooking method, is to pierce a spear with the point of a paring knife — when the spear is crisp-tender, the asparagus is done.

The cooking times that follow are for thick asparagus; skinny asparagus cook faster and should be checked early and often.

TO COOK ASPARAGUS UPRIGHT: Tie the asparagus into bundles — 8 to 12 stalks to a bundle — and stand them up in a tall pot with about 3 inches of boiling salted water in it. Cover and cook; you'll be boiling the base of the asparagus and steaming their tender tips. Start checking the asparagus after 5 minutes.

TO SKILLET-BOIL ASPARAGUS (the method I use most often): Fill a wide skillet with salted water, bring to a boil, and cook the asparagus (loose) in the water until they test done — start testing after 4 minutes.

If you're going to serve the asparagus as a starter, I'd suggest either of the watery methods. But if the asparagus are going to be a side dish to something grilled or something meaty, I'd roast them. Preheat the oven to 450 degrees F and line a baking sheet with parchment, foil, or a silicone baking mat. Lay the (peeled) asparagus out in a single layer, drizzle with a little olive oil, and, using your hands, lift and turn the spears around until they're evenly coated with oil. Sprinkle with sea salt, preferably fleur de sel. Roast the asparagus for about 15 minutes — check on them at the 10-minute mark — or until they pass the knife test.

While steamed and boiled asparagus are superb with creamy sauces and runny eggs, roasted asparagus take best to oil, balsamic vinegar (in moderation), and a sprinkling of grated cheese.

bacon and eggs
and asparagus salad

MAKES 4 SERVINGS

SERVING

A great starter for a spring or summer dinner, the salad can also be the main event at a warm-weather lunch. If you serve it for lunch, think about serving a hunk of cheese (or a small platter of cheeses) as well. Nutty cheeses like Comté, Gruyère, or Parmesan go particularly well with asparagus.

STORING

You can make the vinaigrette days ahead, and it's okay to cook the asparagus, bacon, and eggs a couple of hours ahead, but the eggs' final swirl-around in the bacon fat and the salad's assembly need to be last minute.

ASPARAGUS AND EGGS COULDN'T BE A better pair if they grew out in the field on the same branch. Both are odd flavors in their own ways — neither really resembles any other food — but they come together in classics like asparagus with creamy, eggy hollandaise sauce and asparagus mimosa, in which the spears are showered with sieved hard-boiled egg that resembles the flower. And here they are together again in a dish in which the asparagus are dressed with a sherry vinegar–nut oil vinaigrette, set on a mound of mesclun, and topped with bacon bits, chopped toasted nuts, and a wonderfully soft-boiled egg with a yolk that's runny enough to become a second sauce.

I love the way the eggs for this salad are cooked — they're boiled until they're just barely set, then peeled and rewarmed by rolling them around in bacon fat. I first had eggs cooked like this at Christian Constant's café in Paris and thought that perhaps they were made using the magical immersion circulator. I was delighted to find that I could get a kissing cousin to the eggs using an ordinary saucepan on my ordinary stove.

You can swap these eggs for Ruffly Poached Eggs (page 493) or for old-school Poached Eggs (page 492). Any of these will give you what this salad wants: egg flavor, a soft texture, and a runny yolk to mix with the dressing.

FOR THE VINAIGRETTE

¼ teaspoon Dijon mustard (optional)
1   tablespoon sherry vinegar
1   tablespoon extra-virgin olive oil
1   tablespoon hazelnut oil or walnut oil
    Salt and freshly ground pepper to taste

FOR THE SALAD

4   cold extremely fresh large eggs
20 asparagus spears, preferably thick, trimmed and peeled
6   strips bacon
3   handfuls mesclun or other mixed salad greens, rinsed and dried
    Salt and freshly ground pepper
⅓ cup chopped toasted hazelnuts or walnuts

TO MAKE THE VINAIGRETTE: Put all the ingredients in a small jar, cover, and shake to blend; or use a small bowl and a whisk. If you've used the mustard, the dressing will be fairly well blended; if not, it will blend, then separate — either way, it's fine. Set aside, and shake (or whisk) again before using. *(You can make the vinaigrette up to a week in advance and keep it in the fridge.)*

TO MAKE THE SALAD: Bring a medium saucepan of heavily salted water to a boil. One by one, put the cold eggs on a spoon and slowly and gently lower them into the water (saying a little don't-let-my-egg-break prayer on the way down). Allow the eggs to boil for exactly 6 minutes, then remove the pan from

the heat, lift the eggs into a strainer, and run them under cold water to cool them quickly. Fill the pan with cold water and leave the eggs in the water until needed.

Bring a large skillet of salted water to a boil. Slip the asparagus into the pan and cook for 4 minutes, or until you can pierce the spears with the tip of a paring knife. The asparagus should be cooked through but not at all mushy. Carefully transfer the spears to a plate lined with a double thickness of paper towels and pat them dry.

Pour out the salted water, rinse the skillet to cool it, dry it, and lay the strips of bacon in the pan. Cook over medium-low heat, turning as needed, until the bacon is golden and crisp on both sides. Remove the strips and put them between a double thickness of paper towels; when the bacon is cool, cut it into narrow strips or chop it into bits. Leave 2 tablespoons of the bacon fat in the skillet — you'll use it for the eggs.

When you're ready to serve, very, very carefully shell the eggs. It's a fussy job, because the eggs are so soft, and you might not get the shells off cleanly, but unless you break into the yolks, it will be fine. Rinse the eggs to remove any bits of shell and pat them dry. Warm the bacon fat over medium heat.

While the bacon fat is heating, assemble the salad. You can put it together on a platter or arrange it on individual plates. Either way, season the mesclun with salt and pepper, then toss it with about three-quarters of the vinaigrette, and arrange in the center of the platter or your plates. Toss the asparagus with the remaining vinaigrette (I do this with my fingers) and lay the spears over the greens.

Now return to the skillet. When the fat is warm, gingerly slip the eggs into the skillet and roll them around in the fat for a minute or two, just to coat them with fat, heat them slightly, and color them a little.

Lift the eggs out of the skillet and place them on top of the asparagus. Scatter the bacon and toasted nuts over the salad and serve immediately.

greenskeeping

When you get salad greens from the market, wash them, dry them completely, and put them in a large plastic bag, preferably one that isn't zipper-locked. Leave a few inches of space at the top, draw up the neck of the bag, and then blow enough air into the bag to push out the sides. Keep thinking "balloon," and close the bag at the top with a twist tie.

If your greens were farm-fresh, the carbon dioxide you puffed into the bag will keep them bright and fresh for a week — just remember to breathe new air into the bag each time you open it.

deconstructed BLT and eggs

MAKES **4** SERVINGS

THERE WAS A MOMENT IN FRANCE when everything that could possibly be deconstructed was: Caesar salad was served with its component parts arranged on a plate; ditto the club sandwich; and even regional treasures such as pipérade (page 210), the stewed pepper mix from the Pays Basque, were being taken apart piece by piece and, like Humpty Dumpty, not put back together again. For this dish, I decided to deconstruct a sandwich and saladize it too.

This started out as a BLT *déstructurisé,* made up of bits of crisp bacon, arugula (because it has more flavor than lettuce), and tomatoes, both fresh and sun-dried, all tossed in a vinaigrette and sprinkled with croutons salvaged from stale country bread. At the last minute, thinking that my friends might need something more substantial for lunch, I added the hard-boiled eggs and topped them with a spot of mayonnaise. Adding the eggs made the salad instantly recognizable to my French friends — they looked at the dish and decided that it was deconstructed *oeufs mayonnaise.* If only it were always so easy to cross the cultural divide.

SERVING
I like to bring the arranged salad to the table and toss it there. And, although it already has bread, I still serve bread — it makes it more of a meal, particularly in France.

STORING
You can cook the bacon and make the croutons a couple of hours ahead, hard-boil the eggs up to a day ahead (keep them in the fridge), and make the vinaigrette days ahead. However, once the ingredients are united, it's time to eat.

6	strips bacon
2	big, thick slices country bread, cut into cubes (about 1½ cups)
3	big handfuls arugula, rinsed and dried
3	tablespoons chopped oil-packed sun-dried tomatoes, drained

	Everyday Vinaigrette (page 484)
	About 12 cherry or grape tomatoes, halved
	Salt and freshly ground pepper
8	hard-boiled eggs, halved
2–3	tablespoons mayonnaise, homemade (page 490) or store-bought

Lay the bacon strips in a large skillet and cook them over medium heat, turning occasionally, until the fat is rendered and the bacon is crisp on both sides. Transfer the bacon to a plate lined with a double thickness of paper towels and pat off the excess fat (set the skillet aside). When the bacon is cool, coarsely chop it.

Discard all but about 2 tablespoons fat from the skillet and put the skillet over medium-high heat. When the fat is hot, toss in the bread cubes and cook, stirring, until they're golden. Remove the croutons with a slotted spoon and drain them on paper towels.

To construct the deconstructed salad, put the arugula and sun-dried tomatoes in a large salad bowl — I like to use one that's wide and shallow — and toss with most of the vinaigrette. Turn the fresh tomatoes around with some or all of the remaining vinaigrette (in other words, dress to taste) and strew them over the greens, along with the chopped bacon. Season the salad with salt and pepper. Arrange the eggs, yolks up, over the greens, then give each egg a dab of mayonnaise and a shower of salt and pepper. Scatter over the croutons.

crab and grapefruit salad

MAKES 4 SERVINGS

SERVING

I like to serve this salad *en verrines*, in small glasses, with a little mâche, arugula, or mixed herb salad (a blend of mint, parsley, and cilantro is nice) on top. Mix the greens with olive oil, a squeeze of lemon juice, salt, and pepper. However, the salad can be served without accompaniment. If you'd like to be very à la mode, pair the salad with avocado; see Bonne Idée.

STORING

Enjoy this the instant you make it — it can't be held.

BONNE IDÉE

Crab, Grapefruit, and Avocado Salad. To add avocado to this salad, you can put a layer of guacamole (page 22) in the bottom of the glasses or on top of the crab; you can cube an avocado, toss it with salt, pepper, and a splash of grapefruit juice, and scatter it over the salad; or you can mix a small amount of finely diced avocado into the salad. Avocado turns dark and softens quickly, so add it at the last minute.

A CRAB SALAD LIKE THIS ONE, fanciful and confetti-bright, is a perfect start to anything from a luxurious dinner to a picnic. While there are lots of small additions to the salad — teensy cubes of cucumber, red pepper, and chile, minced mint, and very small pieces of Ruby Red grapefruit — the standout flavor is, just as you want it to be, the crab, sweet and briny.

BE PREPARED: Cut the grapefruit sections a couple of hours, or as many as 6 hours, ahead of time and let them stand between a double layer of paper towels so that the fruit is as dry as possible — a small but crucial step.

1 Ruby Red grapefruit	2 small or 1 fat scallion, white and light green parts only, quartered lengthwise, thinly sliced
1 pound lump crabmeat, picked through for shells and cartilage	½–1 small chile pepper, very finely minced (optional)
1 Kirby cucumber or a 2-inch piece of seedless cucumber, peeled, halved lengthwise, seeded, and cut into ¼-inch dice	About 1½ tablespoons extra-virgin olive oil
	Salt and freshly ground pepper
	Tabasco (optional)
½ red or orange bell pepper, ribs and seeds removed, cut into ¼-inch dice	Fresh lemon juice (optional)
	1 tablespoon minced fresh mint

Cut the grapefruit crosswise in half and carefully cut out the half-segments, slicing along the membranes to release the fruit. Squeeze the juice from the hollowed-out halves and keep it covered in the refrigerator (discard the rinds). Put a double layer of paper towels on a plate or cutting board and arrange the grapefruit segments on the paper. Cover with another double layer of towels and pat the segments lightly. Discard the paper towels, arrange the fruit on a new layer of towels, and cover again. Let the segments sit for at least 2 hours, or for as long as 6 hours; if the towels are very wet, change them again.

When you're ready to make the salad, drain the crabmeat if necessary, turn it out onto a double thickness of paper towels, and pat it dry. Put it in a bowl and add the cucumber, bell pepper, scallion, and chile, if you're using it.

Cut the grapefruit segments into very small pieces, add them to the bowl, and, using a fork (or your fingers), gently toss the ingredients together. Don't overdo it — you want the crab to stay in largish pieces if possible. Add 1 tablespoon of the oil and 1 tablespoon of the reserved grapefruit juice and season with salt and pepper and, if you'd like, a couple of shakes of Tabasco. Taste the salad and decide what you'd like to add, if anything: I usually add a squirt or two of lemon juice for extra pop, or you may need a little more oil. Just pay attention to the amount of liquid you add — you don't want the salad to be wet. When you've got it just the way you want it, stir in the mint and serve.

couscous salad

MAKES **6** SERVINGS

SERVING

As is, the salad makes a great lunch or side dish to grilled fish. Add chicken (see Bonne Idée), and it's an any-time-of-day meal.

STORING

You can put the salad together up to a day ahead and keep it covered in the refrigerator. Leftovers will hold overnight as well.

I T TOOK A REAL EFFORT TO COMMIT this salad to paper, since it's something that I make all the time but never with a recipe. I cook the couscous (the quick-cooking kind) in broth with some spices and then mix it with whatever bits and pieces of fruits and vegetables I've got in the house. It's never the same, always good, and always, because of the cinnamon and turmeric, raisins, nuts, and chickpeas, reminiscent of the traditional North African stew that inspired it.

Adding chicken to the salad makes the dish a complete meal. If you've got leftover chicken, cut the chicken into cubes and stir it into the salad when you stir in the vegetables; if not, the dish is worth cooking chicken for it specifically. See Bonne Idée for chicken that's marinated in olive oil and lemon juice, then grilled, indoors or out.

2 cups chicken broth or vegetable broth

2 tablespoons extra-virgin olive oil, or as needed

2 garlic cloves, split, germ removed, and minced
  Salt

1 tablespoon ground ginger

1 teaspoon turmeric

½ teaspoon ground cinnamon

¼ teaspoon ground cumin

1 10-ounce box quick-cooking couscous

½ cup moist, plump raisins (dark or golden)

1 small cucumber, peeled, halved lengthwise, seeded, and cut into ½-inch cubes

1 red bell pepper, cored, seeded, and cut into ½-inch cubes

1 carrot, trimmed, peeled, quartered lengthwise, and thinly sliced

1 cup thinly sliced sugar snap peas

1 can (about 16 ounces) chickpeas, drained, rinsed, and patted dry
  Finely grated zest of 1 lemon, or as needed

¼ cup fresh lemon juice, or as needed
  Freshly ground pepper

¾ cup loosely packed fresh cilantro leaves, coarsely chopped

½ cup toasted chopped almonds (optional)

Bring the broth, 1 tablespoon of the olive oil, the garlic, 1 teaspoon salt, the ginger, turmeric, cinnamon, and cumin to a boil in a medium saucepan. Whisk the broth just to make sure the spices have dissolved, then stir in the couscous and turn off the heat. Scatter the raisins over the couscous, cover the pan, and let sit for 10 minutes.

Fluff the couscous with a fork (if there are lumps, you may have to break them up with your fingers) and turn it into a large bowl. Stir in the vegetables, chickpeas, and lemon zest.

Put the lemon juice, another teaspoon of salt, and the remaining 1 tablespoon olive oil in a small jar, cover, and shake to blend; or use a small bowl and a whisk. Pour over the couscous and toss well. Taste for salt, and season with pepper; set aside to cool. *(The couscous can be lightly covered and left at room temperature for about 3 hours or covered tightly and refrigerated overnight; bring to room temperature before serving.)*

At serving time, taste again for seasoning — it's almost certain you'll need more salt, and you might want more lemon juice, zest, and olive oil too — and stir in the cilantro and toasted almonds, if you're using them.

grain salads

Walking the grain aisle in any French supermarket is like taking a quick whirl around the world. There's rice from just about every country that grows it; couscous for sure (it's a natural, given that the couscous countries of Algeria and Morocco were once French); tabouleh (also known as bulgur wheat); quinoa, a relatively new addition (it appeared in health food markets before it went mainstream); barley (which turns up in the cooking of Alsace); kasha; and a couple of things we don't see often in the United States: quick-cooking wheat berries and grain mixes that, like the wheat, can go from pantry to table in 10 minutes.

Of course, rice and couscous are the bestsellers, but what I find odd is that the other grains seem to appear more often in restaurant dishes than in home-cooked meals. Not true *chez moi,* where I love using the grains for salads as well as for side dishes.

Grain salads have at least one well-known French precedent, the rice salad, a time-treasured way to make good use of leftovers, but I'm on a mission to get the others into the salad bowl too. Depending on what you add to them, grain salads can be side dishes or mains and served warm, cool, or, best of all, outdoors — they're perfect picnic take-alongs.

BONNE IDÉE

Lemon-Grilled Chicken Breasts. You'll need 6 skinless, boneless chicken cutlets, each about 5 ounces, pounded to a thickness of about ⅓ inch. Pour 2½ tablespoons extra-virgin olive oil and 2 tablespoons fresh lemon juice into a roasting pan or a large plastic bag. Season with salt and pepper and mix well. Drop in the chicken breasts, turn them around so that they're coated with the marinade, and marinate for 30 minutes at room temperature or for up to 3 hours in the refrigerator (bring them to room temperature before cooking). Prepare an outdoor grill, if you've got one, or heat a grill pan over high heat. Remove the cutlets from the marinade and pat dry with paper towels. Grill the chicken until it's opaque at the center, about 4 minutes on a side. Transfer the cutlets to a serving platter, drizzle with olive oil, and sprinkle them, if you'd like, with chopped fresh cilantro. Sometimes I serve the chicken with the couscous and lemon wedges on the side, and sometimes I slice the chicken into strips and put the pieces on top of the salad.

quinoa, fruit, and nut salad

MAKES 4 SERVINGS

SERVING

If you're using salad greens, divide them among four individual bowls, season the greens with salt and pepper, spoon over the quinoa salad, and top each portion with a spoonful of yogurt. If you're not using the greens, simply serve the salad topped with the yogurt.

STORING

The salad is best made a few hours ahead of time and eaten the day it's made. However, leftovers, covered and refrigerated, are very good the next day.

WHEN A FOOD-OBSESSED FRIEND OF MINE was moving from New York to Paris for a couple of months, he wrote to ask if there were things he should bring with him. When I asked what he was thinking about, he wrote back just one word, "quinoa." I informed him it was one less thing he'd have to carry, since quinoa is very easy to get in France — in fact, the ancient, highly nutritious Andean grain is quite trendy. A little nutty and a little wheaty, quinoa can be served hot, but my favorite quinoa dish is this salad, in which the grain is tossed with dried fruits and nuts, finished with herbs and a ginger vinaigrette, and served over greens with tangy chilled yogurt.

BE PREPARED: Start this an hour or so before serving so the flavors blend.

1½ cups quinoa Salt and freshly ground pepper	¼ cup chopped fresh herbs, such as basil, parsley, cilantro, or mint, or a combination
1⅓ cups mixed moist, plump dried fruit, such as cranberries, golden raisins, dark raisins, and/or cut-up apricots	Juice of 1 lemon
	½ teaspoon ground ginger
	3 tablespoons extra-virgin olive oil
1 cup mixed seeds and nuts, such as sunflower and pumpkin seeds, pine nuts, and chopped almonds and/or walnuts	1 tablespoon walnut or hazelnut oil (or another tablespoon of olive oil)
	4 cups mixed salad greens, rinsed and dried (optional)
	1 cup plain yogurt (it can be nonfat), for serving

Rinse the quinoa under cold running water and drain it in a sieve. Bring 3 cups of water to a boil in a medium saucepan, salt the water, and stir in the quinoa. Lower the heat and let the quinoa cook gently for 12 to 15 minutes, or until the grains have expanded — when they're cooked, each little grain will have a thin ring around it. Turn off the heat, cover the pan, and let it sit for 5 minutes. There may still be water in the bottom of the pan, so drain the quinoa in the sieve and cool it to room temperature.

Turn the quinoa into a serving bowl and season it to taste with salt and pepper. Gently stir in the dried fruits, nuts, and herbs.

Put the lemon juice, ginger, olive oil, nut oil, and salt and pepper to taste in a small jar and shake to blend; or whisk together in a small bowl. Pour the vinaigrette over the quinoa and mix well with a large spoon or a rubber spatula. If you've got the time, cover the salad and let it stand at room temperature for at least 1 hour. The salad really benefits from a rest so the flavors can blend.

When you're ready to serve, taste the salad to see if it needs more salt and pepper. Spoon over lightly seasoned greens, if using, and top with the yogurt.

wheat berry and tuna salad

MAYBE ONE DAY WE'LL BE ABLE to get the almost-instant wheat I can find in France, but in the meantime, there are wheat berries, which have a mild nutty flavor, a delightfully chewy texture, and the good manners not to ask anything more from the cook than time. All you have to do is put them in a pot of salted water, cook them until they're tender (set aside a good hour for this), and then use them warm, as a side dish, or cool, in this salad, which includes canned tuna and a cache of colorful vegetables. Topping the salad with tomatoes, avocado, and hard-boiled eggs makes it even more substantial and colorful.

MAKES 4 SERVINGS

1 cup wheat berries

1½ teaspoons Dijon mustard

1½ tablespoons white wine vinegar

4½ tablespoons extra-virgin olive oil, plus about 1 teaspoon for tossing

Salt, preferably sea salt, and freshly ground pepper

Pinch of red pepper flakes

2 celery stalks, trimmed and chopped

1 small onion, chopped

1 red or green bell pepper, cored, seeded, and diced

1 medium red apple, cored and diced

2 5- to 6-ounce cans chunk light tuna packed in oil, drained

4 cups mixed salad greens, rinsed and dried

8 cherry or grape tomatoes, halved

1 avocado, peeled, pitted, and diced

2 hard-boiled eggs, quartered

SERVING
The salad is complete just as it is. You really don't need bread with it — you've already got wheat on the table — but in true French fashion, I always include a basket with bread, and in true French fashion, it's always emptied.

STORING
You can cook the wheat berries up to 1 day ahead and keep them in the fridge (bring them to room temperature before dressing), but the composed salad is really best eaten soon after it's made.

You'll need to get the wheat berries cooked a few hours before assembling the salad: Bring a large pot of salted water to a boil and add the berries, lower the heat so that the water simmers, and cook, stirring occasionally, until the berries are tender but not mushy, 1 to 1¼ hours. Drain, rinse under cold water, drain again, and let cool to room temperature. (*The wheat berries can be cooked ahead, covered, and refrigerated for up to 24 hours; bring to room temperature before using.*)

Put the mustard, vinegar, olive oil, salt and pepper to taste, and red pepper flakes in a small jar and shake to blend; or whisk together in a small bowl.

Put the wheat berries in a large bowl, pour the vinaigrette over them, and mix well with a large spoon or rubber spatula. If you've got the time, cover the berries and let them stand at room temperature for about 1 hour, so that they fully absorb the vinaigrette.

Add the celery, onion, bell pepper, apple, and tuna to the salad and stir everything together gently. Taste and add more salt and pepper as needed.

Put the mixed greens in a large serving bowl or on a platter. Season with salt and pepper and toss with about 1 teaspoon olive oil. Spoon the wheat berry salad over the greens, top with the tomatoes, avocado, and hard-boiled eggs, and season these newcomers with a little salt and pepper.

lentil, lemon, and tuna salad

I'M CRAZY ABOUT THIS SALAD, which is piquant, pungent, surprising, and a serendipitous creation: I'd tasted a lentil cornichon salad at a bistro, and when I wanted to attempt a re-creation, there wasn't a single little pickle lurking anywhere in my fridge. While foraging for a stand-in, I came up with the idea to use tapenade and *citrons confits,* also doing business as Moroccan or preserved lemons. As for the tuna? I can't really explain it. I tasted the salad with the lemon, olive paste, and lentils and the word *tuna* just popped into my brain, and I'm glad it did: it turned out to be what linked all the ingredients together. Although the salad can be served in small portions as a starter, I usually make it for lunch, putting a scoop of it over mixed greens and topping it with halved cherry or grape tomatoes tossed with a little olive oil. Spread on crackers, it also makes a good little nibble with drinks.

The salad starts with cooked lentils du Puy. I use the basic recipe on page 367, but you can cook the lentils any way you wish. If you're lucky enough to have leftover lentils, you'll be that much ahead of the game.

BE PREPARED: While the salad is fine right after it's made, it's better if you refrigerate it for a couple of hours before serving.

2 teaspoons grainy mustard, preferably French	About 3 cups cooked lentils du Puy (see page 367), preferably still warm
2 teaspoons black olive tapenade, homemade (page 487) or store-bought	1 small preserved lemon (see Sources)
2 tablespoons red wine vinegar	2 scallions, white and light green parts only, thinly sliced
3 tablespoons extra-virgin olive oil (you might need a tad more)	1 5- to 6-ounce can chunk light tuna, packed in oil
	Salt and freshly ground pepper

Stir together the mustard and tapenade in a small jar; or whisk together in a small bowl. Add the vinegar and olive oil and shake or whisk until the vinaigrette is well blended. Pour the dressing over the lentils and stir to blend.

You've got a choice about how you want to use the preserved lemon. Most commonly, only the rind is used, but the soft inner pulp can also be stirred into this salad. (I include the pulp.) If you want to use the whole lemon, finely chop it; if you're using just the rind, cut it away from the pulp, discard the pulp, and chop the rind into small bits. Stir the lemon and scallions into the salad.

Drain the tuna and use a fork to flake it over the salad. Season very lightly with salt and generously with pepper, and toss. Taste, and if you think it needs it, stir in a little more olive oil.

You can serve the salad now, but it's better if you cover it and chill for a couple of hours: the rest gives the flavors time to blend. Right before serving, taste again for seasonings and oil.

potato chip tortilla

THIS IS A FAST, FUN, AND FUNNY version of the traditional Basque tortilla made with cubed potatoes (page 142). The French would call this a *clin d'oeil,* or a wink, at the original, and they'd be surprised not only at the potato chips that stand in for the usual sautéed spuds, but at the creator, Jean-François Piège, formerly the chef of Les Ambassadeurs, the Michelin-starred restaurant in Le Crillon. I found the recipe in a French food magazine, played around with it a little, and served it as an hors d'oeuvre at a dinner party in Paris. Not a soul had even an inkling that what they were savoring had been a snack food of a type they'd never eat (or at least never admit to eating).

BE PREPARED: The tortilla is best made ahead and served at room temperature as finger food — convenient for parties.

MAKES 4 LUNCH MAIN-COURSE SERVINGS OR 8 HORS D'OEUVRE SERVINGS

SERVING
Like most Spanish tortillas, this one is good cut into small pieces and served with drinks or quartered and served with a salad for lunch. If you'd like, pair the tortilla with strips of smoked salmon or paper-thin slices of Spanish ham.

STORING
You can make the tortilla several hours ahead of time and, when it's cool, cover it lightly and keep it at room temperature until serving time. Leftovers can be kept covered in the refrigerator — chilled, the tortilla will be quite firm but nice for nibbling.

- 3½ ounces (half a 7-ounce bag) potato chips
- 4 large eggs
- 1 small onion, finely chopped, or 6 scallions, white and light green parts only, thinly sliced (optional)
- ¼ cup minced fresh herbs, such as cilantro, parsley, or basil, or a combination
- 2 garlic cloves, split, germ removed, and finely chopped
- Pinch of piment d'Espelette (see Sources) or cayenne
- Salt and freshly ground pepper
- 1 tablespoon olive oil

Put the potato chips in a bowl, reach in, and crush the chips — a noisy, greasy job that leaves you with potato-chip fingers you'll want to lick.

Put the eggs, onion or scallions (if using), herbs, garlic, and piment d'Espelette or cayenne into another bowl. Season with salt and pepper and whisk to combine. Pour the eggs over the chips and stir to blend well.

You'll need a small skillet that can go under the broiler: 9 inches is about as big as it should be. I use an old-fashioned cast-iron skillet, but a nonstick skillet is also good. (If you're not sure that the handle can go under the broiler, wrap it in foil.) Position a rack under the broiler so that when you slide the skillet onto it, it will be about 6 inches from the heat source. Turn on the broiler.

Place the skillet over medium heat and pour in the olive oil. When the oil is hot, give the eggs and chips a last stir and pour them into the pan. Use a fork to push the mixture out to the edges of the pan if necessary, then turn the heat down to low. Cook the tortilla for 2 to 3 minutes, or until it is set around the edges and the top is almost done (being set is more important than the timing, so just keep watching the eggs). Remove the pan from the heat and run a spatula around the edges and under the tortilla in case it has stuck to the pan.

Slide the pan under the broiler and cook until the top of the tortilla is set, about 1 minute. Slide the tortilla onto a serving platter or board, and serve warm or at room temperature.

basque potato tortilla

MAKES 4 LUNCH MAIN-COURSE SERVINGS OR 8 HORS D'OEUVRE SERVINGS

SERVING

To serve the tortilla as an hors d'oeuvre or as tapas with wine or, in Basque fashion, sangria, cut it into thin wedges, or square the sides and cut it into cubes. If the tortilla is destined for lunch, divide it into quarters and serve it with a tossed green salad. If you'd like, drizzle a little olive oil over each wedge.

STORING

You can make the tortilla several hours ahead and keep it lightly covered at room temperature. Leftovers can be kept covered in the refrigerator — chilling will firm the tortilla, but it will still make a good snack.

BONNE IDÉE

Since this tortilla comes from the land of ham, you might want to add some to the dish. You can stir a small handful of finely diced ham into the eggs and potatoes before cooking the tortilla, or serve the tortilla with a few slices of lightly sautéed Spanish ham or prosciutto. For a more American but equally good touch, serve the tortilla with strips of crisp bacon to nibble alongside. Do that, and you're sure to see why the dish could be a diner special.

WHILE THE IDEA OF A ROOM-TEMPERATURE omelet served with a salad for lunch or in bite-sized pieces as an hors d'oeuvre might rightly put you in mind of the Italian frittata, the first time I had this dish, it had the odd effect of making me think of eggs and hash browns, the classic American diner breakfast. Of course it's the well-browned potatoes and chopped onion that did it.

This particular omelet, so popular in the Basque region of France, goes by its Spanish name, *tortilla*, and everything about it is casual, from the way it is often served (on toothpicks) to the way it is made. Unlike traditional omelets that require close attention and a practiced flick of the wrist for the crucial flip-over, the tortilla needs nothing more than the patience to wait until the eggs cook enough to be run under the broiler.

You do need to be finicky about one thing with this dish: a clean skillet. Make sure that after you cook the potatoes and onion, you wipe the pan clean of any little bits that have stuck to the bottom.

About 3½ tablespoons extra-virgin olive oil	2 garlic cloves, crushed but not peeled (optional)
1 pound starchy potatoes (such as Idaho/russet or Yukon Gold), peeled and cut into ½- to 1-inch cubes	1 rosemary sprig (optional) Salt and freshly ground pepper
1 medium onion, coarsely chopped	9 large eggs, at room temperature Pinch of piment d'Espelette (see Sources) or cayenne

You'll need a heavy skillet with a diameter of 9 to 10 inches — I use an old-fashioned cast-iron skillet. (Smaller is better than larger here.) Choose one with a handle that can go under the broiler. (If you're not sure about the handle, wrap it in aluminum foil.) Pour about 2 tablespoons of the oil into the skillet and warm it over medium heat. Add the potatoes and onion, as well as the garlic and rosemary, if you're using them, and turn the ingredients around until they glisten with oil. Season with salt and pepper, lower the heat, and cook slowly until the potatoes are golden and cooked through, about 20 minutes; you should be able to pierce the potatoes easily with the tip of a knife. Discard the garlic and rosemary, if you used them, and transfer the potatoes and onion to a bowl. Carefully wipe out the skillet with a paper towel. (If anything has stuck to the bottom of the pan, you should wash and dry it — you need a nice clean surface so the tortilla will be easy to unmold.)

Depending on how long your broiler takes to heat, you should turn it on now or when the tortilla has cooked for a few minutes. Before turning it on, position a rack under the broiler so that when you slide the skillet onto it, the pan will be about 6 inches from the heat source.

In a large bowl, beat the eggs with salt and pepper to taste and the piment d'Espelette or cayenne, then stir in the potatoes and onion.

Put the skillet over medium-high heat and pour in about 1½ tablespoons oil. When the oil is hot, add the eggs and potatoes to the pan. Immediately lower the heat and let the eggs cook, undisturbed, for about 2 minutes. Run a silicone spatula or a table knife around the edges of the pan to release the tortilla, then cover the pan and cook slowly for another 8 to 10 minutes, or until the top is almost set — there'll be a circle of liquid or jiggly egg at the center. Every couple of minutes, run your spatula around the sides of the pan and just under the tortilla to keep it from sticking.

Slide the pan under the broiler and cook until the top of the tortilla is set: check it after 1 minute, and then keep checking — it can go fast. Transfer the tortilla to a serving platter and allow it to cool to room temperature before cutting and serving it. (Of course there's nothing to stop you from eating it now, like an omelet.)

Onion-Herb Tortilla. Cook 1½ cups chopped onions in 2 tablespoons olive oil until very soft and lightly golden, about 20 minutes. Mix the onions with about ⅓ cup minced fresh herbs, such as parsley, chives, thyme, and rosemary, let cool slightly, then stir this mix into the eggs; omit the potatoes. Proceed as directed.

Mushroom Tortilla. Cook ½ pound cremini mushrooms, trimmed and sliced, 1 large spring onion or 1 medium yellow onion, chopped, and 2 minced garlic cloves (split and germ removed) in 2 tablespoons olive oil until the mushrooms are cooked through. Add ⅓ cup minced herbs (parsley, chives, thyme, and rosemary), let cool slightly, and then stir into the eggs; omit the potatoes. Proceed as directed.

Spinach–Green Onion Tortilla. Trim and wash 10 ounces spinach. Bring a large pot of salted water to a boil. Drop the spinach into the boiling water and blanch for 2 minutes, then drain and transfer to a bowl of cold water and ice cubes to set the color. Pull the spinach out of the bowl and, working in batches, squeeze it between your palms. Coarsely chop the spinach. Cook 2 large spring onions or 2 bunches scallions, sliced, and 2 minced garlic cloves (split and germ removed) in 2 tablespoons olive oil for 3 minutes. Season with salt and pepper, add the spinach, and cook for 1 minute more; let cool slightly, then stir into the eggs; omit the potatoes. Proceed as directed.

eggplant "tartine" with tomatoes, olives, and cucumbers

MAKES 6 SERVINGS

SERVING

Even though the eggplant is playing the role of bread in this dish, it's nice to have a basket of sliced baguette on the table — you'll want something to sop up the last drop of juice on the plate.

STORING

You can roast the eggplant a few hours ahead and keep the slices at room temperature or refrigerate them. If you'd like, you can serve the eggplant cold, or you can bring it to room temperature. And you can mix the salsa ahead of time, adding everything except the vinegar, salt, and oregano — save those for the last-minute toss. However, once the tartines are assembled, they're best served soon so the eggplant doesn't get soggy.

CALLING THIS DISH A TARTINE, or open-faced sandwich, might stretch the nomenclature given that it's roasted eggplant that stands in for the traditional toasted bread, but I'm doing it in the service of good eating. I'm also following the example of Frédérick Grasser-Hermé, one of France's most creative cooks and the woman who first served me eggplant as a tartine. Inspired by her ingenuity, I created this version, which I've come to think of as slightly Italianate. Here the eggplant is cut into rounds (a little like bruschetta) and topped with a vinegary salsa of chopped tomatoes, capers, and olives (rather like caponata). However, I finish my tartine just as Frédérick did, with thin slices of crunchy cucumbers, a completely unexpected and delightful addition.

1	large eggplant (about 1¾ pounds)
	About 3 tablespoons extra-virgin olive oil, plus more for drizzling
	Salt, preferably fleur de sel, and freshly ground pepper
1	cucumber, peeled, halved lengthwise, and seeded
1	pint grape or cherry tomatoes, quartered lengthwise
2	celery stalks, trimmed and finely diced
½	Vidalia onion or 1 large spring onion, chopped (about ½ cup)
1	garlic clove, split, germ removed, and minced
5	large green olives, pitted and slivered
1	tablespoon capers, rinsed and patted dry
2	tablespoons coarsely chopped fresh oregano
3	tablespoons red wine vinegar
	Pinch of red pepper flakes

Center a rack in the oven and preheat the oven to 375 degrees F. Line a baking sheet with a silicone baking mat, parchment, or nonstick aluminum foil.

Using a vegetable peeler, working from top to bottom, cut away strips of the eggplant's peel at 2-inch intervals. Cut off the top and bottom of the eggplant and cut the eggplant crosswise into 6 slices, each about 1 inch thick. Put the slices on the lined baking sheet and brush each slice with about 1 teaspoon of the olive oil. Season lightly with salt and pepper, and roast the slices for about 45 minutes, or until they are tender all the way through — test with the tip of a knife — and lightly browned. Cool the eggplant on the baking sheet.

Using a mandoline or a Benriner slicer, the slicing blade of a box grater, or a knife, thinly slice the cucumber.

In a large bowl, toss together the tomatoes, celery, onion, garlic, olives, capers, and oregano. Whisk together the vinegar and 1 tablespoon of the olive oil. Pour this dressing over the vegetables, and toss well. Season with the red pepper flakes and salt and pepper.

Arrange the eggplant on plates or a platter, and spoon the tomato salsa over it. Toss the cucumber slices with a drizzle of olive oil, strew them over the tartines, and sprinkle the cucumber with a little salt.

peeling celery

My relationship to celery changed a couple of decades ago when I first saw someone, French, *bien sûr,* peel a celery stalk. When I asked her why, her answer was, "To make it more digestible."

I'm not certain that peeling the curved side of the celery — you do it with a vegetable peeler — makes it more digestible, but it is a pleasure not to have to battle with stringy celery in polite company.

These days, I routinely peel celery if I'm using good-sized hunks of it. If I'm thinly slicing it (and the strings would be short and not too problematic), I peel it only when I'm in the mood.

pumpkin-gorgonzola flans

MAKES **6** SERVINGS

SERVING
I serve these in their cups, but if you want to unmold them, you can — carefully. Run a blunt knife around the edges of the custards, dip the cups into a hot water bath, and turn each flan out onto a small plate. If you unmold the flans, you might want to accompany them with a very lightly dressed herb or baby spinach salad. In true French style, you can serve the flans with a dollop of crème fraîche (or sour cream). The American in me likes to drizzle the teensiest bit of honey or maple syrup over the cream or directly over the flans.

STORING
The flans are best served the day they are made, but they can be kept, lightly covered, at room temperature for about 6 hours before serving.

IF THERE WERE A COMPETITION BETWEEN French and American convenience foods, I'm pretty sure that the French would win. It's hard to compete with readily available all-butter puff pastry, pâte brisée, and sweet tart dough, as well as frozen potato pellets that make fabulous mashed potatoes in minutes, prepared crepes, and chestnuts (whole, pureed, frozen, bottled, and canned). But there's one thing that France doesn't have that we do: canned pumpkin! It's something that really surprises me, since the French are fond of pumpkin, as well as pumpkin's many cousins in the squash family. So, without canned pumpkin, determined French cooks roast or boil the hard-skinned vegetable, puree it, dry it by quickly stirring it around in a hot pan, and then transform it into dishes like this one, rich, custardy individual flans speckled with Gorgonzola and topped with a few chopped walnuts.

The effort needed to start from scratch would be worth the goodness of these flans, but, in fact, all you've got to do is open a can of pumpkin, whir a few things together in a food processor, and slide the flans into the oven. Easy.

1	15-ounce can pumpkin	2	tablespoons chopped toasted walnuts
3	large eggs		
2	large egg yolks		
½	cup heavy cream		Crème fraîche or sour cream,
	Salt and freshly ground pepper		for serving (optional)
3½	ounces Gorgonzola, crumbled (generous ½ cup)		

Center a rack in the oven and preheat the oven to 350 degrees F. Butter six custard cups — I use Pyrex cups with a capacity of 6 ounces — or ramekins, and choose a roasting pan that's large enough to hold the cups comfortably. Line the bottom of the pan with a double layer of paper towels and put the custard cups in the pan. Put a kettle of water on to boil.

Put the pumpkin, eggs, yolks, and cream in a food processor (or use a blender) and whir until well blended. Season with salt and pepper, and pour the custard into the cups. Divide the Gorgonzola among the flans and poke the cheese into the custard a little bit, just to distribute it. Sprinkle the tops of the flans with the walnuts. Pour enough hot water into the roasting pan to come halfway up the sides of the cups.

Bake the flans for 35 to 40 minutes, or until a knife inserted into one comes out almost clean. (Depending on the size and height of your cups, you may need more or less time, so start checking at 25 minutes.) Because you're going to let the flans sit in the water bath, they'll continue to cook, so it's better to err on the side of underbaked. Transfer the roasting pan to a rack and let the flans cool in their water bath to just-warm or to room temperature.

Top with crème fraîche or sour cream, if you like.

cheesy crème brûlée

MAKES 6 SERVINGS

SERVING
The custards should be served as soon as the topping is browned. They need nothing more than a little spoon and a glass of Champagne or white wine.

STORING
You can bake the custards up to 2 days in advance and keep them tightly covered in the refrigerator; bring them to room temperature before finishing them. Once you've topped them, they should be eaten right away.

WHAT COULD BE BETTER THAN COMBINING two of life's great culinary pleasures, crème brûlée and cheese? It's a double serving of voluptuousness, and you don't have to wait for dessert to get it. This recipe is essentially a crème brûlée, but you omit the sugar in the classic cream-and-egg-yolk base and dot the bottom of the ramekins with tiny cubes of cheese that melt and give the custard an even more velvety texture and, of course, a slightly salty tang. Then, instead of finishing the crème with a sugary crust, you sprinkle the top with grated cheese that bubbles, toasts, and browns when brûléed.

This is an elegant starter, the kind that you'd be served in a stylish restaurant, but it's also one that is easily within the reach of any home cook. In fact, because the dish needs to be made ahead, it's ideal for dinner parties: at serving time, all you've got to do is give the topping its final toasting. The best tool for this is a mini propane torch — it does the job fast and gives you the most even finish — but you can melt the cheese and get a nice crust using your broiler.

I like to use a combination of cheeses for this dish, my favorite being Parmesan and Comté. However, since Comté is difficult to find in the United States (and very expensive once found), my American version is Parmesan and cheddar — it may sound like a compromise, but it doesn't taste like one.

About 5 ounces cheese (a combination of Parmesan and Comté or cheddar)
1 cup heavy cream
¾ cup whole milk

3 large egg yolks
Pinch of freshly grated nutmeg
Salt and freshly ground white pepper

Center a rack in the oven and preheat the oven to 200 degrees F. Butter six shallow ramekins. It's important that they be shallow: you want a custard layer that's only ¾ inch thick (my ramekins are 4 inches across and 1 inch high and hold ⅓ cup). Line a baking sheet with a silicone baking mat or parchment paper, and place the ramekins on the sheet.

Cut 3 ounces of the cheese into teensy cubes and divide the cubes evenly among the ramekins. Wrap and refrigerate the rest of the cheese to firm it up for the grating that you'll do later.

Pour the cream and milk into a small saucepan and bring to a boil. Meanwhile, in a medium bowl, vigorously whisk the yolks with the nutmeg and salt and white pepper to taste. Whisking without stopping, dribble a little of the hot cream and milk into the eggs. Continue to whisk and dribble until you've incorporated about a quarter of the liquid and then, still whisking, pour in the remainder in a slow, steady stream. When everything is blended, rap the bowl on the counter a few times to get rid of the bubbles. (If rapping doesn't de-bubble your mixture, spoon off and discard the bubbles.) Divide the custard evenly among the ramekins.

Carefully slide the baking sheet into the oven and bake for 40 to 50 minutes, or until a knife inserted in the center of the custards comes out clean. Transfer the baking sheet to a cooling rack and allow the custards to cool to room temperature. *(Once cooled, the custards can be covered and refrigerated for up to 2 days; bring them to room temperature before continuing.)*

To make the topping, finely grate the remaining 2 ounces of cheese and sprinkle it evenly over the tops of the crèmes. If you've got a mini propane torch, pull it out and use it to brown the cheese evenly. If you're torchless, turn on the broiler and run the custards under it, watching ceaselessly and pulling the crèmes from the heat as soon as the cheese is golden. Serve immediately.

comté cheese

A dense, ivory-colored, nutty-flavored cow's-milk cheese, Comté is made in the Jura, the mountainous region that straddles France and Switzerland. In fact, it's that straddle that accounts for the differences between Comté and the more widely known Gruyère, since the process of making them, the look of the cheeses, and their flavors are almost identical.

The difference? Comté is French, Gruyère is Swiss. For a Comté to comply with the French A.O.C. (Appellation d'Origine Contrôlée) designation, it must have holes (like — dare I say this and confuse things further? — what we call Swiss cheese), while a Gruyère, to be a true Gruyère, must not. Both cheeses are made in large wheels and bought by the thick slice or wedge. They are excellent solo — I always have a Comté or Gruyère on my cheese platter (my favorites are Comtés and Gruyères that have been aged, so that they are firmer and slightly saltier) — and terrific in the kitchen, because they melt smoothly. In fact, they are the cheese of fondue, whose name means melted. You can generally use Comté and Gruyère interchangeably.

cheese soufflé

MAKES 4 TO
6 SERVINGS

SERVING
Serve the instant you lift
the soufflé dish off the
baking sheet. Bring the
soufflé to the table, bow to
the applause, and then use
a large spoon to scoop out
portions.

THIS IS THE CLASSIC, the soufflé that's served in the grandest restaurants and the most legendary bistros throughout France and the one that's got such a reputation for fussiness that novices don't dare attempt it. Really, the soufflé should be ashamed of itself, scaring off cooks for no good reason! There's nothing complicated about the dish, although there are three things you should know: 1) it's important to beat the egg whites until they hold firm peaks, but make sure they're still glossy — it's better to stop just shy of firm than to overbeat the whites and have them separate into little puffs; 2) fold the whites into the soufflé base gently, so you don't knock out all the air you so carefully beat into them — again, less is more, and it's better to have a few streaks of unincorporated whites speckling the batter than to work the mixture too much; and 3) it's crucial to get your guests to the table before you pull the soufflé out of the oven — a soufflé's drama is fleeting.

	Fine dry bread crumbs	Freshly grated nutmeg
2½	cups whole milk	6 large eggs, separated
3	tablespoons unsalted butter	½ pound cheese, such as Gruyère,
6	tablespoons all-purpose flour	Emmenthal, or Swiss, grated
	Salt and freshly ground white	
	pepper	

Position a rack in the lower third of the oven and preheat the oven to 400 degrees F. Give the inside of a 6- to 7-cup soufflé mold a thick coating of butter. Dust with bread crumbs, tap out the excess, and set aside. Line a baking sheet with a silicone baking mat or parchment paper.

Bring the milk to a boil in a medium saucepan; set it aside.

Melt the butter in a medium saucepan over medium heat. Stir in the flour and cook this mixture (a roux) for about 2 minutes, just long enough to rid the flour of its raw taste but not color it. Stirring with a whisk, slowly blend in the hot milk. When all the milk is incorporated and the béchamel is smooth, cook, stirring, for another 8 to 10 minutes, or until the sauce thickens — the whisk will leave tracks. Season the sauce generously with salt and white pepper and a little nutmeg. Pull the pan from the heat and pour the béchamel through a fine-mesh strainer into a medium bowl; allow the béchamel to cool for about 10 minutes. *(At this point, you can pack the béchamel into an airtight container and refrigerate it for up to 3 days; bring it to room temperature before using.)*

One by one, whisk the yolks into the béchamel, then stir in the grated cheese.

Working in a mixer fitted with the whisk attachment or in a bowl with a handheld mixer, whip the egg whites until they hold firm, shiny peaks. Stir one quarter of the whites into the béchamel to lighten it, then use a rubber spatula to gently fold in the remaining whites. Delicately turn the soufflé batter into the prepared mold, put the mold on the baking sheet, and slide the sheet into the oven.

Bake the soufflé for 40 to 50 minutes, or until it is well risen, golden brown, and firm to the touch but still a little jiggly at the center. If, after 25 to 30 minutes (don't even think about opening the oven door before the 25-minute mark), the soufflé is browning too much, carefully open the door and gently slide a piece of aluminum foil over the top.

Serve immediately.

eggs fresh and extra-fresh

"And I'd like six eggs, please, to make a cake," I told the *fromager*. And, even though I'd asked for *moyenne* (medium) eggs, because they correspond best to the large eggs I use in the United States, monsieur pulled a six-pack from the shelf and said, "I'm sorry, I've only got *gros* [large]. The mediums are extra-fresh, and it's not worth paying the higher price if you're going to bake with them."

While it might sound like a marketing expression, in France, "extra-fresh" is a real term on a use-by sticker. Farm eggs will often come with two best-if-used-by dates. One is the fresh-until date, and the other is the extra-fresh-until date, which is about 2½ weeks earlier than the first date and usually about 9 days after the eggs were laid (and, yes, that date is also on the box or stamped on the eggs).

During those precious few days when the eggs are extra-fresh, they're meant to be eaten soft- or medium-boiled, or even raw. Extra-fresh is to eggs what sushi-grade is to fish. If you've got extra-fresh or organic eggs and you want to take full advantage of them, coddle them (page 194), make ruffly eggs (page 493), poach them (page 492), or use them in mayonnaise (page 490) or a mousse (page 421).

muenster cheese soufflés

Soufflés aren't hard to make, but once they come out of the oven, they're prima donnas: they demand to be served immediately, or all of your whipping and folding will fall. If you'd like, serve a little tomato and pepper salad on the side (see Bonne Idée).

BONNE IDÉE
Tomato and Pepper Salad.
This is a nice little salad for any dish that needs a colorful accompaniment, but it's particularly good with the soufflé. Toss together about 20 grape tomatoes, cut in half, ½ red bell pepper and 1 roasted red pepper, both diced, 2 teaspoons extra-virgin olive oil, and a pinch of ground cumin. Season with salt and pepper and, if you think the salad needs it, a drop of white wine vinegar.

IF THE MUENSTER YOU KNOW IS the cheese sold at the supermarket deli counter, you're in for a wonderful surprise. True Muenster, the pride of Alsace, is a cow's-milk cheese that is cosseted to maturity and coveted by connoisseurs. It's one of those cheeses that is famous for its fragrance, which is big and bold (some might say room-clearing), and its flavor, which is far more subtle than you'd expect. It's great on a hunk of rye bread or on a wedge of apple or as the base of this soufflé.

Fine dry bread crumbs	Salt and freshly ground white
About 7 ounces very cold	pepper
French Muenster	¼ teaspoon ground cumin
1¼ cups whole milk	3 large eggs, separated
1½ tablespoons unsalted butter	
3 tablespoons all-purpose flour	

Position a rack in the lower third of the oven and preheat the oven to 400 degrees F. Generously butter the insides of four 8-ounce soufflé molds. Dust with the bread crumbs, tap out the excess, and set aside. Line a baking sheet with a silicone baking mat or parchment paper.

With a sharp paring knife, carefully slice away the rind from the cold cheese. Measure out 4 ounces of cheese (about how much you'll have left once you remove the rind) and cut it into ¼- to ½-inch cubes (you should have 1 cup).

Bring the milk to a boil in a small saucepan; set aside.

Melt the butter in a medium saucepan over medium heat. Whisk in the flour and cook this mixture (a roux) for about 2 minutes, to rid the flour of its raw taste but not color it. Slowly whisk in the hot milk. When all the milk is incorporated and the béchamel is smooth, cook, whisking constantly, for another 5 to 8 minutes, or until the sauce thickens — the whisk will leave tracks. Remove the pan from the heat, season the sauce generously with salt and white pepper, and stir in the cumin. Press the béchamel through a fine-mesh strainer into a bowl and allow it to cool for 10 minutes. *(At this point, the béchamel can be refrigerated for up to 3 days; bring it to room temperature before continuing.)*

One by one, whisk the egg yolks into the béchamel, then stir in the cubes of cheese.

Working in a mixer fitted with the whisk attachment or in a bowl with a handheld mixer, beat the egg whites until they hold firm but still glossy peaks. Stir about one quarter of the whites into the béchamel to lighten it, then use a rubber spatula to gently fold in the remaining whites. Delicately divide the batter among the soufflé molds, filling each mold about three-quarters full. (If you have leftover batter, bake it in another mold or in an ovenproof coffee cup.)

Put the molds on the lined baking sheet, slide it into the oven, and bake the soufflés for 20 to 25 minutes, or until they are well risen, golden brown, and firm to the touch but still a little jiggly at the center. Serve now!

recipe-swap onion "carbonara"

PATRICIA WELLS, COOKBOOK AUTHOR, cooking teacher, and friend, served this to accompany the Christmas goose we had at her house in Provence one year. I was crazy about the recipe, and when I asked if she'd give it to me, she said it was a variation of a recipe originally created by Michel Richard, the French chef who came to America forty years ago as a pastry chef and stayed to create several restaurants and write several books. The recipe is a brilliant play on the classic spaghetti carbonara, but, as Richard jokes, it contains zero carbs, since the pasta is replaced by steamed onions cooked al dente. While missing the carbs, the dish contains everything else that makes a carbonara so impossibly good, that being cream, bacon (or pancetta), butter (Patricia didn't use the butter and the dish was still excellent), Parmesan, and an egg yolk to thicken and smooth the sauce.

I went back to Paris and made the recipe two nights in a row for friends, each time serving it as a starter, my thinking being that the dish was so good it deserved to have the spotlight to itself. I must have been right, because my friends asked me for the recipe just as instantly as I had asked Patricia.

MAKES 6 SERVINGS

SERVING
This needs to be served as soon as the cream-yolk mixture and the Parmesan are stirred in.

STORING
You can steam the onions up to 3 hours ahead, and you can cook the bacon ahead as well, but you need to serve this right away.

BONNE IDÉE
Spaghetti and Onions Carbonara. Michel Richard created this dish to mimic spaghetti, but what he's created is a sauce that's spectacular over pasta. Try it and see if you don't agree.

2 pounds onions, halved, thinly sliced, and separated into half rings	1 large egg yolk
5 strips bacon	1 tablespoon unsalted butter
½ cup cream (Patricia uses light cream)	Salt and freshly ground pepper
	2–3 tablespoons freshly grated Parmesan

The onions need to be steamed, so if you have a large steamer, set it up now; if not, put some water in a large pot, fit the pot with a steaming basket, and bring the water to a simmer. Put the onions in the steamer, cover the pot, and let them steam for 6 minutes, or until they are just "al dente." Remove the basket from the pot. (*You can do this up to 3 hours before serving. Let the onions cool, then cover them lightly.*)

Lay the bacon slices in a cold skillet, place the skillet over medium heat, and cook, turning occasionally, until the bacon is crisp on both sides. Drain the bacon between layers of paper towels, then cut the strips crosswise into slender pieces. (*You can do this ahead as well.*)

Just before you're ready to serve, whisk ¼ cup of the cream and the egg yolk together in a small bowl.

Place a skillet large enough to hold all the ingredients over medium-low heat and add the butter. When it has melted, add the bacon and pour in the remaining ¼ cup cream. Warm it for just 30 seconds, then scrape in the steamed onions, season with salt and pepper, and cook, stirring, until the onions are heated through, 2 to 3 minutes.

Pull the pan from the heat and stir in the reserved cream mixture, as well as the grated Parmesan. Serve immediately.

gérard's mustard tart

MAKES **6** STARTER
SERVINGS OR **4**
MAIN-COURSE
SERVINGS

SERVING
The tart is delicious just
out of the oven, warm,
at room temperature, or
even slightly chilled —
although that wouldn't
be Gérard's preference,
I'm sure. If you're serving
it as a starter, cut it into
6 portions; if it's the main
event, serve it with a lightly
dressed small salad.

STORING
Like all tarts, this is best
soon after it is made, but
leftovers can be covered,
chilled, and nibbled on the
next day.

MY FRIENDS SYLVIE ROUGETET AND GÉRARD JEANNIN are the most
gracious hosts, and you don't have to take my word for it — the people
who've signed the guest book at Les Charmilles, their bed-and-breakfast just
outside Dijon, echo my sentiments all the time. But they're not as lucky as I am.
While they get treated to a hearty breakfast, as a friend, I get to stay for dinner
and play sous-chef to Gérard in the kitchen.

Gérard hasn't had a day of culinary training, but he's an inspired cook and
so organized that I think he could feed a battalion from the cozy confines of
his galley kitchen. It's a pleasure to watch him work — he cooks with his nose,
smelling every ingredient before he tosses it into a bowl, rubbing fresh herbs
between his fingers to bring out their fullest perfume, and leaning over a pot on
the stove to catch the fragrance of a broth as it simmers.

This is the tart Gérard made for Sylvie and me one evening. It's a play on a
traditional tart starring Dijon's most famous export — mustard — and it's both
creamy and piquant, comforting and surprising. It's also not as well known as
it should be. When I returned to Paris, the recipe tucked into my notebook,
I made the tart several times for friends, and each time it was greeted with
delight and puzzlement — I was serving them something they'd never tasted
before. In fact, as Gérard explained to me, the more traditional tart is made
with tomatoes, but he, in his usual fashion, improvised, with carrots and leeks,
since it was fall and tomato season was past.

The original tomato tart is delicious too, so I've included it under Bonne
Idée. No matter which version you make, be sure to use strong mustard from
Dijon. Gérard uses Dijon's two most popular mustards in his tart: smooth,
known around the world as Dijon, and grainy or old-fashioned, known in
France as "*à l'ancienne.*" You can use either one or the other, or you can adjust the
proportions to match your taste, but whatever you do, make sure your mustard
is fresh, bright colored, and powerfully fragrant. Do what Gérard would do:
smell it first. If it just about brings tears to your eyes, it's fresh enough for this
tart.

3 carrots (not too fat), trimmed and peeled	2 tablespoons Dijon mustard, or to taste
3 thin leeks, white and light green parts only, cut lengthwise in half and washed	2 tablespoons grainy mustard, preferably French, or to taste
2 rosemary sprigs	Salt, preferably fleur de sel, and freshly ground white pepper
3 large eggs	1 9- to 9½-inch tart shell made from Tart Dough (page 498), partially baked and cooled
6 tablespoons crème fraîche or heavy cream	

BONNE IDÉE
Tomato-Mustard Tart.
Tomato-Mustard Tart.
This is the original recipe and the one I think you'll make often when ripe, juicy tomatoes are in season. You'll need 1 super-large tomato, 1 or 2 regular-sized tomatoes, 2 or 3 plum tomatoes, or 15 to 20 cherry or grape tomatoes (this has to be approximate because I don't know how big your tomatoes will be). If you've got cherry or grape tomatoes, cut them in half; if you've got round or plum tomatoes, cut them into slices about ⅓ to ½ inch thick. Arrange the halves (cut side down) or slices in the filled tart shell, and don't worry when they sink into the filling; just take care not to put in so many halves or slices that the filling rises above the sides of the crust.

Center a rack in the oven and preheat the oven to 425 degrees F. Line a baking sheet with a silicone baking mat or parchment paper.

Cut the carrots and leeks into slender *bâtons* or sticks: First cut the carrots lengthwise in half, then place the halves cut side down on the cutting board and cut crosswise in half or cut into chunks about 3 inches long. Cut the pieces into ⅛- to ¼-inch-thick matchsticks. If your carrots were fat and you think your matchsticks don't look svelte enough, cut them lengthwise in half. Cut the leeks in the same way.

Fit a steamer basket into a saucepan. Pour in enough water to come almost up to the steamer, cover, and bring to a boil. Drop the carrots, leeks, and 1 rosemary sprig into the basket, cover, and steam until the vegetables are tender enough to be pierced easily with the tip of a knife, 10 to 15 minutes. Drain the vegetables and pat them dry; discard the rosemary sprig.

In a medium bowl, whisk the eggs together with the crème fraîche or heavy cream. Add the mustards, season with salt and white pepper — mustard has a tendency to be salty, so proceed accordingly — and whisk to blend. Taste and see if you want to add a little more of one or the other mustards.

Put the tart pan on the lined baking sheet and pour the filling into the crust. Arrange the vegetables over the filling — they can go in any which way, but they're attractive arranged in spokes coming out from the center of the tart. Top with the remaining rosemary sprig and give the vegetables a sprinkling of salt and a couple of turns of the pepper mill.

Bake the tart for about 30 minutes, or until it is uniformly puffed and lightly browned here and there and a knife inserted into the center of the custard comes out clean. Transfer the tart to a cooling rack and let it rest for 5 minutes before removing the sides of the pan.

Serve hot, warm, or at room temperature (or lightly chilled).

mustard

Mustard is to the French what ketchup is to us: the go-to condiment — it comes to the table at every café, along with the salt and pepper. The best-known mustard is named for the Burgundian city of Dijon (Dijon mustard actually refers to a style of mustard, one that's smooth, sharp, and strong).

Nonetheless, mustard didn't originate in France: it appears to have arrived with the ancient Romans. The fact that the French didn't invent mustard didn't stop them from adopting it and manufacturing their own, and by medieval times, it was a kitchen staple. Pope John XXII, living in Avignon in the fourteenth century, established the position of "Pope's First Mustard Maker," and two centuries later, the Sun King, Louis XIV, took to traveling with his own mustard pot in tow. In fact, mustard pots are traditional wedding presents in France, and you can still bring your own little pot to shops like Maille for a refill.

The two mustards that I keep on hand at all times are Dijon and grainy, known as *moutarde à l'ancienne,* or old-fashioned mustard, but if you're a mustard lover, I urge you to experiment. Mustard with green peppercorns makes a wonderful addition to vinaigrettes, and horseradish mustard is great with steak . . . and frites.

gorgonzola-apple quiche

THE FACT THAT FRANCE IS THE HOME of several magnificent blue cheeses, most notably Roquefort, hasn't stopped sophisticated French cooks and food lovers from falling in love with Gorgonzola dolce, the soft, mild blue cheese from Italy. Along with Parmesan and mozzarella, Gorgonzola turns up in just about every well-stocked *fromagerie* routinely in Paris and reliably in other cities. Gorgonzola has a milder, sweeter, less salty flavor and a softer, creamier consistency than Roquefort, and so it lends itself more readily to smooth concoctions like this quiche.

Like all quiches, this one looks and tastes as if it took a lot of time and skill; unlike many quiches, it offers a double surprise: the mild-sweet-salty pow of the Gorgonzola and the slight crunch of the lightly tart apple. If you're up for a third surprise, try adding some nuts to the mix — toasted walnuts or hazelnuts are especially good.

If you'd like a more traditional quiche — in fact *the* most traditional quiche, quiche Lorraine — take a look at Bonne Idée.

MAKES **6** SERVINGS

SERVING
The quiche can be served hot, warm, or at room temperature, as a starter or the main event at lunch or dinner. If you're serving it as a main course, think about having a green salad to keep it company.

STORING
You can keep the quiche lightly covered on the counter for a few hours if you're going to serve it at room temperature; if you want to keep it overnight, wrap it well and store it in the refrigerator. It's best to bring it to room temperature or to warm it briefly in a moderate oven before serving.

1 tablespoon unsalted butter	½ small apple (a tart-sweet apple, such as Empire or Gala), peeled, cored, and cut into small dice
1 small onion, finely chopped Salt and freshly ground white pepper	
1 9- to 9½-inch tart shell made from Tart Dough (page 498), partially baked and cooled	2 ounces Gorgonzola dolce
	⅔ cup heavy cream
	2 large eggs

Center a rack in the oven and preheat the oven to 400 degrees F. Line a baking sheet with a silicone baking mat or parchment paper.

Melt the butter in a small skillet over low heat and toss in the onion. Season the onion lightly with salt (the Gorgonzola is salty) and white pepper and cook until it is very soft but not at all colored, about 10 minutes; remove from the heat.

Put the tart shell on the lined baking sheet. Spread the onion, with whatever butter remains in the pan, evenly over the bottom of the crust. Scatter the apple over the onion. Cut the Gorgonzola into small cubes and scatter it over the onion and apple. Beat the cream and eggs together until well blended, season with salt and white pepper, and pour into the tart shell.

Gently slide the baking sheet into the oven and bake for 30 to 40 minutes, or until the filling is uniformly puffed (wait for the center to puff), browned, and set. Transfer the quiche to a cooling rack and allow it to cool and gather itself for 5 minutes or so.

Carefully remove the sides of the pan and slide the quiche onto a platter if you want to serve it hot, or onto a rack if you want to cool it. Serve hot, warm, or at room temperature.

BONNE IDÉE
Quiche Lorraine. Omit the apple and replace the Gorgonzola with 2 ounces Gruyère cut into very small thin slices — or grate the cheese. Cook the onion in butter, then transfer it to a bowl. Cut 3 strips cooked bacon into bite-sized pieces. (To be more authentic, start with a 2- to 3-ounce slab of smoked bacon, cut into short slender strips, called lardons. Cook in boiling water for a minute, drain, and pat dry.) To assemble, put the cheese in the bottom of the crust and top with the bacon. Beat together the 2 eggs, ⅔ cup heavy cream, and the cooked onion and pour the mixture over the bacon and cheese. Bake as directed.

quiche maraîchère

MAKES **6** SERVINGS

SERVING

If you're serving the quiche for lunch or as a starter to a light dinner, accompany it with a salad. If it's going to be a nibble with drinks, cut it into wedges that can be eaten as finger food.

STORING

Because this quiche is so good at room temperature, you can make it a few hours ahead and leave it out on the counter. Leftover quiche can be wrapped, refrigerated, and eaten the next day — either warm it briefly in the oven or let it come to room temperature.

WHEN YOU SEE THE WORD *MARAÎCHÈRE,* you know market-fresh produce is in the mix. Here it's in a quiche packed to the brim with celery, leeks, carrots, and little squares of red pepper. It's an unusual quiche in that it's got lots more vegetables than custard and the cheese is on top of it, not inside.

- 1 tablespoon unsalted butter
- 2 celery stalks, trimmed and cut into small dice
- 2 slender leeks, white and light green parts only, quartered lengthwise, washed, and thinly sliced
- 2 slender carrots, trimmed, peeled, and finely diced
- 1 medium red bell pepper, cored, seeded, and finely diced

- Salt and freshly ground pepper
- 1 9- to 9½-inch tart shell made from Tart Dough (page 498), partially baked and cooled
- ⅔ cup heavy cream
- 1 large egg
- 1 large egg yolk
- ⅔ cup grated cheese, preferably Gruyère (cheddar is good too)

Melt the butter in a large skillet over medium-low heat. Toss in the vegetables and cook, stirring, for about 10 minutes, or until they are tender. Season with salt and pepper, then scrape the vegetables into a bowl and let cool.

Center a rack in the oven and preheat the oven to 400 degrees F. Put the crust on a baking sheet lined with a silicone baking mat or parchment paper.

Spoon the vegetables into the tart shell and spread them out — they will just about fill the crust. Whisk the cream, egg, and egg yolk together, season with salt and pepper, and carefully pour over the vegetables. Depending on how your crust baked, you may have too much custard — don't push it. Pour in as much custard as you can without it overflowing and wait a few minutes until it's settled into the crannies, then, if you think it will take it, pour in a little more. Very carefully slide the baking sheet into the oven. (If it's easier for you, put the quiche into the oven without the custard, then pour it in.)

Bake the quiche for 20 minutes. Sprinkle the cheese over the top and bake for another 5 to 10 minutes, or until the cheese is golden and, most important, the filling is uniformly puffed (wait for the center to puff), browned, and set. Transfer the quiche to a rack, remove the sides of the pan, and cool until it's only just warm or until it reaches room temperature before serving.

spinach and bacon quiche

MAKES **6** SERVINGS

SERVING
Like many quiches, this one is excellent hot or only just warm and still very good at room temperature, so when you serve it is up to you.

STORING
Leftover quiche can be covered and kept in the refrigerator; bring to room temperature before serving. If your kitchen is cool, you can cover the quiche and keep it at room temperature overnight. Do that and, if you're like my husband, you might want to have a slice for breakfast.

I WAS SURPRISED TO COME INTO THE KITCHEN early one morning to find my husband happily having a leftover slice of this quiche for breakfast. But really, why not? It's got just about everything a spinach omelet would have — eggs, spinach, bacon, and cheese — and who wouldn't love that for breakfast? (Other than a Frenchman, who'd have a croissant to dunk into his coffee and call it quits.)

While this savory tart qualifies as a quiche, it's unlike most quiches in that cheese is not a primary ingredient. There's more filling than custard in this quiche, a somewhat more chockablock version of those served at lunchtime in the cafés of my Paris neighborhood, and more flavors — you'll catch smoky (the bacon), sweet (the onion and garlic), minerally (the spinach), and creamy (the custard).

1 9- to 9½-inch tart shell made from Tart Dough (page 498), partially baked and cooled	4 strips bacon
	1 small onion, finely chopped
	1 large garlic clove, split, germ removed, and finely chopped
10 ounces ready-to-use baby spinach (or about 1¼ pounds regular spinach, trimmed and washed)	Salt and freshly ground pepper
	2 large eggs
	⅔ cup heavy cream
	¼ cup freshly grated Parmesan

Center a rack in the oven and preheat the oven to 400 degrees F. Put the tart shell on a baking sheet lined with a silicone baking mat or parchment paper.

To cook the spinach, fit a steamer basket into a large pot. Pour in enough water to come almost up to the steamer, cover, and bring to a boil. Add the spinach, cover, and steam just until soft and thoroughly wilted, about 4 minutes. Remove the spinach, drain, and run under very cold water to cool it and set the color.

When the spinach is cool enough not to burn your hands, squeeze it between your palms to get out as much moisture as you can; do this in batches, so you can squeeze harder. Put the clumps of spinach on a cutting board and coarsely chop or thinly slice the spinach.

Put the bacon in a skillet, place the skillet over medium heat, and cook, turning occasionally, until the bacon is crisp on both sides. Transfer the bacon to a plate lined with paper towels to drain, and pat it dry (set the pan aside). Cut the bacon crosswise into thin strips.

Drain off all but 1 tablespoon of the fat from the skillet, return the skillet to medium heat, and toss in the onion and garlic. Season with salt and pepper and cook until soft but not at all colored, about 5 minutes; remove from the heat.

Add the spinach and bacon bits to the pan, toss to blend, and add a little more salt and a few generous grindings of pepper.

Turn the spinach-onion mixture into the crust, spreading it as evenly as you can. Whisk the eggs and cream together until well blended and pour into the tart shell, giving the custard a minute to seep around the spinach and settle in. Sprinkle the top of the quiche with the Parmesan.

Carefully slide the baking sheet into the oven and bake for 30 to 40 minutes, or until the filling is uniformly puffed (wait for the center to puff), browned, and set. Transfer the quiche to a cooling rack, remove the sides of the pan, and allow it to cool and gather itself for at least 5 minutes or so before serving.

mushroom and shallot quiche

MAKES 6 SERVINGS

SERVING
You can pair the quiche with soup or salad or both, but it's also lovely on its own.

STORING
Although it is at its best warm or at room temperature the day it is made, the quiche can be kept in the fridge overnight. Bring it to room temperature or heat it briefly in a moderate oven before serving.

MUSHROOMS AND SHALLOTS ARE A CLASSIC combination and the base of the traditional finely chopped filling called *duxelles*. Here the combo is used to give a deep, earthy flavor to another classic, quiche. Plain white mushrooms make an excellent quiche, but if you use wild mushrooms, or a mix of wild and white, the dish will only be better.

1½ tablespoons unsalted butter
2 shallots, finely chopped
   Salt and freshly ground
   pepper
½ pound mushrooms, trimmed,
   wiped clean, and cut into
   ¼-inch-thick slices
2 tablespoons minced fresh
   thyme

1 9- to 9½-inch tart shell made
   from Tart Dough (page 498),
   partially baked and cooled
¾ cup heavy cream
2 large eggs
2 scallions, white and pale green
   parts only, thinly sliced
2 tablespoons finely grated
   Gruyère

Melt the butter in a large skillet, preferably one that's nonstick. Toss in the shallots, season with salt and pepper, and cook over medium-low heat, stirring, until translucent, about 2 minutes. Add the mushrooms, season again with salt and pepper, turn the heat up to high, and cook, stirring, until they are softened and browned, 5 to 8 minutes. The mushrooms will first sop up all the liquid in the pan, then they'll exude it, then it will disappear. Sprinkle the mushrooms with 1 tablespoon of the thyme and cook for 30 seconds more, then turn the mushrooms into a bowl to cool for at least 15 minutes.

Center a rack in the oven and preheat the oven to 350 degrees F. Put the crust on a baking sheet lined with a silicone baking mat or parchment paper.

Sprinkle the remaining tablespoon of thyme over the bottom of the crust. Spoon over the mushrooms, avoiding any liquid that has accumulated in the bowl. Lightly beat the cream and eggs together just until well blended, season with salt and pepper, and pour over the mushrooms. Top the custard evenly with the sliced scallions and grated cheese.

Carefully slide the baking sheet into the oven and bake for 30 to 35 minutes, or until the custard is uniformly puffed (wait for the center to puff), lightly golden, and set. Transfer the quiche to a rack, remove the sides of the pan, and cool the quiche until it's only just warm or until it reaches room temperature before serving.

creamy mushrooms and eggs

HERE'S AN INSTANCE OF A PROBLEM averted and a recipe created. Friends were coming for dinner, and my plan had been to start the meal with peas, mushrooms, and poached eggs, but minutes before their arrival, I discovered that something had gone wrong with my peas (they were frozen and I'd defrosted them too far in advance). So the choice was: skip the appetizer or punt; I chose to punt. I might have chosen otherwise had I not caught a glimpse of some day-old brioche on the counter and thought about how lovely brioche is with mushrooms. Ten minutes later, I was serving toasted slices of the brioche alongside sautéed mushrooms and shallots, simmered with cream and topped with warm eggs, their yolks soft and runny. At the time, I had only white mushrooms on hand, but making the dish many times after, I confirmed what would be easy to guess: the dish is even tastier when you've got an assortment of mushrooms, some of them wild.

MAKES 4 SERVINGS

SERVING
Place a slice of brioche on each of four salad plates, spoon the mushrooms and shallots over one corner of each slice — it's nice when the mushrooms and cream spill over the edges of the bread onto the center of the plate, and top each with an egg. You can poke the eggs, so that the yolk runs out, or you can leave that little bit of fun to your guests.

STORING
This dish should be made and served *à la minute* — there's no prep ahead of time (unless you make poached eggs) and no leftovers après.

10 ounces mushrooms, preferably a mix of wild and cultivated, caps only, wiped clean	½ cup heavy cream
1 tablespoon unsalted butter	1 teaspoon chopped fresh rosemary
1½ teaspoons olive oil	1 teaspoon chopped fresh mint
1 large shallot, finely minced, rinsed, and patted dry	4 small slices brioche, homemade (page 497) or store-bought, or challah, lightly toasted
Salt and freshly ground pepper	4 Ruffly Poached Eggs (page 493) or Poached Eggs (page 492)

If you have large mushrooms, slice them a scant ¼ inch thick, then cut the slices crosswise in half. If you have smaller mushrooms, leave them whole or slice them in half. What you're looking for is bite-sized pieces — you don't want your guests to have to cut them to eat them.

Put a medium skillet over medium-high heat and add the butter and oil. When the bubbles from the butter have subsided, toss in the shallot and cook, stirring, until glistening and starting to soften, about 2 minutes. Add the mushrooms, season with salt and pepper, and cook, stirring often, until the mushrooms have given up their liquid. Continue cooking and stirring for another 2 minutes or so, until the mushrooms are tender, then pour in the cream. Bring the cream to a boil and cook for 3 minutes or so, until it thickens just a little, then pull the pan from the heat and stir in the rosemary and mint.

Arrange the brioche on salad plates and top with the mushrooms and then the eggs.

tomato-cheese tartlets

MAKES 4 SERVINGS

SERVING
These are a course unto themselves. If you want to add a little salad along with the basil on top of the tartlets, that would be good but not at all necessary.

STORING
The cut-out and pricked dough for the bases can be stored in the freezer for up to 2 months and baked when you need them. The finished tartlets should be eaten as soon after they're assembled as possible, or the pastry will get soggy.

WHEN TOMATOES ARE IN SEASON, the French are as determined as we are to find as many ways as possible to showcase their harvest. You see platters paved with overlapping circles of heirloom tomatoes dressed only with olive oil; tomato and mozzarella salads dotted with thick, syrupy balsamic vinegar; and tarts like these, which can stand alone as lunch.

Like Scallop and Onion Tartes Fines (page 168) and Fresh Tuna, Mozzarella, and Basil Pizza (page 166), these tartlets are built on a base of puff pastry that's been weighted down so that it bakes to a flat crisp. Slices of tomato and cheese — either mozzarella or goat — are spiraled over it. Invisible but providing a lot of flavor is an underlayer of tapenade or pesto. Once the tartlets are assembled, you can serve them immediately or warm them very briefly. In either case, they're best finished with a little olive oil and some fresh basil leaves. If you'd like to make them more like a salad, you can drizzle them with balsamic.

A note on quantities: This is almost as much an idea as it is a recipe. The quantity of puff pastry is exact, but the measurements for the other ingredients are more approximate — you'll have to judge for yourself how many tomatoes and how much cheese you'd like; ditto, how much tapenade or pesto. And, with a recipe like this, you can make more or fewer tartlets, and you can change the size of them — smaller tartlets are nice for aperitifs or picnics.

1 sheet frozen puff pastry (about 8½ ounces), thawed
About ⅓ cup tapenade, homemade (page 487) or store-bought, or pesto, homemade (page 488) or store-bought
4–5 ripe tomatoes, sliced into rounds

1 8-ounce ball mozzarella or about ½ pound fresh goat cheese (preferably in a log, because it's the easiest to slice)
Salt and freshly ground pepper
Olive oil, for drizzling
Fresh basil leaves, for garnish
Balsamic vinegar, for drizzling (optional)

Center a rack in the oven and preheat the oven to 400 degrees F.

Working on a floured surface, roll the puff pastry out into a square that's about 13 inches on a side. Using a plate or saucer with a diameter of about 6 inches as a guide, and the point of a paring knife, score and then cut out 4 rounds of dough. Line a baking sheet with parchment, lay the rounds on it, and prick them well all over with a fork. Put a second sheet of parchment over the rounds and top with another baking sheet to weight the dough down.

Bake the rounds for 15 minutes. Carefully remove the top baking sheet and the parchment — it can be a bit tricky, so protect your hands. If the rounds are well browned and crisp, they are done; if they look a little pale and not thoroughly baked, return them to the oven, uncovered, to finish baking. Put the baking sheet on a cooling rack and allow the crusts to cool until they're just warm or at room temperature. *(You can bake the rounds up to 8 hours ahead and keep them uncovered at room temperature.)*

TO FINISH THE TARTLETS: Spoon a thin layer of tapenade or pesto over each pastry round, leaving a border of about ½ to 1 inch bare. Next, arrange alternating slices of tomato and cheese in a pinwheel pattern, and put a slice of tomato and/or cheese in the center to fill the hole. Now you can season the tartlets with salt and pepper, drizzle them with oil, finish with a basil leaf and a little balsamic, if you like, and serve them. Or you can hold off on the final toppings and warm the tartlets first.

TO WARM THE TARTLETS: After adding the slices of tomato and cheese, put the tartlets on a baking sheet and run them under the broiler (keeping them about 5 inches from the heat) until the cheese just barely starts to melt, about 3 minutes; or warm them in a 425-degree-F oven for about 5 minutes. Season them with salt and pepper, drizzle them with olive oil, and top with fresh basil, and, if you like, a drizzle of balsamic.

fresh tuna, mozzarella, and basil pizza

MAKES 4 SERVINGS

SERVING
It's best to serve the pizza just a few minutes after it comes from the oven, so that the pastry is fresh and flaky and the tuna just a tad warm.

STORING
You can bake the pastry circles up to 8 hours ahead and keep them at room temperature; ditto the sautéed onions. Once the pizzas are assembled, they should be baked immediately and, once baked, served pronto.

GETTING INTO LE COMPTOIR, chef Yves Camdeborde's Paris bistro, is so difficult that nabbing a table comes with bragging rights. Since the place is so small, the food so very, very good, and the reservations policy nonexistent, food lovers from every part of the world are willing to stand in line at all hours and in all weather, and they never complain, because this is one place that consistently lives up to its reputation. My apartment is just down the street from Le Comptoir, and I have a personal policy about the restaurant: if I pass it and there's a table free, I take it.

Camdeborde worked in the kitchens of Le Crillon in the days of Christian Constant's reign (see page 130 for Constant's eggs), when the restaurant had earned the Michelin Guide's top rating of three stars, and he shocked the culinary elite when he decamped to open his own place where, as he said, "neighborhood people could eat great food for the price of a pizza."

Prices have gone up a bit since Yves started, but they are still reasonable. However, whatever pizza he thought his neighborhood friends were eating at the time, it's a sure bet it wasn't like this one. Camdeborde's reading of a pizza is surprising — it's part pissaladière (page 45), part salade Niçoise (page 125), and part pizza, with a large dose of invention tossed in. The pizza is also colorful and easy to make, especially if you bake the (store-bought) puff pastry rounds in advance.

1 sheet frozen puff pastry (about 8½ ounces), thawed
¼ pound fresh mozzarella
  Extra-virgin olive oil
4 large spring onions, trimmed and finely chopped, or 2 medium onions, finely chopped
  Salt and freshly ground pepper
½ pound sushi-grade tuna, in one piece

12 large fresh basil leaves
4 cherry tomatoes, quartered
4 black olives, pitted and quartered
4 small radishes, trimmed and thinly sliced
1 teaspoon finely chopped fresh ginger

Center a rack in the oven and preheat the oven to 400 degrees F.

Working on a lightly floured surface, roll the puff pastry out to a square about 11 inches on a side. Using a 4½-inch cookie cutter, tart ring, or bowl as a guide, and the point of a sharp paring knife, score and then cut out 4 rounds of dough. Line a baking sheet with parchment, lay the rounds on it, and prick them well with a fork. Put a second sheet of parchment over the rounds and top with a second baking sheet to weight the dough down.

Bake the rounds for 15 minutes. Carefully remove the top baking sheet and the parchment — that can be a bit tricky, so protect your hands. If the rounds

are well browned and crisp, they are done; if they look a little pale and are not thoroughly baked, return them to the oven, uncovered, to finish baking. Put the baking sheet on a cooling rack and allow the crusts to cool until they're just warm or at room temperature. *(You can bake the rounds up to 8 hours ahead and keep them covered at room temperature.)*

TO FINISH THE TARTLETS: Cut the mozzarella into 12 thin slices, place them between a double thickness of paper towels, and let them drain while you prepare the rest of the pizza's elements.

If you turned the oven off, bring it back up to 400 degrees F.

Put a medium skillet over medium heat and pour in about 2 teaspoons olive oil. When the oil is warm, toss in the onions and cook, stirring, until they're soft but not colored, about 5 minutes; season with salt and pepper. Pull the pan from the heat and divide the onions among the 4 pastry rounds, spreading them almost to the edge of the circles.

Using a long thin knife, cut the tuna against the grain into 12 thin slices. Brush one side of each slice with a little oil and sprinkle lightly with salt and pepper.

Top each of the pastry rounds with alternating and slightly overlapping slices of tuna (seasoned side up), the mozzarella, and basil, using 3 slices of tuna and cheese and 3 basil leaves for each pizza. Scatter over the tomatoes, olives, and radishes and sprinkle with the ginger. Very sparingly, drizzle each pizza with a little olive oil, and finish with a pinch each of salt and pepper.

Slide the baking sheet back into the oven and heat the pizzas for 2 to 3 minutes, just until the tuna is opaque around the edges — it should remain translucent in the center. Serve warm.

scallop and onion tartes fines

MAKES 4 SERVINGS

SERVING

The tarts are tasty and beautiful on their own; they need nothing but forks and knives.

STORING

You can make the pastry circles up to 8 hours ahead (keep them at room temperature) and you can cook the onions a few hours ahead. It's the scallops that mustn't wait. Although you could cut them a few hours ahead and keep them between sheets of plastic wrap in the fridge, once you put them on the onions, you need to bake the tarts ASAP; and once you've baked them, you need to serve them right away.

I'M NOT SURE WHAT THE PARIS chef Yves Camdeborde had in his mind when he created these paper-thin (or *fine*) puff pastry tarts. Who, except a gifted chef, would think of topping caramely slow-cooked onions with slices of sweet-briny scallops? It's a brilliant combination, a gorgeous dish, and a chef's special that can be re-created perfectly by anyone at home. The tartlets' base is store-bought puff pastry, rolled out, cut, and then baked between two baking sheets to prevent it from doing the very thing it's designed to do: puff.

I find one thing particularly marvelous about this tart: the texture of the scallops. Fresh raw scallops have a smooth and velvety texture that's often difficult to maintain in cooking. No problem here — the thinly sliced scallops are arranged in lovely overlapping circles on top of the onions, and then the tarts are slid into a hot oven for just a few minutes, just the right amount of time to ever so gently warm the scallops and to set their texture at a smidgen past raw. A drizzle of olive oil, and the tarts are ready to serve.

1 sheet frozen puff pastry (about 8½ ounces), thawed	¾ pound onions (about 2 medium), thinly sliced or finely chopped
4 strips bacon or 3 slices pancetta	Salt and freshly ground pepper
1 tablespoon unsalted butter	1 pound dry-packed sea scallops Extra-virgin olive oil

Center a rack in the oven and preheat the oven to 400 degrees F.

Working on a floured surface, roll the puff pastry out into a square that's about 13 inches on a side. Using a plate or saucer with a diameter of about 6 inches as a guide, and the point of a sharp paring knife, score and then cut out 4 rounds of dough. Line a baking sheet with parchment, lay the rounds on it, and prick them well all over with a fork. Put a second sheet of parchment over the rounds and top with another baking sheet to weight the dough down.

Bake the rounds for 15 minutes. Carefully remove the top baking sheet and the parchment — it can be a bit tricky, so protect your hands. If the rounds are well browned and crisp, they are done; if they look a little pale and not thoroughly baked, return them to the oven, uncovered, to finish baking. Put the baking sheet on a cooling rack and allow to cool. (*You can bake the rounds up to 8 hours ahead and keep them uncovered at room temperature.*)

Place the bacon strips or pancetta in a skillet, put the skillet over medium-low heat, and cook, turning occasionally, until the bacon is crisp on both sides. Transfer to a plate lined with a double layer of paper towels, cover with another double layer of paper towels, and pat dry (set the pan aside). Cut the bacon crosswise into slender strips.

Pour out all but 1 tablespoon of the fat from the skillet, put the skillet over low heat, and add the butter. When it's melted, toss in the onions, season with salt and pepper, and cook, turning frequently, until they are soft and caramel brown. Be patient — this will take about 20 minutes. Stir in the bacon bits, and taste for salt and pepper. Remove from the heat.

TO FINISH THE TARTS: If you turned the oven off, bring it back up to 400 degrees F.

Remove the little muscle that's attached to the side of each scallop and lay the scallops on a cutting board. Using a sharp paring knife, slice the scallops horizontally into thin petals — you'll probably get 3 slices from each scallop.

Divide the onion-bacon mixture among the 4 crusts, using the back of a spoon to spread the onions evenly all the way to the edges. Using an equal number of scallop slices for each tart, arrange the scallops in concentric circles over the onions, slightly overlapping the slices. Season the scallops with salt and pepper and drizzle each tart with a little olive oil.

Slide the baking sheet into the oven for 3 to 4 minutes, just long enough to warm the scallops. Serve immediately.

smoked salmon waffles

MAKES **8** WAFFLES
(ABOUT **7** INCHES
IN DIAMETER)

SERVING
You can arrange the waffles
in the kitchen, topping
them with crème fraîche or
sour cream and the salmon
roe, if you're using it; you
can just put out the waffles
and fixings and let your
guests make their own; or
you can go fancy and make
mini waffles that can be
stacked. They'll be delicious
no matter how you serve
them.

STORING
Waffles are best eaten hot
off the iron, although they
can be kept for about 20
minutes in a 200-degree-F
oven. You can freeze freshly
made or leftover waffles.
Layer them between sheets
of wax paper and wrap
them airtight. To revive
them, thaw, then reheat
and recrisp them in a
toaster or toaster oven.

WAFFLES ARE A SPECIALTY of the north of France, the area that borders Belgium, beloved throughout the country, and, odd as it seems to us, almost never served in the morning. For the French, waffles are often a snack — you can buy them on the street from the same vendors who make crepes — most often a dessert (like Waffles and Cream, page 416), and sometimes a savory starter or nibble, which is the perfect role for these chic waffles studded with smoked salmon.

The batter is flavored with chives and scallions, along with the salmon. I use a standard waffle iron, but in Paris restaurants, waffles are often served as mini versions made by pouring small polka dots of batter onto the iron. Whether you make the waffles small or large (then cut them into smaller wedges), they're lovely topped with a dollop of crème fraîche or sour cream and lovelier still when finished with a few beads of salmon roe.

1¾ cups all-purpose flour	5 scallions, white and light green parts only, halved lengthwise and thinly sliced
2 teaspoons baking powder	
1¼ teaspoons salt, or to taste	
¼ teaspoon freshly ground pepper, or to taste	3 tablespoons snipped fresh chives (or more scallions), plus more for sprinkling
1¾ cups whole milk	
2 large eggs	
6 tablespoons (¾ stick) unsalted butter, melted	Crème fraîche or sour cream, for serving
3 ounces thinly sliced smoked salmon, cut into thin strips or slivers	Salmon roe, for topping (optional)

Whisk the flour, baking powder, salt, and pepper together in a medium bowl. In another bowl or a large measuring cup with a spout, whisk together the milk, eggs, and melted butter. Pour the liquid ingredients over the dry and stir everything together gently — it's better to have a few lumps than it is to beat the batter. Stir in the smoked salmon, scallions, and chives. *(You can cover the batter and leave it at room temperature for up to 1 hour before waffling; stir well before using.)*

When you're ready to make the waffles, preheat a waffle iron according to the manufacturer's directions. If your iron is not nonstick, brush it lightly with oil or spritz it with vegetable cooking spray. If you'd like to keep the waffles warm while you're making the full batch, center a rack in the oven and preheat the oven to 200 degrees F; line a baking sheet with a silicone baking mat or parchment paper.

When the iron is hot, pour about ½ cup batter over the grids, using a spatula to spread it evenly across the surface — you want a thin layer. (Precisely how much batter you need will depend on the size of your iron.) Let the batter bake for about 30 seconds before closing the lid and baking the waffle until it is well

browned on the underside — that's the side that will always be brownest and most beautiful, no matter what you do. To keep the waffles warm if you're not serving as you go, place them on the baking sheet and slide them into the oven. Continue until you've cooked all the batter.

Cut the waffles into quarters and arrange the quarters on plates. Top each one with crème fraîche or sour cream, salmon roe, if you're using it, and a sprinkling of chives. Or, if you've made mini waffles, you can create millefeuilles with them, sandwiching the waffles with cream. Count on 3 little waffle stacks per serving.

buckwheat blini with smoked salmon and crème fraîche

MAKES **6** SERVINGS

SERVING

I like to top the warm blini with the works: a thin slice of smoked salmon, a spoonful of crème fraîche, a little salmon roe, and a small feather of fresh dill.

STORING

You can make the batter a day ahead, and you can also make the blini a day in advance. To reheat them, arrange them on a baking sheet lined with a silicone baking mat or parchment paper, brush them lightly with melted butter, and warm them in a 350-degree-F oven for 10 to 15 minutes.

WHILE BLINI MAY CONJURE UP THOUGHTS of Russia and a picture of tins piled high with caviar and ice buckets packed with vodka, the word is as much a part of the cocktail vocabulary in France as it is in Russia, or in the United States, for that matter. And the buckwheat that's used to give the blini a lovely brown color and a deep nutty flavor is also very French — it's the flour of choice for Brittany's savory crepes. In fact, blini are so popular in France that even small convenience stores stock them in their refrigerator cases, and while they don't usually sell caviar, they often have other things, like taramasalata (carp roe), lumpfish roe, and smoked salmon, that make excellent toppers.

Making your own blini at home is both fun and easy, if not as spur-of-the-moment as getting them from the nearby 7-Eleven (or 8 à Huit, the French equivalent), since these are yeast-raised pancakes and you've got to give the leavening a little time to build up its puff power. But the time is short — let the batter rest for an hour and a half, and you're good to go; let it rest overnight, and the blini will have even more flavor.

I usually serve the blini topped with smoked salmon, the smallest dab of crème fraîche, some salmon roe, and feathery dill, but the possibilities are wide and the choice all yours.

BE PREPARED: The batter needs to rise for 60 to 90 minutes.

1½ cups whole milk	2 teaspoons active dry yeast
4 tablespoons (½ stick) unsalted butter, cut into 8 pieces	½ teaspoon salt
	3 large eggs, lightly beaten
¾ cup all-purpose flour	Thinly sliced smoked salmon, crème fraîche, salmon roe (optional), and small sprigs of dill, for topping
½ cup buckwheat flour	
2 tablespoons sugar	

Warm the milk and butter in a saucepan over low heat (or in a microwave oven) until the butter is melted and the milk feels warm to the touch — you're aiming for 110 degrees F. (If you overshoot the temperature, just let the mixture cool down.)

Whisk together the all-purpose flour, buckwheat flour, sugar, yeast, and salt in a medium bowl. Pour the warm milk and butter over the dry ingredients and whisk gently only until you have a smooth batter. Cover the bowl with plastic wrap, put it in a warm, draft-free place, and let rise for 60 to 90 minutes, or until it is bubbly and doubled in volume. (*The batter can be kept, covered, in the refrigerator overnight. If you chill the batter, let it stand at room temperature for about 20 minutes before proceeding.*)

Whisk the batter and stir in the beaten eggs.

Lightly butter, oil, or spray a blini pan, griddle, or skillet and place it over medium heat. (Electric griddles should be preheated to 350 degrees F.) If you're not going to serve each batch as it is cooked, center a rack in the oven and preheat the oven to 200 degrees F; line a baking sheet with a silicone baking mat or parchment paper.

Drop 2 tablespoons of the batter into the pan for each blini, leaving room between the dollops of batter for spreading. When the undersides of the blini are golden and the tops are dotted with bubbles that pop, flip over the blini and bake until the other side is light brown. (The second side always cooks faster than the first side and it's never as pretty — it's just a fact of pancaking.) You can dress the blini now, hot off the griddle, or put them on the baking sheet, cover lightly, and keep them in the preheated oven while you make the rest of the batch.

To serve, top the blini with smoked salmon, crème fraîche, salmon roe (if using), and dill.

tuna-packed piquillo peppers

MAKES 6 SERVINGS

SERVING
These need nothing more
than a glass of wine and
maybe a bit of bread to
wipe the plate.

STORING
You can stuff the peppers
ahead of time and keep
them covered in the
refrigerator for up to
6 hours.

WITH THEIR BELLIES FULL OF SAVORY tuna speckled with capers, olives, and mint, these bright red piquillo peppers have the look of a surprise package. On its own, the tuna mix is a good spread for thin slices of toasted baguettes or crackers, but paired with the sweet, smoky peppers and warmed ever so slightly just before serving, the blend seems almost exotic. It's the peppers that do that — they can make just about anything special.

If you were in Spain, where piquillo peppers grow, or in France's Pays Basque, where they're a staple, stuffed peppers like these would be considered tapas, tasty little somethings to have with drinks, and there's no reason not to consider them as such no matter where you live. But because they are knife-and-fork morsels, I like to serve them when my guests are at the table and can maneuver their silverware and enjoy their wine without juggling either.

Depending on how and when you're serving these, you may want to double this recipe.

1 5- to 6-ounce can chunk light tuna packed in oil, drained Grated zest of ½ lemon	2 teaspoons finely minced fresh mint or parsley
1 tablespoon capers, rinsed, patted dry, and chopped	1 tablespoon fresh lemon juice (more or less to taste) About 2 tablespoons extra-virgin olive oil
1 tablespoon minced shallot (about ¼ large), rinsed and patted dry	Salt and freshly ground pepper
4 Niçoise olives, pitted and chopped, or 1 tablespoon chopped black or green olives	6 piquillo peppers (see Sources), drained and patted dry

Put the tuna in a bowl and toss it lightly with a fork to break it up. While you can mash it, I think it's nice when it's still a little flaky. Stir in the lemon zest, capers, shallot, olives, and mint or parsley. Add 2 teaspoons of the lemon juice and 1 tablespoon of the olive oil, as well as some pepper, and taste. You'll probably want another teaspoon of lemon juice and you might want another teaspoon of oil — it will depend on the tuna and your taste. If you think the mix needs salt, add it now.

With your fingers, gently open the peppers, and fill each with a tablespoon or so of the filling. The peppers should be plump but not packed to the brim. Put them in a lightly oiled small baking pan (it's okay if they're touching one another) or lay them on a lightly oiled foil-lined baking sheet. Save any leftover filling to use as a spread. (*You can cover the peppers and keep them at room temperature for a couple of hours, or refrigerate them for up to 6 hours. If possible, bring the peppers to room temperature before heating them.*)

Just before you're ready to serve, position a rack 4 inches from the broiler and turn on the broiler. (You can skip the broiling and serve the peppers at room temperature, if you like, but a little bit of heat really brings the flavors together.) Drizzle a few teaspoons of olive oil over the peppers and place them under the broiler. Broil for 5 to 10 minutes, just until they're warmed through. Serve immediately.

piquillo peppers

If piquillo peppers existed only because it's fun to say their name — "peek-*ee*-oh" — that would be fine with me. But, in fact, saying their name can get you not just the amusement of alliteration, but the pleasure of enjoying a pepper that's slightly smoky, pleasantly sweet, and a beautiful scarlet color.

The peppers, which are used abundantly in Basque cuisine as well as in the kitchens of knowing cooks all over France, are not French natives, but come from Navarre, just over the border in Spain. What makes them so special is that they're fire-roasted, peeled, and packed in bottles (sometimes in cans) — they aren't a vegetable that you buy fresh at the market. They are about 2 inches from their rounded tips to their broad tops, their flesh is firm, and they are capacious enough to hold a plump tablespoon of stuffing.

And, in fact, stuffing the peppers is a great way to showcase them, as is adding them to a salad.

Look for piquillos that have the D.O. (Denomination of Origin), symbol, attesting to the fact that they were grown and grilled in Navarre. The peppers are not inexpensive, but they are distinctive — and very delicious too.

winter ceviche

WHEN PARIS-BASED BLOGGER MEG ZIMBECK brought this scallop ceviche to a potluck dinner, I was impressed by the way she had managed to take an essentially Latin-American dish known for its heat and acidity and mold it to match the tamer French palate. Where a south-of-the-border ceviche might have chiles, Meg used shallots; where there might have been crunchy vegetables, she added grapes; where cilantro might have joined the mix, Meg chose tarragon, a quintessentially French herb; and where tartness would have reigned, a tangy sweetness (citrus mellowed by mango nectar) held sway. It was a brilliant mix, but in typical Meg fashion, when she sent me the recipe, she called it Strange, Made-Up Winter Ceviche, a witty name that shortchanged both the recipe and her culinary imagination.

This dish is easily multiplied, so it's great for parties, especially during the holidays.

BE PREPARED: The scallops should marinate for at least 1 hour.

MAKES 4 SERVINGS

SERVING
As soon as you've arranged the plates, serve — you don't want the tarragon to lose its punch.

STORING
While the scallops must marinate for at least 1 hour, storing is not a possibility.

½ shallot, thinly sliced, rinsed, and patted dry
½ teaspoon sherry vinegar
Fleur de sel or other sea salt and freshly ground pepper
Finely grated zest and juice of 1 lemon
Finely grated zest and juice of 1 lime
½ cup mango nectar
1 tablespoon brown sugar
12 bay scallops, tough side muscle removed (or 4 sea scallops, side muscle removed and quartered)
1 cup fresh tarragon leaves
2 teaspoons extra-virgin olive oil
12 seedless grapes, halved (or quartered, if they're very large)

Put the shallot in a small bowl with the vinegar, a teensy pinch of sea salt, and a little pepper and stir to moisten. Cover the bowl and leave at room temperature.

Whisk together the lemon and lime zest and juice, mango nectar, brown sugar, and a dash of salt and pepper in a bowl. Add the scallops, turn them around in the marinade, cover, and refrigerate for at least 1 hour, or for up to 4 hours.

When you're ready to serve, put the tarragon leaves in a small bowl, drizzle with the olive oil, and season with salt and pepper. Divide the leaves among four small bowls.

Remove the scallops from the marinade, divide them among the bowls, and, if they need it, season them with salt and pepper. Quickly dip the grapes into the marinade and scatter them evenly around the scallops. Finish the dish with the shallot. You can serve the dish just as it is, or you can spoon a little marinade into each bowl — I spoon in more than a little marinade, because I'm addicted to it.

tuna and mango ceviche

MAKES 4 SERVINGS

SERVING
I like to serve the ceviche in martini glasses or brandy snifters, but it's also nice spooned into small bowls.

STORING
The ceviche is at its peak 1 hour after you mix it. You can keep it chilled for another hour, but if you wait too long, the lime juice will "cook" away the texture of the fish, mango, and avocado.

INSPIRED BY THE CUISINE OF SENEGAL, the West African nation that was once a French colony, this dish is built on two of Senegal's important exports, mangoes and avocados. It's flavored with rum, a drink the French became attached to in the Antilles and brought with them to Africa, and is a takeoff on an entrée that originally included grilled *gambas* (shrimp). In this version, tuna replaces the shrimp and the ingredients are tossed together and marinated. If you want to, you can make the dish with shrimp (smallish shrimp are the best), or you can sear the tuna (or shrimp) and arrange it on top of the rum-dressed mango and avocado, ingredients so similar in texture that it's surprising they're not used together more often (see Bonne Idée).

The French aren't particularly fond of hot and spicy food — heat and spice are not wine-friendly — but the foods of Africa (and the Antilles, for that matter) have some heat, and hot pepper or Tabasco sauce is not a stranger in those kitchens, so feel free to hot-up the dish to taste. Depending on my audience, I toss a minced hot pepper or an extra splash of Tabasco into the mix. Turning up the heat seems also to turn up the mango's sweetness, the avocado's smoothness, and the tuna's richness.

BE PREPARED: The ceviche should marinate for 1 hour.

2 limes
1 large mango, peeled, pitted, and cut into ½-inch cubes
1 large avocado, peeled, pitted, and cut into ½-inch cubes
1 small red onion, halved, thinly sliced, rinsed, and patted dry
2 quarter-sized slices fresh ginger, peeled and minced

1 small red chile pepper, minced (optional)
½ pound sushi-grade tuna, cut into ½-inch cubes
4 teaspoons extra-virgin olive oil
1 tablespoon white rum
Tabasco to taste
Salt and freshly ground pepper
Fresh cilantro leaves, for garnish

Finely grate the zest of both limes into a medium bowl. Cut one of the limes crosswise in half and cut out sections of fruit from the membranes from one half. Cut the segments into very small cubes. Toss the fruit into the bowl and squeeze the juice from the other half of the lime into the bowl. Add the mango, avocado, onion, ginger, chile (if you're using it), and tuna and stir everything together very gently with a rubber spatula.

Squeeze the juice from the remaining lime into a small bowl and whisk in the olive oil and rum. Season with Tabasco, salt, and pepper and pour the vinaigrette over the tuna mixture, again stirring very lightly so you don't crush the avocado. Taste for seasoning — you'll have another opportunity to season the ceviche, so don't overdo it now — then cover the bowl tightly and chill for 1 hour.

At serving time, adjust the salt, pepper, and Tabasco if you think it's necessary, and give the ceviche another stir. Serve immediately, garnished with a few cilantro leaves.

BONNE IDÉE

Seared Tuna or Shrimp with Mango and Avocado.

I serve this as a main course, and I make it with 2 mangoes and 2 avocados. If tuna's going to star, I use 1 pound tuna; if shrimp is taking the lead, I use jumbo shrimp and figure on 5 to a person. Cut the tuna into 1- to 2-inch cubes, or peel the shrimp, leaving on the tail shell, if you'd like, and devein. Make the lime vinaigrette, using the juice of 1 lime; set aside. Slice the mangoes and avocados into thin slices or strips and arrange them in overlapping circles on a platter. Scatter over the onion, ginger, and chile pepper (if using). Toss the tuna or shrimp with salt, pepper, and, if you'd like, some red pepper flakes. Heat 1 tablespoon mild oil (such as grapeseed or canola) in a large skillet (nonstick is best here) or wok, and when it's almost shimmering, toss in the seafood. (You may need to do this in batches.) Cook the tuna for about 1 minute on a side until seared on the outside and rare within, the shrimp about 2 minutes, until just cooked through. Spoon the seafood into the center of the platter, dress the mango and avocado with the lime vinaigrette, giving the tuna or shrimp a splash, and serve immediately, garnished with cilantro leaves. If you've got a little leftover vinaigrette, pass it at the table.

salmon tartare

MAKES 4 SERVINGS

SERVING
This is a dish unto itself; it needs nothing else.

STORING
You can get the salmon and tomatoes ready a few hours ahead of time, but the tartare depends on freshness, and the closer to serving time that you prepare things, the better it will be.

OR ALL THE YEARS THAT I'VE been cooking, I still get excited when I can make a dish that not only tastes like something I've had in a restaurant, but looks like it too. And if it's easy and quick to get it perfect, as it is with this triple-layer tartare, then so much the better. Salmon tartares of many varieties, all based on well-seasoned chopped or cubed raw salmon, turn up regularly on the menus of both fancy restaurants and cozy bistros. Sometimes the salmon appears solo, like a classic beef tartare; sometimes there's a little puff of micro greens or herbs to keep it company; and sometimes the salmon is teamed with other colorful ingredients, so that every forkful brings a lively mix of flavors, colors, and textures. This tartare, which includes avocado, tomatoes, lime, mint, and chives, is one of the lively ones and one of the most beautiful. I build the layers — avocado, then salmon, then sliced grape tomatoes — in a 4-inch round pancake ring, but you can do it in ramekins or bowls, or in martini or Cognac glasses, which make a gorgeous presentation.

While you can cut the salmon and tomatoes a little ahead of time and mix them with most of the seasonings, you shouldn't add the lime juice, lime segments, or salt until the very last minute, because the acid in the lime "cooks" the salmon, whitening its color and tightening its texture. If you add the juice ahead of time, it will not only diminish the fresh look and taste of the tartare but turn your tartare into a ceviche — not a terrible thing, but not what this dish is about.

One last thing: the size of the portions. I use a quarter pound of salmon per person, which makes a generous starter or a perfect main course for a lunch that includes salad, cheese, and great bread. Because this is a DIY construction project, you can easily adjust the serving size to fit your meal.

2	limes	1	tablespoon minced fresh mint
1	pound salmon fillet, cut from the thick center portion, skin removed	4	teaspoons extra-virgin olive oil
			Salt and freshly ground pepper
			Tabasco
2	scallions, white and light green parts only, quartered lengthwise and thinly sliced	20	grape tomatoes
		2	Hass avocados
			Pistachio oil (see Sources; optional)
2	tablespoons finely snipped fresh chives		

Have at hand a 4-inch-diameter pancake ring (or tart or flan ring) — or use four rings, if you've got them — or four 1-cup ramekins or bowls lined with plastic wrap or four martini or Cognac glasses.

Grate the zest from 1 of the limes onto a sheet of wax paper. Using a sharp knife, peel the lime, removing all the white pith. Working over a bowl to catch the juice, very carefully cut out the sections of fruit, separating them from the membranes. Squeeze the juice from the membranes into the bowl; set aside. Cut the segments crosswise in half.

Cut the salmon into ½-inch cubes and toss into a bowl. Add the scallions, half of the grated lime zest, 2 teaspoons of the chives, 1 teaspoon of the mint, and 2 teaspoons of the olive oil. Season with salt and pepper and give the mix a splash of Tabasco. Stir the ingredients together gently and cover the bowl. *(You can prepare the salmon to this point 2 hours ahead; refrigerate until needed.)*

Slice each grape tomato crosswise into thirds and toss into a bowl. Add 2 teaspoons of the chives, 1 teaspoon of the mint, and the remaining 2 teaspoons olive oil and stir to mix. If you're going to assemble the tartare now, season with salt and pepper; if you're going to wait, add only pepper. *(You can prepare the tomatoes to this point an hour or so before you're ready to serve; keep covered at room temperature.)*

Just before you're ready to serve the tartare, prepare the avocados. Remove the pits and peel, and cut the fruit into ½-inch cubes. Put the pieces in a bowl. Halve the remaining lime to use for juice; have the reserved juice from the first lime at hand. Gently — you don't want to mash the avocado — stir in the remaining lime zest, some lime juice (I taste as I go and usually use the juice from a half or whole lime), the remaining 2 teaspoons chives, and the last teaspoon mint. Add a splash of Tabasco and season with salt and pepper.

Stir the lime segments into the salmon, add a little lime juice — a quarter to a half lime might be enough, but add more or less to match your taste — and season with salt. Taste a salmon cube and see if it needs more salt, pepper, Tabasco, or lime juice. Add some salt to the tomatoes if you haven't already done so.

If you're using a pancake ring (or rings), place a ring on a serving plate or salad plate and add one quarter of the avocado mixture, nudging it to fill the circle. Next add an even layer of one quarter of the salmon. At this point, the mixture has probably topped the ring — that's fine. Carefully lay one quarter of the tomatoes over the salmon, pressing them gently so they stay put. It's okay if the top of the tartare is rounded — it's pretty like that. Carefully remove the ring (if you don't have enough rings to go around), and construct the next plate. Continue until you've constructed all 4 tartares (lift off the rings if necessary).

If you're using ramekins or bowls lined with plastic wrap, put the tomatoes in first, then the salmon, and then the avocado. Tamp the layers down very, very gently, then invert each ramekin or bowl onto a plate, lift it off, and remove the plastic.

If you're using glasses, just layer the ingredients as you would with a ring.

Drizzle a few drops — really, just drops — of pistachio oil over and around the tartares, if you'd like, and serve.

salmon and potatoes in a jar

MAKES 6
APPETIZER
SERVINGS OR
4 LUNCH MAIN-
COURSE SERVINGS

SERVING
I like to bring the jars to the table and pass them around with lemon or lime wedges — the salmon is nice with a squirt of juice — along with some rye, pumpernickel, or other dark bread and a hunk of butter. You could pass around a lightly dressed green salad too.

STRADDLING A SPACE BETWEEN GRAVLAX AND TARTARE, this dish is a never-fail knockout, even when you serve it, as I often do, to savvy Parisians who know it's a modern version of a humble bistro classic, herring and potatoes. Packed into canning jars or crocks, which look great when you bring them to the table, this is really two dishes in one: there are boiled potatoes marinated in aromatic oil and chunks of salmon cured in sugar and salt, just like gravlax, then marinated. The dish is simple in every way — the only cooking involves boiling the potatoes. But you must have patience, since you have to wait a day or two before you can dig in. However, the duo is always surprising, especially to people who know the original from restaurants; they'll invariably give you cheers for serving something most people think can only be made by a chef.

The recipe will work with any cut of salmon, but it's best (and looks best) if you use a piece cut from the thick center portion of the fillet. With a center cut, you can slice meaty chunks of salmon that will all cure evenly.

Finally, don't be frightened by the amount of olive oil in the recipe — it's a lot, but you won't be eating it all. Although you need a large quantity of oil to cover both the salmon and potatoes, neither of them will absorb much. You can use the leftover potato oil to season or cook other vegetables or to make a vinaigrette, and the salmon oil to make a vinaigrette or even a mayonnaise for other fish dishes or salads.

BE PREPARED: You'll need to start at least 1 day ahead.

2 tablespoons kosher salt or other coarse salt	2 large carrots, trimmed, peeled, halved lengthwise, and thinly sliced
1 tablespoon sugar	
1 1-pound salmon fillet, cut from the thickest portion of the fish, skinned	1–2 small onions, red or yellow, halved and thinly sliced
	About 4 cups olive oil
1 pound fingerlings or other small potatoes, scrubbed	Salt
20 coriander seeds	3 tablespoons distilled white vinegar or white wine vinegar
20 black peppercorns	
4 bay leaves, halved	Lemon or lime wedges, for serving
8 thyme sprigs	

AT LEAST 1 DAY BEFORE SERVING: Stir the salt and sugar together in a bowl. Slice the salmon into 12 equal pieces, toss the pieces into the bowl, and gently turn the salmon around to coat it evenly. (It's easiest to use your hands for this.) Arrange the salmon snugly in a bowl or terrine (you can layer it), cover tightly with plastic wrap, and refrigerate for at least 12 hours, or for up to 18 hours.

THE FOLLOWING DAY: Have two quart-sized canning jars or crocks ready. (If you've got really small fingerling potatoes, they might fit into a pint jar.)

BONNE IDÉE
Roasted Cured Salmon.
Rather than marinating the salt-sugar-cured salmon, you can roast it. The salmon will be firm on the outside, rosy pink and satiny inside. To serve 4, use 4 pieces of center-cut salmon fillet, each 5 to 6 ounces, and cure them for 12 to 18 hours in a mix of 3 tablespoons coarse salt and 2 tablespoons sugar. When you're ready to cook the salmon, rinse the pieces well and pat them dry. Center a rack in the oven and preheat the oven to 425 degrees F. Put the salmon on a foil-lined baking sheet and roast for 5 to 7 minutes, or until a knife inserted into the fillets reveals flesh that is set but still very pink. Serve the salmon with a gloss of melted butter or olive oil and, if you'd like, a salsa (page 305), a mango chatini (page 489), some pesto (page 488), or a parsley coulis (page 76).

Alternatively, you can use terrines, bowls, or even heavy-duty zipper-lock plastic bags.

Bring a large pot of salted water to a boil. Toss the potatoes into the pot and cook until they can be pierced easily with the point of a knife, 10 to 20 minutes, depending on their size. Drain the potatoes and, if you'd like, peel them. (I usually leave the skin on.)

Rinse the salmon under cold water (discard the brine) and pat dry.

Divide the spices, herbs, carrots, and onions in half. Start packing the salmon into one of the canning jars, using half the aromatics. Make a layer of salmon and cover it with some of the coriander and peppercorns, a piece of bay leaf, a little thyme, and some carrot and onion; continue until all the salmon is in the jar. If you can arrange it, it's nice to finish with a layer of spices, herbs, carrot, and onion. Pour in enough of the olive oil to cover the ingredients and seal the jar.

Pack the potatoes, whole or cut into chunks, into the second jar following the same method, but this time adding a pinch of salt to each layer (potatoes have a way of gobbling up salt). When the potatoes are packed and you've added the oil, pour in the vinegar, seal the jar, and shake it gently a couple of times to mix the vinegar into the oil. (If you've packed your potatoes in another kind of container, just swish the ingredients around as best you can.)

Put both jars in the refrigerator and chill for at least 6 hours, or for up to 3 days.

Serve, directly from the jars if you like, with lemon or lime wedges.

crab-avocado "ravioli"

IF EVER A DISH TOOK A COUNTRY by storm, this was it. It comes from chef Pascal Barbot of L'Astrance, in Paris, and it was on his menu when the restaurant opened in 2001. These days, L'Astrance has three Michelin stars and all of France has this "ravioli" (you find variations of it everywhere).

There isn't a sheet of pasta to be found in this dish; instead, you've got two very thin slices of avocado cradling a zesty crab salad. I'm crazy about the way Barbot cuts an avocado: he uses a mandoline to get thin, even slices, and he neither peels nor pits the fruit before he cuts, a nifty technique that ensures that the slices will keep their shape. If you don't have a mandoline or a Benriner slicer, you can do this by hand.

At L'Astrance, the crab salad is mixed with lime zest and juice, chives, and almond oil. I make the salad with the lime, but I add minced shallot and cilantro. The playful ravioli construction is so good that it'll stand up to just about any kind of variation that suits your taste.

MAKES 4 SERVINGS

SERVING
These need nothing as an accompaniment or garnish.

STORING
You can make the crab salad about an hour in advance — but don't add the lime juice until you're ready for the salad. The avocado must be used as soon as it's sliced.

½ pound crabmeat, preferably jumbo lump, picked over for cartilage and shells
Fleur de sel or other sea salt
Grated zest and juice of ½ lime (or maybe a squirt more juice)
½ shallot, finely chopped, rinsed, and patted dry

1 tablespoon minced fresh cilantro
About 2 tablespoons sweet almond oil (see Sources) or extra-virgin olive oil (optional)
2–3 large ripe but firm Hass avocados
Freshly ground white pepper

Put the crab in a bowl and, using a fork (or your fingers), toss it lightly with a pinch or two of sea salt and the lime zest. Mix in the shallot and cilantro and then a little of the lime juice. Taste for salt and lime juice. If you like, gently stir in a little of the almond or olive oil.

Without peeling or pitting them, slice 2 of the avocados on a mandoline. If you're working with a mandoline or a Benriner slicer, you'll be slicing right through the pits. Ideally, you'll get 12 slices with pit and 12 without from the 2 avocados; if you can't (and this might be the case if you're hand slicing), slice another. Use a paring knife or your fingers to remove the peel and pit from each slice. If you're cutting the avocados by hand, peel and halve them, remove the pit, and slice.

It's best to build the ravioli on individual plates, 3 ravioli per person. Choose one of the large slices of avocado — the ones with holes from the pit — for the base of each one, and fill the holes with a scoop of crab salad. Top with a smaller slice of avocado, season with salt, a little white pepper, and a tiny drizzle of lime juice, and finish with a drizzle of almond or olive oil, if you like.

Serve the ravioli the instant you've finished making them, since avocados blacken unattractively if they're left exposed to the air for even a few minutes.

shrimp-filled zucchini blossoms

MAKES 4 SERVINGS

SERVING
These should be served as soon as possible after they're cooked, either plain or with mayo, tartar sauce, or even bottled cocktail or chili sauce — not thoroughly French, but delicious.

STORING
You can make the tempura batter up to 1 hour ahead and keep it covered in the refrigerator.

WE WERE IN THE MIDDLE OF LUNCH when the chef started delivering a little extra surprise to each of his eight or so tables. The restaurant was the former Spring, in Paris; the chef was the super-talented Daniel Rose, one of the very few American chefs to win accolades in France; and the surprise was beautiful zucchini blossom beignets, or fritters, coated with tempura batter and filled with langoustine, a luxe crustacean that Americans know as crayfish or Dublin prawns. The fritters were burn-your-fingers hot, having just emerged from their fry, fabulous and simple in the extreme.

I loved them, but I knew I wouldn't be serving these bonbons often if I had to fill them with langoustine. I've been making them with shrimp, and they've been playing to cheers. (See Bonne Idées for other good fillings.)

These were served without additions at Spring, but they could be served with mayonnaise or even tartar sauce. Or you could serve them the way similar zucchini fritters were presented at Ostapé in Basque Country — accompanied by a little tomato salad consisting of diced tomatoes (peeled and seeded) seasoned with fleur de sel and tossed with fruity olive oil.

A note on the tempura batter: You can buy tempura-batter mix in a box, but the batter is simplicity itself to make. While the traditional French recipe for tempura usually includes cold water and ice cubes, I've found that club soda or seltzer makes a terrific batter, so I'm giving you my recipe.

FOR THE BATTER
¾ cup all-purpose flour
1½ teaspoons baking powder
½ teaspoon salt
    Freshly ground pepper
1 cup very cold club soda or seltzer, or as needed

FOR THE FRITTERS
12 zucchini blossoms
12 medium or large shrimp, peeled and deveined

Salt and freshly ground pepper
Peanut oil, for frying
Fleur de sel or other sea salt, for sprinkling

Mayonnaise, homemade (page 490) or store-bought, tartar sauce, or cocktail or chili sauce, for serving (optional)

TO MAKE THE BATTER: Whisk together the flour, baking powder, salt, and a grind or two of pepper in a bowl, then whisk in the club soda or seltzer. The batter will have the consistency of heavy cream. If you're not using it right away, cover and keep it in the fridge. *(The batter can be refrigerated for up to 1 hour.)*

TO MAKE THE FRITTERS: Wipe the blossoms with a lightly dampened paper towel, or, if they've got some dirt stuck to them, use a little brush to flick it off: you don't want to wash the blossoms and risk waterlogging them. Gently pry the blossoms open, reach in, with your fingers, a paring knife, or tweezers, and pull out the pistils and stamens. It's a touchy job, and you might tear a blossom or two, but that's okay — the shrimp and the batter will repair everything.

Season the shrimp with a little salt and pepper. Tuck 1 shrimp into each blossom and twist the top of the blossom gently to seal it (don't fuss too much if you don't have enough blossom to twist; the shrimp is not at risk of falling out).

Take a look at your tempura batter — if it has thickened considerably from sitting in the refrigerator, thin it as needed with a little more soda or seltzer or some cold water.

Pour about ½ inch of oil into a large skillet and heat it until it's very hot but not smoking. Line a plate with a double layer of paper towels. One by one, working in batches (you don't want to crowd the pan and lower the oil's temperature), run the blossoms through the batter, coating them on all sides, then drop them into the hot oil. Fry the fritters for a minute or two on the first side and a scant minute on the other — the coating should be golden brown. As each fritter is cooked, drain it on the paper towels and season it with a little fleur de sel. Serve immediately, with mayonnaise or tartar, cocktail, or chili sauce, if desired.

BONNE IDÉE
Ricotta-Filled Zucchini Blossoms. Put ¾ cup ricotta cheese, 1 large egg yolk, 1 shallot, finely minced, rinsed, and dried, and 2 tablespoons minced mixed fresh herbs, such as basil, mint, and parsley (or use 2 tablespoons of just one of these), in a bowl and whisk energetically — you want the ricotta to be nice and smooth. Season well with salt and pepper (think about adding a dash of cayenne or a few red pepper flakes), divide the filling among the blossoms, and fry as directed.

ANOTHER BONNE IDÉE
Zucchini Blossoms Filled with Goat-Cheese Tapenade. Put ¾ cup very soft goat cheese, at room temperature, 1 large egg yolk, 1½ tablespoons tapenade, black or green (homemade, page 487, or store-bought), 1 tablespoon minced fresh basil, and the finely grated zest of ½ lemon in a bowl and whisk energetically — the mixture should be very smooth. Season with pepper and only a dash or two of salt (tapenade is salty), divide the filling among the blossoms, and fry as directed.

sardine escabeche

MAKES 6 SERVINGS

SERVING

Bring the escabeche to the table as is and have lemon wedges and bread at the ready, so that guests can squeeze as much juice as they want over the fish and use the bread to get up every last drop of sauce. It's not at all traditional, but it is nice to serve a small salad on the side of the escabeche. If you do, use a drizzle of the escabeche soaking sauce to dress the greens.

STORING

Covered tightly, the escabeche will keep for about 3 days in the refrigerator.

BONNE IDÉE

Shrimp Escabeche. Replace the sardines with 1 pound shrimp, peeled and deveined. Don't dredge the shrimp in flour; just sauté them very quickly in a little of the olive oil, season them with salt and pepper, and proceed with the recipe.

JUST BECAUSE ESCABECHE, a dish of marinated fish — in this case, sardines — vegetables, and aromatics, wasn't invented in France, it doesn't mean the French haven't taken it into their hearts and made it their own. When the weather's warm, it's popular all over the country, but you can find it anytime and everywhere in the southwest corner of France, on the frontier of the dish's homeland, Spain.

When you see the word *escabeche,* you know that there'll be olive oil and a not insubstantial quantity of vinegar (or maybe wine), since the dish was originally used to preserve fish. In fact, I got a lesson about the dish's roots the first time I served a version of it to a group of Parisians, one of whom was a chef. I offered the dish with apologies because I thought my initial attempt was too vinegary.

"How long has the escabeche been in the refrigerator?" the chef asked. When I told her "eighteen hours," she knowingly concluded, "That's the problem — you're supposed to wait eight days!"

I'm sure she's right and sure that in eight days the vinegar would have done a fine job of softening the sardines and rendering the carrots tender enough for babies — and that, having done all this work, the vinegar would have lost its bite. But who can wait eight days? Definitely not me! So I changed the recipe, cooking the sardines a little longer at the start so I wouldn't have to wait more than half a day to dig in. And, since I cut down the vinegar's work, I could also cut down its quantity.

It's escabeche for the modern world, and a quick check shows I'm not the only one without the patience to wait — this is how escabeche is made all around the country.

BE PREPARED: You'll need to marinate the sardines for at least 6 hours, or, better yet, overnight.

1 cup extra-virgin olive oil	2 carrots, trimmed, peeled, and thinly sliced
All-purpose flour, for dredging	
Salt and freshly ground white pepper	2 celery stalks, trimmed and thinly sliced
12 ultrafresh sardines, filleted, tails removed if necessary	4 garlic cloves, split, germ removed, and slivered
1 rosemary sprig	2 dried red chiles or ¼ teaspoon red pepper flakes
1 thyme sprig	1 tablespoon tomato paste or ketchup
2 bay leaves, halved	½ teaspoon sugar
4 oil-packed sun-dried tomatoes, drained and slivered (optional)	¼ teaspoon coriander seeds
	½ cup distilled white vinegar
1 medium onion, halved lengthwise and thinly sliced	Lemon wedges, for serving
	Bread, for serving

Pour 2 tablespoons of the olive oil into a large skillet, preferably nonstick, and warm it over medium heat. Put the flour for dredging on a plate or sheet of wax paper, season it with salt and white pepper, and dredge the sardine fillets in the flour, shaking off the excess. Slip the sardines into the hot oil (don't crowd the pan — sauté the fish in batches if necessary) and cook for 2 minutes on a side, or until the flour is lightly browned and the sardines are just barely cooked through. Transfer the sardines to a plate covered with a double layer of paper towels and gently pat off any excess oil. Repeat with any remaining sardines.

Arrange the sardines in an overlapping pattern in an oval gratin dish, a Pyrex pie plate, or another rimmed serving dish. Scatter the rosemary, thyme, bay leaves, and sun-dried tomato slivers, if you're using them, over the fillets.

Wipe out the skillet, pour in another 2 tablespoons of the oil, and return the pan to medium-low heat. When the oil is hot, toss in the onion, carrots, celery, and garlic and cook, stirring, for about 10 minutes, until the vegetables are almost cooked through but not colored. Add the remaining ¾ cup oil, along with the remaining ingredients, 1 teaspoon salt, and white pepper to taste, bring just to a simmer, and cook for 5 minutes.

Pour the hot mixture over the sardines. Jiggle things around if necessary to make certain that the fillets are covered in oil and that the vegetables are evenly strewn over the fish, then cover the dish with plastic wrap. Allow the escabeche to cool to room temperature, then put it in the refrigerator for at least 6 hours, or, better yet, overnight.

Serve chilled, with lemon wedges and bread.

chicken liver gâteaux
with pickled onions

MAKES **6** SERVINGS

SERVING

If you're serving the cakes on a bed of greens, toss the salad with a little vinaigrette and divide it among the plates. Place a cake in the center of each plate and top with some pickled onions.

STORING

The cakes can be baked, cooled, covered tightly, and chilled overnight before serving. Dunk the cups in hot water to unmold them. Alternatively, they can be cooled, unmolded, and frozen on a baking sheet until solid, then wrapped airtight and kept frozen for up to 2 months; defrost overnight in the refrigerator before serving.

THE FRENCH SEEM TO KNOW a million things to do with livers of every variety — some of them rough and rustic, like the chunky pâtés you find at charcuteries, and some elegant and quite pretty, like these little upside-down *gâteaux,* a specialty of Lyon, where they're most often served with tomato sauce (see Bonne Idée). In truth, these are more custard than cake, but the idea of having cake at the start of the meal is too irresistible. Made quickly and simply by whirring chicken livers with cream, eggs, herbs, and a little brandy in a blender, the cakes are baked in a water bath, then topped with some quickly pickled onions (a little treat you might want to make often for topping everything from salads to burgers) and, if you'd like, served on a handful of mixed salad greens. Done this way, with the lettuce leaves forming a ruff around the cakes, the dish looks restaurant-fancy.

A note on temperature: These cakes are meant to be served soon after they emerge from their water bath, but I think they're also good when they're just slightly warm or at room temperature. In fact, they're fine cold too, when they're more like pâté than custard.

FOR THE ONIONS
- 5 black peppercorns
- 5 coriander seeds
- 1 clove
- 1 cup cider vinegar
- ⅓ cup water
- ⅓ cup sugar
- 1 onion, thinly sliced and rinsed

FOR THE CAKES
- ½ pound chicken livers, veins and any fat or green spots removed
- 3 large eggs
- 3 large egg yolks

- ½ cup heavy cream
- ½ cup whole milk
- 2 teaspoons brandy, such as Cognac or Armagnac
- ½ teaspoon minced fresh thyme
- ½ teaspoon minced fresh sage
- ½ teaspoon minced fresh rosemary
- 1 teaspoon salt
- ¼ teaspoon freshly ground pepper

FOR SERVING (OPTIONAL)
Handful of mixed greens, frisée, or spinach, rinsed and dried
Everyday Vinaigrette (page 484)

TO MAKE THE ONIONS: Put the peppercorns, coriander, and clove in a tea infuser or wrap them in a small piece of cheesecloth and tie up the bundle with kitchen twine. Put the spices, vinegar, water, and sugar in a medium saucepan and bring to a boil, stirring to dissolve the sugar. Lower the temperature so that the pickling mix just simmers and cook for 5 minutes.

Drop in the onion slices and simmer for 10 minutes, then turn off the heat. Allow the onions to cool to room temperature in the liquid. If you'll be using

BONNE IDÉE
Chicken Liver Gâteaux with Tomato Sauce Lyonnaise.
Cook 1 chopped onion and a couple of chopped garlic cloves, split and germ removed, in 2 tablespoons of olive oil in a saucepan until softened. Add a can (about 15 ounces) crushed tomatoes to the pan, along with 2 parsley sprigs, 1 thyme sprig, 1 bay leaf, and some salt and pepper. Bring to a boil, then lower the heat and simmer very gently for about 3 minutes. Pluck out the bay leaf and the thyme branch, if you can, then puree the sauce in a blender or food processor and adjust the seasonings. When you're ready to serve, reheat the sauce. Put a few spoonfuls of sauce in the center of each plate and top with a warm *gâteau*. Instead of the pickled onions, you can finish with a little bouquet of parsley leaves tossed with a drop of olive oil.

them right away, drain them; if not, put the onions and liquid in a covered jar and refrigerate until needed. *(The onions can be refrigerated for up to a week.)*

TO MAKE THE CAKES: Center a rack in the oven and preheat the oven to 350 degrees F. Butter six 6-ounce ramekins or custard cups. Line a roasting pan with a double layer of paper towels. Have a kettle of hot water on the stove.

Put all of the ingredients in a blender or food processor and whir until the mixture is smooth, about 2 minutes, scraping down the sides of the jar or work bowl a couple of times to ensure that everything gets mixed. Pour the custard into the cups or ramekins (they'll be about three-quarters full) and rap each one on the counter to de-bubble the mixture. Put the cups in the roasting pan and slide the pan onto the oven rack. Pour enough hot water into the roaster to come about halfway up the sides of the cups.

Bake the cakes for 30 to 40 minutes, or until the custard is set and no longer jiggly; a knife inserted in the center of the cakes should come out clean. Carefully transfer the cakes to a cooling rack and let them rest for about 10 minutes before unmolding them.

If you'd like to serve the cakes on a bed of greens, toss the greens with a little vinaigrette and arrange on six plates.

To unmold the cakes, run a blunt knife around the edges of each cup and turn the cake out onto a plate, lined with salad or not. Top the cakes with the onions or place them alongside and serve.

a taste for innards

Lots of people say innards of all kinds are an acquired taste. I can think of four ways to have acquired the taste: **1)** Mom served them to you when you were young; **2)** you grew up on a farm; **3)** one of the little body parts was slipped into a dish without your knowing it and — shazam! — you loved it; or **4)** you were born with the I-love-innards gene, in which case, you're probably French and maybe even from some deep-in-the-country part of the Southwest, like the Auvergne — where a friend and I were invited to a gala dinner hosted by the city's chamber of commerce. I was the only non-Française present, and the city fathers were pleased to be able to offer me their region's best. Here is the menu we were served.

APERITIF: Puff pastry tidbits with a kir made with chestnut liqueur (this is the land of chestnuts)

APPETIZER: A selection of local charcuterie, including pork saucisson, blue cheese roulade, and *pâté de tête de veau* (an ingredient that's never translated from the French because most foreigners don't want to know they're eating calf's head)

FIRST COURSE: Stuffed cabbage with morel cream sauce — the cabbage was Savoy and the stuffing was *ris de veau* (another normally untranslated ingredient because "thymus gland" sounds so ugly)

MAIN COURSE: *Aligot,* the regional specialty of mashed potatoes and cheese, and *langue de veau* (yup, calf's tongue)

CHEESE: Cantal (a firm, rich cow's milk cheese)

DESSERT: Frozen walnut soufflé (the Auvergne is also walnut-rich)

I looked around the table at my eleven other dinnermates eating with gusto and polishing off the last of each sauce with a little hunk of bread, and I did the same — and enjoyed every bite.

I can't think of how I acquired this taste. Maybe I was born with it. Maybe I'm French. Of course, the fact that I'm not a great scarf-knotter argues against it. Maybe the scarf gene is recessive — or shy.

cabbage and foie gras bundles

MAKES 4 SERVINGS

THESE CAN BE AN ELEGANT DINNER-PARTY starter or an hors d'oeuvre for a Champagne soirée. As basic as they are — they're just small pieces of foie gras wrapped in curly cabbage leaves and steamed — that's how chic they are: when it comes to sensuousness, there's little that can compete with warm, almost-liquid foie gras.

A shopping note: Buy a small terrine of foie gras made from whole pieces of foie gras, not a mousse or pâté made from ground or chopped foie gras.

12 large cabbage leaves, preferably Savoy	Extra-virgin olive oil
6 ounces foie gras terrine (see above)	Fleur de sel

SERVING
These need nothing but some Champagne or Sauternes.

STORING
You can construct the bundles a few hours in advance and keep them covered in the refrigerator. Once the bundles are steamed, they should be served immediately, so that everyone can enjoy the lovely texture of the softened foie gras.

Bring a large pot of salted water to a boil. Two by two, drop the cabbage leaves into the water and cook until they are pliable, a matter of minutes. When the leaves are cool enough to handle, pat them dry and cut away the tough part of the center rib.

To cut the foie gras, run a slender knife under hot water, wipe it dry, and slice the foie gras into 12 pieces. Place a piece of foie gras near the bottom of each cabbage leaf. Lift the bottom of each leaf over the foie gras, turn to cover the foie gras again, fold in the sides of the leaf, and finish the bundle by rolling the foie gras to the end of the leaf.

Place a steamer over boiling water in a large pot, and have a plate lined with a couple of layers of paper towels at hand. Just before you're ready to serve, arrange the bundles seam side down in the steamer, cover the pot, and steam for 5 minutes. Carefully transfer the bundles to the paper-towel-lined plate and pat them dry.

Divide the bundles among four plates, drizzle a very little bit of olive oil over each one, sprinkle with a few grains of fleur de sel, and serve immediately.

coddled eggs with foie gras

MAKES 4 SERVINGS

SERVING
You can serve the eggs with buttered toast — either 1-inch-wide strips or little points — but I think the eggs are perfect straight up.

STORING
Although the eggs must be served piping hot, you can prepare the molds a few hours in advance and keep them well covered in the refrigerator; bring them to room temperature before steaming.

IN THE EARLY 1900S, when the Lost Generation of writers and artists — legends like Hemingway, Fitzgerald, Picasso, and even on occasion James Joyce — wanted to see one another, catch up on news, or make news, they'd often head for the sprawling terrace of Le Dôme, which still holds down an impressively large and sunny corner on Paris's boulevard Montparnasse. Down the street from La Coupole and across from Le Sélect and La Rotonde, the cafés of Hemingway's *A Moveable Feast,* Le Dôme is still a destination for travelers from around the world. Most come for the restaurant's impeccable fish, and while that draws me as well, I go for the added pleasure of conversing with M. Jacques Drouot, the maître d'hôtel. Monsieur Jacques, as he's known, is a man of many parts: a top-notch host, he is also a deep-sea diver, an accomplished photographer, and a passionate cook. For me, the most enjoyable time to go to Le Dôme is Wednesday evening, because M. Jacques will have had Tuesday off and spent that entire day cooking, making Wednesday the ideal time to get a full report on his adventures.

Coddled eggs with foie gras is a recipe M. Jacques related to me one Wednesday evening. It's a dish that's both simple and luxurious — I think eggs by themselves are luxurious, and when paired with a tidbit of foie gras mousse or pâté (and all you need is a tidbit per egg), they border on opulent. And if you add black truffle, as M. Jacques does in the winter . . . !

I used to make this recipe in the oven, until my friend the cookbook author and teacher Patricia Wells showed me that eggs coddle perfectly in a steamer. Oven-coddling is easy; steam-coddling is even easier.

As elegant as these eggs are, they're among the simplest starters you can make for a dinner party, since you can have them ready to cook hours in advance. However, you'll want to serve them the instant you lift them out of the steamer, so have everyone at the table.

1	¼-pound slice foie gras pâté or mousse	¼	cup heavy cream
4	absolutely fresh (preferably organic) large or extra-large eggs	4	slices black truffle, cut into slivers (optional)
	Salt and freshly ground white pepper	2	teaspoons finely chopped fresh tarragon
		2	teaspoons finely chopped fresh parsley

Lightly butter four individual soufflé molds or ramekins (4-ounce molds look prettiest for this dish, but any mold with a capacity of between 4 and 6 ounces will work). Set up your steamer — if you don't have a steamer with a large base (a bamboo steamer set over a wok is ideal), a pasta pot with an insert will work, as will a rack set in a large skillet with a lid. Bring the water in the steamer to a simmer.

Slice the pâté or mousse into 4 pieces and cut each piece into quarters. Divide the pâté among the molds. Carefully break 1 egg into each mold (the yolks should remain unbroken), season with salt and white pepper, and spoon 1 tablespoon of the cream over each egg white — you can cover the yolks, but I think it's prettier to leave them bare (it also makes it easier to check on doneness). Scatter an equal amount of truffle strips, if you're lucky enough to have them, over each egg, then sprinkle with the tarragon and parsley. (*You can prepare the ramekins to this point, cover them, and keep them in the refrigerator for a few hours; bring them to room temperature before cooking.*)

Make sure that the water in the steamer is simmering, then settle the molds into the steamer and cover the pot. Steam the eggs for about 5 minutes, or until the whites are opaque but the yolks are still runny. Remove the molds from the pan, dry the bottoms, place each mold on a plate, and serve immediately.

truffles

It would be hard to underestimate the French sentiment for black truffles, specifically *Tuber melanosporum,* the gnarly fungi ferreted out from under oak trees by pigs and dogs in the South of France and bought and sold in village markets the way drugs are probably bartered elsewhere in the world.

In the truffle-blessed town of Richerenches, in Provence, the Saturday market looks more like a used-car lot than a venue where tens of thousands of dollars will trade hands in the course of a few hours. Buyers park along the sides of the street, while anyone with a truffle to sell, professional or lucky farmer, walks from car to car looking for his best deal. It's fascinating, and as quaint as it sounds, and it's also big business.

I got a hint of just how big the business is when I attended the Truffle Mass at Richerenches's Catholic Church held at the end of January. When the alms basket was passed on that Sunday, it wasn't coins that were tossed into it, but truffles, lots of them and some of them the size of my fist. After the Mass, everyone gathered outside the *hôtel de ville* (town hall), wine and canapés were passed, and the truffles were auctioned off, with the proceeds — they topped 1,000,000 euros — going to the church.

Even people who have truffles growing in their backyards understand how rare and valuable they are and put them in the same class as caviar and lobster, saving them for special occasions or using them sparingly where their powerful aroma — dark, woodsy, slightly musky, and very sexy — can be most appreciated.

If you buy a truffle (see Sources, page 514), store it in a container of rice or a jar full of eggs until you're ready for it (it should be used in a couple of days), and you'll get a bonus: the rice or eggs will take on the flavor and aroma of truffles.

The taste and fragrance of black truffles are enhanced by warmth, but they can be destroyed by too much heat, so it's best to slice or shave the truffle into a dish just before it's finished cooking or as you're bringing it to the table. If you have only a few bits of truffles, even little shavings, you can work them into some softened butter, and you'll have a terrific topping for mashed potatoes, steak, or toast.

chicken and duck

ROAST CHICKEN FOR
LES PARESSEUX (PAGE 200)

chicken and duck

roast chicken for les paresseux

SERVING
After you've grabbed the juice-soaked bread and chicken liver, if you have it, for yourself (see headnote), carve the chicken and serve it with the pan sauce and roasted vegetables, if you made them. If you roasted only the chicken, you can serve it with any kind of green vegetable or a simple salad.

STORING
Leftover chicken can be covered and refrigerated for 3 to 4 days.

LES PARESSEUX ARE LAZY PEOPLE, and this is a recipe perfect for them — and the rest of us too — because once you put the chicken in the oven, you've got nothing more to do but pull it out when the timer buzzes ninety minutes or so later. You can roast the chicken by itself, but if you've got some garlic and onions, herbs, and a few root vegetables in the bin, adding them to the pot can only make dinner more delicious.

Because the chicken stays in one place — it isn't turned or basted — you can do what I think of as the bread trick. Before you put the chicken in the pot, you put a slice of bread (or two slices of baguette) in the center of the pot and then rest the bird on it. As the chicken roasts, the bread will imbibe its juices and, after a while, crisp and become a treat so tasty that even the most generous person won't want to share it — you have my permission to keep it all to yourself (I do). If you want to make a good thing even better, tuck the liver into the bird's cavity, and when it's cooked, mash and spread it over the juicy piece of bread, drizzle it with some of the fat from the pot, and sprinkle it with salt.

One last thing: the chicken is made in a Dutch oven, so there are no splatters, a boon to the lazy and the energetic alike. The photo is on page 198.

Olive oil	1 garlic head, cut horizontally in half, unpeeled
1 thick slice bread or 2 slices baguette	About ⅔ cup dry white wine or water (optional)
1 chicken, 4½ to 5 pounds, preferably organic (reserve the liver if it came with the chicken), at room temperature	4 baby potatoes, scrubbed and quartered (optional)
Salt and freshly ground pepper	2 carrots, trimmed, peeled, and cut into thick chunks (optional)
2 sprigs each rosemary, thyme, and oregano	4 shallots, left whole, or 1 onion, quartered (optional)

Center a rack in the oven and preheat the oven to 450 degrees F.

Rub the inside of a Dutch oven or other large high-sided casserole with oil and place the bread in the center of the pot. Season the chicken inside and out with salt and pepper. Put the liver, if you've got it, inside the chicken and toss in a half sprig of each of the herbs as well as one half of the garlic. Put the chicken in the pot, resting it on the bread. Put the other garlic half in the pot, along with the remaining herbs, and pour in a few tablespoons each of oil and the wine or water, if you're using it. Slide the pot into the oven.

If you'd like to roast the vegetables with the chicken, wait until the chicken has roasted for 45 minutes. Then toss the potatoes, carrots, and shallots with enough olive oil to give them a shine, season generously with salt and pepper, and scatter them around the chicken. Roast the chicken undisturbed for about 45 minutes more — a total of about 90 minutes — or until the skin is crackly and crisp and the juices run clear when you pierce the thickest part of the thigh with the tip of a knife. Remove the chicken from the oven.

If you're feeling really lazy, you can leave the chicken in the pot for 5 to 10 minutes to rest before serving. If you've got a bit more get-up-and-go, to get the juices back into the breast meat, put a cereal bowl at one end of a large platter and transfer the chicken, breast side down, to the platter. Let it rest under a foil tent, tail leaning on the bowl and pointing up, for 5 to 10 minutes before serving.

Should you want a little pan sauce — and you'll only get a little — spoon the vegetables, if you've got them, into a bowl, remove the bread, and skim off as much of the fat remaining in the pot as possible. Put the pot over high heat, and when the liquid boils, pour in about ½ cup wine or water and cook, scraping up whatever bits may have stuck to the bottom of the pot. Remove from the heat.

Carve the chicken and serve with the sauce, if you made it.

to wash or not to wash chicken?

Years ago I was cooking dinner for Jacques Pépin in our house near his in Connecticut. When Jacques arrived, I was in the kitchen giving the chicken we'd be having for dinner a nice bath, making sure to rinse it all over, inside, outside, and behind its wings. "What are you doing?" the normally soft-spoken chef exclaimed rather loudly.

"Washing the chicken. Don't you wash your chicken?" I asked.

His answer was succinct: "Chickens from Bresse don't need to be washed."

I should think they don't. The Bresse chicken — Bresse being both the breed of the chicken and its hometown (a town close to Jacques's birthplace) — is a French national treasure. Not only is it red (its crown), white (its body), and blue (its feet), but it's raised according to such exacting standards that each one is tagged with a number (and a very high price). But my chicken had just come from the local butcher and didn't have such a pedigree.

Still, why was I washing it? My mother didn't wash her chicken. I'd never seen any cook in France scrub a bird, whether the bird came from Bresse or the supermarket. What was I doing? I was following the then-current food-safety advice.

Now that advice has changed. These days, the prevailing wisdom is that chicken shouldn't be given a precook rinse, because the same bacteria that we're trying to wash away cross-contaminates whatever tools come in contact with it and whatever gets splashed by the wash-up water in the process. And besides, whatever we try to wash away will be done in when the bird is cooked.

So now, even if our chickens don't come from Bresse, we can treat them the same way.

hurry-up-and-wait
roast chicken

MAKES 4 SERVINGS

SERVING
If you were having this chicken in France on a Sunday afternoon, you'd face a mutiny if you didn't serve it with roasted potatoes (see Bonne Idée), but if you're in any other country, or it's any other day, feel free to accompany it with any kind of vegetable or even just a salad of mixed greens, preferably some with character.

STORING
Cooled to room temperature and well wrapped, the leftover chicken makes great sandwiches, salads, or snacks the following day.

IN FRANCE, THE LAND OF PEDIGREED CHICKENS (chickens are often bought by breed at the market), a roast chicken is a beloved staple — it's the most traditional dish for Sunday lunch. Yet the country's little secret is that often home cooks don't even roast the birds themselves: they buy them hot off the butcher's rotisserie, and the small potatoes that are cooked on the drip tray under the chicken are included. Still, I've never met a French cook who can't roast a chicken; I just haven't met one who fussed over her prowess.

And if, like me, the cook follows the lead of one of France's greatest chefs, Joël Robuchon, prowess is unnecessary. The chef advises turning the chicken during its roast and then letting it rest just about standing on its head so that the juices return to the breast, the part that cooks fastest and is usually the driest. The method, which is easy — except for the part where you have to turn the bird over (I use silicone mitts) — produces a remarkably moist chicken.

The hurry-up part is the high temperature at which the chicken cooks; the wait part is the rest period, the 15 minutes or so during which the bird does a headstand. Whatever you do, don't skip the wait — it makes all the difference in the juciness of the breasts.

If you want to add herbs or roast vegetables along with the bird, take a look at Bonne Idée for a few tips.

About 2 tablespoons butter (salted or unsalted), at room temperature, 2 tablespoons olive oil, or a combination, plus (optional) 1 tablespoon cold butter if making the sauce	1 chicken, about 4 pounds, preferably organic, at room temperature Salt and freshly ground pepper ¾–1 cup water or a combination of water and dry white wine

Center a rack in the oven and preheat the oven to 450 degrees F. Choose a suitable pan — a metal roasting pan, a cast-iron skillet, or a Dutch oven — what's important is that it be sturdy and, unless you're roasting vegetables along with the chicken, not oversized. Lightly grease the bottom and sides of the pan with some of the butter and/or oil.

Tie the chicken's legs together and fold the wings back, then rub the remaining butter and/or oil over the chicken. Season the chicken with salt and pepper.

Put the chicken on its side in the pan and roast undisturbed for 25 minutes. Turn the bird over onto its other side: if you have silicone mitts or silicone pot holders, grab them for the job; if not, use two wooden spoons or a pair of pancake turners. Give the chicken another 25 minutes in the oven. For the final flip, turn it onto its back and roast it, breast side up, for another 10 minutes, or until the skin is golden and the juices run clear when you pierce the thickest part of the thigh with the tip of a knife.

While the chicken is finishing up in the oven, prepare for its resting headstand: have at the ready a platter or a rimmed dish that can hold the bird comfortably and a small bowl.

Pull the pan from the oven and transfer the chicken, breast side down, to the platter. Lift the chicken's tail in the air, slide the bowl under it, and balance the bird so that it's resting at an angle. Cover the chicken loosely with aluminum foil and let it rest for 10 to 20 minutes so that the juices can resettle themselves in the breast.

If you'd like to make a little sauce, spoon the fat off the liquid in the pan, put the pan over medium heat, and add the water or water and wine, scraping up whatever solids have stuck to the bottom of the pan. Boil the sauce for a few minutes, taste, and season with salt and pepper. If you'd like, cut the tablespoon of cold butter into bits and, off the heat, swirl it into the sauce.

Carve the chicken and serve it with the sauce, if you made it.

BONNE IDÉE

There are so many ways you can play around with roast chicken. To get you started, think about putting a small bouquet of fresh herbs and a few wedges of lemon or orange inside it before roasting (a few garlic cloves are nice too); working some herb butter under the skin, pressing on the softened butter so that it covers the breast and the chubby part of the thighs; and/or surrounding the chicken with some vegetables. If you're going to add vegetables to the roasting pan, it's best to keep them small and to slice them so they are all about the same size. I like to add small potatoes (or potatoes cut into small chunks), carrot slices, small onions, and mushrooms. I toss them in olive oil so that they're glossy, season them with salt and freshly ground pepper, and often mix sprigs of fresh herbs with them as well. Scatter them around the chicken, taking care not to crowd the pan — remember you need room to turn the chicken — and be sure to add a little water or wine so that the vegetables don't stick before the chicken starts letting go of some of its juices.

m. jacques' armagnac chicken

MAKES 4 SERVINGS

SERVING
You can bring the chicken to the table whole, surrounded by the vegetables, and carve it in public, or you can do what I do, which is to cut the chicken into quarters in the kitchen, then separate the wings from the breasts and the thighs from the legs. I arrange the pieces in a large shallow serving bowl, spoon the vegetables into the center, moisten everything with a little of the sauce, and then pour the remainder of the elixir into a sauceboat to pass at the table.

STORING
I can't imagine that you'll have anything left over, but if you do, you can reheat the chicken and vegetables — make sure there's some sauce, so nothing dries out — covered in a microwave oven.

BONNE IDÉE
Armagnac and prunes are a classic combination in France. If you'd like, you can toss 8 to 12 prunes, pitted or not, into the pot along with the herbs. If your prunes are pitted and soft, they might pretty much melt during the cooking, but they'll make a sweet, lovely addition to the mix.

THIS RECIPE, *UNE PETITE MERVEILLE* (a little marvel), as the French would say, was given to me years ago by Jacques Drouot, the maître d' hôtel at the famous Le Dôme brasserie in Paris and an inspired home cook. I've been making it regularly ever since. It's one of those remarkable dishes that is comforting, yet more sophisticated than you'd expect (or really have any right to demand, given the basic ingredients and even more basic cooking method).

Here's the recipe at its simplest: You put a chicken and some onions, carrots, and potatoes in a heavy casserole, add Armagnac, slap on the cover, and roast at a high temperature for 60 minutes or so. (One Christmas, after getting the bird into the oven, I took a leisurely mid-meal walk with my friends.) When it's done, you pull the pot out of the oven, lift the lid and admire how golden and gorgeous the chicken is, stir in some water, and march to the dining room. Of course, you'll be pleasantly dizzy by the time you get there — the combination of pride and a deeply aromatic sauce can do that — but you'll be delighted to serve the chicken with its tender roasted vegetables and the sauce. Oh, that sauce: it's just a little sweet and really rather complex — you've got the chicken and vegetable juices, of course, but it's the soft, pruney flavor of the Armagnac that's so intriguing. That you made it by stirring the pan juices with water is just another of this dish's *merveilles*.

1 tablespoon olive oil or vegetable oil	1 thyme sprig
8 small thin-skinned potatoes, scrubbed and halved lengthwise	1 rosemary sprig
	1 bay leaf
3 medium onions, halved and thinly sliced	1 chicken, about 3½ pounds, preferably organic, trussed (or wings turned under and feet tied together with kitchen string), at room temperature
2 carrots, trimmed, peeled, and thickly sliced on the diagonal	
Salt and freshly ground white pepper	½ cup Armagnac (Cognac or other brandy)
	1 cup water

Center a rack in the oven and preheat the oven to 450 degrees F. You'll need a heavy casserole with a tight-fitting cover, one large enough to hold the chicken snugly but still leave room for the vegetables. (I use an enameled cast-iron Dutch oven.)

Put the casserole over medium heat and pour in the oil. When it's warm, toss in the vegetables and turn them around in the oil for a minute or two until they glisten; season with salt and white pepper. Stir in the herbs and push everything toward the sides of the pot to make way for the chicken. Rub the chicken all over with salt and white pepper, nestle it in the pot, and pour the Armagnac around it. Leave the pot on the heat for a minute to warm the Armagnac, then cover it tightly — if your lid is shaky, cover the pot with a piece of aluminum foil and then put the cover in place.

Slide the casserole into the oven and let the chicken roast undisturbed for 60 minutes.

Transfer the pot to the stove, and carefully remove the lid and the foil, if you used it — make sure to open the lid away from you, because there will be a lot of steam. After admiring the beautifully browned chicken, very carefully transfer it to a warm platter or, better yet, a bowl; cover loosely with a foil tent.

Using a spoon, skim off the fat that will have risen to the top of the cooking liquid and discard it; pick out the bay leaf and discard it too. Turn the heat to medium, stir the vegetables gently to dislodge any that might have stuck to the bottom of the pot, and add the water, stirring to blend it with the pan juices. Simmer for about 5 minutes, or until the sauce thickens ever so slightly, then taste for salt and pepper.

Carve the chicken and serve with the vegetables and sauce.

armagnac

Like Cognac, whiskey, and bourbon, Armagnac is a distilled (highly alcoholic) spirit. It is made from three types of white grapes — Folle Blanche, Ugni Blanc, and Colombard — and aged in oak casks in Gascony, the region in Southwest France best known as home to the Three Musketeers. It's enjoyed most often, just as Cognac is, as a digestive after dinner.

Armagnac is a wonderful spirit to cook with — and a good sip-along with rich desserts, especially the Coupétade (page 419), since it contains prunes, another specialty of the region, and one that goes so well with Armagnac. Armagnac is not inexpensive (bottles sell from about $30 to well over $100), but stored upright (never on its side) away from light and heat, it will keep

almost forever, even after you've opened it.

You can replace Armagnac with Cognac or brandy in most recipes. The spirits are not the same, but they all add character to a dish.

chicken in a pot: the garlic and lemon version

MAKES 4 SERVINGS

SERVING
If the chicken is cut up, you can just serve it and the vegetables from the pot. If the chicken is whole, you can quarter it and return the pieces to the pot or arrange the chicken and vegetables on a serving platter. Either way, you don't need to serve anything else but some country bread, which is good for two things: spreading with the sweet garlic popped from the skins and dunking into the cooking broth. One of the reasons I like to bring the pot to the table is because it makes for easy dipping.

STORING
If you have any leftover chicken, vegetables, and broth (what we call "goop" in our house), they can be reheated gently in the top of a double boiler or in a microwave oven.

I CAN'T REMEMBER EXACTLY WHEN I FIRST made a chicken cooked in a casserole that was sealed tighter than the ancient pyramids, but I do remember that it was called Chicken with 40 Cloves of Garlic and that the recipe came from Richard Olney's deservedly classic cookbook *Simple French Food*. In his version of this traditional dish, the chicken is cut up and tucked into a casserole with four heads of garlic, separated into cloves but not peeled; dried herbs; a bouquet garni; and some olive oil. Everything is turned around until it's all mixed up, the casserole is sealed tight with a flour-and-water dough, and the whole is slid into the oven to bake until the chicken is done and the garlic is cooked through, sweet and soft enough to spread on bread. It's a masterpiece of simplicity, and when the seal is cracked at the table, the pouf of fragrant steam is mildly theatrical and completely intoxicating.

Olney's recipe was the first of I-can't-even-count-how-many chickens in a pot I've made. I've cooked chickens whole and in pieces, with a garden's worth of vegetables and with only garlic, with hot spices and with fragrant herbs, with and without wine, and with and without the dough seal (with is better). I've cooked the chicken in a heavy Dutch oven (my favorite), a speckled enamel roaster (not the best), and a clay cooker (my second favorite; if you use a clay cooker, though, omit the dough seal — the clay is too fragile). And I've cooked it in every season — it's just as good in the summer as in winter.

This, my garlic and lemon rendition, was inspired by a dish made by Antoine Westermann, a chef with a Michelin three-star restaurant in Alsace and a bistro in Paris. That there's nothing Alsatian about his use of Moroccan preserved lemons and nothing particularly French about the addition of sweet potatoes makes the dish even more fun.

½ preserved lemon (see Sources), rinsed well	4 celery stalks, trimmed, peeled, and quartered
1 cup water	4 garlic heads, cloves separated but not peeled
¼ cup sugar	Salt and freshly ground pepper
5 tablespoons extra-virgin olive oil	3 thyme sprigs
2 large sweet potatoes, peeled and each cut into 8 same-sized pieces (you can use white potatoes, if you prefer)	3 parsley sprigs
	2 rosemary sprigs
	1 chicken, about 4 pounds, preferably organic, whole or cut into 8 pieces, at room temperature
16 small white onions, yellow onions, or shallots	1 cup chicken broth
8 carrots, trimmed, peeled, and quartered	½ cup dry white wine
	About 1½ cups all-purpose flour
	About ¾ cup hot water

Center a rack in the oven and preheat the oven to 450 degrees F.

Using a paring knife, slice the peel from the preserved lemon and cut it into small squares; discard the pulp. Bring the water and sugar to a boil in a small saucepan, drop in the peel, and cook for 1 minute; drain and set aside.

Heat 2 tablespoons of the olive oil in a large skillet over high heat. Add the vegetables and garlic, season with salt and pepper, and sauté until the vegetables are brown on all sides. (If necessary, do this in 2 batches.) Spoon the vegetables

BONNE IDÉE
You can save yourself a
little time and some cleanup by using store-bought
pizza dough to seal the pot.
If you use pizza dough, it
will rise around the pot.

into a 4½- to 5-quart Dutch oven or other pot with a lid and stir in the herbs and the preserved lemon.

Return the skillet to the heat, add another tablespoon of oil, and brown the chicken on all sides, seasoning it with salt and pepper as it cooks. Tuck the chicken into the casserole, surrounding it with the vegetables. Mix together the broth, wine, and the remaining olive oil and pour over the chicken and vegetables.

Put 1½ cups flour in a medium bowl and add enough hot water to make a malleable dough. Dust a work surface with a little flour, turn out the dough, and, working with your hands, roll the dough into a sausage. Place the dough on the rim of the pot — if it breaks, just piece it together — and press the lid onto the dough to seal the pot.

Slide the pot into the oven and bake for 55 minutes.

Now you have a choice — you can break the seal in the kitchen or do it at the table, where it's bound to make a mess, but where everyone will have the pleasure of sharing that first fragrant whiff as you lift the lid with a flourish. Whether at the table or in the kitchen, the best tool to break the seal is the least attractive — a screwdriver. Use the point of the screwdriver as a lever to separate the lid from the dough.

Depending on whether your chicken was whole or cut up, you might have to do some in-the-kitchen carving, but in the end, you want to make sure that the vegetables and the delicious broth are on the table with the chicken.

preserved lemons

Known as *citrons confits* in France, preserved lemons are a Moroccan and Middle Eastern specialty made by cutting deep slits in lemons and burying them in salt and their own juices for at least three weeks. The result is a pickled or brined lemon, prized for its rind (often the pulp isn't used), which is soft and has a sharp and, yes, salty flavor.

Preserved lemons are good with chicken and with meaty fish, like tuna and swordfish; they're also wonderful with bitter greens and even beets.

CHICKEN BASQUAISE (PAGE 210)

chicken basquaise

MAKES 4 SERVINGS

SERVING

The colorful chicken and pipérade is best served on top of plain white rice. If you'd like, dust the top of the dish with some minced fresh basil or cilantro. In the Basque tradition, have a small bowl of piment d'Espelette on the table or fill a small pepper grinder or shaker with the piment.

STORING

The pipérade can be made ahead and kept in the refrigerator for up to 4 days or packed airtight and frozen for up to 2 months. The pipérade and chicken can also be made ahead and refrigerated for a couple of days or frozen for a couple of months; defrost overnight in the refrigerator.

WHENEVER YOU SEE THE TERM *BASQUAISE,* or "in the Basque style," on a menu, you can be pretty sure that the dish contains a ragout of red and green peppers, onions, tomatoes, and a hit of heat, usually from the region's famous chile, the piment d'Espelette. Called *pipérade,* the mélange turns up alongside rice (think "Spanish rice"), mixed with scrambled eggs (when, just to confuse things, the finished dish of peppers and eggs is also called *pipérade*), and as the base of a stew that can include tuna, a treasured catch along the Basque coast, or, as it does here, chicken. In other words, with a pot of pipérade, you can play mix-and-match for a couple of meals, which is what I've been doing ever since my first trip through French Basque Country.

I've taken to the Basque custom of putting a little bowl of piment d'Espelette on the table instead of the usual peppermill. The mildly hot red pepper takes its name from the village of Espelette, where the freshly harvested chiles are tied into braids and hung to dry against the walls of the whitewashed houses before they're ground. Piment d'Espelette is available at specialty stores and online, and no matter where you buy it, even in Espelette, it's expensive — fortunately, a pinch packs a lot of flavor. If you don't have piment d'Espelette, don't let it stop you from making the pipérade; use Anaheim chile powder (or even regular chili powder) instead.

You can prepare the pipérade without peeling the peppers; however, as they cook, the skins will separate from the flesh. If you don't mind a few floating skins, skip the peeling (it's what I do). If you'd rather peel the peppers, you've got a couple of options: You can use a serrated swivel-blade vegetable peeler to remove the peels, or you can roast the peppers just until the skins can be easily removed, but not until the flesh becomes soft. The fastest and easiest way to do this is to char the peppers over a gas burner or on an electric burner. As soon as the skin warms and blisters enough for you to remove it, you're on your way. The photo is on page 209.

FOR THE PIPÉRADE

- 2 big Spanish or Vidalia onions
- 3 tablespoons olive oil
- 4 green bell peppers, peeled if you like
- 2 red bell peppers, peeled if you like
- 3 mild chiles (or another red bell pepper)
- 6 tomatoes, peeled and cut into chunks
- 2–4 garlic cloves (to taste), split, germ removed, and minced
- 2 teaspoons sea salt, or more to taste
- Pinch of sugar
- 2 thyme sprigs
- 1 bay leaf
- ¼–½ teaspoon piment d'Espelette (see headnote and Sources), Anaheim or other pure chile powder, or chili powder
- Freshly ground pepper

FOR THE CHICKEN

1 chicken, about 4 pounds,
 preferably organic, cut into
 8 pieces, or 8 chicken thighs,
 at room temperature
2 tablespoons olive oil

Salt and freshly ground pepper
¾ cup dry white wine

White rice, for serving
Minced fresh basil and/or
 cilantro, for garnish (optional)

TO MAKE THE PIPÉRADE: Cut the onions in half from top to bottom. Lay each piece flat side down and cut in half again from top to bottom, stopping just short of the root end; cut each half onion crosswise into thin slices.

Put a Dutch oven or large high-sided skillet with a cover over medium heat and pour in 2 tablespoons of the oil. Warm the oil for a minute, then toss in the onions and cook, stirring, for 10 minutes, or until softened but not colored.

Meanwhile, cut the peppers and chiles in half, trim the tops, remove the cores, and remove the seeds. Cut the bell peppers lengthwise into strips about ½ inch wide. Thinly slice the chiles.

Add the remaining tablespoon of oil to the pot, stir in the peppers and chiles, cover, and reduce the heat to medium-low. Cook and stir for another 20 minutes, or until all the vegetables are quite soft.

Add the tomatoes, garlic, salt, sugar, thyme, bay leaf, piment d'Espelette or chile powder, and freshly ground pepper to taste, stir well, cover, and cook for 10 minutes more. Remove the cover and let the pipérade simmer for another 15 minutes. You'll have a fair amount of liquid in the pot, and that's fine. Remove the thyme and bay leaf. Taste and add more salt, pepper, or piment d'Espelette if you think it needs it.

If you'd like to make the pipérade and eggs (see Bonne Idée), use a slotted spoon to transfer 2 cups of the pepper mixture to a bowl. Spoon in a little of the cooking liquid, and refrigerate until needed. (*You can pack all of the pipérade airtight and keep it refrigerated for up to 4 days.*)

TO MAKE THE CHICKEN: Pat the chicken pieces dry. Warm the oil in a Dutch oven or other heavy casserole over medium-high heat. Add a couple of chicken pieces, skin side down (don't crowd the chicken — do this in batches), and cook until the skin is golden, about 5 minutes. Turn the pieces over and cook for another 3 minutes. Transfer the pieces to a bowl, season with salt and pepper, and continue until all the chicken is browned.

Discard the oil, set the pot over high heat, pour in the wine, and use a wooden spoon to scrape up any bits that might have stuck to the bottom. Let the wine bubble away until it cooks down to about 2 tablespoons. Return the chicken to the pot, add any juices that have accumulated in the bowl, and spoon in the pipérade. Bring the mixture to a boil, then reduce the heat so that the pipérade just simmers, cover the pot, and simmer gently for 40 minutes, or until the chicken is cooked through. Taste for salt and pepper and adjust the seasonings as needed.

Serve over white rice, sprinkled with the basil and/or cilantro, if using.

BONNE IDÉE

Pipérade and Eggs. The traditional way to make pipérade and eggs is to heat the pipérade, stir beaten eggs into the mixture, and cook until the eggs are scrambled. Inevitably and invariably the eggs curdle, but no one (at least no one Basque) seems to mind. If you'd like uncurdled eggs, warm 2 cups pipérade in a saucepan. Meanwhile, beat 6 eggs with a little salt and pepper in a bowl. Heat 2 tablespoons unsalted butter in a large nonstick skillet over medium heat, and when the bubbles subside, pour in the eggs. Cook the eggs, stirring, until they form soft curds. Spoon the pipérade into four shallow soup plates and, with the back of a spoon, make a little well in the center of each. Fill each well with some scrambled eggs. Drizzle the eggs and pipérade sparingly with olive oil, dust with minced basil or cilantro, if you'd like, and serve immediately, with slices of warm toasted country bread rubbed with garlic and moistened with oil.

chicken tagine with sweet potatoes and prunes

MAKES 4 SERVINGS

SERVING
Because of the sweet potatoes, you really don't have to serve anything else with the tagine — it's a true one-pot meal. However, since the sauce is so good, it's hard not to want to pour it over something more. Couscous is a natural choice, and a fine rice, like basmati or jasmine, is also very good, but my personal favorite is quinoa: I think the grain's toastiness goes really well with the tagine's spices.

STORING
As with so many braised dishes, this one reheats well the following day.

FALLING DEFINITIVELY ON THE SWEET SIDE of the sweet-savory continuum, this tagine seduces with its haunting fragrances and conquers with its mix of spices, fruit, and vegetables. As is often true in tagines, it is built on a base of onions, cooked slowly, slowly, slowly, not to color them, but to concentrate their flavor, just about melt them really, and to get them ready to welcome the spices — saffron, cinnamon (if you can find full-flavored and slightly spicy Vietnamese cinnamon, it's lovely here), star anise, and bay. While this is a powerful blend, gentle cooking renders it mild and pleasantly puzzling; it won't be easy to put your finger on which of the spices is urging you to have another taste. The sweet potatoes and prunes only add to the exoticism.

About ¼ cup olive oil	⅛ teaspoon ground cinnamon
2 large white onions, halved lengthwise and thinly sliced	Pinch of cayenne
½ cup plus 1 tablespoon water	1 star anise point
Salt	1 bay leaf
1 chicken, about 4 pounds, preferably organic, cut into 8 pieces, or 8 chicken thighs, patted dry, at room temperature	2 tablespoons honey
	1 cup chicken broth
	12 pitted prunes
	1 pound sweet potatoes, peeled and cut into 2-inch cubes
Freshly ground pepper	
2 large pinches of saffron threads	Toasted chopped walnuts, for serving (optional)

Pour 2 tablespoons of the oil into the base of a large tagine or a Dutch oven and warm over low heat. Add the onions, stirring to coat them with oil, then mix in 1 tablespoon of the water, season with salt, and cover the pot. Cook the onions gently for about 30 minutes, stirring occasionally, until they are very soft but not colored.

Meanwhile, brown the chicken. Heat a tablespoon or two of oil in a large skillet, preferably nonstick, over medium heat. Slip the chicken into the pan, skin side down (don't crowd the pan — if it isn't large enough to hold the pieces comfortably, work in batches), and cook the chicken for about 4 minutes on a side, or until golden. Transfer the chicken to a plate and season with salt and pepper.

When the onions are softened, add the saffron, crushing it between your fingers as you sprinkle it in, the rest of the spices, the bay leaf, honey, broth, and the remaining ½ cup water and stir to blend. Scatter the prunes over the mixture, then top with the chicken pieces, skin side up. Strew the potato cubes over the chicken and bring the liquid to a boil. Adjust the heat so that the

broth simmers gently but steadily, cover, and cook for about 45 minutes, or until the chicken is cooked through and the potatoes are tender. Wait until you hit the 45-minute mark before lifting the lid — the tagine should bubble away undisturbed.

Taste the pan juices, and if you'd like to concentrate the flavors, remove the chicken and vegetables to a serving bowl, cover, and keep warm. Boil the liquid for a few minutes, keeping in mind that this is really a *jus,* not a sauce, and it's meant to be thin. If you removed the chicken and accompaniments, pour the *jus* over them; if everything is still in the tagine or casserole, you can leave them there for serving.

In either case, taste for salt and pepper, scatter over the chopped walnuts, if you're using them, and serve.

chicken couscous

You can put everything on
the table and let guests
serve themselves, or you
can serve each guest
couscous (the pasta),
chicken, and vegetables
in shallow soup plates.
The couscous can be a
base for the stew, or it can
go alongside. Pour some
broth over each serving.
When it comes to the hot
sauce, let guests decide
for themselves. Put a small
bowl of broth next to each
serving and let guests add
as much harissa as they'd
like to the broth and then
pour it over their couscous.
Pass the raisins at the
table.

If it's more convenient
for you to work in stages,
make the dish up to the
point where you remove
some broth to cook the
couscous. Refrigerate the
broth and the chicken with
the vegetables separately,
then finish the dish the
next day. If you've made
the whole dish and have
leftovers, reheat them
gently — the grain and
vegetables will be a little
soft, but they'll still be tasty.

COUSCOUS IS THE NAME OF BOTH a teensy-grained semolina pasta and
the fragrantly spiced North African stew that's served with it. Most times,
the stew is spooned into one bowl, the couscous into another, and the broth
from the stew into a third; the harissa comes to the table in a small pot, and
there might even be a bowl of raisins and one of almonds too. You take some
stew and some couscous and then, if you like it spicy, put a little harissa in the
ladle or a small bowl, add some broth, swish it around, and pour the broth over
your fixings. The raisins and nuts are for sprinkling. It's a congenial dish and,
like other participatory dishes, one that's great for a crowd.

Truly traditional couscous is a complex affair requiring a couscoussière, a
large two-level pot that allows you to cook the stew in the bottom and let its
moisture steam the grain above, and a special technique for hand-raking the
semolina. It's a long process, and one that I find beautiful to watch, but it's not
one that most people do at home. For homemade couscous, French cooks, like
Americans, turn to instant couscous that can be cooked in broth in less than
five minutes. You can make this delicious couscous in about an hour, not that
you'll want to rush — the aroma of a couscous in progress is enticing.

1 tablespoon grated fresh ginger and/or 2½ teaspoons ground ginger (or to taste)	2 leeks, white and light green parts only, split lengthwise, washed, and cut into 2-inch lengths
¾ teaspoon ground cumin	8 small white onions
½ teaspoon turmeric	2 celery stalks, trimmed, peeled, and cut into 2-inch lengths
¼ teaspoon saffron threads, pinched between your fingers (optional)	2 carrots, trimmed, peeled, and cut into 2-inch lengths
⅛ teaspoon ground cinnamon	2 medium turnips, trimmed, peeled, and quartered
3 garlic cloves, split, germ removed, and finely chopped	1½ cups quick-cooking couscous
Salt and freshly ground pepper	2 slender zucchini, trimmed and cut into 2-inch lengths
2–3 tablespoons unsalted butter	1 15- to 16-ounce can chickpeas, drained and rinsed
1 chicken, about 4 pounds, preferably organic, cut into 8 pieces, or 8 chicken thighs, patted dry, at room temperature	
	Harissa (see Sources) for serving
6 cups chicken broth	Moist, plump golden raisins, for serving (optional)

Mix the ginger (fresh and ground, if you're using both), cumin, turmeric, saffron
(if using), cinnamon, garlic, and salt and pepper to taste in a small bowl.

Put a large Dutch oven or soup pot over medium heat and add the butter.

When it's melted, put the chicken pieces in the pot (working in batches, if necessary) and sprinkle over the spice/herb mix. Cook, turning the pieces so that they pick up the seasonings in the bottom of the pot, just until they lose their raw texture — you don't have to brown them.

Pour the broth into the pot, increase the heat, and bring to a boil. Lower the heat to keep the broth at a gentle but steady simmer, add the leeks, onions, celery, carrots, and turnips, and cook until the vegetables can be easily pierced with the tip of a knife, about 15 minutes. (*You can make the couscous to this point up to a day ahead; refrigerate the broth separately from the chicken and vegetables, and reunite and reheat them before finishing the dish.*)

Taste for salt and pepper and season as needed. Transfer 3 cups of the broth to a medium saucepan and bring to a boil. Pour in the couscous and let the broth simmer gently for a minute, then stir, turn off the heat, cover the pan, and allow the couscous to absorb the broth, about 5 minutes.

To finish the stew, drop in the zucchini and chickpeas and cook for about 5 minutes, or until the zucchini is tender.

Serve the stew while it's piping hot. Each person should have a plate of couscous with chicken, vegetables, and broth, with small bowls of broth, harissa, and raisins (if using) within easy reach.

chicken breasts diable

*D*IABLE IS THE FRENCH WORD FOR DEVIL, and when you see it on a menu, you can be sure that the dish includes mustard, usually *la moutarde forte de Dijon,* strong Dijon mustard, which is about as hot as condiments in the French kitchen get. You can pretty much count on the presence of bread crumbs too. In the most traditional reading of *poulet à la diable,* the on-the-bone chicken pieces are painted with smooth Dijon mustard, coated with bread crumbs, drizzled with melted butter, and roasted. In my quicker version, you sauté chicken cutlets, then make a pan sauce with shallots and garlic, white wine, cream, and mustard. With a small tweak, you can turn this dish into steak diable (see Bonne Idée).

MAKES 4 SERVINGS

SERVING
Arrange the chicken on a warm serving platter or on individual plates and spoon an equal amount of sauce over each piece. I like to serve the devilish chicken with Garlicky Crumb-Coated Broccoli (page 334) or simply steamed carrots, tossed with a little butter and minced fresh parsley or thyme.

STORING
Chicken diable is not a dish to hold on to — enjoy it as soon as it's made.

4	skinless, boneless chicken breast halves, preferably organic, without tenders, pounded lightly, at room temperature
1	tablespoon unsalted butter
	About 1 tablespoon olive oil
	Salt and freshly ground pepper
1	medium shallot, finely chopped, rinsed, and patted dry

1	garlic clove, split, germ removed, and finely chopped
⅓	cup dry white wine
½	cup heavy cream
3	tablespoons Dijon or grainy mustard, preferably French, or a bit more
1–2	teaspoons Worcestershire sauce

Center a rack in the oven and preheat the oven to 200 degrees F. Pat the chicken breasts dry.

Put a large skillet over medium-high heat and add the butter and 1 tablespoon oil. When the butter is melted, slip the chicken pieces into the pan. (If your pan isn't large enough to hold all the pieces at one time, cook the chicken in batches or work in two skillets.) Adjust the heat so that the butter doesn't burn, and cook the chicken until it's well browned on the underside, about 4 minutes. Turn the pieces over and cook until the other side is also well browned and the chicken is cooked through — cut into a piece to check. If the pan dries out, drizzle in just a touch more oil. Transfer the breasts to a heatproof plate (one with a rim to catch the juices), season with salt and pepper, cover lightly with a foil tent, and keep warm in the oven while you prepare the sauce.

Lower the heat to medium, toss the shallot and garlic into the pan, and season lightly with salt and pepper. Cook, stirring, just until they soften, about 2 minutes. Pour in the wine, and when it starts to bubble, stir it around so that you can pick up whatever little bits might have stuck to the bottom of the skillet. Let the wine boil for a few seconds, then pour in the heavy cream. As soon as it reaches a boil, stir in the mustard and 1 teaspoon Worcestershire sauce. Taste and decide if you want more mustard, Worcestershire, or pepper (you probably won't need more salt, since the mustard is salty).

Remove the chicken from the oven, pour any juices on the plate into the skillet, and stir the sauce again. Serve the chicken with the sauce.

BONNE IDÉE
Filet Mignon Diable. **Bring the filets mignons to room temperature, then pat each piece dry between paper towels, and sear on both sides in the butter and oil. Beef needs less skillet time than chicken, so start checking after 2 minutes on a side. When the beef is cooked to your liking, transfer it to a plate, season with salt and pepper, cover it loosely, and put it in the 200-degree-F oven. Cook the shallot and garlic in the fat that remains in the skillet, then pour in ¼ cup dry white wine and 2 tablespoons Cognac, Armagnac, or other brandy. Let boil for 1 minute as you scrape up whatever bits are stuck to the skillet, then add the heavy cream, followed by the mustard and Worcestershire sauce. Pour the juices around the beef into the skillet, give the sauce one last stir, and serve, spooning the sauce over the beef.**

chicken, apples, and cream à la normande

MAKES 4 SERVINGS

SERVING
Sometimes I put the chicken with its wonderful cream sauce over Lemon-Steamed Spinach (page 331) — I like the plain, mineral flavor of the spinach against the sweetness of the apple and onion. Sometimes I pair it with steamed broccoli tossed with olive oil or with Pancetta Green Beans (page 333), and sometimes I just let it play by itself — it's got enough flavor, texture, and nuance to stand alone.

STORING
If you have leftovers, they can be reheated gently the next day.

WHEN YOU FIND A DISH with apples and cream, it's likely to be *à la Normande,* a tribute to Normandy. Running from the western edges of Paris to the English Channel, the region is famed for apples, cider, brandy-like Calvados (which is made from apples), cream (including thick, spoonable crème fraîche), Camembert, and butter. Not bad for a little corner of the country. In this instance, it's chicken breasts that get the Norman treatment (although it could be pork; see Bonne Idée), and in addition to the apples and cream, there's Calvados and mushrooms, which are also local to the area. The dish is a slightly sweet, decidedly rich mix that's more luxurious, far fancier, and much prettier than either its ingredient list or the brief time it takes you to pull it together would lead you to believe.

All-purpose flour, for dredging	1 medium onion, finely chopped
Salt and freshly ground pepper	8 mushrooms, stemmed, wiped
4 skinless, boneless chicken	clean, thinly sliced, and slices
breast halves, preferably	cut crosswise in half
organic, without tenders,	⅓ cup chicken broth
at room temperature	2 tablespoons Calvados, apple
1–2 tablespoons unsalted butter	jack, or brandy
1–2 tablespoons olive oil	⅔ cup heavy cream
1 large apple, peeled, cored, and	
cut into 1-inch chunks	

Put some flour on a plate and season it with salt and pepper. Pat the chicken pieces dry and run them through the flour, coating both sides lightly and tapping off the excess.

Put a large deep skillet over medium-high heat (I like nonstick) and add 1 tablespoon each butter and oil. When the butter is melted, slip the chicken into the pan (if your pan isn't large enough to accommodate all 4 pieces, do this in 2 batches, or use two skillets). Cook for 3 minutes, to brown the undersides, then turn over and cook for 3 minutes more. (Return all the chicken to the pan if you cooked it in batches.)

If you're low on butter and oil, add a little more now, then toss in the apple, onion, and mushrooms. Season with salt and pepper and turn the new additions around so that they're well mixed and glossy with butter and oil. Cook for 1 minute, then pour in the broth. When the broth bubbles, reduce the heat — you want to keep it at a slow simmer — and cook for about 10 minutes, or until the chicken is almost cooked through. (Cooking time will depend on the thickness of your chicken pieces; start checking at the 6-minute mark.)

Turn the heat up again, pour in the Calvados, and boil until it's almost evaporated, about 1 minute. Add the cream and, keeping the heat on high, cook until the cream reduces by about one quarter, a matter of a few minutes. (If you're concerned that your chicken will overcook, transfer it to a serving platter and keep it warm, covered lightly.) Taste the sauce for salt and pepper. If you removed the chicken, pour the sauce over it; if the dish is still intact, arrange it on a platter.

BONNE IDÉE

Pork à la Normande. Swap the chicken breasts for pork cutlets (they should take 15 minutes, more or less, to cook through, depending on their thickness), and keep everything else in the recipe. If you'd like, because pork and sage are such a lovely combination, you can add a little finely chopped fresh sage to the flour that you use to dredge the meat.

cinnamon-crunch chicken

MAKES 4 SERVINGS

SERVING
My favorite side dish is Lemon-Steamed Spinach (page 331) mixed with nothing but salt and pepper and, if you'd like, a little freshly grated nutmeg. Since the dish is sweet and a little rich, it's nice to have something very basic as a go-with.

STORING
The dish is quickly made and should be eaten as soon as it's ready.

MY FRIEND ALICE VASSEUR has a most expressive face. Her smiles and frowns are oversized, and when she's excited, her eyes widen and her brows look like they're going to take off. And so there we were, having tea in my Paris kitchen on a chilly winter afternoon, when all of a sudden her face lit up and she exclaimed, "I forgot to tell you what I made last night — it's so easy and so good, and my friends loved it: chicken with speculoos!"

Speculoos (also spelled speculaas) are thin, buttery cinnamon and spice cookies that, although crunchy, melt in your mouth like shortbread. They're a specialty of northern France, Belgium, and Holland, most popular at Christmastime, but available year-round, even in American supermarkets (look for LU Cinnamon Sugar Spice Biscuits or LU Bastogne), and they are paired most often — when they're not served alongside tea or coffee (they're great dunkers) — with foie gras or something gamy. Using the cookies with chicken was a leap and Alice's little stroke of brilliance.

This dish has only three main ingredients, chicken breasts, crème fraîche, and speculoos, and it takes just 10 minutes to prepare, but it's not only unusual and delicious, it's also a recipe that perfectly represents French home cooking today: it makes supermarket ingredients look stylish and taste haute.

Crème fraîche is really what you should use here, as much for its tang as for its heatability. If you must, you can substitute heavy cream, but not sour cream, which will curdle and break over heat. And, while I love homemade speculoos (page 406), this recipe is best with store-bought.

2	speculoos (LU Cinnamon Sugar Spice Biscuits or LU Bastogne)	Salt and freshly ground pepper
1	cup crème fraîche (see above)	4 skinless, boneless chicken breast halves, preferably organic, without tenders, at room temperature
		1–2 tablespoons unsalted butter or olive oil

Using a long serrated knife, chop the cookies unevenly so that you've got some cookie powder, some cookie crumbs, and some cookie bits. Stir the cookies into the crème fraîche and season with salt and pepper.

Pat the chicken breasts dry and slice them crosswise into strips about a scant inch wide.

Place a large skillet, preferably nonstick, over medium-high heat and add 1 tablespoon butter or oil. When it's hot, toss in the chicken strips and sauté, adding more butter or oil if necessary, until the chicken is lightly colored on all sides and almost cooked through, about 7 minutes.

Season the chicken with salt and pepper and add the cookie mixture to the pan. Bring to a boil and cook for another minute, stirring, or until the chicken is coated and completely cooked. Taste for salt and pepper, and serve.

curried chicken, peppers, and peas en papillote

I CAN'T EVEN COUNT THE NUMBER OF TIMES I've made this dish, but each time I do, I have the same reaction: I wonder how anything this good and this pretty can be this easy. It takes about five minutes to assemble and needs absolutely none of your attention while it cooks, yet it comes out of the oven full of flavor, fragrant, beautifully colorful, and ready to serve alone or with a little white rice. Normally I use nonstick foil to make the cooking packets, but if I'm serving this at a dinner party (don't think it isn't dinner-party-worthy just because it's easy), I make the papillotes from parchment paper and bring the pouches to the table, so that each guest can have the pleasure of opening the packet and getting that first heady whiff of aromatic steam.

A word on multiplying the recipe: With anything cooked *en papillote,* it's easy to increase or decrease the number of servings. However, if you do increase them, you shouldn't put all the packets on one baking sheet. Four packs to a sheet is the max; you need to leave room for heat circulation and papillote puffing.

MAKES 4 SERVINGS

SERVING
You can put each packet on a plate or in a shallow soup plate and have your guests open them at the table, or you can open them in the kitchen and plate them there. White rice seems like the most traditional accompaniment (consider Cardamom Rice Pilaf, page 382), but couscous or quinoa are very good too.

STORING
You can assemble the packets a few hours ahead of time and refrigerate them; just add another minute or two to the baking time.

2	large skinless, boneless chicken breast halves, preferably organic, at room temperature
12	thin slices red onion, halved
½	red bell pepper, cored, seeded, and diced

1	cup peas (fresh or frozen)
4	teaspoons olive oil
1	teaspoon curry powder
	Salt and freshly ground pepper

Center a rack in the oven and preheat the oven to 400 degrees F. Cut four 12-inch squares of nonstick aluminum foil. Have a baking sheet at hand.

Cut the chicken into long strips and then cut the strips crosswise in half. Put the chicken and all the other ingredients in a bowl, seasoning them with salt and pepper, and stir until the curry powder has evenly colored the chicken and vegetables. Spoon an equal amount of the mix onto the center of each piece of foil. Draw up the edges of the foil and seal the packets well, but don't crimp the foil very close to the chicken — you want to leave room around the ingredients so they can steam. Put the packets on the baking sheet. *(You can assemble the packets up to 4 hours ahead and refrigerate; bake for a few more minutes.)*

Bake the papillotes for 17 to 20 minutes, or until the chicken is cooked through — carefully open a packet and cut into a piece of chicken to test.

Serve the packets immediately, bringing them to the table straight from the oven or opening them in the kitchen and arranging the chicken and vegetables on individual plates.

chicken b'stilla

MAKES 6 SERVINGS

SERVING
B'stilla needs no accompaniments.

STORING
You can make the chicken and sauce up to a day ahead and keep it covered and chilled until you're ready to construct the b'stilla; however, once the b'stilla is baked, it's best served that day. If you've got any left over, cover and refrigerate it; let it come to room temperature before serving, or reheat it in a 325-degree-F oven — the pastry will not be as flaky, but the dish will still be satisfying.

B'STILLA (OR PASTILLA, AS IT'S SOMETIMES WRITTEN) is one of the legendary dishes of Morocco and something that the French have adapted infinitely to make their own. Essentially a covered pie constructed from see-through-thin flaky pastry, the sweetly spiced dish is traditionally made with pigeon, but I've seen it made in Paris with guinea hen, quail, chicken, and even fish. This version stars chicken spiced with ginger, cinnamon, coriander, and saffron; uses filo dough for the pastry, which is perfect for the pie; and has, as it does in Morocco, a dusting of cinnamon sugar over the crust.

It takes time to make a b'stilla — the chicken must marinate and then be cooked ahead, and the construction is a tad artsy-craftsy — but the dish is worth the effort, especially if you're having a party. Aside from being do-aheadable (always a plus), it's beautiful and, since it's meant to be eaten with your hands, fun to eat. Actually, it's also meant to be eaten at the start of a multi-course meal, but no one will fault you for following my lead and bringing it to the table as the *plat de résistance*.

BE PREPARED: The chicken needs to marinate for an hour.

8 chicken thighs, preferably organic, skinned	2 tablespoons honey Freshly ground pepper
2 large onions, coarsely chopped	1 tablespoon chopped fresh cilantro
3 garlic cloves, split, germ removed, and chopped	1 tablespoon chopped fresh parsley
¾ teaspoon ground ginger	8 sheets filo (each 9 x 14 inches)
¾ teaspoon ground coriander	About 6 tablespoons unsalted butter, melted
¾ teaspoon ground cinnamon Big pinch of saffron threads	3 ounces sliced almonds (a scant cup), toasted and chopped
2½ cups chicken broth Salt	
3 tablespoons fresh lemon juice	Cinnamon sugar, for dusting
3 large eggs	

Put the chicken pieces, onions, garlic, and spices into a Dutch oven or other large casserole and give everything a good stir (I do this with my hands). Cover and let the chicken marinate for 1 hour at room temperature. *(If it's more convenient for you, the chicken can be marinated in the refrigerator for as long as 1 day.)*

Add the chicken broth and 1 teaspoon salt to the pot and bring to a boil over high heat. Lower the heat so that the liquid simmers, cover the pot, and cook for 1 hour, at which point the chicken should be falling-off-the-bone tender.

Using a slotted spoon, transfer the chicken to a bowl. Strain the broth, saving both the liquid and the onions. When the chicken is cool enough to handle, remove the meat from the bones and cut it into small cubes or shred it.

Clean the Dutch oven and pour the broth back into it, or pour the broth into a medium saucepan. Whisk in the lemon juice, bring to a boil, and cook until you have about 1 cup liquid. Reduce the heat to low.

Beat the eggs with the honey, and, whisking all the while, pour into the broth. Heat, whisking constantly, until the sauce thickens enough that your whisk leaves tracks in it, about 5 minutes. Pull the pan from the heat and season the sauce with salt and pepper.

Stir the chicken and reserved onions into the sauce, along with the cilantro and parsley. *(You can make the chicken and sauce up to 1 day ahead and keep it covered and refrigerated.)*

Center a rack in the oven and preheat the oven to 400 degrees F. Line a baking sheet with foil.

Place the filo sheets between sheets of wax paper and cover with a kitchen towel. Brush a 9-inch round cake pan, one that's 2 inches tall, with melted butter. Brush 1 sheet of filo with butter and center it in the pan, so that the excess hangs over the edges. Brush another sheet and press it into the pan so that it's perpendicular to the first sheet and forms a plus sign. Place a third and then a fourth buttered sheet into the pan so that they form an X; the overhang from all of the sheets should cover the edges of the pan.

Sprinkle half of the almonds over the filo. Spoon in the saucy chicken, spreading it evenly across the pan, and top with the rest of the almonds. Fold the overhanging filo over the chicken.

Butter the remaining 4 sheets of filo, stacking them one on top of the other on the work surface. Using a pot lid or the bottom of a tart pan as a guide, cut out a 10- to 11-inch circle. Center the circle over the cake pan and gently tuck the edges of the dough into the pan, working your way around it as though you were making a bed. Brush the top of the b'stilla with a little butter and sprinkle with some cinnamon sugar. Place the pan on the baking sheet.

Bake the b'stilla for 20 minutes, then lower the temperature to 350 degrees F and bake for 20 minutes more. If the top seems to be getting too brown at any point, cover it loosely with foil. Transfer the b'stilla to a cooling rack and let rest for about 5 minutes.

Lay a piece of parchment over a cutting board, and have a serving platter at hand. Turn the b'stilla out onto the parchment-lined board and then invert it onto the serving platter, so that it's right side up. Serve the b'stilla now, cutting it into wedges, or serve it warm or at room temperature.

olive-olive cornish hens

THIS IS ONE OF THE EASIEST WAYS I know to make a really good dinner really fast. Cornish hens are quick-cookers in general, but prepared as they are here, split in half and flattened, their time in the oven is even shorter. The French call this preparation *en crapaudine,* which translates roughly to "like a toad," which is what the flattened hens, with their legs splayed and their wings sticking out, resemble. It's not the most appetizing description for a dish, I know (the British word for the technique, *spatchcocked,* doesn't sound any more appealing), but cutting the hens like this halves their cooking time and gives you crisp skin all around.

For this version of *poussin en crapaudine,* I work some tapenade under the hens' skin and give them an olive oil massage, a squirt of lemon juice, and just 30 minutes in the oven.

Depending on what else you've got on the menu, 1 hen will serve 1 or 2 people. To serve 4 people, just cut the roasted hens in half. You can also double the recipe.

MAKES 2 TO
4 SERVINGS

SERVING
I like to serve the birds almost au naturel: If the pan juices aren't burned, I may spoon a little of them over the hens, but usually I just moisten the hens with a few drops of olive oil and surround them with lemon wedges. A squeeze of lemon is really all the dressing these birds need.

STORING
Any leftovers make good snacking the next day.

---

2 Cornish hens, preferably organic, at room temperature	Olive oil
	Fresh lemon juice
	Salt and freshly ground pepper
About 2 teaspoons tapenade, black (my first choice) or green, homemade (page 487) or store-bought	Lemon wedges, for serving

---

Center a rack in the oven and preheat the oven to 500 degrees F. Oil a shallow roasting pan or your broiler pan. (For easier cleanup, line the pan with nonstick aluminum foil and oil that.)

Working with 1 hen at a time, using kitchen shears or a chef's knife, cut down along both sides of the backbone to remove it. Discard the bone (or put it into your scraps-for-stock pile) and turn the bird breast side up on the cutting board. Now, putting your weight into it, press the heel of your hand against the middle of the hen's breastbone, crack the bone, and flatten the bird. With that bit of rough work done, gently loosen the skin from the flesh, separating it just enough to get to the breast meat and the chubby part of the thighs. Using your fingers, work half of the tapenade under the skin — you don't need much of the tapenade in any one place; a little, when heated, goes a long way.

Transfer the hens to the roasting pan, skin side up, and give the skin a rubdown with some olive oil. Sprinkle over some lemon juice, season with salt and pepper, and slide the pan into the oven.

Roast the hens undisturbed for 25 to 30 minutes, until the skin is deeply golden and crisp and the juices run clear when you prick the thighs.

If you're serving 4, cut the birds in half by slicing them along the breastbone. Serve with lemon wedges and, if you'd like, a drizzle of olive oil.

sausage-stuffed cornish hens

MAKES 2 TO
4 SERVINGS

SERVING
If you're going to split
the hens, cut them in
half along the breast and
backbone with kitchen
shears or a good strong
knife, then tuck half the
stuffing under each half. If
you've made a pan sauce,
just pour a little of it over
each serving.

STORING
If you've got leftovers,
remove the stuffing from
the hens and keep it and
the bird(s) covered in the
fridge — it makes for great
next-day snacking.

OUR READILY AVAILABLE CORNISH HENS ARE perfect stand-ins for the slightly smaller French *poussins,* or baby chickens. They're good little birds to cook on busy weeknights, since they're tasty, versatile, and in and out of the oven in about 40 minutes — and that's with stuffing (here a simple mix of bread and sausage). While a French cook might make even quicker work of this dish, because she can pick up her ready-made sausage stuffing from the butcher, this stuffing can still be put together in a flash, adding only a few extra minutes to your American kitchen time.

A word on serving size: Depending on what else you've got on the menu, 1 hen will serve either 1 or 2 people. If you decide to make 2 hens for 4, roast the hens, then cut them in half along the breast and backbones. Of course, you can also double the recipe; in that case, use two skillets or a larger roaster.

2 Cornish hens, preferably organic (livers reserved if included), at room temperature About 2 tablespoons olive oil About 1½ tablespoons unsalted butter, plus (optional) 1 tablespoon cold butter if making the sauce 1 garlic clove, split, germ removed, and finely chopped	1 shallot or ½ small onion, finely chopped, rinsed, and dried ¼ pound sausage, casings removed if necessary (you can use sweet or hot sausage or a mixture) ½ slice stale bread, crust removed, cut into small cubes 1 large egg, lightly beaten 2 tablespoons minced fresh parsley Salt and freshly ground pepper ½ cup dry white wine (optional)

Center a rack in the oven and preheat the oven to 425 degrees F. Lightly butter or oil an oven-going skillet (I use my old cast-iron skillet) or a small roaster.

If you were lucky enough to get hens with livers, rinse and dry the livers, cut away any veins and green spots, and coarsely chop them.

Heat 2 teaspoons of the oil and ½ tablespoon of the butter in a medium skillet over medium heat. Toss in the garlic and shallot or onion and stir everything around for a minute or so. Add the livers, if you've got them, and stir for another minute. Toss in the sausage and cook for 1 to 2 minutes, breaking up any lumps. Remove from the heat and let cool for a couple of minutes, then stir in the bread, beaten egg, and parsley; season with salt and pepper.

Salt and pepper the insides of the hens and spoon in the stuffing, taking care not to pack it in too tightly or too fully. Rub the hens with a couple teaspoons of olive oil and a tablespoon or so of butter, then season them generously with salt and pepper.

Put them in the skillet and slide the pan into the oven — if you'd like, you can roast the hens using the side-side-back method: lay them on their sides in the skillet and give them 15 minutes of roasting time, turn them over onto their other sides and give them another 15 minutes, and then finish by roasting them for 10 minutes on their backs. However you roast them, cook for 40 minutes, or until the juices run clear when you prick their thighs at the thickest part.

When the hens are ready, give them a little feet-in-the-air rest: transfer them to a platter, put a bowl at one end of the platter, turn the birds over, breast side down, and rest their legs on the bowl. Cover them lightly with a foil tent and leave them like this for about 5 minutes, or while you make the sauce, if you'd like.

To make a pan *jus,* cut the tablespoon of cold butter into quarters. Pour off the fat in the skillet (or roaster) and put the pan over medium-high heat. When it's hot, pour in the wine and let it bubble away until it's reduced by about half. Pull the pan from the heat and swirl in the pieces of cold butter. Check for salt and pepper.

Serve the hens with the sauce, if you made it.

duck breasts: the basics

If you're like me, seared duck breast isn't the first thing that jumps to mind when you think of fast food. Consider it another culinary tic that proves we're not French.

For us, duck is often thought of as a fancy restaurant dish; for the French, it's something that can be seared, sauced, and served in under 30 minutes on a weeknight, which explains why there are so many simple duck dishes in every home cook's recipe box.

In France, you'd buy a *magret de canard,* and it would come from a Moulard, a duck that's a cross between a Muscovy and a Pekin (Long Island) duck. The entire Moulard is used: The legs make duck confit (a dish in which the legs are cooked in their own fat and then preserved in that fat). The breast, which is often aged for a few days, is prized for its dark, flavorful meat, sometimes likened to that of a tender steak, as well as for its thick layer of fat, which is rendered in cooking (the cooked breast is actually quite low in calories) and saved because it's so good for frying potatoes.

You can find Moulard breasts here (see Sources), but most of our markets offer Muscovy ducks, a very lean breed, or Pekins, another lean breed. Neither is as succulent as the Moulard, but either will make a terrific dinner. And any of the breasts, once seared (see page 229 for the easy technique) and rested (an important part of cooking duck breasts), will take to a sweet-sour finish. Almost without fail, recipes for *magret de canard* include something acidic, usually vinegar, and something sweet, often honey and just as often fruit, or both honey and fruit. The combinations are classic for good reason — they play perfect point-counterpoint with the duck's rich meatiness.

When you get duck breasts in a restaurant, they're always served sliced — the breasts are cut on the diagonal into slices about ½ inch thick — with the slices overlapping each other just a bit. At home, you might not want to arrange it that way on individual plates, but it's good to slice the duck anyway, since slicing on the diagonal makes it more tender.

A note on size: American duck breasts can weigh from about 5 ounces to almost 1 pound. The smaller breasts are single-serves, while the large ones are generous but right for 2 people. Sometimes I cook an extra breast so I'll have leftovers, and, of course, if there are any leftover slices, I keep them. The meat can be diced and added to lentils, white beans, or potatoes, the way you'd add bacon; incorporated into a salad; or used to make a great sandwich.

twenty-minute honey-glazed duck breasts

Here's when I had my duck-as-an-everyday-food epiphany: hurrying through the rue des Carmes market one Saturday, I grabbed a couple of duck breasts and then cooked them in under 20 minutes, and I thought, "I may never resort to pasta and cheese again."

In this dish, the breasts are seared in a casserole, wrapped in foil for a short rest, and reheated for a minute in a mix of honey, balsamic vinegar, lime juice, and a bit of the duck fat. Served with country bread and a salad, which you can put together while the ducks are resting (and which you can toss with a little of the fat, if you'd like), you've got the kind of meal that would make you happy were it served to you at your favorite bistro. But unless that bistro is next door, it would take you longer to get there than to make this satisfying meal.

MAKES 4 SERVINGS

2 large duck breasts, preferably from a Moulard, or 4 small duck breasts (about 2 pounds total), at room temperature

Salt and freshly ground pepper
2 tablespoons balsamic vinegar
1 tablespoon honey
Juice of 1 lime

Preheat the oven to 250 degrees F.

Using the point of a sharp knife, score the duck skin in a crosshatch pattern, cutting deeply into the layer of fat but taking care not to nick the meat. Season both sides of the breasts with salt and pepper.

Heat a Dutch oven over medium-high heat. (You can cook the breasts in a skillet, but a casserole does a better job of containing the fat spatters. A cast-iron casserole is perfect.) When a few drops of water sprinkled into the pot dance and evaporate quickly, put the breasts in the casserole skin side down — stand away, because the fat will spatter. Cook for 8 minutes, or until the skin is brown and crisp. Turn the pieces over and cook for 3 minutes more for very rare breasts, which will cook a tad more during their rest in the oven. If you'd like the meat slightly more cooked, keep the breasts in the pot for up to 2 minutes longer. (Cook any longer, and they will really be well-done, which is not what's best for a duck breast.)

Lift the breasts out of the pot and onto a sheet of aluminum foil. Seal the breasts loosely in the foil and put them on a baking sheet in the oven for 5 minutes to rest and finish cooking. (Now's a good time to make a salad.)

Pour off almost all the fat from the pot (you should have just a teaspoon or two left in the pot), and put the pot over medium heat. When the fat is warm, stir in the balsamic, honey, and lime juice, as well as the duck juices that have accumulated in the foil packet, and cook, stirring, for 1 minute. Return the breasts to the pot and reheat them, about 30 seconds on each side.

Slice the duck and serve drizzled with the sauce.

SERVING
Transfer the breasts to a cutting board and, working on the diagonal, cut each breast into ½-inch-thick slices. Drizzle with the sauce and serve immediately. I usually serve the duck with nothing more than a salad — frisée or arugula — but if you're not on a 20-minute timetable, it would be great to add either some Broth-Braised Potatoes (page 358) or a half-portion of Endives, Apples, and Grapes (page 338) to each plate.

STORING
If you have leftover duck, it can be refrigerated for up to 2 days, wrapped well; use it in salads or sandwiches. Sliced into thin strips, it adds flavor, texture, and a touch of heartiness to soups.

duck breasts
with fresh peaches

Cut each duck breast on
the diagonal into slices
about ½ inch thick. Fan
out the pieces on serving
plates, spoon over the
sauce, and arrange the
peach halves around
the meat. Sprinkle the
duck and peaches with
thyme leaves, if you're
using them, and serve
immediately.

STORING
The dish is quick and
should be cooked *à la
minute*. If you want to get
a head start on it, though,
you can make the sauce up
to a day ahead, pour it into
a covered container, and
keep it refrigerated until
serving time, when you
can reheat it in the pot. If
you have any leftover duck,
wrap it well and refrigerate
it — it's great in salads and
sandwiches (use it the way
you'd use leftover steak).

THE FRENCH SEEM TO HAVE A HUNDRED WAYS to sauce a duck breast, almost all of them sweet and savory and fruity and almost all of them very good. This recipe, which came to me from my first-ever French friend, Anne Noblet, who begged it from her brother Hervé's friend Françoise Maloberti, is indeed sweet (honey and port), savory (balsamic vinegar, white wine vinegar, and thyme), and fruity (peach) and is indeed very, very good. It's also simple and, like the best duck breast recipes, looks fancier and more time-consuming than it is — always a neat trick. When I got the recipe, I told myself that I would make it only at the height of summer, when peaches are at their most perfect, and that I would retire the recipe at the end of the season, an idea that struck me as righteous, responsible, and culinarily sound. But I liked the sauce so much that I never put the recipe away; instead, I found other fruits and herbs that I could easily slip in as the seasons changed. For a few examples, see Bonne Idée.

2 large duck breasts, preferably
  from a Moulard, or 4 small
  duck breasts (about 2 pounds
  total), at room temperature
  Salt and freshly ground pepper
1 thyme sprig
3 garlic cloves, lightly smashed,
  not peeled
4 ripe but still firm peaches,
  peeled, halved, and pits
  removed

1 teaspoon honey
2 tablespoons ruby port
2 tablespoons balsamic vinegar
2 tablespoons white wine vinegar
1½ tablespoons cold unsalted
  butter, cut into 4 pieces

Fresh thyme leaves, for garnish
  (optional)

Preheat the oven to 250 degrees F.

Using the point of a sharp knife, score the duck skin in a crosshatch pattern, cutting deeply into the layer of fat but taking care not to nick the meat. Season the duck breasts on both sides with salt and pepper.

Heat a Dutch oven over medium-high heat. (You can cook the breasts in a skillet, but a casserole does a better job of containing the fat spatters. A cast-iron casserole is perfect.) When a few drops of water sprinkled into the pot dance and evaporate quickly, put the breasts in the casserole skin side down — stand away, because the fat will spatter. Cook for 8 minutes, or until the skin is brown and crisp. Turn the pieces over and cook for 3 minutes more for very rare breasts, which will cook a tad more during their rest in the oven. If you'd like the meat slightly more cooked, keep the breasts in the pot for up to 2 minutes longer. (Cook any longer, and they will really be well-done, which is not what's best for a duck breast.)

Lift the breasts out of the pot and onto a sheet of aluminum foil. Seal the breasts loosely in the foil and put them in the oven on a baking sheet for 5 minutes to rest and finish cooking.

Pour off all but a scant tablespoon of fat from the pot and put the pot over medium heat. Toss in the thyme sprig and garlic, stir to coat with fat, and then add the peaches. Lower the heat and cook the peaches gently for about 5 minutes, or until they are golden. Transfer the peaches to a plate and keep warm (in the oven, if you like); discard the thyme and garlic.

Pour out whatever fat remains in the pot and put the pot over low heat. Add the honey and cook just until it melts, a minute or so. Pour in the port and vinegars and bring to a boil. Season with salt and pepper, lower the heat, and, using a whisk, energetically stir in the butter piece by piece until you have a smooth sauce.

Open the foil packet and pour whatever juices have accumulated around the duck breasts into the sauce, whisking to incorporate them. Slide the duck breasts into the pot and turn them around in the sauce, about 30 seconds on each side, to reheat them.

Slice the duck and serve with the sauce and peaches, sprinkled with thyme, if you like.

BONNE IDÉE
Without changing the major ingredients in the recipe, you can take this dish through the seasons by varying the fruit. In the early fall, substitute fresh figs for the peaches; later in the fall, use small pears (like Seckel pears — just make sure they cook through) or slices of firm Fuyu persimmons. In the winter, dried fruits, such as prunes, figs, or apricots, are nice as long as they're really soft — you might want to steam them briefly if they're hard at the start. And in late spring, you can use raspberries. If you decide on berries, think about replacing the white wine vinegar with a berry vinegar.

pan-seared duck breasts
with kumquats

MAKES 4 SERVINGS

SERVING
Cut each duck breast on
the diagonal into slices
about ½ inch thick. Fan
the slices out on individual
plates, pour a little sauce
over each breast, sprinkle
over the candied kumquats,
and dust each breast with a
little crushed black pepper.
Serve immediately.

STORING
You can make the
kumquats and the sauce
days ahead. If you have
any leftover duck, wrap it
well and refrigerate it —
it is great in salads and
sandwiches (use it the way
you'd use leftover steak).

DUCK À L'ORANGE, A DUCK ROASTED with oranges, is one of the great classics of traditional dressy French cuisine. In the 1950s and '60s, it was one of the standards against which serious home cooks in America measured themselves, but today it's almost never made at home in France or the United States and rarely found in restaurants.

The dish, which was daunting — you had to deal with a whole duck and a whole lot of fat — may have lost its following, but the combination of duck and orange is too good not to live on, so here's a more manageable version. This rendition delivers both the duck and the orange, but it features just the meaty breast and amps up the citrus flavor by using kumquat, orange's smaller, more exotic, more acidic cousin. It's a great addition to the sauce, which is made from wine, vinegar, broth, and cracked spices.

For added doability, the kumquats can be candied and the sauce made a few days ahead.

FOR THE KUMQUATS
1 cup water
½ cup sugar
12 kumquats, each cut crosswise
   into 4 slices and seeded

FOR THE SAUCE
1½ cups red wine (a fruity wine is
   good here)
3 tablespoons balsamic vinegar
3 small shallots, coarsely
   chopped
15 black peppercorns, bruised
8 coriander seeds, bruised
¾ cup fresh orange juice

2 cups chicken broth
3 tablespoons kumquat syrup
   (from cooking kumquats)
Salt and freshly ground pepper

FOR THE DUCK BREASTS
2 large duck breasts, preferably
   from a Moulard, or 4 small
   duck breasts (about 2 pounds
   total), at room temperature
Salt and freshly ground pepper

Crushed black pepper, for
   garnish

TO MAKE THE KUMQUATS: Bring the water and sugar to a boil in a small saucepan, stirring to make certain the sugar dissolves. Add the kumquats, lower the heat so that the syrup simmers gently, and cook for about 10 minutes, or until the kumquats are tender and translucent. Set aside to cool. (*The kumquats can be made up to 5 days ahead and kept in a sealed container in the refrigerator; bring to room temperature before using.*)

TO MAKE THE SAUCE: Put the wine, balsamic vinegar, shallots, peppercorns, and coriander in a medium saucepan, bring to a boil over high heat, and cook until the liquid is reduced by half. Add the orange juice, return the mixture to a boil, and cook for 5 minutes. Add the chicken broth, bring to a boil, and continue to cook at a boil until reduced to about 2 cups of liquid. Strain the sauce and set aside while you prepare the duck breasts. *(You can cover and refrigerate the sauce for up to 2 days.)*

TO MAKE THE DUCK: Preheat the oven to 250 degrees F.

Using the point of a sharp knife, score the duck skin in a crosshatch pattern, cutting deeply into the layer of fat but taking care not to nick the meat. Season the duck breasts on both sides with salt and pepper.

Heat a Dutch oven over medium-high heat. (You can cook the breasts in a skillet, but a casserole does a better job of containing fat spatters. A cast-iron casserole is perfect.) When a few drops of water sprinkled into the pot dance and evaporate quickly, put the breasts in the casserole skin side down — stand away, because the fat will spatter. Cook for 8 minutes, or until the skin is brown and crisp. Turn the pieces over and cook on the meat side for 3 minutes more for very rare breasts, which will cook a little more while they rest in the oven. If you'd like the meat slightly more cooked, keep the breasts in the pot for up to 2 minutes longer. (Cook any longer, and they will really be well-done, which is not what's best for a duck breast.)

Lift the breasts out of the pot and onto a sheet of aluminum foil. Seal the breasts loosely in the foil and put them in the oven on a baking sheet for 5 minutes to rest and finish cooking.

Pour off all but about a tablespoon of the fat from the pot, and set the pot over medium heat. Add the sauce and bring it to a boil, then stir in the 3 tablespoons kumquat syrup. Open the foil packet and pour whatever juices have accumulated around the duck breasts into the pot. Bring the sauce to a boil again; taste for salt and pepper. Return the breasts to the pot and turn them around in the sauce to reheat them, about 30 seconds on each side.

Slice the duck and serve with the sauce and candied kumquats; garnish the duck with crushed pepper.

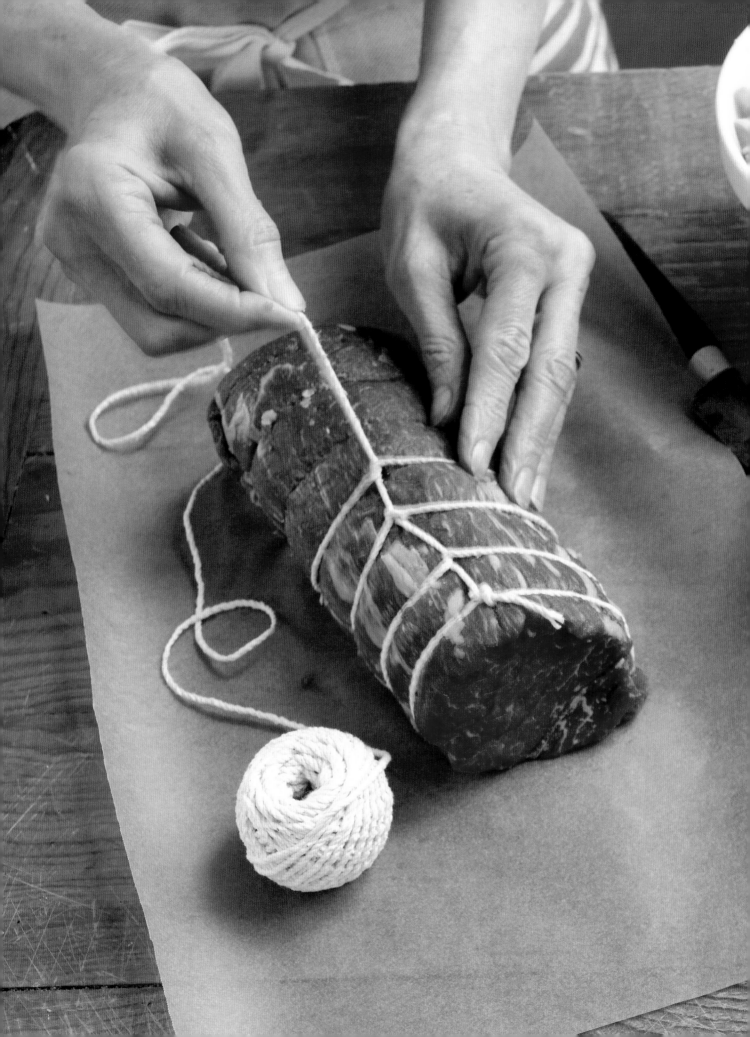

beef, veal, pork, and lamb

BISTROT PAUL BERT PEPPER STEAK (PAGE 238)

beef, veal, pork, and lamb

bistrot paul bert pepper steak

MAKES 4 SERVINGS

SERVING
Transfer the steaks to warm dinner plates, spoon over the sauce, and head for the table. At Bistrot Paul Bert, the steak comes with frites (see box, opposite page), always a good idea, but other good ideas include Salty-Sweet Potato Far (page 359), Celery Root Puree (page 354), simple Broth-Braised Potatoes (page 358), or anything steamed and green.

STORING
No do-aheads here, and usually no leftovers either.

BISTROT PAUL BERT IS ONE OF MY FAVORITE family-owned restaurants in Paris. It's got just the right hum and just the right bustle, and it looks as though it was lifted from everyone's dream of what the perfect French bistro should look like — there are red leather banquettes and a big wooden bar with a zinc countertop and a wine list that would be the envy of much, much grander restaurants. Most important, the food is great. The owner, Bertrand Auboyneau, and his wife, whose family are third-generation oyster growers from Brittany, search out small farmers and producers, know all their suppliers, dote on everything they serve, and don't shy away from offering their opinions on what you should eat and drink, and how. While the menu on the chalkboard changes daily, the tagline doesn't: *Ici les viandes sont servies bleues, saignantes, ou malcuites.* To translate: We serve meat blue [just barely warm in the center], rare, or badly cooked! That doesn't mean you can't get a well-done steak at Paul Bert; it just means it'll come with attitude.

But if you love beef (cooked to any degree of doneness), you'll love the way the Bistrot serves its pepper steak. Bertrand uses a fillet, or tenderloin (although the cooking method and wonderful sauce work with other cuts — I often use it with a not-too-thick rib-eye steak), presses cracked pepper all over it, pan-sears it, and makes a quick sauce of Cognac and cream. When he gave me the recipe, he wrote that the cream should be thick and that "it should come from the nearest farm." And Bertrand's cream really does come from a farm just outside of Paris. The photo is on page 236.

About 1 tablespoon black peppercorns, preferably Sarawak pepper (that's what's used at Paul Bert; see Sources), or a mix of peppercorns	1 tablespoon mild oil (such as grapeseed or canola)
	½ tablespoon unsalted butter
	¼ cup Cognac, or other brandy (plus a splash more if desired)
4 filets mignons, 1 to 1½ inches thick, at room temperature	½ cup heavy cream
	Salt

The peppercorns need to be coarsely cracked, a job that's done quickly and easily with a mortar and pestle. Lacking that, put the peppercorns in a kitchen towel so they don't go flying about, and give them a couple of bashes with the bottom of a heavy skillet or the heel or back of a knife. Sprinkle some peppercorns on both sides of each steak, and use the palm of your hand to press them into the meat.

Put a heavy-bottomed skillet over high heat — I use a cast-iron pan — and add the oil and butter. When the butter has melted, slip in the steaks and cook them for 2 to 3 minutes for rare steaks, or a minute or so longer if you like your beef more well-done. Flip them over and give them another 2 to 3 minutes in the pan, then transfer them to a warm plate and cover them loosely with a foil tent.

Pour off all of the fat in the pan, but leave any bits of steak that have stuck to the bottom; let the pan cool for a minute or so. Now you've got a decision to make: to flame the Cognac or to just let it boil down. If you decide to flame it, pour it into the pan, stand back, and set a match to the Cognac. When the flames have subsided, stir to scrape up whatever bits of meat are in the pan. If you just want to boil the Cognac, put the pan over medium heat, pour in the Cognac, and let cook until it's almost evaporated; scrape up whatever bits of steak have stuck to the pan.

When you've reduced the Cognac, lower the heat and add the cream. Swirl the pan and let the cream bubble gently for 2 to 3 minutes. Now, Bertrand says, "Salt with care, and that's it!" And that can be it, but if you'd like just a slightly stronger flavor of Cognac, when you pull the pan from the heat, swirl in 1 more teaspoon.

Spoon the sauce over the steaks and serve immediately.

les frites

The kindest thing I can say about my relationship to homemade French fries is that it's complicated. When I was thirteen and burned down my parents' kitchen, it was French fries I'd been trying to make. And when I started cooking with French chefs, every time I'd ask for the best recipe for *frites,* they'd make the whole process seem so complex that my eyes would glaze over even before the first potato was peeled. But then Bertrand Auboyneau of Bistrot Paul Bert sent me his recipe for steak and *frites,* and all was revealed.

"To make good frites," he wrote, "there are two secrets: choose the good kind of potatoes and never let them sit in water."

For most of us in America, "the good kind of potatoes" is Idaho (russet). You can fry Yukon Golds or even sweet potatoes, but Idaho potatoes will get you closest to French *frites.*

As for letting them sit in water — don't! Peel the potatoes close to frying time and then pat them dry. Rinse them if you want to, but make certain that they're completely dry for the fry.

Now, about that fry . . . Bertrand didn't dub his two-step frying method a secret, because it's considered standard operating procedure among ace potato fryers.

In the first step, the potatoes are fried in oil at a relatively low temperature, 325 degrees F, so that they cook almost completely (they should be the potato equivalent of al dente pasta) but don't color — in other words, they're blanched in the oil. Blanch the potatoes, drain them very well, and allow them to cool. You can do this up to a few hours before you're ready to give them their final fry.

The second step should be done at serving time: heat the oil to 375 degrees F and fry the (dry) blanched potatoes until they are cooked through, beautifully browned, and crisp.

"After that," wrote Bertrand, "put them in a bowl with paper to dry them, add salt, and serve."

And here's my two cents: 1) Make sure you're using a type of oil that can stand the heat of frying: peanut or canola oil will work well; and 2) Don't crowd the pot — fry in small batches, so that the temperature of the oil remains as constant as possible.

Voilà! It's not much of a recipe, I know, but follow it, and your *frites* will be *splendide.*

BONNE IDÉE

Bistrot Paul Bert's Steak à la Bourguignonne. Steak in a red wine sauce with garlic and shallots is a bistro classic, especially if the meat is a hanger steak, a muscular, full-flavored cut that is best cooked rare. This technique and the sauce are also good with rib-eye or boneless New York strip steak and filet mignon. Season the steaks with salt and pepper (don't coat them with cracked pepper) and cook them as you would the pepper steak. When you've poured off the fat and cooled the pan, toss in 1 tablespoon unsalted butter. Put the pan over medium heat, and when the butter melts, add 1 to 2 minced garlic cloves and 1 to 2 minced shallots (this is a to-taste situation) and cook just until they soften, about 3 minutes. Pour in ⅔ cup dry red wine, turn up the heat, and let the wine boil until it has reduced by half. If any juices accumulated around the steaks while they rested, pour them into the sauce. If you'd like, when you pull the pan from the heat, swirl in 1 tablespoon cold butter, cut into bits. Spoon the sauce over the steak.

café salle pleyel hamburger

MAKES 4 SERVINGS

SERVING
At Café Salle Pleyel, Heinz ketchup was served with the hamburgers, but only on request and, as it turned out, only rarely — with its onion jam, pickles, and great flavor, the burgers didn't need much of anything else.

STORING
You can make the onion marmalade a couple of days ahead and keep it covered and chilled; ditto the sun-dried tomato mixture.

WHEN MY FRIEND HÉLÈNE SAMUEL, who created the stunning café in Paris's newly renovated Salle Pleyel concert hall, decided to put a hamburger on the menu, she gave it a lot of thought. She knew she was playing with an American icon, and she wanted to honor it, but she also wanted to make it understandable — and appealing — to her French diners, almost all of whom, on hearing the word *hamburger,* would think "McDonald's." In the end, what she and her chef for that opening year, Sonia Ezgulian, came up with was a hamburger that any red-blooded American would be happy to sit down to and any French gourmet would be happy to claim for his country. It's got the sesame seed bun and the dill pickles, but it's also got a very French seasoning blend: capers, cornichons, tarragon, and sun-dried tomatoes (who needs ketchup?); a red onion marmalade; and, standing in for the American cheese, some shards of Parmesan — neither French nor American, but just perfect with beef. At home, I often serve the burger with my own quick-pickled cucumbers (page 340).

It didn't take long for the burger to become the café's bestseller and a media darling. Hélène had started a craze so widespread that it ended up as a page-one style story in the *New York Times,* and one of Hélène's comments was chosen as the paper's "Quotation of the Day." Asked why the hamburger was so popular in Paris, she said: "It has the taste of the forbidden, the illicit — the subversive, even." She might just as easily have said, "Because it's so delicious," but that wouldn't have been nearly as quotable.

FOR THE ONION MARMALADE
- 1 medium red onion, finely chopped
- 1 cup water
- 1 teaspoon ground coriander
- 1 tablespoon unsalted butter
- Salt and freshly ground pepper

FOR THE BURGERS
- About ⅓ cup oil-packed sun-dried tomatoes, drained and coarsely chopped or sliced
- ¼ cup drained capers
- 6 cornichons
- ¼ cup fresh tarragon leaves
- ½ cup fresh parsley leaves

- 1½ pounds ground beef, preferably sirloin, or a mix of sirloin and chuck, at room temperature
- Salt and freshly ground pepper
- 1 tablespoon grapeseed oil or peanut oil
- 2 ounces Parmesan, cut into ribbons with a vegetable peeler (to make about ½ cup)

FOR SERVING
- 4 sesame seed hamburger buns, toasted
- 2 dill pickles, cut lengthwise into ribbons with a vegetable peeler
- Ketchup (very optional)

TO MAKE THE ONION MARMALADE: In a small saucepan, stir together the onion and water. Add the coriander and butter, season with salt and pepper, and bring to a boil. Lower the heat to medium-low and simmer, stirring regularly, for about 20 minutes, or until the mixture is soft and jammy; you'll have about

⅓ cup marmalade. Scrape the marmalade into a bowl, cover with plastic, and set aside. *(You can make the marmalade up to 2 days ahead and keep it tightly covered in the refrigerator; bring to room temperature before using.)*

TO MAKE THE BURGERS: Using a mini food processor and the pulse button, chop the tomatoes, capers, cornichons, tarragon, and parsley. (Or chop the ingredients by hand, using a large chef's knife.) Put the beef in a large bowl, scrape the tomato mixture over it, and season with salt and pepper (there may be enough salt from the capers and cornichons). Using your hands, mix everything together lightly, then shape the mixture into 4 patties, about ¾ inch thick.

Choose a large heavy-bottomed skillet (cast-iron is great here), pour in the oil, and put it over medium heat. When the oil is really hot, slip in the burgers. (Alternatively, you can cook them in a grill pan or on a grill — do that, and you won't need the oil.) Cook the hamburgers for 2 minutes on a side if you want them rare (the French preference), 3 minutes if you want them medium-rare. You can cook them longer if that's the way you like your burgers, but there isn't much fat in these burgers, so they may get a little dry if you go beyond medium-rare. Transfer to a platter and immediately top them with the cheese.

Spread the bottoms of the buns with a little onion marmalade and divide the dill pickles among them. Put the burgers on the pickles and close up the sandwiches. Serve with ketchup, if you like.

MY GO-TO BEEF DAUBE (PAGE 244)

my go-to beef daube

MAKES **6** SERVINGS

SERVING
I like to use shallow soup plates or small cast-iron *cocottes* for this stew. Spoon the daube out into the little casseroles and let each guest dig into one.

STORING
Like all stews, this can be kept in the refrigerator for about 3 days or frozen for up to 2 months. If you are preparing the daube ahead, don't reduce the sauce, just cool the daube and chill it. Then, at serving time, lift off the fat (an easy job when the daube's been chilled), reduce the sauce, and season it one last time.

WE ALL NEED A GREAT BEEF STEW in our cooking back pocket, and this one's mine. It's fairly classic in its preparation — the meat is browned, then piled into a sturdy pot and slow-roasted with a lot of red wine, a splash of brandy, and some onions, garlic, carrots, and a little herb bouquet to keep it company. It finishes spoon-tender, sweet and winey through and through, and burnished the color of great-grandma's armoire.

I call this dish a *daube,* which means it's a stew cooked in wine and also means that it's made in a *daubière,* or a deep casserole, in my case, an enamel-coated cast-iron Dutch oven. However, a French friend took issue with the name and claimed that what I make, while *très délicieuse,* is not a daube, but *boeuf aux carottes,* or beef and carrots. She's not wrong, but I'm stubbornly sticking with *daube* because it gives me the leeway to play around.

My first-choice cut for this stew is chuck, which I buy whole and cut into 2- to 3-inch cubes myself. Since the meat is going to cook leisurely and soften, it's good to have larger pieces — larger than the chunks that are usually cut for stews — that will hold their shape better. (If you've got a butcher, you can ask to have the meat cut at the shop.) My favorite go-alongs are mashed potatoes (page 355), celery root puree (page 354), or spaetzle (page 372).

If you're serving a crowd, you can certainly double the recipe, but if the crowd is larger than a dozen, I'd suggest you divide the daube between two pots, or put it in a large roasting pan and stir it a few times while it's in the oven.

BE PREPARED: See Storing for how to make the daube ahead — a good idea.

4 slices thick-cut bacon, cut crosswise into 1-inch-wide pieces	1½ pounds carrots, trimmed, peeled, halved crosswise, and halved or quartered lengthwise, depending on thickness
1 3½-pound beef chuck roast, fat and any sinews removed, cut into 2- to 3-inch cubes	½ pound parsnips, trimmed, peeled, halved crosswise, and quartered lengthwise (optional)
2 tablespoons mild oil (such as grapeseed or canola) Salt and freshly ground pepper	¼ cup Cognac or other brandy
2 yellow onions or 1 Spanish onion, quartered and thinly sliced	1 750-ml bottle fruity red wine (I know this may sound sacrilegious, but a Central Coast Syrah is great here)
6 shallots, thinly sliced	A bouquet garni — 2 thyme sprigs, 2 parsley sprigs, 1 rosemary sprig, and the leaves from 1 celery stalk, tied together in a dampened piece of cheesecloth
1 garlic head, halved horizontally, only loose papery peel removed	

Center a rack in the oven and preheat the oven to 350 degrees F.

Put a Dutch oven over medium heat and toss in the bacon. Cook, stirring, just until the bacon browns, then transfer to a bowl.

Dry the beef between sheets of paper towels. Add 1 tablespoon of the oil to the bacon fat in the pot and warm it over medium-high heat, then brown the beef, in batches, on all sides. Don't crowd the pot — if you try to cook too many pieces at once, you'll steam the meat rather than brown it — and make sure that each piece gets good color. Transfer the browned meat to the bowl with the bacon and season lightly with salt and pepper.

Pour off the oil in the pot (don't remove any browned bits stuck to the bottom), add the remaining tablespoon of oil, and warm it over medium heat. Add the onions and shallots, season lightly with salt and pepper, and cook, stirring, until the onions soften, about 8 minutes. Toss in the garlic, carrots, and parsnips, if you're using them, and give everything a few good turns to cover all the ingredients with a little oil. Pour in the brandy, turn up the heat, and stir well to loosen whatever may be clinging to the bottom of the pot. Let the brandy boil for a minute, then return the beef and bacon to the pot, pour in the wine, and toss in the bouquet garni. Once again, give everything a good stir.

When the wine comes to a boil, cover the pot tightly with a piece of aluminum foil and the lid. Slide the daube into the oven and allow it to braise undisturbed for 1 hour.

Pull the pot out of the oven, remove the lid and foil, and stir everything up once. If it looks as if the liquid is reducing by a great deal (unlikely), add just enough water to cover the ingredients. Re-cover the pot with the foil and lid, slip it back into the oven, and cook for another 1½ hours (total time is 2½ hours). At this point, the meat should be fork-tender — if it's not, give it another 30 minutes or so in the oven.

Taste the sauce. If you'd like it a little more concentrated (usually I think it's just fine as is), pour it into a saucepan, put it over high heat, and boil it down until it's just the way you like it. When the sauce meets your approval, taste it for salt and pepper. (If you're going to reduce the sauce, make certain not to salt it until it's reduced.) Fish out the bouquet garni and garlic and, using a large serving spoon, skim off the surface fat.

Serve the beef and vegetables moistened with the sauce.

beef cheek daube with carrots and elbow macaroni

I'D BEEN LOVING BEEF CHEEKS IN RESTAURANTS for years before I bought a pair and cooked them for myself. Why was I so surprised to discover that they were really big? I must have been seduced by the cuteness of their name into thinking of them as little puffs of meat. It wasn't until I hefted them out of my market sack and laid them on the cutting board that I thought, of course they're big — cows are big! And the flavor of their cheeks is as big as their size. This is hearty, rich, rustic fare of the first order, even if some pretty fancy chefs in both France and America have given them favored-ingredient status.

One of those chefs is Yves Camdeborde, the Michelin-restaurant-trained Parisian chef who is credited with starting the neo-bistro craze. (In neo-bistros, the look is casual, the prices are low, and the food is as high quality and as finely prepared as it is in the luxe restaurants all the neo-bistro chefs originally cooked in.) Camdeborde, whose Le Comptoir bistro has been known to be booked months in advance, keeps these braised beef cheeks on his menu year-round — they're so beloved he can't possibly scratch them even at the height of summer.

Camdeborde's daube has two nice additions: chocolate and macaroni. The chocolate is stirred in at the end, and it's not so much a surprise as a mystery — the flavor's not easily picked up; the macaroni is just right and lighter than the more expected potatoes.

If you can't find beef cheeks — they're not an easy grab, given that each cow has only two and you're competing for them against the chefs in your neighborhood — buy a piece of chuck, remove any large hunks of fat, and cut the meat into four pieces.

2 beef cheeks (about 1 pound each) or 2 pounds boneless beef chuck roast, excess fat removed
3 tablespoons grapeseed oil or peanut oil
Salt and freshly ground pepper
¾ pound carrots, trimmed, peeled, and cut into thin rounds
1 large onion, chopped

3 strips bacon, cut crosswise into thin strips
2 tablespoons all-purpose flour
½ cup water
2 cups hearty red wine, such as Syrah
1 cup beef broth (it can be canned or made from bouillon cubes or beef stock base)
½ pound elbow macaroni
¾ ounce bittersweet chocolate, finely chopped

Center a rack in the oven and preheat the oven to 325 degrees F.

If you've got beef cheeks, cut them in half; if you've got chuck, cut the meat into 4 pieces. Pat the meat dry between sheets of paper towels.

In a large Dutch oven or other oven-going casserole with a cover, heat 2 tablespoons of the oil over high heat. When the oil is just about shimmering, add the beef. You don't want to crowd the pot, so do this in 2 batches if necessary. Brown the meat well on one side, 3 minutes or so, then turn and brown the other side. Lift the meat out of the pot and into a bowl, and season well with salt and pepper.

Pour out the oil and carefully wipe the bottom of the pot. Put the pot over low heat and add the last tablespoon of oil. When it's warm, add the carrots, onion, and bacon and cook, stirring frequently, for about 10 minutes, or until the vegetables are almost soft; season with salt and pepper. Sprinkle the flour over the ingredients, turn the heat up just a tad, and cook, stirring, for about 2 minutes, to lightly toast the flour; you'll have a flour film on the bottom of the pot, and that's fine. Pour in the water and, with a wooden spoon, stir to scrape up any bits on the bottom of the pot. Raise the heat and cook away the water (it will boil away rapidly), then pour in the wine and broth and stir.

Return the meat to the pot, adding any juices that have accumulated in the bowl, and bring to a boil. Boil for a couple of minutes, then seal the pot tightly with aluminum foil, settle the cover over the foil, and slide the pot into the oven. Let the daube braise for about 2 hours, or until fork-tender, undisturbed.

Shortly before the daube is ready, put a big pot of salted water on to boil. Add the macaroni and cook until it is 3 minutes shy of done. Drain.

When the meat is done, pull the pot out of the oven, skim off whatever fat has accumulated at the surface of the daube, and stir in the chocolate. Taste for salt and pepper and bring to a gentle simmer.

Stir the macaroni into the daube and finish cooking it, then serve.

boeuf à la ficelle *(beef on a string)*

MAKES 6 SERVINGS

SERVING
I like to use shallow soup plates for this dish and arrange them in the kitchen. Carve the beef so the slices are ¼ to ½ inch thick and put a slice or two in each plate. Add the vegetables and ladle a little hot broth either around the meat or, for those who like their meat more well done, over it. Bring the plates to the table and let your guests season their servings to taste with fleur de sel, Dijon and grainy mustard, horseradish, and pepper from the mill.

STORING
The bouillon can be made ahead and refrigerated for up to 3 days or frozen for up to 2 months, and the vegetables can be poached a few hours in advance. It's best to cook the beef right before serving, but leftovers can be covered and refrigerated for up to a couple of days and used for sandwiches or salads.

THIS IS THE MAIN COURSE OF CHOICE for my New Year's Eve dinners because it's got everything going for it in the party-food department. It's wonderfully satisfying, elegant, universally appreciated (among carnivores, of course), expandable — you can make it for twenty as easily as you can for two — and ninety percent do-aheadable, so you need to be away from the action for only a few minutes just before serving.

The dish is a pared-down, luxury edition of pot-au-feu, the traditional one-pot meal that usually includes several cuts of meat cooked in bouillon. Here you've got just one piece of meat, a fillet of beef, tied with a length of kitchen twine that's got a tail long enough to grab, so that you can pull the beef from the broth and rightly call the dish "beef on a string." This version also has a handful of root vegetables that poach in the bouillon, which is made from bones, vegetables, and, yes, a couple of bouillon cubes. (See the story about making this in Paris on page 251.) The bouillon is prepared ahead, days ahead if you can manage it, and the vegetables can also be made ahead. At serving time, all you've got to do is poach the meat lightly and gently. And there's never a need to worry about whether guests want their meat rare or well-done: you poach the beef until rare, let it rest, and then, at serving time, pour hot bouillon around the beef for the rare-lovers, or over it, to cook it a bit more, for those who like their meat better done.

Traditionally the bouillon is served as a first course and the meat and vegetables as the main, but I like to serve slices of the beef in shallow soup plates surrounded by the vegetables and finished with a small ladleful of broth. Using just a bit of the bouillon moistens the dish perfectly and gives it a lovely look, while leaving some to be turned into soup the next day. Actually, speaking about holding back, you might hope for leftover beef as well — it's wonderful in Next-Day Beef Salad (page 260).

If you want to multiply the number of servings, keep the same amount of bouillon but double the amount of beef to serve 12; to serve even more (I've made this for a dinner party of 26), you should double the bouillon as well, or poach the beef in batches.

If your beef isn't already tied crosswise at intervals, do this at home using kitchen twine. The crosswise ties will hold it in shape while it poaches. To make the traditional string that gives this dish its name, tie the beef lengthwise — you can tuck this lengthwise string under the knots made by the crosswise strings — and leave a long piece of the twine free. You'll use this string to pull the beef out of the broth.

5 parsley sprigs

2 thyme sprigs

2 bay leaves

2 celery stalks with leaves

2 tablespoons mild oil (such as grapeseed or canola)

3 big veal or marrow bones

1 oxtail

2 big onions, unpeeled, halved

¼ teaspoon sugar

About 5 quarts water

3 leeks, dark green parts only (reserve the white and light green parts), washed

2 carrots, trimmed and cut in half crosswise

1 garlic head, only the loose papery peel removed, halved horizontally

1 2-inch chunk fresh ginger, peeled and halved

1 star anise (optional)

1 teaspoon black peppercorns

2 beef bouillon cubes

1 tablespoon tomato paste

1 tablespoon coarse salt

FOR THE VEGETABLES AND BEEF

6 small potatoes, scrubbed and halved

6 small turnips, trimmed, peeled, and halved

6 carrots, trimmed, peeled, and cut crosswise into thirds

1 pound celery root, trimmed, peeled, and cut into 2-inch cubes

Reserved white and light green parts of the 3 leeks, split lengthwise, washed, and cut into 2-inch lengths

6 shallots, peeled and halved

1 1½-pound beef tenderloin roast, all fat removed, tied with twine (leave a long tail of string), at room temperature

FOR SERVING

Fleur de sel or other sea salt

Dijon and grainy mustard, preferably French

Horseradish, preferably grated fresh

A peppermill filled with black peppercorns

TO MAKE THE BOUILLON: Gather together the parsley, thyme, and bay leaves, tuck them between the celery stalks, and tie up the bundle with kitchen string.

Put a large soup pot over medium-high heat and add the oil. Drop in the bones, oxtail, and onions (if you can get everything in without crowding the pot, go for it; if not, do this in batches), sprinkle over the sugar, and brown the bones and onions, stirring as needed. When all the ingredients are as deeply browned as you can get them — even blackened — transfer to a bowl, and pour out and discard the fat.

Put the pot back over medium heat and, standing away, pour a cup or two of water into the pot. Using a wooden or metal spoon, scrape up all the goop that formed on the bottom of the pot, a satisfying job, since you get all the color and flavor from the sticky bits and the scraping does a good job of cleaning the pot too. Pour in 4½ quarts water and toss in all the remaining ingredients, including the celery bundle, bones, oxtail, and onions. Bring to a boil, skimming off the scum that bubbles to the top, then lower the heat to a simmer, and cook the bouillon, uncovered, skimming often, for 1 hour.

Strain the bouillon into a bowl and discard the solids — they've done their job. *(The bouillon can be cooled and refrigerated for up to 3 days or frozen for up to 2 months. Once the bouillon is cooled, skim off any fat — it will have floated to the top.)*

TO COOK THE VEGETABLES AND BEEF: Return the bouillon to the pot and bring it to a boil. Lower the heat to a simmer and add the potatoes, turnips, carrots, and celery root. After 10 minutes, add the leeks and shallots and cook for 10 minutes more. Check that the vegetables are cooked and, when they are tender, using a slotted spoon, lift them out of the bouillon and into a large bowl. Cover and set aside while you poach the beef. (*The vegetables can be cooked a few hours ahead, moistened with a little bouillon, covered, and refrigerated until you're ready for them.*)

Drop the beef into the simmering bouillon, keeping the string out of the broth (you can tie it to the pot's handle) and poach for 15 minutes — it will be very rare in the center. Pull the beef from the pot using the string; transfer it to a plate, cover with foil, and allow to rest for 5 to 10 minutes. (If you want the beef more well done, you can poach it longer or, better yet, pour some of the hot broth over it at serving time.)

Meanwhile, reheat the vegetables in the bouillon. Cut the beef into slices about ¼ to ½ inch thick. For each portion, put a slice or two of beef in the center of a shallow soup plate, surround it with some poached vegetables, and moisten with bouillon. Have fleur de sel, Dijon and grainy mustard, horseradish, and a peppermill on the table so your guests can season their own dishes.

beef on a string, say what?

I had waited patiently in line at the butcher's counter at La Grande Épicerie, Paris's premier supermarket, and now it was my turn. I leaned across the counter and told the butcher that I wanted enough *boeuf à la ficelle,* or beef on a string, for eight guests. He gave me a questioning "Eh?" and said, "You need *jarret de veau,*" which is veal knuckle and not at all what I needed.

"No," I said, politely but firmly. "That's fine for pot-au-feu, but I'm making *boeuf à la ficelle* and need something more tender." "I can't understand you," he huffed and started to move on to someone else.

While my French isn't flawless, it had been years since someone couldn't understand me, especially when I was speaking kitchen French. Knowing that I was about to be dismissed and seeing that I was upset, the woman next to me told the butcher that, indeed, *jarret de veau* was completely wrong and that Madame (that would be *moi*) was correct in asking for something

more tender. Even the other butcher at the counter came over and whispered the "tender" word to his associate. But my guy repeated that he couldn't understand me, turned his shoulder to me, and addressed himself to the next customer, the nice woman to my left. She shrugged at me, said she was sorry, and proceeded to order a roast for dinner. Bruised, I stomped off furious. Couldn't understand me? Harummpf.

I finished gathering the rest of the fixings for dinner and looked over at the now quiet butcher counter. Only the whispering butcher was there, so I approached and started to repeat my request. "I know, I know," he said, "you're making *boeuf à la ficelle* for eight tonight." He then hefted a gorgeous hunk of fillet of beef, cut off a length, and tied it, as it must be tied for this dish, with a long loop of string, the loop I would use to lower the beef into the simmering broth and to lift it out minutes later.

I thanked him — lots — and then, wanting to say something about his fellow butcher, I said, in a roundabout and typically French way, "I really appreciate your having been so patient with me." Bingo — he knew just what I meant. "Madame," he replied, "you must forgive my colleague. He couldn't help you because he had no idea what you were making for dinner. In fact, I'm surprised that you, an American, know *boeuf à la ficelle.* Here in France, we think of it as *une recette perdue.*"

Une recette perdue, a lost recipe. I was fascinated by the idea.

Clearly, the recipe wasn't lost to the woman who'd waited in the line with me. In fact, she confided a bit of culinary advice, suggesting that I add a spoonful of tomato paste to the bouillon, just as her mother did. Oh, and a couple of bouillon cubes too. Later that night, after following her advice, I was sorry I couldn't call to thank her — it was just the right touch.

boeuf à la mode *(aka great pot roast)*

MAKES 6 SERVINGS

SERVING
The roast is good with steamed carrots, simply cooked rice, buttered noodles, steamed potatoes, or mashed potatoes (everyone's favorite).

STORING
Like most braises, this one is good (actually even better) a day or two later. Keep the *boeuf à la mode* well covered in the refrigerator and, before serving, spoon off the fat and heat the sauce through (with the vegetables, if you haven't discarded them) either on the stovetop or in the oven. You can also pack the dish airtight and freeze it for up to 2 months.

THE FRENCH HAVE TONS OF WAYS of taking inexpensive, often tough cuts of meat and turning them into dishes so tasty the mere mention of them can make you smile — and *boeuf à la mode* is one of those dishes. It's essentially a pot roast, and although it's French through and through, it seems to remind everyone from everywhere of granny's slow-cooked roast. (Even my grandmother might have thought of this dish as kinfolk to her brisket.)

What makes this an "à la mode" and not a stew is the fact that the beef is cooked in a hunk, not in chunks. The roast is marinated overnight and, in the process, tenderized, then browned well and simmered gently in the oven in a combination of herbs and vegetables, wine and Cognac, and a surprise ingredient: anchovies. As assertive as they are straight out of the can, they are mild, even unrecognizable, in this dish, adding subtle depth.

After hours in the oven, the beef is tender and the sauce richly flavored and just as richly colored. You can skim off the surface fat, slice the roast, and head for the table, or you can hold the dish for a day or two.

BE PREPARED: The roast must be marinated overnight. And, like so many slow-cooked dishes, this one benefits from an overnight rest, making it as great for parties as it is for cozy family meals.

1 chuck, round, or rump roast, about 4 pounds, trimmed but not completely devoid of fat	1 750-ml bottle hearty, fruity red wine
Salt and freshly ground pepper	1 tablespoon olive oil
1 onion, halved and thinly sliced	4 cups beef broth (it can be canned or made from bouillon cubes or beef stock base)
1 carrot, trimmed, peeled, and cut into chunks	3 tablespoons grapeseed oil, canola oil, or peanut oil
1 celery stalk, trimmed, peeled and cut into chunks (save the leaves)	3 tablespoons Cognac or other brandy
A bouquet garni — 2 thyme sprigs, 2 parsley sprigs, 1 rosemary sprig, 1 bay leaf, and the leaves from the celery stalk, tied together in a piece of dampened cheesecloth	4 anchovies, drained, rinsed, and patted dry
	2 tablespoons tomato paste

Give the roast a salt-and-pepper massage and put it in a casserole, bowl, or sturdy zipper-lock plastic bag that can hold it, the vegetables, and the wine. Toss in the onion, carrot, celery, and bouquet garni, then pour in the wine and olive oil. Mix everything together as best you can, cover the container or seal the bag, and put it in the refrigerator to marinate overnight. (If you can, turn the roast from time to time so that the wine permeates it evenly.)

The next day, remove the beef from the marinade and, if you've got the time, let it come to room temperature.

Meanwhile, strain the marinade, reserving the vegetables and bouquet garni, and pour the liquid into a medium saucepan. Bring to a boil over high heat and cook until reduced by half, about 10 minutes. Add the beef broth and bring back to a boil, then remove the pan from the heat.

Center a rack in the oven and preheat the oven to 350 degrees F. Have a heavy 4- to 5-quart Dutch oven or casserole with a cover at the ready.

Using paper towels, pat the beef dry as best you can. Put a heavy skillet over medium-high heat and pour in 2 tablespoons of the grapeseed, canola, or peanut oil. When it's hot, put the roast in the pan and sear it on all sides, making sure you get good color and a little crust on it. Transfer the roast to the Dutch oven and season it with salt and pepper; discard the oil.

Return the skillet to medium heat, pour in the last tablespoon of oil, and toss in the drained vegetables. Cook, stirring, until the vegetables are softened, about 10 minutes. (Because the vegetables won't be perfectly dry, you might not be able to brown them, but pan-cooking will give them a roasted flavor.) Season with salt and pepper, pour in the Cognac, and stir and scrape to loosen any bits that may have stuck to the bottom of the pan. Transfer everything to the Dutch oven.

Once again, put the skillet over medium heat. Pour in about ½ cup of the wine-broth mixture and stir in the anchovies and tomato paste. Cook, stirring, until the anchovies "melt," a matter of minutes. Pour in the rest of the wine-broth mixture and stir to blend, then toss in the reserved bouquet garni, season with salt and pepper, and transfer to the Dutch oven.

Put the Dutch oven over medium-high heat, and when the liquid comes to a boil, cover the pot tightly with a piece of aluminum foil and the lid. Slide the beef into the oven and allow it to braise undisturbed for 1 hour.

Pull the pot out of the oven, remove the lid and foil, and turn the meat over. (This step really isn't necessary, so if you're not around to do it, don't worry about it.) Re-cover the pot with the foil and lid, slip it back into the oven, and cook for another 1½ to 2 hours (total time is 2½ to 3 hours), or until the meat is fork-tender.

Taste the sauce, and if you'd like it a little more concentrated (usually I think it's fine as is), pour it into a saucepan, put it over high heat, and boil the sauce down until it's just the way you like it. (If you're going to reduce the sauce, don't salt it until it's reduced.) Using a large serving spoon, skim off the surface fat and taste for salt and pepper.

Strain the sauce (if you haven't already done this to boil it down) and discard the cooked vegetables (something my husband never lets me do, because he loves the mushy carrots).

You can serve the roast now or cool it (if you cool it, leave the fat and skim it off when it's cold — it's much easier to do it then) and serve it later (see Storing).

Slice the beef and, if necessary, rewarm it in the sauce.

short ribs in red wine and port

MAKES **6** SERVINGS

SERVING
Braised short ribs are a natural with mashed potatoes (always my first choice), noodles, rice, or celery root puree (page 354).

STORING
You can make the short ribs 2 to 3 days ahead and keep them covered in the refrigerator (don't strain the sauce or broil the cooked ribs until just before serving). Leftovers can be covered and refrigerated for up to 2 days.

UNTIL A FEW YEARS AGO, when American super-chefs decided that short ribs were cool and turned them into a trendy cut of meat, the richly marbled rectangles of beef-on-the-bone were cheaper than a box of Cheerios. That their price increased a bit is the downside of their fame; the upside is that they're now available just about everywhere, including supermarkets.

Short ribs are a homey cut of beef and, like other homey cuts, made to braise. In fact, I don't think I've ever seen them cooked any other way. Certainly it's how my friends in Paris make them. I follow their lead and braise the short ribs for a long time, at a low temperature and in leisure — I don't shake, stir, or disturb them in any other way while they simmer gently in their big casserole. But I take liberties with the seasonings, adding ginger and star anise to the brew, and instead of the usual shower of chopped parsley, I finish the dish with a play on gremolata: chopped garlic, cilantro, and clementine, tangerine, or orange zest. I like the freshness these ingredients add to the long-cooked meat. The photo is on page 256.

BE PREPARED: If you can, make the short ribs a day ahead and refrigerate them.

FOR THE SHORT RIBS

- 2 parsley sprigs
- 2 thyme sprigs
- 2 bay leaves
- 1 rosemary sprig
- 1 star anise
- 2 celery stalks, trimmed and thinly sliced (reserve leaves from 1 stalk)
- 12 short ribs, each with 1 bone (about 9 pounds)
  Salt and freshly ground pepper
- 2 tablespoons mild oil (such as grapeseed or canola)
- 2 big onions, chopped
- 2 carrots, trimmed, peeled, and sliced
- 1 parsley root or parsnip, trimmed, peeled, and sliced (optional)
- 1 1½-inch piece fresh ginger, peeled and coarsely chopped
- 5 big garlic cloves, split, germ removed, and coarsely chopped
- 2 tablespoons tomato paste
- 1 750-ml bottle fruity red wine (I like a California Syrah)
- 1½ cups ruby port
- 4–6 cups beef broth (it can be made with bouillon cubes), as needed

FOR THE GREMOLATA
Finely chopped zest of 2 tangerines, 2 clementines, or 1 orange
- 2 garlic cloves, split, germ removed, and finely chopped
- 3 tablespoons finely chopped fresh cilantro (or, if you prefer, parsley or mint)

TO MAKE THE SHORT RIBS: Position a rack in the top third of the oven and preheat the broiler. (If you've got a broiler that's below the oven, arrange the rack so that it's as far from the broiler as your setup allows; 6 inches would be good.) Line a baking sheet with foil. Dampen a piece of cheesecloth and use it and some kitchen twine to bundle up the parsley, thyme, bay, rosemary, star anise, and celery leaves; set the bouquet garni aside.

Pat the short ribs dry with paper towels and arrange them bone side up on the foil-lined baking sheet. Broil for about 5 minutes. Carefully, using tongs, flip the ribs over and return them to the broiler for another 10 minutes, or until they are browned and sizzling. If any of the pieces look uncooked on any side, turn them around and broil until browned. Transfer the ribs to a large bowl and season with salt and pepper. Center a rack in the oven and turn the oven down to 350 degrees F.

Pour the oil into a casserole large enough to hold all the ingredients (I use an enameled cast-iron Dutch oven) and place over medium heat. Toss the vegetables, ginger, and garlic into the pot, season lightly with salt and pepper, and cook, stirring, until softened and just a little browned, about 10 minutes. Add the tomato paste, lower the heat, and cook, stirring constantly, for another 2 minutes. Pour in the wine and port, add the bouquet garni, increase the heat to high, bring to a boil, and boil until the liquid is reduced by about one third.

Return the meat to the casserole — I like to put it in bone side up — and pour in 4 cups beef broth. The meat should be almost covered; if it's not, pour in some more broth. Cover tightly with foil and then with the lid and slide it into the oven. Cook, undisturbed, for 2 hours.

Remove the lid and rearrange the foil so that it covers the casserole loosely — you want some steam to escape. Return to the oven and cook for 1 hour more, then pull the casserole from the oven.

If you've got the time, cool and then chill the ribs overnight; the next day, spoon off the congealed fat and transfer the ribs bone side down to a shallow roasting pan that will hold them snugly. (If the bones fall off the meat, as they usually do, discard them.) Strain the sauce, pressing on the solids to get all the liquid from them, and discard the solids.

Or, if you're continuing with the recipe sans refrigerating, transfer the ribs, bone side down, to a shallow roasting pan. Pour the sauce through a strainer into a large measuring cup or bowl; press on the solids to get all the liquid from them, then discard them. Skim off as much fat from the sauce as you can.

Preheat the broiler, positioning a rack as you did before. Pour some of the sauce over the ribs to moisten and coat them, then broil the ribs for 5 to 8 minutes, turning once or twice, until they are glazed.

Meanwhile, return the remaining sauce to the casserole or pour into a saucepan and bring to a boil. If you think the sauce needs to intensify a bit, boil it for a few minutes to reduce it. It is very thin, and unless you reduce it to a few spoonfuls, boiling it won't thicken it much. Taste and season with salt and pepper if needed.

TO MAKE THE GREMOLATA: Mix together the zest, garlic, and cilantro.

Transfer the ribs to a serving platter and spoon over some sauce; pass the rest of the sauce at the table. Top the ribs with the gremolata, or let your guests serve themselves.

SHORT RIBS IN RED WINE AND PORT (PAGE 254)

HACHIS PARMENTIER (PAGE 258)

hachis parmentier

MAKES 4
GENEROUS
SERVINGS

SERVING
Bring the hachis
Parmentier to the table and
spoon out portions there.
The dish needs nothing
more than a green salad
to make it a full and very
satisfying meal.

STORING
It's easy to make this
dish in stages: the beef
and bouillon can be
made up to a day ahead
and kept covered in the
refrigerator, and the filling
can be prepared a few
hours ahead and kept
covered in the fridge. You
can even assemble the
entire pie ahead and keep
it chilled for a few hours
before baking it (directly
from the refrigerator if
your casserole can stand
the temperature change)
— of course, you'll have
to bake it a little longer.
If you've got leftovers,
you can reheat them in a
350-degree-F oven.

MANY, MANY YEARS AGO, I was lucky enough to have Daniel Boulud, a chef from Lyon who's made his life in New York City, cook a meal especially for me and my husband. It was luxurious, and at the end of it, after thanking Daniel endlessly, I asked him what *he* was going to have for dinner. "Hachis Parmentier," he said with the kind of anticipatory delight usually seen only in children who've been told they can have ice cream. We had just had lobster and truffles, but Daniel was about to have the French version of shepherd's pie, and you could tell that he was going to love it.

Hachis Parmentier is a well-seasoned meat-and-mashed-potato pie that is customarily made with leftovers from a boiled beef dinner, like pot-au-feu. If you have leftover beef and broth from anything you've made, go ahead and use it. Or, if you'd like to shortcut the process, make Quick Hachis Parmentier; see Bonne Idée. But if you start from scratch and make your own bouillon, and if you add tasty sausage (not completely traditional), you'll have the kind of hachis Parmentier that would delight even Daniel Boulud.

You can use chuck, as you would for a stew, but one day my stateside butcher suggested I use cube steak, a cut I'd never cooked with. It's an inexpensive, thin, tenderized cut (its surface is scored, almost as though it's been run through a grinder) that cooks quickly and works perfectly here. If you use it, just cut it into 2-inch pieces before boiling it; if you use another type of beef, you should cut it into smaller pieces and you might want to cook it for another 30 minutes.

FOR THE BEEF AND BOUILLON

- 1 pound cube steak or boneless beef chuck (see above), cut into small pieces
- 1 small onion, sliced
- 1 small carrot, trimmed, peeled, and cut into 1-inch-long pieces
- 1 small celery stalk, trimmed and cut into 1-inch-long pieces
- 2 garlic cloves, smashed and peeled
- 2 parsley sprigs
- 1 bay leaf
- 1 teaspoon salt
- ¼ teaspoon black peppercorns
- 6 cups water
- ½ beef bouillon cube (optional)

FOR THE FILLING

- 1½ tablespoons olive oil
- ½ pound sausage, sweet or spicy, removed from casings if necessary
- 1 teaspoon tomato paste
  Salt and freshly ground pepper

FOR THE TOPPING

- 2 pounds Idaho (russet) potatoes, peeled and quartered
- ½ cup whole milk
- ¼ cup heavy cream
- 3 tablespoons unsalted butter, at room temperature, plus 1 tablespoon butter, cut into bits
  Salt and freshly ground pepper
- ½ cup grated Gruyère, Comté, or Emmenthal
- 2 tablespoons freshly grated Parmesan (optional)

TO MAKE THE BEEF: Put all the ingredients except the bouillon cube in a Dutch oven or soup pot and bring to a boil, skimming off the foam and solids that bubble to the surface. Lower the heat and simmer gently for 1½ hours. The broth will have a mild flavor, and that's fine for this dish, but if you want to pump it up, you can stir in the half bouillon cube — taste the broth at the midway point and decide.

Drain the meat, reserving the broth. Transfer the meat to a cutting board and discard the vegetables, or if they've still got some flavor to spare, hold on to them for the filling. Traditionally hachis Parmentier is vegetableless, but that shouldn't stop you from salvaging and using the vegetables. Strain the broth. *(The beef and bouillon can be made up to 1 day ahead, covered, and refrigerated.)*

Using a chef's knife, chop the beef into tiny pieces. You could do this in a food processor, but the texture of your hachis Parmentier will be more interesting if you chop it by hand, an easy and quick job.

TO MAKE THE FILLING: Butter a 2-quart oven-going casserole — a Pyrex deep-dish pie plate is just the right size for this.

Put a large skillet over medium heat and pour in the olive oil. When it's hot, add the sausage and cook, breaking up the clumps of meat, until the sausage is just pink. Add the chopped beef and tomato paste and stir to mix everything well. Stir in 1 cup of the bouillon and bring to a boil. You want to have just enough bouillon in the pan to moisten the filling and to bubble up gently wherever there's a little room; if you think you need more (a smidgen more is better than too little), add it now. Season with salt and pepper, especially pepper. If you've kept any of the vegetables from the bouillon, cut them into small cubes and stir them into the filling before you put the filling in the casserole. Scrape the filling into the casserole and cover it lightly; set aside while you prepare the potatoes. *(You can make the dish to this point up to a few hours ahead; cover the casserole with foil and refrigerate.)*

TO MAKE THE TOPPING: Have ready a potato ricer or food mill (first choices), a masher, or a fork.

Put the potatoes in a large pot of generously salted cold water and bring to a boil. Cook until the potatoes are tender enough to be pierced easily with the tip of a knife, about 20 minutes; drain them well.

Meanwhile, center a rack in the oven and preheat the oven to 400 degrees F. Line a baking sheet with foil or a silicone baking mat (you'll use it as a drip catcher).

Warm the milk and cream.

Run the potatoes through the ricer or food mill into a bowl, or mash them well. Using a wooden spoon or a sturdy spatula, stir in the milk and cream, then blend in the 3 tablespoons butter. Season to taste with salt and pepper.

Spoon the potatoes over the filling, spreading them evenly and making sure they reach to the edges of the casserole. Sprinkle the grated Gruyère, Comté, or Emmenthal over the top of the pie, dust with the Parmesan (if using), and scatter over the bits of butter. Place the dish on the lined baking sheet.

Bake for 30 minutes, or until the filling is bubbling steadily and the potatoes have developed a golden brown crust (the best part). Serve.

BONNE IDÉE
Quick Hachis Parmentier. You can make a very good hachis Parmentier using ground beef and store-bought beef broth. Use 1 pound ground beef instead of the steak, and when you add it to the sausage in the skillet, think about adding some finely chopped fresh parsley and maybe a little minced fresh thyme. You can also sauté 1 or 2 minced garlic cloves, split and germ removed, in the olive oil before the sausage goes into the skillet. (The herbs and garlic help mimic the aromatics in the bouillon.) Moisten the filling with the broth, and you're good to go.

next-day beef salad

MAKES 4 SERVINGS

SERVING
The salad needs only a loaf
of bread, but serving a little
soft cheese on the side — a
very un-French thing to do
— is a nice touch.

STORING
Eat up and enjoy.

I'VE BEEN COOKING FOR DECADES, but every time I make something delicious from leftovers, I'm as proud as a kitchen newcomer. I was particularly proud of this beef salad the first time I made it. In fact, I was so happy with it that now I actually go out and buy the "leftovers" so that I can make it for lunch or an informal supper.

The original leftover beef came from a Saturday night's boeuf à la ficelle for a crowd. Channeling my inner French homemaker — my French friends would never, ever let a scrap of anything good languish, spoil, or be tossed — and scavenging the refrigerator's shelves and the basket of vegetables on the counter, I discovered that I had a plethora of made-for-salad things at my fingertips. The challenge was not to add so many of them that the dish would lose its integrity, a danger when you're doing a refrigerator sweep.

In the end, my salad included green olives (part of Saturday's predinner nibbles), cornichons (a fridge staple for me), capers, tomatoes, bell pepper, hot pepper, onion, apple, and a dressing of (store-bought) mayonnaise and mustard. Served over arugula, it was a great one-plate meal.

I'm giving you a "real" recipe for this salad, but you should treat it as a base to riff on, which is what I do. Depending on what you've got at hand, you can add cubes of Gruyère, mozzarella, or Gouda; top it with shards of Parmesan; toss in minced fresh tarragon, basil, chives, and/or chopped garlic; or stir in chopped cooked potatoes or even hard-boiled eggs. And feel free to up the quantity of olives, skip the capers, or play around in any other way to make the salad your own and to help you use up the tidbits tucked away in your fridge.

6 tablespoons mayonnaise, homemade (page 490) or store-bought	10–15 cornichons, drained and thinly sliced
1½ tablespoons grainy mustard, preferably French	10 grape tomatoes, sliced
1½ teaspoons Dijon mustard (optional)	1 red bell pepper, cored, seeded, and finely diced
About 1 pound cooked beef, either roast beef or leftovers from Boeuf à la Ficelle (page 248), cut into small cubes (½ to ¾ inch)	1–2 red chile peppers, seeded and finely sliced (you can use pickled peppers, if you'd like)
	1 tart apple, peeled or not, cored and diced
1–2 spring onions, trimmed, halved lengthwise, and finely chopped, or 2–4 scallions, white and light green parts only, thinly sliced	1–1½ tablespoons drained capers Salt and freshly ground black pepper
20 green olives (I like Picholine), pitted and cut into slivers	Arugula, spinach, or mixed salad greens, for serving Olive oil, for the greens (optional)

In a small bowl, stir the mayonnaise and grainy mustard together. Taste the dressing and, if you think you want a little more heat, blend in the Dijon mustard.

Toss all the remaining ingredients except the salt and pepper into a large bowl and stir to mix. Spoon the dressing over the salad and, using a rubber spatula, stir together well. Season generously with salt and pepper.

Line a serving bowl or plate with the arugula or other greens (there's really no need to dress them, although you can toss them with a little olive oil, if you'd like to) and mound the beef salad over it.

spring onions

Looking like fat scallions and sometimes marketed as Texas or salad onions, spring onions are white with long, thick (scallion-like) green stalks. They might have a skin that needs to be peeled away, and, depending on their age and variety, they'll be mild or strong, although never as strong as bulb onions, which is one reason I like to use them. Another is their texture — firmer than scallions, softer than onions, and therefore very good raw.

While it is only the onion bulb that is called for in most recipes, you can chop the light green parts of the stalks into salads or use the darker parts to add more flavor to soups — just toss the stalks into the pot the way you would leek greens.

If you can't get spring onions, substitute white onions or, for salads, scallions or sweet onions like Vidalia, Maui, or Texas Sweets.

green-as-spring veal stew

MAKES 6 SERVINGS

SERVING
Martine often serves the veal with simple steamed potatoes — an ideal accompaniment — but it's good with rice or noodles too. Anything that benefits from a little sauce will be welcome with this dish.

STORING
While you can cook the veal in the broth as much as a day ahead, once you've made the sauce, you should get the dish to the table.

I OWE THE INSPIRATION FOR THIS STEW to my close friend Martine Collet, who was the first to make a version of it for me. It's intriguing for its bold use of leafy vegetables and herbs: a combination of arugula, spinach, parsley, dill, and tarragon.

The ingredients for this stew are available year-round, but the dish is truly meant for spring, the best season for veal and the time when the stew's vibrant color and deep vegetal flavor will match the landscape. That said, it would be awfully nice to bring this to the table in the depths of winter, when we all need to be reminded that spring will come — eventually.

A word on the crème fraîche: It's good to have the thickness and no-worries heatability of crème fraîche in this dish, but you can replace it with easier-to-find heavy cream (in which case, you might want to be generous with the lemon juice, to give the dish the tang it needs) or even sour cream. If you're using sour cream, you have to be careful not to let it boil — too much heat, and sour cream (unlike crème fraîche) will separate.

3	pounds veal for stew, cut into 2-inch cubes	1	bay leaf
2	cups chicken broth		Salt and freshly ground white pepper
2	cups water	2½	cups packed arugula leaves
3	carrots, trimmed, peeled, and quartered	2	cups packed spinach leaves
2	celery stalks, trimmed, peeled, and quartered	1	cup small fresh dill fronds
		½	cup fresh parsley leaves
1	onion, quartered	¼	cup fresh tarragon leaves
3	garlic cloves, smashed and peeled		Scant ¾ cup crème fraîche, homemade (page 491) or store-bought (see above)
2	thyme sprigs	1–2	tablespoons fresh lemon juice

Bring a large pot of water to a boil. Drop in the cubes of veal and boil for just 1 minute to rid the meat of impurities that might later cloud your sauce. Drain and rinse the meat.

In a Dutch oven or other large casserole with a tight-fitting lid, stir together the broth, water, carrots, celery, onion, garlic, thyme, and bay leaf. Season the mix with salt and white pepper and bring to a boil. Stir in the veal and bring the broth back to a boil, then cover the pot (if your lid is a little shaky, seal the pot with foil and then top with the lid) and lower the heat to a gentle simmer. Cook the veal for 1½ hours. *(You can make the dish up to this point and, once cooled, refrigerate it for a few hours, or for as long as overnight; reheat gently until the meat is heated through before continuing.)*

Transfer the meat to a bowl, cover, and keep it warm while you work on the sauce.

Remove the vegetables and herbs from the broth (you can fish them out with a slotted spoon or strain the broth and return it to the pot) and discard them. Bring the broth to a boil and boil until reduced to about 1½ cups.

Toss in all the greens and fresh herbs and cook for 1 minute. Puree the mixture using a handheld blender, a regular blender, or a food processor; if necessary, return the sauce to the pot. Whisk in the crème fraîche and 1 tablespoon lemon juice. Taste the sauce, add more lemon juice, if you'd like, and season as needed with salt and white pepper.

Return the meat to the pot, give the pot a stir, and gently heat everything through before serving.

veal marengo

MAKES 4 SERVINGS

SERVING
While I often arrange individual dinner plates in the kitchen, I like to serve this dish family-style, bringing it to the table on a large platter with the veal on one side and the parsleyed potatoes on the other.

STORING
You can make the dish up to a day ahead. Reheat it in a covered skillet over low heat — it's good to do this with a parchment circle in place. However, it's best to boil and butter-glaze the potatoes right before serving.

THESE DAYS, IT'S NATURAL TO CALL something a classic that it's easy to forget the dishes that, having truly stood the test of time, not only deserve the title, but might even define it. One of those dishes is veal Marengo. Found on menus all over France, it was first made in 1800 by Napoleon Bonaparte's chef in honor of the general's success at the Battle of Marengo, fought against the Austrians on Italian soil. Some believe that the dish was created with supplies that were at hand, and that's plausible, since, minus the garnish of mushrooms, baby onions, and parsleyed potatoes, the ingredients are basic: cubes of veal, tomatoes, onions, and white wine.

This rendition of veal Marengo comes from Le Cordon Bleu in Paris and specifically the notebook of my friend Alice Vasseur, who was a student there when she was just eight years old. And, yes, the kids got to cook with wine.

FOR THE VEAL
All-purpose flour, for dredging
Salt and freshly ground pepper
1¾ pounds boneless veal shoulder, cut into 2-inch cubes
2 tablespoons mild oil (such as grapeseed or canola)
2 tablespoons unsalted butter
1 medium onion, coarsely chopped
¾ cup drained canned diced tomatoes (or peeled, seeded, and chopped fresh tomatoes)
2 tablespoons tomato paste
¾ cup dry white wine

A bouquet garni — 2 thyme sprigs, 2 parsley sprigs, 1 rosemary sprig, and 1 bay leaf, tied together in a piece of dampened cheesecloth

FOR THE VEGETABLES
About 3 tablespoons unsalted butter
12 cipolline or small white boiling onions
Salt and freshly ground pepper
1 cup water
8 white mushrooms, caps only, wiped clean and halved
8 baby potatoes, peeled or unpeeled

Chopped fresh parsley, for garnish

Center a rack in the oven and preheat the oven to 325 degrees F. Have a large oven-going skillet with a lid at hand. Cut a parchment paper circle large enough to cover the pan.

Season some flour with salt and pepper. Pat the veal cubes dry between sheets of paper towels and run the veal through the flour, coating all sides and tapping to shake off the excess.

Put the skillet over medium-high heat and add the oil. When it's hot, slip in some of the veal cubes — you don't want to crowd the pan, so you may need

to cook the veal in batches. Cook the cubes just until they're brown on all sides, then transfer them to a plate.

Discard whatever oil remains in the pan, return the pan to medium heat, and add the butter. When it melts, toss in the onion and cook, stirring, until it softens, about 5 minutes. Stir in the tomatoes, tomato paste, wine, and bouquet garni. Add the veal and give everything a good stir, stirring up whatever bits may have stuck to the pan, and bring just to a boil. Taste for salt and pepper.

Cover the pan with the parchment circle (this will keep the liquids from evaporating) and the lid, and put it in the oven. Cook for 30 minutes, undisturbed.

MEANWHILE, MAKE THE VEGETABLES: Melt 1 tablespoon of the butter in a small saucepan. Toss in the onions and turn them around in the butter until they're glossy. Season with salt and pepper, then pour in the water and bring to a boil. Lower the heat to a simmer and cook the onions until they are tender enough to be pierced with the tip of a knife, at which point the water should have evaporated. If the onions are cooked and you still have water in the pan, boil it away. Set the glazed onions aside.

Melt 1 tablespoon of the butter in a small skillet over medium heat. Add the mushrooms, season with salt and pepper, and cook, stirring, until they soften, about 5 minutes. If the pan goes dry, add a bit more butter. Set the mushrooms aside.

Put a pot of salted water on to boil for the potatoes.

Remove the skillet of veal from the oven. To make veal Marengo the traditional way, transfer the veal cubes to a bowl, cover, and keep them warm. Remove and discard the bouquet garni, then strain the sauce; discard the chopped onion. (If you don't want to fuss with this step, you can skip it.) Return the veal to the pan if you removed it, and add the glazed onions and mushrooms. Bring the sauce to a simmer over low heat (you won't have a lot of sauce, but that's fine), cover the pan, and allow the dish to bubble away very gently for 10 minutes or so while you cook the potatoes.

Drop the potatoes into the boiling water and cook until you can pierce them easily with the tip of a knife, about 10 minutes; drain well.

Put the potato pot back over low heat and add the remaining 1 tablespoon butter. When the butter has melted, return the potatoes to the pot — be gentle with them now that they're cooked — and turn them around in the butter until they're coated. If necessary, add a little more butter.

Spoon the veal, onions, and mushrooms into the center of a heated serving platter or four dinner plates, surround with the boiled potatoes, and finish with a flurry of chopped parsley, giving the lion's share of the parsley to the taters.

VEAL CHOPS WITH ROSEMARY BUTTER (PAGE 268) AND GO-WITH-EVERYTHING CELERY ROOT PUREE (PAGE 354)

veal chops
with rosemary butter

MAKES 4 SERVINGS

SERVING
You can never go wrong
serving a veal chop with
potatoes — it's a classic
combination — but for
a change, try the chops
with Celery Root Puree
(page 354).

STORING
The butter can be made
ahead and refrigerated for
1 week or frozen for up to
3 months, and the chops
can be seasoned up to
1 day ahead and stored in
the fridge.

VEAL CHOPS ARE AS EXPENSIVE IN FRANCE as they are in America, but here's the nice thing: you don't have to do much to make them great. In fact, with veal chops, the less-is-more adage is the one to follow. For this dish, a favorite of mine because it's quick and easy, the chops are pan-roasted, sauced with a mix of white wine and chicken broth, and topped with a pat of made-in-advance rosemary butter.

There's only one caveat about cooking veal — don't cook it too much. It's delicate, and if you overcook it, its texture will be too tight. Start with the chops at room temperature, and they'll need only about 2 minutes on a side to be perfect.

BE PREPARED: Make the rosemary butter and season the chops a day in advance, and they'll both have more flavor. Just make sure to take the chops out of the refrigerator at least 1 hour before you plan to cook them.

FOR THE ROSEMARY BUTTER	FOR THE CHOPS
4 tablespoons (½ stick) unsalted butter, at room temperature	4 veal rib chops, each about 12 ounces and 1 inch thick, at room temperature
1 teaspoon chopped fresh rosemary	3–4 tablespoons extra-virgin olive oil
½ teaspoon chopped fresh thyme	1 teaspoon minced fresh rosemary, plus 1 rosemary sprig
Generous pinch of salt	¾ teaspoon minced fresh thyme
	Salt and freshly ground pepper
	1 large garlic clove, smashed (there's no need to peel it)
	3 tablespoons dry white wine
	3 tablespoons chicken broth (you can make this from a bouillon cube)

TO MAKE THE ROSEMARY BUTTER: Using a rubber spatula, beat the butter in a small bowl until it is smooth and very creamy. Stir in the rosemary, thyme, and salt, and turn the butter out onto a piece of plastic wrap. Use the plastic to shape the butter into a log about 1½ inches in diameter. Wrap the log well and chill it for at least 2 hours. (*Wrapped airtight, the butter can be refrigerated for 1 week or frozen for up to 3 months.*)

TO MAKE THE CHOPS: Put the chops in a large baking dish (a Pyrex pan is perfect), drizzle with 1 to 2 tablespoons of the olive oil, sprinkle with the minced rosemary and thyme, and season with salt and pepper. Rub the oil and seasonings into both sides of the chops. (*You can season the chops up to 1 day ahead; cover and keep them in the refrigerator. Let stand for 1 hour at room temperature before cooking.*)

Put a large heavy skillet over medium-high heat, pour in 2 tablespoons olive oil, add the rosemary sprig and smashed garlic, and cook, stirring, until the garlic is fragrant but not browned, about 2 minutes. Pull out and discard the rosemary and garlic and raise the heat to high. Slip the chops into the pan and cook for 2 minutes, or until the undersides of the chops are golden brown. Turn and cook for 2 minutes more (or until an instant-read thermometer inserted into the center of a chop reads 130 degrees F). Transfer the chops to a warm serving platter and cover loosely with a foil tent.

Pour out whatever fat remains in the skillet and put the skillet over medium-high heat. Add the wine and cook, stirring to scrape up any browned bits that have stuck to the bottom of the pan, until only about 2 teaspoons remain, about 30 seconds. Add the chicken broth and cook until you have about 2 tablespoons liquid in the skillet, about 30 seconds. Remove from the heat and drizzle the sauce over the chops.

Divide the rosemary butter into 4 pieces and top each chop with a pat; serve immediately.

with knife and fork: two-fisted eating

The French eat the way most Europeans do: efficiently, with a marked economy of motion. In America we cut food using a fork in our left hand and a knife in our right, then put the knife down, transfer the fork to our right hand, place our left hand in our lap, and direct the fork mouthward. It's a complicated ballet that we never think about once we've learned the steps. The French cut the food with a fork in their left hand and a knife in their right, then they eat the food from the fork, rarely relinquishing the knife. It's still a ballet; it's just

that the French dance the allegro movement.

And when the knife and fork are put down, they're arranged as sign language: leaving the knife and fork separated, the knife on the right side of the plate, the fork on the left, ready to be picked up and used, says, "I'm still eating," while bringing the knife and fork together, so that they're parallel to one another, says, "I'm finished."

While we're at the table, here's another little difference: the French keep both hands on the table at all times. Elbows are allowed between

courses and among good friends, but no matter where and with whom, you take a poker-game position, keeping both hands from mid-forearm up in view at all times. I'm not sure about the custom's origin — it might have had to do with trust, or a lack of it, in an earlier era — but now that I've gotten used to it, I like it.

With both hands at the ready, it's easy to jump into an animated conversation, easier still to lift a hand to your lips, make a little kiss motion, and compliment the cook for a dish well made.

osso buco à l'arman

MAKES 4 SERVINGS

SERVING
Osso buco and rice is both perfect and traditional. In Italy, the dish would be paired with a saffron risotto, but Arman's choice was rice cooked with orange zest, and it's my favorite accompaniment as well (see Another Bonne Idée, page 272). If you'd like, prepare an orange-basil gremolata (see Bonne Idée) to sprinkle over the osso buco or to bring to the table for individual sprinkling.

STORING
Like most braised dishes, osso buco is a good keeper. You can make the dish up to 2 days ahead, chill it, and then reheat it gently on top of the stove or in a 325-degree-F oven. It can also be frozen: cool the dish (or the leftovers), pack airtight, and freeze for up to 2 months.

BONNE IDÉE
Orange-Basil Gremolata. While you can certainly make this from fresh zest, it's foolish not to use the zest you blanched for the sauce. Pat the zest dry and finely chop enough of it to measure about ¼ cup. Toss the zest with 1 garlic clove, split, germ removed, and minced, 3 tablespoons minced fresh basil, salt (fleur de sel would be nice), and freshly ground pepper. You can make this about an hour or so before serving time, but keep it tightly covered with plastic wrap so that it stays moist.

THE ITALIANS GOT TO NAME THIS DISH, but that doesn't mean the French don't make it regularly and make it their own. *Osso buco,* meaning "bone with a hole," is the heart of this dish and also gives it its name. Cut crosswise from a veal shank, thick slices of osso buco are round, with meaty nuggets surrounding the central hole, which is filled with marrow — and treasured.

A gently braised dish, osso buco is often finished at the last minute with a shower of gremolata, traditionally a mix of garlic, lemon zest, and parsley. In this rendition, a recipe given to me by the late French artist Arman, the veal, simmered in an orange and tomato sauce, is served with rice beneath and nothing above. However, taking artistic license (something I'm certain Arman would have granted me), I top the veal with a gremolata that mimics the dish's seasonings — orange zest, garlic, and minced basil (see Bonne Idée). Since you'll only be using the zest, think about making an Orange and Olive Salad (page 117) with the fruit.

A word on the veal: Because the meat around the bone doesn't form a solid piece — the nuggets, encircled by connective tissue, press against one another like pieces in a jigsaw puzzle — it's best to tie kitchen twine around the circumference of each slice to hold it neatly in place during cooking. If you buy your veal shanks from a butcher, the odds are he'll tie the rounds without your even having to ask.

If you'd like to serve 6, add 2 more pieces of osso buco without making any other adjustments to the recipe — there'll be enough of the delicious sauce to go around.

4 navel oranges, rinsed and dried	2 teaspoons herbes de Provence
2 cups water	1 28-ounce can whole tomatoes in tomato puree
About ⅓ cup olive oil	5 medium tomatoes, sliced
2 medium onions, coarsely chopped	2 chicken bouillon cubes, dissolved in ¼ cup boiling water
2 garlic cloves, crushed and peeled	Salt and freshly ground pepper
1 tablespoon chopped fresh thyme (Arman used 2 teaspoons dried)	4 veal shanks, sawed into 2- to 3-inch lengths (osso buco)
1 tablespoon chopped fresh basil (Arman used 2 teaspoons dried)	4 large carrots, trimmed, peeled, and thinly sliced

Remove the zest from the oranges with a vegetable peeler, taking care not to get any of the cottony white pith. Pour the water into a saucepan, drop in the zest, bring to a boil, and boil for 5 minutes. Lower the heat so that the water just simmers and cook for another 5 minutes. Set aside.

Put a Dutch oven or a very large oven-going skillet with a lid over medium heat and pour in 2 tablespoons of the olive oil. Add the onions, garlic, and herbs and cook, stirring, for 5 minutes, just to soften. Using scissors, reach into the can of tomatoes and snip the tomatoes into pieces. Add the fresh and canned tomatoes, liquid included, the bouillon, and 2 tablespoons of the water in which the zest cooked — hold on to the rest of the liquid; you'll need it later. Bring the sauce to a boil, season with salt and pepper, reduce the heat, and let it simmer gently while you brown the veal.

Center a rack in the oven and preheat the oven to 325 degrees F.

Set a large heavy-bottomed skillet over medium-high heat and pour in 3 tablespoons of the olive oil. Pat the veal dry and season sparingly with pepper. Working in batches if necessary, slip the pieces into the pan and brown them lightly on both sides. (If you're working in batches, you'll probably have to add more oil.) As each piece of meat is browned, lift it out of the skillet with a slotted spatula (let the fat drip back into the pan) and lower it into the simmering sauce.

Pour off the fat in the skillet and pour in the remainder of the liquid in which the zest cooked — reserve the zest. Turn the heat up and cook for a minute, stirring to get up whatever little bits of meat have stuck to the pan, then pour the pan juices into the Dutch oven. Add 8 to 10 strips of the zest to the pot (you can save the rest for pilaf and gremolata; see the Bonne Idées) and, using a wooden spoon or spatula, mix everything together as best you can — you won't be mixing as much as gently sloshing, but that's fine. Scatter the carrots over the veal.

Cut a circle of parchment paper or two circles of wax paper (it's good to have a double layer) just large enough to fit inside the Dutch oven and lay the paper on top of the osso buco. Simmer for 5 minutes more, then settle the lid on the pot and slide it into the oven.

Braise the osso buco undisturbed for 2 hours, at which point the meat should be fork-tender. Carefully lift off the pot's lid and the parchment paper and, with a large spoon, skim as much fat from the surface of the sauce as possible before serving.

ANOTHER
BONNE IDÉE
Orange (or Lemon) Rice Pilaf.
Because there's a lot of orange zest left over from the veal, I usually use it to make this pilaf, but you can use lemon zest or a mix of orange and lemon zest. Set a medium saucepan over low heat and pour in 2 tablespoons olive oil. When it's warm, stir in 1 onion, finely chopped, and about 3 tablespoons finely chopped orange zest (if you use the zest you cooked for the osso buco's sauce, just pat it dry). Season with salt and freshly ground pepper and cook gently, stirring occasionally, for about 3 minutes, or until the onion is soft and translucent. Increase the heat to medium, add 1 cup basmati or other long-grain white rice, and stir it around until it is coated with oil, about 1 minute. Pour in 2 cups chicken broth and stir. Bring the broth to a boil, add a little more salt and pepper if you think it's needed, and stir, then reduce the heat to low, cover, and cook until the rice has absorbed all the liquid. (White basmati rice usually needs about 11 minutes, but rice varies, so check the package and, most important, the pan.) Remove from the heat, let sit for 2 minutes, and then fluff the rice with a fork. If you'd like, you can stir a little chopped fresh basil into the rice.

fresh orange pork tenderloin

IKE US, THE FRENCH LOVE TO PAIR pork tenderloin with fruits (dried and fresh), with sauces (sweet and sticky), and with herbs and spices (mild and hot). But here's a recipe that strikes me as being a little different. It's got some spice — cardamom — and it's got fruit, but the fruit is orange, which gives the dish a light, refreshing feel. Like most pork tenderloin recipes, this one is quick enough to make on a busy weekday.

MAKES **4** SERVINGS

SERVING
The pork and oranges are good with potatoes or rice, but they're particularly nice paired with Broth-Braised Potatoes and Fennel (page 358) or Celery Root Puree (page 354).

STORING
This dish is best served as soon as it's made — because there isn't much sauce, it doesn't reheat very well. But any leftover pork can be used for sandwiches or salads.

- 4 large oranges (navels are good)
- 1 large pork tenderloin, about 1½ pounds, or 2 smaller tenderloins, each about 12 ounces, at room temperature
- 1 tablespoon unsalted butter, plus more if needed
- 1 tablespoon mild oil (such as grapeseed or canola), plus more if needed

- Salt and freshly ground pepper
- 1 medium onion, finely chopped, or 4 spring onions, trimmed and finely chopped, or 8 scallions, white and light green parts only, finely chopped
- Seeds from 4 cardamom pods, bruised with the flat side of a knife

Peel 2 of the oranges all the way down to the flesh, then cut between the membranes to release the segments. Cut the segments crosswise in half. Remove the zest from the other 2 oranges with a zester or vegetable peeler, being careful to avoid the white cottony pith if using a peeler; if you removed the zest with a peeler, slice the strips into long thin strands. Cut the zest into pieces 1 to 2 inches long. Squeeze the juice from the 2 zested oranges.

Cut a large tenderloin into 8 pieces or smaller ones into 4 pieces each. Try to get the thickness of the pieces as even as possible, so they will all cook in the same amount of time. Pat the slices dry between paper towels.

Put a large skillet over medium-high heat and add the butter and oil. When the mixture is hot, add the pork slices, without crowding, and brown them for 2 to 3 minutes on each side; season with salt and pepper when you turn the pieces over. (If putting all the pork in the pan would crowd it, brown the pieces in 2 batches, adding more butter and oil if necessary, then return all the pork to the pan.) Add the orange zest, juice, onion, and cardamom, season everything with salt and pepper, and give the pan a stir. When the sauce produces one little bubble, reduce the heat to low and cover the pan. Cook the pork at the gentlest simmer for 10 minutes.

Add the orange segments, cover, and continue to simmer for 3 minutes more, or until the pork is tender and cooked through.

Remove the lid, and if you think the sauce needs to be cooked down a bit, transfer the pork and orange segments to a warm serving platter and boil the sauce until it reaches the consistency you want. Taste for salt and pepper and serve immediately.

coconut-lemongrass-braised pork

MAKES 6 SERVINGS

SERVING
Because the sauce is so good and so plentiful, you'll want something to capture it — bread is an option, of course, but boiled rice or egg noodles are naturals as well.

STORING
Like all stews, this one is very good the next day. If you want to make it ahead, cook the pork for a slightly shorter time, so that you don't overcook it when you reheat it. If you've got leftovers, remove the pork, reheat the sauce, and when it's hot, add the pork and simmer just long enough to warm it through.

MARIE NAËL, A PARIS RESIDENT and an energetic blogger, is a rare breed of professional chef — one who cooks for many during the day and returns home to cook for two every night. We met at a photography atelier and have exchanged culinary notes ever since. I love how imaginative she is and how willing she is to tweak classics, jump cuisinary borders, and play around in the kitchen. You can get a sense of her style in this recipe, which was originally made with a hunk of wild boar she had in the freezer. Lacking a tucked-away morsel of boar, I made it with a much tamer pork butt and had the feeling that no matter what cut I'd used, I would have ended up with a winning dish. It's hard to go wrong with a sauce based on coconut milk, cardamom, coriander, curry, and fresh lemongrass. In fact, it's so hard to go wrong that I've even made the recipe with chicken instead of pork.

In Marie's recipe, an assortment of root vegetables is cooked separately and added to the stew at the last minute. When I've had time to do that, I've been delighted; when I haven't, I've added frozen peas to the pot at the last minute or just left the braise pristine.

2	tablespoons grapeseed oil or olive oil	2	strips lemon zest, white pith removed
3	pounds boneless pork (pork butt is good here), cut into 1- to 2-inch cubes and patted dry, at room temperature	½	lemongrass stalk, tender center part only, pounded to crush it a bit
	Coarse salt, such as *sel gris* or kosher salt, and freshly ground pepper	1	15½-ounce can unsweetened coconut milk, well stirred, plus more if needed
2	teaspoons turmeric	1½	cups water
1¼	teaspoons curry powder (Marie suggests mild; I often use Madras)	3	small potatoes, scrubbed or peeled and halved (optional)
	Seeds from 6 cardamom pods	3	small carrots, trimmed, peeled, and halved (optional)
6	white peppercorns	3	small onions, halved (optional)
6	coriander seeds	½	small celery root, trimmed, peeled, and cubed (optional)
		1	teaspoon honey (optional)

Center a rack in the oven and preheat the oven to 300 degrees F.

Put a large skillet, preferably nonstick, over high heat and add the oil. When it's hot, toss in some of the pork — don't crowd the pan — and cook, stirring, until the pieces are golden on all sides. As the pieces are done, lift them out of the pot and place in a Dutch oven or other oven-going stew pot; season lightly with salt and pepper. Continue to brown the remainder of the pork.

Put the Dutch oven over medium heat and add the spices, lemon zest, lemongrass, and 1 teaspoon salt. Stir everything around until the spices are toasty — you'll smell them — and then stir in the coconut milk and water. Bring to a boil, cover the pot well, and slide it into the oven.

Allow the stew to braise undisturbed for 30 to 40 minutes, or until the pork is tender and cooked through. (*If you plan to make the dish ahead, cook the pork for 15 to 20 minutes.*)

While the stew is in the oven, cook the vegetables, if you're using them: Bring a large pot of salted water to a boil and add the potatoes, carrots, onions, and celery root. Keep an eye on the pot, and remove the vegetables with a slotted spoon as they're tender. Transfer the vegetables to a bowl and set aside until the pork is cooked.

When the pork is done, put the Dutch oven over medium heat, add the vegetables, if you've got them, and bring the liquid to a boil. Reduce the heat to a gentle simmer and simmer just until the vegetables are heated through. If you think the sauce needs it, you can add a little more stirred coconut milk to the pot — it will heighten the braise's coconut flavor and thin the sauce (which is not particularly thick). Taste for salt and pepper, add a teaspoon of honey, if you'd like, and serve.

chard-stuffed pork roast

MAKES 6 SERVINGS

SERVING

The roast doesn't make its own sauce, and it really doesn't need a sauce per se, but it's very good with mustard — grainy or honey mustard, or a mixture of Dijon mustard and crème fraîche.

STORING

If you've got some roast left over, let it cool, wrap it well, and keep it refrigerated for up to 3 days. Chilled, it makes great sandwiches.

ALTHOUGH THIS ROAST IS FESTIVE ENOUGH to be served at a party, it's quick and easy enough to be supper on a busy weeknight. The stuffing is chard sautéed with onions and garlic and mixed with raisins — pork and dried fruits are made for each other. And, rather than the stuffing being worked precisely (and fussily) into the center of the roast, the loin is butterflied, the filling is spooned on, and the whole is tied up with kitchen string, making it more rustic but no less appealing than the precisely stuffed roasts displayed in every French butcher shop. I love the way this roast looks, particularly when the filling is made with bright-colored red or rainbow chard. And it's great for the holidays when, in very non-Gallic style, you can replace the raisins with dried cranberries and serve the pork with a chunky cranberry sauce.

3 large Swiss chard stalks	¼ cup moist, plump golden or
2 tablespoons olive oil	dark raisins
1 small onion, finely chopped	Red pepper flakes
2 garlic cloves, split, germ	½ teaspoon black peppercorns
removed, and finely	½ teaspoon coriander seeds
chopped	1 2½-pound pork loin roast, at
Salt and freshly ground	room temperature
pepper	

Cut ½ inch or so off the bottoms of the stalks of chard, then cut the leaves away from the ribs and thinly slice the ribs and stalks. Shred the leaves by rolling them up like a cigar and slicing them crosswise (or chop the leaves).

Heat 1 tablespoon of the olive oil in a large skillet over medium heat. Add the onion and garlic, season with a little salt and pepper, and cook, stirring, until the onion is almost softened, about 3 minutes. Toss in half of the chard and stir it around; when it wilts enough to free up some space in the skillet, add the rest of it. Continue to cook and stir until the chard is tender, a total of about 5 minutes. Scrape the mixture into a bowl, stir in the raisins and a good pinch of red pepper flakes, and season with salt and pepper.

Center a rack in the oven and preheat the oven to 375 degrees F.

Pound the peppercorns and coriander in a mortar and pestle just until they crack (don't pulverize them), or put them between sheets of wax paper and bash them with the bottom of a skillet or the heel or back of a chef's knife.

Put the pork loin fat side up on a cutting board. Using a long sharp knife, cut it in half along one side without cutting all the way through; leave about ¼ inch intact. Open the roast like a book, and spoon the stuffing onto it. Tie the roast at intervals with kitchen twine, tucking in the stuffing that pops out as you go, or close the flap with toothpicks or skewers. Rub the pork with the remaining tablespoon of olive oil, season with salt, and pat the crushed peppercorns and coriander over it. Settle the loin fat side up in a roasting pan or other pan that's just big enough to hold it comfortably — I use a 9-inch cast-iron skillet.

Roast undisturbed until an instant-read thermometer inserted into the thick part of the loin — not into the stuffing — registers 140 degrees F. Because pork is so variable, you should start checking the temperature after 25 minutes, but it's likely the roast will need about 40 minutes in the oven. Pull the pan from the oven, cover the roast lightly with a foil tent, and let it rest in a warm place for 15 minutes, during which time the roast will continue to cook and the juices will settle. The roast will still be pinkish at the center (it might also be red, if you've used red chard, but that's something else); if that's not the way you like your pork, roast it a bit longer before resting it.

Slice the roast with a careful sawing motion, so that the stuffing remains encased by the meat.

pork roast with mangoes and lychees

MAKES 4 TO 6
SERVINGS

SERVING
Alec serves his pork with
sticky rice, but I like it as
much with Cardamom
Rice Pilaf (page 382) —
the citrusy flavor of the
cardamom is really nice
with the fruit in the sauce
— or Orange Rice Pilaf
(see Another Bonne Idée,
page 272).

STORING
Leftovers can be covered
and refrigerated overnight,
then reheated very gently
the following day, but it's
likely that the pork will
be a tad overcooked. You
can use the pork chilled
in salads or let it come
to room temperature
and make open-faced
sandwiches. Do that, and
you should reheat the
sauce and spoon it over
the sandwiches. Speaking
of the sauce, it's great over
pasta.

MY FRIEND ALEC LOBRANO IS THE MAN thousands turn to when they want advice on where to eat in Paris. The author of *Hungry for Paris* and a longtime contributor to *Gourmet* magazine, he's been the go-to guy on the Paris scene for more than twenty-five years. Yet while Alec can detect and describe the nuances of French cuisine from classic to nouvelle, when he's cooking at home, he's apt to serve his French friends something from his earlier life in America, often this sweet-and-sharp pork loin, a dish with roots in the Dominican Republic.

Alec tells a wonderful story of moving to New York's Upper West Side in 1977, where he shared an apartment with a friend who was as broke as he was, and discovering a neighborhood Dominican bar where the air-conditioning was reliable, the beer cheap, and the welcome — once the crowd got used to the gringos — warm, so warm that when Dominican Independence Day rolled around, Alec found himself invited to celebrate with the bar's owner. It was there that he had a version of this dish: pork and mangoes in a wine and vinegar sauce with soy and honey. It must have been love at first taste, because he has carried the memory and the recipe with him ever since, first to London and then to Paris, where it seems perfectly at home.

Alec told me that when he re-created this roast, he added the lychees, which, as he says, "have the oddball fun of standing in for the fat that's missing from a pork loin. People always think that the lychees are fat and push them to one side, so I love revealing the trompe l'oeil and insisting they try at least one."

1	2- to 2½-pound pork loin roast, at room temperature		Juice of 1 lime
2	tablespoons olive oil	3	tablespoons honey
	Salt and freshly ground pepper	½–1	teaspoon piment d'Espelette (see Sources) or chili powder
1	large onion, finely chopped	1	bay leaf
5	garlic cloves, split, germ removed, and thinly sliced	2	thyme sprigs
3	tablespoons red wine vinegar	1	ripe mango, peeled, pitted, and cut into thin strips
½	cup dry white wine	10	lychees, peeled and pitted if fresh, drained if canned
3	tablespoons soy sauce		

Center a rack in the oven and preheat the oven to 300 degrees F.

Pat the roast dry with paper towels. Place a Dutch oven or other heavy oven-going casserole over medium-high heat and pour in 1 tablespoon of the oil. When it's hot, put the pork fat side down in the pot and cook for a couple of minutes, until the fat is browned, then turn it over and brown the other side. Transfer the roast to a plate, season with salt and pepper, and discard the oil.

Return the pot to the stove, this time over low heat, and add the remaining tablespoon of oil. When it's warm, toss in the onion and garlic, season with salt and pepper, and cook, stirring, for about 3 minutes, or until the onion is translucent. Turn up the heat and pour in the vinegar — stand back, the scent of hot vinegar is very strong. When the vinegar has almost evaporated, a matter of a minute or two, pour in the wine. Let the wine bubble for 30 seconds or so, then add the soy, lime juice, and honey. Bring to a boil, stir in the piment d'Espelette or chili powder, add the bay leaf, thyme, mango, and lychees, and give the pot another minute at the boil. Add the roast fat side up, baste with the sauce, cover the casserole, and slide it into the oven.

Allow the roast to braise gently for 30 minutes, then check its temperature: you're looking for it to measure 140 degrees F at its center on an instant-read thermometer. The roast is likely to need a total of 40 to 50 minutes in the oven, but it's important to check early, since pork varies. Pull the pot from the oven, transfer the roast to a cutting board, cover it lightly with a foil tent, and let it rest for 5 to 10 minutes, during which time it will continue to cook (its temperature will probably rise another 5 degrees or so).

While the roast is resting, taste the sauce. If you'd like to concentrate the flavors even more, boil it for a couple of minutes. Don't forget to check for salt and pepper.

Slice the roast and serve with the sauce.

cola and jam spareribs

The French would eat these with a knife and fork and deftly get every last morsel of meat from every bone, but if you're not French, or you're among family and friends, you can eat them the good old-fashioned American way — i.e., with your fingers and a stack of paper napkins at the ready.

STORING
The ribs can be made a day ahead and kept covered in the refrigerator overnight. Reheat them in a 250-degree-F oven before serving.

A FEW YEARS AGO, I HAD A DINNER in a tiny restaurant in Tours, in the Loire Valley, and was tickled to discover that the chef had spent some time in Kentucky and that, while there, he'd developed a fondness for Coca-Cola and barbecue. Being a smart guy and a good cook, he didn't take long to figure out that he could have his Coke and eat it too if he used it to baste barbecued ribs. Coke (particularly Coca-Cola Light) is very popular in France, and meaty individual spareribs, or *travers de porc,* are a familiar French cut, often served lacquered Asian-style, braised like a stew, or grilled or oven-glazed, as these ribs are. I couldn't pry the recipe for the ribs from the chef, but I was able to come up with a version that I think he would like.

BE PREPARED: If you've got the time, it's good to marinate the ribs for at least a few hours; if you're short on time, just rub and go.

⅓	cup apricot jam	½	teaspoon ground ginger
⅓	cup orange juice		Salt and freshly ground pepper
	Juice of 1 lemon	1	rack spareribs, about 3 pounds
1½	teaspoons Chinese five-spice powder	1	cup Coca-Cola

Center a rack in the oven and preheat the oven to 350 degrees F. (Or, if you will be using two pans — see below — and can't fit them both on the same rack, position the racks to divide the oven into thirds.)

Stir the apricot jam and orange juice together and heat them for 1 minute in a microwave oven, or warm them in a saucepan, just until the mixture simmers. Let cool a little, then stir in the lemon juice.

Mix the five-spice powder, ginger, and some salt and pepper together.

Cut the rack of ribs in half. Working your knife in between every 2 or 3 ribs, make a slash to separate them a bit. (This will help keep the ribs flat when you roast them.) Rub the ribs with the spice mix and then with the jam. (If you want to marinate the ribs, cover and refrigerate them for a few hours, or for as long as overnight.)

If you've got a roasting pan large enough to hold both pieces of pork, use it; if not, put each piece in its own baking pan. (I use Pyrex baking dishes.) Pour a few tablespoons of water around the ribs and slide them into the oven.

Bake the spareribs for 45 minutes, then baste them and add a little more water if you think the pan looks dry or if the marinade is sticking and blackening. Roast for another 45 minutes, basting occasionally.

Pour the Coca-Cola around the ribs and then baste every 5 minutes or so for 30 minutes. (The total baking time is about 2 hours.) At this point, the ribs will be cooked through, juicy and glazed. If you'd like them more well-done or the glaze darker, run the ribs under the broiler to finish them.

These are at their best warm or at room temperature, so give them a little rest after they come out of the oven, then cut the ribs apart.

navarin printanier

MEANT TO BE MADE WITH FRESHLY DUG spring vegetables (that's the *printanier* part), this lamb stew (*navarin*) is a classic, a staple of the Easter season and another of those slowly braised dishes that make French cooking timelessly appealing. The lamb is browned stovetop and then simmered gently with its springtime companions: onions, small potatoes, carrots, and turnips. When the sauce is a burnished mahogany color and both the lamb and the vegetables are fork-tender, you finish the stew with a standard bearer of spring vegetables: peas. That almost everyone uses frozen peas is a truth rarely uttered but one not to be ashamed of. So many French cooks, chefs included, have told me that they can never get fresh peas as good, or as consistently good, as what they buy frozen, and I've always nodded in agreement.

This recipe came to me fourth-hand. It was my friend Betty Rosbottom, cookbook author and part-time Paris resident, who gave it to me, explaining that she'd gotten it from her friend Catherine Lafarge, who had begged the recipe from her mother, so that she could keep alive her culinary memories of a Parisian childhood.

SERVING

An all-in-one meal, this really needs nothing more than what's in the pot. Ladle the meat, vegetables, and beautiful sauce into shallow soup plates. If you feel you must do something, dust each serving with a little minced parsley.

STORING

You can make the navarin, without the peas, up to 2 days ahead and keep it covered in the refrigerator. Reheat the navarin, covered, in a 350-degree-F oven for about 30 minutes, then add the peas and let them cook. The stew can also be packed airtight and frozen for up to 2 months.

About 2 tablespoons olive oil

3 pounds boneless lamb shoulder, excess fat removed, cut into 1½-inch cubes, and patted dry

3 tablespoons all-purpose flour
Salt and freshly ground pepper
About 4 cups beef broth

3 tablespoons tomato paste

3 medium garlic cloves, split and germ removed

2 parsley sprigs

1 thyme sprig, leaves only, minced

1 bay leaf, cut in half

12 small white onions, not peeled

2 tablespoons unsalted butter

3 medium carrots, trimmed, peeled, and sliced ½ inch thick on the diagonal

1 medium turnip, trimmed, peeled, cut into ½-inch-thick wedges, and wedges cut crosswise in half

1 tablespoon sugar

½ pound small red-skin or Yukon Gold potatoes, scrubbed and quartered

1¼ cups fresh or thawed frozen peas

Put a Dutch oven or other large high-sided pot over medium-high heat and pour in 2 tablespoons oil. When it's hot, add some of the lamb pieces — you want to have a single layer of lamb and you don't want to crowd the pot, so do this in batches. Brown the meat on all sides, about 5 minutes, then transfer to a plate. Continue until all the lamb has been browned, adding more oil to the pot if needed.

Pour out the oil and return the meat to the pot. Put the pot over medium-high heat again, sprinkle the meat with the flour, and season generously with salt and pepper. Cook, stirring, for 2 minutes, then add 4 cups broth, the tomato

BEEF, VEAL, PORK, AND LAMB **281**

paste, garlic, parsley, thyme, and bay leaf. Give everything a good stir and bring the broth to a boil. Reduce the heat, cover the pot, and simmer the navarin gently for 45 minutes.

Meanwhile, work on the vegetables: Bring a saucepan of water to a boil, drop in the onions, and cook for just a minute. Drain the onions, slice off the root and stem ends, and slip off their skins.

Set a large skillet over high heat and add the butter. When it's hot, add the onions, carrots, and turnip and cook, stirring, for 2 minutes. Sprinkle the sugar over the vegetables and stir for a minute or so, then reduce the heat a bit and cook, stirring often, until the vegetables are browned, about 10 minutes — they should be well colored but not soft. Set aside.

Position a rack in the lower third of the oven and preheat the oven to 400 degrees F.

When the lamb has simmered for 45 minutes, add the sautéed vegetables, as well as the potatoes, and simmer, still covered, for another 15 minutes.

Slide the pot into the oven and braise for 30 to 40 minutes, or until the lamb is fork-tender.

Fish out and discard the parsley and bay leaf and stir in the peas. If the peas are fresh, give them 3 to 4 minutes; if they've been frozen, give them just a minute or two. Taste the stew for salt and pepper, and if you think the sauce is too thick, thin it with a little more broth.

Ladle into soup plates and serve.

braised cardamom-curry lamb

IF YOU'VE GOT SNOW OUTSIDE AND A POT of this lamb stew braising inside, you're set for the perfect evening. Cardamom and curry, a mix the French would call *à l'indienne,* give this braise deep flavor and the kind of warm fragrance that pulls people to the kitchen and makes even well-behaved guests want to lift the lid on the pot and get a sneak peek of what's for dinner. It's not just the cardamom and curry that draw you in, it's the mint and honey and the figs too. The ingredients are a little Indian and a little North African; the way the dish is made is a little like a French stew and a little like a Moroccan tagine.

MAKES 6 SERVINGS

1   small bunch mint (about 6 sprigs)
      About 2 tablespoons olive oil
2   large onions, finely chopped
6   garlic cloves, crushed and peeled
2½ tablespoons curry powder (I use Madras)
½   teaspoon ground cardamom
4   crushed cardamom pods (optional)
3   pounds boneless lamb shoulder, fat removed, cut into 1-inch cubes, and patted dry

      Salt and freshly ground pepper
¾   cup water
1½ teaspoons honey (optional)
3   dried figs, quartered
3   tablespoons golden raisins (optional)
9   small potatoes (I use baby Yukon Golds), peeled and halved
3   tart-sweet apples, such as Gala or Fuji, peeled, quartered, and cored

Tie the mint stems in a bundle with kitchen twine. Pull off the mint leaves (reserve the stems) and chop them.

Put a Dutch oven or other large heavy-bottomed casserole over low heat and pour in 2 tablespoons olive oil. When it's hot, stir in the onions, garlic, curry, cardamom powder, and pods, if you're using them. Heat, stirring, just until the onions are translucent and soft, about 10 minutes.

Toss in the lamb, turn the heat up a little, and cook, turning often, until the meat colors (if the mixture looks a little dry or if the meat is sticking to the pot, add a drizzle more olive oil). Season with salt and pepper, then pour in the water, toss in the mint bundle, and stir in half of the chopped mint, the honey (if using), figs, and raisins, if you're using them. Scatter the potatoes and apples over the meat, season with salt and pepper, and bring to a boil. Lower the heat to a gentle simmer, put a piece of aluminum foil over the casserole, and cover it with the lid.

Braise for 1 hour and 15 to 30 minutes, or until the meat and potatoes are tender enough to be pierced easily with the tip of knife.

Taste the *jus* and add more salt and pepper, if needed. Sprinkle over the remaining chopped mint.

SERVING
Because the lamb curry has potatoes, it really doesn't need to be served with anything else — it can simply be ladled into shallow soup plates and served with a sliced baguette for sopping up sauce. However, I think it's nice to have something green on the table, maybe broccoli or peas, and even with the potatoes, I like to put the stew on a small bed of rice (brown or white), kasha, or egg noodles. . . . After all, it's winter, and we need hearty food to keep us warm.

STORING
Like all good stews, this one can be made ahead, cooled, and stored, covered, in the refrigerator; reheat gently the next day. The apples may get a little mushy, but that's okay — they'll make the sauce even tastier. You can also pack the stew into an airtight container and freeze it for up to 2 months.

lamb and dried apricot tagine

MAKES 4 SERVINGS

SERVING

While you could serve the tagine solo, it would be a shame not to offer something to go with the wonderful sauce. I serve either couscous (cooked without spices in chicken broth or water) or white rice.

STORING

Like most braised dishes, this is a good keeper. You can make it a day or two ahead and, when it's cool, cover it well and keep it in the refrigerator. If you make the dish ahead, refrain from adding the toasted almonds until you reheat the tagine for serving, and hold off on the last dusting of cilantro until ready to serve.

THE FIRST TIME I MADE THIS TAGINE, I made a mistake: I stayed in the kitchen while it simmered slowly in the oven, and the smell of the spices — ginger and cumin, cinnamon, dried chiles, coriander, and saffron — drove me nuts. I was so dizzy, to say nothing of hungry, by the time I pulled the pot out of the oven that I might just as well have spent the time spinning in circles.

The recipe comes from Françoise Maloberti, a gifted home cook, to whom, after you've made it, you'll be as grateful as I am. Like many Moroccan tagines, this one is *aigre-doux*, or sour-sweet, and studded with fruit — here, plumped dried apricots. Because of the toasted almonds that are cooked in the tagine for the last few minutes, and because of the hot peppers and saffron, the dish is reminiscent of couscous, which is a tagine's first cousin. It's not surprising that the best (and easiest) accompaniment you can offer is a spoonful of plain couscous, a pasta that's got texture, a mild flavor, and, most important, a remarkable capacity for soaking up good sauces.

While Françoise uses peeled, seeded, and chopped tomatoes, I often use canned diced, which put the tagine in the realm of easily doable in winter.

2 chicken bouillon cubes and 1¾ cups boiling water (what Françoise uses) or 1¾ cups chicken broth	1 14½-ounce can diced tomatoes, drained, or 4 medium tomatoes, peeled, seeded, and chopped
¼ pound moist, plump dried apricots (I use Turkish)	1–2 small dried chile peppers
About 6 tablespoons olive oil	1 tablespoon coriander seeds, cracked
About 1¾ pounds boneless lamb shoulder, fat removed, cut into 1½-inch cubes	2 pinches of saffron threads
Salt and freshly ground pepper	½ teaspoon finely grated fresh ginger
4 medium onions, coarsely chopped	½ teaspoon ground cumin
4 garlic cloves, split, germ removed, and finely chopped	¼ teaspoon ground cinnamon
	About ¼ cup chopped fresh cilantro
	½ cup toasted sliced almonds
	Couscous or rice, for serving (optional)

Center a rack in the oven and preheat the oven to 325 degrees F.

If you're using the bouillon cubes, drop them into a medium bowl and pour over the boiling water; stir to dissolve. If you're using chicken broth, bring it to a boil, then pour it into a bowl. Add the apricots to the bowl and let them soak and plump while you prepare the rest of the tagine.

Put the base of a tagine, a high-sided heavy skillet, or a Dutch oven over medium-high heat and pour in 3 tablespoons of the oil. Pat the pieces of lamb dry between paper towels, then drop them into the hot oil (don't crowd the

pan — work in batches if necessary) and brown on all sides, about 4 minutes. With a slotted spoon, lift the meat out of the pan and onto a plate. Season the lamb with salt and pepper. Pour out the fat in the pan, leaving whatever bits may have stuck.

Return the pan to the stove, reduce the heat to low, and add 2 more tablespoons olive oil. When the oil is warm, stir in the onions and garlic and cook, stirring, for about 5 minutes, just to get them started on the road to softening. Add the tomatoes, season with salt and pepper, and cook, stirring often, for 10 minutes, adding a little more oil if needed.

Drain the apricots and add the chicken bouillon/broth to the pan, along with the chile(s), coriander, saffron — crush it between your fingers as you sprinkle it in — ginger, cumin, cinnamon, and 2 tablespoons of the cilantro. Stir to mix and dissolve the spices, then season with salt and pepper. Spoon the meat and any juices on the plate over the vegetables and top with the apricots. Seal the pan with aluminum foil, clap on the lid, and slide it into the oven.

Bake the tagine for 1 hour. Carefully lift the lid and foil and scatter the almonds over the meat. Re-cover the pan and bake the tagine for 15 minutes more. (Sometimes I skip this step and just save the toasted almonds to sprinkle over the tagine at serving time.)

If you cooked the braise in a tagine, sprinkle the remaining 2 tablespoons cilantro over the meat, bring the tagine to the table, and serve directly from the pan. If you used a skillet or Dutch oven, transfer the tagine to a warm large serving platter and dust with the cilantro. Serve with couscous or rice, if you like.

fish and shellfish

ALMOND FLOUNDER MEUNIÈRE (PAGE 290)

fish and shellfish

almond flounder meunière

MAKES 2 SERVINGS

SERVING

The flounder is good with simple sides, like boiled potatoes — roll them around in a little butter and sprinkle them with chives before serving — steamed spinach (page 331), or broccoli. I often pair the fish with braised fennel (see Bonne Idée, page 358), or as untraditional a match as it is, Matafan (page 356).

STORING

Although you could make the nut mixture earlier in the day or even the day before, the fillets should be enjoyed as soon as they're cooked. These portions are small, so it's doubtful you'll have leftovers, but if you do, you'll be surprised how good the fish is when you make it into a sandwich with sliced tomatoes on toasted white or egg bread spread with mayonnaise, Rouille (see Bonne Idée, page 491), or mayo mixed with a dab of Sriracha.

THIS DISH IS AN INVENTIVE crossbreeding of two classic dishes: sole amandine, in which the fish is finished with sautéed sliced almonds, and sole meunière, in which the fish, often whole, is sautéed in browned butter. In my version, I use baby flounder (easier to find in the market here than true sole), lightly coat the fillets with ground almonds, sauté them in browned butter, and serve them with toasted almonds and a sprinkling of parsley (borrowed from the meunière). It's a marriage of equal partners and one that I think would easily win familial approval on both sides of the aisle.

A word on quantity: Since I usually make this for my husband and myself, I've given you a recipe that serves two, but of course the recipe can be multiplied. If you have to prepare the fillets in batches, though, it's best to lightly cover the sautéed fillets and keep them in a 300-degree-F oven while you fry the remaining fish. The photo is on page 288.

⅓ cup ground almonds	About 2 tablespoons cold
1 tablespoon all-purpose flour	butter, preferably salted (you'll
Grated zest of ½ lemon	need more if you're cooking
Salt and freshly ground	in batches)
pepper	
4 baby flounder fillets, about	Lemon wedges, for serving
3 ounces each	Toasted sliced almonds, for
1 large egg yolk, lightly beaten	garnish
	Chopped fresh parsley, for
	garnish

Whisk the ground almonds, flour, and zest together, then season the mix with salt and pepper. Pat the fish fillets dry and, using a pastry brush, lightly coat one side of each fillet with a little of the beaten yolk. (I coat the side that would have had skin.) Dip the coated side of each fillet into the nut mixture.

Put a large nonstick skillet over medium heat. Add 1 tablespoon of the butter and a small pinch of salt, if your butter isn't salted, and cook the butter until it turns light brown, about 3 minutes. Slip the fillets into the skillet nut side down, without crowding, lower the heat, and cook for 3 minutes or so, until the coating is golden and the fish is cooked halfway through. Season the exposed side of each fillet with salt and pepper, add another ½ tablespoon cold butter to the pan, and very gently turn the fillets over. Cook, spooning some of the browned butter over the fillets once or twice, until the fish is opaque throughout, about 2 minutes more. If it looks like the pan is dry, add a little more butter. (If you weren't able to cook all the fillets in one pan, keep the cooked fish warm while you sauté the remaining fillets; see headnote.)

Give each fillet a squirt of lemon juice, then scatter over some toasted almonds and parsley. Have more lemon wedges at the table so you can give the fish another squeeze or two if needed.

skate with capers, cornichons, and brown butter sauce

HAPED LIKE A RUFFLE-EDGED FAN and tufted like a quilt, skate looks like an art school project. In French, skate is called *raie* (pronounced "ray"), and it is, indeed, a member of the stingray family, which explains why the edible part, the wing, has that beautiful triangular shape. Skate's most usual companion is black butter, a misnomer really, since the butter is cooked until it's a toasty brown and smells vaguely of hazelnuts before it gets a splash of vinegar and is poured over the fish. It's a terrific dish (see Bonne Idée), one often served with capers, and it inspired me to create this sassier version in which the golden butter and capers team up with cornichons and mustard.

MAKES 4 SERVINGS

SERVING
It's always nice to give the skate a soft pillow to rest on: think mashed potatoes (page 357) or Celery Root Puree (page 354). Choose something on the subtle side, and don't go for anything salty, since the vinegar, cornichons, and capers have enough to carry the plate.

STORING
Eat the skate as soon as it's sauced, and don't give a thought to leftovers.

All-purpose flour, for dredging	About 8 tablespoons (1 stick) unsalted butter
Salt and freshly ground pepper	¼ cup sherry vinegar
4 cleaned and boned skate wings or sections of wings, about 6 ounces each, patted dry	1 tablespoon grainy mustard, preferably French
	12 cornichons, rinsed and thinly sliced
	1½ tablespoons capers, rinsed

Center a rack in the oven and preheat the oven to 200 degrees F. Have a heatproof platter at hand.

Put about ½ cup flour on a plate or sheet of wax paper and season with salt and pepper. Run both sides of the skate wings through the flour and tap off the excess.

Place a large heavy-bottomed skillet over medium-high heat and drop in 2 tablespoons of the butter. When it melts and the bubbles calm down, slip in the skate. (If your pan can't comfortably hold all the wings at one time, do them in batches.) Cook the wings for about 3 minutes on a side, adding a little more butter if needed — the wings should be browned and opaque all the way through. Carefully transfer them to the heatproof platter, cover them with a foil tent, and keep warm in the oven while you make the sauce.

Pour out the butter remaining in the skillet and give the skillet a quick wipe with a paper towel. Return the skillet to medium heat and drop in the remaining 6 tablespoons butter. Cook the butter, swirling the pan, until it starts to turn a light brown — you might just catch the scent of hazelnuts. Add the vinegar and swirl the pan, then stir in the mustard, cornichons, and capers. Pull the skate out of the oven, spoon over the sauce, and head for the table.

BONNE IDÉE
Poached Skate and Beurre Noisette. Put the skate in a high-sided skillet or a Dutch oven and cover with cold water. Slice 2 peeled carrots, 1 onion, and 1 celery stalk and add them to the pot, along with a couple of black peppercorns, 2 bay leaves, and a pinch of salt. Bring to a boil, then lower the heat and simmer gently until the skate is cooked through and opaque; check after 10 minutes. Carefully lift the skate with a slotted spatula onto a heated platter and cover lightly. To make the sauce, melt 8 tablespoons (1 stick) unsalted butter in a skillet over low heat until it bubbles and foams and turns a light nutty brown. Pour in ¼ cup sherry vinegar. Swirl and drop in 3 to 4 tablespoons rinsed capers. Spoon the sauce over the skate and serve immediately.

cod and spinach roulades

MAKES 4 SERVINGS

SERVING
I don't usually serve anything on the same plate as the roulades or even alongside them. They're so dramatic that they can hold center stage on their own.

STORING
You can make the roulades a few hours ahead of time and keep them refrigerated until ready to steam. Leftover roulades can be chilled and served over salad the next day.

DISHES LIKE THIS ONE — a light, elegant fish mousse filled with lemony spinach, rolled into a chubby sausage shape, and steamed — used to be prepared by chefs in tall white toques working in grand French restaurants surrounded by scores of apprentices, who could do the kind of tedious work once required to get the mousse perfectly smooth. Now we press the button on the food processor, and in under five minutes, it's done . . . not that you have to tell anyone.

I make these roulades with cod, but you can use any mild-flavored white fish. I stuff them with a quickly made mix of fresh spinach (you can use frozen), onion, garlic, and the peel from a small preserved lemon, but, again, you can play around with this. Because the mousse is so light and its texture so smooth, you don't want anything that can't be pureed, but you do want something with a little personality. Chard, basil, arugula, roasted peppers, sun-dried tomatoes, even tapenade are all good starting points for the filling.

This recipe is in the spirit of Lyon's famed pike dumplings, *quenelles de brochet,* which are poached and then finished in any of a number of ways: with Nantua sauce, based on béchamel; classic béchamel; or beurre blanc. *Chez moi,* I use a very thin sauce of fresh tomatoes and lemon, but just a drizzle of fruity olive oil or a bit of pesto is fine too. If you want something gorgeous, use a few spoonfuls of Cheating-on-Winter Pea Soup (page 59) as the sauce.

FOR THE OPTIONAL
TOMATO-LEMON SAUCE
1 tablespoon unsalted butter
¾ pound ripe tomatoes, peeled, preferably, and seeded
1 garlic clove, split, germ removed, and sliced
  Peel from ½ small preserved lemon (see Sources; reserve the other half), finely chopped
  Salt and freshly ground pepper

FOR THE FILLING
1 tablespoon unsalted butter
1 small onion, finely chopped
1 small garlic clove, split, germ removed, and finely chopped

5–6 ounces baby spinach
1 tablespoon water
  Reserved peel from ½ small preserved lemon, finely chopped
  Salt and freshly ground pepper

FOR THE ROULADES
10 ounces cold skinless, boneless cod or other white fish fillet
2 large egg whites
½ cup very cold heavy cream
  Salt and freshly ground pepper

  Basil Pesto, homemade (page 488) or store-bought, for serving (optional)
  Extra-virgin olive oil, for serving (optional)

TO MAKE THE OPTIONAL SAUCE: Melt the butter in a large skillet over medium-low heat. Add the tomatoes and garlic and cook, stirring, for about 8 minutes, until the tomatoes are softened.

Spoon the sauce into a food processor (a mini will work for this) or blender and puree until it's as smooth as you'd like it — it can be a little chunky, if that's your preference. Toss in the preserved lemon peel and pulse briefly, then season with salt and pepper. *(The sauce can be made up to 1 day ahead and refrigerated.)*

TO MAKE THE FILLING: Melt the butter in a large skillet over medium heat. Toss in the onion and garlic and cook, stirring, just until they soften a bit, 2 to 3 minutes. Add the spinach and water and continue to cook and stir until the spinach wilts and softens, about 2 minutes.

Using a slotted spoon or a skimmer, lift the spinach out of the skillet, allowing it to drain, and onto a cutting board. Finely chop the spinach, then put it into a bowl, stir in the preserved lemon peel, and season with salt and pepper.

TO MAKE THE ROULADES: Cut the cod into small pieces and put them in a food processor, along with the egg whites and cream. Pulse and then process, scraping down the sides of the bowl frequently, until you have a thick, smooth, but very sticky mousse. Season with salt and lots of pepper.

For each roulade, tear off a piece of plastic wrap that's about a foot long and position it with a long side toward you. Using a rubber spatula, put one quarter of the fish mousse in the center of the plastic and spread it into a rectangle about 3 x 5 inches (long side toward you). It will be pretty thin and it probably won't be very even, but that's okay. Spoon one quarter of the spinach filling lengthwise across the center of the mousse, cajoling the filling into a band that fills the center third of the rectangle. Using the plastic to help you, roll the package into a sausage. Because the mousse is so sticky, you probably won't be able to completely hide the filling inside the sausage, but it's fine if you can see a strip of spinach peeking out the ends of the mousse. Draw the plastic up around the roulade and tighten and twist it at the ends, like a firecracker. Repeat with the remaining mousse and filling, making 4 roulades. *(The roulades can be made up to 4 hours ahead and refrigerated.)*

When you're ready to cook the roulades, set up a steamer: put a little water in the bottom of a pot and place a rack or steaming tray above it, or use a pasta pot with an insert, and bring to a boil. Place the quartet of roulades on the steamer, cover the pot, and steam for 10 minutes, at which point the mousse will feel springy to the touch.

Meanwhile, if you made the sauce, reheat it over gentle heat or in a microwave oven.

Gently transfer the roulades to a board (they're pretty fragile) and use scissors to snip the plastic so that you can peel it away. With a sharp knife and a gentle motion, slash each roulade diagonally into quarters, taking care not to cut all the way through.

If you're using the sauce, spoon a thin layer of it into the bottom of four warm shallow soup plates, gently fan the roulades out, and place them on top of the sauce. If you're using pesto or olive oil, fan the roulades and drizzle the pesto or oil over them.

monkfish and double carrots

MAKES 4 SERVINGS

SERVING
If you want to make this special dish even more special, start with a spoonful of Celery Root Puree (page 354) or mashed potatoes (page 357) on each plate, then add the carrots, monkfish, sauce, and bacon.

STORING
You can make the carrots a few hours ahead of time and then, right before serving, reheat them and finish the sauce with the last tablespoon of butter.

BONNE IDÉE
Scallops, Shrimp, or Flounder with Double Carrots. You can replace the monkfish medallions with sea scallops — figure 4 scallops per person and cook them for just 2 minutes on a side; with jumbo shrimp — figure about 5 per person — cook for about 2 minutes on a side; or 4 flounder fillets, 4 to 5 ounces each. For flounder, pat the fillets dry, dredge them in flour seasoned with salt and pepper, and sauté them until they are golden on both sides and just cooked through, about 3 minutes on a side.

WITH ITS TRANSLUCENT WHITE MEAT and firm texture, monkfish has sometimes been called "poor man's lobster." (Because of its diet of shellfish, it even tastes faintly like lobster.) An ugly fish, it was almost never found on restaurant menus in America and only rarely in France, where chefs, like home cooks, might prepare it for their families, but not their guests. Now, a decade or so later, monkfish, or *lotte,* is so popular that it costs more than lobster!

Like lobster, *lotte* takes to gentle cooking and works well with vegetables and herbs. Here medallions of monkfish, cut from the tail, are quickly sautéed and served with a light carrot sauce, an accompaniment that's really good with other kinds of fish and shellfish, including shrimp, scallops, and even flounder fillets (see Bonne Idée).

While chefs vie for monkfish cheeks and liver, it's the tail that's the meatiest and most prized part of the fish. It should not be cooked until it has been skinned, and trust me, you don't want to be the one doing the skinning — ask your fishmonger to take on the task.

FOR THE CARROTS	FOR THE MONKFISH
1 cup carrot juice (store-bought is fine)	4 strips bacon
2 tablespoons cold unsalted butter	1 tablespoon unsalted butter
1 tablespoon extra-virgin olive oil	4 monkfish medallions, 5–6 ounces each
2 rosemary sprigs	Salt and freshly ground pepper
1 pound carrots, trimmed, peeled, and cut into ½-inch-thick coins	
Salt and freshly ground pepper	

TO MAKE THE CARROTS: Put the carrot juice, 1 tablespoon of the butter, the olive oil, and rosemary in a medium saucepan and bring to a boil. Add the carrots, season with salt and pepper, cover the pan, reduce the heat to low, and cook at a simmer for 10 minutes.

Remove the lid and, still over low heat, continue to cook the carrots until they're tender enough to be pierced easily with the tip of a knife. Take the pan off the burner. *(The carrots can be made to this point up to 3 hours ahead, covered, and refrigerated.)*

MEANWHILE, MAKE THE MONKFISH: Place the bacon in a large skillet over medium heat and cook until the bacon is browned on one side. Carefully turn the strips over and cook until browned on the second side. Lift the bacon onto a plate lined with a double layer of paper towels, and blot away as much fat as you can (set the skillet aside). Cut the bacon into thin strips or crumble it.

Pour off all but about 2 teaspoons of the fat from the skillet. Add the butter

and put the skillet over medium-high heat. When the bubbles from the melted butter have subsided, slip in the pieces of monkfish. Cook for 4 minutes, then flip the pieces over, season with salt and pepper, and cook for another 4 minutes or so — you want the fish to be brown on the outside and opaque in the center. Remove the fish from the skillet and keep it lightly covered in a warm place while you finish the carrots (a matter of minutes).

TO FINISH THE CARROTS: Cut the remaining tablespoon of cold butter into 3 pieces. Bring the carrots back to a boil, then, using a slotted spoon, transfer the carrots to a bowl. Remove the saucepan from the heat and, one by one, swirl in the pieces of butter. Taste for salt and pepper and remove the rosemary sprigs.

Divide the carrots among four warm dinner plates. Spoon over some of the sauce, top the carrots with the monkfish, drizzle with the remaining sauce, and finish with the bacon bits.

mediterranean swordfish
with frilly herb salad

MAKES 4 SERVINGS

WHEN I FIRST HEARD THE WORD *ESPADON* ("*es*-pa-*dahn*"), I thought it was the title for a medieval cavalier, and I guess I wasn't so far off, since the rightful owner of the name, the swordfish, might easily be considered a swashbuckler of sorts. For sure, it grabs pride of place (along with tuna) in the Paris fishmongers' stalls: it's a big fish and is often settled on the highest mound of ice the vendor has. The swordfish sold in France is normally fished from the Mediterranean Sea, and its color is often grayer than that of our American catch. And where we would normally buy inch-thick steaks of the fish to grill, the French are more likely to ask for a slice maybe half that thickness that can be quickly cooked in a skillet. (If you'd like to go American and grill a thicker piece of fish, see Bonne Idée.)

Whether your fish comes from the North Atlantic or the warm Mediterranean, the marinade will give it the fragrance and flavor of the Riviera. A combination of rosemary, lemons, capers, chiles, and olive oil, it does double duty: it moistens and boldly flavors the swordfish, then it turns into a sauce, so that every last drop of goodness is captured.

While the fish and its salty-tangy sauce are good with almost any kind of side dish, from simply grilled vegetables to mashed potatoes, no matter what you choose as a go-along, I hope you'll also make the herb salad — it's the perfect finish for the fish. You can mix the herbs while the fish is marinating, but wait until the last minute to toss the delicate leaves with the oil and lemon juice, so you preserve their flavor and frilliness.

BE PREPARED: The fish needs to marinate for an hour.

FOR THE SWORDFISH
Finely grated zest of 2 lemons
About ¼ cup fresh lemon juice
1 small onion, quartered and thinly sliced
2 tablespoons capers
4 teaspoons caper juice (from the jar)
6 tablespoons extra-virgin olive oil, plus 1–2 tablespoons for sautéing
1 teaspoon sea salt
Big pinch of piment d'Espelette (see Sources) or red pepper flakes
Teensy pinch of sugar

4 teaspoons minced fresh rosemary
4 swordfish steaks, ½ to ¾ inch thick, about 5 ounces each

FOR THE HERB SALAD
2 cups loosely packed fresh parsley leaves (from 1 big bunch parsley)
½ cup loosely packed mixed fresh herb leaves, such as oregano, marjoram, tarragon (just a little), thyme (also just a little), and chervil (if you can find it)
1 teaspoon fresh lemon juice
1 teaspoon extra-virgin olive oil
Salt and freshly ground pepper

SERVING
The fish goes well with a side of Pancetta Green Beans (page 333) or the more substantial Lemon-Barley Pilaf (page 383), but if I'm serving it during the summer, my favorite accompaniment is a dish from the fish's neighborhood, Tomatoes Provençal (page 344). And, for summer, both the swordfish and the tomatoes are excellent at room temperature, making them perfect for outdoor eating.

STORING
You can marinate the fish up to 4 hours in advance (keep it in the refrigerator and bring it to room temperature before cooking it), and you can toss the herbs together a few hours in advance as well (chill them in a plastic bag). If you'd like, you can even sauté the fish ahead of time and serve it at room temperature. If you've got fish left over, cover it well, store it in the fridge, and use it to make a salad the next day. It's particularly good with arugula, red onions, and tomatoes; dress the salad with any leftover marinade, or lemon juice and olive oil, or, best choice, tapenade (homemade, page 487, or store-bought) thinned with some olive oil. What could be more Mediterranean?

BONNE IDÉE
Grilled Swordfish. Heat your barbecue to high and brush the rack with oil. Scrape the marinade from the fish, lightly pat it dry, and grill for 2 minutes on one side, then carefully turn it over to cook for another 2 minutes on the other. Nick the fish so that you can check that it's opaque at the center; if it's not, cook for another minute or so until done. If you're using thicker (about 1 inch) American-style steaks, you'll probably need to grill them for 4 to 5 minutes on each side — check at the 4-minute mark. Serve with the warmed marinade and salad.

TO MARINATE THE SWORDFISH: Whisk together all the ingredients except 2 teaspoons of the rosemary and the swordfish in a nonreactive 9-x-13-inch baking pan (I use a Pyrex roaster), or put them in a jumbo zipper-lock plastic bag and shake them around. Put the swordfish in the pan or bag and turn it so that it's well coated with the marinade. Cover with plastic or seal the bag and marinate the fish, turning it a couple of times, for 1 hour at room temperature. *(The fish can marinate for up to 4 hours in the refrigerator; bring to room temperature before proceeding.)*

TO MAKE THE SALAD: Toss all the herbs together in a bowl. Hold off on dressing the salad.

TO COOK THE SWORDFISH: Remove the fish from the marinade and scrape any ingredients that have stuck to the fish back into the marinade; reserve the marinade. Using paper towels, lightly pat the fish dry.

In a large skillet (nonstick is good), warm 1 tablespoon olive oil over high heat. When it's hot, slip in the swordfish. (If your skillet isn't large enough to hold the 4 pieces, cook the fish in 2 batches, adding more oil to the pan as needed.) Cook for 3 minutes, then carefully turn the fish over and cook for 2 to 3 minutes on the other side. You want the fish to be opaque in the center — swordfish is not one of those fish best served rare. Make a small cut in the center of the fish to check for doneness; depending on the thickness of your fish, you may need to cook it a little longer. Transfer the fish to a platter and cover loosely.

Heat the reserved marinade in a microwave oven or in a small saucepan over medium heat until it's hot but not boiling. Drizzle it over the swordfish and sprinkle with the remaining 2 teaspoons minced rosemary.

Toss the herb salad with the lemon juice and olive oil, season with salt and pepper, and top each piece of fish with a little mound of salad.

piment d'espelette

A chile pepper from the Pays Basque whose name is protected under an A.O.C. (appellation d'origine contrôlée), piment d'Espelette is both mildly sweet and mildly hot. When you're in the Pays Basque, it may be the only pepper you'll get.

From simple cafés to elegant restaurants, you'll find the dried ground chile in a teensy bowl with a spoon; occasionally it will be served in a peppermill. And if you go to Espelette, the *piment*'s hometown, in the fall, you'll see the peppers drying everywhere, hanging against the whitewashed walls of houses. The sight looks as if it was stage-directed for tourists, but the method is as practical as it is picturesque.

salmon with basil tapenade

THE FIRST TIME I TASTED SALMON with piquant black olive tapenade, I had one of those aha moments: they're the proverbial match made in heaven. For this recipe, the tapenade is used as both a stuffing — it goes into a pocket cut into the salmon — and a little sauce. If you'd like, serve the salmon with a tomato and red pepper salsa (page 305) or even a mango mix (see the chatini on page 489), but it's delicious and quite elegant on its own.

¼ cup Black Olive Tapenade, homemade (page 487) or store-bought
¼ cup minced fresh basil and/ or mint
Grated zest and juice of 1 lemon

Freshly ground pepper
4 pieces salmon fillets, cut from the thick center portion, skin-on, 5 ounces each
Salt
About ⅓ cup olive oil

MAKES 4 SERVINGS

SERVING
This dish is really good over steamed spinach (page 331) or alongside green beans (page 333), which have an affinity for tapenade (think salade Niçoise).

STORING
While the fish should be served as soon as it's cooked, you can make the tapenade mixture 1 to 2 days ahead and keep it covered in the refrigerator.

Center a rack in the oven and preheat the oven to 450 degrees F. Pull out an ovenproof skillet that can hold the 4 salmon fillets, or choose a skillet to use stovetop and a baking pan for the oven.

In a small bowl, stir together the tapenade, 2 tablespoons of the herbs, and half the lemon zest and juice. Season with pepper — you probably won't need salt, since the tapenade is salty. Spoon out a generous tablespoon of the tapenade and keep it aside to make the sauce. Put the remaining tapenade into a small zipper-lock plastic bag, seal the bag, and snip off a small corner. (*The tapenade mixture can be made up to 2 days ahead and refrigerated.*)

You need to cut 2 pockets to fill with tapenade in each salmon fillet, and the pockets should run parallel to the skin. The easiest way to do this is to put the fillets on a cutting board, skin side down, and, using a paring knife or a long thin knife, slice through the fish to create 2 slits, each about 1 inch long, on either side of the center of the fillet. Squeeze a little of the tapenade into each pocket, "massaging" the salmon if necessary so that the tapenade fills the pockets evenly but isn't squirting out the sides. Season the fillets lightly with salt and pepper.

Heat 2 tablespoons of the olive oil in the skillet over high heat. When it's hot, slip the fish into the pan, top side down, and cook for 2 minutes, then turn the fillets over and cook for 2 more minutes — this will give the fish nice color. Slide the skillet into the oven, or transfer the fish to the baking pan, and roast the fillets for 6 minutes, at which point they should still be just the slightest bit jiggly in the center. Put the skillet or pan in a warm place, cover the fillets lightly with foil, and let rest for 5 minutes.

Meanwhile, to make the sauce, stir 3 to 4 tablespoons of olive oil into the reserved tapenade (it will look like a thin vinaigrette with speckles of olive). Season to taste with more lemon zest and juice, stir in the remaining 2 tablespoons herbs, and finish with salt and pepper.

Serve the salmon with the sauce spooned over it.

BONNE IDÉE
Salmon is such a team player that it can easily be paired with finely chopped or pureed sun-dried tomatoes pepped up with herbs and lemon juice — make the tomato sauce just as you would the tapenade sauce; or with a mix of roasted garlic and white bean puree — this is great with the tapenade sauce; or with a riff on the recipe's tapenade, with finely chopped preserved lemon peel (see Sources) and a tiny bit of the lemon's liquid instead of the fresh zest and juice, and rosemary instead of basil or mint.

roasted salmon and lentils

MAKES 4 SERVINGS

SERVING
This is a complete meal —
and a very good one.

STORING
Any leftover salmon will be
good at room temperature
the next day. Should
you have leftover lentils,
keep them covered in the
refrigerator, and reheat
them gently in a saucepan
on the stove or in a
microwave oven; add some
of the reserved broth, if you
kept it, or water to the pan
or bowl.

LENTILS ARE SO DARK AND EARTHY that you might think they're only meant to go with meat, but it turns out they're a terrific mate for salmon, something bistro cooks figured out a while ago. The combination of rich, slightly sweet pink salmon on top of the minerally lentils is not just satisfying, it's good-looking too. And it's easy to put together, since the lentils can be prepared ahead and the salmon needs less than a quarter of an hour of high-heat roasting. Like many simple dishes, this one takes to tweaking, even to deluxeing — I've seen it made grand with the addition of truffles, which are wonderful with both lentils and salmon. While you might not have a hunk of black truffle available to chop and add to the lentils or to shave over the salmon when it's hot from the oven, you can get a hint of the effect by finishing the dish with a few drops of very fine truffle oil. And when I say a few drops, I mean it: with truffle oil, quality is a must, and restraint an imperative.

1 cup lentils du Puy (French green lentils)	Salt
1 clove	1 1¼-pound piece salmon fillet, cut from the thick center portion, skin on, at room temperature
1 small onion	
1 medium carrot, trimmed, peeled, and cut into 4–6 pieces	
	Olive oil
	Freshly ground pepper
1 celery stalk, trimmed and cut into 4–6 pieces	
1 bay leaf	Chopped fresh parsley and/or snipped fresh chives, for garnish (optional)
3½ cups chicken broth, vegetable broth, or water	

Put the lentils in a strainer, pick through them, and discard any bits of stone that might have escaped the packers; rinse under cold running water.

Turn the lentils into a medium saucepan, cover them with cold water, bring to a boil, and cook for 2 minutes; drain the lentils in the strainer. Rinse the lentils again and rinse out the saucepan.

Press the clove into the onion and toss the onion, carrot, celery, and bay leaf into the pan. Pour in the broth, stir in the lentils, and bring to a boil. Lower the heat to a steady simmer and cook for 25 to 30 minutes, or until the lentils are almost tender. As the lentils cook, skim off the dark foam that rises to the top. Season with salt and cook until they're tender, 5 to 10 minutes more.

While the lentils are cooking, center a rack in the oven and preheat the oven to 475 degrees F. Line a baking sheet with foil.

Place a strainer over a large measuring cup and drain the lentils, reserving the broth; set the pan aside. Pick out the vegetables and discard the clove and bay leaf; if you'd like to serve the carrots, celery, and onion with the lentils (I always do, although they are very soft), cut them into very small dice. Rinse out the saucepan.

Put the salmon on the foil-lined baking sheet, rub a little olive oil over the top, and season with salt and pepper. Slide the baking sheet into the oven and roast the salmon for about 12 minutes, or until it is firm on the outside and still pink and just the tiniest bit jiggly at the center (nick the thickest part with a slender knife to test). If the salmon is done before you've finished the lentils, cover it lightly with a foil tent and leave it on the counter to rest.

Meanwhile, put ¾ cup of the cooked lentils into a food processor (a mini processor is fine) or blender and add ½ cup of the reserved broth. Whir for a minute or so, until the lentils are reduced to a puree, then scrape the puree and the remaining cooked lentils back into the saucepan. Pour in another ½ cup broth, add the diced vegetables, if you kept them, and season with salt and pepper as needed. (*You can make the lentils to this point and keep them, covered, at room temperature for a few hours or in the refrigerator overnight.*)

Return the saucepan to medium heat and cook, stirring, only until the lentils are warmed through again.

Divide the lentils among four warm shallow soup plates. Slice the salmon into 4 portions and place a piece in the center of each plate. Drizzle the salmon and lentils very lightly with olive oil, dust the top of the fish with parsley and/ or chives, if you'd like, and serve immediately.

salmon and tomatoes en papillote

MAKES 4 SERVINGS

SERVING
You can put the packets on dinner plates and open them at the table or open them in the kitchen and arrange the ingredients on plates. If you plate the fish, you might want to finish each dish with a little minced fresh basil or some snipped fresh chives.

STORING
You can construct the packets up to 6 hours ahead and refrigerate them until 30 minutes before it's time to bake them. If the packets still feel cold when you're ready to slide them into the oven, add a minute to the baking time.

SALMON, SO RICH IN THE OILS that are good for us, is an ideal candidate to cook *en papillote,* in foil packets, because those healthful oils are also helpful in cooking — they self-baste the fish while it's in its little pouch.

I often make this recipe for lunch or when we've got friends coming for dinner and I don't have much time to either shop or prep. The ingredients are always available — salmon is as easy to get in Paris as it is in Peoria, and grape tomatoes are sweet and at hand throughout the year. The time needed to get everything together is under thirty minutes (even if you take the optional step of pan-roasting the tomatoes), plus you can do everything ahead if you want to. The packets look like presents, and no one knows what's in them until they're opened.

Not surprisingly, this technique and combination of ingredients work well with other fish — try it with cod or sea bass (choose a nice thick cut, and the baking time will be the same). Also keep in mind that you can easily increase or decrease the number of servings (I sometimes make this for just myself). The only caveat is that you've got to leave space between the packets, so if you're going to make more than four papillotes, arrange the extras on another baking sheet.

About 2½ tablespoons extra-virgin olive oil, or a few spoonfuls more to taste

16 grape tomatoes or small cherry tomatoes

24 large fresh basil leaves
Salt and freshly ground white pepper

4 pieces salmon fillets (skinless or not), cut from the thick center portion, 5 ounces each

2 spring onions, trimmed and thinly sliced, or 4 scallions, white and light green parts only, thinly sliced (optional)

1 lemon

4 thyme or rosemary sprigs

Center a rack in the oven and preheat the oven to 475 degrees F. Have a baking sheet at hand. Cut four 12-inch squares of foil (I like to use nonstick foil for this).

If you'd like to sear the tomatoes (it's not necessary but will intensify their flavor), warm 1 tablespoon of the olive oil in a small skillet over medium-high heat and cook the tomatoes, turning them as needed, just until their skins are wrinkled and bubbly, about 3 minutes. Remove from the heat.

Put 5 basil leaves in the center of each piece of foil. Sprinkle the basil with a little salt and white pepper, top with a piece of salmon (if the salmon has skin, lay it skin side down), drizzle a teaspoon or so of oil over each piece, and season the fish with salt and white pepper. Put the tomatoes on one side of the salmon and grate the lemon zest over everything. If you're using the spring onions or scallions, scatter them over the fish and tomatoes. Give the salmon a squirt of lemon juice, then cut 8 thin slices from the lemon and put 2 slices on top of each piece of fish. Finish with a basil leaf and a sprig of thyme or rosemary; moisten with olive oil.

Seal the packets, making sure they are airtight and that there's puff space between the fish and the top of its cocoon. *(The packets can be assembled up to 6 hours ahead and refrigerated; remove from the refrigerator 30 minutes before baking.)*

Put the packets on the baking sheet, slide the setup into the oven, and bake for 10 minutes if you like your fish slightly jiggly in the center (great for salmon), or for 2 minutes longer if you want your fish more well done.

Serve the salmon immediately, either *en papillote* or spooned onto plates.

spice-crusted tuna

MAKES 4 SERVINGS

SERVING
I usually drizzle the tuna
with olive oil and serve it
with lemon wedges, but
it's equally good with a
spoonful of warmed crème
fraîche, and it's very nice
with any kind of vegetable
or tropical fruit salsa or
chutney. Serving the tuna
with some guacamole
(page 22) would be
unorthodox but delicious
nonetheless, especially in
summer.

STORING
The tuna is very good at
room temperature and,
should you have leftovers,
it's delicious sliced and
served over a green salad.

THE LATIN QUARTER BISTRO LE PRÉ VERRE made a huge splash when it opened with a menu built around spices — not just a pinch of this and a dash of that, but bold ones that played the dramatic lead in every dish. While this would not be out of the ordinary for us Americans, who are used to incendiary foods from all parts of the world, it was news to the French, who normally keep their food tame, the better to appreciate the wine that goes with it. Happily, the team at Le Pré Verre found wines from France's own Southwest to match their dishes spice for spice, and they quickly won a cosmopolitan clientele and a following for what became their signature dish, spice-crusted tuna.

I don't know exactly what Le Pré Verre's tuna was patted down with — my guess is black, green, white, and pink peppercorns; coriander; fennel; cumin; ginger; and maybe some Szechuan pepper too — and the team wasn't telling, but over the years, I've come up with this recipe for my own pared-down, not nearly as hot version that's simple, quick to make, great tasting, and perfect with red wine.

Seeds from 6 cardamom pods	4 pieces tuna, about ½ inch thick, 5–6 ounces each
2 teaspoons white peppercorns	About 3 tablespoons extra-virgin olive oil
2 teaspoons coriander seeds	
4 thin slices peeled fresh ginger	
Salt, preferably fleur de sel	Lemon wedges, for serving

If you have a mortar and pestle, put the cardamom, peppercorns, coriander, ginger, and a generous pinch of salt in the mortar and, using the pestle, pound the spices until they are coarsely broken. You don't want to pulverize them; part of the excitement of the dish is in the spices being discernible. If you don't have a mortar and pestle, crush the spices in a mini processor or blender, or finely chop the ginger and crush the other spices by wrapping them in a kitchen towel and bashing them with the bottom of a heavy skillet or the heel or back of a chef's knife.

Rub the tuna with a little olive oil. Sprinkle the crushed spices evenly over both sides of each piece of fish, then press the spices into the fish, patting just firmly enough so they stick.

Put a large skillet over high heat (a nonstick skillet works nicely) and pour in 2 tablespoons olive oil. When the oil is hot, add the tuna and cook for 2 minutes, then flip the fish over and cook for about 2 minutes more — a generous third of the center of the tuna should remain pink. Of course, if you like your tuna better cooked, go ahead and give each side a little more time in the pan.

Serve with just a drizzle of olive oil and lemon wedges for squeezing.

tuna confit with black olive tapenade and tomato salsa

USUALLY THE WORD *CONFIT* REFERS TO DUCK CONFIT, a dish from France's Southwest in which duck legs are salted and then cooked in their own fat, a way to both preserve and flavor them. It's a very old technique, but it's trendy these days, especially in Paris bistros, where chefs are likely to confit fish as well as fowl solely for the purpose of flavoring it.

I've seen chefs confit cod and halibut, but the dish I like best is tuna confit: a thick slice of tuna spends the night in a bath of extra-virgin olive oil, herbs, spices, sun-dried tomatoes, salted lemons, and aromatic garlic and onions, then, in true confit fashion, is cooked slowly, so that in the end you can call its texture velvety without being accused of exaggeration. Surprisingly, even though the tuna is oven-poached in a cup of oil, it isn't oily. In fact, most of the oil you start with will be left over, and you'll be glad: it makes a great vinaigrette for a salad, especially one like salade Niçoise.

Speaking of things from the South of France, the confit is served with a Provençal black olive tapenade and a tomato salsa, which can be tossed together quickly a couple of hours before dinner. When you've got the tuna, tapenade, and tomatoes, you've got a complete meal that's casually elegant and equally good straight from the oven, at room temperature, or chilled.

BE PREPARED: The tuna needs to marinate for at least 6 hours, or for as long as overnight, and then come to room temperature before it goes into the oven.

MAKES 4 SERVINGS

SERVING
I serve this in shallow soup plates, and while it's fine as is, it's really nice set over a bed of mashed potatoes (page 357) or Celery Root Puree (page 354).

STORING
Any leftover confit and marinade can be covered well and kept in the refrigerator for up to 2 days. Serve it chilled or at room temperature (my preference), or use it in Salade Niçoise (page 125).

FOR THE TUNA

1 1-pound piece tuna, about 1 inch thick

2 small (or 1 large) preserved lemons (see Sources), halved, seeds removed, and thinly sliced, plus 1 tablespoon liquid from the preserved lemons

6 sun-dried tomatoes (dry or oil-packed), cut into short slender strips

3 garlic cloves, smashed and peeled

2 spring onions, trimmed and thinly sliced, or 1 small white onion, thinly sliced

1 celery stalk, trimmed and thinly sliced

3 parsley sprigs, leaves only, chopped

1 thyme sprig, leaves only, chopped

1 rosemary sprig, leaves only, chopped

1½ teaspoons fleur de sel or 1 teaspoon fine sea salt

½ teaspoon red pepper flakes, or to taste

Finely grated zest and juice of 2 lemons

About 1 cup extra-virgin olive oil

½ pint grape tomatoes, halved

½ red bell pepper, cored, seeded, and finely chopped

1 tablespoon minced preserved lemon

3 Peppadew peppers or sweet pickled cherry peppers, finely chopped (optional)

1 tablespoon extra-virgin olive oil

1½ teaspoons liquid from the preserved lemons

Pinch of piment d'Espelette (see Sources) or cayenne

Fleur de sel or other sea salt to taste

Black olive tapenade, home-made (page 487) or store-bought, for serving

TO MAKE THE TUNA: Cut the tuna crosswise in half, so that it will fit into a 9-x-5-inch nonreactive loaf pan (I use Pyrex). You can use a nonreactive 9-inch square pan, but depending on the size of the tuna, you might have to use a little more oil to cover it.

Put all the ingredients except the tuna, lemon juice, liquid from the preserved lemons, and olive oil into the pan and mix them together well. Add the tuna and use your hands to turn it around in the seasonings so that it's evenly coated on all sides.

Whisk the lemon juice, preserved lemon juice, and 1 cup olive oil in a bowl and pour over the tuna. If the oil doesn't cover the tuna, add a little more. Stir to mix up the seasonings a bit, cover the pan tightly with plastic wrap, and refrigerate for at least 6 hours, or as long as overnight.

An hour or so before you're ready to cook the fish, remove it from the refrigerator and let it come to room temperature. (You can make the tomato salsa now and keep it covered on the counter.)

Center a rack in the oven and preheat the oven to 225 degrees F. Line a baking sheet with a silicone baking mat or foil.

Remove the plastic wrap and give the liquid and seasonings another stir. Put the pan on the baking sheet and cover it with a new sheet of plastic wrap (the temperature is so low that the wrap is in no danger of melting) or seal the pan with a sheet of nonstick aluminum foil. (Don't use regular aluminum foil, because if it comes in contact with the acidic marinade, it will turn black and discolor the fish.)

Slow-bake the tuna for 1 hour. When confited, the tuna will be firm, but it may still be rosy in the center.

MEANWHILE, MAKE THE TOMATO SALSA: Put all the ingredients in a bowl and stir to combine. *(The salsa can be made up to 2 hours ahead and kept covered at room temperature.)*

TO SERVE: The tuna can be served warm or left to cool to room temperature. Carefully transfer the tuna to a cutting board. Cut it into long slices, the way you'd cut beef, and transfer to plates. Spoon over some of the lemon, sun-dried tomatoes, and other seasonings, as well as a generous spoonful or two of the cooking liquid. Top with the salsa and a dab of the tapenade. (You can pass more at the table.)

seafood pot-au-feu

MAKES 4 SERVINGS

SERVING
Because this is really a stew, it's best served in wide shallow soup plates. I like to arrange the plates in the kitchen, but it's just as nice to bring the pot to the table and serve from there. Serve with forks, knives, and soupspoons.

STORING
While you can cook the vegetables a little ahead of time, the dish should be served as soon as the fish is poached. If there's leftover poached fish, make it part of a salad the next day.

THINK OF THIS AS THE CLASSIC POT-AU-FEU'S lighter, brighter, quicker cousin, a dish for the spring and summer. Also think of it as a fooler, since as light as it is (there's just about no fat in the mix), its flavors are deep and complex, the happy result of poaching a succession of ingredients in a simple broth. First come the vegetables — potatoes, onions, carrots, leeks, mushrooms, and bright green sugar snaps — each one adding a layer of flavor; then comes the seafood — salmon, scallops, and mussels — each adding a little richness and a lot of interest.

Because this dish is simple, relatively fast to put together (the cooking time is counted in minutes, not pot-au-feu's usual hours), and invariably beautiful, it feels a little like a cheat. The first time I served it, a friend asked if it was as difficult and time-consuming to make as it looked. He seemed mildly disappointed when I confessed that it was really rather easy. I think he wanted to feel that I'd fussed a little more for him. If your conscience gets the best of you and you feel like you've got to fuss, make an aïoli or pesto — or both — to serve alongside.

For an even lighter version, try the all-vegetable pot-au-feu on page 378.

3 cups chicken broth
1 cup water
1 bay leaf
½ teaspoon grated fresh ginger or 1 teaspoon ground ginger
1 strip lemon zest
Salt and freshly ground white pepper
½ pound potatoes (new potatoes or small Yukon Golds), scrubbed
2 spring onions, trimmed, or 4 scallions, white and light green parts only
2 carrots, trimmed and peeled
1 leek, white and light green parts only

4 mushrooms, cleaned and trimmed
1 pound mussels, scrubbed, debearded if necessary
1 pound skinless salmon fillet, cut from the thickest part of the fish
12 sea scallops, side muscle removed
½ pound sugar snap peas

Aïoli, homemade (see Bonne Idées, page 490) or store-bought, and/or pesto, home-made (page 488) or store-bought, for serving (optional)

Pour the chicken broth and water into a Dutch oven or large high-sided skillet with a cover (I often use a nonstick pan that's shaped like a wok). Toss in the bay leaf, ginger, zest, some salt (start with ½ teaspoon), and a little white pepper. Bring to a boil, lower the heat, cover the pot, and simmer for 5 minutes.

You'll be cutting the vegetables and poaching them in succession, so while the broth is simmering, start by halving the new potatoes or cutting the Yukon

Golds into cubes about 2 inches on a side. Add the potatoes to the pot, cover, and simmer for 5 minutes.

Meanwhile, cut the spring onions or scallions lengthwise in half and rinse them to make sure they're free of dirt, then cut each half lengthwise into thirds (they won't hold together, and that's okay). If your carrots are thick, cut them in half the long way, then cut them crosswise into quarters; if they're slender, just quarter them. Cut the leek lengthwise in half, rinse it under cold running water to get all the dirt out from between the layers, and then cut each piece crosswise into quarters.

Add this batch of vegetables to the pot, cover, and simmer for 5 minutes. While the vegetables are cooking, thinly slice the mushrooms, then toss them in and cook for 5 minutes more. Using a slotted spoon or skimmer, transfer the vegetables to a bowl and cover. (*You can make the pot-au-feu up to this point a few hours ahead. Cover the broth and the vegetables and refrigerate until needed. When you're ready to continue, bring the vegetables to room temperature and the broth to a boil.*)

With the broth at a light simmer, add the mussels. Cover and cook just until the mussels open — check after 3 minutes. Using a slotted spoon, transfer the mussels to a bowl as they open. When the mussels are cool enough to handle, remove them from their shells and discard the shells; pour any liquid that has accumulated in the bottom of the bowl into the broth; discard any mussels that do not open.

Cut the salmon into 4 even pieces (I cut the fillet in half lengthwise and crosswise, making a cross, so that each piece has a thick meaty section). Slip them into the broth, cover, and poach for 6 minutes. Taste the broth and add a little more salt and white pepper, if you'd like. Add the scallops to the pot, followed by the mussels, the sugar snap peas, and the reserved vegetables. Cover and give everything another 2 to 3 minutes to warm up.

To serve, fish out the vegetables with the skimmer or slotted spoon — the mussels might come along with the vegetables. Top each serving with a piece of salmon and 3 scallops, and spoon over some broth. If you're serving aïoli and/or pesto, you can either put some directly on the fish or mix it into the broth.

mussels

For the first half of my life, I thought of mussels as the kind of dish my mother would have told me to avoid on a first date; now I think of them as just fine for dates and dinner parties. I owe the flip to a woman of a certain age who, unbeknownst to herself, taught me how to turn the admittedly messy job of eating mussels into an act acceptable in polite society.

We were in a small seaside restaurant in Cannes, and Mme. Mussel was at a table directly in our line of vision. She was beautifully dressed, perfectly coiffed, freshly manicured, and a regular — you could tell by the way she was greeted and the fact that her *coupe de Champagne* was brought to her the instant she was settled. But she wouldn't have held our attention had it not been for the mussels.

Mussel dishes like moules marinière (page 312), and any of its many cousins, are always served with a small two-pronged fork, so you can pull the mollusk out of its shell, and a bowl for the discarded shells, which, in my case, always ends up looking like something an angry tide dragged in. That is, until I started mimicking Madame, whose discard bowl could have been shot for the cover of a fancy food magazine. Here's what she did: As she finished each mussel, she'd fit the small end of the shell into the mouth of a shell already in the bowl. And when she'd circled the rim, she'd start on the next circle, forming the shells into a spiraling conga line that, when she'd finished her dish, looked like a necklace from some exotic island. It made the whole act of eating with your fingers seem elegant.

Of course, this technique works only if you've got patience, but here patience is rewarded: the shell game takes seconds longer than just tossing the empties, but it makes the pleasure of the dish last longer.

Here's one more mussel-eating tip (not as refined as the necklace trick, but neat in its own way): Choose a small mussel as your first and pluck the meat out with your fork, then retire the fork and use that shell as pincers for the rest of the dish. The shells are as efficient as the fork and far more fun.

moules marinière

MAKES 4 MAIN-
COURSE SERVINGS
OR 6 STARTER
SERVINGS

SERVING

Don't wait even a second to get this to the table — the hotter the mussels, the better. I like to serve them straight from the pot, making sure that everyone's bowl has a pile of mussels, which should be eaten with fingers, and some sauce, which can be eaten with a spoon or just sopped up with bread. Have a bowl for the empty shells on the table.

STORING

If there are mussels left over, remove them from their shells, wrap them well, and keep them covered in the refrigerator to be used in a salad the following day. Mussels are a classic addition to a salad of leftover rice mixed with herbs, vinaigrette, and, often, peas.

IF FRESH MUSSELS ARE AN EASY FIND in your neighborhood, then *moules marinière,* or fisherman's mussels, may slip right into your repertoire of great dishes that are simple enough to pull together on a weeknight. Once the onions and garlic are chopped, you're only about ten minutes away from dinner and a meal that is beautiful — I love the look of a big casserole chock-full of mussels, bluish black, shiny, and piled into the pot every which way, so you glimpse some open and filled with bits of herbs, others shells up and glistening with sauce — aromatic, healthful and fun to eat. Anytime you talk about mussels, you're talking about an elbows-on-the-table meal and messy fingers.

In this traditional and most basic mussel dish, onion and garlic, along with shallots, if you've got them, are softened in a spoonful of oil before you add white wine, herbs, and the mussels, clap the lid on the pot, and wait a few minutes until they steam open, the sign that they're done. Bay leaf, parsley, and thyme are the usual herbs, but in the summer, when my garden is in bloom, I often pick a few leaves of lemon verbena to add to the mix; in winter, I get that little hit of citrus flavor by adding strips of lemon zest.

I confess to using whatever white wine I've got in the house or open in the fridge, and the *moules marinière* is always good. However, if you want the dish to be super-good, I suggest a soft white wine that's not exceedingly dry — an Alsatian Riesling is perfect. Also, I'm not sure what made me do this originally, but years ago, I dropped a quarter of a chicken bouillon cube into the pot; I liked the subtle bit of extra flavor it added and have been doing it ever since.

1	tablespoon olive oil or unsalted butter	¾	cup dry white wine
1	medium onion, finely chopped	¼	chicken bouillon cube (optional)
2	shallots, finely chopped, rinsed, and dried (optional)	2	thyme sprigs
		2	parsley sprigs
4	garlic cloves, split, germ removed, and thinly sliced	1	bay leaf
	Salt and freshly ground pepper	2	strips lemon zest (optional)
		4	pounds mussels, scrubbed, debearded if necessary

In a large Dutch oven or other heavy-bottomed casserole, warm the oil or melt the butter over low heat. Toss in the onion, shallots (if you're using them), and garlic and turn them until they're glistening. Season with salt and pepper and cook, stirring, for about 3 minutes, just to soften the onion. Pour in the wine, increase the heat to medium, add the bouillon cube (if you're using it), the herbs, and the (optional) zest, and simmer for 3 minutes.

Add the mussels and stir them around in the liquid as best you can (if you can't, that's okay). Increase the heat to high and bring to a boil, then cover the pot, adjust the heat so the liquid simmers steadily, and cook for 3 minutes. (If the pot is large enough, I sometimes give the mussels one stir during this time, or I shake the pot to mix the mussels, but it's not really necessary.)

Turn the heat off, keep the lid on the pot, and let the mussels rest for another minute (or more, if need be) so they finish opening. Once they're opened, they should be served immediately.

curried mussels

MAKES 4 MAIN-
COURSE SERVINGS
OR 6 STARTER
SERVINGS

SERVING
Mussels must be hot, and they must be eaten with your fingers. As far as I know, finger-licking is both expected and appreciated. And dunking, normally unacceptable public behavior, is not just tolerated, it's relished, so make sure there's plenty of bread on the table, along with a bowl for the shells.

STORING
You can't keep this dish, but if there are mussels left over, remove them from their shells, wrap them well, and keep them covered in the refrigerator to be used in a salad the following day.

IT TOOK A LACK OF IMAGINATION and a serious lack of energy to discover Horse's Tavern, a place that's been in Paris for years and one I'd passed hundreds of times without ever having the least interest in going in. It's at the Carrefour de l'Odéon, steps from a clutch of cinemas, and catercorner from one of my favorite bistros, Le Comptoir, and it's built on a jut of street that gives it a wraparound terrace (worth more than gold in Paris) and great light. Despite its advantages, it never called to me. And then one night, a day or so after we'd moved into our new apartment, my husband, son, and I found ourselves still unpacking cartons at 11:00 p.m. and starving. With no kitchen to speak of and not enough oomph to have pulled together a dinner even if the cupboards had been stocked, we trudged out into the night in search of a simple meal. All of a sudden the Tavern, just up the street from our new place, looked very appealing. It was still open, they were still serving, and there was a table on the terrace. A quick look around told us that *moules-frites,* or mussels and fries, was both the house specialty and the crowd's choice, so we joined the crowd.

At Horse's Tavern, the fries are served with mayonnaise and the mussels are served with a bucket that's hooked onto the side of the table. While it's meant to hold your empties, it's large enough to hold a magnum of Champagne. Everything is oversized there, but that first night, and on nights after, I managed to finish the casserole of mussels and fill up the bucket. It was easy — munch a mussel, eat a fry, sip some wine, chat, repeat, and some time later, you become a member of the clean-plate club.

Like so many places around town that serve *moules-frites,* Horse's Tavern offers basic moules marinière (see page 312 for my version) and a variation or two, including the one that's become my regular: curried mussels. At first blush, the idea of curry might seem foreign to French food, but the spice blend has a home in the cooking of Brittany, a historic port region, a spice-route stop, and an area that treasures mussels. In fact, one of the defining dishes of Brittany is *mouclade,* which features mussels in a thick curried egg-yolk-and-cream-enriched sauce. This dish is lighter than *mouclade,* a little richer than moules marinière, and a winner served with either fries or bread, the usual accompaniment at our house.

1	tablespoon unsalted butter	Salt and freshly ground pepper
1	medium onion, finely chopped	¾ cup dry white wine
2	shallots, finely chopped, rinsed, and dried	1 thyme sprig
2	teaspoons curry powder	1 parsley sprig
1	small chile pepper, left whole, or a pinch of red pepper flakes	1 bay leaf
		4 pounds mussels, scrubbed, debearded if necessary
		⅔ cup heavy cream

In a large Dutch oven or other heavy-bottomed casserole, melt the butter over low heat. Toss in the onion and shallots and turn them until they're glistening with butter. Sprinkle over the curry powder, add the chile pepper or pepper flakes, season with salt and pepper, and cook, stirring, for about 3 minutes, just to soften the onion and toast the curry powder. Pour in the wine, increase the heat to medium, add the thyme, parsley, and bay, and simmer for 3 minutes more.

Add the mussels to the pot and stir them around in the liquid as best you can (if you can't, that's okay). Increase the heat to high, bring the liquid to a boil, cover the pot, and cook for 3 minutes. (If the pot is large enough, I sometimes give the mussels one stir during this time, or I shake the pot to mix the mussels, but it's not really necessary.) Turn the heat off, keep the lid on the pot, and let the mussels rest for another minute (or more, if need be) so they finish opening.

Using a large slotted spoon, transfer the mussels to a heatproof bowl. Cover well and keep in a warm place while you finish the sauce. If you'd like a more refined sauce, strain the broth, discarding the solids, rinse out and dry the Dutch oven, and return the sauce to the pot — but I always go for the chunky, unrefined sauce.

Bring the sauce to a boil over high heat and cook for 2 minutes. Pour in the cream and boil for another 3 minutes. Taste for salt and pepper, return the mussels to the pot, and stir them around. Discard the chile pepper, if you used one. Transfer the mussels and sauce to a warm serving bowl, or bring the pot to the table and serve from it.

mussels and chorizo
with or without pasta

MAKES 6 SERVINGS
WITH PASTA OR
4 WITHOUT

SERVING
If you're serving the mussels with the pasta, put the hot fettuccine in a warm bowl and top with the mussels and their sauce. Sans pasta, keep the mussels in the pot or transfer them to a big bowl, and have plenty of bread on hand. In either case, have a bowl on the table for the empty shells.

STORING
If you've got leftovers, remove the mussels from their shells and use them in a salad the next day. Leftover sauce can be reheated gently and spooned over pasta, with or without the shelled mussels.

CHORIZO HAS ITS OWN PLACE in the lineup of French sausages and its own fan club of knowing French gourmets, who love its heat and smokiness, both of which are front and center in this somewhat Basquaise mussel dish. It's terrific served over pasta or just with hunks of bread for sauce dunking. Either way, it's a pretty messy affair, but one worth the game. If you're topping pasta with the mussels and finger licking isn't your favorite sport, you can pluck the mussels from their shells as soon as they're cooked and give them a quick toss in the tomato sauce before serving.

2 tablespoons extra-virgin olive oil

1 red bell pepper, cored, seeded, and finely chopped

1 medium onion, finely chopped

4 garlic cloves, split, germ removed, and finely chopped

2 thyme sprigs
Salt and freshly ground pepper

2 14½-ounce cans diced tomatoes, drained

1 ½-pound piece (cooked) chorizo, cut lengthwise in half and sliced ¼ to ½ inch thick

4 pounds mussels, scrubbed, debearded if necessary

¾ cup dry white wine

1 pound fettuccine, just cooked (optional)
Bread, for serving (optional)

Warm the olive oil over medium heat in a large Dutch oven or casserole that will hold all the ingredients. Add the bell pepper, onion, garlic, thyme, 1 teaspoon salt, and some pepper and cook, stirring, until the vegetables are soft, about 5 minutes. Mix in the tomatoes and chorizo and cook and stir for another 5 minutes, or until they are warmed through.

Turn the mussels into the pot, pour in the wine, increase the heat to high, and give the pot a good stir. Cover and cook for 3 minutes more. (You can stir the mussels once during this time or shake the pot, but it's not really necessary.) Turn off the heat, keep the lid on the pot, and let the mussels rest for another minute (or more, if need be) so they finish opening.

Once they are open, the mussels should be served immediately with, if you'd like, hot fettuccine or lots of bread.

scallops with caramel-orange sauce

I WAS INSPIRED TO CREATE THIS DISH after having two sweet-savory dishes at two fancy restaurants in Paris: the first dish was a soft-boiled egg sauced with maple syrup, served at Alain Passard's Arpège, and the other was a foie gras crème brûlée dreamed up by Jean-Georges Vongerichten at Market.

Those dishes were completely surprising, and so is this one. In fact, everything about this recipe is unexpected, including the fact that I made it. A savory sauce based on caramel and paired with seafood sounded a little fussy for my style. But it turned out to be so good — and it takes less time to make than a hamburger.

The scallops are cooked quickly in a little oil over high heat with nothing more than salt and pepper. They're sweet, firm on the outside, and velvety within — perfect. But they're not really the main event — the drama is in the sauce, which is slightly syrupy, slightly sweet-sour (or sour-sweet, *aigre-doux*, as the French say), and derived from a preparation called a *gastrique,* essentially a reduction of caramelized sugar and vinegar. In my version, the sauce (which takes only 10 minutes) can be made a day ahead, and the vinegar, which would supply the acidity for a *gastrique,* is replaced by white wine and fresh orange juice.

MAKES 4 SERVINGS

SERVING
The scallops are good served with a simple green vegetable, such as steamed green beans or asparagus, and any grain, but for something a little different, I urge you to pair them with Spiced Butter-Glazed Carrots (page 335).

STORING
While the scallops must be eaten as soon as they're cooked, the caramel sauce can be kept covered in the refrigerator for up to 2 days.

2 tablespoons sugar	½–1 tablespoon olive oil
½ cup dry white wine	Salt and freshly ground white pepper
Juice of 1 large orange (generous ⅓ cup)	1 tablespoon cold unsalted butter, cut into 3 pieces
1 pound sea scallops	

Sprinkle the sugar into a small saucepan. Place the pan over medium-high heat and warm the sugar until it starts to melt and color. As soon as you see it turn brown, begin to gently swirl the pan. When the sugar has turned a deep caramel color (you can put a drop of sugar on a white plate to test the color), about 3 minutes, stand back and add the white wine and orange juice. It may bubble and spatter, so watch out. Turn the heat up to high, stir with a wooden spoon, and boil the sauce until it is reduced by half — you should have about ⅓ cup. Pull the pan from the heat and set it aside. *(You can make the sauce up to 2 days ahead and keep it covered in the refrigerator.)*

Pat the scallops dry between paper towels. Slice or pull off the little muscle attached to the sides of the scallops. Have a warm serving platter and a small strainer at the ready.

Put the saucepan with the caramel sauce over very low heat so that it can warm while you cook the scallops.

Put a heavy-bottomed skillet over high heat. When the pan is hot, pour in

1½ teapoons olive oil and swirl to coat the bottom. Add the scallops, season them with salt and white pepper, and cook, without moving them, for 2 minutes. Flip the scallops over, season with salt and white pepper, add a little more oil if needed, and cook for another 1 to 2 minutes, or until the scallops are firm on the outside and just barely opaque in the center — nick one to test. Transfer the scallops to the serving platter.

Check that the caramel sauce is hot — give it more heat if necessary. Pull the pan from the heat and toss in the butter, bit by bit, swirling the pan until the butter is melted and the sauce is glistening. Season the sauce with salt and white pepper, then pour it through the strainer into a sauceboat or pitcher.

Drizzle some of the sauce over the scallops and pass the rest at the table.

BONNE IDÉE

Candied Orange Zest. If you want to dress the dish up a tad, top the scallops with strips of candied orange zest. Before you squeeze the juice from the orange, cut off the zest using a zester, a vegetable peeler, or a knife — avoid the cottony white pith. If you didn't use a zester, cut the zest into very thin strips. Bring a small saucepan of water to a boil, toss in the zest, and boil for 1 minute, then drain in a strainer and rinse under cold water. Put ¾ cup water and ½ cup sugar in the pan and cook, stirring, until the sugar is dissolved and the syrup is boiling. Add the zest, reduce the heat to as low as possible, and cook for 15 to 20 minutes, or until the zest is soft. At serving time, remove the zest with chopsticks or a slotted spoon and strew it over the caramel-sauced scallops.

warm scallop salad with corn, nectarines, and basil

MAKES 6 SERVINGS

SERVING
I like to arrange this salad on individual plates, but it can certainly be served family-style.

STORING
You can make the lime dressing and basil coulis the day before, but everything else should be prepared as close to serving time as possible.

TO INCLUDE THIS RECIPE IN A BOOK of French recipes is cheating just a little, because it is a dish that I serve in Connecticut when everything that makes it fabulous — corn, tomatoes, basil, and nectarines — is at its ripest, sweetest, and most plentiful. It sneaked into this collection because I slipped it into a meal in Paris, where my friends considered it *exotique*.

If you think the exotic part is the inclusion of the nectarines with vegetables and scallops, you think wrong. The French take that in stride, especially since the nouvelle cuisine of the 1970s. No, the exotic was our beloved corn.

Corn is not unheard of in France, but it's not nearly as esteemed there as it is here (it's considered good fodder for livestock), and when it turns up in dishes, it usually comes straight from a can and goes into a salad. In fact, when I made this salad in Paris, the corn came from a can. Needless to say, it didn't have the taste, texture, or wonderful aroma of our terrific corn, but the dish was good enough to make the point that the vegetable can be taken seriously and, more important, good enough to make everyone around the table happy.

FOR THE LIME DRESSING
Finely grated zest of 1 lime
3 tablespoons fresh lime juice (from 2 limes)
Pinch of sea salt
Pinch of piment d'Espelette (see Sources) or chili powder
3 tablespoons extra-virgin olive oil

FOR THE BASIL COULIS
¾ cup loosely packed fresh basil leaves, coarsely chopped
¼ cup extra-virgin olive oil
Sea salt

FOR THE SALAD
3 ripe but firm nectarines, halved and pitted
24 sea scallops, side muscles removed, patted dry
Fleur de sel or other sea salt and freshly ground white pepper
About 1 tablespoon olive oil, if you're pan-searing the scallops
3 ears corn, husked, silk removed, and kernels cut from the cobs (about 1½ cups)
24 cherry tomatoes or grape tomatoes, halved (or 3 ripe tomatoes, cut into small chunks)
6 large fresh basil leaves, shredded

TO MAKE THE DRESSING: Put all the ingredients in a small jar, cover, and shake to blend. Or whisk the zest, juice, salt, and piment d'Espelette or chili powder together in a small bowl, then slowly whisk in the olive oil. *(The dressing can be made the night before and kept covered in the refrigerator; bring it to room temperature before using.)*

TO MAKE THE BASIL COULIS: If you have the time, blanch the basil for 30 seconds in boiling water, drop it into a bowl of ice and water, chill for a few minutes, then dry it, so the coulis will be bright green. Put the basil, olive oil, and a pinch of salt in a mini processor or blender and whir to puree; set aside. *(The coulis can be made ahead and kept covered in the refrigerator overnight; bring to room temperature before using.)*

TO MAKE THE SALAD: If you're grilling the scallops, preheat the grill. If you're pan-searing them, heat a large heavy-bottomed pan over high heat — a cast-iron skillet is good here; a large griddle is great too.

If you're grilling, arrange the nectarines, cut side down, and the scallops on the grill and cook for 1½ minutes. Turn the scallops — leave the nectarines undisturbed — season the scallops with salt and white pepper, and grill for another 1½ minutes; the scallops should be firm but still translucent at their centers. If you're pan-searing, add just enough oil to lightly coat the bottom of the pan and, over medium-high heat and working in batches so that nothing is crowded, first cook the nectarines until they are warmed through, about 3 minutes, then remove and keep warm. (If you're using a griddle, you might not have to oil it — it will depend on how well seasoned it is.) Then sear the scallops for 1½ minutes on each side, seasoning them with salt and white pepper when you turn them. Keep warm.

To serve, put the corn in a small bowl and toss with a spoonful of lime dressing — you want to use only enough to moisten the kernels. Taste for salt and pepper. Put the tomatoes in another bowl and season with salt and pepper. Put 4 scallops in the center of each plate. Surround the scallops with the corn kernels, scatter the tomatoes over the corn, and put 1 nectarine half at the side of each plate. Spoon some lime dressing over the scallops, then top them with basil coulis; dot the corn and tomatoes with a little coulis too, if you'd like. Sprinkle the shredded basil over the corn and tomatoes and serve.

shrimp and cellophane noodles

MAKES 4 SERVINGS

SERVING

This is a complete meal in a bowl and needs nothing more than wine or beer to go with it. But it's also a dish that lends itself to accompaniments. I sometimes put small bowls of chopped salted peanuts, sliced scallions, and Fried Garlic Petals (see Bonne Idée, page 127) on the table, so that my guests can add crunch and extra zip to the dish as they go.

STORING

Like all stir-fries, this is meant to be eaten as soon as it's done, and it's best that way. However, like so many noodle dishes, the leftovers are good the next day, eaten while you're standing at the kitchen counter.

AS ASSIDUOUSLY AS THEY GUARD THE PURITY of their family specialties, the French are unabashedly freewheeling with recipes from other cultures. They'll stir Parmesan into a pot of rice and call it risotto, slice a tomato paper-thin and dub it carpaccio, add a pinch of curry powder to a stew and tag it *à l'indienne,* and make anything in a wok and call it Asian. It may be a little cavalier, but the food that comes out of this open-spirited stab at fusion is often so good that only a prig would fuss over the nomenclature. Certainly no one would complain if faced with this just-remotely Chinese mix of shrimp, dried mushrooms, and slithery, translucent noodles tossed with a tomato sauce that gets its spunk from a spoonful of Chinese five-spice powder, a mix of ginger, cloves, cinnamon, pepper, and star anise. The flavor is haunting and mysterious — no one ever guesses what it is.

This dish was created by my friend Hélène Samuel and was first served chez Hélène as part of an all-orange meal. I can't remember the reason she decided to serve us only orange food (aside from the fact that she's crazy about the color), but I do remember that we started with an orange salad, had the shrimp, and finished the meal with a carrot cake. I asked for this recipe before I walked out the door.

1 ounce dried Chinese tree ear mushrooms	2 tablespoons peanut oil or grape seed oil
3 ounces cellophane noodles (aka Chinese vermicelli or glass noodles)	1 small onion, finely chopped
	3 small garlic cloves, split, germ removed, and finely chopped
1 tablespoon Asian toasted sesame oil, or a little more to taste	1 pound large shrimp, peeled and deveined
1 teaspoon Chinese five-spice powder	Salt and freshly ground white pepper
1 teaspoon sugar Pinch of cayenne or other hot red pepper	2 cups tomato puree
	2–3 tablespoons minced fresh cilantro

About 30 minutes before you're ready to cook, soak the dried mushrooms in a large quantity of warm water until soft. Drain, rinse, and pat the mushrooms dry. Chop them or cut them into shreds.

Soak the noodles in hot water, following the directions on the package (usually for about 10 minutes). When the noodles are soft and slippery, drain and snip them into easy-to-eat lengths (I cut them into thirds). Toss them with 1 tablespoon sesame oil.

Bring a medium saucepan of water to a boil and keep it at a simmer. Have a strainer at hand.

Mix the five-spice powder, sugar, and cayenne together.

Put a wok or large skillet over medium heat and pour in the peanut or grapeseed oil. When it's hot, toss in the onion and cook for a minute or so, just until it's translucent, then add the rehydrated mushrooms and garlic and cook, stirring, for another 30 seconds. Turn up the heat and add the shrimp to the pan, followed quickly by the spice mixture. Season generously with salt and white pepper and cook, stirring often, until the shrimp just start to turn pink, about 30 seconds. Pour in the tomato puree and cook, stirring, for about 2 minutes, or until the shrimp are fully cooked. Taste for salt, pepper, and cayenne, then turn off the heat.

Slide the cellophane noodles into the simmering water, turn up the heat, and cook for 1 minute. Drain the noodles in the strainer, shake to dry them well, and turn them into a serving bowl; if you'd like, toss them with a little more sesame oil.

Pour the shrimp and sauce over the noodles, sprinkle the cilantro over the shrimp, and serve immediately, with chopsticks or forks.

vanilla-butter-braised lobster

MAKES 4 SERVINGS

SERVING
My favorite way to serve this elegant dish is to pair it with Lemon-Steamed Spinach (page 331). I put a small bed of spinach in the center of each of four shallow soup plates, top with the lobster, making sure it's seasoned with salt and pepper, and spoon over some of the vanilla butter. I finish each plate with a piece of vanilla bean — it's not edible, but it is beautiful and aromatic.

STORING
The lobster can be parcooked a day ahead, and the butter can be clarified a week ahead and flavored the day before. Once the elements are united and the dish is completed, it should be savored immediately, with no thoughts of leftovers.

I THINK IT WAS THE LEGENDARY AND REBELLIOUS Paris chef Alain Senderens who first thought to pair lobster with vanilla, and I can imagine that he might have had to cajole his guests to go for the nouvelle duo. I can also imagine that once they did, they'd have been won over immediately. Tasting luxurious sweet lobster with powerfully fragrant sweet vanilla is one of those eureka moments: you know in an instant that the combination is inspired.

Senderens' first foray into vanilla-lobster land was roasted lobster with a vanilla beurre blanc, and that gave me the idea to infuse clarified butter with vanilla and to gently and quickly braise lobster tails and claws in it. The dish looks and tastes as though it were made in a top chef's kitchen, when, in fact, it requires no complicated techniques or equipment. It is, however, expensive — lobster, butter, and vanilla are all luxe ingredients. But if you're looking for a special-occasion dish, make this recipe.

Even though you use only part of each lobster, I like to buy whole lobsters for the dish and boil them just long enough to remove the meat from the tails and claws (I pick out the body meat and enjoy it for myself). If you want to make this dish even simpler to prepare, you can start with lobster tails (2 per person), either freshly cooked by the fishmonger or defrosted frozen lobster.

I prefer vanilla beans (plumpness and pliability, along with fragrance, are your signs that the beans are in prime condition), but you can use pure vanilla extract — imitation will spoil the dish.

As for the butter, you need the full amount called for to poach the lobsters properly, but you'll be left with plenty, which you can use in mashed potatoes, or for sautéing seafood, or as a great dipping sauce for soft-shelled crabs or boiled lobster.

BE PREPARED: The recipe is long but not complicated, and you can precook the lobsters and clarify and flavor the butter ahead of time, so read it through first and plan a schedule that works for you.

4	live lobsters, 1¼ to 1½ pounds each	2	plump, pliable vanilla beans (first choice) or 1½ table-spoons pure vanilla extract
1½	pounds (6 sticks) unsalted butter		Fleur de sel or other sea salt
			Freshly ground white pepper

To get the lobsters ready for braising, have a nutcracker, a lobster pick or a pointy skewer, kitchen shears, and a heavy chef's knife at hand, along with a few kitchen towels. I'd suggest that even if you never wear an apron, you make an exception and don one now.

Bring a big pot of generously salted water to a boil. You can precook the lobsters all at once, but since it's easier to remove the meat from them when they're still warm, it's better to work with one or two at a time. Plunge the lobsters headfirst into the water and cook for 3 minutes. Pull them out of the water with tongs, holding the lobsters over the pot so that most of the water drips off them, then transfer them to a tray or large pan. (I put the lobsters on a cooling rack over a baking sheet.) Protecting your hands with dish towels, break off the claws where they meet the body, and return them to the pot to boil for another 3 minutes.

Now set to work separating the meat from the shells. Using the knife (or your hands), remove each tail from the body and lay it down on a cutting board. Using whatever tool works best for you (I grab the shears at this point), cut down the center of the tail without cutting into the meat and then, using your fingers, pull the meat from the tail in one piece. To release the claw meat, use the nutcracker to break the shells, then, if necessary, run a table knife (or a marrow spoon, if you've got one) between the meat and the shell to free the meat. Now use the pick to remove the knuckle meat, and enjoy it — it's your reward for the work you've done and your encouragement to keep going.

Put all the tail and claw meat in a bowl and cover with plastic wrap. *(You can prepare the lobster up to a day ahead and keep it covered in the refrigerator.)* As for the rest, you can munch on the bodies or freeze them and the shells for soup.

Cut the butter into pieces and drop them into a small saucepan. Place the saucepan over very low heat and melt the butter slowly — don't rush the process. When the butter is melted, leave it over the heat for a few minutes more while you carefully skim off and discard the foam that has risen to the top. Remove the pan from the heat, place it on a trivet, and let it sit for 3 minutes or so.

Very slowly and gently pour the clear yellow liquid — the clarified butter — into a container (I use a Pyrex measuring cup), stopping as soon as the white milk solids start to creep up to the edge of the pan. If you've poured a little too quickly, let the clarified butter rest for a moment and then repeat the pouring process. Alternatively, you can pour the butter through a fine-mesh strainer lined with dampened cheesecloth to catch the solids. *(You can clarify the butter up to a week ahead and keep it tightly covered in the refrigerator.)*

Put the butter into a saucepan that will just hold it and the lobster meat — the smaller the diameter the better, so the butter will cover more of the lobster when you add it. (I use a 6-inch-wide 3-quart pan.) Cut the vanilla beans lengthwise in half and scrape the pulp and seeds into the pan, then drop in the beans themselves, or add the vanilla extract, and add a pinch of fleur de sel. Once again over the lowest possible heat, warm the butter for 10 minutes — it shouldn't boil, although you might get a bubble or two — then turn off the heat and let the butter stand for another 10 minutes. *(You can flavor the butter up to a day ahead and keep it covered in the refrigerator.)*

To braise the lobsters, bring the lobster meat to room temperature if it was refrigerated. Return the pan with the butter and vanilla to low heat, and when it is hot — about 160 degrees F on an instant-read thermometer — drop in the lobster. The butter should cover most of the lobster; if you've got a little piece above the butter, turn it after a minute. Cook the lobster for 4 minutes, or until it is opaque — if you're not sure that the lobster is done, make a small cut in a tail. Lift the lobster out of the butter, reserve the butter for another use, and season the lobster with fleur de sel and white pepper. Serve now!

vegetables and grains

(mostly sides, but a few mains too)

WARM-WEATHER VEGETABLE POT-AU-FEU (PAGE 378)

vegetables and grains *(mostly sides, but a few mains too)*

asparagus and bits of bacon

MAKES 4 SERVINGS

SERVING
Arrange the asparagus on a serving plate. Lift the bacon and onion out of the skillet with a slotted spoon and spoon them across the asparagus.

STORING
This is a make-and-eat recipe.

T OSS BOILED ASPARAGUS WITH NUT OIL and lemon juice, then top the spears with onion and bacon, and you get sophisticated flavor, texture, and looks — all in about 10 minutes.

2 teaspoons hazelnut oil or walnut oil, or more to taste
1 teaspoon fresh lemon juice, or more to taste
3 thick strips bacon
½ small onion, finely chopped, rinsed, and dried

20–24 asparagus stalks (preferably thick stalks), trimmed and peeled
Salt and freshly ground pepper

Stir together the nut oil and lemon juice; set aside.

Put the bacon in a large skillet, set over medium heat, and cook, turning occasionally, until both sides are well browned. Drain the bacon well, and pour off all but 1 teaspoon of the bacon fat from the skillet; set aside.

Cut the bacon into ¼-inch dice and combine with the onion.

Bring a large skillet of salted water to a boil. Put the asparagus in the pan and cook until a knife pierces the stalks easily, about 4 minutes. Drain, pat the asparagus dry between paper towels, and gently toss with the oil and lemon juice. Season generously with salt and pepper; taste and add more oil or juice if needed.

While the asparagus is cooking, heat the bacon fat remaining in the skillet until warm. Add the bacon bits and onion and stir to warm slightly and coat with oil (you don't want to color or cook the onion).

To serve, drain the bacon and onion and spoon them over the asparagus.

lemon-steamed spinach

HERE'S A SMART, IF TOPSY-TURVY, way to perfectly steam and season spinach. It's topsy-turvy because you season the spinach before you steam it, and it's smart because it solves the problem of how to toss spinach with flavorings once it's wilted. What I do is mix the cleaned spinach with salt, pepper, olive oil, and grated lemon zest, as though I were making a salad, then steam the leaves and just lift them out of the pot and onto plates. Nothing could be simpler, and the best part is that the preseasoning sticks — the flavor and fragrance of the grated lemon really stand out after steaming.

You can cook the spinach in any kind of steamer or steaming basket, but ever since my friend Patricia Wells told me she uses her pasta pot, which has a perforated insert, as a steamer, I've been doing it too. It's perfect for the job.

MAKES 4 SERVINGS

1¼ pounds (two 10-ounce bags) baby spinach (precleaned and trimmed)	1–1½ tablespoons extra-virgin olive oil Grated zest of 1 lemon Salt and freshly ground pepper

Have your steamer set up and ready to go — make sure you don't fill the pot with so much water that it will boil up into the steaming basket.

Put the spinach in a bowl and toss it with 1 tablespoon of the oil, the zest, and salt and pepper to taste. Taste for seasoning and, if the spinach looks dry, add some or all of the remaining olive oil.

Turn the spinach into the pot, cover, and steam for 3 minutes — the spinach will probably need another minute or two before it's tender, but it's a good idea to check early and to give it a turn. The spinach should be served as soon as it's cooked.

SERVING
The easiest way to dish out the spinach is to lift it from the steamer with a pair of tongs: hold it above the steamer, letting some of the moisture drip back into the pot, and then put it onto a serving platter or individual plates. The spinach is good on its own, but it's great as a little cushion for dishes like Cinnamon-Crunch Chicken (page 220), Salmon with Basil Tapenade (page 299), or, best of all, Vanilla-Butter-Braised Lobster (page 324).

STORING
It's best to eat the spinach immediately after steaming, but if you have a little left over, you can reheat it gently in a microwave oven or steamer.

beets: *four ways to cook them*

For years, every time I'd return from a trip to France, I'd call Julia Child to report on my adventures. Of course, she'd always ask me what I'd cooked and what I'd eaten, and she'd often ask, with a winsome sigh, if the food was still wonderful. Then one day she asked a question that came completely out of the blue but was so Julia: "Can you still get cooked beets at the market?" she asked, adding, "I've always loved that and can't understand why we don't do that here." Indeed.

Yes, you can still get cooked beets at the market, any market. Usually the beets are the big fat round kind, cooked au naturel with not a lick of seasoning (a tabula rasa for your own recipes) and stacked up with their skins still intact. They're displayed in boxes alongside the fresh produce, and when you ask for one, the vendor grabs a fork, spears it, and plops it into a plastic bag — one you hope keeps your ruby treasure safe until you get home, because beet juice, as beautiful as it is, might just as well be sold as dye.

Of course, in season, you can also get fresh beets at the French market. They come in all sizes and now in a rainbow of colors. But judging by the salads I see around town and the dishes my friends make, red remains the favorite hue and ready-cooked the ingredient of choice for salads.

Because my local markets stateside rarely have cooked beets (some markets in New York City import vacuum-packed shelf-stable beets from France), I cook the beets myself so that I can make salads. Depending on the time I have, I roast the beets, steam them, boil them, or, fastest of all, cook them in the microwave. Steaming is simple, boiling is traditional, and microwaving is better than you'd expect. Roasting gives you the deepest flavor, but I wouldn't turn on my oven just to cook beets.

GETTING READY: If your beets are still attached to their greens, cut them loose, leaving just an inch or two of stalk; save the greens for another use. Scrub — not just rinse, but really rub and scrub — the beets clean under running water. If you've got a vegetable brush, use it.

TO ROAST BEETS: Center a rack in the oven and preheat the oven to 425 degrees F. Put the beets in a baking dish, pour in a little water (just a few spoonfuls), cover the dish with foil, and stab a little hole in it. Roast for 30 to 60 minutes, depending on the size of the beets, until you can pierce them easily with a knife. Slip off the skins when the beets are cool enough to handle.

TO STEAM BEETS: Arrange a steaming basket in a saucepan and add enough water to the pan to come about 1 inch below the basket; bring to a boil. Put the beets in the basket, cover the pan, and steam until the beets can be easily pierced with the tip of a knife, 20 to 30 minutes for small beets, up to 1 hour for giant beets. Make sure to add more water as needed. When they're cool enough to handle, peel them.

TO BOIL BEETS: Bring a large pot of salted water to a boil. Drop in the beets and boil until they are tender enough to be pierced with the tip of a knife. Drain the beets, and when you can handle them (you can rinse them under cold water to speed the cooling), peel them.

TO MICROWAVE BEETS: Put the beets in a microwave-safe container with a few drops of water, cover, and cook on high power for 10 minutes. (If the beets are very small, they may need just 8 minutes.) Remove all the beets that can be easily pierced with the tip of a knife; if there are some that are still too firm, return them to the oven and cook them in 30-second spurts until tender. When the beets are cool enough to handle, peel them.

pancetta green beans

THIS SIMPLE DISH IS MADE SPECIAL with the addition of a little sautéed pancetta. It adds a speck of saltiness, another texture, and elements of elegance and surprise.

¾ pound green beans, trimmed
2 ounces pancetta, coarsely chopped

½ tablespoon unsalted butter
Salt and freshly ground pepper
Walnut oil (my preference) or extra-virgin olive oil

MAKES **4** SERVINGS

SERVING
Get the beans to the table while they're hot and serve them alongside steaks, roasts, chops, or chicken.

STORING
Leftover beans can be kept covered in the refrigerator overnight. Reheat them gently, or serve them at room temperature with a splash of sherry vinegar or fresh lemon juice.

Bring a large pot of salted water to a boil, and fill a bowl with ice cubes and cold water. Toss the beans into the boiling water and cook just until crisp-tender, about 5 minutes. Drain, transfer to the ice-water bath, and cool for 2 minutes; drain and pat dry.

Heat a large skillet over medium heat. Add the pancetta and sauté until frizzled and crisp, about 2 minutes. Using a slotted spoon, transfer the pancetta to a plate lined with paper towels and pat dry. Drain all but 1 tablespoon of fat from the skillet.

Return the skillet to medium heat and add the butter. When the fat is hot, toss in the beans and cook, stirring, until heated through. Season with salt and pepper and stir in the pancetta. Remove from the heat and drizzle the beans with a little oil.

at the market: leave it to the experts

On the last day of my first trip to France, I was severely scolded by a fruit vendor because I'd dared to pick my own plum. I was startled, embarrassed, and a bit surprised that my always-on-my-side husband didn't leap forward to defend me. It was only after I'd apologized to the vendor and allowed him to choose a pair of plums for me that Michael pointed to the big sign just inches above the fruit, a sign that said, *"Ne Touchez Pas"* in big letters and "Don't Touch the Fruit" in even bigger letters.

Away from the scene of the crime, I realized that the vendor's scolding was a matter of pride: he knew his fruit, knew what he had on the stands that day, and knew that it was his job to choose just the right fruit for each of his clients.

When it's done well, this kind of service is a delight — you feel special and, most important, you get the best food. At the *fromagerie* — still a don't-touch kind of place — the cheesemonger asks you when you plan to serve a particular cheese, and then he presses and prods as many as need be to get you the one that will reach its perfect moment of readiness at just the right hour.

It's the same story at the fruit stand. At the height of melon season on the rue de Buci, near my apartment, I ask the vendor for one melon, please. "When will you be serving it?" he queries.

To my answer, "Tonight," he asks, "At what time?"

I play the straight guy and tell him, "9:00 p.m."

He starts hefting the melons, discarding each in turn, until he finds what I presume to be the ideal one for me. He moves it from hand to hand, furrows his brow, and says with deep seriousness, "I hope this one will be good — it really won't be ready until 9:15."

garlicky crumb-coated broccoli

MAKES **6** SERVINGS

SERVING
The broccoli is particularly good with fish or chicken, grilled or sautéed, and nice alongside omelets.

STORING
You can steam the broccoli a few hours ahead, but once you've coated the stalks with crumbs, get the dish to the table.

ROLLING BROCCOLI AROUND IN SOME BUTTERY bread crumbs flavored with garlic, lemon, and herbs is quick, easy, and transformative: the everyday vegetable is suddenly ready for company.

1½–2 pounds broccoli, trimmed and cut into 6 stalks	3 small garlic cloves, split, germ removed, and finely chopped
Salt and freshly ground pepper	½ cup plain dry bread crumbs
4 tablespoons (½ stick) unsalted butter	Finely chopped or coarsely grated zest of 1 lemon
	2 tablespoons minced fresh mint or parsley

In a steamer or a pot fitted with a steaming basket, steam the broccoli, covered, until the stalks are just tender, 7 to 9 minutes. You should be able to pierce the stalks with the tip of a knife. Transfer to a plate lined with a double thickness of paper towels, drain, and pat dry. Season the broccoli with salt and pepper and set aside.

Put a large skillet, preferably nonstick, over medium-low heat and add the butter. When the butter's melted, add the garlic and cook for about 2 minutes, just until it is softened but not colored. Add the bread crumbs, season with salt and pepper, and toss the crumbs with the garlic until they are well blended, moistened with butter, and toasted, about 2 minutes. Stir in the zest and mint or parsley.

Add the broccoli and turn it around to coat the florets with crumbs. Transfer the broccoli to a serving platter and spoon over any crumbs that remain in the skillet. Serve immediately.

spiced butter-glazed carrots

CARROTS, SO SWEET ON THEIR OWN, are an easygoing mate to ingredients both sweet and savory. Here, in addition to onion and garlic, the carrots are cooked with a fair amount of ginger and a few cardamom seeds, which add a kind of citrusy brightness that's both welcoming and elusive. To get the most flavor from the cardamom, bruise the seeds just a little with a mortar and pestle, or give them a smash with the heel or back of a chef's knife.

MAKES 6 SERVINGS

SERVING
Prepared this way, carrots are a utility player: they're as good with light dishes like fish and chicken as they are with meat.

STORING
Although these are best served soon after they're glazed, leftovers can be refrigerated overnight and gently reheated the next day.

2 tablespoons unsalted butter
1 small onion, finely chopped
1 ½-inch piece fresh ginger, peeled and thinly sliced
1 garlic clove, split, germ removed, and thinly sliced
Seeds from 4 cardamom pods, bruised (see headnote)
Salt and freshly ground white pepper
12 medium carrots (about 1½ pounds), trimmed, peeled, and cut on the diagonal into pieces about 2 inches long
1 cup chicken broth

Melt the butter in a medium saucepan over medium heat. Stir in the onion, ginger, garlic, and cardamom seeds, season very lightly with salt and white pepper, and cook, stirring, until the vegetables soften, about 5 minutes. Add the carrots and stir to coat them with the butter. Pour in the chicken broth and bring to a boil, then lower the heat so that the broth is at a simmer. Cover the saucepan and cook until the carrots are just tender, 10 to 15 minutes.

Remove the cover, raise the heat, and cook until the broth almost completely evaporates and all that remains is the spiced butter glazing the carrots. Season with salt and white pepper and serve.

boulevard raspail
corn on the cob

MAKES 4 SERVINGS

SERVING
While I find it impossible to imagine most French people picking up an ear of corn and munching on it — the mere mention of this to my French friends produced such looks of alarm that I've never served them corn on the cob — that's the best way to eat it, as Americans know so well. Slather the corn with butter, salt and pepper it amply, and enjoy. If you insist on eating it the French way, cut the kernels from the cob and serve them in a bowl.

STORING
Fresh corn is meant to be eaten freshly cooked.

THE SUNDAY ORGANIC MARKET on the boulevard Raspail is probably the most expensive in Paris, in part because it's organic (one of only two outdoor markets in the city that are *biologique*), in part because it's in a high-rent district, and maybe in part because the people-watching is so good. It was here that I fell into conversation with the actress Juliette Binoche over a basket of muffins made by a longtime Paris resident. Despite the fact that the market is narrow and terribly cold and dark in winter, it's always crowded, and the lines for the best vendors are always long.

I'm not the world's most patient waiter, and one very cold day, when the line was at a standstill, I had to remind myself that the attentive service the woman at the head of it was receiving was what so endeared the markets to me. Finally, after what had to have been a full five-minute conversation, the vendor handed a small paper bag over to the woman. I couldn't imagine what she had bought. It's rare to leave a vegetable stall with just one package, unless you're buying wild mushrooms, truffles, or the first of the season's berries, none of which were on offer that day.

My turn came and went, and I continued along my way. In the course of finishing my shopping, I ran into the woman who'd held up the line. I stopped her, excused myself for being so bold, and explained that I was curious about what advice the vendor had given her about her purchase. "Whatever did you buy?" I asked. "Oh," she exclaimed, "look!" And, with great delight and excitement, she pulled out two (out-of-season, imported, and slightly shriveled) ears of corn, complete with husks. Had she purchased diamonds, she couldn't have been more pleased and I couldn't have been more surprised: you don't see much corn on the cob in France, where it's long been considered fit only for feeding animals. When corn turns up in French recipes, it's usually in salads, and almost always kernel corn straight from the can. "What are you going to do with the corn?" was my next question, to which the woman replied, "I'm going to cook it exactly as the vegetable lady told me to."

Well, the vegetable lady may have been selling corn that no corn-loving American would buy, but she certainly knew how to cook it. Here's her recipe.

4–8 ears corn in the husk	Salt and freshly ground pepper
Butter	

Center a rack in the oven and preheat the oven to 400 degrees F.

Place the unhusked ears of corn on the oven rack and roast the corn for 40 minutes, turning it at the 20-minute mark. Working over a trash bin and wearing good oven mitts, shuck the corn and pull away and discard the silk.

Serve on the cob or cut the kernels off the cob and put them in a bowl. On or off the cob, serve the corn hot with butter, salt, and pepper.

corn pancakes

WHILE WE'RE APT TO DISMISS CANNED CORN, the French use it happily and unapologetically, most commonly in salads, but also sometimes incorporating it into dishes like these small savory pancakes, which make me wonder why they weren't invented stateside.

I first had them at a French country inn a few decades ago, and because they were made with the canned stuff, I figured I wasn't going to see the dish again anytime soon back in America, a hunch that proved true. It took years until I had them here, and when I did, they were prepared by a French chef, the now world-famous Jean-Georges Vongerichten, who made them soon after he arrived on our shores. When I told him how delighted I was to have them (he paired the cakes with crème fraîche and caviar), he looked puzzled. With an offhand shrug, he told me, "They're something my mother made all the time." Lucky kid.

MAKES 6 SERVINGS

SERVING
These make a terrific accompaniment, instead of potatoes, rice, or noodles, to roast chicken or beef or even the Thanksgiving turkey. Or do as Jean-Georges did and serve the pancakes as an hors d'oeuvre with crème fraîche and caviar, salmon roe, or smoked salmon.

STORING
You can make the pancakes a few hours ahead, keep them covered at room temperature, and reheat them before serving (in a conventional or microwave oven). Or you can pack them airtight (separate the pancakes with small squares of parchment or wax paper) and freeze them for up to 2 months, then reheat them as needed.

1	15- to 16-ounce can corn kernels (preferably without sugar or corn syrup), drained
2	large eggs
6	tablespoons all-purpose flour
¾	teaspoon salt
	Mild oil (such as grapeseed or canola), for frying

Preheat the oven to 250 degrees F. Line a baking sheet with a silicone baking mat or foil, and line a plate with paper towels.

Put the corn, eggs, flour, and salt in a blender or a food processor and whir until everything's well mixed and fairly smooth. The mixture won't be completely smooth, and that's just fine.

Put a large heavy-bottomed skillet, preferably nonstick, over medium heat and pour in about 3 tablespoons oil. When the oil is hot, drop in the batter by tablespoonfuls, pressing gently to round the pancakes. Cook for about 2 minutes, until the undersides are golden, then flip them over and cook the other side for a minute or so more, until it too is golden. Transfer the pancakes to the paper-towel-lined plate, cover with more towels, and pat off the excess oil. Transfer them to the baking sheet, cover loosely with foil, and keep them warm in the oven while you continue to make pancakes, adding more oil to the pan as needed.

endives, apples, and grapes

MAKES 4 STARTER
OR SIDE-DISH
SERVINGS OR 2
MAIN-COURSE
SERVINGS

SERVING
You can serve this as a first course or as a side dish to chicken or fish that isn't heavily sauced; something grilled would be just right. It is also a great main course (if you want to double the recipe, make it in two skillets) followed by bread and cheese — think blue cheese.

STORING
This really should be served as soon as it's cooked. I've reheated leftovers briefly in the microwave oven, and they've been okay, but not nearly as good as they were the day before; endive has a tendency to become more bitter when it's reheated.

BONNE IDÉE
Thanksgiving Squash and Apples. A squash or pumpkin rendition is splendid for the holidays. Here's the combination I make most often: 4 thin (1- to 1½-inch-thick) wedges pumpkin or squash (I use Red Kuri squash, which doesn't need to be peeled), 12 to 16 cooked chestnuts (I use jarred), 1 apple (or pear), 4 clusters grapes, and sprigs of rosemary, thyme, or, best of all, sage for the herb. You can drizzle warm maple syrup over this — and it's also good topped with toasted pecans, with a spoonful of a cranberry-orange relish alongside.

IF YOU'VE NEVER PUT COOKED ENDIVE at the top of your favorites list, or if you've never even cooked endive, it's probably because you didn't have this recipe to turn to. It came from Alain Passard, the Michelin three-star chef who has a magical garden outside Paris. Passard, obsessed with vegetables, turned the Parisian haute cuisine establishment on its head when he announced that he would serve only vegetables grown on his farm and that he would serve them simply. When Passard said simply, he truly meant it: dishes might be as basic as one potato (a perfect one, to be sure) baked in a salt crust and served, sauceless and unaccompanied, the instant it emerged from the oven. Prices for these little treasures might be as high as those for truffles and foie gras. Such boldness bordered on scandal, but soon Passard's passion for vegetables and his sure hand with his harvest became the standard by which vegetable cooking was judged.

This recipe, recommended to me by my friend Meg Zimbeck, could not be simpler or more sublime. The fruits and endive are cooked slowly in salted butter — you turn them just once — until they are soft and caramelized. That's it, except for scraping up the cooking sugars, and you need nothing more. The endive, known for its bitterness, keeps its hallmark flavor, but the apples and grapes become even sweeter under heat, so that sometimes you bounce between bitter and sweet and sometimes the flavors meld. It's a remarkable dish.

This is the kind of recipe you'll be able to play with, but I urge you to hold on to the grapes — they're completely unexpected and so good that they just about steal the show.

2	plump endives, trimmed	4	small clusters white or green grapes (in France, I like to use Muscat grapes)
1	tart-sweet apple, such as Fuji or Gala		
1½	tablespoons salted butter (if you can find butter with sea salt crystals, use it)	4	small rosemary sprigs Salt, preferably fleur de sel, and freshly ground pepper

Cut the endives lengthwise in half. Cut the apple into quarters and remove the core. Peel off a thin strip of skin down the center of each quarter.

Put a large skillet (nonstick is best) over low heat and toss in the butter. When it's melted, put the endive into the pan cut side down and the apples skin side up. Add the grapes, scatter over the rosemary, and cook, undisturbed, for 20 minutes, at which point the underside of the endives will have caramelized and the apples and grapes will be soft and perhaps browned. Gently turn everything over, baste with any liquid in the pan, and cook for 20 minutes more.

Transfer the ingredients to a warm serving platter or to individual plates and, using a sturdy wooden or silicone spoon, scrape up the cooking sugars sticking to the bottom of the pan. You might want to pour a few spoonfuls of water into the pan to help you nab the sugars and make a spare amount of sauce. Season the endive with salt and pepper, spoon over the *jus,* and serve.

crunchy ginger-pickled cucumbers

MAKES 4 SERVINGS

SERVING
I think the pickles are best chilled, but they're fine at room temperature too, which is part of what makes them good picnic fare, and they're good at any temperature with the Café Salle Pleyel Hamburger (page 240).

STORING
The cucumbers are at their crunchiest the day they are made, but they're still very tasty a day later. If you're going to keep them overnight, drain off most of the pickling liquid and store the cucumbers in an airtight container in the fridge.

THE NEXT TIME YOU'RE GOING TO BE eating outdoors, think about these — they can up the piquancy quotient of any picnic hamper, since they're a hotter, hunkier take on traditional thinly sliced cucumbers in vinegar. In this version, the cucumbers (I like to use the seedless kind) are halved the long way, quartered, and cut into chunks small enough to eat in polite company but hearty enough to give you a good dose of the salad's sharp mix of minced ginger, hot pepper, and, of course, vinegar — either plain, unfancy white, or, if you're feeling a bit exotic, seasoned rice vinegar.

BE PREPARED: The pickles need to chill for at least 2 hours before serving.

1 seedless cucumber or 2 long regular cucumbers, peeled	¼ teaspoon sugar if you're using white vinegar
½ teaspoon sea salt	Pinch of red pepper flakes
1 tablespoon minced fresh ginger	Minced fresh cilantro, parsley, or chives, for garnish
¼ cup distilled white vinegar or seasoned rice vinegar	(optional)

If you're using a seedless cucumber, cut it into quarters the long way, then cut each quarter into chunks 1 to 1½ inches long. If you're using regular cucumbers, cut them in half the long way, scoop out the seeds with a small spoon, then cut the halves in half the long way and slice into chunks. Toss the chunks into a bowl, sprinkle with the salt, and stir to blend. Let the cucumbers stand, stirring occasionally, for about 30 minutes, then drain off the liquid.

Add the rest of the ingredients except the chopped herbs to the bowl and stir. Chill the pickles for at least 2 hours (4 to 6 hours is better), or for as long as overnight, before serving.

Just before serving, sprinkle with herbs, if desired.

pipérade stir-fry

STRICTLY SPEAKING, THIS IS NOT A PIPÉRADE, the Basque specialty of soft sautéed bell peppers with a little piment d'Espelette tossed in (see page 210 for a real pipérade), just my invention based on most of the ingredients that go into the classic. This is essentially a stir-fry in which colorful peppers are quickly cooked and then finished, very untraditionally, with vinegar, giving them a sharp edge and making them the ideal topping or sidekick for grilled foods or for any of the foods that would normally be paired with the classic: chicken, tuna, shrimp, chorizo, or eggs, for example. Think of it as a salsa from Southwest France.

MAKES 4 SERVINGS

SERVING
This mix goes well with grilled foods like chicken, meaty fish (try it with Spice-Crusted Tuna, page 304), and, best of all, steak. Serve the peppers family-style, or use them to top or go alongside the main course.

STORING
The peppers can be made up to 1 day ahead and kept tightly covered in the refrigerator; bring to room temperature and check for salt and pepper before serving.

2 red bell peppers	¼ cup red wine vinegar
1 green bell pepper	½ small red onion
1 yellow bell pepper	1 garlic clove, split, germ removed, and minced
1 orange bell pepper	
2 tablespoons extra-virgin olive oil	⅛ teaspoon piment d'Espelette (see Sources) or ¼ habanero chile, finely chopped
Salt and freshly ground pepper	

Cut the tops and bottoms off the peppers, and cut the peppers lengthwise in half. Remove the seeds, cut away the ribs, and slice the peppers into long strips about ¾ inch wide.

Put a wok or a large skillet, preferably nonstick, over high heat and add the oil. When it's hot, toss in the peppers, season with salt and pepper, and cook, stirring often, for 6 to 8 minutes, or until crisp-tender. Add the vinegar and cook, stirring, for another 2 to 3 minutes, until the vinegar caramelizes and coats the peppers. Transfer the peppers to a large bowl and let them come to room temperature.

Cut the onion half lengthwise in half, then slice it very thinly. Rinse the slices briefly under cold water, drain, and pat dry between paper towels.

Toss the onion, along with the garlic and piment d'Espelette or chile, into the bowl with the peppers and season with salt and pepper.

slow-roasted tomatoes

MAKES ABOUT
4 SERVINGS

SERVING
Think of these more as a
condiment than a side dish
and serve them whenever
you want a touch of color,
an extra hit of flavor, and
another texture.

STORING
If just cooled on the baking
sheet, the tomatoes should
be used within a few hours;
topped with oil and packed
in a jar, they will keep in the
refrigerator for a few weeks.

SLOW-ROASTED TOMATOES, OR *TOMATES CONFITES*, are somewhere between fresh tomatoes and sun-dried tomatoes and are the best thing you can do with any tomato that isn't as flavorful as you'd like it to be. (That said, don't let having good tomatoes stop you from roasting them — the time in the oven only makes them better.) By drizzling the tomatoes with oil and roasting them long and slow, you concentrate and deepen their flavor (I consider it a mini magic trick). And, if you don't use them right away, you can cover them with oil and get a bonus: tomato-infused olive oil.

Freshly made, the tomatoes are standouts in warm salads or tucked into whole fish bound for the oven or grill. If the tomatoes have been packed in oil, I stir them into simple pasta dishes, chop them to go into spreads and dips (see Eggplant Caviar, page 23), or spoon them and a little of their oil over grilled, sautéed, or steamed chicken, salmon, or tuna.

1 pint cherry or grape tomatoes	About 2 teaspoons extra-virgin olive oil, plus (optional) additional oil for storing
Pinch of fleur de sel or fine sea salt	1–2 rosemary or thyme sprigs (optional)
Pinch of freshly ground pepper	1–2 garlic cloves, smashed but not peeled (optional)

Center a rack in the oven and preheat the oven to 225 degrees F. Line a baking sheet with a silicone baking mat or parchment paper.

Cut the tomatoes in half — I cut cherry tomatoes crosswise (around their waists) and grape tomatoes from top to bottom — and place them cut side up on the lined baking sheet. Sprinkle with the salt and pepper and drizzle with the olive oil. There's no need to use a lot of oil — just enough so that the tomato tops glisten. (If you'd like, you can brush on the oil.) If you're using the herbs and/or garlic, scatter them over the tomatoes.

Slide the baking sheet into the oven and roast the tomatoes for about 3 hours. When they're done, they will be shriveled and a little dry looking, but press them gently, and you'll see that they've still got some juice.

Use the tomatoes immediately, or cool them on the baking sheet. If you're not using them now, pack them in a jar along with the garlic and herbs, if you used them, and cover them with olive oil.

tomatoes provençal

MAKES 6 SERVINGS

SERVING
I can't think of a dish that doesn't go with these tomatoes, from omelets and salads to roasted chicken, chops, and vegetables. You can serve tomatoes Provençal as a side dish, but because they're very good at room temperature, they're great on a buffet or in a picnic basket, or brought to a friend's for a potluck meal. Coarsely chopped, the tomatoes and their oil make a very good sauce for pasta.

STORING
The tomatoes can be covered and kept in the refrigerator overnight; serve cold, or allow them to come to room temperature, or reheat them gently.

EVERY FRENCH COOK WHO MAKES OVEN-ROASTED herb-topped tomatoes has his or her own recipe, but the fact is it needs no recipe at all. There are a few givens — the tomatoes, to be sure; olive oil to moisten them and make a little basting sauce; herbs to top them; and garlic to set your culinary compass to the South of France — but which herbs you use, how you cut the tomatoes, whether you roast them until they're almost melted or leave them a little firmer are all up to you.

Many recipes for tomatoes Provençal call for cutting the tomatoes in half, removing the seeds, and making a copious topping, really a stuffing, of herbs, garlic, and bread crumbs. As delicious as that is, it's not my favorite way to play the recipe — I prefer the rusticity of leaving in the tomatoes' juicy innards, and I don't use bread crumbs, because I like a dish with more emphasis on the tomatoes and herbs. But I've no doubt that after you make this once, you'll find your own version.

One last word: of course, everything will be better if you use ripe tomatoes, but because of the bold-flavored herbs and garlic, this is a recipe you can turn to even when tomatoes are not at their prime.

About 2 tablespoons extra-virgin olive oil	2 garlic cloves (or more or less), split, germ removed, and finely chopped
6 ripe tomatoes, about 4 ounces each	2–3 tablespoons minced mixed fresh herbs, such as parsley, basil, rosemary, oregano, thyme, and/or chives
Salt and freshly ground pepper	

Center a rack in the oven and preheat the oven to 375 degrees F. Use a little of the olive oil to grease a 9-inch pie plate or other baking dish that can hold the 12 tomato halves in a single layer.

Core the tomatoes and then slice them crosswise in half. If you want to scoop out the seeds, go ahead, but again, it's not necessary. Season the cut sides of the tomatoes with salt and pepper, and arrange them in the pie plate. (It's okay if the halves jostle one another and tilt on their sides a bit — precision isn't crucial here.)

Toss the garlic and minced herbs into a small bowl, season with salt and pepper, and, using your fingers, mix to blend. Sprinkle the topping over the tomatoes, making sure that each tomato gets its share, then drizzle the tomatoes and topping with olive oil. Don't drench the tomatoes, but don't be stingy either — you want the topping to be lightly moistened, and it's good to have some oil in the bottom of the pan.

Roast the tomatoes for 25 to 30 minutes. Spoon some of the accumulated juices over the tomatoes, and continue to roast for another 20 to 30 minutes, until the tomatoes are very tender and easily pierced with the tip of a knife. If you like your tomatoes firmer, take a look at them at the 20-minute mark and decide if they're done enough for you.

When you remove the pan from the oven, baste the tomatoes again.

Tomato Provençal Tian. The tian is named for the pottery dish, like a deep-dish pie plate, that holds the tomatoes. Slice the tomatoes crosswise into thirds and arrange them in slightly overlapping circles in an oiled 9-inch pie plate. (You may need more or fewer than 6 tomatoes.) Cover the tomatoes with the herb-garlic mixture (you may need a little more), drizzle generously with oil, and roast. If you like, a few minutes before the tomatoes are ready to come out of the oven, dust the top of the tian with grated Parmesan or Gruyère. For a browner top, run the pan under the broiler before serving. If you use the cheese, the dish is better served hot than cold.

chanterelles with napa and nuts

MAKES 4 SIDE-
DISH OR STARTER
SERVINGS

SERVING
You need to get the mushrooms to the table quickly, since they're best served hot. If, for some reason, they've had to wait, you can give them a very quick reheat (see Storing) to bring them back up to temperature. Serve them as an accompaniment to steaks, roasts, or sautéed meat or as a starter, in which case you can add a pouf of herb salad.

STORING
Best eaten as soon as they're made, the mushrooms can be reheated quickly in a skillet over high heat if necessary. You might have to add a bit more bouillon or a splash of water.

BONNE IDÉE
Chanterelles for Chicken or Fish. Replace the beef bouillon with an equal amount of chicken bouillon and omit the soy sauce. If you'd like, you can add a few white grapes to the mix: Halve and seed the grapes. Add them when the mushrooms are almost soft and cook for 1 minute, then proceed with the recipe.

THIS DISH COMES FROM LA FERRANDAISE, a wonderful bistro around the corner from our apartment. Chanterelles, the thin-stemmed, fan-shaped golden mushrooms known as *girolles* in France, are quickly sautéed, cooked to tenderness in broth, and then strewn with finely shredded Napa cabbage, chopped hazelnuts, and fresh parsley. The cabbage, so unexpected, is sweet and bold, the nuts are a little crunchy, and the parsley adds some freshness. At La Ferrandaise, the mushrooms are cooked in a *jus de viande,* a rich, meaty broth that chefs have on hand all the time. At home, to keep the rapidity of the dish's preparation as well as its flavor and spirit, I use a beef broth made with that most relied-upon French shortcut, a bouillon cube, which I fortify with a drop of soy sauce.

When I first had this dish, it was as a starter — the mushrooms were spooned into a soup plate and presented on their own — but it's also good served alongside something substantial. In fact, with just a switch of bouillon, from beef to chicken, the dish goes from deep and dark to soft and light, and from perfect with a big roast to just right with chicken or fish; see Bonne Idée for the how-to.

This dish was created for chanterelles and is really best with them. However, if chanterelles aren't available, you can make the dish with assorted wild mushrooms or even white mushrooms, any of which might not cook up in the same way as chanterelles, so be prepared to make adjustments in the amounts of oil and liquid needed.

¾	pound chanterelles	Salt and freshly ground pepper
½	beef bouillon cube	⅓ cup finely shredded Napa cabbage
½	cup boiling water	
	Scant ½ teaspoon soy sauce	2 tablespoons chopped toasted hazelnuts
1–2	tablespoons extra-virgin olive oil	1 tablespoon chopped fresh parsley
1	shallot, finely chopped, rinsed, and dried	

If your mushrooms are not very dirty, you can clean them using a little brush or a damp cloth or paper towel. If they're really dirty, you may need to rinse them — just make sure to dry them well. Trim the bottom of the stems if they seem tough, and if the mushrooms are very large, slice them in half lengthwise. Dissolve the bouillon cube in the boiling water, and stir in the soy sauce.

Pour 1 tablespoon oil into a large skillet or, better yet, a wok (or wok-shaped pan), and warm over medium heat. Add the shallot and cook, stirring, until it softens, about 2 minutes. Turn up the heat to medium-high and, if the pan seems dry, add some more oil. Add the mushrooms and stir to coat them with

oil. Season with salt and pepper and sauté the mushrooms for a minute, then add the bouillon and bring to a boil. If the mushrooms haven't released much liquid, cook them, covered, for about 2 minutes, until they're just tender; if they have given up a lot of liquid, cook them uncovered. (If you have really a lot of liquid, unusual but possible, remove the mushrooms with a slotted spoon and reduce the liquid. Then, when you add the cabbage, return the mushrooms to the pan.) In either case, at the point where the mushrooms offer just a little resistance when poked with the tip of a knife, 2 to 3 minutes into the cooking, uncover them if they were covered and boil down the bouillon until just a couple of tablespoons remain. Add the cabbage and stir to mix. Cook for about 30 seconds, turn off the heat, stir in the hazelnuts and parsley, and serve.

baby bok choy, sugar snaps, and garlic en papillote

MAKES 4 SERVINGS

SERVING
The vegetables should be served as soon as you pull the packets from the oven. You can put each packet on a plate or in a shallow soup plate and open them at the table, or you can open them in the kitchen and plate them there. Have minced fresh mint for dusting each portion on the table, if you'd like. While this is perfect as a side dish — it's particularly good with fish — I think it's so pretty and so tasty that I often serve it as a starter.

STORING
You can assemble the packets a few hours ahead of time and refrigerate them; just add another minute or two to the oven time.

I FIND IT BOTH DELIGHTFUL AND ODD that I've never been served baby bok choy at a single Parisian dinner party, since it's a vegetable that I can count on finding at just about every market. Who, besides *moi,* is buying it? Most often used in Chinese cooking, baby bok choy takes perfectly to the French technique of cooking *en papillote* — oven-steaming keeps the bok choy's pale celadon color, the delicacy of its leaves (I love the slight furling at their edges), and the firmness of its bulbous body. While you can cook bok choy with Asian flavorings — toss it with soy, ginger, garlic, and one drop of sesame oil — I like to give it a more Europe-in-the-spring accent by having it share the pouch with bright green sugar snaps, baby white onions, and slim, slim slices of garlic. Finishing it with olive oil, mint, and orange zest makes this pure invention taste as though it might have come from somewhere along the French-Italian border.

32 sugar snap peas	4 teaspoons olive oil
2 baby bok choy	4 mint sprigs, plus (optional)
12 baby white onions, halved	minced fresh mint for garnish
1 garlic clove, peeled	Salt and freshly ground pepper
Zest of ½ small orange	

Center a rack in the oven and preheat the oven to 400 degrees F. Cut four 12-inch squares of nonstick aluminum foil, and have a baking sheet at hand.

If necessary, string the sugar snaps by pulling on the little bit of "string" sticking out from one end of the pea, then pull the string across the top of the pod. Cut the sugar snaps crosswise in half and toss them into a bowl. Quarter the bok choy lengthwise and add to the bowl, along with the onions.

If you'd like, you can finely chop the garlic, but I prefer to slice it. If you use a garlic mandoline (a mini mandoline), a Benriner slicer, or a regular mandoline, you'll get lovely, petal-thin slices of garlic; if you're sans mandoline, cut the garlic into slivers with a small, very sharp knife. Toss the garlic into the bowl. As for the orange zest, I like to have skinny ribbons of zest for this dish, so I use a zester — a little scraper with tiny holes in the top that removes the zest in strands — but you can remove the zest with a vegetable peeler and chop it, or you can grate it. Toss the zest into the bowl, pour in the olive oil, add the mint sprigs, and season generously with salt and pepper.

Spoon an equal amount of the mix onto the center of each piece of foil. Draw up the edges of the foil and seal the packets well, but don't crimp the foil too close to the vegetables — you want to leave room around the ingredients so they can steam. Put the packets on the baking sheet.

Bake the *papillotes* for 15 minutes, or until the bok choy is tender — carefully

open a packet and poke a piece with the tip of a knife to test.

Serve the vegetables in their packets, or spoon them into individual bowls. Have a bowl of minced fresh mint on the table, if desired, so each serving can be garnished to taste.

swiss chard pancakes

MAKES ABOUT
FORTY 5-INCH
PANCAKES;
12 SIDE-DISH OR
STARTER SERVINGS
OR 8 MAIN-
COURSE SERVINGS

SERVING
Traditionally, *farçous* are served with a salad as a main course, but you could serve fewer per portion as a starter or omit the salad and serve them as a side dish. If you want to serve the *farçous* as an hors d'oeuvre, you might want to include a dipping sauce or topping of crème fraîche, *cervelle de canut* (page 20), or plain yogurt. You might also think about drizzling them with a little basil or parsley coulis (see Bonne Idée, page 488) — they don't really need the coulis, but it's a good combination.

STORING
You can make the *farçous* a few hours ahead, keep them covered at room temperature, and reheat them in a conventional oven or microwave before serving. Or you can pack them airtight (make sure to separate them with small squares of wax or parchment paper) and freeze them, then reheat as needed.

MY FRIEND DIDIER FRAYSSOU, a wine master who can match any dish to its soul-mate wine, has a quality I adore in French men: a sophisticated palate and a love of his mom's home cooking. I don't think I'd known him five minutes before he started telling me about his mother's *farçous,* a type of crepe or galette that's loaded with greens, most especially Swiss chard. Didier comes from Laguiole in the Auvergne, but *farçous* are a staple throughout Southwest France, where all the moms have their own way of making them.

In French homes, *farçous* are a robust main course, most often served with a salad. Served as supper, the pancakes are usually fairly big, sometimes even as large as a skillet, but they can be made smaller (my preference) and served as an hors d'oeuvre, starter, or side dish. And while I'm sure that moms all over France insist that their combination of chard and herbs is the best (if not the only acceptable one), I'm equally sure that thrifty cooks vary the recipe without apology, adding whatever herbs they can snip from the garden or scavenge from the refrigerator bin and opting for another onion instead of a shallot if that's what they have on hand. I like the addition of parsley and chives to the pancakes, but if you've got rosemary or thyme instead, or if you prefer basil or sage, feel free to play around. I'm sure that somewhere in the rule book it says that *farçous* can only be made with Swiss chard, but spinach, however unorthodox, is also awfully good.

This makes a lot of pancakes, but they freeze perfectly, so I always make the full recipe. If you think this is going to be too much for you, cut the recipe in half and use 1 egg and 1 yolk.

2	cups whole milk	
2½	cups all-purpose flour	
3	large eggs	
1	small onion, coarsely chopped	
1	shallot, coarsely chopped, rinsed, and patted dry	
2	garlic cloves, split, germ removed, and coarsely chopped	

	Leaves from 10 parsley sprigs
10	fresh chives, snipped
	Salt and freshly ground pepper
5	large or 10 small Swiss chard leaves, center ribs removed, washed, and dried
	About ½ cup grapeseed, peanut, or vegetable oil

Preheat the oven to 250 degrees F. Line a baking sheet with foil, and line a plate with paper towels.

Put everything except the Swiss chard and oil in a blender or food processor, making sure you season the mix generously with salt and pepper, and whir until the batter is smooth. (If your machine won't handle this quantity, work in batches.) Little by little, add the chard to the mix and whir to incorporate it. There's no need to pulverize the chard — having some strands is nice.

Pour ¼ to ½ inch of oil into a large skillet and place the skillet over medium-high heat. When the oil is hot (a drop of batter should seize immediately), spoon in a scant ¼ cup batter for each pancake — don't crowd the pan: depending on the size of the pan, 4 pancakes is probably max per batch. Cook the pancakes for about 3 minutes, until the underside is nicely browned and the edges are browned and curled. Flip the pancakes over and cook for another 2 minutes or so. Transfer the pancakes to the paper-towel-lined plate, cover with more towels, and pat off the excess oil. Place them on the foil-lined baking sheet and keep warm in the oven while you continue to make pancakes, adding more oil to the pan as needed.

brown-sugar squash and brussels sprouts en papillote

MAKES 4 SERVINGS

SERVING

The vegetables should be served as soon as they're cooked. You have a choice: you can open the packets in the kitchen and spoon the vegetables and their *jus* onto dinner plates or bring the sealed packets to the table on the plates and let each guest have the pleasure of savoring that first fragrant puff of steam that's released when the seal is broken.

STORING

You can make the packets a few hours ahead and keep them in the refrigerator; bake them directly from the fridge, adding a couple of minutes to their cooking time.

IT'S EASY TO GET CARRIED AWAY in the Paris markets. Everything is displayed so fetchingly, and while you're waiting for the vendor, you watch what everyone else is buying, talk to a few people, spy one or two things in the back of the stall — and then, when it's your turn, you buy very little that's on your list and everything that's caught your eye in the past few minutes. That's how you end up with a little of this and a little of that in the vegetable bin, and it's how new dishes are created. As you can see from the ingredient list, this dish was created in late fall. What pleased me most about this serendipitous side was the play between earthy and sweet. I don't think I'd ever have put the squash and Brussels sprouts together if they weren't packed into the bin side by side. And it was just a stroke of luck that I had both an apple and fresh sage, which is perfect with the vegetables and fruit.

1	pound peeled butternut squash, cubed	4	teaspoons olive oil
			Salt and freshly ground pepper
16	small Brussels sprouts, halved	1	teaspoon brown sugar, or more to taste
1	apple, peeled, cored, and cubed	4	fresh sage leaves

Preheat the oven to 400 degrees F. Cut four 12-inch squares of nonstick aluminum foil, and have a baking sheet at hand.

Toss the squash, Brussels sprouts, apple, and olive oil together in a bowl. Season with salt and pepper, and spoon an equal amount of the mixture onto each piece of foil. Sprinkle a little bit of brown sugar over each bundle — you can use more brown sugar if you'd like — and top with a sage leaf. Draw up the edges of the foil and seal the packets well, leaving room around the ingredients so they can steam. Put the packets on the baking sheet.

Bake for 25 minutes, or until the vegetables are tender. You can open a packet to test.

roasted jerusalem artichokes with garlic

MAKES 4 SERVINGS

FOR REASONS THAT ARE NOT CLEAR TO ME, Jerusalem artichokes are usually pureed. They're pushed through a food mill or beaten in a mixer and served like mashed potatoes or pureed into a soup (see page 76 for one of my favorite Jerusalem artichoke soups). These knobbly vegetables, which look a little like darker, rougher-skinned relatives of ginger, are sold mostly under the name of sunchokes in the United States — they're actually sunflower tubers. When they're pureed, you catch their artichokeness, but when they're roasted, they're more difficult to place: their flavor is mostly toasty and sweet, and their texture, so crunchy when raw, becomes soft and light, like the inside of a perfectly cooked French fry.

For this dish, the roasted artichokes are paired with another full-flavored ingredient: garlic. When you slice the garlic into translucent petals (I do this with a small mandoline made specifically for garlic or with a Benriner slicer), it browns and crisps in the oven and emerges tasting like the best snack food you've ever had. It's tempting to want to pick the petals out of the roasting dish and nibble them, but don't — as good as they are alone, they're so much better with their culinary companion, the sunchokes.

SERVING
These are meant to be served hot from the oven. If the chokes look a tad dry to you, drizzle them with a little extra-virgin olive oil or let your guests do that themselves.

STORING
It's best to enjoy these freshly roasted.

1¼	pounds Jerusalem artichokes (sunchokes), well scrubbed
	About 2 tablespoons olive oil
4	garlic cloves, split, germ removed, and very thinly sliced (see above)
4	thyme sprigs
4	rosemary sprigs
	Salt and freshly ground pepper

Center a rack in the oven and preheat the oven to 400 degrees F. Lightly oil a 9-inch pie plate or similar-sized baking dish.

This dish is really best if you peel the Jerusalem artichokes, a job that can be a little fussy. It's easiest to peel the gnarly hunks with a swivel-blade vegetable peeler (i.e., a peeler with a blade that moves around), so it can get in and out of the artichokes' nooks and crannies. If all you've got is a fixed-blade peeler, do the best you can without making yourself crazy, and leave whatever peel is too hard to reach — the peel is edible, so there are no worries on that count. Cut the sunchokes into quarters. I cut lengthwise quarters, but you can cut them crosswise if you prefer that look.

Put all of the ingredients in the pie plate — be generous with the salt and pepper — and, using your hands, toss everything together until the slices of artichokes are glistening with oil.

Roast for 35 to 45 minutes, turning the artichokes once after 20 minutes, if you think of it, until they're lightly browned at the tips and you can pierce their middles easily with the point of a small knife.

go-with-everything celery root puree

MAKES **6** SERVINGS

SERVING
Like mashed potatoes, this puree is fine served in a bowl that can be passed at the table, but, again like mashed potatoes, it's also a good base, so think of it when you want to serve a one-dish main course — you can never go wrong with a combo like celery root puree topped with short ribs.

STORING
Leftover puree can be refrigerated for up to 3 days or packed airtight and frozen for up to 2 months. To reheat, warm the puree in the top of a double boiler or in a microwave oven.

EIGHT TIMES OUT OF TEN, when I pick up celery root in a market in the United States, someone asks me what it is. I rarely see recipes for it, and I can't remember when I was ever served celery root in a friend's home. Not so in France, where the sweet, fresh, and just-a-little-green flavor of celery root is prized, mostly for its role in *céleri rémoulade* (shredded celery root mixed with a zesty mayonnaise dressing) but also in soups and stews — it can be added to any stew in which you're using other root vegetables, like potatoes, turnips, or parsnips.

For this recipe, the celery root is cooked, then whirred in a food processor. The result is a smooth ivory puree with a soft, surprising flavor — you'll think it's celery, but you won't be sure. Because the flavor is subtle, complex, and just a little sweet, the puree is the perfect accompaniment to fish, meat, or poultry, whether it's a main dish that is robust and big flavored or one that is light and mild.

3 cups whole milk	1 small onion, quartered
3 cups water	5 tablespoons unsalted butter,
Salt	cut into 5 pieces, at room
2 celery roots, about 1¼	temperature
pounds each, peeled and	Freshly ground white pepper
cut into 2-inch cubes	
1 medium Idaho (russet)	Snipped fresh chives, pistachio
potato (about 10 ounces),	oil (see Sources), or browned
peeled and cut into 2-inch	butter (see below), for serving
cubes	(optional)

Bring the milk, water, and 1 tablespoon salt to a boil in a large pot — keep an eye on the pot, because milk has a tendency to bubble up furiously. Drop in the celery root, potato, and onion, adjust the heat so that the liquid simmers steadily, and cook for about 30 minutes, or until the vegetables are tender and can be pierced easily with the point of a knife. Drain, discard the liquid, and shake the colander well to remove as much liquid as possible.

In a food processor, in batches if necessary, puree the vegetables until perfectly smooth. Add the butter and whir until completely incorporated. Taste and add salt and white pepper as needed.

Transfer the puree to a warm serving bowl and, if you'd like, top with a generous shower of snipped chives or a drizzle of pistachio oil or butter that's been cooked over low heat until its color is honey brown. Serve immediately.

mashed potatoes
mine, michael's, and those of a burgundy chef

In our house, it's my husband who usually makes the mashed potatoes, or what the French call *purée*. (Never mind that almost any fruit or vegetable can be pureed; when you hear the word in France, the odds are that potatoes are involved.)

My own recipe is straightforward: For 4 people, I take about 2 pounds of Idaho (russet) or Yukon Gold potatoes, peel them, cut them into chunks, and cook them in a large pot of generously salted boiling water. When they're soft enough to break when poked with a knife, I drain them, put them back into the pot, and toss them around over low heat to dry them. To mash them, I use a food mill, which is what many of my French friends use, or a ricer, a tool that turns ordinary boiled potatoes into short, ricelike, fluffy strands.

Following advice I first heard from Julia Child, I stir warm milk into the potatoes. (The quantity depends some on your potatoes and mostly on the consistency you want, but have at least ½ cup at hand.) Then, when the potatoes are the way I like them, I start adding butter a tablespoon at a time, tasting as I go and usually going not further than 3 to 4 tablespoons.

Michael, however, thinks my potatoes aren't rich enough. I like a puree that retains some starch and graininess, while he likes it to be flawlessly smooth, the kind of smooth you can only get if you're profligate with the butter and carefree with the cream. When Michael's on KP, he boils the potatoes the way I do, but he mashes them using the paddle attachment of a stand mixer. Where I add milk, he adds heavy cream, lots of it, since he likes his puree fairly thin. Finally, in goes the butter, again, lots of it, usually twice as much as I add, making the potatoes slightly stretchy and exceedingly luxurious.

Michael's platonic ideal of mashed potatoes is the puree we had in a now-defunct restaurant near Beaune in Burgundy. He loved them so much that he ordered seconds and begged the owner to give us the chef's secret for the richness and startling smoothness. *"C'est simple,"* she said, "the puree's more butter than potatoes!"

If you're hesitant, just add as much butter as your conscience allows, then close your eyes and, while adding another pat or three, think of the legendary chef Fernand Point. His guiding principle was *simple* too: "Butter, butter, and more butter."

matafan
(fluffy mashed potato pancakes)

MAKES 4 SIDE-
DISH SERVINGS OR
8 HORS-D'OEUVRE
SERVINGS

SERVING

Matafan should be served hot, although they don't lose their appeal when they're only just warm. If you're serving *matafan* as a side dish, you don't need to fancy them up, although a quick brush of melted butter never did anything any harm. And, as my husband will tell you, they're not half bad with maple syrup. If you're serving them as an hors d'oeuvre or even a starter, you might top them with crème fraîche and caviar, a spoonful of *cervelle de canut* (page 20), a little cottage cheese and cracked pepper, or a green salad dressed with a sharp vinaigrette.

STORING

You can keep the batter in the refrigerator for a few hours, and once the pancakes are made, you can keep them warm in a 200-degree-F oven for about 20 minutes if you cover them loosely with foil. You can also pack the pancakes airtight — make sure to separate them with sheets of wax or parchment paper — and freeze them for up to 2 months. Defrost them on the counter or in a microwave oven and warm them in a moderate oven or, for a little crispness, pop them into the toaster.

ACROSS BETWEEN PANCAKES AND BLINI, a side dish, snack, or starter, *matafan* used to be eaten in the morning in the hopes of staving off belly rumbling before lunch. (*Mat* is short for *matín,* or morning, and *fan* is what *faím,* the word for hungry, sounds like.) The first time I made *matafan,* my plan was to serve the little mashed potato pancakes as an hors d'oeuvre, something to nibble with white wine and tide everyone over until dinner, but they barely made it out of the kitchen. No sooner did I flip one cake from the frying pan onto a plate than someone would come into the kitchen and snatch it. I had made them blini-size and wanted to serve them with a bit of crème fraîche and salmon roe, but I gave up when Michael pulled out the maple syrup (something I always keep in Paris) and started dipping the *matafan* into it. I have to admit, it was a great combination.

To get the best texture, you should use Idaho (russet) potatoes, and you should follow the instructions and bake them on a bed of salt. Salt-baking the potatoes dries them out and makes them easy to blend with the other ingredients. I tried making *matafan* with yellow potatoes, specifically Yukon Golds, and I tried boiling the potatoes (so much faster) and then drying them by tossing them around in a saucepan over heat, but the pancakes weren't the same. Also, if you've got a potato ricer or a food mill, pull it out — it will give you the best texture for these cakes.

I serve mini *matafan* as a nibble with an aperitif, in pancake size as a side dish with anything that's got a sauce (it's great with Boeuf à la Mode, page 252), and in any size as the base for a salad at lunch, when I pile dressed greens on top of the pancakes.

Kosher or other coarse salt, for baking the potatoes	½ cup all-purpose flour
2 large Idaho (russet) potatoes (1½ pounds total), scrubbed and dried	¼ cup hot whole milk
	Salt and freshly ground white pepper
4 large eggs; 2 separated	Butter, for cooking the pancakes

Center a rack in the oven and preheat the oven to 400 degrees F. Choose a small baking dish (it needs to be just slightly larger than the potatoes), or use a foil pan, and pour in ¼ inch of kosher salt. The salt bed doesn't have to cover the whole pan; it should be just as large as the 2 potatoes side by side with a little breathing room between them. Put the spuds on the salt.

Bake the potatoes for 1½ hours — they will be very dry and the skin will be very hard. Set the potatoes on a rack, and as soon as you can bear to handle them, cut them in half and scoop out the flesh. Run the potato innards through a ricer or food mill — first choices — into a bowl, or push the flesh through a strainer (tedious but effective).

Using a sturdy spatula or a wooden spoon, beat in the 2 whole eggs and the 2 egg yolks one at a time. Stir in half of the flour, followed by all of the warm milk, and then the last of the flour. Season the batter generously with salt and white pepper.

With an electric mixer, beat the 2 egg whites with a pinch of salt until they form firm but still glossy peaks. Stir about one quarter of the whites into the *matafan* batter, then add the remaining whites to the bowl and gently fold them in. *(You can cover the batter at this point and chill it for a few hours.)*

When you're ready to cook the *matafan,* place a heavy-bottomed skillet, preferably nonstick, or a griddle over medium heat. Put 2 teaspoons butter into the skillet or lightly butter the griddle, and when the bubbles subside, start making the pancakes. For regular-sized cakes, use about ¼ cup batter; for blini-sized pancakes, use about 2 tablespoons. Spoon the batter into the pan (or onto the griddle) — nudge it gently to round the cakes — and cook for 2 minutes, or until the bubbles that form on top of the pancakes have popped, then flip the cakes over and cook for another minute, or until the underside is nicely browned. Transfer the finished pancakes to a plate, cover loosely with foil, and continue flipping the cakes until you've used all the batter. (If you want to hold these until serving time, you can keep them in a 200-degree-F oven for about 20 minutes.)

broth-braised potatoes

MAKES 4 SERVINGS

SERVING
While the braised potatoes are good with any kind of roasted or pan-seared meat, I think they're particularly good with "white" foods like chicken or mild fish fillets.

STORING
The potatoes should be served as soon as they're ready. However, if you've got any leftover spuds, you can use them in a salad. Or turn them into hash browns by cutting them into smaller cubes and browning them in oil with chopped onions and, if you'd like, a little bacon.

BONNE IDÉE
Broth-Braised Fennel. Trim 4 bulbs of baby fennel and halve them, or trim 2 small fennel bulbs and quarter them lengthwise, and braise them in the same way as the potatoes. The fennel usually cooks faster than potatoes, so check for tenderness at the 10-minute mark.

THINK OF THESE AS ENERGIZED BOILED POTATOES. They get the same high marks as boiled potatoes for playing well with others and extra points for having more flavor, since they're cooked in chicken broth infused with garlic, herbs, lemon zest, and olive oil. The broth et al bring up the sweetness of the potatoes and add a touch of intrigue to a dependable dish. This treatment works best with small potatoes, like fingerlings, baby Yukon Golds, or new potatoes, but you can cut larger potatoes into smaller cubes.

1	cup chicken broth	2	thyme or rosemary sprigs or
½	cup water		2 fresh sage leaves
1	tablespoon extra-virgin olive oil		Salt and freshly ground pepper
2	garlic cloves, split and germ removed	12	fingerling, new, or baby potatoes, scrubbed or peeled and cut in half (or about 1¼ pounds large Yukon Gold potatoes, peeled and cut into about 3-inch cubes)
1	strip lemon zest		
1	bay leaf		

Put all the ingredients except the potatoes in a medium saucepan with a cover, seasoning the broth well with salt and pepper. Bring to a boil, cover, reduce the heat, and simmer for 5 minutes. Add the potatoes, cover, and simmer until they can be pierced easily with the tip of a knife, about 15 minutes. The time will vary with the type and size of the potatoes, so check a little before the 15-minute mark and then check frequently after it.

If you'd like to serve some of the cooking liquid with the potatoes, lift the potatoes from the pan with a slotted spoon — put them in a warm bowl and cover them — and turn the heat up under the broth. Cook the broth for a few minutes, until it reduces slightly and the flavors are more concentrated. Taste for salt and pepper.

salty-sweet potato far

MAKES **6** TO **8** SIDE-DISH SERVINGS OR **3** OR **4** MAIN-COURSE SERVINGS

THE CLASSIC *FAR BRETON*, a custardy cake with prunes, raisins, and rum, has been a favorite of mine since a friend of ours from southern Brittany made it for us more than thirty years ago. Until a recent trip to the region, I had no idea that the *far* had a salty sister. The base is still a crepe batter and there are still prunes and raisins, but instead of sugar, there are bits of bacon and lots of grated potatoes. It's a substantial go-along — a little like a German kugel — that pairs surprisingly well with dishes as varied as saucy beef stew and simply grilled salmon, but it's so deliciously quirky that since I discovered it, I've been serving it with a salad and calling it supper.

I usually bake the *far* in a deep-dish Pyrex pie plate, but if you've got an oven-going pottery or ceramic dish of similar volume, use it — you'll love the way the golden, puffed, and slightly craggy-topped *far* looks in a rustic dish.

SERVING
The *far* should be served piping hot, as a side dish or as the main event of a casual meal.

STORING
Though *far* is best right after it's made, leftovers can be kept covered in the refrigerator or on the counter overnight and served at room temperature the following day.

¼ pound slab bacon, cut into lardons (pieces about 1 inch long and ¼ to ½ inch thick)

1¾ cups all-purpose flour

1⅓ cups whole milk

2 large eggs

½ teaspoon salt

¼ teaspoon freshly ground pepper

1¼ pounds all-purpose potatoes, scrubbed or peeled and coarsely grated into a bowl

8 plump, moist pitted prunes, halved

⅔ cup plump, moist raisins

2 tablespoons cold butter, preferably salted

Center a rack in the oven and preheat the oven to 425 degrees F. Line a baking sheet with a silicone baking mat or parchment paper. Generously butter a 9-inch deep-dish pie plate (or a similar-sized baking dish; 2-quart capacity is right); set the pan on the baking sheet.

Put a heavy skillet over medium-low heat and toss in the bacon matchsticks. Cook slowly, turning as needed, until the lardons are nicely browned. Lift the lardons out of the pan and drain on a double layer of paper towels.

Put the flour, milk, eggs, salt, and pepper in a bowl and beat with a whisk until the batter is lumpless. Lift the grated potatoes out of their bowl, squeeze them gently between your hands — you want to rid them of excess moisture, not pack them together — and stir them into the batter. Add the lardons, prunes, and raisins, stir to blend, and turn the batter into the prepared pan. Cut 1 tablespoon of the butter into bits and scatter them over the *far*.

Bake for 45 minutes, then lower the oven temperature to 350 degrees F. Cut the remaining tablespoon of butter into bits, dot the top of the *far* with the butter, and continue baking for about 30 minutes more. When done, the top will be golden (if it looks as though the *far* is browning too quickly, cover it loosely with a foil tent), the butter will be bubbling all around the edges, and a knife inserted into the center of the *far* will come out clean.

Remove the *far* from the oven and serve immediately.

potato gratin (*pommes dauphinois*)

MAKES **8** SERVINGS

SERVING
Bring the gratin to the table to cut — it's too pretty to leave in the kitchen.

STORING
This should be eaten soon after it's baked. You can reheat it, but it will lose some of its creaminess and almost all of the sheen that freshly melted cheese has.

AFTER *POMMES FRITES* (French fries, see box, page 239), this may be the most famous potato dish in France. While the recipe for *pommes dauphinois* can have a few flourishes, it is basic: layers of thinly sliced potatoes soaked in cream, topped with cheese, and baked until the potatoes absorb the cream and the cheese melts and bubbles and forms a little crust, or *gratin*.

The gratin is named and claimed by the former Dauphiné province of France (now part of Burgundy), but its reputation is international and its popularity extreme, particularly in cold climes. When we were in Megève, a movie-perfect skiing village in the French Alps, almost every dish, no matter what it was, came with a hefty serving of *pommes dauphinois*. And, in case you're wondering, a serving of potato gratin, even a small serving, is hefty — it's the nature of the dish and part of what makes it so remarkably satisfying. Besides, if you've been schussing the Alps all day, potatoes, cream, and cheese are just what you need.

There's really no reason to embellish this dish, but then there's really no reason not to, since potatoes and cream take so nicely to so many things, like mushrooms or spinach or a companion cheese. See Bonne Idée for a few suggestions for personalizing the gratin (and maybe using up some leftovers in the process).

1¾ cups heavy cream	Light cream or whole milk, if needed
3 garlic cloves, split, germ removed, and finely chopped	Small thyme or rosemary sprigs (optional)
2–2¼ pounds Idaho (russet) potatoes	¼ pound cheese, preferably Gruyère, grated (about 1 cup)
Salt and freshly ground pepper	

Center a rack in the oven and preheat the oven to 350 degrees F. Line a baking sheet with a silicone baking mat or parchment. Generously butter a 9-inch deep-dish pie plate (a Pyrex pan is perfect) or other 2-quart baking pan and put it on the baking sheet.

Put the heavy cream and garlic in a saucepan and bring to a gentle simmer over low heat. Keep it warm while you work on the potatoes.

If you've got a mandoline or a Benriner slicer, now's the time to get it out; if not, you can use the thin slicing blade of a food processor or a sturdy sharp knife. One by one, peel the potatoes and slice them into rounds about ⅛ inch thick. As each potato is cut, arrange the slices in slightly overlapping concentric circles in the pie plate (or rows, if your pan isn't round), season with salt and pepper, and spoon over some of the warm garlic-infused cream, lightly pressing down on the potatoes with the back of the spoon so that the cream works its way around all of the slices. Continue until you've filled the pan. If you're shy of a little garlic-infused cream — you want the cream to just peek out around the edges of the pan — pour over a little light cream or milk. If you're using the herbs,

BONNE IDÉE
If you want a dash of color, substitute an equal weight of sweet potatoes for an Idaho or two or sneak in a layer of cooked chopped spinach or chard, sautéed mushrooms, or steamed small broccoli florets. Bits of cooked bacon or strips of lightly sautéed pancetta are natural go-withs as well. And while Gruyère or Emmenthal is traditional, there's no reason not to mix things up and add Parmesan or even a blue cheese, like Gorgonzola. If you've got odd chunks of cheese in the fridge, use Gruyère or Emmenthal as the base and add the other cheeses to it.

strew them over the potatoes. Dust the top of the gratin with the grated cheese.

Slide the gratin (on the baking sheet) into the oven and bake for 45 minutes, then check the gratin: if you can poke a knife through the potatoes and easily reach the bottom of the pan, the gratin is done; if the potatoes need more time but the gratin is getting too brown, cover the top loosely with foil and bake until the potatoes are tender, another 15 minutes or so.

Remove the gratin from the oven and let it rest in a very warm place (or in the turned-off oven with the door open) for 5 to 10 minutes before you serve it, just so the bubbles can settle down and the potatoes can absorb the maximum amount of cream.

cauliflower-bacon gratin

MAKES ABOUT
10 SIDE-DISH
SERVINGS OR 5
MAIN-COURSE
SERVINGS

SERVING
The gratin is best just from the oven or warm, but like a quiche, it can be enjoyed at room temperature. Serve it alongside anything roasted — it's nice with something a little rich like a roast — or have it with a salad and call it supper.

STORING
You really should eat the gratin the day it is made, but if you've got leftovers, cover and refrigerate them, then let them come to room temperature or warm them briefly and gently in the oven or microwave.

BONNE IDÉE
You can replace the bacon with cubes of ham. You can certainly add herbs or spices to the mix — thyme is good, but so is curry. And you can add a companion vegetable — quickly sautéed onions come to mind, but there's no reason not to have the cauliflower share the stage with its more colorful cousin, broccoli.

IF THE FRENCH CELEBRATED THANKSGIVING, I'm sure they'd find a place at the table for this gratin. Simply made, appealingly rustic, and very tasty, it can sit alongside a main course or, with a little salad (and maybe even some cranberry sauce), take the stage alone for brunch, lunch, or supper. The recipe was given to me more than twenty-five years ago, and after making it the first time, I wrote in the margin that it was a little like a quiche (it's really only the addition of flour that sets it apart from a quiche filling) and in some ways like a pudding, in that it's rich, soft, and creamy. It's a classic — it was popular when it was first passed along to me, and it's a recipe that's still treasured today.

1 cauliflower	⅔ cup whole milk
¼ pound bacon, cut crosswise into slender strips	Salt and freshly ground pepper
⅓ cup all-purpose flour	Freshly grated nutmeg
5 large eggs, lightly beaten	3 ounces Gruyère (you can use
1 cup heavy cream	Emmenthal, or even Swiss in a pinch), grated

Center a rack in the oven and preheat the oven to 425 degrees F. Line a baking sheet with a silicone baking mat or parchment paper. Generously butter an oven-going pan that holds about 2½ quarts. (It's not elegant and it's a tad too big, but a 9-x-13-inch Pyrex pan is fine.) Put the dish on the baking sheet.

Put a large pot of salted water on to boil. Pull or cut the florets from the cauliflower, leaving about an inch or so of stem. Drop the florets into the boiling water and cook for 10 minutes. Drain, rinse the cauliflower under cold running water to cool it down, and pat it dry. (Alternatively, you can steam the florets over salted water. When they're fork-tender, drain and pat dry.)

While the cauliflower is cooking, toss the bacon strips into a heavy skillet, put the skillet over medium heat, and cook just until the bacon is browned but not crisp. Drain and pat dry.

Spread the cauliflower out in the buttered pan, and scatter over the bacon bits.

Put the flour in a bowl and gradually whisk in the eggs. When the flour and eggs are blended, whisk in the cream and milk. Season the mixture with salt, pepper, and nutmeg and stir in about two thirds of the cheese. Pour the mixture over the cauliflower, shake the pan a little so that the liquid settles between the florets, and scatter over the remaining cheese.

Bake the gratin for about 25 minutes, or until it is puffed and golden and a knife inserted into the center comes out clean. If the top isn't as brown as you'd like it to be, run it under the broiler for a couple of minutes.

pumpkin stuffed with everything good

MAKES 2 VERY
GENEROUS
SERVINGS OR
4 MORE GENTEEL
SERVINGS

SERVING
You have choices: you
can cut wedges of the
pumpkin and filling; you
can spoon out portions of
the filling, making sure to
get a generous amount of
pumpkin into the spoonful;
or you can dig into the
pumpkin with a big spoon,
pull the pumpkin meat
into the filling, and then
mix everything up. I'm a
fan of the pull-and-mix
option. Served in hearty
portions followed by a
salad, the pumpkin is a
perfect cold-weather main
course; served in generous
spoonfuls or wedges, it's
just right alongside the
Thanksgiving turkey.

STORING
It's really best to eat this as
soon as it's ready. However,
if you've got leftovers, you
can scoop them out of
the pumpkin, mix them
up, cover, and chill them;
reheat them the next day.

SHORTLY AFTER I WAS GIVEN THIS RECIPE, I started keeping a list of whom I'd made it for — because I loved it so much, I was sure that if I didn't keep track, I'd end up serving the dish to the same people over and over. The idea for it came from my friend Hélène Samuel's sister, Catherine, whose husband grows pumpkins on his farm just outside Lyon. Catherine sent me a charming outline of the recipe, and as soon as I'd baked my first pumpkin, I realized that an outline is about the best you can do with this dish. It's a hollowed-out pumpkin stuffed with bread, cheese, garlic, and cream, and since pumpkins come in unpredictable sizes, cheeses and breads differ, and baking times depend on how long it takes for the pumpkin to get soft enough to pierce with a knife, being precise is impossible.

As Catherine said when she turned this family favorite over to me, "I hope you will put the recipe to good use, knowing that it's destined to evolve . . . and maybe even be improved."

Well, I've certainly been putting it to good use, and it has evolved, although I'm not sure that it's been improved, since every time I make it, it's different, but still wonderful. My guess is that you'll have the same feeling once you start playing around with this "outline." See Bonne Idée for some hints on variations.

And speaking of playing around, you might consider serving this alongside the Thanksgiving turkey or even instead of it — omit the bacon, and you've got a great vegetarian main course.

1 pumpkin, about 3 pounds Salt and freshly ground pepper	4 strips bacon, cooked until crisp, drained, and chopped (my addition)
¼ pound stale bread, thinly sliced and cut into ½-inch chunks	About ¼ cup snipped fresh chives or sliced scallions (my addition)
¼ pound cheese, such as Gruyère, Emmenthal, ched- dar, or a combination, cut into ½-inch chunks	1 tablespoon minced fresh thyme (my addition) About ⅓ cup heavy cream Pinch of freshly grated nutmeg
2–4 garlic cloves (to taste), split, germ removed, and coarsely chopped	

Center a rack in the oven and preheat the oven to 350 degrees F. Line a baking sheet with a silicone baking mat or parchment, or find a Dutch oven with a diameter that's just a tiny bit larger than your pumpkin. If you bake the pumpkin in a casserole, it will keep its shape, but it might stick to the casserole, so you'll

There are many ways to vary this arts-and-crafts project. Instead of bread, I've filled the pumpkin with cooked rice — when it's baked, it's almost risotto-like. And, with either bread or rice, on different occasions I've added cooked spinach, kale, chard, or peas (the peas came straight from the freezer). I've made it without bacon, and I've also made and loved, loved, loved it with cooked sausage meat; cubes of ham are another good idea. Nuts are a great addition, as are chunks of apple or pear or pieces of chestnut.

have to serve it from the pot — which is an appealingly homey way to serve it. If you bake it on a baking sheet, you can present it freestanding, but maneuvering a heavy stuffed pumpkin with a softened shell isn't so easy. However, since I love the way the unencumbered pumpkin looks in the center of the table, I've always taken my chances with the baked-on-a-sheet method, and so far, I've been lucky.

Using a very sturdy knife — and caution — cut a cap out of the top of the pumpkin (think Halloween jack-o'-lantern). It's easiest to work your knife around the top of the pumpkin at a 45-degree angle. You want to cut off enough of the top to make it easy for you to work inside the pumpkin. Clear away the seeds and strings from the cap and from inside the pumpkin. Season the inside of the pumpkin generously with salt and pepper, and put it on the baking sheet or in the pot.

Toss the bread, cheese, garlic, bacon, and herbs together in a bowl. Season with pepper — you probably have enough salt from the bacon and cheese, but taste to be sure — and pack the mix into the pumpkin. The pumpkin should be well filled — you might have a little too much filling, or you might need to add to it. Stir the cream with the nutmeg and some salt and pepper and pour it into the pumpkin. Again, you might have too much or too little — you don't want the ingredients to swim in cream, but you do want them nicely moistened. (But it's hard to go wrong here.)

Put the cap in place and bake the pumpkin for about 2 hours — check after 90 minutes — or until everything inside the pumpkin is bubbling and the flesh of the pumpkin is tender enough to be pierced easily with the tip of a knife. Because the pumpkin will have exuded liquid, I like to remove the cap during the last 20 minutes or so, so that the liquid can bake away and the top of the stuffing can brown a little.

When the pumpkin is ready, carefully, very carefully — it's heavy, hot, and wobbly — bring it to the table or transfer it to a platter that you'll bring to the table.

french lentils: *a basic recipe*

THE BEST FRENCH LENTILS, called *lentilles du Puy,* look like members of an entirely different branch of the family that gives us the colorful pale green, yellow, and orange lentils so vital to Indian cooking. In fact, they've been granted A.O.C. (*appellation d'origine contrôlée*) status, the French government's assurance that the product is unique to the area in which it's grown, in this case a section of the Auvergne in central France. The lentils are small, slightly oval, beautifully thin around the edges, elegantly rounded in the center, smooth like river stones, and, depending on how you look at them, dark green or slate gray.

The lentils cook quickly and become tender, not mushy. They don't need to be soaked, but I've found that you get the cleanest flavor when you boil them for a couple of minutes and then give them a rinse before cooking them for real. And although the lentils can be simmered in water, they develop an even deeper flavor when they're cooked in broth.

This is a basic recipe. Once the lentils are tender, you can serve them as a side dish straight from the pot, maybe with just a drizzle of oil — olive oil is a good choice, but nut oils, like walnut or hazelnut, accentuate the lentils' earthiness — and perhaps a splash of vinegar or lemon juice. (Because lentils have such a deep, tied-to-the-earth flavor, they pair perfectly with brighter, zestier, more acidic ingredients.) Or you can season them with a vinaigrette and serve them as a side dish or a salad. Lentil salads are good warm or at room temperature, but no matter the temperature, you should dress them when they're hot, because that's when they absorb a vinaigrette best. For lentil salad recipes, see Bonne Idée and page 140.

MAKES **4** SERVINGS

SERVING
Warm lentils make a terrific side dish — they're particularly good with salmon or simply sautéed or grilled chicken breasts (see Bonne Idée, page 137). Cooled and tossed with vinaigrette, they make a very good salad (see Bonne Idée).

STORING
Once cooled, the lentils and their liquid can be packed airtight and kept chilled for up to 3 days. Warm in a covered saucepan over gentle heat.

1 cup French green lentils (lentilles du Puy)	1 garlic clove, smashed, peeled, and germ removed
1 clove	1 bay leaf
1 small onion	3½ cups chicken broth, vegetable broth, or water
1 medium carrot, trimmed, peeled, and cut into 4–6 pieces	Salt and freshly ground pepper
1 celery stalk, trimmed, peeled, and cut into 4–6 pieces	1 tablespoon Cognac or other brandy (optional)
	1 shallot, finely chopped, rinsed, and patted dry (optional)

Put the lentils in a strainer and pick through them, discarding any bits of stone that might have escaped the packers; rinse under cold running water.

Turn the lentils into a medium saucepan, cover them with cold water, bring to a boil, and cook for 2 minutes; spill the lentils out into the strainer. Drain, rinse the lentils again, and rinse out the saucepan.

Press the clove into the onion and toss the onion, carrot, celery, garlic, and bay leaf into the pan. Pour in the broth or water, stir in the lentils, and bring to

BONNE IDÉE
Classic Lentil Salad. While the lentils are cooking, make a vinaigrette by shaking or whisking together 1 teaspoon Dijon mustard, 1 tablespoon sherry vinegar, 2 tablespoons walnut or hazelnut oil, 1 tablespoon extra-virgin olive oil, and salt and freshly ground pepper to taste. Stir into the lentils while they are still warm. If you'd like, finish the salad with a generous amount of chopped fresh parsley. Other good additions include bacon bits; finely diced vegetables — raw, lightly steamed, or quickly sautéed; cheese — goat cheese, soft or crumbly, is particularly good; and yogurt, especially a thick Greek yogurt.

ANOTHER
BONNE IDÉE
Bacon is a natural with lentils. Stir small pieces of cooked bacon into warm lentils or, if you're making a salad, use a little of the bacon fat to replace some of the oil in the vinaigrette.

a boil. Lower the heat to a steady simmer and cook for 25 to 30 minutes, or until the lentils are almost tender. As the lentils cook, skim off the solids that rise to the top and stir as needed. Season with salt and pepper and cook until the lentils are tender, another 5 to 10 minutes, then pour in the Cognac, if you're using it. Give everything a good stir and another minute over the heat.

Drain the lentils, reserving the cooking liquid if you're going to want to reheat them. Remove the vegetables and either discard them all or discard the clove and bay leaf and finely chop the vegetables, which will be soft but tasty; stir the vegetables back into the lentils if you're using them. Stir in the shallot, if you'd like (I think it adds a lot to the mix).

The lentils are ready to be served now, or set aside and reheated over low heat in the liquid you've reserved, or used in other recipes.

dressy pasta "risotto"

IN TRUTH, THIS IS A RISOTTO the way that finely sliced apples are a carpaccio, which means not at all, but these days the definition of a dish — particularly one that didn't originate in France — is often applied loosely and with a dash of poetic license. This faux risotto (it's really macaroni mixed with cheese) is simple and quick to make, yet chic enough to be served at fancy dinner parties.

As with so many French dishes, the native preference is to make the chicken broth with bouillon cubes. Of course, if you have homemade stock, you should use it, but if you're stockless, go with the cubes; they're just fine in this dish.

MAKES 4 SIDE-DISH OR STARTER SERVINGS

2 tablespoons unsalted butter	1⅓ cups tubetti (my preference) or
1 small onion, finely chopped	elbow macaroni (traditional)
Salt and freshly ground	½ cup heavy cream
pepper	½ cup freshly grated Parmesan
3¾ cups chicken broth or	3½ tablespoons mascarpone
3¾ cups water and	
2 chicken bouillon cubes	

Melt the butter in a large skillet or saucepan over medium-low heat. Toss in the onion, season with salt and pepper, and cook, stirring, until soft and translucent, about 10 minutes. (Or, if you'd like, go ahead and cook the onion until it's golden.) Pour in the chicken broth or water and bring to a boil; if you're using bouillon cubes, drop them in now and stir to dissolve. Add the pasta, stir it around, and let it cook at a steady simmer until it has absorbed almost all the broth, 20 to 25 minutes. (There should be just ¼ inch or less of liquid bubbling at the bottom of the pan.)

Pour in the cream and allow it to simmer for about 3 minutes, until it thickens slightly. Stir in the Parmesan and mascarpone, cook for 1 minute, and taste for salt and pepper (it should be generously peppered). Pull the pan from the heat, cover, and let rest for 3 minutes before serving.

ANOTHER BONNE IDÉE
Sophie-Charlotte's Macaroni Risotto.

When my friend Sophie-Charlotte Guitter gave me this recipe, she told me it was one that her little children really loved. Heat 2 tablespoons olive oil in a large skillet or saucepan, add 1 onion, finely chopped, and cook until soft. Add 1½ cups elbow macaroni and stir to coat with the oil and onion. Pour in about 3½ cups beef broth (or chicken or vegetable) and bring to a boil. Cover the pan, lower the heat so that the liquid simmers, and cook until the pasta is done, about 15 minutes. (Check as the pasta cooks to see if you need to add some more broth; you may need up to ½ cup more.) Stir in 2 tablespoons butter, cut into bits, and dust with about ½ cup freshly grated Parmesan. Season with salt and freshly ground pepper. Sophie-Charlotte says that to vary the recipe, you can add a couple of tablespoons of white wine to the pan when the onions are cooked and boil it away before adding the macaroni, or stir in cooked bacon, mushrooms, or leeks.

SERVING
You can certainly serve this as a side dish to a roast of almost any kind, including chicken — think of it as fancy mac 'n' cheese — but it's elegant enough to be served on its own as a starter. It can be served plain or with a dusting of parsley or a little more Parmesan; of course, if you have some truffles to grate over each portion . . .

STORING
This is meant to be eaten as soon as you uncover the pan and finished on the spot.

BONNE IDÉE
About 30 minutes before you start the pasta, bring the cream — plus another 2 tablespoonfuls — to a boil in a saucepan and drop in some dried mushrooms, chopped fresh thyme or rosemary, black truffle peelings, or even a spoonful or two of crushed black peppercorns. Turn off the heat, cover the pan, and let the cream infuse for 20 minutes or more. Strain the cream before you pour it into the pasta pan (check the amount — if you don't have ½ cup, top it off) and proceed with the recipe.

beggar's linguine

WOULD HAVE LOVED THIS DISH THE FIRST TIME I had it, no matter what. The fact that I tasted it when I was cold and jet-lagged and hungry added to its initial appeal — it was the perfect comfort food for that moment. However, I've made it many times since, and it's never failed to make me happy. The dish comes from La Ferrandaise, the bistro around the corner from our apartment, and I first had it when my friend Hélène Samuel and I had walked in and just about pleaded for a table, since it was thirty seconds before the kitchen was to close. Always gracious, the owner seated us, suggested a few dishes, and poured us glasses of wine to both welcome and warm us. Looking back, it seems only natural that, having begged for a meal, our first dish was *linguine mendiant.*

Mendiant translates as beggar, but the word is actually used more often to describe a delicious bonbon, a chocolate disk topped with nuts and dried fruits, sometimes accented with candied orange zest. The fruits and nuts on the candies were originally chosen to represent the four mendicant monastic orders: dried figs for the Franciscans, raisins for the Dominicans, hazelnuts for the Augustinians, and almonds for the Carmelites. While you might find this combination today, you'll also find *mendiants* with pistachios or walnuts, dried apricots or lemon zest, or whatever fruit the chocolatier prefers.

Anyone can imagine how good the mix would be with chocolate, but it takes a very creative culinary mind to imagine the concoction as a savory dish, and that's just what the chef did when he mixed pasta with browned butter, chopped almonds, pistachios, raisins, snipped dried figs, grated Parmesan, and a pinch of orange zest. If I didn't know the origin of the dish, I'd have thought that the name meant that people begged to have it often.

1 box (14–16 ounces) linguine	¼ cup plump, moist raisins (golden raisins are nice)
12 tablespoons (1½ sticks) unsalted butter	Salt and freshly ground pepper
⅓ cup shelled pistachios, coarsely chopped	½ cup freshly grated Parmesan (or more or less to taste)
⅓ cup almonds, coarsely chopped	Grated zest of ½ orange (or more to taste)
8 plump dried Mission figs or 3 dried Kadota figs, finely chopped	Minced fresh chives and/or parsley, for serving (optional)

Cook the linguine according to the package directions; drain it well.

Meanwhile, about 5 minutes before the pasta is ready, melt the butter in a large high-sided skillet or casserole over medium heat. (You're going to add the pasta to this pan, so make sure it's large enough.) When the butter is melted and golden, stir in the nuts, figs, and raisins. Allow the butter to bubble and boil — you want it to cook to a lovely light brown, or to turn into *beurre noisette,* butter with the color and fragrance of hazelnuts.

When the butter has reached just the color you want, add the pasta and stir it around in the butter to coat it evenly and to tangle it up with the bits of fruit and nuts; season with salt and a generous amount of pepper.

Turn the pasta into a serving bowl and add the grated cheese. Toss and turn the pasta to incorporate the cheese, then dust the top with the orange zest and chives and/or parsley, if you're using them. Taste and add more cheese and/or zest if you'd like.

Bring the pasta to the table immediately and, just before you're ready to dish out the first serving, give it one more toss to mix in the zest and (optional) herbs.

herb-speckled spaetzle

MAKES 4 SIDE-
DISH SERVINGS OR
2 MAIN-COURSE
SERVINGS

SERVING

There isn't much that isn't good with spaetzle, from delicate sautéed fish fillets to he-man grilled steak. Sometimes I make the spaetzle the main course of a light supper or a lunch, topped with a few slices of crumbled well-cooked bacon and served with a green salad and a hunk of cheese.

STORING

The just-boiled spaetzle can be cooled to room temperature, covered well, and refrigerated overnight. While the spaetzle is best just after it's been cooked with the broth, leftovers can be refrigerated and reheated the next day. I've had the best results sprinkling the spaetzle with a little water and reheating it, covered, in the top of a double boiler or covering it and giving it a couple of minutes in the microwave oven — the time you'll need to bring it up to temperature will depend on how much spaetzle you've got left over.

FRANCE IS NOT A PASTA COUNTRY, but then spaetzle, a chewy, baby-sized pasta, comes from Alsace, and Alsace is not the main branch on the French family tree. Holding down a long swath of eastern France and sharing its extensive frontier with Germany, Alsace was passed back and forth between the two countries up until the middle of the last century, and you can taste this teeter-tottering of allegiance in the region's robust food. You can also see it in the names of many of the dishes — just looking at the word *spaetzle,* you know it's not bred-in-the-bone French.

The egg dough for spaetzle is quickly mixed by hand, and it's shaped and cooked by pushing it through the coarse holes of a grater, a slotted spoon, or a colander (or a special spaetzle maker) into a pot of boiling water, a process that can be a little messy.

Since it is plain, in the way pasta is plain, spaetzle is versatile: it can be served in soup, like dumplings, or tossed with a little butter and served as a side dish. It can also be mixed with other ingredients — a temptation I rarely resist. Here I've flecked the dough with herbs and given the dish a touch more dash by adding mushrooms and onion and cooking everything in some chicken broth. It's pasta with enough flavor to hold its own alongside any main course, even a deep, dark, winey beef daube (page 244).

2¼ cups all-purpose flour Salt and freshly ground white pepper	4 tablespoons (½ stick) unsalted butter
⅛ teaspoon freshly grated nutmeg	2 tablespoons extra-virgin olive oil
¾ cup whole milk	½ pound white mushrooms, cleaned, trimmed, and thinly sliced
3 large eggs	1 onion, finely chopped
3 tablespoons finely chopped mixed fresh herbs (my favorite combination is the leaves from 4 parsley sprigs, 4 thyme sprigs, 2 small rosemary sprigs, and 10 chives) or parsley	¾–1 cup chicken broth

In a large bowl, whisk together the flour, 1 teaspoon salt, ¼ teaspoon white pepper, and the nutmeg. In a large measuring cup, whisk together the milk and eggs. Slowly pour the liquid ingredients over the dry ingredients, stirring with a wooden spatula or spoon. Continue to stir until you have a soft, sticky, thick, but wet dough. Stir in 1½ tablespoons of the herbs.

Have a large buttered bowl at the ready.

Bring a large pot of salted water to a boil. Using a spaetzle maker, the large holes of a box or flat (easier) grater, a large slotted spoon, or a colander, push small batches of the dough through the holes into the water. Stir, let the spaetzle float to the surface, and boil for about 2 minutes. Remove the spaetzle with a skimmer or slotted spoon and toss into the buttered bowl. Repeat until all the dough is used. *(The spaetzle can be cooled and kept covered at room temperature for a few hours or refrigerated overnight.)*

At serving time, heat 2 tablespoons of the butter and 1 tablespoon of the olive oil in a large skillet over medium heat. Add the mushrooms, season with salt and white pepper, and cook, stirring, until they soften, about 5 minutes. Add the onion, season, and cook just until it softens, about 5 minutes more. Add the remaining 2 tablespoons butter and 1 tablespoon oil, and toss in the spaetzle. Cook, stirring, until the spaetzle is heated through and starting to brown, 5 to 10 minutes.

Pour ¾ cup chicken broth over the spaetzle and cook just until it almost evaporates. If you think you'd like the spaeztle to be softer and even moister, add up to ¼ cup more broth and cook it down. Taste for salt and pepper, stir in the remaining 1½ tablespoons herbs, and serve immediately.

gnocchi à la parisienne

MAKES **6** MAIN-
COURSE SERVINGS

SERVING
Gnocchi à la Parisienne is
a dish that doesn't wait.
As soon as it comes out
of the oven, it should go
directly to the table. Like
macaroni and cheese, this
needs nothing but a hearty
appetite.

STORING
You can make the
béchamel sauce and the
dough for the gnocchi
ahead of time (you can
freeze the shaped gnocchi
for up to 2 months — pack
them airtight once frozen
hard, and boil without
defrosting). Once the dish
is baked, though, it's meant
to be eaten immediately
and fully — leftovers won't
keep.

THIS RECIPE COMES FROM MY LONGTIME FRIEND Paule Caillat, who handed it over to me with a story. It seems that when Paule, the Parisienne behind Promenades Gourmandes' market tours and cooking classes, was getting married, her husband's family wanted to be certain she'd be ready to cook the kind of food he liked, and so they passed their family recipes along to her. Among the several she received was this one, taught to her by Tante Léo, for a dish that is most definitely Parisian but contains nothing that we know as gnocchi. Standing in for the potato dumplings is *pâte à choux,* or cream puff dough, which is poached just the way gnocchi are, and then baked under a blanket of creamy béchamel. It is, as Paule told me, a filling dish of the comfort-food variety best served in winter.

Under the title of the recipe, Paule wrote, "a Caillat family classic," but my guess is that gnocchi à la Parisienne must have found its way into the classic category in other French families, since Paule's recipe originally came from Le Cordon Bleu. It was there, before World War II, that Tante Léo learned it while she was in training to become a *cuisinière en maison bourgeoise,* a cook in a bourgeoisie home.

Paule gave me this recipe one afternoon over lunch, and as she talked about it, she annotated it for me. Her little *trucs,* or tricks of the trade, are included in this version.

A word on timing: If you're not going to rest the dough for a couple of hours, you might want to make the béchamel sauce first.

FOR THE GNOCCHI DOUGH
- 1¼ cups water
- 7 tablespoons unsalted butter, cut into small pieces
- ½ teaspoon salt
- 1¼ cups all-purpose flour
- 4 large eggs, at room temperature

FOR THE BÉCHAMEL
- 2 cups whole milk
- 2½ tablespoons unsalted butter

- 6 tablespoons all-purpose flour
- Salt and freshly ground pepper
- Freshly grated nutmeg
- 2 tablespoons freshly grated Parmesan (Paule's addition)
- About ¾ cup grated cheese (Paule uses a mixture of Parmesan and Comté here, although originally the cheese was Gruyère or Emmenthal)
- 2 tablespoons unsalted butter, cut into bits

TO MAKE THE GNOCCHI DOUGH: Bring the water, butter, and salt to a boil in a medium saucepan. Add the flour all at once, and as soon as the water starts to boil again, remove the pan from the heat, even if the butter hasn't melted.

Using a wooden spoon, stir everything together well, then put the pan back over medium heat. Keep stirring energetically and constantly until you have a dough that forms a ball and leaves a light film on the bottom of the pan, about 2 minutes.

Turn the dough into a bowl or the bowl of a mixer and, with a wooden spoon or a mixer (either handheld or stand), beat in the eggs one at a time. Make sure each egg is fully incorporated before you add the next one. (Paule says that Tante Léo would mix 3 eggs and the yolk of the fourth, then she'd beat the egg white until it held peaks and fold it into the dough to make the gnocchi even lighter.)

You can make the gnocchi now (see below), or you can do what Tante Léo used to do: cover the dough with a kitchen towel and let it rest at room temperature for up to 2 hours. *(Alternatively, you can form the gnocchi, put them on a lined baking sheet, and freeze them; then, when they are solid, pack them into an airtight container and freeze for up to 2 months.)*

TO MAKE THE BÉCHAMEL: Put the milk in a medium saucepan over medium-low heat and heat until it is just about to boil. You want to scald the milk, which means that little bubbles will form around the edges of the pan, but the milk shouldn't boil.

Meanwhile, in a medium heavy-bottomed saucepan, melt the butter over medium-low heat. Grab a wooden spoon, add the flour to the pan, and cook for 2 minutes, stirring constantly so that the flour absorbs the butter but doesn't brown. (You're making a roux and cooking the flour to get rid of its raw taste.) Stir in the hot milk and, still stirring without stopping, increase the heat to medium and bring to a boil. Season with salt, pepper, and a pinch of nutmeg. Reduce the heat to low and cook, stirring, for 3 minutes more. Pull the pan from the heat, scrape the sauce into a bowl, and press a piece of plastic wrap against the surface to keep a skin from forming.

TO COOK AND BAKE THE GNOCCHI: Center a rack in the oven and preheat the oven to 350 degrees F. Butter a 9-inch deep-dish pie plate (a Pyrex pan is perfect) and dust it with the 2 tablespoons Parmesan. Bring a large pot of salted water to a boil, then lower the heat so that the water is at a simmer.

Drop teaspoonfuls of the dough into the water, and when the balls rise to the surface, let them float for a minute before lifting them out of the water with a slotted spoon and draining them on a kitchen towel or a double layer of paper towels. Do this in batches — you don't want to crowd the pot or lower the temperature of the water too much or too fast.

Spoon a thin layer of béchamel over the bottom of the pie plate. Put the gnocchi into the pan and pour over the remaining béchamel. Cover the béchamel evenly with the ¾ cup cheese, then dot with the butter.

Slide the pan into the oven and bake for 10 minutes. Raise the oven temperature to 400 degrees F and bake for another 10 to 15 minutes, or until the béchamel is bubbly and browned. If the sauce is bubbling but the cheese isn't as golden brown as you'd like, run the dish under the broiler.

storzapretis

(aka corsican spinach and mint gnocchi)

MAKES **6** SIDE-
DISH OR STARTER
SERVINGS OR
4 MAIN-COURSE
SERVINGS

SERVING
I like to serve these as a first course on their own, but they can certainly be a side dish or a main course, in which case I think they're great with a big leafy green salad.

STORING
Once formed, the storzapretis can be refrigerated overnight. They can also be frozen; when they're solid, transfer to an airtight container and keep in the freezer for up to 2 months. When you're ready to cook them, drop them into boiling salted water without defrosting — just adjust the poaching time as necessary.

TECHNICALLY CORSICA IS CONSIDERED a region of France, like Normandy or Brittany, but when it comes to things culinary, it might as well have rogue-nation status. The island, afloat in the Mediterranean and separated from Italian Sardinia by a spit of water about as wide as a strand of fettuccine, is inhabited by people who have their own way of cooking and their own dialect to describe it and everything else, which explains why when Laëtitia Ghipponi, the blithe spirit who helps make Bistrot Paul Bert such a remarkable place, told me she'd send me her father's recipe for *les storzapretis,* I didn't have a clue as to what she was talking about. It was only after a quick study of the ingredient list and instructions that I realized that what Laëtitia and her father make is as close a relative as I can think of to ricotta gnocchi.

In Corsica, rather than ricotta, storzapretis would be made with *brocciu,* the island's own fresh sheep's-milk cheese. If you can find it — it's sometimes available at very good cheese shops in the United States — by all means use it; if not, choose a thick whole-milk ricotta, or allow your ricotta to drain in a cheesecloth-lined strainer for a couple of hours before you use it.

Laëtitia's storzapretis are speckled with chopped spinach, accented with fresh mint (my usual choice) or marjoram, both native to Corsica's hillsides, and then baked under a light blanket of tomato sauce and grated cheese. They can be served as either a starter or a main course; it's a question of how large you make the portions.

10 ounces spinach, trimmed	1 bunch mint or marjoram, leaves only, finely chopped (about 1 cup)
1 pound whole-milk ricotta or fresh brocciu, if you can get it	
1 large egg	2 tablespoons all-purpose flour, plus more for shaping
5 ounces cheese, such as Gruyère or Emmenthal or a combination of Gruyère and Parmesan, grated (about 1¼ cups)	Salt and freshly ground pepper
	Olive oil
	1½ cups tomato sauce (you can use a good-quality bottled marinara sauce)

Wash the spinach in several changes of cool water — fresh spinach can be sandy — and when it's clean, toss it into a large pot, with the water still clinging to the leaves. Place the pot over medium-low heat, cover, and cook the spinach, turning often, until it is soft, about 5 minutes. Turn the spinach into a colander and shake out as much of the water as possible.

When the spinach is cool enough to handle, press out the remainder of the water (or as much as you can) by squeezing small bunches of the spinach between your palms or by twisting them in a kitchen towel. Coarsely chop the spinach, toss it into a bowl, and use your fingers to pull the clumps of spinach apart as best as you can.

With a sturdy rubber spatula or a wooden spoon, beat the ricotta or *brocciu* into the spinach, followed by the egg. Stir in half of the grated cheese and the mint or marjoram, sprinkle over the flour, season with salt and pepper, and blend. You'll have a soft, malleable mixture.

Line a baking sheet or tray that will fit in the fridge or freezer with plastic wrap. Make a mound of about ¼ cup flour on your work surface.

Working with two soupspoons, scoop up a tablespoonful of the cheese mixture with one spoon and then scrape the mix from one spoon to the other until you've formed a cohesive quenelle. Drop the quenelle into the mound of flour, cover it with flour, and then toss it gently from hand to hand to shake off the excess. After working the mixture this way, your quenelle will probably look like a large, slightly misshapen bullet, and that's just fine. Put the nugget on the lined sheet and continue until you've used all the dough; you'll have about 3 dozen storzapretis. Chill or freeze the storzapretis for about 30 minutes, just to firm them a bit. *(Once they are firm, you can cover and refrigerate them overnight or freeze them, packed airtight, for up to 2 months.)*

Center a rack in the oven and preheat the oven to 425 degrees F. Lightly oil a 7-x-11-inch or 9-x-13-inch baking dish (glass, porcelain, or pottery, since the tomato sauce might react with a metal pan).

Bring a large pot of salted water to a boil, and have a big bowl of ice and cold water nearby.

Remove the storzapretis from the refrigerator or freezer. Lower the heat under the pot so that the water is at a simmer, and carefully drop some storzapretis into the pot — don't crowd the pot; the storzapretis need room to float around (figure on cooking about 8 at a time if your pot is large). The nuggets will sink to the bottom of the pot and then pop to the top. After they do, let them gently bob around in the pot for 5 minutes, then lift them out of the simmering water with a skimmer or slotted spoon and drop them into the ice water to cool rapidly. Continue poaching and cooling the rest.

Drain the storzapretis, dry between sheets of paper towels — be careful, they're soft and fragile — and arrange them in the oiled pan. Pour the tomato sauce over the storzapretis, top with the remaining grated cheese, and slide the pan into the oven.

Bake for about 15 minutes, until the sauce is bubbling hot, the cheese melted, and the storzapretis heated through. Serve immediately.

warm-weather vegetable pot-au-feu

MAKES 4 MAIN-
COURSE SERVINGS

SERVING
This has to be piping hot
— accompany the pot-
au-feu with bread and the
instruction that the egg
should be cut into at once,
so that the yolk can mix
with the broth.

STORING
This is not a dish for
keeping.

TRADITIONAL POT-AU-FEU, a mix of hearty cuts of meat, root vegetables, and a warming-down-to-your-toes broth, is an unequivocally wintry dish, perfect after a mountain hike or a day in the great outdoors. But it's a dish with too many possibilities to be shelved when the weather changes, which is why some form of pot-au-feu is made year-round, its concept remaining constant, the ingredients taking seasonal star turns: meat in fall and winter, fish (page 308) or vegetables in spring and summer.

The underpinnings of classic pot-au-feu, the onions, carrots, leeks, and potatoes, are here, but in their young spring form. And in this can-be-vegetarian version, they cook briefly, keep their colors, and share their light broth with asparagus and spinach, harbingers of warmer times.

My recipe should be a jumping-off point for you. Choose whatever is young and fresh at your market. Because you add the vegetables in succession, you can easily use ingredients with widely different cooking times. Green beans or peas are a good addition, as are newly dug turnips, small pieces of squash (acorn, pattypan, or zucchini), tiny tomatoes, and corn cut from the cob.

You could omit the poached or soft-boiled eggs, but I hope you won't — they add richness to an otherwise lean but tasty broth. And, while the herb coulis is optional, again, I hope you'll include it — it tilts the dish a little toward Provence, and what could be nicer when the temperature registers sultry? The photo is on page 328.

2 tablespoons extra-virgin olive oil

2 garlic cloves, split, germ removed, and thinly sliced

1 onion, preferably a spring or Texas onion, thinly sliced

1 leek, white and light green parts only, quartered length-wise, and rinsed
Salt and freshly ground white pepper

6 small new potatoes, scrubbed and cut into ½-inch-thick slices

4 slender carrots, trimmed, peeled, and cut on the diagonal into ½-inch-thick pieces

3 cups vegetable broth or chicken broth

1 strip lemon or orange zest (optional)

1 2-inch-long piece lemongrass, split lengthwise (optional)

8 asparagus stalks, trimmed and peeled

4 large shiitakes, stemmed, cleaned, and sliced

½ pound spinach, stemmed and washed

4 large eggs, poached (page 492) or boiled (page 130)

Basil, cilantro, or parsley coulis (see Bonne Idée, page 488) and/or chopped fresh herbs, for serving (optional)

In a large high-sided skillet or, if you've got one, a woklike stir-fry pan, warm the olive oil over medium-low heat. Toss in the garlic and cook for just 1 minute. Add the onion and leek, turning them in the oil, and season with salt and white pepper. Cook, stirring gently, just until the onion and leek soften slightly, about 5 minutes. Stir in the potatoes and carrots, then pour in the broth. If you're using zest and/or lemongrass, toss them in now too. Increase the heat and bring the broth to a boil, then lower the heat and simmer gently, uncovered, until the vegetables are just short of tender, about 10 minutes. *(You can make the pot-au-feu to this point up to 3 hours in advance; cover and refrigerate. When you're ready to continue, bring the broth back to a boil, lower the heat so that it simmers, and cook gently until everything is heated through.)*

While the vegetables are simmering, bring a skillet of water to a boil — you'll use the pan to reheat the eggs right before serving.

With the pot-au-feu at a gentle simmer, drop in the asparagus and shiitakes and cook until tender, about 4 minutes. Scatter the spinach over the vegetables and cook for another 2 minutes, just until slightly wilted. Taste for salt and white pepper.

Slip the eggs into the skillet of simmering water and give them just a couple of minutes to warm while you spoon out the pot-au-feu.

Ladle the vegetables and broth into shallow soup plates, dot with the basil, cilantro, or parsley puree and/or scatter with the chopped herbs, and finish each with a poached or boiled egg. Serve immediately.

creamy, cheesy, garlicky rice with spinach

MAKES 4 SIDE-
DISH SERVINGS OR
2 MAIN-COURSE
SERVINGS

SERVING
Everyone — French, Italian, or American — would agree that you've got to serve the rice the instant it's ready: it must be eaten *chaud, caldo,* hot! You could sprinkle the creamy rice with a little Parmesan, which would be somewhat traditional but not necessary. Or, if the rice is the main course, you can top it with a little fresh spinach salad dressed with olive oil and balsamic, which bucks tradition but is delicious.

STORING
You can make the spinach ahead, but the rice is best served soon after it's made.

"NEVER ORDER A RISOTTO IN A FRENCH RESTAURANT," warned my Italian friend. "The French don't have a clue about what it should be." To hear my friend tell it, it was almost as though the French were physically incapable of making risotto, or maybe even genetically unable to get it right. Since my husband adores risotto, he never heeded the caution; instead, he ordered it every time he'd see it on a menu and was always disappointed. It wasn't that the dish wasn't good — it was invariably delicious — it was just that it wasn't risotto. Why, I wondered, didn't the French just call their dish creamy rice and be done with it?

I thought of this again recently when I added a splash of heavy cream to a pot of rice (Arborio, aka risotto rice), cheese, and spinach. I used the rice to stuff some peppers (see Bonne Idée), and when I served it, my husband said, "The risotto is great!" — leading me to believe that either he'd joined ranks with the French or that good creamy rice is good no matter what you call it.

3¼–3½ cups chicken broth or vegetable broth

1 cup Arborio or other round risotto rice

10 ounces spinach, trimmed
Salt

1 tablespoon unsalted butter

1 medium onion, finely chopped

2 garlic cloves, split, germ removed, and finely chopped
Freshly ground pepper

¼ pound Gruyère, Emmenthal, or Swiss cheese, grated (about 1 cup)
About ¼ cup heavy cream

In a medium saucepan with a tight-fitting lid, bring 3¼ cups broth to a boil. Stir in the rice, cover the pot, lower the heat, and simmer until almost all of the broth has been absorbed and the rice is almost tender. Turn off the heat and let the rice finish cooking on its own.

While the rice is cooking, make the spinach: Rinse the spinach well, shake off the water, and toss it, with whatever water still clings to the leaves, into a large (about 4-quart) pot. Sprinkle with salt, stir, cover the pot, and cook over medium-low heat, turning often, until the spinach is tender, about 5 minutes. It will wilt, and you'll have just a handful in the bottom of the pot. Drain the spinach, and when it's cool enough to handle, squeeze it dry between your palms. (Do this in batches, and squeeze hard.) Coarsely chop the spinach. (*You can make the spinach up to a day ahead and keep it tightly covered in the refrigerator.*)

Wipe out the spinach pot, put it over medium-low heat, and melt the butter in it. Add the onion and garlic, season with salt and pepper, and cook slowly until the vegetables soften and become translucent, about 5 minutes. Turn the rice and spinach into the pot and stir well. Add the cheese and ¼ cup cream, season generously with salt and pepper, and give everything a few good turns to blend the elements. If the mix seems a little dry, stir in a little more broth or a splash more heavy cream. Serve immediately.

Rice-Packed Peppers. This amount of cheesy rice is enough to stuff 4 good-sized bell peppers. Milder peppers — red, yellow, orange, or purple — are best, but you can use green peppers. Preheat the oven to 400 degrees F. Pull out a baking pan that can hold the peppers snugly, and rub it with butter or olive oil. Cut the cap (stem end) off the peppers and use a paring knife to scrape away the seeds and remove the inside ribs. Spoon the rice into the peppers — you'll have enough to really pack the peppers — replace the caps, and stand the peppers upright in the baking pan. Pour about ½ cup water into the pan, cover the pan loosely with foil, and bake for 45 minutes. Remove the foil and let the peppers bake for another 15 minutes. You can serve the peppers as is, drizzle the filling with olive oil, or make a pesto (page 488), replacing the basil with spinach, to pass at the table.

cardamom rice pilaf

MAKES 4 SERVINGS

SERVING
Although this pilaf is a great companion to saucy dishes, it has enough flavor to stand on its own, so don't hesitate to serve it alongside simple roasted or grilled chicken, fish, or meats.

STORING
Rice is never the same the day after, but if you want to reheat the pilaf, the best way is to splash it with a little water, cover it, and warm it in the microwave oven. Chilled leftover rice can be used to make a salad (dress it with a lemon juice vinaigrette) or to stuff tomatoes.

ADDING CARDAMOM TO RICE GIVES it a faint Indian accent, but that doesn't keep it from being the perfect accompaniment to dishes like Chicken Tagine with Sweet Potatoes and Prunes (page 212), Coconut-Lemongrass-Braised Pork (page 274), or Salmon and Tomatoes en Papillote (page 302). Cardamom, once seemingly exotic, is now available in the spice section of most supermarkets. Whether you find white or green cardamom (I prefer green), what you're after are the little seeds within the dried, reedy pods — they're the keepers of the spice's citrusy freshness. (Save the pods and steep them in your tea, or toss them into the rice, but tell your guests to avoid eating them.) If you want to get even more flavor from the seeds, tap them lightly using a mortar and pestle or the heel or back of a heavy knife.

1 tablespoon olive oil	2 cups chicken broth, vegetable
1 small onion, finely chopped	broth, or water
Seeds from 7 cardamom	1 teaspoon finely chopped or
pods, bruised (see above)	coarsely grated lemon zest
1 cup long-grain white rice,	Salt and freshly ground pepper
such as basmati	

Put a medium saucepan over low heat and pour in the oil. When it's hot, add the onion and cardamom seeds and cook, stirring, for about 3 minutes, until the onion is translucent and everything's nicely coated with oil. Increase the heat to medium, add the rice, and cook and stir until it is warmed through and it, too, is glossy with oil, another minute or so.

Turn up the heat, pour in the broth or water — stand back, it may sputter — stir, and bring to a boil. Toss in the lemon zest, season with salt and pepper, and give everything a last stir. Lower the heat, cover the pan, and cook the rice until it's tender and has absorbed all (or almost all) of the liquid, 10 to 15 minutes, depending on the rice you've used. (White basmati rice usually cooks in about 11 minutes, but you should check the package so you'll have an idea of when to start testing.)

Remove the pan from the heat and let the rice sit for 2 minutes before fluffing it with a fork and serving.

lemon barley pilaf

Barley's an odd-man-out kind of grain in the French kitchen. It's readily available and easy to prepare, yet it appears only now and then on the dining room table — but when it does, it's greeted with smiles, polished off, and sent on its way with comments like, "It's really so good, I don't know why I don't have it more often." In this rendition (which anyone will want to have more often), the barley is cooked in broth, mixed with a few colorful vegetables, and finished with freshly grated lemon zest. It's a lively way to serve an earthy grain.

MAKES 4 SERVINGS

SERVING
This dish is best served hot alongside chicken, veal, pork, or fish.

STORING
Leftover pilaf can be kept covered in the refrigerator overnight and reheated or served at room temperature the next day.

1 tablespoon unsalted butter	1 small carrot, trimmed, peeled, and cut into small cubes
1 small onion, finely chopped	
Salt and freshly ground pepper	½ red bell pepper, cored, seeded, and cut into small cubes
½ cup pearl barley	4 scallions, white and light green parts only, sliced
1¾ cups chicken broth	
½ cup water	Grated zest of ½ lemon
1 bay leaf	

Melt the butter in a medium saucepan over medium heat. Add the onion, season lightly with salt and pepper, stir to coat with butter, and cook and stir until it is soft but not colored, 3 to 5 minutes. Add the barley and cook, stirring, for 3 minutes. Raise the heat, pour in the broth and water, toss in the bay leaf, and bring to a boil. Give everything a good stir, reduce the heat so that the broth simmers, cover the pan, and cook for 30 minutes, or until the barley is almost tender (it should retain a bit of chew).

Sprinkle over the carrot, cover again, and cook for 5 minutes. Add the red pepper, stir the pilaf, cover the pan, and turn off the heat. Allow the pilaf to rest for 5 to 10 minutes.

Stir in the scallions and grated lemon zest, remove the bay leaf, and taste for salt and pepper before serving.

BONNE IDÉE
Chicken, Ham, and Barley Salad. Cool the pilaf to room temperature, and stir in 2 cups diced cooked chicken, 1 cup diced ham, 1 cup peas (fresh, boiled for 1 minute, or frozen, thawed and patted dry), and 3 scallions, white and light green parts only, sliced. Puree 1 packed cup fresh mint leaves with ⅓ cup extra-virgin olive oil and pour the coulis over the salad. Stir to blend, and season with salt, pepper, and fresh lemon juice. Serve over arugula or spinach that's been lightly seasoned and drizzled with a little oil.

desserts

CHOCOLATE ÉCLAIRS WITH THICK GANACHE (PAGE 474)

desserts

a short primer on
the do's and don'ts of cheese

The first time I went to the grand annual agricultural fair held in Paris, I was reminded of Charles de Gaulle's remark that it was impossible to govern a land with 264 cheeses. My next thought was that the great general vastly underestimated his country's output of what is often considered milk's greatest achievement.

Cheese is so important in France that it's its own course, coming between *le plat de résistance* (aka the main course) and dessert, or sometimes replacing dessert. Depending on the meal and the occasion, the cheese course might be as simple as one perfect cheese — in the winter, when Mont d'Or, a soft-enough-to-serve-with-a-spoon cheese, is in season, I often serve it by itself. Or the course can be an elaborate spread including goat, cow, and sheep milk cheeses, soft and hard cheeses, mild and strong cheeses, and at least one blue-veined cheese.

With a cheese platter, variety is key, but timing is all — each cheese should be at just the proper stage of ripeness, and of course, all the cheeses should be served at room temperature. If a cheese is too cold, you lose the nuance of its texture, and you won't get the full measure of its aroma.

I love the elegance of a cheese platter, and I also like the rituals that attend it, at least I like them now that I know them. Trust me, it's easy for a newcomer to get tripped up.

If you're having cheese in a fine restaurant, you can relax — everything will be taken care of for you. The cheese waiter will wheel over the cart, explain each cheese, ask you what you want, and suggest a cheese or two if, judging from what you've chosen, he thinks you'll like it (or if he thinks you're missing a genre). As he cuts, he'll arrange the cheeses around the plate and point out to you the order in which you should eat them. In general, you start with the most delicate cheeses and work your way around the plate until you come to the really strong ones.

You almost always start with a soft goat cheese and finish with a blue.

One evening in Paris many years ago, I was having dinner alone at a restaurant that specialized in cheese. After a cheese-centric starter and main, it was time for the traditional cheese course. I chose what I wanted from the cart and checked with the waiter about where I should start my *dégustation*. No sooner did he point to the 12 o'clock spot on my plate (the usual starting point), than the gentleman at an adjoining table excused himself for interrupting and piped in that he thought the cheese at 3 o'clock really should be the first bite. "*Mais non, mais non*," said the woman at the table to my left, insisting that while the 12 o'clock cheese was fine for the opener, the cheese at 7 o'clock was seriously misplaced. After a lot of talk and a little rearranging, I was given permission to eat — and I was also given a taxi ride home by my two new friends.

Things get a little more complicated when you're served a cheese course at someone's home or at a bistro where there's a communal cheese platter and you're encouraged to serve yourself and pass the platter on to the next table. This is where you can easily commit the most common and most serious of cheese crimes: slicing the cheese in the wrong direction.

Faced with a triangular piece of ripe, runny Brie, you might cut the tip off the cheese and think nothing of it, but your host, while too polite to say anything, may think you were badly brought up or perhaps a little selfish for taking the best part for yourself. (Although, in truth, most French people go easy on us Americans, understanding that cheese is not really in our culture.) The rule of thumb with cheese is to cut it so that the piece that's left on the platter is more or less the same shape as the original piece — unless the cheese is round, like a Camembert, in which case you cut it like a pie. Keeping the form is easy with a triangle of Brie and harder, but happily a little less important, with

certain big wedge-shaped cheeses. When in doubt, smile and ask for help or consult the book a friend gave me: *L'Art de Couper le Fromage (The Art of Cutting Cheese)*, a 64-page book with diagrams rivaling those that appeared in my dreaded elementary geometry text.

When the platter is in front of you, take as much as you want, but plan ahead — taking seconds of cheese is just not done. While it's a compliment to take more of the main course, taking another serving of cheese is impolite, because the cheese is not something your hosts made themselves.

When you're the one serving the cheese, you have only to select perfect cheeses, allow them to reach their correct temperature, and serve them with the right accompaniments — which would be bread and wine. The baguette or country bread that you served with dinner is fine, but it's also nice to serve what the French call a "fantasy" bread, one made with nuts or dried fruits.

As for the wine. . . . It used to be simple and pretty much unquestioned: you had red wine, usually left over from the main course. But times have changed. While red wine is still the most common

accompaniment to cheese — and you'll never hear anyone squawk about it — white wine is becoming the drink of choice for many contemporary diners. Precedents for this are the pairing of goat cheeses from the Loire Valley with white wines from the region, most especially Sancerre; the happy marriage of Roquefort with sweet, syrupy Sauternes; and the match between nutty Comté, made in the Jura, with wines carrying the mountainous region's appellation. But now you see white wines with all kinds of cheeses. In fact, the sommelier from an haute Paris restaurant told me that he did a cheese-and-wine tasting with the staff and that in 80 percent of the cases, white wine was the winning choice.

I've timidly mentioned this to a few of my most old-fashioned French friends, i.e., those who serve red wine with every dish (never changing the wine during the meal), and the response has been consistent: as they poured red wine for cheese, they've said, "Perhaps it could be so," leaving me to believe that things might not change chez them, but that *chez moi*, as long as I don't snip the nose off the Brie, I can pour them some white.

long and slow apples

MAKES 4 SERVINGS

SERVING
The apples are great warm, at room temperature, or chilled, topped with a thick layer of whipped cream and served with a spoon.

STORING
Once cooled, the apples can be kept covered in the refrigerator for up to 3 days.

PIERRE HERMÉ TAUGHT ME A VERSION of this recipe over a decade ago, and when I made it and called to tell him he was a genius, he said, "Not me. We've got Edouard Nignon to thank for this — he created it over a hundred years ago." It's a brilliantly simple recipe, and once you know it, you'll find it turning up in various guises in places where pastry chefs aced their history classes. (I found it at Jean-Georges Vongerichten's restaurant in New York City and in Alain Ducasse's in Paris.) Known most widely as *pommes confites,* the recipe entails nothing more than cutting apples as thin as you can (a mandoline is great here), layering them with a gossamer slick of butter and a sprinkling of sugar, weighting them down, and baking them for a long time. Until you've had it, you can't imagine how glorious this dish is.

Traditionally *pommes confites* was made in a roasting pan, baked for ten hours, and cooled for another ten. (When I included this recipe in my first book with Pierre Hermé, I called it Twenty-Hour Apples; see Bonne Idée.) Because I'm more impatient than I used to be — and because a roasting pan full of apples is often too many apples at my house — I've tinkered with the recipe to make mini versions that can be baked in small custard cups and, if you like, unmolded to make the very homey dessert a little dressier. And while I was tinkering, I added a little spice as well — a small touch that brings the dessert gently into the twenty-first century.

FOR THE APPLES

¼ cup sugar

⅛ teaspoon ground ginger
Pinch of ground coriander

4 medium apples, such as Gala or Fuji, peeled

3 tablespoons unsalted butter, melted

Zest of 1 small orange, removed with a vegetable peeler, then very finely chopped (optional)

FOR THE TOPPING

⅓ cup very cold heavy cream

1 tablespoon confectioners' sugar
Small pinch of ground ginger

¼ teaspoon pure vanilla extract

TO MAKE THE APPLES: Center a rack in the oven and preheat the oven to 300 degrees F. Butter four 6-ounce ramekins or heatproof cups (Pyrex custard cups work well). Line a baking sheet with a silicone baking mat or parchment paper.

Put the sugar, ginger, and coriander in a small bowl and whisk to blend.

The apples need to be sliced as thin as possible: First cut them in half from top to bottom and remove the cores with a melon baller, or excavate them with the tip of a small knife. If you have a mandoline or Benriner slicer, use it to slice the apples crosswise ⅛ to 1/16 inch thick. If not, do this with a knife — just set the apple halves cut side down on a board and slice crosswise.

Arrange a thin layer of apple slices in each ramekin, brush with a little melted butter, sprinkle with a little spiced sugar, and scatter over a small pinch of orange zest, if you're using it. Continue to make layers of apples, butter, spiced sugar, and orange zest until you've used all the apples. Wrap each ramekin in plastic (don't worry, the plastic won't melt) and then foil and use a small knife to pierce both the plastic and foil in about 4 places. Put the ramekins on the baking sheet and weight each ramekin down. I use more ramekins or heatproof coffee cups for the job; you don't need anything too heavy, but you do want to press the apples a bit while they're baking.

Bake the apples for 2 hours, undisturbed. Transfer the baking sheet to a cooling rack and let the ramekins rest with the weights in place until they cool down a little, or until they reach room temperature. Remove the weights and the wrapping. If the juices have run over the sides of the ramekins, wipe them clean.

Serve warm, at room temperature, or chilled. If you want to serve the apples chilled, cover each one with a clean piece of plastic wrap and refrigerate for at least 4 hours, or, better yet, overnight. If you want to unmold the apples, run a small knife around the edges of each ramekin, cover with a small plate, turn over, and lift off the ramekin.

RIGHT BEFORE SERVING, MAKE THE TOPPING: Whip the cream just until it holds soft peaks, then beat in the confectioners' sugar, ginger, and vanilla. Spread some cream over each ramekin.

BONNE IDÉE
Twenty-Hour Apples

Butter an 8-inch square nonreactive baking dish (glass or ceramic is good here), and line a baking sheet with a silicone baking mat or parchment paper. You'll need 8 to 10 large apples, peeled, cut in half from blossom to stem, cored, and cut crosswise into very thin slices. As you cut, keep the shape of each half intact so that when you're done, you can press on it and fan out the slices. Place the fanned slices in the buttered pan, continuing until you've covered the base of the pan. Generously brush the layer with melted unsalted butter (you'll need 4 to 6 tablespoons total) and sprinkle evenly with a thin coating of sugar (as much as ½ cup sugar total). Toss a few strands of grated orange zest over the apples (the zest from 1 orange), and continue making layers. The apples will probably mound above the edge of the pan, and that's just fine. Double-wrap the pan with plastic wrap, covering the top and bottom, and prick the plastic in about 6 places. Top with weights (I use cans of tomatoes) — don't cover all the air holes — put the pan on the lined baking sheet, and bake for 10 hours in a 175-degree-F oven. (Don't worry — the plastic won't melt.) Let the apples cool to room temperature, still wrapped and weighted, then move the whole setup into the refrigerator and chill the apples for 10 hours. To serve, cut into squares — you'll have enough for about 10 servings — and top with whipped cream, if you like.

compote de pommes two ways

MAKES ABOUT
4 SERVINGS

SERVING
The lighter *compote de pommes* makes a good dessert mixed with a little crème fraîche or yogurt and served with cookies, while the darker compote is great in crepes. (It's also nice spread over the base of the *tarte fine,* see Bonne Idée, page 459, before the apple slices are added.)

STORING
Either compote can be kept tightly covered in the refrigerator for at least 1 week.

IT'S SURPRISING HOW POPULAR *COMPOTE DE POMMES,* or applesauce, is in France. It's one of the first foods babies get to eat, but it's also a household standby; a small bowlful topped with a little crème fraîche or mixed with yogurt makes a dessert, as does a few spoonfuls savored with a couple of cookies. When Marie-Cécile Noblet came to live with us to be the au pair to our then ten-month-old son, one of the first things she did was make *compote de pommes* for the little one. While her chocolate rice pudding became my husband's all-time favorite dessert, the fact that the applesauce was for the kid never stopped him from dipping into the stash. As for me, I was always looking for ways to bake with it (see Bonne Idée).

Compote de pommes can be as simple as cooking cut-up apples with a little water (to keep them from scorching) until they're soft enough to mash with a spoon or as sophisticated as cooking them until they're dark and caramelish (halfway between applesauce and apple butter), then mixing them with salted butter, to make a treat that's a specialty of both Normandy (which is just about synonymous with apples) and Brittany (where salted butter reigns).

If you decide to make the darker compote, you can double the recipe — you'll be cooking the apples for a long time (getting the texture you want can take over 30 minutes), so you might want to maximize your effort.

2 pounds (about 6 medium) apples, preferably red apples like Empire, Cortland, or McIntosh	1–4 tablespoons sugar (optional)
About ¼ cup water	½ teaspoon pure vanilla extract (optional)
1 tablespoon brown sugar	2 tablespoons salted butter, for thicker compote (optional)

I like to make my applesauce with chunks of apples (peel and cores intact), and then run the sauce through a food mill, which purees and strains the fruit at the same time. If you don't have a food mill, it's easier to peel and core the apples at the start. Cut the fruit into chunks and toss them into a medium saucepan — one with a heavy bottom works best here.

Stir in ¼ cup water and the brown sugar and put the pan over medium-low heat. Cook, stirring frequently — stay close, because the juices can bubble up — until the apples are soft enough to be crushed with the back of a spoon. If the pan looks too dry, add a little more water as you cook and stir. Count on about 15 to 20 minutes to get to the mashable stage.

If you want regular *compote de pommes,* remove the pan from the heat and run the compote through a food mill. If you're without a mill, push it through a strainer — or don't: chunky applesauce is great. Should the applesauce seem too thin to you, pour it back into the pan and cook, stirring constantly, for a few minutes, until the sauce is thick enough to mound on a spoon. Scoop the applesauce into a bowl. If you're making the regular compote, taste it now, and if you'd like it sweeter, add some of the granulated sugar. Now's also the time to add the vanilla, if you want it.

If you want to cook the compote down so that it's thicker and jammier, it's best to strain it first — but don't add the sugar or vanilla. Return the compote to the saucepan, put the pan over the lowest possible heat, and cook, stirring and scraping the bottom of the pan often, until you have a thick, spreadable mixture. (This can take more than 30 minutes for a single recipe and more than an hour if you've doubled it, so be patient.) Be careful: the apples will sputter, and they're very, very hot! Alternatively, you can put the pan in a 250-degree-F oven and bake the compote, stirring every 10 minutes or so, until it's thick. Let cool slightly, and when the compote is no longer burn-your-tongue hot, taste it for sugar — but cooked down like this, it will probably be sweet enough — and add the vanilla, if you'd like. Stir in the butter, if you're using it.

Whichever compote you've made, press a piece of plastic wrap against the surface and chill.

what's good for the apple is good for the pear

Apples and pears could not look, taste, or feel more different, but when you're baking, you might just think of them as fraternal twins. With very few exceptions, when a recipe calls for apples, you can swap them for pears. That means that an apple tart, tarte Tatin, turnover, or even compote can be made with pears. The only thing you have to remember is that a ripe, juicy, fragrant pear is more fragile than just about any apple in the bushel, so it might need a gentler touch and a slightly shorter time in, under, or over heat. It might even need a tad less sugar, so taste as you go.

BONNE IDÉE

Apple Turnovers. Chaussons aux pommes made with puff pastry, about the size of the palm of your hand, are a morning treat throughout France. My own preference is for pastries that are more petite. To make 8 turnovers, you'll need 2 sheets of frozen puff pastry, thawed. One at a time, roll each sheet out into an 11-inch square and then, using a 4½-inch saucer as a guide, cut out 4 circles. Spoon a tablespoon or so of compote (the lighter compote is better here) into the center of each one. Paint the edges of each circle with a little beaten egg and fold the dough over to make a half-moon shape, pressing with your fingertips to seal the edges. Crimp the edges with the tines of a fork and brush the tops with egg. Sprinkle a little sugar over the turnovers and use the point of a paring knife to poke 2 holes in each pastry. Put the turnovers on a baking sheet lined with a silicone baking mat or parchment paper and bake in a 400-degree-F oven for 20 to 25 minutes, or until they're puffed and golden and a little of the applesauce is bubbling up through the steam vents. Transfer them to racks and let them cool to just warm or room temperature.

baked apples filled
with fruits and nuts

MAKES 4 SERVINGS

SERVING
Drizzle the apples with some of the pan sauce, and then, if you like, spoon over some yogurt, heavy cream, whipped or not (there's something nice about plain cream with these apples), crème fraîche, or vanilla ice cream.

STORING
The apples are softer and more comforting served warm, but they're still very good at room temperature (covered lightly, they can stay on the counter for several hours) or even chilled. If you've got leftovers, cover them, put them in the refrigerator, and have them for breakfast the next day.

BAKED APPLES, OR *POMMES AU FOUR* (apples in the oven), are the kind of dessert you might believe the French pop out of the womb knowing how to make. In fact, baked apples are less a recipe than a construction: you core some apples, stuff their hollows with dried fruits, nuts, honey, and butter, and then slide them into the oven. Which fruits and nuts? It's up to you. Cinnamon or no cinnamon? Again, your choice. Hot? Warm? Chilled, with heavy cream? No one will tell you definitively. I love sweets like these, and clearly the French do too, because when I bake these apples for my friends there, invariably, no matter their age, they start to tell me about how their grandmothers made them.

When I first made this dessert in Paris, I asked the apple man at the market which fruit to use. His suggestion was Canada or Boskoop, two varieties I've never seen in America, so when I returned to the U.S., I decided to use what my own grandmother had used: big old-fashioned red baking apples, like Rome Beauty or Cortland. But, like the rest of this recipe, even the apples are up for grabs. You can make these with "regular" apples, like Gala, Empire, or Jonagold. Everyday eating apples are smaller than big bakers, so they'll take less filling and need less time in the oven, but these are easy adjustments to make as you go.

A word of advice: Make a thin cut around the tummy of each apple to keep it from bursting.

 4 apples, preferably Rome Beauty or Cortland (or your favorite apple)
 1 slice lemon
   About ½ cup coarsely chopped dried assorted fruits, such as raisins, figs, prunes, dates, apricots, and/or cherries (if you prefer, use just one kind of fruit)
   About 2 tablespoons coarsely chopped nuts

 1½ tablespoons honey, or to taste
   Pinch of fleur de sel (optional)
   Pinch of ground cinnamon, nutmeg, or ginger (optional)
 4 tablespoons (½ stick) unsalted butter
 ⅔ cup apple cider or water

   Plain or vanilla yogurt, heavy cream, crème fraîche, or vanilla ice cream, for topping (optional)

Center a rack in the oven and preheat the oven to 350 degrees F. Have a baking dish at hand: you want a dish that can hold the apples comfortably but snugly (a 9- or 10-inch deep-dish Pyrex pie pan works well).

Core the apples, making sure not to cut through the bottoms. Peel the apples down to the halfway mark; don't toss away the peels. Make a very shallow cut around each apple at the point where the peel begins. Rub the cut parts of the apples with the slice of lemon.

In a small bowl, mix together the dried fruits, nuts, and honey; add the salt and spice, if you're using them. Cut 2 tablespoons of the butter into 8 pieces and put a piece of butter inside each apple. Divide the fruit-and-nut mixture among the apples, then top each with another piece of butter.

Arrange the apples in the baking dish and pour in the cider or water. Cut the remaining 2 tablespoons butter into bits and scatter the bits over the cider, then toss in the reserved peels (if they're very long, just cut them into manageable strips).

Slide the baking dish into the oven and bake the apples, basting them every 15 minutes, for 50 to 75 minutes, until they are tender. (I can't give you a more precise estimate of the time because it will depend on the size and type of your apples — so check early and often.) Don't go for al dente — the apples should be spoon-tender.

Transfer the apples to a serving platter or individual small bowls. If you'd like, pour the baking juices into a saucepan and boil for a few minutes to make a more concentrated sauce; set aside. Let the apples cool for about 10 minutes, or until they reach room temperature.

Serve the apples moistened with the pan sauce, and, if desired, topped with yogurt, cream, crème fraîche, or ice cream.

BONNE IDÉE

Pommes au Four Meringuées. I normally do nothing more to my *pommes au four* but fill them with fruit, but my French neighbors turn this nursery sweet into dinner-party fare by topping each apple with a pouf of meringue. Bake the apples as directed, and then crown them with meringue (beat 2 large egg whites with a scant ½ cup sugar until they form firm, glossy peaks) and run them under the broiler to brown their tops; or, if you've got a blowtorch, use it to color the meringue.

spice-poached apples or pears

MAKES **6** SERVINGS

SERVING
The fruit can be served, with its syrup, when it's just slightly warm or at room temperature. You can certainly serve the fruit cold, but the flavors are fuller when it's on the warm side.

STORING
You can make the fruit up to 3 days ahead. Pack the fruit and syrup into a covered container and refrigerate.

BONNE IDÉE
When the weather is warm, you can use the basic syrup (with or without the spices, although I'd keep the vanilla) to poach stone fruits like plums, apricots, or cherries — just keep a close watch on these soft fruits, because they cook faster than apples or pears.

COOKED FRUITS AND SIMMERED COMPOTES are among the simplest of French family sweets, and the most comforting too. While they're usually served with little more than heavy cream, crème fraîche, or plain yogurt, I like to pair these holiday-spiced fruits with rice pudding (page 429) or French toast (page 418), moistening the pudding or toast with the poaching syrup and then spooning over the fruit.

½ cup honey
⅓ cup sugar
3 cups water
   Zest and juice of ½ orange, zest removed in wide strips with a vegetable peeler
   Zest and juice of ½ lemon, zest removed in wide strips with a vegetable peeler

2 pieces star anise
1 piece thin cinnamon stick (about 1½ inches long)
1 piece vanilla bean (about 2 inches long), split (see box)
3 medium apples or pears, peeled, halved, and cored

Put all the ingredients except the fruit in a large saucepan, turn the heat to medium-high, and bring to a boil. As soon as the liquid boils, reduce the heat to medium-low and simmer the syrup for 5 minutes.

Carefully drop the apples or pears into the pan and bring the syrup back to a simmer. Cover the pan and cook until the fruit can be pierced easily with a thin knife, 10 to 15 minutes, depending on the fruit; check early and often. Using a slotted spoon, transfer the apples or pears to a bowl.

Turn up the heat and boil the syrup for another 10 minutes, at which point you'll have about 1¼ cups. Pour the syrup over the fruit, cover, and let cool until slightly warm or at room temperature.

vanilla beans

Vanilla beans should be plump and pliable, bendable actually, and moist. It's the pulp you're meant to use, so lay the bean on a cutting board and, with a sharp paring knife, slice it lengthwise in half, then use the knife to scrape out the seedy pulp. Don't toss the bean — stick it in a jar of sugar, and soon you'll have vanilla sugar; or dry it on the counter or in a low oven, then toss it and some sugar into a food processor and process until the bean is pulverized. Alternatively, you can use the pod to flavor anything you're poaching.

roasted rhubarb

R HUBARB'S A WIMP. It's tall and straight and firm on the stalk, but give it a little heat, and after a couple of minutes, it's gone to mush. It is much more appealing when it retains a little of its natural structure, as it does when it's roasted, the simplest method I've ever learned to prepare rhubarb so that it cooks through, sweetens, and stays almost intact.

Served with a little cream or yogurt, roasted rhubarb is the kind of sweet you'd have after a weekday meal. But spoon it over a slice of cake — the Visitandine (page 436), for example — and this homey dessert becomes company fare.

1   pound trimmed rhubarb

½   cup sugar

Grated zest of ½ orange (you
    can use the zest of 1 lemon,
    if you like)

Honey (optional)

Center a rack in the oven and preheat the oven to 400 degrees F.

Cut the rhubarb into pieces about 1½ inches long, and toss them into a baking pan that will hold them comfortably. (I use a Pyrex pie plate.) Sprinkle over the sugar and zest and stir everything around until the rhubarb is covered with sugar. Let the mix rest for 5 minutes, or just long enough for a little syrup to start to develop.

Cover the pan with foil and roast the rhubarb for 15 minutes. Take a peek, and if the sugar isn't almost completely melted, stir, re-cover the pan with the foil, and roast for a few minutes more. Once the sugar is melted, take off the foil and roast the rhubarb for another 5 minutes, or until the syrup is bubbling.

Remove the pan from the oven and let the rhubarb cool just enough for you to taste it. If you don't think the mix is sweet enough, add a little honey.

MAKES **4** SERVINGS

SERVING
You can serve roasted rhubarb warm, at room temperature, or chilled; under yogurt, heavy cream, or crème fraîche; over ice cream; under, over, or around cake; or on its own. It's also good with rice pudding (page 429).

STORING
The rhubarb can be refrigerated in a covered container for at least a week.

citrus-berry terrine

WHILE AMERICANS OF ALL STRIPES tend to turn snobby at the mere mention of gelatin, the French accept gelatin with the same equanimity with which they accept salt and pepper: as just another ingredient. Gelatin is a staple in the French pastry kitchen, where it's used to stabilize whipped cream, make Bavarian cream, and hold up a mousse destined to go between layers of cake. *À la maison,* it's often used to make fresh-flavored, rather elegant gelées, the Gallic version of homemade Jell-O.

When the weather turns warm, gelées appear more often, sometimes savory, but usually sweet and fruity, like this terrine that straddles the seasons. While it's got lots of berries, its base is citrus. Like most gelées, it's beautiful.

BE PREPARED: You'll need to chill the gelatin mixture for 2 hours and the terrine for at least 4 hours.

MAKES
10 SERVINGS

SERVING
The terrine should be served in thick slices. If you'd like, you can dress each serving with more berries (I like to serve it with cold berries, which I toss with a pinch of sugar just before I spoon them out) or pour over a spoonful or two of sweetened pureed raspberries.

STORING
The terrine can be kept covered in the refrigerator for up to 3 days. If you've got some gelée left over, press a piece of plastic wrap against the cut surface before you cover the terrine.

Segments from 2 navel oranges, cut into bite-sized pieces
Segments from 1 pink grapefruit, cut into bite-sized pieces
⅓ cup cold water
2 packets unflavored gelatin
2 cups orange or grapefruit juice

⅓ cup sugar
About 3 cups mixed fresh blueberries, raspberries, and blackberries (if you want to add strawberries, look for small berries or cut larger ones into bite-sized pieces)

Put a double layer of paper towels on a cutting board and spread the citrus pieces out on the paper. Cover with another double layer of towels and set the pieces aside until you're ready for them. If the paper gets very wet, change it.

Put the cold water in a large bowl, sprinkle over the gelatin, and let it soften.

Meanwhile, bring the juice and sugar to a boil in a medium saucepan, stirring to dissolve the sugar. Pour some of the juice over the gelatin, gently stir to dissolve, and then stir in the rest of the juice. Put the gelatin mixture in the refrigerator and let it chill, stirring occasionally, until it thickens slightly, about 2 hours. You're looking for a mixture with the texture of egg whites.

Rinse a 9-x-5-inch loaf pan with cold water and shake out the excess. (I use a Pyrex pan.) Gently stir the citrus segments and the berries into the lightly thickened gelatin mixture, and scrape everything into the pan. Jiggle the pan a little to settle the gel, and chill for at least 4 hours, or for up to overnight.

When you're ready to serve the terrine, dip the pan into a bowl or sinkful of hot water for a few seconds, and run a blunt knife around the edges of the pan. Wipe the pan and unmold the terrine onto a platter.

salted butter break-ups

MAKES 4 SERVINGS

SERVING
If fun is what you're after, bring the break-up to the table whole and let everyone break off pieces big and small; if order suits you better, break up the cookie in the kitchen and serve the pieces on a plate.

STORING
You can make the dough up to 3 days ahead and keep it in the refrigerator, or you can wrap it airtight and freeze it for up to 2 months. The baked cookie will keep in an airtight container for about 3 days.

EVEN IF THIS WEREN'T WONDERFULLY GOOD — and it is — I'd want to make it just because it's so much fun to serve. Essentially a large, buttery, flaky, salty-sweet rectangular cookie with a pretty little crosshatch pattern on top, it is put in the center of the table, and guests serve themselves by reaching over and breaking off pieces of the sweet. Yes, it's messy — it's impossible for this to be a crumbless endeavor — but everyone, young and old, easygoing and stuffy, likes it. For neatness's sake, you could break the cookie up in the kitchen, or you could even cut it into cookie shapes after you roll it out, but that wouldn't be as amusing, would it?

Called *broyé* in French, meaning crushed, the cookie is a tradition in the Poitou region, a part of western France where butter is prized. Butteriness is one of the cookie's defining characteristics, and saltiness is another — it's undeniably salty, and now and again, you can even feel the salt on your tongue. In France, the cookie is made with *sel gris,* a moist, slightly gray (*gris*) sea salt with crystals that are large enough to be picked up individually. If you can't find *sel gris,* go with kosher or another coarse salt.

BE PREPARED: The dough should be chilled for 1 hour.

1¾ cups all-purpose flour	9 tablespoons cold unsalted
⅔ cup sugar	butter, cut into 18 pieces
¾–1 teaspoon *sel gris* (see above)	3–5 tablespoons cold water
or kosher salt	1 egg yolk, for the glaze

Put the flour, sugar, and salt in a food processor and pulse to combine. Drop in the pieces of butter and pulse until the mixture looks like coarse meal — you'll have both big pea-sized pieces and small flakes. With the machine running, start adding the cold water gradually: add just enough water to produce a dough that almost forms a ball. When you reach into the bowl to feel the dough, it should be very malleable.

Scrape the dough onto a work surface, form it into a square, and pat it down to flatten it a bit. Wrap the dough in plastic and chill it for about 1 hour. *(The dough can be refrigerated for up to 3 days or wrapped airtight and frozen for up to 2 months.)*

When you're ready to bake, center a rack in the oven and preheat the oven to 350 degrees F. Line a baking sheet with a silicone baking mat or parchment paper.

Remove the dough from the fridge and, if it's very hard, bash it a few times with your rolling pin to soften it. Put the dough between sheets of plastic wrap or wax paper and roll it into a rectangle that's about ¼ inch thick and about 5 x 11 inches; accuracy and neatness don't count for a lot here. Transfer the dough to the lined baking sheet.

Beat the egg yolk with a few drops of cold water and, using a pastry brush, paint the top surface of the dough with the egg glaze. Using the back of a table fork, decorate the cookie in a crosshatch pattern.

Bake the cookie for 30 to 40 minutes, or until it is golden. It will be firm to the touch but have a little spring when pressed in the center — the perfect break-up is crisp on the outside and still tender within. Transfer the baking sheet to a rack and allow the cookie to cool to room temperature.

cocoa sablés

MAKES ABOUT
36 COOKIES

SERVING
These cookies can be served alone, with tea, or, better still, with espresso or milk, but they're also nice spread with jam or ice cream.

STORING
The logs of dough, without the egg wash and sugar, can be kept in the refrigerator for up to 3 days or wrapped airtight and frozen for up to 2 months. You can slice and bake the cookies straight from the freezer; just add a minute or two to the baking time.

SABLÉ MEANS SANDY, AND IT DESCRIBES the slightly crumbly texture of the French shortbread that bears its name. What it doesn't even hint at is how rich a sablé usually is — the best sablés have a no-two-ways-about-it butteriness that defines the genre as much as the texture does. In fact, without the butter, you wouldn't get the texture. Whether the sablé melts in your mouth, as this one does, or has the bit of crunch you get with a sablé Breton (see Bonne Idée, page 465), depends on the amounts of flour, butter, and sugar and on whether or not you add the eggs, but in the end, every card-carrying sablé has that distinctive crumbliness at its core.

This slice-and-bake sablé is a slight variation of one of Pierre Hermé's. It should be made with deep, dark cocoa powder, and to get the loveliest texture, the dough should be worked as little as possible. I've added some very finely chopped chocolate to the recipe — just enough to speckle the cookies and deepen the flavor — but it's an optional flavoring. Also optional is the sparkle edging, a crunchy white ringlet obtained by brushing the logs of dough with egg and rolling them in sugar, preferably decorating sugar, before cutting them and sending them into the oven.

Finally, I like to make these cookies thick — I slice them at ½-inch intervals — because I think you can appreciate their texture best when you've got something substantial to bite into, but you can make them thinner, of course. Do that, and they'll make fine ice cream sandwiches. (Try them with Ben & Jerry's Coffee Heath Bar Crunch.)

BE PREPARED: You'll need to chill the dough for at least 3 hours.

2¾	cups all-purpose flour	1	teaspoon pure vanilla extract
⅓	cup unsweetened cocoa powder, preferably Dutch-processed	¼	pound semisweet or bittersweet chocolate, finely chopped (optional)
½	teaspoon salt		
2½	sticks (10 ounces) unsalted butter, at room temperature	1	large egg (optional)
⅔	cup sugar		Decorating sugar (optional)

Whisk the flour, cocoa, and salt together.

In the bowl of a stand mixer fitted with the paddle attachment or in a large bowl with a hand mixer, beat the butter on medium speed until soft and smooth. Gradually add the sugar and keep beating, scraping the bowl as needed, until the mixture is creamy but not airy. (You want to be beating, not whipping.) Mix in the vanilla. Reduce the mixer speed to low and add the flour mixture in 3 additions, mixing just until the ingredients are incorporated — no more. If you're using the chopped chocolate, stir it in now, using a large rubber spatula.

Scrape the dough onto a cutting board and divide it in half. Roll each piece into a log that's about 1¾ inches in diameter. (Rolled to this diameter, the baked cookies will be about 2½ inches across. If you'd prefer larger or smaller cookies, shape the logs accordingly.) Wrap the logs in plastic wrap and chill for at least 3 hours. *(The dough can be refrigerated for up to 3 days or wrapped airtight and frozen for up to 2 months.)*

When you're ready to bake, position the racks to divide the oven into thirds and preheat the oven to 350 degrees F. Line two baking sheets with silicone baking mats or parchment paper.

If you want to sugar-crust the cookies, beat the egg in a small bowl. Put some decorating sugar on a piece of wax paper. Brush the logs with the beaten egg and then roll them around in the sugar, pressing the sugar gently to get it to stick evenly.

Slice the logs into ½-inch-thick cookies. (If you'd like thinner cookies, cut them ⅓ inch thick. You can cut them a hair thinner, but those won't hold up for ice cream sandwiches. If you do make thinner cookies, make sure to reduce the baking time.) Arrange the cookies on the baking sheets, leaving a generous inch of space between the rounds.

Bake the cookies for 15 to 18 minutes, rotating the sheets from top to bottom and front to back at the midway point, until the cookies are just firm to the touch. Transfer them to racks to cool to room temperature.

If you've got any dough left over, slice and bake it, making sure your baking sheets are cool first.

BONNE IDÉE

Classic Butter Sablés.
These are made with a mixture of confectioners' and granulated sugar, but the method of mixing, shaping, and sugaring the logs is the same as that for the chocolate cookies. Beat 2 sticks (8 ounces) unsalted butter, at room temperature, together with ½ cup sugar, ¼ cup confectioners' sugar, sifted, and ½ teaspoon salt until the mixture is creamy but not airy. One by one, with the mixer on low speed, beat in 2 large egg yolks. Keeping the mixer on its lowest speed, blend in 2 cups all-purpose flour, mixing only until the flour disappears into the soft dough. Divide the dough in half, shape into logs about 9 inches long, wrap in plastic, and chill for at least 3 hours or freeze. When you're ready to bake, brush the logs with a beaten egg and roll in sugar, if you'd like. Cut the dough into ½-inch-thick rounds and bake on baking sheets lined with silicone baking mats or parchment in a 350-degree-F oven for 17 to 20 minutes, or until the cookies are just golden around the edges but still pale on top.

almond-orange tuiles

MAKES ABOUT
36 TUILES

SERVING
Thin, fragile tuiles are naturally elegant and so should be served either as the sole sweet (the better to appreciate their loveliness), with tea or coffee, or alongside something as creamy as they are crisp. They're perfect with ice cream, chocolate mousse (page 421), and crème brûlée (page 422).

STORING
Humidity is the great enemy of tuiles — just the least bit of moisture will cause them to soften and wilt — but if your kitchen is cool and dry, you can keep the cookies overnight (maybe even a bit longer). Put them on a lined baking sheet — there's no need to cover them — or keep them in a tin. They can't be frozen, but because you can keep the dough in the refrigerator for up to 3 days, you can make as many tuiles as you want whenever you need them.

TUILES ARE AMONG THE PRETTIEST COOKIES in the French repertoire. Named for the curved clay roof tiles of Provençal farmhouses, they're lacy, fragile, light, and, as their name suggests, curved. They look complicated but are in fact easy to make, since the batter spreads and rounds on its own in the oven and then all you have to do to get the beautiful curved shape is to lay the cookies over a rolling pin to cool — or you can just leave them flat.

There are many recipes for tuiles, but this one has a special place in my heart because it came to me unexpectedly. My husband, friends, and I were having dinner at La Robe et le Palais, a small bistro near Paris's Palais de Justice, where we chose crème brûlée for dessert. Because it had a little twist, I asked our waiter if he could possibly get the chef to tell him how he made it. Instead of returning with a description, the waiter returned with the chef, Yannis Théodore, who was delighted to share his secret (the recipe is on page 422). "And the tuiles that accompanied the crème brûlée, did we want to know about them too?" he asked. They were made with chopped almonds, and they had a slight tang, in part a product of the sugar in the dough having caramelized, but there was something else, not as easily discernible. "Orange juice!" exclaimed the chef. And then he dashed away and quickly returned with a little plastic container filled with the dough for his tuiles. He handed me the tub, wrote the recipe on a small scrap of paper, and said, "I hope you'll enjoy these at home," and off he went. The gesture was sweet, generous, and spontaneous, and the tuiles were wonderful. I made a batch with his dough the following day and have been using his recipe to make batch after batch ever since.

BE PREPARED: The dough really needs an overnight rest before baking, so plan accordingly.

½ cup sugar	3½ tablespoons orange juice
¼ cup minus 1 teaspoon all-purpose flour	4 tablespoons (½ stick) unsalted butter, melted and cooled
3½ ounces blanched almonds, finely chopped (a scant cup)	

Whisk the sugar, flour, and almonds together in a small bowl. Stir in the orange juice. Switch to a rubber spatula and stir in the melted butter. Press a piece of plastic wrap against the surface of the dough and chill it overnight. (*The dough can be refrigerated, well covered, for up to 3 days.*)

When you're ready to bake, center a rack in the oven and preheat the oven to 325 degrees F. Have one or two baking sheets at the ready; you don't need to line or butter the sheets. If you'd like to curve the tuiles, set a rolling pin (or an empty wine bottle) on the counter.

For each tuile, scoop out 1 teaspoonful of dough and roll it lightly between your palms into a ball. Arrange on the baking sheet(s), leaving 2 inches of spread space between the balls of dough.

Bake the tuiles, one sheet at a time, for 10 to 12 minutes, rotating the sheet at the midway mark. When done, the dough, which will have bubbled, will have calmed down, spread into pretty rounds, and become golden and honeycombed. Pull the sheet from the oven and let the cookies rest for a few seconds, then, using a wide metal spatula, lift the cookies from the sheet: the best way to do this is to carefully work the spatula under a cookie edge, then push the spatula beneath the cookie with a quick jerk. If the cookie crumples a bit, as it might, don't worry — it will straighten out on the rolling pin (or the cooling rack if you're not curving the cookies). Moving quickly, place the cookies over the rolling pin to curve them. Transfer the cookies to a flat surface after they have set — they set in under a minute. If the cookies cool and stick stubbornly to the baking sheet, slide the sheet into the oven for another minute to warm the cookies, then remove them. If you want flat cookies, just cool them on a rack.

If you are using the same baking sheet to make another batch of cookies, make certain it is clean and cool before spooning on the dough.

speculoos

MAKES ABOUT
70 COOKIES

SERVING
The cookies are just right
with coffee, made for
espresso and tea, and really
good nibbled as a snack.

STORING
The dough can be wrapped
airtight and kept in the
refrigerator for up to
3 days or in the freezer for
up to 2 months. Kept in
an airtight container, the
cookies will be fine for a
week or more.

SPECULOOS ARE CRISP BROWN-SUGAR COOKIES that can be big or small (I make them very small), thin or thick (mine are medium-thin), and spicy or spicier (I lean toward spicier). In general, the predominant spice is cinnamon — indeed, some recipes I've seen use cinnamon alone — but a little ginger and a pinch of cloves make the cookies slightly more complex.

As far as I know, there's no law against eating speculoos in March or June or even September, but no matter when you have them, their smell will hint of Christmas and their flavor will just about exclaim it. In fact, in their native Belgium, they are the cookie that celebrates the name day of Saint Nicholas, the man we know as Father Christmas, or Santa Claus.

These cookies keep really well, making them perfect to pack up in tins and give as Christmas presents.

BE PREPARED: The rolled-out dough needs to be chilled for at least 3 hours.

1⅔	cups all-purpose flour	⅛	teaspoon ground cloves
¼	teaspoon salt	7	tablespoons unsalted butter,
¼	teaspoon baking soda		at room temperature
2½	teaspoons ground cinnamon	½	cup sugar
¼	teaspoon ground ginger	½	cup packed light brown sugar

Whisk the flour, salt, baking soda, and spices together in a bowl.

In the bowl of a stand mixer fitted with the paddle attachment or in a bowl with a hand mixer, beat the butter at medium speed until creamy. Add the sugars and beat until well blended, about 2 minutes. With the mixer on the lowest speed, add the dry ingredients in 3 additions, mixing only until the flour disappears into the soft dough. You may have some flour at the bottom of the bowl, or the dough may not be entirely smooth, but that's normal. Using your hands (always my first choice) or a spatula, reach into the bowl and knead or stir the dough 2 or 3 times, just enough to eliminate any dry spots.

Divide the dough in half. (The dough is very soft, even after you refrigerate it for several hours, so if your kitchen is hot, you might want to divide the dough into thirds — that way it won't take you as long to cut out the cookies and the dough won't soften as much.) Working with 1 piece of dough at a time, roll the dough between two sheets of wax paper or plastic wrap until you have a circle that's a scant ¼ inch thick. As you're rolling, turn the dough over a couple of times and pull away the paper or plastic, so you don't end up rolling creases into the dough. Put the rolled-out rounds of dough on a tray or cutting board and refrigerate for at least 3 hours. *(The dough can be refrigerated for up to 3 days or frozen, well wrapped, for up to 2 months.)*

When you're ready to bake, center a rack in the oven and preheat the oven to 350 degrees F. Line a baking sheet with a silicone baking mat or parchment paper.

Choose a cookie cutter — I use a scalloped cutter that's 1¼ inches in diameter — and remove 1 circle of dough from the refrigerator. Peel off the top piece of wax paper or plastic and cut out as many cookies as you can from the dough, carefully lifting the cutouts onto the lined baking sheet. Collect the scraps and set them aside to combine with the scraps from the second piece of dough.

Bake the cookies for 8 to 10 minutes, or until they are lightly golden and just slightly brown around the edges. Allow the cookies to rest on the baking sheet for a couple of minutes before transferring them to a cooling rack to cool.

Repeat with the second round of dough, making certain the baking sheet is cool before you put the cutouts on it. To use the scraps, press them together, roll them into a circle, and chill before cutting and baking.

BONNE IDÉE
If you roll the dough thinner (and bake the cookies for a shorter time), the speculoos will make great sandwich cookies. Try them with Nutella, dulce de leche, or bittersweet ganache (page 467). Or bring some raspberry or apricot jam to a boil with a tiny splash of water (you can do this in a microwave oven), and when the jam cools and thickens a bit, use it as a filling.

honey-spiced madeleines

MAKES 12 LARGE
MADELEINES OR
MORE THAN 36
MINI MADELEINES

SERVING
Like traditional madeleines, these are good with tea, but because of the spices, they're also very good with espresso. And, as unorthodox as the combination may be, they pair well with single-malt whisky or Armagnac.

STORING
Although the batter can be made up to a day ahead, madeleines are really best served just warm or at room temperature the day they are made. Leftovers should be kept in a closely covered container. If you've had them long enough for them to have gone stale, dunk them in whatever you're drinking.

THIS IS NOT YOUR TYPICAL MADELEINE, nor Proust's either. Although it's based on the classic (for that recipe, turn to Bonne Idée), it's my own invention, created to be served over the holidays, when spices like ginger, cinnamon, and cloves are most appreciated in both France and America. Like traditional madeleines, these require a light hand when folding the flour and butter into the egg and spice mixture. And the batter can be prepared ahead, even spooned into the molds, and baked *à la minute,* so that you can serve the little cakes warm. While I don't usually recommend serving a cake until it's thoroughly cooled, madeleines are the exception: for reasons inexplicable, ever-so-slightly warm is the perfect temperature for madeleines, particularly if they are small.

Although most often considered a cookie, a madeleine is more rightly a cake, since it's made from a batter very much like the one used for a génoise, which explains its lovely, fine-grained crumb. It is always made in a shell-shaped pan, now called a madeleine pan; the scallop shape was once associated with medieval religious pilgrims. And, in addition to having taste and literary celebrity on its side, it's got history too: the cookie was given its name about 250 years ago by Stanislas Leszczynski, king of Poland, who enjoyed the cakes, made by Madeleine, a home baker in the village of Commercy, when he was in France.

BE PREPARED: You'll need to chill the batter for at least 3 hours.

¾	cup all-purpose flour		Finely grated zest of ½ orange
½	teaspoon baking powder	2	large eggs, at room temperature
½	teaspoon ground ginger	2	tablespoons honey
¼	teaspoon ground cinnamon	1	teaspoon pure vanilla extract
⅛	teaspoon ground cloves (or a little less, if you prefer)	6	tablespoons (¾ stick) unsalted butter, melted and cooled
	Pinch of salt		
	Pinch of freshly ground pepper		Confectioners' sugar, for dusting
⅓	cup sugar		

Whisk together the flour, baking powder, spices, salt, and pepper.

In the bowl of a stand mixer or in a large bowl, rub the sugar and orange zest together with your fingertips until the sugar is moist and fragrant. Fit the stand mixer with the whisk attachment or use a hand mixer or a whisk. Add the eggs to the bowl and beat until the mixture is light colored, fluffy, and thickened, about 2 minutes. Beat in the honey, then the vanilla. Switch to a rubber spatula and very gently fold in the dry ingredients, followed by the melted butter.

You can use the batter now, but it's better if you give it a little rest. Or, for real convenience, you can spoon the batter into buttered-and-floured madeleine molds (see below for instructions on prepping the pans), cover, and

BONNE IDÉE
Classic Madeleines. These are the madeleines you find in just about every pastry shop throughout France. To make 12 large or 36 mini madeleines, whisk together ⅔ cup all-purpose flour, ¾ teaspoon baking powder, and a pinch of salt. Put ½ cup sugar and the finely grated zest of 1 lemon in the bowl of a stand mixer or a large bowl and use your fingers to rub them together until the sugar is moist and fragrant. Add 2 large eggs to the bowl and beat, using the whisk attachment or a hand mixer or whisk, for 2 minutes, or until the batter is light colored, fluffy, and thick. Beat in 2 teaspoons pure vanilla extract, then, using a rubber spatula, fold in the dry ingredients followed by 6 tablespoons (¾ stick) melted and cooled unsalted butter. From here, follow the directions for Honey-Spiced Madeleines.

chill, then bake the cookies directly from the fridge. In either case, press a piece of plastic wrap against the surface of the batter and refrigerate it for at least 3 hours, or overnight.

When you're ready to bake, center a rack in the oven and preheat the oven to 400 degrees F. Butter 12 regular madeleine molds (or 36 mini molds), dust them with flour, and tap out the excess. (If you have a nonstick madeleine mold, butter and flour it or give it a light coating of vegetable cooking spray. If your pan is silicone, you can leave it as is or, just to be sure, give it a light butter-and-flour coating.) Place the pan(s) on a baking sheet and spoon the batter into the molds, filling each one to the top.

Bake large madeleines for 11 to 13 minutes, minis for 8 to 10 minutes, or until they are golden and the tops spring back when prodded gently. Remove the pan(s) from the oven and release the madeleines from the molds by rapping the edge of the pan against the counter. Gently pry any recalcitrant madeleines from the pan using your fingers or a butter knife. Transfer the cookies to a rack to cool to just warm or room temperature.

Just before serving, dust with confectioners' sugar.

croquants

MAKES ABOUT
34 COOKIES

SERVING
These are fabulous with
ice cream, but they're
also just right with coffee,
particularly strong dark
espresso.

STORING
The cookies will keep for
a week or so in a covered
container if you can
manage to keep them cool
and dry, especially dry.
Don't put them in a plastic
bag, and don't wrap them
in plastic wrap, or they'll go
crunchless.

IF CRUNCHY IS YOUR FAVORITE TEXTURE, then this may become your favorite cookie. Named for its texture (*croquant* means crunchy), the cookie is so crisp that there's no way to eat it silently — each bite comes with its own culinary equivalent of a brass band. The cookies are simplicity itself, yet I can never seem to get enough of them. They are made with (unwhipped) egg whites, a fair amount of sugar (they're very sweet), a small amount of flour, and lots of big pieces of nuts. Although they sound as if they might be meringues, they're not. They're light and airy, less fragile than they look, and, because the nuts are kept large, remarkably flavorful.

Croquants are a popular cookie in France. They can be bought in cellophane bags at supermarkets and specialty shops, and they're served with ice cream at Paris's most famous *glacier,* Berthillon. One day, when I was baking these cookies at home, it struck me why Berthillon makes them a specialty: with all the egg yolks they use to churn ice cream, they had to find something wonderful to do with all the whites. *Voilà! Les croquants!*

You can use just about any nut you like, as long as you keep the pieces hefty. I like them the size of chocolate chips. Unskinned hazelnuts and almonds, singly or in combination, are the most popular. But one day, when I was without either of these nuts, I used salted cashews, and they became our house favorite.

3½ ounces nuts (about 1 cup; see above), very coarsely chopped	2 large egg whites
1¼ cups sugar	½ cup plus 1 tablespoon all-purpose flour, sifted

Center a rack in the oven and preheat the oven to 400 degrees F. Line a couple of baking sheets with parchment paper. (You can use nonstick foil or silicone baking mats, but the silicone doesn't work as well as parchment here.)

Put the nuts and sugar in a medium bowl and, using a rubber spatula, stir to mix. Add the egg whites and stir so that the nuts are evenly coated. Add the flour and stir to blend. You'll have a thick mix, not quite batter, not quite dough, and not quite what you'd expect for a cookie, but that's fine.

Measure out 1 teaspoon dough for each cookie and put the little mounds on the lined baking sheet, making sure to leave about 2 inches between them. Pat each mound of dough gently just to round it.

Bake the cookies for 8 minutes, rotating the sheet at the midway mark, or until they are puffed, crackled, and nicely browned. Transfer the baking sheet to a cooling rack and let the cookies stand for about 10 minutes, or until you can easily peel them away from the parchment. Allow the cookies to cool to room temperature on the cooling rack; make sure they're in a dry place — as with meringues, humidity will quickly turn these chewy.

Repeat with the remaining dough, baking each batch on a cool baking sheet.

butter and rum crepes, fancy and plain

CREPES ARE A HIGH/LOW SWEET. They can be the finish of a luxe meal or a snack you pick up at an outdoor stand and eat on the run. Perhaps the most famous crepe dish is crepes Suzette, a dish that's attributed to a mistake. In 1895, Henri Charpentier, who would later become a great chef, was a young waiter in Monte Carlo charged with serving crepes to the Prince of Wales, who would later become the King of England. In that age of tableside service, Charpentier had a pan of liqueurs at the ready to make a sauce for the guests, when the alcohol went up in flames. The waiter may have been young, but he was resourceful — he quickly slid the crepes into the pan of boiling liqueur, swirled them around, and, with extraordinary élan, presented them as Crepes Princesse, honoring Suzanne, Edward's daughter, who was at the table. Later the name was changed to Suzette, ostensibly at the prince's request.

Not surprisingly, the paper-thin pancakes get simpler treatment on Paris streets, where crepe stands are abundant. Often you'll see a stand about the size of a telephone booth attached to a café or on a street corner, and when you go to markets, you'll find mobile crepe and waffle trucks, usually with lines of eager snackers in front of them. The most popular toppings for snack crepes are sugar and butter (put a pat of butter on a hot crepe, spread it as it melts, and sprinkle with sugar), jam or marmalade, Grand Marnier (a splash creates a crepes Suzette moment), Nutella, or, for a splurge, Nutella topped with thin slices of banana. The crepes are made on large round griddles: the batter is smoothed over them with a long wooden spatula, and then, when both sides of the crepe are cooked and the topping has been added, the spatula is used to fold the crepe into quarters. You end up with a four-layer triangle of crepe that, wrapped in a piece of waxy paper, is not just delicious, but the best hand warmer on a winter's day.

Usually street-corner crepes are made with the simplest ingredients, but when you're making crepes at home, there's no reason not to make them with a little extra butter and a spoonful of dark rum, so that even if all you do is sprinkle them with sugar, you've got crepes with a lot of flavor.

If you'd like to do more than sugar the crepes, you can fold them into triangles, fill them with lemon curd (delicious but optional), and drizzle over a sauce with all the flavors of the original Suzette. The sauce comes from Pierre Hermé, and while it's simpler than the classic, it's no less seductive.

BE PREPARED: Crepe batter is very quick to make, but it absolutely must rest in the refrigerator before you use it — it needs the rest and chill to become perfectly blended and to thicken. Two hours is the minimum; 12 hours or more is ideal.

MAKES ABOUT
10 CREPES

SERVING
Although you can certainly eat crepes out of hand and imagine yourself on the streets of Paris, I serve these as a plated dessert because I'm crazy about the impossible-to-eat-on-the-run sauce. Whether filled with lemon curd or just sprinkled with sugar, the crepes should be folded into triangles and drizzled with the sauce.

STORING
You can make the crepe batter and sauce a day ahead and keep them covered in the refrigerator; reheat the sauce gently before using. You can even make the crepes ahead. Let cool, then wrap them airtight and keep them in the refrigerator for up to 1 day or in the freezer for up to 2 months; if you want to freeze the crepes, stack them, putting a piece of wax paper between each crepe, and then wrap them airtight. Thaw, still wrapped, in the refrigerator. To reheat the crepes, wrap them in aluminum foil — it's best to make 2 packets — and put them in a 350-degree-F oven for about 5 minutes.

2 tablespoons sugar, plus more
   for sprinkling
   Finely grated zest of ½ lemon
   Finely grated zest of ¼ orange
   Pinch of salt
2 large eggs
¾ cup whole milk, plus a little
   more if needed
1 tablespoon dark rum or 1½
   teaspoons pure vanilla
   extract
2 teaspoons Grand Marnier
   (optional)

3 tablespoons unsalted butter,
   melted
½ cup all-purpose flour
   Canola oil or other flavorless oil,
   for the pan

⅓ cup honey
⅓ cup fresh orange juice
¼ cup fresh lemon juice
7 tablespoons unsalted butter,
   at cool room temperature

Lemon Curd (page 507)

TO MAKE THE CREPES: If you'd like, put the sugar and zests into a bowl and rub the ingredients together with your fingertips until the sugar is moist and very fragrant. (This is a great technique for getting all of the flavor from the zests' volatile oils into the sugar.) Rubbed or not, put the sugar and zests in a blender or food processor. Add the salt, eggs, milk, rum or vanilla, and Grand Marnier, if you're using it, and whir to blend. Pour in the butter and whir until the mixture is well blended. Add the flour and pulse the machine to incorporate it. Make certain the flour is blended, but don't mix the batter too much. Pour the batter into a pitcher or a large measuring cup with a spout, cover, and refrigerate for at least 2 hours. *(The batter can be refrigerated for up to 1 day.)*

When you're ready to make the crepes, sprinkle a dinner plate with sugar, and keep the sugar bowl close by. Check the batter: it should be just a bit thicker than heavy cream. If it seems a little too thick — it should pour easily — thin it with milk, stirring it in a drop at a time.

To make the crepes, you'll need a seasoned or nonstick 7½-inch-diameter crepe pan or a similar-sized skillet. Rub the pan with a lightly oiled crumpled paper towel and put the pan over medium heat. When it's hot, lift it from the heat and pour in 2 to 3 tablespoons of batter; as soon as the batter is in the pan, swirl the pan to spread the batter in a thin, even layer. If you're new at this, the easiest thing is to pour in more batter than you need, quickly swirl the pan, and then pour the excess batter back into the pitcher. Return the pan to the heat — use a small spatula to cut off the tail that formed if you poured back the batter — and cook until the top of the crepe is set. Run the spatula — an offset icing spatula is great for crepe making — around the edges of the crepe and take a look at the underside: if it's browned, flip it over, a job best done with your fingers. Cook until the underside is speckled with brown spots (it will never be as brown or as pretty as the first side). Transfer the crepe to the sugared plate, sprinkle it lightly with sugar, and continue with the rest of the batter. The crepes can be used now or held for later (see Storing).

TO MAKE THE SAUCE: If you have an immersion blender, this is a good job for it; if not, use a whisk. Melt the honey in a microwave oven or in a saucepan over low heat. Cool the honey for 5 minutes, then add the orange and lemon juices. Blend or whisk in the butter, adding it a tablespoon at a time. You'll have a smooth, slightly thickened sauce. *(The sauce can be refrigerated overnight; reheat before serving.)*

If you want to fill the crepes, spoon some lemon curd onto the upper-right-hand quarter of each crepe, fold the crepe up from the bottom, so you cover the filling, and finish by folding the left half of the crepe over the right, forming a triangle. If you're not filling the crepes, fold them in quarters. Arrange the crepes on plates, drizzle the sauce over them, and serve immediately.

BONNE IDÉE
Gâteau de Crepes

Instead of wrapping your crepes around a filling, you can stack the crepes, layering them with some filling, and make a cake that's unfailingly impressive. Traditionally a crepe cake is made with about 20 crepes (so you'll need to double the crepe recipe) and layered with vanilla pastry cream (page 505). You can use chocolate pastry cream (page 506) or the same lemon curd (page 507) used for the Suzette-type crepes, or you can alternate layers of pastry cream and curd or use pastry cream or curd on half the crepes and jam on the others. You can layer the crepes with bittersweet ganache (page 467) or ganache and Nutella. Whatever you do, you should assemble the *gâteau* in advance so that you can give it at least 4 hours in the refrigerator before serving. To finish the cake in style, sprinkle the top of the (cold) *gâteau* with an even coating of brown sugar and use a blowtorch to caramelize the sugar. Wait for the sugar to cool before you bring the cake out to applause. If you don't have a torch, just dust the top of the *gâteau* with confectioners' sugar.

nutella tartine

IT IS IMPOSSIBLE TO OVERESTIMATE the French love of Nutella, the chocolate and hazelnut spread invented in Italy about seventy years ago and eaten with gusto all over most of Europe. If you think about how attached we Americans are to peanut butter, you'll have an idea of how much the French love Nutella. It's a perennial at crepe stands all over the country, sometimes along with bananas. Spread on a slice of bread, it's often the after-school snack of choice (see box).

And just as American chefs have been known to use peanut butter to create grown-up desserts that recapture the pleasures of childhood, so French chefs are always finding surprising ways to make Nutella chic. Here's Pierre Hermé's reading of the after-school treat *pain au chocolat:* the bread is brioche (or challah), the chocolate is Nutella, and the surprise is orange marmalade.

For another sophisticated use of Nutella, look at the ganache tart with a hidden layer of the chocolate and hazelnut spread (see Bonne Idée, page 468).

MAKES **4** SERVINGS

SERVING
Although it's a play on an after-school snack, this tartine is also made for a strong espresso.

STORING
No leftovers except the crumbs.

¼ cup Nutella	¼ cup bitter orange marmalade
4 slices Brioche (see Bonne Idée, page 497) or challah	Fleur de sel
1½ tablespoons unsalted butter, melted	Hazelnuts, toasted, loose skins rubbed off in a towel, and coarsely chopped, for topping

Preheat the broiler. Line a baking sheet (or the broiler pan) with aluminum foil.

Put the Nutella in a heatproof bowl set over a pan of simmering water and heat, stirring frequently, just until it is softened and warm.

Brush one side of each slice of bread with melted butter, and put the bread, buttered side up, on the baking sheet. Run the bread under the broiler; pull it out when the slices are golden. Spread the marmalade over the hot bread and then, using the tines of a fork, generously drizzle each tartine with some warm Nutella. Top with a few grains of fleur de sel and some chopped hazelnuts.

bread and chocolate

A chocolate sandwich sounds like something someone with a serious sweet tooth or a love of carbs would have to sneak-eat, but the combination is a classic after-school snack, the French version of milk and cookies. It's sometimes served open-faced and sometimes made as a real sandwich, but most often nowadays, it is a pâtisserie-bought *pain au chocolat,* a croissant with a rectangle of chocolate in the middle. The treat is so woven into the culture that it's one of the first things that comes to mind when you mention *goûter,* or afternoon snack.

waffles and cream

MAKES 4 SERVINGS

SERVING

My favorite way to serve these waffles is with cream and caramel sauce, but they're awfully good with ice cream . . . and with chocolate sauce. . . . No matter what you serve them with, you should dust the waffles with confectioners' sugar and cut them in half or in quarters. Dividing the waffles seems to make the pleasure last longer.

STORING

In a pinch, you can freeze the waffles and reheat them in a toaster or toaster oven, but that would be a shame, because they'd lose some of their lightness. These are really meant to be enjoyed as soon as they're made.

THE TEXTURE OF THIS LIGHT, thin, crisp, flavorful, and very buttery waffle is remarkable and puzzling — you've got to wonder how anything with so much butter can be so light. The lightness comes not from leavening, but from beaten egg whites, and the crispness from butter.

I can remember when we first tasted this waffle. Michael had ordered it for dessert at Ghislaine Arabian's restaurant in Paris, and after he'd taken the first bite, you could see that he wanted to proclaim its goodness but that he didn't want the exclamation to get in the way of his enjoying the waffle while it was warm and the accompanying ice cream was cold.

When Ghislaine sent me the recipe, I was sure there was a mistake, because when you fold the ingredients into the whipped egg whites, there's so much more liquid than whites that the first thing that comes to mind is "floating islands." And the batter's thin, closer to a crepe batter than the usual waffle mixture. But I should never have doubted a star chef who, although she made her name in Paris, comes from Belgium, the land of waffles.

At the restaurant, Ghislaine served her waffle dusted with confectioners' sugar and accompanied by ice cream. But the waffle can also have a little whipped cream and some chocolate sauce. Or it can be served in the style of the Parisian chef Christian Constant, who cuts his waffles in half, tops each half with whipped cream, and sends out the plate with a little pitcher of caramel sauce.

9 tablespoons unsalted butter, melted	Confectioners' sugar, for dusting
⅔ cup whole milk, warmed	Whipped cream or ice cream, for serving
½ cup all-purpose flour	Warm Caramel Sauce (page 510)
1 tablespoon sugar	and/or Bittersweet Chocolate
¼ teaspoon salt	Sauce (page 508; optional)
1 teaspoon pure vanilla extract	
2 large egg whites, preferably at room temperature	

Preheat a waffle iron. A Belgian waffle iron, one that has deep-pocketed grids, will live up to the treat's origins, but any waffle iron will produce good crispy waffles from this recipe. Just keep in mind that there isn't a standard capacity for irons, so depending on your iron, you might get a bigger or smaller waffle.

Put the butter and milk in a bowl and whisk together. Whisk in the flour until the mixture is fairly smooth — don't worry about a few small lumps — then whisk in the sugar, salt, and vanilla.

In a clean dry bowl, beat the egg whites with an electric mixer until they hold firm, glossy peaks. Fold the flour mixture into the beaten whites — don't be discouraged when you get a very thin batter dotted with clumps of whites that refuse to be folded in neatly.

Pour one quarter of the batter onto your hot waffle iron and use a metal spatula to spread it evenly over the grids. (Since I don't know the size of your waffler, here's what I suggest: pour the batter onto the center of the waffle iron, and then if it needs spreading, spread it out evenly by working the flat of your spatula in concentric circles. If you end up shy of the waffler's border, that's fine — you'll have pretty ruffly edges on your waffles.) Bake the waffle for about 2 minutes, or until the underside is nicely browned (again, the timing will depend on your waffler), then turn the waffle over and bake until golden. Transfer to a plate. Repeat with the remaining batter.

Dust the waffles with confectioners' sugar and serve with ice cream and, if you like, caramel sauce and/or chocolate sauce.

sugar-crusted french toast

MAKES **6** SERVINGS

SERVING

Just because the French wouldn't serve this dessert with maple syrup doesn't mean you can't, but you might also want to try serving it with jam, a fruit coulis, some crème fraîche or whipped cream, or fruit. My favorite fruit accompaniments are Roasted Rhubarb (page 397) in spring and summer and Spice-Poached Apples or Pears (page 396) in fall and winter. With either of these, you'll have a wonderful fruit syrup to pour over the *pain perdu*.

STORING

French toast must be served immediately. If you need to keep the toast warm for just a short while, put the slices on a heatproof platter, cover loosely with a foil tent, and put into a 200-degree-F oven.

CALLED *PAIN PERDU*, OR LOST BREAD, French toast is a dish born of thrift, a way to make a sweet and delicious dessert — and it's always dessert in France, never breakfast — from something that might otherwise be tossed out: stale bread. Never mind that these days the best French toast, like this sugar-crusted version, uses ingredients that cost more than the bread they're meant to rescue. If you've got an egg bread, like brioche or challah, that can be cut thick, you'll have a dessert that will be not only splendid but also typically French. (If you've got a presliced loaf, the slices will be thinner but fine; just soak and cook the bread for less time.)

When I'm in Paris, I might, in fact, have enough leftover brioche to make French toast, but when I'm in the U.S., it's a rare day when there's a loaf of brioche or challah that's *perdu,* and so when I want French toast, I have to go out and buy bread specifically for the purpose. I almost never plan far enough in advance to let the bread go stale, and if you're like me, you'll have to stale the bread yourself. Before you're ready to soak it, either toast it very, very lightly or, better yet, lay the slices out on a baking sheet and put them in a 200-degree-F oven just until they're slightly dry.

6 large eggs	6 slices (a scant inch thick) stale
3 large egg yolks	Brioche (see Bonne Idée, page
2 cups whole milk	497) or challah
1½ cups heavy cream	About 6 tablespoons (¾ stick)
About 1⅓ cups sugar	unsalted butter
1 tablespoon pure vanilla	
extract	Confectioners' sugar, for
½ teaspoon salt	dusting

In a 9-x-13-inch baking pan (Pyrex is good for this), whisk together the eggs, yolks, milk, cream, ⅔ cup of the sugar, the vanilla, and salt. Add as many slices of bread as you can to the pan — you'll be working in batches — and allow the bread to soak for about 3 minutes on each side.

Put a large nonstick skillet over medium-low heat and add about 2 tablespoons of the butter. When it melts and the bubbles subside, sprinkle the pan evenly with about 1½ tablespoons sugar and add as many slices of soaked bread as you can without crowding the pan. Cook the bread until it is deeply golden and crusty on the underside, then sprinkle the tops of the slices with sugar to lightly coat them and carefully flip them over; cook until the second side is equally browned and crusty. Transfer to a platter, cover loosely with foil, and keep warm while you cook the remaining bread. Before adding more slices of soaked bread, wipe the pan clean and add fresh butter and sugar.

Right before you serve the French toast, dust the slices with confectioners' sugar.

coupétade *(french-toast pudding)*

EVERY ONCE IN A WHILE, YOU COME ACROSS an idea that's just so right, it makes you wonder why you haven't heard about it before, why it's not everywhere in the world, and why you didn't think of it yourself. The *coupétade,* a very simple dessert from central France (the name comes from *coupet,* the pottery dish in which it is traditionally baked), raises all these questions. In its most sublime incarnation, it combines two fabulous dishes — French toast and bread pudding — in a way that's so natural you might assume they were first joined at the dawn of time.

For the best *coupétade,* you first make French toast using a rich buttery bread, like brioche or challah, and a batter with enough sugar in it to caramelize both sides of the bread as it cooks. The French toast is particularly good, and served alone, it would be a worthy dessert, but the *coupétade* goes one step further, soaking the already soaked French toast in another egg-and-milk bath and then baking it into a pudding. (There are *coupétades* that skip the French toast part, but the combo *coupétade* is the heart-winner.) Yes, it's as rich as it sounds; it's also as good as you'd expect.

MAKES **6** SERVINGS

SERVING
The *coupétade* is meant to be served cold, but I think it's very good at room temperature too. Although it can come to the table unadorned, just like "normal" French toast, it benefits from a drizzle of pure maple syrup.

STORING
Although it is best served the day it is made, the *coupétade* can be cooled to room temperature, covered well, and refrigerated overnight. If you keep it too long, the custard may break and weep — not a pretty sight, but not a fatal one: weepy custard is perfectly edible.

FOR THE FRENCH TOAST

- 3 large eggs
- ½ cup sugar
- ½ cup whole milk
  About 4 tablespoons (½ stick) butter (it can be salted)
- 8 slices (a scant ½ inch thick) stale bread, preferably Brioche (page 496) or challah

- 12 plump, moist pitted prunes or dried apricots, halved
- ⅓ cup plump, moist raisins (dark or golden), dried cranberries, or dried cherries

FOR THE CUSTARD

- 4 large eggs
- 1 cup sugar
- 2½ teaspoons pure vanilla extract
- 2 cups whole milk

Generously butter a 9-x-13-inch baking pan. Have a roasting pan at hand that's large enough to hold the baking pan, and line a plate with a double thickness of paper towels.

TO MAKE THE FRENCH TOAST: In a large bowl, whisk the eggs, sugar, and milk together until smooth and well blended.

Put a large skillet over medium heat and toss in 2 tablespoons of the butter. While it's melting, soak 2 or 3 slices of bread in the egg mixture (how many slices you soak at a time will depend on how many slices you can fit in your skillet), making sure that each side gets a soak. When the butter bubbles have subsided, add the bread to the pan, and put more slices into the bowl to soak. Cook the bread for 2 to 3 minutes on each side, or until both sides are golden and crusty. Transfer to the paper-towel-lined plate and continue soaking and sautéing the pieces of bread, adding more butter to the skillet as needed, until you've cooked the lot.

Cut the slices of bread in half on the diagonal, so you have 16 triangles, and arrange them in the baking pan. Don't worry about being even, just tuck the slices in as best you can. Then nestle the fruit pieces under, over, and between the triangles.

Center a rack in the oven and preheat the oven to 325 degrees F.

TO MAKE THE CUSTARD: Whisk together the eggs and sugar in a bowl until foamy. Beat in the vanilla, then whisk in the milk until the mixture is smooth.

Place the baking pan in the roasting pan and slowly pour the custard over the bread and fruit. Allow the pudding to stand for 10 minutes to give the custard a little time to start soaking into the bread.

Pour enough hot water into the roaster to come about halfway up the sides of the baking pan and very, very carefully slide the setup into the oven. Bake the *coupétade* for 1½ to 1¾ hours, or until the custard is set — a knife inserted into the custard will come out clean. Transfer the baking pan to a rack and allow the *coupétade* to come to room temperature.

Traditionally the *coupétade* is chilled before serving, but it's also delicious at room temperature.

top-secret chocolate mousse

THERE WAS A MOMENT WHEN I WAS CONVINCED that all Parisian dinner-party givers either had the same magic touch with chocolate mousse or bought their great mousse from the same place and passed it off as their own. And I was almost right, but it took me years to discover the truth: just about every perfect mousse I ever had at a friend's house was made following the recipe on the back of a bar of Nestlé Dessert Chocolate. Everyone made it, but no one admitted to it — not even when asked point-blank for the recipe. In the end, it was my friend Martine Collet who clued me in, handing me a bar of the chocolate, pointing to the recipe, and exclaiming "*Voilà!*" as she kissed me on both cheeks. It felt like a rite of passage.

If you make the recipe as written below, you'll have the quintessential French dinner-party mousse; if you add your own little touches, you'll be doing exactly what my French friends do (see Bonne Idée for some hints).

The recipe can easily be doubled.

3½	ounces bittersweet chocolate, coarsely chopped	Pinch of salt
3	large eggs, separated, at room temperature	1½ teaspoons sugar
		Whipped cream or crème fraîche, for serving (optional)

Gently melt the chocolate in a heatproof bowl over a saucepan of simmering water or in a microwave oven on medium power.

If necessary, transfer the chocolate to a bowl that can hold all the ingredients. Using a whisk, stir the egg yolks into the chocolate one at a time.

In the bowl of a stand mixer fitted with the whisk attachment or in a bowl with a hand mixer, beat the egg whites with the salt until they start to form peaks. Beating all the while, gradually add the sugar. Continue to beat until the whites are shiny and hold medium-firm peaks.

Spoon about one quarter of the whites over the melted chocolate and stir with the whisk until the mixture is almost smooth. (Stirring in a bit of the whites lightens the chocolate and makes the next step easier.) Spoon the rest of the whites over the chocolate and, using the whisk or a large rubber spatula, very carefully fold them in. Be as thorough as you can without overworking the mixture — it's better to have a few white streaks than to beat the bubbles out of the mousse by overmixing (actually, I find the streaks appealing).

Spoon the mousse into a serving bowl or individual bowls and serve it now, or cover it and keep it in the refrigerator until you're ready for dessert. Serve with whipped cream or crème fraîche, if you like.

MAKES 4 SERVINGS

SERVING
Before the mousse sets, spoon it into individual cups — I love the way the mousse looks in martini glasses — or put it in a pretty serving bowl. I like to top it with lightly whipped heavy cream or crème fraîche. You don't have to stop there — the mousse is delicious with fresh berries, chocolate shavings, crushed candied nuts, nut brittle, or even pulverized Heath Bar bits.

STORING
Covered well, the mousse will keep overnight in the refrigerator, although it does get denser as it stands.

BONNE IDÉE
To give the mousse a mocha flavor, add 1 tablespoon strong coffee to the bowl with the chocolate to be melted. Alternatively, you can add another flavor when you whisk in the egg yolks, such as 1 teaspoon pure vanilla extract, ½ teaspoon pure almond extract, ⅛ teaspoon pure peppermint extract, or a drop or two of pure orange oil.

crème brûlée

MAKES **6** SERVINGS

SERVING
You can serve the crèmes as soon as the caramelized sugar is cool enough to eat, or you can chill the sugar-topped custards and serve them cold. Do that, and the top may not be as crackly, but there are many who prefer it that way. At La Robe et le Palais, every crème brûlée comes with a beautiful almond and orange tuile; you'll find the recipe on page 404.

STORING
The custard for crème brûlée must be made ahead so it has plenty of time to chill — you can make it up to 2 days in advance and keep it covered in the refrigerator — and the baked crèmes, which also must be cold, can be kept covered in the refrigerator for up to 2 days, but once you've caramelized the sugar on top, your storage time is limited.

WE WERE FOUR PEOPLE FOR DINNER at the Paris bistro La Robe et le Palais, and we had eaten heartily and drunk just as lustily, so when it came time for dessert, we decided to restrain ourselves and order just one crème brûlée for the table. Congratulating ourselves for being *sage,* or wise, we each took a small spoonful — just to be polite, of course — and then we took another set of spoonfuls . . . and then we ordered a couple more. When a crème brûlée is made well, it is a sublime dessert.

For a crème brûlée, made well means that there's a nice balance between eggs and cream, that the vanilla is pure, the custard voluptuous, and the burnt-sugar topping crackly. In chef Yannis Théodore's crème brûlée, the brûléed sugar covered the crème and the crème covered a spoonful of jam that had melted and formed a little sauce under the dessert. As soon as I tasted it, I knew I'd be making crème brûlée with jam *chez moi.*

If you have a propane torch, now's the time to use it. If you don't, you can get a sugar crust on the custards by running the thoroughly chilled crèmes under the broiler. The crust won't be as even, but it will crackle and taste like caramel, the two great pleasures of brûléed sugar.

About the dishes for crème brûlée: they should be shallow. The best ones, round or oval, are about 1 inch high and 4 inches in diameter. You'll be pouring ½ cup of liquid into each dish, so make sure your dishes can hold that with a little room to spare.

BE PREPARED: The custards need to chill for at least 3 hours.

2 tablespoons jam or jelly, such as strawberry, raspberry, or marmalade	⅓ cup sugar
	2 teaspoons pure vanilla extract
1¼ cups heavy cream	Brownulated or strained brown sugar (preferably dark brown), for topping
½ cup whole milk	
3 large egg yolks	

Center a rack in the oven and preheat the oven to 200 degrees F. Line a baking sheet with a silicone baking mat or parchment paper and put six baking dishes (see above) on it. Have a sieve at hand.

Spoon 1 teaspoon of the jam or jelly into each baking dish and use the back of the spoon to spread it out — don't worry about getting it even or smooth, you just want to minimize the mound in the center.

Mix the cream and milk together and bring just to a boil in a microwave oven, or do this on the stovetop.

Put a 1- or 2-quart measuring cup with a spout (or a medium bowl) on a folded kitchen towel, to keep it from sliding around, add the yolks and sugar, and whisk well to blend. Whisking constantly, add about one quarter of the hot milk mixture little by little — it's important to add the hot liquid gradually so you don't cook the eggs. Once you get the yolks tempered (i.e., acclimatized to the heat), you can whisk in the remainder of the liquid in a slow but more steady stream. Whisk in the vanilla. *(The custard can be made up to 2 days ahead and kept covered in the refrigerator.)*

Rap the measuring cup against the counter to de-bubble the mixture. If you've got a lot of bubbles, you might want to skim off the foam. (The foam won't disappear in the oven, and it will cause the top of your custard to have tiny holes. It's not serious, but it's not so pretty.) Strain the custard into the baking dishes and very carefully slide the baking sheet into the oven.

Bake the crèmes for 50 to 60 minutes, or until the centers are just set — if you tap the sides of the dishes, the custards should hold firm or jiggle just a tad. Lift the dishes onto a cooling rack (a pancake turner is good for this job) and allow them to cool to room temperature.

When the crèmes are cool, cover them with plastic wrap and chill them until they're thoroughly cold — at least 3 hours, preferably longer. To caramelize the sugar in the next step, the custards must be thoroughly chilled. *(The custards can be kept covered in the refrigerator for up to 2 days.)*

TO USE A BLOWTORCH TO CARAMELIZE THE SUGAR: Work with one crème at a time. Sprinkle the top of the custard evenly with brownulated or brown sugar — you'll need about 1 tablespoon for each dish — and then caramelize the sugar, torching it until it bubbles and browns. Wait until the bubbles subside before serving the crèmes.

TO USE THE BROILER TO CARAMELIZE THE SUGAR: Preheat the broiler and fill a shallow broiler pan with ice cubes. Sprinkle each custard evenly with about 1 tablespoon brownulated or brown sugar, put the baking dishes on the bed of ice, and run them under the broiler. Stand guard at the oven so you don't overdo this — depending on your broiler, it can take seconds or minutes to caramelize the sugar. When the sugar bubbles and browns, pull out the pan, transfer the crèmes to a kitchen towel to dry the bottoms, and let them settle down before serving.

BONNE IDÉE

Berry Crème Non-Brûlée. Because the custard for crème brûlée is so delicious, it's nice to serve it without the sugar topping from time to time. When I do this, I pretend that each little crème is like a fruit tart. I put a few berries — raspberries, blueberries, and blackberries work best (strawberries are too watery) — in the bottom of each dish instead of jam or jelly before I add the custard. Then, when the crèmes are baked, chilled, and ready to serve, I top each one with fresh berries and dust the fruit with confectioners' sugar or drizzle it with warmed (liquefied) jam or jelly. If you'd like, when you make the custard, you can decrease the amount of vanilla and flavor the custard very lightly with kirsch or a berry eau de vie.

coeur à la crème

A COUPLE OF YEARS AGO, I WAS RUMMAGING through a storage bin at the back of a closet and I came across my coeur à la crème mold, a heart-shaped white porcelain mold with small holes in the base and little feet to lift it up. The mold is designed to hold a mixture of sweetened cream cheese (in France, it would be fromage blanc) and heavy cream that needs to drain, thus the perforated bottom and the elevation. (If you don't have a mold, don't fret — you can make coeur à la crème in a strainer.) That I'd turned up the mold just before Valentine's Day made the find that much more fortuitous, so I washed it off and set to work to make the dessert for which it was created, one I'd neither made nor thought about for a very long time. I couldn't find my old coeur à la crème recipe, so I made up a new one and did something I don't think I'd done before — I whipped the heavy cream and folded it into the cream cheese. The result was terrific: an indulgently luxurious coeur à la crème with a texture so light you could fool yourself into thinking you were eating sweetened air.

Coeur à la crème is usually served with a fruit sauce. Because my version usually includes a few spoonfuls of framboise, a raspberry liqueur, raspberry coulis is just right with it. But you can serve the dessert with another fruit coulis, berries, jam (dilute it with a little water and add a shot of liqueur, if you'd like), honey, chocolate sauce, or even very un-French maple syrup.

BE PREPARED: The coeur à la crème needs at least 12 hours to drain — overnight is better.

MAKES 6 SERVINGS

SERVING
Drizzle the coeur à la crème with whatever topping you've chosen, surround with berries, if you're offering them, and bring the dessert to the table. If you've made one large coeur à la crème, present it in its beautiful entirety and then slice it as you would a cake.

STORING
The coeur à la crème can be made up to 3 days in advance and kept covered in the refrigerator.

1	8-ounce package cream cheese (you can use lower-fat Neufchâtel, if you'd like)
¾	cup confectioners' sugar, sifted
	Pinch of salt
1½	teaspoons pure vanilla extract
2	teaspoons framboise, crème de cassis, kirsch, or dark rum (optional)

1½	cups cold heavy cream
	Raspberry coulis (see Bonne Idée, page 444), fruit sauce, jam, honey, Bittersweet Chocolate Sauce (page 508), or maple syrup, for topping
	Berries, for serving (optional)

Line six small coeur à la crème molds with a double layer of dampened cheesecloth, letting the excess hang over the sides of the molds. Alternatively, you can use a large coeur à la crème mold (if your mold has a 3-cup capacity, you may have some of the mixture left over, which you can put in a small lined strainer) or a large cheesecloth-lined strainer.

In the bowl of a stand mixer fitted with the paddle attachment or in a large bowl with a hand mixer, beat the cream cheese until it is smooth and velvety, scraping down the bowl as needed. Gradually beat in the confectioners' sugar and salt and continue to beat until the cream cheese is again very smooth. Beat in the vanilla and framboise, other liqueur, or rum, if you're using it.

If you're using a stand mixer, scrape the cream cheese into another bowl; pour the heavy cream into the bowl (no need to wash it), fit the mixer with the whisk attachment, and whip the cream until it's just shy of holding firm peaks. If you're using a hand mixer, pour the heavy cream into another bowl and whip it. Using a flexible spatula, gently stir about one quarter of the whipped cream into the cream cheese mixture to lighten it, then carefully fold in the remaining cream.

Divide the mixture among the individual molds or scrape it into your large mold. Fold the excess cheesecloth over the top of the mixture and put the mold(s) on a baking sheet with a rim or a plate to catch the liquid that will drain. Or, if you're making your coeur à la crème in a strainer, cover it with the excess cheesecloth and set the strainer over a bowl. Chill the coeur à la crème for at least 12 hours, or, better yet, overnight.

When you're ready to serve, unfold the cheesecloth and turn the coeur à la crème out onto individual plates or a serving platter. Serve with the topping of your choice, and berries, if you'd like.

floating islands

FLOATING ISLANDS, OR *ÎLES FLOTTANTES,* is one of those desserts that a French woman of a certain age can probably whip up with her eyes closed — certainly she can do it without a recipe. Traditionally made by poaching puffs of meringue, the islands, and then floating them in a sea of crème anglaise, it's a sweet most French people remember from their childhoods and lots of tourists remember from bistros.

For years I made this dessert just the way I was taught to: I prepared a meringue, scooped it by the spoonful, and dropped the puffs into a pot of simmering milk, where they poached for 2 minutes. The method is classic, simple, and foolproof, and the dessert is luscious. But recently I learned another way to make the islands — in the oven. This is not a completely untraditional method, just one that wasn't used as much, since an oven wasn't always a given. If you bake the meringues, you can make individual islands, just as you do when you poach them, but you can also make a dramatic meringue "cake," from which you can slice tall wedges.

The first time I had a wedge-shaped island was at the Paris bistro Le Hide, where the chef served the meringue on a shallow pool of vanilla crème anglaise and finished the dish with a scoop of chocolate ice cream. At first it seemed a little odd, then it seemed amusing — after all, ice cream is simply frozen crème anglaise — and then it seemed just right and just delicious.

I haven't given up poaching meringue (you can find that recipe in Bonne Idée), but when I've got a crowd, I'm more likely to bake it — and just as likely to serve the meringue with a drizzle of hot fudge or caramel sauce (in addition to the crème anglaise, of course). Not so traditional, but so very good.

BE PREPARED: You'll need to chill the meringue for at least an hour.

MAKES **8** SERVINGS

SERVING
Baked meringue afloat in crème anglaise is a thing of beauty unto itself, but if you want to go all out, put a small scoop of chocolate ice cream alongside the meringue and finish the dessert with just a drizzle of hot fudge or caramel sauce.

STORING
The meringue can be made up to 4 hours ahead and kept chilled, and the crème anglaise, which should be served cold, can be prepared up to 3 days ahead, but everything must be assembled at serving time, and leftovers cannot be saved.

FOR THE MERINGUE
- 6 large egg whites, at room temperature
- Pinch of salt
- ½ cup sugar
- ½ teaspoon pure vanilla extract

FOR SERVING
- Crème Anglaise (page 504), chilled
- Chocolate ice cream, home-made (page 513) or store-bought; optional
- Hot Fudge Sauce (page 509) or Warm Caramel Sauce (page 510); optional

TO MAKE THE MERINGUE: Center a rack in the oven and preheat the oven to 250 degrees F. Butter a 9-inch springform pan, dust the inside with sugar, and tap out the excess. Wrap the base of the springform pan in aluminum foil — you'll need to use two pieces — so the bottom is fully encased and the foil comes up the sides of the pan. Have a roasting pan at the ready.

In the bowl of a stand mixer fitted with the whisk attachment or in a large bowl with a hand mixer, beat the egg whites with the salt at medium speed until

BONNE IDÉE
Milk-Poached Meringue Puffs. Spread a kitchen towel out on the counter near the stove and have a large slotted spoon at the ready. Bring 2 cups whole milk to a boil in a saucepan. Beat 4 large egg whites in a large bowl with a pinch of salt, and when they're opaque, gradually add ¼ cup sugar and beat until the whites are firm and glossy. Scoop up some meringue — you'll be able to make 12 islands — and drop the puff into the simmering milk. Add a few more puffs (don't crowd the pan), and poach for 1 minute. Gently flip the puffs over and poach for 1 minute more. Lift the puffs out of the milk and onto the towel. When all the puffs are poached and cooled, transfer them to a baking sheet lined with a silicone baking mat or parchment paper and chill for at least 1 hour, or for up to 4 hours.

they turn opaque and just start to thicken. Continuing to beat, gradually add the sugar. When the sugar is incorporated, add the vanilla and then beat until you have whites that hold firm peaks but are still glossy. Scrape the meringue into the pan and, using a rubber spatula, gently spread it so that it fills the pan — you might need to cajole it to the edge of the pan; smooth the top. Put the springform in the roasting pan, fill the roasting pan with enough hot water so that it comes halfway up the sides of the springform, and carefully slide the roaster into the oven.

Bake the meringue for about 40 minutes, or until it has risen (it will rise above the top of the pan) and is firm to the touch. Remove the roasting pan from the oven and very carefully lift the springform out of the water bath. Pay attention — the foil may be holding some hot water. Put the springform in the sink, remove the foil, shake out any water that might have seeped in, and then replace the foil. (The butter and sugar lining the pan form a syrup that can be drippy, so it's good to keep the foil in place until you're ready to serve.)

Let the meringue cool to room temperature, then chill it for at least 1 hour. *(The meringue can be refrigerated for up to 4 hours.)*

When you're ready to serve, put the pan back in the sink and remove the foil and the sides of the springform. If any syrup has formed, spill it out. Using two large spatulas or pancake turners, lift the meringue onto a cutting board. The easiest way to cut the meringue into wedges is to treat it like an angel food cake and use a pronged angel-food slicer or a table fork, piercing the "cake" with the tines until you can lift away a wedge.

For each serving, spoon enough crème anglaise over the bottom of a dinner plate or a shallow soup plate to cover it, and settle an island in the crème sea. If desired, add a small scoop of ice cream and a drizzle of sauce. Serve immediately, with dessert spoons or soupspoons.

rice pudding
and caramel apples

S OLD-FASHIONED AS RICE PUDDING, or *riz au lait,* is, it is never out of
style in France. Little children grow up on it, adults crave it for comfort,
and bistros all across the country serve it year-round. At Guy Savoy's chic
bistro Atelier Maître Albert, across from Notre-Dame, rice pudding is served
in beautiful little canning jars. At the trendy Parisian bistro Itinéraires, the
rice pudding is served in martini glasses with a little surprise at the bottom
— caramel sauce, which was the inspiration for this recipe. And in a rustic
bistro in the mountains surrounding the French Alpine village of Megève, the
rice pudding was brought to the table in a bowl as big as a washbasin. Our
instructions: take as much as we wanted.

I like to use Arborio rice for pudding because, precooked for 10 minutes
in water, then cooked in milk, it becomes wonderfully creamy yet retains just
the slightest bit of chewiness. However, you can make the pudding with long-
grain white, basmati, or jasmine rice — just keep an eye on the pan, because the
cooking times will vary.

Riz au lait is often served unembellished, especially at home, but like vanilla
ice cream, its plainness makes it a good match to sauces and fruits. Here I pair
it with apples (or pears) in a caramel sauce — I love the two together — but
you can also serve the pudding with a fruit coulis, caramel sauce (page 510), a
drizzle of maple syrup, or fresh berries.

MAKES **4** TO
6 SERVINGS

SERVING
I usually arrange individual
servings of this dessert
in the kitchen, layering
the caramel sauce, rice
pudding, apples, and more
sauce in small bowls or
glasses, but sometimes
when I've got a lot of
people around the table,
I set out the pudding and
apple bowls and let my
guests serve themselves.
Either way, I like to top off
the dessert with whipped
cream.

STORING
The pudding can be made
up to 3 days ahead and
kept, tightly covered, in the
refrigerator. The apples are
really best the day they are
made, but leftovers will
keep in the fridge for a day
or so; warm them gently
before serving.

FOR THE PUDDING
Pinch of salt
½ cup Arborio rice
4 cups whole milk
⅓ cup sugar
1½–2 teaspoons pure vanilla extract

FOR THE APPLES
2 sweet apples, such as Gala,
Braeburn, or Jonagold,
peeled
¼ cup sugar

Fresh lemon juice
1 tablespoon unsalted butter,
cut into 3 pieces, at room
temperature
½ cup apple cider, at room
temperature
Pinch of salt
½ cup heavy cream, at room
temperature

Lightly whipped cream, for
topping (optional)

TO MAKE THE RICE PUDDING: Bring about 3 cups water and the salt to a boil in a
medium to large saucepan. (I like to use a narrow 4-quart pan for this.) Stir in
the rice and boil for 10 minutes. Drain, and rinse out the pan.

Put the milk and sugar in the pan and bring to a boil. Stir in the rice,
reduce the heat to medium/medium-low, and cook at a steady simmer, stirring
frequently. Pay particular attention at the beginning, because the milk has a
tendency to bubble up exuberantly and will bubble over even a tall pot if you

don't catch it and stir it down in time. And be vigilant during the last 10 minutes, so you don't burn or overcook the rice. The pudding should cook for 30 to 50 minutes — I'm giving you a lot of leeway, because you might be using a wide pan in which the milk boils away fast. Cook until the rice is very tender, the pudding has thickened a little, and most of the milk has been absorbed. Don't cook until all the milk has been absorbed — if you do that, you'll have a stiff pudding. Remove the pan from the heat and stir in the vanilla extract — this really is a matter of taste. If you're going to chill the pudding, you should use more extract than if you are serving it at room temperature, since cold mutes flavors.

Scrape the pudding into a heatproof bowl, press a piece of plastic wrap against the surface, and let cool to room temperature; the pudding will thicken as it cools. If you'd like, you can chill the pudding. *(The pudding can be refrigerated, tightly covered, for up to 3 days.)*

TO MAKE THE APPLES: Cut each apple from top to bottom into quarters and core the pieces. Slice each quarter lengthwise into 3 or 4 pieces, each about ¼ inch thick, then cut each piece crosswise into thirds. Set aside.

Sprinkle the sugar into the center of a medium nonstick skillet. Moisten with a splash of lemon juice and turn the heat to medium-high. When the sugar melts, bubbles, and starts to color, either tilt the pan or stir the sugar with a fork or wooden spoon. As soon as the sugar is a nice amber color, pull the pan from the heat. Stand away, because the mixture will spatter, and add the butter, swirling to mix it in.

Put the skillet on medium heat, pour in the cider, and add the salt. Bring the cider to a boil, then add the apples. Cook, stirring often, for 5 minutes, or until the apples are tender. Pour in the heavy cream and boil for 1 minute more, then turn the apples and caramel sauce into a heatproof bowl and allow to cool. The apples are ready to serve when they are just slightly warm or at room temperature. (Don't taste them as soon as they're cooked: the caramel is dangerously hot.)

Put a little of the caramel sauce in the bottom of each bowl or glass, top with rice pudding, and finish with apples and a little more sauce. If you'd like, add a dollop of whipped cream.

MARIE-HÉLÈNE'S APPLE CAKE (PAGE 432)

marie-hélène's apple cake

MAKES **8** SERVINGS

SERVING
The cake can be served warm or at room temperature, with or without a little softly whipped barely sweetened heavy cream or a spoonful of ice cream. Marie-Hélène served her cake with cinnamon ice cream, and it was a terrific combination.

STORING
The cake will keep for about 2 days at room temperature and, according to my husband, gets more comforting with each passing day. However long you keep the cake, it's best not to cover it — it's too moist. Leave the cake on its plate and just press a piece of plastic wrap or wax paper against the cut surfaces.

MY FRIEND MARIE-HÉLÈNE BRUNET-LHOSTE is a woman who knows her way around food. She's a top editor of the Louis Vuitton City Guides (and one of the restaurant critics for the Paris edition), so she eats at scores of restaurants every year, and she's a terrific hostess, so she cooks at home often and with great generosity. There's no question that she's a great cook, but for me, she's the most frustrating kind of cook: she never follows a recipe (in fact, I don't think there's a cookbook to be found on her packed bookshelves), never takes a note about what she does, and while she's always happy to share her cooking tips, she can never give you a real recipe — she just doesn't know it.

I've watched her in her kitchen, in the hopes of nabbing a recipe by observation, but it's impossible. Like so many really good cooks, Marie-Hélène starts off with a set of ingredients that could be annotated and recipe-ized, but once she starts mixing, stirring, boiling, baking, or sautéing, she makes so many mid-cooking adjustments that you just have to throw up your hands and content yourself with being the lucky recipient.

And so it was with this apple cake, which is more apple than cake, rather plain but very appealing in its simplicity (the chunks of apple make a bumpy, golden top), and so satisfying that we all went back for seconds. Despite knowing that it was futile, I asked for the recipe, and of course, Marie-Hélène didn't really know.

"It's got two eggs, sugar, flour, and melted butter — oh, and rum," she said. "I mix the eggs and sugar together, and then I add some flour, some butter, some flour, and some butter." When I asked how much flour and butter, I got a genuinely apologetic shrug, and when I asked what kind of apples she used, the answer was, *divers,* or different kinds.

Since there were only a few major ingredients, I thought I could figure out the recipe — and I did! (Although not on the first — or second — shot.) I've added baking powder to the mix (and I have a feeling Marie-Hélène might have too) and a drizzle of vanilla, which you can skip if you want. What you don't want to skip is the pleasure of having *divers* apples. It's really nice to mix up the fruit, so that you have some apples that are crisp, some soft, some sweet, and some tart.

¾	cup all-purpose flour	¾	cup sugar
¾	teaspoon baking powder	3	tablespoons dark rum
	Pinch of salt	½	teaspoon pure vanilla extract
4	large apples (if you can, choose 4 different kinds)	8	tablespoons (1 stick) unsalted butter, melted and cooled
2	large eggs		

Center a rack in the oven and preheat the oven to 350 degrees F. Generously butter an 8-inch springform pan. Line a baking sheet with a silicone baking mat or parchment paper and put the springform on it.

Whisk the flour, baking powder, and salt together in a small bowl.

Peel the apples, cut them in half, and remove the cores. Cut the apples into 1- to 2-inch chunks.

In a medium bowl, beat the eggs with a whisk until they're foamy. Pour in the sugar and whisk for a minute or so to blend. Whisk in the rum and vanilla. Whisk in half the flour and, when it is incorporated, add half the melted butter, followed by the rest of the flour and the remaining butter, mixing gently after each addition so that you have a smooth, rather thick batter. Switch to a rubber spatula and fold in the apples, turning the fruit so that it's coated with batter. Scrape the mix into the pan and poke it around a little with the spatula so that it's evenish.

Slide the pan into the oven and bake for 50 to 60 minutes, or until the top of the cake is golden brown and a knife inserted deep into the center comes out clean; the cake may pull away from the sides of the pan. Transfer to a cooling rack and let rest for 5 minutes.

Carefully run a blunt knife around the edges of the cake and remove the sides of the springform pan. (Open the springform slowly, and before it's fully opened, make sure there aren't any apples stuck to it.) Allow the cake to cool until it is just slightly warm or at room temperature. If you want to remove the cake from the bottom of the springform pan, wait until the cake is almost cooled, then run a long spatula between the cake and the pan, cover the top of the cake with a piece of parchment or wax paper, and invert it onto a rack. Carefully remove the bottom of the pan and turn the cake over onto a serving dish.

quatre-quarts

MAKES **6** SERVINGS

SERVING
The cake is best when it is only ever so slightly warm or at room temperature. Serve it in wedges as a snack or top it with fruit, sauces, or ice cream and serve it for dessert.

STORING
Once cooled, the cake can be wrapped airtight and kept for up to 3 days at room temperature. Stale cake is delicious lightly toasted.

THE DIRECT TRANSLATION OF *QUATRE-QUARTS* IS four-fourths, or 4/4. Like our American pound cake, the *quatre-quarts* is based on equal measures of four ingredients: eggs, flour, sugar, and butter. In fact, many of the French recipes for this very basic cake have ingredient lists that read something like this: weigh the eggs, then measure out equal amounts of flour, sugar, and butter. Because of the differences between French and American flours, I've had to tweak the measurements a little, but what you'll get in the end will be just the same as what mothers across France get when they make this as an after-school treat for their kids: a cake with a lovely crumb, a light spring, the comforting flavor of basic ingredients, and a look so sweet and plain that you'd think the cake had the word *home* etched into its slightly domed top.

As with any recipe that's been made for as long as this one has, and is made by as many people as this one is, there are lots of opinions abroad about the way things should be done. I'm told there's a school of bakers that doesn't separate the eggs, but I don't hold with that. Whipping the whites is an extra step, but worth the extra effort. And I'm not sure there are many bakers who sprinkle the tops of their cakes with brown sugar, but it creates such a nice glaze and such a nice little bit of unexpected sweetness that I make it a standard practice.

Like many French cakes, this one is dry by our standards, but dry is just fine when you're serving it with tea or coffee and is absolutely perfect when you want to dress it up a little, as is often done, with saucy sugared berries, jam, any kind of fruit coulis, a dollop of whipped cream, a spoonful of crème fraîche, or ice cream and chocolate sauce.

1 cup all-purpose flour	8 tablespoons (1 stick) unsalted
1 teaspoon baking powder	butter, melted and cooled
Pinch of salt	1–2 teaspoons pure vanilla extract
3 large eggs, separated, at	or 2–3 teaspoons dark rum or
room temperature	Cognac (optional)
¾ cup sugar	About 1 tablespoon lump-free
	light brown sugar, for topping

Center a rack in the oven and preheat the oven to 350 degrees F. Butter an 8-x-2-inch round cake pan or an 8-inch springform pan, dust the inside with flour, and tap out the excess. Line a baking sheet with a silicone baking mat or parchment paper.

Whisk together the flour, baking powder, and salt. In the bowl of a stand mixer fitted with the whisk attachment or in a large bowl with a hand mixer, whip the egg whites until they hold firm peaks but are still glossy.

In a large bowl, beat the egg yolks and sugar together with a whisk until they are thick and pale. Pour in the melted butter and the vanilla or alcohol, if you're using it, and whisk gently until you have a satiny batter. Gently whisk in the flour mixture. Switch to a rubber spatula and stir one quarter of the egg whites into the batter — there's no need to be thorough — then lightly fold in the remainder of the whipped whites. Scrape the batter into the pan, put the pan on the lined baking sheet, and sprinkle the top of the cake with the brown sugar.

Bake for 20 to 25 minutes, or until the cake is golden and starting to pull away from the sides of the pan; a knife inserted into the center should come out clean. Transfer the pan to a cooling rack and let the cake rest for about 10 minutes.

If you used a regular cake pan, run a blunt knife around the edge of the pan and unmold the cake onto the cooling rack, turn the cake right side up, and let it cool to room temperature on the rack. If you used a springform pan, remove the sides of the pan and either leave the cake on the base or turn the cake over, remove the base, and turn the cake right side up to cool on the rack.

visitandine

MAKES **8** SERVINGS

SERVING

Cut in wedges, the cake makes a good finger sweet at teatime. Make two cakes, and you can layer them with jam and top with whipped cream and maybe some berries. The cake just about defines versatility, so have fun with it.

STORING

Covered, the cake will keep at room temperature for at least 3 days. The *visitandine* is still good when it goes a little stale, particularly if you dunk it into tea or milky coffee.

IF MY FRIEND CLAUDINE MARTINA, a teacher from Angers, had given me this recipe years ago, my baking career might have ended — I would have found a way to use this recipe for just about everything. The *visitandine* is a simple, very white cake with an elegant small-grained crumb, a lovely springy sponge, and a pure butter-and-sugar flavor that makes it perfect plain or paired with jam, fruit, chocolate, citrus curds, cream, frosting, or glaze. In fact, even though it's totally French, it's outstanding as the base for an all-American strawberry shortcake.

Except for the fact that Claudine beats her egg whites (there are no yolks in the recipe), something that not everyone does with the *visitandine,* the recipe is very similar to the one for Coconut Friands (page 456) and not that dissimilar from the one for Financiers (page 454), a centuries-old recipe in which the whites are heated. *Visitandine* is in all likelihood as old as, or older than, these recipes. Named for a Catholic religious order founded in France, the cake was probably baked by the nuns as a means of supporting themselves when they were a cloistered contemplative community.

If you find *visitandines* in pastry shops in France, you might find them baked in madeleine molds, financier pans, tins that turn out little mini-muffin cakes, or small fluted tartlet pans. Claudine bakes hers as a cake in a large porcelain tart pan. Following her lead, I use a 10-inch glass pie plate. About using her *plat à tarte,* Claudine says, "I like it because I get a nice flat *galette,*" which is exactly what I like about using the pie plate.

About the butter: If you'd like, you can brown it, turning it into *beurre noisette,* which gives it hints of caramel and hazelnuts *(noisettes),* a nice flavor addition to this cake. Turn the heat up under the melted butter so that it boils gently and, never taking your eyes off the pan, continue to simmer the butter until it turns a golden brown. As soon as you get the color you want, remove the pan from the heat and pour the butter into a heatproof bowl to stop the cooking and cool it down.

4 large egg whites, preferably at room temperature	7 tablespoons unsalted butter, melted and cooled slightly (see above)
¾ cup all-purpose flour	1 teaspoon pure vanilla extract
⅔ cup sugar	
Pinch of salt	

Center a rack in the oven and preheat the oven to 350 degrees F. Choose a pan: I often use a 10-inch Pyrex pie plate, but you can use a springform, layer cake, or fluted porcelain or glass quiche pan of similar size. (If your pan is a little smaller, you'll have to bake the *visitandine* a little longer; if it's larger, bake it a little less.) Whatever you choose, butter the pan well and line it with a circle of parchment paper cut to fit the base of the pan; butter the parchment.

In the bowl of a stand mixer fitted with the whisk attachment or in a large

bowl with a hand mixer, whip the egg whites until they hold firm peaks but are still glossy.

In another bowl, whisk together the flour, sugar, and salt. Pour in the melted butter, followed by the vanilla, and, using the whisk, stir until the ingredients are fully blended. The mixture will clump together and look slightly hopeless, but press on, stirring it gently to mix. Staying with the whisk, slide about one quarter of the beaten whites out of their bowl and onto the batter (it looks more like a dough now) and use the whisk to stir them in. Be gentle, but don't be concerned about knocking the air out of the whites — it's inevitable. With this portion of the whites in, the batter will be loose enough that you can use the whisk to fold in the remaining whites. Scrape the batter into the pan and jiggle the pan to even the top.

Bake the cake for 33 to 38 minutes (remember to check earlier if your pan is larger than 10 inches), or until it's beautifully browned and starting to pull away from the sides of the pan; a knife inserted into the center should come out clean. As soon as the cake comes from the oven, run a blunt knife around the edge. Let the cake cool on a cooling rack for about 3 minutes, then invert it, pull off the parchment, and let it cool to room temperature on the rack.

caramel-topped semolina cake

MAKES **8** SERVINGS

SERVING
Once the cake is cool, cut it into slices and serve it with the caramel sauce that has pooled on the plate. Traditionally this cake is served with a spoonful of crème anglaise (page 504), a very nice addition. For something a little less rich, pair the cake with fresh fruit; it's particularly good with pineapple.

STORING
Although the cake is meant to be served at room temperature, it will keep, covered, in the refrigerator overnight and can be served chilled — the caramel will remain saucy — or brought to room temperature.

I T WAS SUMMER AND SUNNY, and my husband, Michael, and I were having lunch outdoors at a tiny bistro off the picturesque and often-pictured Place Dauphine in Paris. Someone had told me that Yves Montand lived in one of the stone buildings surrounding the square, and I was secretly hoping that he'd stroll past us at any moment. What I wasn't expecting was that we'd finish our meal with a dessert that was completely new to me: it was a simple puddingish cake, almost like fine-grained polenta, dotted with raisins and coated in caramel, like a flan.

Although my French friends had childhood memories of the cake and loved it, no one could tell me what was in it, because the only way they'd ever seen it made — or made it themselves — was from a supermarket mix.

It took me a while to find out that the semolina that gives the cake its name is farina, best known in our country under the brand name Cream of Wheat, the breakfast cereal. Now that I know, I make the cake often, usually to serve after a light meal. The traditional addition is golden raisins — they're even included in the boxed mix — but bits of any dried fruit are fine, as are diced apple or pear sautéed in a little butter beforehand, or even small pieces of mango.

By the way, I tried the cake from the mix — it doesn't hold a candle to this homemade version.

FOR THE CAKE
- 2 cups whole milk
- ¼ teaspoon salt
- ⅓ cup farina or Cream of Wheat
- ⅓ cup sugar
- 1 teaspoon pure vanilla extract
- 2 large eggs, lightly beaten

- ½ cup plump, moist golden raisins (or other dried fruit, cut into small bits)

FOR THE CARAMEL
- ⅓ cup sugar
- 3 tablespoons water
- Squeeze of fresh lemon juice

Center a rack in the oven and preheat the oven to 350 degrees F. Have an 8-inch round cake pan (preferably one with sides at least 1½ inches high) at hand.

TO MAKE THE CAKE: Bring the milk and salt just to a boil in a medium saucepan. At the sign of the first bubble, lower the heat, pour in the farina, and stir with a wooden spoon. Keep stirring, adjusting the heat so that the farina doesn't scorch, until the mixture thickens — check the cereal box for approximate cooking times. Remove the pan from the heat and stir in the sugar and vanilla. Let the mixture cool for about 15 minutes.

WHILE THE FARINA COOLS, MAKE THE CARAMEL: Slide the cake pan into the oven to warm — warming it makes getting an even layer of caramel a snap.

Put the sugar, water, and lemon juice in a small skillet or saucepan over high heat. Stir to moisten the sugar, then allow the mixture to come to a boil. As the sugar starts to take on color, swirl the pan gently so that it heats evenly. Keep a close watch on the pan, and when the sugar turns deep amber (about

5 minutes) — you can test the color by dropping a bit of caramel onto a white plate — remove the pan from the heat. Pour the caramel into the warm cake pan and tilt the pan until you get an even coating.

TO FINISH THE CAKE: Stir the beaten eggs and raisins into the cooled farina mixture, and scrape the batter into the caramelized cake pan. Slide the pan into the oven and bake until the cake firms and puffs and a knife inserted into the center comes out clean, 25 to 35 minutes.

Invert a serving plate with a rim over the cake pan and, working carefully — the caramel is very, very hot — turn the pan over onto the plate and lift it off, allowing the caramel sauce to run down the sides of the cake. Let the cake cool to room temperature before serving.

ispahan loaf cake

MAKES **8** SERVINGS

SERVING

The cake should be cut into thick slices, so that each slice has some berries, and served with coffee, tea, or Champagne. Although there's nothing that says you can't serve it with a raspberry coulis or even a little whipped cream or crème fraîche and berries, it's really perfect plain. Since the pink color makes it festive and party-ish, it's a great cake for Valentine's Day.

STORING

The cake is a good keeper. It can be kept, wrapped in plastic wrap, at room temperature for at least 4 days.

ISPAHAN (OR ISFAHAN) IS THE NAME of both a profoundly fragrant rose and the once-capital of Persia. And while we Americans might not ever mention the name, many Parisians have it on the tips of their tongues daily, thanks to the pastry genius Pierre Hermé, whose collection of Ispahan desserts is among his best sellers.

The first of Pierre's Ispahan sweets was a *macaron:* two disks of rose-colored almond-meringue cookies sandwiching a rose-flavored cream studded with lychees and raspberries. It was topped with a fresh rose petal, held to the *macaron* by a tiny drop of sugar syrup that looked like dew, and it was stunning. This is the pastry that started the rose fever that spread throughout France. Today every *grande pâtisserie* has something made with rose, and if your local pâtisserie doesn't, you can get your Ispahan fix at the supermarket: there's now a rose-raspberry-lychee yogurt.

Among all the members of the Ispahan family, this loaf cake is perhaps the simplest for home bakers to re-create. There's nothing unusual or difficult about the recipe — all the surprises are in the finished cake: the color is pink, the flavor is haunting, and the crumb is soft, tight, and pleasantly springy, a result of the cake being leavened by whipped egg whites. And then there are the fresh raspberries — they dot the interior of the cake and permeate it with both their distinctive flavor and their perfume. It's a remarkable cake.

About the rose flavoring: The cake must be made with rose syrup, *not* rose water. Monin is the brand that Pierre recommends, and it is the one most easily found in the United States. However, if you know a store that specializes in products from the Middle East, you may be able to find another brand of high-quality syrup there. In addition, the cake uses a little rose extract (and a little is all you need); I use an extract made by Star Kay White. These ingredients are expensive, but they keep for a long time, and I'm convinced that if you make this cake once, you'll make it many times thereafter.

2½ tablespoons rose syrup (see above and Sources)	12 tablespoons (1½ sticks) unsalted butter, at room temperature
2 tablespoons whole milk	¼ teaspoon rose extract (see headnote and Sources)
2 cups almond flour	
1 cup confectioners' sugar	
3 large eggs, separated, plus 1 large egg at room temperature	½ cup plus 1 tablespoon all-purpose flour
2½ tablespoons sugar	1 pint raspberries

Center a rack in the oven and preheat the oven to 350 degrees F. Generously butter a 9-x-5-inch loaf pan, dust the inside with flour, and tap out the excess.

Stir the rose syrup into the milk. Put the almond flour and confectioners' sugar in a sieve set over a bowl and stir the ingredients to pass them through it. Whisk them together.

In the bowl of a stand mixer fitted with the whisk attachment or in a large bowl with a hand mixer, beat the egg whites just until they start to hold their shape, then gradually add the sugar, beating until the whites hold firm, glossy peaks. If you need the mixer bowl, gently slide the whites into another bowl. (There's no need to wash the mixer bowl.)

Put the butter and almond-flour mixture in the mixer bowl or another large bowl and, using the paddle attachment or a hand mixer, beat at medium-high speed, scraping the bowl as needed, for 3 minutes, or until very smooth. Working at medium speed, add the 3 egg yolks one at a time, beating for about 1 minute after each addition, then beat in the whole egg. Add the rose-flavored milk, as well as the rose extract, and beat for 1 minute more.

Give the egg whites a quick turn with a whisk and stir one quarter to one third of them into the batter to lighten it. Switch to a rubber spatula and, working with a light touch, alternately fold the remaining whites and the all-purpose flour into the batter: do this as quickly and gently as you can, folding in the flour in about 3 additions and the whites in 2.

Scrape one third of the batter into the prepared loaf pan and spread to even it. Make 3 rows of berries down the length of the pan — don't let the berries touch the sides of the pan — then cover the berries with half of the remaining batter. Make 3 more rows of berries and carefully cover these with the last of the batter.

Lower the oven temperature to 300 degrees, and bake the cake for 55 to 65 minutes, or until a knife inserted into the center comes out clean. The top of the cake should be a lovely brown and feel springy to the touch, and the cake will have started to pull away from the sides of the pan. Transfer the cake to a cooling rack and let it rest for about 3 minutes, then unmold it, invert it, and let it cool to room temperature on the rack.

blueberry-mascarpone roulade

MAKES 8 TO
10 SERVINGS

SERVING
If you'd like, you can serve the cake with a berry coulis. Puree some blueberries in a blender or food processor with a little sugar or some of the leftover syrup; strain before using.

STORING
The blueberries and syrup can be prepared up to a day ahead. Covered, the roulade can be kept for up to 6 hours in the refrigerator. Just be certain to keep it away from food with strong odors.

ROULADES, OR JELLY ROLLS, AS WE CALL THEM, are just what you'd hope homemade cakes would be: tasty, beautiful, and fun to make. They're also easy. For proof, I offer the fact that roulades are something the French make at home often, and they're far less ambitious about home baking than we are. (Jelly rolls, homemade or store-bought, are so popular that even the most casual French home-goods store carries a cake plate made for a roulade.)

Like all jelly rolls, this one is made with a sponge cake, here the same sponge you'd use if you were making ladyfingers. (If you want to make ladyfingers, see Bonne Idée.) But instead of being rolled up with jelly, this cake is filled with a mixture of blueberry-speckled sweetened mascarpone and whipped cream, one very similar to a charlotte filling I learned from Pierre Hermé. It's a dessert that manages to be both homey and sophisticated at the same time.

Dropping the berries into hot syrup plumps the fruit, sweetens it slightly, and softens it just slightly.

BE PREPARED: The filled roulade needs to chill for at least 2 hours.

FOR THE BERRIES
- 2 cups water
- 1 cup sugar
- 1 pint blueberries

Confectioners' sugar, for dusting

FOR THE ROULADE
- ½ cup all-purpose flour
- ¼ cup cornstarch
- 6 large eggs, separated, at room temperature
- ⅔ cup sugar

FOR THE FILLING
- ½ cup mascarpone
- ⅓ cup confectioners' sugar
- ½ teaspoon pure vanilla extract
- ¾ cup cold heavy cream

TO MAKE THE BERRIES: Bring the water and sugar to a boil in a medium saucepan, stirring to dissolve the sugar. Add the blueberries and immediately remove the pan from the heat. Let cool to room temperature, then chill until needed. (*You can make the berries up to a day ahead and keep them well covered in the refrigerator.*)

TO MAKE THE ROULADE: Center a rack in the oven and preheat the oven to 400 degrees F. You have a choice about how to make the roulade. If you've got a large cookie sheet, take a large piece of parchment paper, draw a rectangle on one side that's about 12 x 17 inches, flip the paper over, and put it on the sheet. If you've got a rimmed baking sheet, one that's in the neighborhood of 12 x 17, just line it with parchment. Have a clean kitchen towel and some confectioners' sugar at the ready.

Sift the flour and cornstarch onto a piece of wax or parchment paper. (Using paper makes it easy to funnel the dry ingredients into the bowl.)

Put the egg whites into the clean dry bowl of a stand mixer fitted with the whisk attachment or into a large clean dry bowl that you can use with a hand mixer and whip the whites until they are opaque and just starting to thicken and hold their shape. Little by little, whip in the granulated sugar, and when it's fully incorporated, beat at medium-high to high speed for another couple of minutes. You want the meringue to be very firm.

Put the yolks in a bowl and whisk them for about 1 minute, until smooth. Gently scoop out about one quarter of the meringue and whisk it into the yolks to lighten them. Don't worry if the whites deflate some; they'll still do their job. Now scrape the lightened yolks onto the meringue, then put the dry ingredients over the yolks. With a large rubber spatula, gently fold all the ingredients together. Work as gingerly as you can — of course, no matter how careful you are, you're going to knock some air out of the meringue — and get the batter as well blended as you can, but keep in mind that it's perfectly fine to have patches of egg white here and there. It's better to have spots of egg white than to have a deflated batter. Turn the batter out onto the prepared pan. If you're using a large parchment-lined cookie sheet, fill in the area of your penciled rectangle with batter, spreading the batter so that it is the same thickness overall. Don't worry about scraggly edges — you can trim them later. If you're using a rimmed pan, smooth the batter to cover the pan evenly.

Bake the sponge for 8 to 10 minutes, or until it is uniformly puffed, crusted, slightly spongy to the touch, and lightly golden (if the cake is in a rimmed pan, it will be just starting to come away from the sides). Transfer the pan to a cooling rack.

Dust the kitchen towel with confectioners' sugar — be generous. If the cake is free-form, run a long metal spatula, preferably offset, under the cake to loosen it from the parchment, then invert it onto the sugar-dusted kitchen towel. If the cake is in a rimmed pan, run a blunt knife around the sides of the cake, then invert the cake onto the sugared cloth. Gently peel away the parchment paper.

Position the cake so that you've got a long side closest to you, and roll the cake up snugly in the towel. Allow the rolled-up cake to cool to room temperature.

TO MAKE THE FILLING: Before you start, drain the blueberries — you want them to be as dry as possible. (Hold onto the syrup, it's a good sweetener for lemonade and sparkling water.)

Put the mascarpone in a bowl and sift or strain the confectioners' sugar over it. Gently whisk together, then stir in the vanilla. (Don't beat the mascarpone, or it will become too thick; just stir it to loosen it.)

Whip the cream in the bowl of a stand mixer fitted with the whisk attachment or in a large bowl with a hand mixer until it holds firm peaks. Using a rubber spatula, stir a scant quarter of the cream into the mascarpone, then gently fold in the rest. When the whipped cream is almost incorporated, add the berries and fold them in.

TO ASSEMBLE THE CAKE: Unroll the cake, leaving it on the kitchen towel. Scoop the filling onto the cake, spreading it evenly and leaving an inch or so bare around the cake's perimeter. Using the towel to help you, gently lift and

BONNE IDÉE

Ladyfingers. Fit a pastry bag with a ½-inch plain tip and line a baking sheet with parchment. (Parchment works better than a silicone baking mat here.) Fill the bag with half of the sponge batter and pipe out fingers of dough about 4 inches long and an inch or so wide. (Or make them any length or width you want.) If you want to do this the way the pros do, pipe the logs side by side, so that they're touching — you'll separate them après baking; if not, pipe individual logs. Continue until you've piped as many ladyfingers as you'd like, using the remaining batter. (You can also use the batter to pipe circles.) Dust the tops of the fingers lightly with confectioners' sugar and let them rest on the counter for 15 minutes while you preheat the oven to 400 degrees F. (If you've piped out two sheets of fingers, position the oven racks so that they divide the oven into thirds.) Just before you're ready to bake, give the little cakes another light dusting of confectioners' sugar. Bake the ladyfingers for 8 to 10 minutes, or until they're a pale golden color — they shouldn't color much. When they're done, lift the parchment from the baking sheet(s) onto a cooling rack and let the fingers cool to room temperature. When you're ready for the ladyfingers, run a long metal spatula, preferably offset, under them to ease them off the parchment, then, if necessary, use a pizza cutter (my first choice) or a long sharp knife to cut individual ladyfingers.

ANOTHER
BONNE IDÉE
Raspberry Tiramisu en Verrine. The name *tiramisu* is used in France for just about any combination that has ladyfingers and mascarpone, and most of the combos are pretty tasty. Many of the versions star strawberries or raspberries. Here's one that's made in a *verrine*, or short glass, a presentation style that started several years ago and seems only to get more popular with time. You can use either a sponge sheet or ladyfingers for the cake part of the tiramisu. Whichever you use, cut it to fit inside the glasses. For each portion (depending on the size of the glasses, you'll probably have enough filling for 4 to 6 portions), put a round of cake in the bottom of the glass. Brush the cake with a little kirsch, framboise, or crème de cassis, an optional but delicious step.

Spread a little raspberry coulis over the cake. (Make the coulis by pureeing fresh or frozen raspberries, straining it — or not — and then sweetening it to taste.)

Spoon on a layer of the mascarpone cream filling (make it without the blueberries) and then top with fresh raspberries. Repeat with another set of cake, optional liqueur, coulis, cream, and berries. Chill well before serving with a dusting of confectioners' sugar.

roll the cake, starting with the long side farthest from you and finishing so that the seam is on the bottom; you'll probably be able to roll the cake one and a half times. You've got a choice now: you can leave the cake in its towel wrapper and move it to a cake plate or cutting board later, or you can unwrap it and put it on the plate or board now. Whatever you decide, the cake should be refrigerated (if the cake is not in the towel, cover it) for at least 2 hours; longer is better.

Just before serving, cut the ragged ends off the cake, trimming them just far enough to expose the filling. (I use a long knife with wide wavy serrations.) Dust the top of the cake with confectioners' sugar, and off you go.

michel rostang's double chocolate mousse cake

MAKES **6** SERVINGS

SERVING
Whipped cream or ice cream is never a bad idea with chocolate cake.

STORING
You must bake the base of the cake ahead, and the mousse can be kept chilled for several hours. Once baked, the cake can be covered and kept in the refrigerator for a day or two or wrapped airtight and frozen for up to 2 months; thaw the cake in its wrapper.

BONNE IDÉE
Michel Rostang's Double Chocolate Mousse Tartlets. **To make individual tartlets, you'll need six 3½-inch metal dessert rings, each about 2 inches high. Place the rings on a baking sheet lined with a silicone baking mat or parchment paper, then divide one third of the mousse among the six rings. Bake the tartlet bases in a 400-degree-F oven for 8 minutes if you're going to serve the tartlets warm, for 13 minutes if you're going to serve them cold. Proceed as directed. If you're serving the tartlets cold, the easiest way to remove the dessert rings is to warm them with a hair dryer and then to slide the rings up and off.**

THE TECHNIQUE FOR MAKING THIS DESSERT is ingenious. You prepare a chocolate mousse and bake some of it so that it firms, takes on a little chewiness, and, after puffing, sinks in the center to form a kind of bowl. Then you mound the remaining mousse over the "crust" and chill it — or bake it again. Either way, you get a sweet that's elegant, luscious, and intriguing, because each layer has a different texture.

This is a recipe I learned in the late 1980s from the Michelin-starred chef Michel Rostang. By the time he taught it to me, it was already a classic at his restaurant — and it still is today. Chez Rostang, the dessert is made in individual portions and called a *tarte*. Because the metal dessert rings the chef uses are hard to find, I've reworked the recipe so that it can be made in an 8-inch springform pan. Made like that, it's more a *gâteau* than a tart, but it remains delicious.

Quite by accident, I made a third variation of this recipe and ended up liking it best of all: I baked the cake and chilled it overnight, rather than serving it warm. Done this way, the difference between the layers is even more distinct and the mousse layer is considerably more luxurious.

I've given you all three variations in the recipe and the fourth, for the individual desserts, as well (see Bonne Idée).

BE PREPARED: You'll need to chill the base of the cake for at least an hour.

¼ pound bittersweet chocolate, coarsely chopped	⅔ cup sugar
	2 pinches of salt
⅓ cup hot espresso or very strong coffee	4 large eggs, separated
7 tablespoons unsalted butter, at room temperature	Cocoa powder, for dusting

Center a rack in the oven and preheat the oven to 400 degrees F. Generously butter the sides of an 8-inch springform pan (you won't be using the base). Line a baking sheet with a silicone baking mat or parchment paper and put the springform ring on it.

Melt the chocolate, stirring occasionally, in a large bowl set over a pan of simmering water (the bowl should not be touching the water). When it's smooth, whisk in the espresso or coffee. Remove the pan from the heat and mix in the butter tablespoon by tablespoon. Gently whisk in the sugar and a pinch of salt, then add the yolks one at a time. You'll have a lovely, velvety mix.

In the bowl of a stand mixer fitted with the whisk attachment or in a large bowl with a hand mixer, whip the egg whites with another pinch of salt until they are firm but still glossy. Very gingerly whisk about one quarter of the

whites into the chocolate mixture, just to lighten it. Switch to a rubber spatula and gently fold the remainder of the whites into the chocolate.

Scrape a generous one third of the mixture into the buttered ring of the pan. Cover and refrigerate the remaining mousse.

Bake the cake for 15 minutes, at which point it will be puffed. Transfer the baking sheet to a cooling rack and let the cake cool to room temperature (see below if serving the cake cold) — when there'll be a dip in the center of it. Then chill the base, still on the baking sheet, for at least an hour if you want to serve the cake warm.

TO SERVE THE CAKE COLD: Wait for the bottom layer to cool completely (you can put it in the refrigerator), then scrape the remaining mousse into the pan. Cover the pan and refrigerate for at least 6 hours, or for as long as overnight. Transfer the springform to a serving plate and remove the ring (run a blunt knife around the edge, with the ring still in place, or warm the pan with a hair dryer). Dust the cake with cocoa powder.

TO SERVE THE CAKE WARM: Preheat the oven to 400 degrees F. Scrape the chilled mousse onto the chilled base, still on the baking sheet. Bake the cake for about 30 minutes, or until the top is puffed and dry — it will crack, and that's both fine and attractive — and a knife inserted inside a crack comes out almost dry.

Transfer the baking sheet to a cooling rack and wait for 5 minutes, then run a blunt knife around the edges of the cake and remove the sides of the pan. The cake will sink, so just let it settle for another 5 minutes. Transfer to a serving plate and dust with cocoa powder.

TO SERVE THE CAKE BAKED AND CHILLED (THE WAY I PREFER IT): Bake the cake filled with the chilled mousse as directed for warm cake above, then cool it to room temperature and chill it for at least 4 hours. Remove the sides of the springform pan (run a blunt knife around the edges or warm the pan with a hair dryer), carefully transfer the cake to a serving platter, and dust the top with cocoa powder.

tourteau de chèvre

I CAN STILL REMEMBER HOW EXCITED I WAS when I first saw a *tourteau de chèvre*. It was over thirty years ago, and I was in Paris for the first time. I'd gone to a cheese shop to buy a slice of Brie, a cheese I couldn't wait to taste on native soil, and there, sitting to the side of the cool marble counters, was something that didn't look like anything I'd ever seen before. It was round on the sides and ballooned on top, a top that was as black as ash. Of course, I bought one, and when Michael and I tasted it, we fell in love with it — but we still didn't know what it was. The blackened top didn't taste burnt, the tender interior was not really sweet, but not savory either, and it wasn't clearly one flavor or another. And was that a crust on the bottom and up the sides? Was it cheese? Did you have it before a meal? Or was it a cake you had for dessert? As part of the cheese course? We reasoned it had to be cheese, since it was only sold in *fromageries,* but everything about it was a mystery, and neither of us spoke French well enough to ask for an explanation or to understand one had it been forthcoming. It wasn't until we got back to New York that I discovered that it was a cheesecake (of sorts) and that the cheese was *chèvre,* goat cheese.

This creation is so unlike what we know as cheesecake in America that I hesitate to use the name for fear of misleading you. Unlike just about everything in the American cheesecake family, the *tourteau* is not soft, creamy, moist, or even rich. Instead, it's a fairly dry cake (it's most like a sponge cake) that you cut into wedges and eat out of hand.

It turns out that a *tourteau de chèvre* is easily within the grasp of us ordinary mortals. We can't get the spherical shape, and the *noir* top doesn't seem possible in our ovens, but what we can make is so good, and the joy of making it at home so great, that the other stuff seems unimportant. I offer it here as a dessert, but I'm urging you to also give it a try with drinks before dinner.

About the goat cheese: You want to use a soft goat cheese without a crust. If you've got a very fresh cheese with a lot of moisture, it's best to put it in a strainer and allow it to drain for a few hours before you start making the *tourteau.*

MAKES **6** SERVINGS

SERVING
Try the *tourteau* with white wine as an aperitif, in the afternoon with tea, with coffee in the morning, anytime as a snack, or as dessert, in which case it's nice with a drizzle of honey and some fresh fruit.

STORING
The *tourteau*, which is not moist to begin with, can be covered tightly and kept at room temperature for a day or two.

Tart Dough (page 498) or Sweet Tart Dough (page 500), chilled and ready to roll

5 large eggs, separated, at room temperature
Pinch of salt

½ cup plus 2 tablespoons sugar

9 ounces soft goat cheese (see above; a log of crustless goat cheese is fine)

3 tablespoons cornstarch

½ teaspoon pure vanilla extract or orange-flower water or 2 teaspoons Cognac (optional)

Center a rack in the oven and preheat the oven to 400 degrees F. Generously butter an 8-inch springform pan. Line a baking sheet with a silicone baking mat or parchment paper.

On a lightly floured surface, roll the dough out into a circle that's about 10½ inches in diameter. Fit the dough into the springform pan, pressing it against the bottom and up the sides. It will pleat and fold in on itself as it climbs the sides — do the best you can to straighten it out, but don't worry about it, since perfection is impossible here and not really important. If the dough is uneven, you can trim it, but again, that's not crucial. (Once baked, the crust seems to melt into the cake, so you never really see the edges.) Put the springform in the fridge while you make the filling.

In the bowl of a stand mixer fitted with the whisk attachment or in a large bowl with a hand mixer, whip the egg whites with the salt until they start to form soft peaks. Still whipping, gradually add 2 tablespoons of the sugar, and beat until the whites hold firm but still glossy peaks. If the whites are in the bowl of your stand mixer, transfer them gingerly to another bowl.

With the mixer — use the paddle attachment now, if you've got one — beat the egg yolks, goat cheese, the remaining ½ cup sugar, the cornstarch, and flavoring, if you're using any, until very smooth and creamy, about a minute or two. Switch to a rubber spatula and stir one quarter of the whites into the mixture to lighten it, then gently fold in the rest of the whites. Scrape the batter into the crust and put the springform pan on the lined baking sheet.

Bake for 15 minutes, then turn the oven temperature down to 350 degrees F. Continue to bake for about 35 minutes more, or until the top, which will have cracked, is dark brown and firm; a thin knife inserted into the center of the cake should come out clean. Transfer the pan to a cooling rack and let the *tourteau* rest for 10 minutes.

Carefully remove the sides of the springform. Cool the cake to room temperature before serving. The cake will deflate as it cools.

whole-cherry clafoutis

SERVING
Serve with spoons and a warning about the pits (and bowls for them) — it really doesn't need anything else.

STORING
Like most pudding-ish sweets, this one's best the day it is made. If you've got leftovers, cover and chill them and have them the next day. The cold clafoutis will be different but still good.

ONCE WHILE TRAVELING IN FRANCE, I fell into conversation with a woman about how she makes clafoutis (cla-foo-*tee*), the most famous dessert from her own region, the Limousin. "I always use whole cherries," she said, "it's the tradition." I'd been told this before and had read it many times — the theory is that the cherries retain more of their flavor (and, of course, their juice) if you keep the pits, but I'd never had the chance to ask a native from the land of clafoutis the polite and proper way to dispose of those pits. "You put them in the pit bowl," she declared. And what is the pit bowl? "It's the bowl my great-grandmother used for pits. It goes in the center of the table, and everyone deposits the pits in it." I'd only just met the woman, so I didn't think it was right to quiz her on how the pits got from the clafoutis eater's mouth to the bowl. I'm sure they were conveyed on a dessert spoon, but isn't it easy to imagine kids having a little fun shortcutting the spoon?

Technically clafoutis is considered a cake, but as you'll see, it's more like a pudding, a firm, eggy, flour-based pudding that, when cut into wedges, stands up straight on the plate. This is not at all what I was told a clafoutis should be when I took my first class from a French pastry chef. Then I was taught to make the clafoutis sans flour, like a rich, jiggly custard, and to bake it in a tart crust. I love that style of clafoutis and continue to make it often (see Bonne Idée), but it's not the true clafoutis, the one that caused so much is-it-cake-or-is-it-pudding fuss that the question went to the lofty Académie Française, the keeper of the French language, for arbitration. (That's how the clafoutis was finally deemed a cake.)

This recipe would meet Académie Française standards. It uses whole cherries, is made without a crust, and is baked until firm. However, since everyone outside the Limousin plays around with the sweet, you can too. You can replace the fresh cherries with frozen (don't thaw them before baking) or *griottes* (sour cherries in syrup; drain before baking); you can use a mix of berries — blueberries and raspberries are particularly good; or you can use dried fruit — prunes soaked in Armagnac make a terrific clafoutis.

1	pound sweet cherries, stemmed but not pitted (see above)	½	cup all-purpose flour
		¾	cup whole milk
3	large eggs	½	cup heavy cream
½	cup sugar		
	Pinch of salt		Confectioners' sugar, for dusting
2	teaspoons pure vanilla extract		

Center a rack in the oven and preheat the oven to 350 degrees F. Generously butter a 9-inch deep-dish pie pan (or another baking pan with a 2-quart capacity).

Put the cherries in the pie pan — they should fit in a single layer.

In a medium bowl, whisk the eggs until they're foamy, then add the sugar and whisk for a minute or so. Whisk in the salt and vanilla. Add the flour and whisk vigorously — usually you should be gentle when incorporating flour, but this is an exception — until the batter is smooth. Still whisking (less energetically), gradually pour in the milk and cream and whisk until well blended. Rap the bowl against the counter to knock out any bubbles and pour the batter over the cherries.

Bake the clafoutis for 35 to 45 minutes, or until it's puffed and lightly browned and, most important, a knife inserted into the center comes out clean. Transfer the clafoutis to a cooling rack and allow it to cool until it's only the least bit warm, or until it comes to room temperature.

Dust the clafoutis with confectioners' sugar right before you bring it to the table.

BONNE IDÉE

Clafoutis Tart. When you make clafoutis as a tart, you don't use any flour in the mixture. Once baked, the clafoutis is most like a creamy custard. Have ready a 9- to 9½-inch partially baked tart shell, made with Sweet Tart Dough (page 500), on a lined baking sheet. To make the batter, whisk together 3 large eggs, ⅓ cup sugar, a pinch of salt, 1 cup heavy cream, and 2 teaspoons pure vanilla extract in a bowl, adding the ingredients in order and whisking each until blended. Cover the bottom of the tart shell with ¾ pound cherries (or other fruit; see headnote) and pour in the custard. You may have too much, in which case, just pour in enough to reach almost to the top of the crust. Bake in a 400-degree-F oven for 10 minutes. Then, if you have extra batter, pour in as much of it as you can. Continue to bake until the custard is just set in the center, another 15 minutes or so. Serve slightly warm or at room temperature, dusted with confectioners' sugar.

financiers

MAKES 12
RECTANGULAR
CAKES OR ABOUT
18 MINI-MUFFIN
CAKES

SERVING
These are made for coffee or tea (especially tea) and are good with jam.

STORING
While you can keep the batter in the refrigerator for up to 3 days, once you've baked the financiers, you should serve them that day. However, financiers can be wrapped airtight and frozen for up to 2 months; allow them to thaw in the wrapper.

BONNE IDÉE
Fruit Financiers. Adding a little fresh fruit to financiers is a nice touch. Fill the molds so that they're just a little shy of the rims, then put a little piece of fruit in the center of each mold — raspberries (this is my favorite add-in) or slivers of peaches, apricots, or plums.

W HILE FINANCIERS ARE A TREAT ALL OVER FRANCE, they are Paris born and bred. The small cakes were invented at Pâtisserie Lasne, which was a favorite of the stockbrokers who worked at the nearby Bourse. The brokers, *financiers,* would rush in every day in search of a sweet and rush out, brushing little bits of it off their suits as they went. It was Lasne's genius to realize that what his clients needed was "fast food": a pastry that the hurried brokers could eat without knife, fork, or fear of telltale crumbs. What he created was a gold ingot–shaped cake that could be eaten on the run. That it was as rich as the brokers he made it for might have been done for his own amusement, but it's part of what has sustained the financier's place in the pastry hall of fame for well over 100 years.

What makes the small cakes rich is butter — lots of it — cooked until it's lightly browned, and ground nuts. The most usual nut for the job is almond, but hazelnuts make perfect financiers as well. (I've also had pistachio financiers that were delicious, but they were made with pistachio paste, an expensive ingredient more easily found by professionals.) And because the batter is made with (unwhipped) egg whites, it has a tight crumb and a light spring that is especially appealing.

The best way to make financiers is to prepare the batter one day and bake it the next; however, if you're in as much of a rush to get your sweet as the Parisian stockbrokers were, you can do everything at once, only stopping for an hour to let the warm batter chill.

The classic pan for a financier is a shallow rectangle with slightly flared sides (mine are 3¾ x 2 x ⅝ inches and each holds 3 tablespoons), but a mini-muffin tin will give you delicious tea cakes.

This recipe is based on one Jean-Luc Poujauran taught me. Jean-Luc once had Paris's cutest pastry shop. The shop remains (it's on the rue Jean Nicot), but Jean-Luc is no longer there — he's in a nearby bakery making bread for some of the city's best restaurants.

BE PREPARED: The batter needs to chill for at least an hour.

12	tablespoons (1½ sticks) unsalted butter	1	cup almond flour
		6	large egg whites
1	cup sugar	⅔	cup all-purpose flour

Financiers can be made with "normal" melted butter, but if you follow tradition and brown the butter, you'll give the cakes an extra layer of flavor. To make *beurre noisette* (hazelnut butter), cut the butter into pieces, toss it into a small saucepan, and bring it to a gentle boil over medium heat. Once the butter boils, keep a close eye on it — you want it to turn a golden brown. If you get a deeper color, you'll get more flavor, but you have to be careful not to let the butter go black — something that can happen quickly. When you've got the color you want (and perhaps the fragrance of hazelnuts), pull the pan from the heat and set it aside in a warm place.

Put the sugar and almond flour in a medium saucepan and stir to mix. Add the egg whites, stir, and place the pan over low heat. Again, never leaving the pan unattended, stir with a wooden spoon or silicone spatula for about 2 minutes, until the mixture is slightly white, runny, and hot to the touch. Remove the pan from the heat and stir in the all-purpose flour, then gradually blend in the melted butter.

Scrape the batter into a heatproof bowl and press a piece of plastic wrap against the surface of the batter. Chill the batter for at least 1 hour, or, better yet, overnight. *(You can keep the batter in the fridge for up to 3 days.)*

When you're ready to bake, center a rack in the oven and preheat the oven to 400 degrees F. Generously butter 12 rectangular financier molds or 18 mini-muffin molds, dust with flour, and tap out the excess. Place the molds on a baking sheet. (If you don't have enough molds, bake the financiers in batches, cooling the tins between batches.)

Fill each mold almost to the top. Bake the financiers for about 13 minutes. The rectangular molds might take a little longer to bake and the mini muffins might take a little less time: the cakes should be golden, springy to the touch, and easy to pull away from the sides of the pan. Unmold the cakes as soon as you remove the pans from the oven — if necessary, run a blunt knife around the edges of the cakes to help ease them out of the pans. Transfer the cakes to a cooling rack and allow them to cool to room temperature.

ANOTHER BONNE IDÉE
Chocolate Financiers.

This recipe was given to me many years ago by Jean-Paul Hévin, one of Paris's most admired chocolatiers. The texture of these is more cakelike, and they're very chocolatey. Melt 4½ tablespoons unsalted butter as directed, stopping when the butter is a light golden color. Bring ⅔ cup heavy cream to a full boil and pour it over 5 ounces finely chopped bittersweet chocolate in a bowl. Stir just until you have a smooth, shiny ganache. In another bowl, whisk together ½ cup confectioners' sugar, sifted, ⅓ cup almond flour, 4½ tablespoons all-purpose flour, ⅛ teaspoon baking powder, and a pinch of salt. Whisk 3 egg whites together just until they're foamy, then pour them over the dry ingredients. Using a spatula, gently stir in the whites, followed by the melted butter. Add this mixture to the ganache and, using a light touch, blend. Spoon the batter into 15 buttered-and-floured financier molds or about 24 mini-muffin molds (if you don't have enough tins, bake the financiers in batches, cooling the tins between batches), filling the molds to about the three-quarter mark. Bake in the center of a 350-degree-F oven for 13 to 15 minutes (the mini muffins might need a little less time). The tops of the cakes should be dry, and a toothpick inserted in the center should come out clean. Cool the cakes for 3 minutes before unmolding them.

coconut friands

MAKES ABOUT 20
TEA CAKES

SERVING
Best with coffee or tea,
these are also good with a
little jam.

STORING
Well covered, the batter can
be kept in the refrigerator
for up to 3 days. You can
also hold the baked cakes
for that long or even a
little longer — they're
remarkably keepable;
store them in an airtight
container at room
temperature.

BONNE IDÉE
Fruited Friands. Add a
small bit of fruit to the
friands right before you
bake them. Place a fresh
raspberry or slivers of soft
fruits like peaches, plums,
apricots, or figs in the
center of each mold. Bits
of candied orange zest or
even stem ginger (ginger
preserved in syrup) are also
very good.

FRIANDS ARE VERY SIMILAR TO FINANCIERS, but here, instead of the traditional ground nuts, these little cakes have unsweetened coconut. It was my good friend the pastry chef and cookbook author Nick Malgieri, a veteran of kitchens in the South of France, who told me to add coconut, and I'm grateful to him for the recipe. The coconut is a good change-up, creating a not-too-sweet little tea cake that is good with tea, also nice with espresso, and lovely served alongside fresh fruit.

If pastry isn't your strong suit, take heart — friands are simple. They're made by hand in minutes, require no techniques more complicated than stirring, and are baked in a mini-muffin tin, the kind you can pick up in the supermarket.

4 large egg whites, preferably at room temperature	½ cup all-purpose flour
1½ cups shredded dried coconut, preferably unsweetened	½ teaspoon pure vanilla extract
	¼ teaspoon salt
⅔ cup sugar	8 tablespoons (1 stick) unsalted butter, melted

Center a rack in the oven and preheat the oven to 350 degrees F. If you've got two 12-cup mini-muffin tins, butter them both or fit them with paper liners; if you've only got one, butter or line it, and bake the friands in batches. (In the tins I use, each mold holds a scant 2½ tablespoons, and I can get 20 friands from the batter.)

Put the egg whites in a bowl and whisk them until they're smooth and a little foamy. One by one, whisk in the remaining ingredients gently, being particularly gentle with the flour and butter. You'll have a thick batter with a nice satiny shine. (*If it's more convenient, you can press a piece of plastic against the batter and refrigerate it for up to 3 days.*)

Spoon the batter into the muffin tins, filling them almost to the top, and put the tins on a baking sheet.

Bake the friands for 17 to 20 minutes, rotating the baking sheet at the midway mark. When they are done, it will be easy to pull the little cakes away from the sides of the pan, and they'll be springy to the touch; poke a toothpick in the center of one of them, and it will come out clean. As soon as you remove the pans from the oven, unmold the friands. If they're a little reluctant to come out of the molds, just rap the edges of the muffin tins against the counter. Cool the cakes right side up on cooling racks.

caramel-almond custard tart

EVERYTHING ABOUT THIS TART WAS CLASSIC until I played around with it. The simple custard filling is a French standard, rather like a sweet quiche, and one that's used all the time with fruit. But I've also seen it paired with nuts, and it was a nut tart that I was preparing to make when I decided to take out a bit of the sugar and caramelize it. It changed the tart completely and, I think, quite wonderfully. If you love caramel, as I do, you'll love this new version; if you're not a fan, go to Bonne Idée, where you'll find the original. You can make this tart with chopped walnuts or pecans instead of almonds; just be sure to lightly toast them beforehand so that they keep their interesting texture during baking.

MAKES **6** SERVINGS

1　9- to 9½-inch tart shell made with Sweet Tart Dough (page 500), partially baked and cooled

¾　cup sugar
2　tablespoons water

⅔　cup heavy cream, at room temperature
2　large eggs
　　Pinch of salt
¾　cup plus 2 tablespoons whole milk
3½　ounces (about 1 cup) sliced almonds, lightly toasted

SERVING
Even though the tart has cream in it, it's awfully good with a little sweetened whipped cream or, better yet, a scoop of crème fraîche. The tart is best at room temperature, when the custard is most satiny, but it can be served chilled.

STORING
Best served the day it is made — when both the custard and the crust are at their finest and their two different textures are most apparent — the tart can be kept covered in the refrigerator overnight if necessary.

Center a rack in the oven and preheat the oven to 350 degrees F. Line a baking sheet with a silicone baking mat or parchment paper and put the tart shell on the baking sheet. Have a white saucer at hand.

To make the caramel, put ¼ cup of the sugar in a medium heavy-bottomed saucepan, add the water, and place the pan over medium-high heat. Allow the sugar to melt and come to a boil. If the sugar is coloring unevenly, swirl the mixture gently to even it out. Watching the pan like a hawk, let the sugar bubble until it turns a deep amber color — test the color by putting a drop of the caramel on the white saucer. The sugar will smoke, and that's disconcerting but fine. Turn the heat down and, being careful to stand away from the pan — this is an imperative — pour in the cream. The sugar, which is seriously hot, will sputter and bubble, and it may even seize, but as the cream heats, it will calm down and smooth out. Remove the pan from the heat.

In a large bowl, whisk the eggs until they are foamy, then beat in the remaining ½ cup sugar and the salt and whisk for 1 minute. Stir in the milk, followed by the caramel cream.

Scatter the nuts over the bottom of the tart shell, then pour in the custard. Carefully slide the baking sheet into the oven and immediately reduce the oven temperature to 300 degrees F. Bake the tart for 35 to 45 minutes, or until the filling is uniformly puffed (make sure the center puffs) and feels firm at the center. Transfer the tart to a cooling rack and let cool to room temperature.

Remove the sides of the pan, slide the tart off the bottom of the pan (if you can't do this easily, don't bother with this step), and slice.

BONNE IDÉE
Almond Custard Tart. Do not caramelize the sugar; instead, beat the eggs with the full ¾ cup sugar. If you like, add 1 teaspoon pure vanilla extract and ⅛ teaspoon pure almond extract to the custard. If you're making the tart in summer, think about serving it with fresh berries, lightly sweetened or not.

crispy, crackly apple-almond tart

MAKES **8** SERVINGS

SERVING
The tart can be cut into rectangles and served warm or at room temperature. If it's at room temperature, you can eat it with your fingers at the dinner table — it will be messy but fun — or have it as a snack. The tart is good with lightly sweetened whipped cream or crème fraîche or with ice cream, but it's also delicious plain.

STORING
The almond cream can be made up to 3 days ahead. Although it's really best soon after it's made, the tart can be kept at room temperature for several hours. If you think it's gotten a little soggy — and it might if it's humid — reheat it on a baking sheet in a 350-degree-F oven for about 10 minutes.

DINNER CHEZ MY FRIENDS THE COLLETS is always a treat. The food is always good, and the conversation is always wide-ranging, interesting, and nonstop, which explains why my husband and I never leave their place until way after midnight, even on school nights. On one such late night, Michael, Joshua (our son), and I were walking back to our apartment and hitting the highlights of the evening: all the stories and the tart, the tart, the tart.

The base is eight sheets of filo dough, each brushed with butter and sprinkled with sugar. Then there's a kind of almond cream, one that's quickly whisked together (although it should chill for at least 3 hours), and, finally, the fruit. Here it's made with apples, but it's also good with figs, pears, or plums. When you pull the tart out of the oven, it's gorgeous — the crust is crispy, the almond topping has puffed around the fruit, and the fruit has softened as it baked. I give the whole thing a quick brush with a little melted jelly, just to make it shine, and, like Martine, I always bring it to the table uncut. There's something so exciting about bringing something big to the table, and this tart is big. Because it's so thin and crackly, you get to eat it out of hand, a rare thing at the French dinner table and a surefire recipe for giggles and crumbs.

BE PREPARED: The almond cream needs to be chilled for at least 3 hours.

FOR THE ALMOND CREAM	
1¼	cups almond flour
¼	cup sugar
1	large egg
½	teaspoon pure vanilla extract
	Pinch of salt
5	tablespoons heavy cream

FOR THE TART	
8	sheets filo dough (each 9 x 14 inches)
4	tablespoons (½ stick) unsalted butter, melted
	About 1 tablespoon sugar
3	medium sweet apples, such as Gala, peeled
2	teaspoons water
	About ½ cup apple jelly or strained apricot jam, for glazing

TO MAKE THE ALMOND CREAM: Whisk the almond flour and sugar together in a bowl.

In another bowl, beat the egg, vanilla, and salt together. Whisk in half of the almond flour mixture, and when it's well combined, whisk in the heavy cream. Finish by whisking in the remaining almond mixture. Press a piece of plastic wrap against the surface of the almond cream and chill it for at least 3 hours. (*The almond cream can be refrigerated for up to 3 days.*)

When you're ready to construct and bake the tart, center a rack in the oven and preheat the oven to 350 degrees F. Line a baking sheet with a silicone baking mat or parchment paper.

Place one piece of filo dough on the lined baking sheet (keep the remaining pieces of filo covered with plastic wrap), brush it with melted butter, and sprinkle it with sugar. Cover with another sheet of dough, then butter and sugar the sheet. Continue until you've stacked, buttered, and sugared all 8 sheets. Using a small offset spatula or the back of a spoon, very gently spread the almond cream over the top of the filo: you can leave a slim border of uncovered dough on all sides — it will curl in the oven and that's rather nice — or you can spread the almond topping all the way to the edges. Work slowly and be gentle, since filo is extremely delicate — if it tears (and it probably will), patch it with almond cream. Cover the tart lightly with plastic wrap while you cut the apples.

Slice each apple in half from top to bottom and remove the core. Cut each half lengthwise into very thin slices, keeping the slices together — you should get about 14 slices per half — then use the palm of your hand to flatten and fan them. Arrange the fanned-out apples on top of the almond cream, placing them in 3 long rows down the length of the tart or in as many short crosswise rows as you can fit. Keep the rows fairly close together, but allow a little almond cream to peek out between them.

Bake the tart for 30 to 35 minutes, or until the apples are tender when pierced with the tip of a knife and the almond cream is set. Transfer the baking sheet to a cooling rack.

Stir the water into the apple jelly or apricot jam and bring it to a boil in a saucepan over medium heat or in a microwave oven. Gently brush the glaze over the entire tart. Using a cookie sheet or two large metal spatulas or pancake turners, transfer the tart to a serving platter or cutting board. Serve warm or at room temperature.

BONNE IDÉE
Because nuts are so accommodating, this tart lends itself to being made with many different fruits. You can use pears, and you can also use grapes, plums, apricots, figs, peaches, or nectarines. If you're using juicy fruits, like plums and peaches, cut the fruit in half and place it cut side up on the cream. And as good as almonds are in the topping, they're not your only choice: you can use hazelnuts (skinned), walnuts, pecans, or even a mix of nuts in their place.

ANOTHER BONNE IDÉE
Apple Tartes Fines.

Also crispy and crackly, these small tarts, made on puff pastry bases, were inspired by the wonderful tart at the Paris bistro L'Avant-Goût. To make 4 individual tarts, roll out a sheet of puff pastry (about 8 ounces) until it's about ⅛ inch thick. (If you're using a sheet of Pepperidge Farm dough, roll it into a square that's about 13 inches on a side.) Use a saucer to cut out 4 rounds of dough, 4 to 6 inches in diameter. Transfer the rounds to a lined baking sheet and prick them all over with a fork; chill the rounds while you prepare the apples. Peel and core 3 firm sweet apples, such as Granny Smith or Fuji (you might need a couple more), then cut them into long, thin wedges. Arrange the apples attractively over the pastry rounds, leaving just a narrow border bare. (I usually make slightly overlapping concentric circles.) Beat 1 egg with ½ teaspoon cold water and brush this wash over the apples. Sprinkle the apples with sugar, and, if you'd like, brush the edges of the tarts with a little milk and sprinkle sugar over the edges as well. Bake the tarts in a 400-degree-F oven for about 30 minutes (check a few minutes before), or until the borders of the pastry are puffed and the apples are soft and browned at their edges. If you'd like the apples to be even darker, protect the edges of the pastry with foil and run the tarts under the broiler just to get a little more color. These are meant to be served hot or warm — with olive oil ice cream (page 479).

orange-almond tart

MAKES **6** SERVINGS

SERVING
Tarts like this are usually served with nothing else on the plate, but lightly whipped cream is never unwelcome.

STORING
While the crust, oranges, and almond cream can all be prepared ahead, the tart should be served the day it is made.

BONNE IDÉE
Poached Pear and Almond Tart. To my mind, this is the most classic of the French almond cream tarts. You can make the tart with 6 canned pear halves, or you can poach the pears yourself: Make a poaching syrup by bringing 4 cups water, 1¼ cups sugar, and the juice of 1 lemon to a boil in a medium saucepan. Peel 3 firm but ripe pears and drop them into the syrup. Lower the heat and gently poach the pears until you can easily pierce them with the tip of a knife, about 15 minutes; cool the pears in the syrup. Pat the pears dry, cut them in half from top to bottom, and remove the cores. Thinly slice each pear half crosswise, keeping the slices together. One by one, slide a spatula under each pear half, press down on the pear to fan the slices slightly, and place over the almond cream, wider ends toward the edges of the crust so that the fruit forms spokes.

THIS TART IS VERY LIKE ONE that can usually be found in the top row of Gérard Mulot's pâtisserie window, the long side window on the rue Lobineau. It's held that place for years, and if all remains right with the world, it will be there for years more. It's a classic with an unexpected twist. The truly classic part is the lovely *pâte sablée* crust and the almond cream filling. The surprise is that the fruit that's baked into the filling is orange, not a fruit that usually jumps to mind when you think of a tart, particularly one that is baked. It's an inspired idea.

Almond cream, which is not really a cream but is very creamy, is a *pâtissier's* building block for baked fruit tarts. It's easily made, it's very flavorful, and it bakes to a beautiful brown, puffing around whatever fruit you've topped it with. And you can top almond cream with almost any fruit. Perhaps the most classic French almond cream tart is the one made with sliced pears (see Bonne Idée), but you can use apples, cherries, figs (particularly wonderful), peaches (peeled), nectarines, apricots, or plums (I love this tart with plums, especially Italian prune plums, or what the French call *quetsches,* a favorite in Alsace). Or, in keeping with the spirit of M. Mulot's tart, you can use ruby grapefruit or even lemon segments. It's customary to add a splash of dark rum to almond cream, but if you change the fruit, you might also change the alcohol, substituting Cognac, another brandy, or an eau de vie, such as kirsch with cherries or Quetsche (plum) with plums.

BE PREPARED: To get the most flavor and texture from the fruit, it's important to dry the cut segments for at least 1 hour; several hours is better. It's a fussy step that makes a difference.

FOR THE ORANGES	
4	navel or other meaty oranges

FOR THE ALMOND CREAM	
6	tablespoons (¾ stick) unsalted butter, at room temperature
⅔	cup sugar
¾	cup almond flour
2	teaspoons all-purpose flour
1	teaspoon cornstarch
1	large egg

2	teaspoons dark rum or 1 teaspoon pure vanilla extract
1	9- to 9½-inch tart shell made with Sweet Tart Dough (page 500), partially baked and cooled
	Confectioners' sugar, for dusting, or about ¼ cup apple jelly and ½ teaspoon water, for glazing

TO PREPARE THE ORANGES: Using a sharp knife (I use a chef's knife), cut a thin slice off the top and bottom of each orange so that it can stand upright. Working from top to bottom and following the curve of the fruit, use the knife to remove the peel in wide bands, cutting down to the fruit. You want to expose the juicy fruit, so take the thinnest little bit of fruit away with each strip of peel.

ANOTHER
BONNE IDÉE
Sugar Baby Plum Tart.
One of my favorite almond cream tarts is topped with a fruit we don't find in America: mirabelles. Mirabelles are tiny, very sweet yellow-pink plums that are about the size of plump cherries. They're beloved in their native region, Alsace, where, in addition to being used in this tart, they are made into mirabelle eau de vie. In the United States, I use Methany plums or Sugar Plums to make the tart. (You can use any small, sweet plums that are in your market.) Cut the plums in half, pit them, and dot the top of the almond cream with them. If you have Mirabelle eau de vie, add a teaspoon to the almond cream instead of the rum.

Carefully run the knife down the connective membranes to release the orange segments one by one. Place the segments between triple layers of paper towels and let them dry for at least 1 hour, or for several hours, or even overnight. If you have the chance and the towels seem saturated, change them.

TO MAKE THE ALMOND CREAM: Put the butter and sugar in a food processor and process until the mixture is smooth and satiny. Add the almond flour and process until well blended. Add the all-purpose flour and cornstarch, and process, then add the egg. Process for about 15 seconds more, or until the almond cream is homogeneous. Add the rum or vanilla and process just to blend. (If you prefer, you can make the cream in a mixer fitted with the whisk attachment or in a bowl with a rubber spatula. In either case, add the ingredients in the same order.) You can use the almond cream immediately or scrape it into a container and refrigerate it until firm, about 2 hours. It's better if you can allow the cream to chill, but it's not imperative. *(The cream can be refrigerated, tightly covered, for up to 3 days.)*

When you're ready to bake, center a rack in the oven and preheat the oven to 350 degrees F. Line a baking sheet with a silicone baking mat or parchment paper and put the tart shell on it.

Stir the almond cream, then turn it into the crust, smoothing the top. Arrange the orange slices in a decorative pattern over the top. M. Mulot arranges them in a spiral, working from the center out, but they can be arranged in concentric circles. Whatever you do, don't cover every bit of the cream — it will bubble and rise as it bakes, and it's nice to leave space for it to come up around the fruit.

Bake the tart for 50 to 60 minutes, or until the cream has risen and turned golden brown. If you slip a knife into the cream, it should come out clean. Transfer the tart to a cooling rack and cool to room temperature.

Right before serving, dust the tart with confectioners' sugar. Or, if you prefer, prepare a glaze by bringing the apple jelly and water to a boil (you can do this in a microwave oven or saucepan). Brush the glaze over the surface of the tart.

Remove the sides of the pan, slide the tart off the bottom of the pan (if you can't do this easily, don't bother with this step), and slice.

SABLÉ BRETON GALETTE WITH BERRIES (PAGE 464)

sablé breton galette
with berries

MAKES **6** SERVINGS

SERVING

Cut the galette into wedges and serve as is — nothing more is needed.

STORING

You can make the sablé dough up to 3 days ahead and keep it well wrapped in the refrigerator, and you can bake the galette a day or two ahead and keep it at room temperature. (I put it back in the tart pan and cover the pan with foil.) However, once you put the curd over the galette and top it with berries, it's best to serve it quickly. If you have to, you can keep the finished galette in the refrigerator for an hour or two, but the base will soften a bit.

BRITTANY, THE NORTHWESTERN REGION OF FRANCE, is known for its oysters, envied for its fleur de sel, beloved for its crepes and its caramels, and unusual for its use of salted butter. It is the only part of France where salted butter is the norm. It's salted butter with breakfast, salted butter on dark bread with oysters, salted butter on crepes, salted butter in those famous caramels, and salted butter in the region's renowned butter cookie, *le sablé Breton*.

The sablé is a sweet shortbread that's buttery and noticeably salty. Because we don't get butter that's as salty as Breton butter, when I'm in the United States, I make the cookie with unsalted butter and add fleur de sel (or fine sea salt) so that I can get the salt level just right. In this version of the sablé, the dough is purposely very soft (it's too soft to roll and cut for cookies) so that it can be patted and pressed into a tart pan, baked, and used as the base of a really beautiful berry dessert.

I like to spread the galette with lemon curd and top it with sliced strawberries or whole raspberries, but it is equally good with whipped cream or ice cream in place of the curd. In fact, it's good on its own — just cut it into wedges and nibble. If you're not serving a group, leave the galette plain, and when you need a slice or three of tart, cut the galette and top it on the spot. The photo is on page 463.

If you'd like to make *sablé Breton* cookies, see Bonne Idée.

BE PREPARED: The dough needs to chill for at least 3 hours.

FOR THE GALETTE	FOR THE TOPPING
1 cup all-purpose flour	About 1 cup lemon curd,
1¼ teaspoons baking powder	homemade (page 507) or
10 tablespoons (1¼ sticks)	store-bought
unsalted butter, at room	About 3 cups berries
temperature	(strawberries, raspberries, or
⅔ cup sugar	blueberries, or a mix)
½ teaspoon fleur de sel or	About ¼ cup red currant jelly,
¼ teaspoon fine sea salt	for glazing (optional)
1 large egg	Confectioners' sugar, for
	dusting (optional)

TO MAKE THE GALETTE: Whisk the flour and baking powder together.

In the bowl of a stand mixer fitted with the paddle attachment or in a large bowl with a hand mixer, beat the butter on medium speed until soft and creamy. Add the sugar and salt and beat for another 2 minutes, or until the mixture is very smooth. Beat in the egg and mix for 2 minutes more. Reduce the mixer speed to low, add the flour mixture, and mix only until it is blended — you'll have a very soft dough.

Working with a rubber spatula, give the dough a few turns to make sure you've picked up all the dry ingredients at the bottom of the bowl, then scrape the dough onto a piece of wax paper or plastic wrap. Press down on the dough to form it into a disk, wrap it well, and chill it for at least 3 hours. *(The dough can be refrigerated for up to 3 days.)*

When you are ready to bake the galette, center a rack in the oven and preheat the oven to 325 degrees F. Butter a 9- to 9½-inch fluted tart pan with a removable bottom and put it on a baking sheet lined with a silicone baking mat or parchment paper.

To get the dough going, put it between two pieces of wax paper or plastic wrap and roll it into a circle. If it's too difficult to roll — it's soft and it has a tendency to break — skip the rolling part and go directly to the patting part: Put the dough in the center of the tart pan and pat and press it into an even layer. Don't press the dough up the sides of the pan — you want as flat a surface as you can get. Place the pan on the baking sheet.

Bake the galette for 40 to 45 minutes, or until the top is golden brown and the edges come away from the sides of the pan; if you press the galette gently, it won't feel completely firm, but that's just fine. Transfer the pan to a cooling rack and let the galette rest for 3 minutes or so, then invert it onto another rack, invert again onto a rack so that it's right side up, and let cool to room temperature.

JUST BEFORE YOU'RE READY TO SERVE, TOP THE GALETTE: Put the galette on a flat serving plate and spoon over as much lemon curd as you'd like, spreading it in swirls but leaving a little border around the edge bare (the curd will spread when you cut the base). If you're using strawberries, hull them, leave them whole or slice them in half, and arrange attractively over the curd. If you've got raspberries or blueberries or a mélange, scatter the berries over the curd or arrange them neatly in pretty circles.

If you want to give the galette a little glaze, warm the currant jelly with a tiny splash of water until it liquefies (you can do this in a microwave oven or a saucepan). Either drizzle the glaze over the berries — this is my preferred technique — or use a pastry brush or feather to paint the berries with the jelly.

If you haven't glazed the berries, you might want to give them a dusting of confectioners' sugar just before you bring the galette to the table.

BONNE IDÉE

Sablé Breton Cookies. Increase the amount of flour to 1¼ cups, decrease the butter to 8 tablespoons (1 stick), and use 2 large egg yolks instead of the egg. When the dough is mixed, it will be much firmer than the galette dough. Divide the dough in half and roll each half into a log, to make slice-and-bake cookies, or pat the halves into disks, to make cut-out cookies. Either way, wrap the dough and chill it for at least 6 hours, or for up to 3 days.

When you're ready to bake, center a rack in the oven and preheat the oven to 325 degrees F. Line two baking sheets with silicone baking mats or parchment paper. If you've made logs, slice the dough ⅓ inch thick. If you've got disks, let them stand just until you can roll the dough out, then roll it to about ¼ inch thick. (Thicker is better than thinner here.) Cut out the cookies and place them 2 inches apart on the baking sheets. Bake them, one sheet at a time, for 11 to 14 minutes, or until they are firm but not browned. Allow them to rest on the baking sheets for a few minutes, then transfer them to racks to cool. Repeat with the remaining dough. I usually cut out cookies with a 2-inch-diameter fluted cutter and get between 24 and 30 cookies (including cookies cut from rerolled scraps).

double chocolate
and banana tart

THE INSPIRATION FOR THIS TART COMES from one that the chocolatier Christian Constant made for the world-famous designer Sonia Rykiel. In Paris, Madame Rykiel is celebrated almost as much for being a founding member of Le Club des Croqueurs de Chocolat (The Chocolate Connoisseurs' Club) — an exclusive association with strict membership rules and delicious meetings — as she is for creating coveted clothing. Being a friend of Rykiel and knowing of her love of both chocolate and bananas, Constant created a stunning tart for her that was filled with bittersweet chocolate ganache and topped with concentric circles of sliced bananas. It's a beauty and a recipe I've played with over the years. This rendition is a double-the-pleasure tart: both the filling and the crust are chocolate. (I use a chocolate shortbread cookie dough as a crust.) The bananas appear twice as well — in M. Constant's original sunburst topping and, caramelized in butter and sugar, scattered over the crust and covered with the ganache, only to be revealed with the first slice.

For a completely different way to enjoy the ganache in this tart, see Bonne Idée for a Chocolate Nutella Tart.

MAKES 6 SERVINGS

SERVING
The tart can be served as soon as the glaze cools, but I prefer it at cool room temperature, which is when you get the best contrast between the cookie crust and the velvety ganache. It's also superb cold, and since chocolate melts at body temperature, it won't stay cold or firm for long.

STORING
The tart should be eaten the day you make it, but you can prepare the caramelized bananas a couple of hours ahead. You can also prepare the ganache ahead: It can be packed airtight and refrigerated for up to 2 days or frozen for up to 3 months. (Thaw in the container overnight in the fridge.) Reheat the ganache gently in a microwave oven before pouring it into the crust.

FOR THE CARAMELIZED
BANANAS

1   ripe but firm banana
    Fresh lemon juice
1½ tablespoons unsalted butter
3½ tablespoons sugar

FOR THE BITTERSWEET
GANACHE

½   pound bittersweet chocolate, very finely chopped
1   cup plus 2 tablespoons heavy cream

4   tablespoons (½ stick) unsalted butter, cut into 4 pieces, at room temperature

1   9- to 9½-inch tart shell made with Chocolate Shortbread Dough (see Bonne Idée, page 501), fully baked and cooled

FOR THE BANANA TOPPING

½   cup apricot jam, strained
2–3 ripe but firm bananas
    Fresh lemon juice

TO MAKE THE CARAMELIZED BANANAS: Line a plate with parchment paper. Cut the banana into ⅛-inch-thick slices — it's nice to cut on the bias — and toss the slices with lemon juice to keep them from blackening.

Put a large skillet — nonstick is perfect — over high heat and toss in the butter. When it melts and starts to bubble, add the bananas, turning them so that they're coated with butter. Sprinkle the sugar over the bananas and cook, still over high heat, turning, until they're golden and caramel-coated on both sides. Transfer the bananas to the parchment-lined plate and pat them gently

BONNE IDÉE

Chocolate Nutella Tart.
The inspiration for this tart
comes from the famous
Parisian pastry chef Pierre
Hermé, who makes a baked
ganache tart with a hidden
layer of Nutella beneath
the chocolate. You can get
that taste combination by
spreading ⅔ cup Nutella
over the bottom of the
baked tart shell and chilling
the tart for about 1 hour,
then pouring over the
ganache and allowing it
to set as directed. In the
original, the tart is topped
with coarsely chopped
toasted hazelnuts, a key
ingredient in Nutella. Since
both Nutella and chocolate
are so good with bananas,
you might want to finish
this tart with the bananas
too.

on both sides with paper towels to remove any excess butter. Cool to room temperature. *(The bananas can be caramelized a couple of hours ahead and kept at room temperature.)*

TO MAKE THE BITTERSWEET GANACHE: Put the chocolate in a heatproof bowl.

Bring the cream to a boil in a small saucepan, then pour it over the chocolate. Let the mixture sit for 30 seconds or so, then, with a whisk or spatula, gently stir the chocolate and cream together: the best way to do this is to stir in small circles, starting at the center of the bowl and working your way out in increasingly larger circles. Stir gently, and when the ganache is smooth and shiny, stir in the butter, piece by piece. *(The ganache can be refrigerated for up to 2 days or frozen for up to 2 months; reheat gently in a microwave before proceeding.)*

Arrange the caramelized bananas in an even layer over the bottom of the crust, then pour over the ganache. Hold the tart pan with both hands and rotate it lightly from side to side to encourage the ganache to even out, then slide the tart into the fridge to set the ganache, 30 to 60 minutes. *(You can refrigerate the tart until serving time; just be certain to cover it once the chocolate has set.)*

TO MAKE THE TOPPING: Bring the apricot jam to a boil in a small saucepan or in a microwave oven.

Peel the bananas and cut them on the bias into slices that are a scant ¼ inch thick. Toss them lightly with just the slightest bit of lemon juice — the juice will keep them from blackening, but you don't want them to be so wet that they dribble on the ganache. Arrange the banana slices in concentric circles over the top of the tart — start at the outer edge and slightly overlap the slices in a circle, then continue building concentric circles, having each circle slightly overlap its neighbor. Brush the bananas with a thin coating of the hot jam, glazing them evenly. Allow the glaze to cool and set.

When you're ready to serve, remove the sides of the pan and slide the tart off the bottom of the pan (if you can't do this easily, skip it), and slice.

cheesecake tart

I DON'T UNDERSTAND WHY THIS TART hasn't become more popular here — it's simple, creamy, slightly tangy, and much like our own beloved cheesecake. Baked in a shortbreadlike tart shell and traditionally studded with plump raisins, the filling puffs, then forms a thin layer that almost melds with the crust. A mixture of cottage cheese and sour cream whirred together gives you the same smoothness and zest as the traditional fromage blanc.

This recipe comes from the notebook my friend Alice Vasseur kept when she was seven years old and taking after-school classes at Le Cordon Bleu.

MAKES **6** SERVINGS

SERVING
With its mix of sweetness and zest, this cheese tart works well with tea or espresso and is especially good with a honey-ish dessert wine.

STORING
The tart should be served the day it is made, but it has its day-after fans who enjoy it chilled.

BONNE IDÉE
You can use dried cranberries or snippets of dried apricot instead of the raisins.

1	9- to 9½-inch tart shell made with Sweet Tart Dough (page 500), partially baked and cooled		strainer for 30 minutes) or 1⅓ cups fromage blanc
3	tablespoons plump, moist raisins (or other dried fruit, chopped if necessary)	3	tablespoons sour cream, if you're using cottage cheese
3	tablespoons cornstarch	3	large egg yolks
3	tablespoons whole milk	3	tablespoons sugar
1¼	cups cottage cheese (drained in a cheesecloth-lined		Pinch of salt
		1–2	teaspoons pure vanilla extract
			Finely grated zest of ½ lemon
			Apricot jam, for glazing
			Confectioners' sugar, for dusting

Center a rack in the oven and preheat the oven to 350 degrees F. Line a baking sheet with a silicone baking mat or parchment paper and put the tart shell on the baking sheet. Scatter the raisins evenly over the bottom of the shell.

Put the cornstarch in a small bowl, pour in the milk, and stir to blend — the cornstarch will dissolve. Set aside.

If you're using cottage cheese, scrape the cottage cheese and sour cream into a food processor and whir for about 2 minutes, or until the mixture is perfectly smooth and satiny. Add the yolks and sugar and process for 1 minute more. Add the salt, vanilla, zest, and reserved milk mixture and pulse just to blend. If you are using fromage blanc, omit the sour cream and use the food processor or simply whisk the ingredients together in a bowl. Pour the filling into the crust.

Slide the baking sheet into the oven and bake the tart for 50 to 60 minutes, or until the top is lightly browned and puffed all over (you want the center to puff, not just the sides). Transfer the baking sheet to a cooling rack and let the tart cool until it is slightly warm or at room temperature.

If you'd like to glaze the tart, warm the apricot jam with a splash of water in a microwave oven or a small saucepan. When the jam liquefies, use a pastry brush to paint a very thin layer of the jam over the top of the tart. Alternatively, dust the cooled tart with confectioners' sugar.

gâteau basque

SERVING
I think the cake is best plain, but a little whipped cream or a scoop of ice cream is always nice on simple sweets.

STORING
The dough can be made up to 3 days ahead. Wrapped well, the jam-filled cake will keep for a day or so at room temperature. You can keep the cream-filled cake overnight in the refrigerator, but because refrigeration can dry cakes, I think it's best to serve the cream-filled cake the day it is made.

I'M SURE THERE ARE DIFFERENT KINDS OF PASTRIES in the shops throughout the Pays Basque, but as I think back to my travels there, I can't conjure up anything but the pride of the region, the *gâteau Basque*. It was everywhere — in pâtisseries, of course, and also at outdoor markets: you'd see a vendor with a long table covered with *gâteaux Basque* and then, ten feet away, another vendor with another long table and more *gâteaux Basque*. Outside the village of Sare, there was even a museum dedicated to the cake. It was there, under the tutelage of the museum's founder, Bixente Marichular, that I learned to make a *gâteau Basque*.

The simplest way to describe this sweet is to liken it to a double-crusted tart, one in which the crust is like butter cookies and the filling is either pastry cream or thick cherry jam, preferably made from the region's dark cherries grown in Itxassou. (Marichular would insist that that's the only kind of jam that can be used.) Traditionally, when pastry cream is the filling, the top crust is brushed with an egg wash and decorated with a crosshatch pattern etched into the dough with the tines of a fork. When there's jam within, the top is finished with a Basque cross, which looks like an elongated S bisected by a sideways S. However, since I love the look of the *gâteau* with the crosshatch and the taste of it with the jam, I often play mix-and-match with tradition.

In another region, this *gâteau* might be called a galette or a torte, but for the Basque people, it's a cake, and it's a daily treat. Because the cake is so much like a cookie, it's perfect snack food, great for a picnic, and ideal for brunch. And since it's not overly sweet, it's not too much to think about sneaking a sliver of a slice in with that first cup of coffee in the morning.

BE PREPARED: You'll need to refrigerate the dough for at least 3 hours.

2 cups all-purpose flour	1 large egg, at room temperature
¾ teaspoon baking powder	½ teaspoon pure vanilla extract
½ teaspoon salt	
10 tablespoons (1¼ sticks) unsalted butter, at room temperature	¾–1 cup thick cherry jam or Vanilla Pastry Cream (page 505)
¼ cup packed light brown sugar	1 egg, beaten with a splash of water, for glazing
¼ cup sugar	

Whisk together the flour, baking powder, and salt.

In the bowl of a stand mixer fitted with the paddle attachment or in a bowl with a hand mixer, beat the butter and both sugars together on medium speed for about 3 minutes, or until smooth. Add the egg and beat for another 2 minutes or so, scraping down the sides of the bowl as needed. The mixture may look curdled, but that's okay. Reduce the mixer speed to low, beat in the vanilla, and add the dry ingredients in 2 or 3 additions, mixing only until they're fully incorporated.

Place a large sheet of plastic wrap or wax paper on your work surface and put half of the very soft, sticky dough in the center of the sheet. Cover with another piece of plastic or wax paper, then roll the dough into a circle just a little larger than 8 inches in diameter. As you're rolling, turn the dough over and lift the plastic or paper frequently so that you don't roll it into the dough and form creases. Repeat with the other half of the dough. Put the dough, still covered with the plastic wrap or wax paper, on a cutting board or baking sheet and refrigerate it for at least 3 hours (or for up to 3 days).

When you're ready to assemble and bake the *gâteau*, center a rack in the oven and preheat the oven to 350 degrees F. Generously butter an 8-x-2-inch round cake pan.

Remove the rounds of dough from the refrigerator and let them rest on the counter for a couple of minutes before peeling away the plastic or wax paper. Fit one round into the pan — if it breaks, just press the pieces together. If there's a little extra dough running up the sides of the pan, you can either fold it over or trim it so that it's even. Spoon ¾ cup of the jam or pastry cream onto the dough, starting in the center and leaving 1 inch of dough bare around the border. Add more filling if you don't think it will squish out the sides when you press down on it with the top layer of dough. (I find that ¾ cup is usually just the right amount, but if you're using a very thick jam, you might want a bit more.)

Moisten the bare ring of dough at the edge with a little water and top with the second piece of dough, pressing down around the edges to seal it. If you'd like, work your finger between the top round of dough and the edge of the pan, so that you tuck the dough under a little. Because of the softness of the dough, even if you only press the layers together very lightly, they'll fuse as they bake. But no matter how you press them together, it seems inevitable that a little of the filling will escape.

Brush the top of the dough with the egg glaze and use the tips of the tines of a fork to etch a crosshatch pattern in the top.

Bake the cake for 40 to 45 minutes, or until the top is golden brown. Transfer the cake to a cooling rack and let it rest for 5 minutes.

Carefully run a blunt knife around the edge of the cake. Turn the cake over onto a cooling rack and then quickly and carefully invert it onto another rack so that it can cool to room temperature right side up.

vanilla éclairs

FAUCHON, THE SPECIALTY FOOD EMPORIUM IN PARIS whose teas and coffees, biscuits, and cookies are found around the world, was started in 1886 but has managed to remain fashionable through the years, in part by drawing on tradition and then turning that tradition upside down. That's what the shop has done with the éclair, a pastry that's older than it is. These days, when you pass Fauchon's window on the place de la Madeleine, you might see an éclair glazed with zebra stripes, leopard spots, or even the face of the Mona Lisa. Although the pastry chefs have used the éclair as a canvas for their whims and changing inspirations, they haven't changed the basic recipe, the one Carême invented so many years ago.

Antonin Carême, considered the father of modern pastry, was the first to pipe *pâte à choux* into long fingerlike shapes. Once the pastry was baked, he sliced the strips in half, filled them with pastry cream, and glazed their tops, creating an enduring classic, which he christened *éclairs* (*éclair* means lightning). No one's certain why he called the slender pastries lightning. Some say the name was inspired by the sweet's shape, others say it came from the way light plays off the shiny glaze. I hold with the camp convinced that the name described the way an éclair is eaten — lightning fast.

Interestingly, no matter how avant-garde éclairs get these days, the most beloved remain the most traditional: vanilla, chocolate, and coffee. I'm giving you the recipe for vanilla éclairs here, but variations are both easy and encouraged; see Bonne Idée.

BE PREPARED: The éclairs need to be chilled for at least 1 hour before serving.

FOR THE ÉCLAIRS
1 recipe Cream Puff Dough (page 502), still warm

FOR THE FILLING
1 recipe Vanilla Pastry Cream (page 505), chilled

FOR THE GLAZE
About 1½ cups confectioners' sugar, sifted
About 2 tablespoons whole milk
A squeeze of fresh lemon juice

TO MAKE THE ÉCLAIRS: Position the racks to divide the oven into thirds and preheat the oven to 375 degrees F. Line two baking sheets with silicone baking mats or parchment paper. Fit a large pastry bag with a large (⅔-inch-diameter) plain tip. (You can also pipe the éclairs with a star tip; the star makes a pretty éclair, but it's not easy to glaze the ridges.)

Fill the pastry bag with half of the dough and pipe out strips of dough that are 4 to 4½ inches long onto the first baking sheet; keep the strips about 2 inches apart so the éclairs will have room to puff. Pipe the other half of the dough onto the second baking sheet. (*The éclairs can be frozen for up to 2 months.*)

Bake the éclairs for 10 minutes, then rotate the pans from front to back and top to bottom. Continue baking for another 7 minutes, then wedge the handle

MAKES ABOUT
20 ÉCLAIRS

SERVING
Although éclairs can easily be finger food, they are usually served on plates with small forks and knives.

STORING
You can pipe out the cream puff dough and freeze the "fingers" on the baking sheets until they are firm, then pack them airtight and freeze for up to 2 months. When you're ready to bake them, arrange the éclairs on the baking sheets and bake without defrosting; add a few extra minutes to the baking time. The pastry cream can be made ahead and kept refrigerated for up to 3 days. Only the glaze must be used as soon as it's made, but once you've spread it over the pastry, the éclairs should chill for at least 1 hour (or up to 8 hours), making this sweet very do-aheadable.

BONNE IDÉE
Profiteroles. To make this extremely popular dessert, form the dough into puffs (see page 502 for instructions) and bake as directed. When they're cool, slice the top third off each puff and fill the bottom with ice cream; freeze in an airtight container until needed. Profiteroles are best when they've had a couple of minutes to warm up from their freeze. Serve 2 or 3 to a plate, and just before you bring them to the table, pour a generous amount of Bittersweet Chocolate Sauce (page 508) over each one.

ANOTHER
BONNE IDÉE

Coffee Éclairs, Chocolate Éclairs with Thick Ganache, and Some More Ideas.
To make coffee pastry cream to fill the éclairs, make a coffee extract by dissolving 2 tablespoons instant coffee or espresso in 2 tablespoons boiling water. Add 1 tablespoon of this mixture to a recipe of Vanilla Pastry Cream, then taste and add more, if you like. To make a coffee glaze, swap espresso for the milk.

If it's chocolate you want, use Chocolate Pastry Cream (page 506) for the filling and a thick ganache for the glaze: Bring ¾ cup heavy cream to a boil. Pour the cream over ¾ pound bittersweet chocolate, very finely chopped, and wait for 30 seconds, then gently stir to blend. Chill the ganache for about 20 minutes, or until it thickens enough for you to spread it smoothly over the éclairs.

Éclairs can also be filled with whipped cream, ice cream, or a mixture of lemon curd (page 507) and whipped cream (very untraditional).

of a wooden spoon into the oven door so it stays slightly ajar, and bake for 3 minutes more, or until the éclairs are golden, firm, and puffed (total baking time is about 20 minutes). Transfer the éclairs to a rack and cool to room temperature. *(If the room is cool and dry, the éclairs can stay out for a few hours before being filled.)*

TO FILL THE ÉCLAIRS: Cut the éclairs horizontally in half — they'll probably have puff marks around their middles, showing just where they want to be cut. I use a serrated knife and a gentle sawing motion. Lift off the tops.

Whisk the pastry cream lightly to loosen it a bit, spoon it into a pastry bag fitted with a large plain tip, and pipe enough into each éclair base to fill it. Or skip the pastry bag and fill the éclairs using a spoon. *(You'll have pastry cream left over, which you can cover and keep refrigerated for up to 3 days.)* Put the filled bases on a baking sheet, cover them lightly, and refrigerate while you make the glaze.

TO MAKE THE GLAZE: Put 1½ cups confectioners' sugar in a medium bowl and add 1½ tablespoons of the milk, as well as the lemon juice. Whisk gently to combine the ingredients. If the glaze seems too thick, add more milk drop by drop; if too thin, add more sugar a pinch at a time. What you're looking for is a smooth glaze that can be spread evenly over the éclairs.

Using a small icing spatula or a butter knife, glaze the tops of the éclairs, then settle the tops gently over the filled bases. Refrigerate the éclairs for at least 1 hour (or up to 8 hours) before serving.

paris-brest

EVERY FOUR YEARS, THE UNION DES AUDAX FRANÇAIS organizes an amateur bicycle race that goes from Paris to Brest, and every day in Paris, Brest, and all over France, the Paris-Brest turns up for dessert. Created to celebrate the race, the first one of which was held in 1891, the dessert is a cream puff ring (made from *pâte à choux*) meant to evoke a bicycle wheel, split in half, filled with cream, and topped with toasted sliced almonds. I've seen Paris-Brest filled with whipped cream, buttercream, crème Chiboust (pastry cream lightened with cooked meringue), and almond praline pastry cream, which I think of as the truest filling and the one often referred to as crème Paris-Brest. The pastry is wonderful-looking — truly a party dessert — and not difficult to make, since, like a bicycle race, it's done in stages.

If you'd like, you can make smaller rings — that's what's often done in pâtisseries and restaurants. (I always order the Paris-Brest at Bistrot Paul Bert, where although they say it's a single serving, one is enough for a whole table, no matter how many you've got at the table.)

BE PREPARED: You'll need to refrigerate the Paris-Brest for at least 1 hour before serving.

MAKES 8 SERVINGS

SERVING
In France the pastry is served plain or with a drizzle of Crème Anglaise (page 504), but that doesn't mean that in America we can't serve it with a little Bittersweet Chocolate Sauce (page 508) on the plate.

STORING
You can make the caramelized almonds several days ahead, and the pastry cream can be made up to 3 days ahead and kept covered in the refrigerator, but don't combine the two until you need the filling. The cream puff ring can also be made a few hours ahead. And you can fill the Paris-Brest up to 8 hours ahead and keep it chilled, but this is a pastry that should be enjoyed the day it is made.

FOR THE CARAMELIZED ALMONDS

- 3 tablespoons sugar
- 2 tablespoons water
- ½ cup blanched almonds, at room temperature

FOR THE RING

- 1 recipe Cream Puff Dough (page 502), still warm
  About ½ cup sliced almonds

- 1 recipe Vanilla Pastry Cream (page 505), chilled

  Confectioners' sugar, for dusting

TO MAKE THE CARAMELIZED ALMONDS: Line a baking sheet with a silicone baking mat or parchment paper. Put the sugar and water in a small saucepan, preferably nonstick, over medium-high heat and cook to dissolve the sugar. Swirl the pan to make sure that all the sugar is dissolved, then bring the mixture to a boil and cook until the sugar is a medium caramel color. Add the nuts and, using a wooden spoon or spatula, stir without stopping until the sugar turns a dark caramel color and coats the nuts. Turn the nuts out onto the baking sheet, spreading them out as best you can, and allow them to cool to room temperature.

When the nuts are completely cool, put them in a food processor and pulse until they are very finely chopped. Keep the nuts in a cool, dry place — *not* the refrigerator — until needed (or for up to several days).

When you are ready to fill the Paris-Brest, whisk the pastry cream to loosen it, then stir in the caramelized almonds.

TO MAKE THE RING: Center a rack in the oven and preheat the oven to 425 degrees F. Draw an 8-inch circle on a piece of parchment paper, turn the paper over, and use it to line a baking sheet. Fit a large pastry bag with a large (⅔-inch-diameter) plain or star tip.

Spoon the warm dough into the pastry bag and, keeping the tip 1 to 2 inches above the circle's outline, pipe a ring of dough about 1 inch thick. Pipe a second ring of dough inside the first ring and just touching it (the rings will merge when you bake them, and that's just what you want). Pipe a third ring of dough on top of the first two rings, piping along the seam where the bottom circles meet. (If you have any extra dough, pipe out as many cream puffs as you can — they'll be the baker's treat.) Sprinkle the top of the ring with the sliced almonds and slide the baking sheet into the oven.

Bake for 15 minutes, then reduce the oven temperature to 375 degrees F and bake the ring for another 20 to 25 minutes, until it is puffed, brown, and firm (total baking time is 35 to 40 minutes — although the puffs might be done sooner). Transfer the ring to a cooling rack and allow it to cool to room temperature.

TO CONSTRUCT THE PARIS-BREST: Using a serrated knife and a very gentle sawing motion, slice off the top third of the cream-puff ring in one piece (you'll see the seam that forms a natural guide for cutting). Put the base on a cake dish and, if there's some soft dough in the base, gently pull it out with your fingers (discard or munch). Spoon the pastry cream into the base, then settle the top of the Paris-Brest in place. Refrigerate for at least 1 hour (or up to 8 hours) before serving.

At serving time, dust the top of the Paris-Brest generously with confectioners' sugar.

peach melba

NELLIE MELBA, AN OPERA SINGER in the late nineteenth century, must have been quite a woman. Not only is Melba toast named for her, but peach Melba too. Both the dry toast and the beloved ice cream sundae were created by Auguste Escoffier, one of France's best-known chefs (and the man credited with codifying all of *la cuisine française*), when he was directing the vast kitchens of the Savoy Hotel in London. The cultured chef had heard Melba perform at Covent Gardens, and learning that she had a fondness for ice cream, he created the sundae, taking care to arrange it so that it wouldn't be frightfully cold, a hazard to her vocal cords. Given her fear of chill, it's not certain that Melba got to enjoy the dessert, but there's nothing to stop us from the pleasure that comes from working your long spoon down to the bottom of the glass and bringing it up with a little of the sundae's vanilla ice cream, raspberry sauce, poached peaches, and toasted almonds.

MAKES 4 SERVINGS

SERVING
Peach Melba is an elegant dessert alone, but I like to have something a little crunchy to go with it, so I often put out a plate of Almond-Orange Tuiles (page 404) or Croquants (page 410).

STORING
You can poach the peaches and make the raspberry sauce up to 3 days ahead and keep them covered in the refrigerator, but you've got to dig into the assembled treat as soon as you top it with the last berry.

BONNE IDÉE
Raspberry-Cassis Ice Cream. On its own, this is a lovely ice cream with deep fruit flavor, but in Peach Melba, it becomes sublime. Follow the instructions for making Vanilla Ice Cream (page 511) up to the point where you cool the custard. Defrost and drain one 12-ounce bag frozen red raspberries (unsweetened and not in syrup) and put the berries, 2 tablespoons sugar, and 2½ tablespoons crème de cassis into a blender (first choice) or a food processor. Let everything sit for 10 minutes, then whir to puree the berries; strain and discard the seeds. Stir the puree into the vanilla ice cream base and churn following your ice cream maker's instructions. Freeze until scoopable, and use in the Peach Melba or serve with anything chocolate.

FOR THE PEACHES

- 4 ripe but firm peaches
- 2 cups water
- ¾ cup sugar (you can add up to ¼ cup more sugar if your peaches aren't super-sweet)
- 10 fresh lemon verbena leaves (optional)
- 3 fat strips lemon zest (removed with a vegetable peeler)
- ½ vanilla bean, split and scraped (see box, page 396), or ½ teaspoon pure vanilla extract
- 2 tablespoons crème de cassis, crème de framboise, or Chambord
- Fresh lemon juice to taste

FOR THE RASPBERRY SAUCE

- ½ pint raspberries

FOR SERVING

- Vanilla ice cream, homemade (page 511) or store-bought
- Lightly sweetened lightly whipped cream
- Raspberries (optional)
- Toasted sliced or slivered almonds (optional)

TO POACH THE PEACHES: Bring a 2- to 3-quart saucepan of water to a boil. Drop in the peaches and count to 20, then, using a slotted spoon, transfer them gently to a bowl. When they're cool enough to handle, slip off the skins. If some of the skin just won't come off, use a vegetable peeler or paring knife.

Empty the pan, add the water and sugar, and bring to a boil, stirring until the sugar dissolves. Add the lemon verbena (if you're using it), the lemon zest, and vanilla bean and seeds. (If you're using vanilla extract, you'll add it later.) Bring back to a boil, then lower the heat and simmer for 5 minutes. Drop in the peaches and poach them gently for 10 minutes. (If there isn't enough liquid to immerse the peaches, cover the pan and turn the peaches frequently.)

Carefully transfer the peaches (not the syrup) to a container or bowl that will hold them and the liquid. Stir the vanilla extract, if you're using it, and the

liqueur into the syrup. Taste and add a little lemon juice, if needed, then pour the syrup over the peaches and allow the peaches to cool in the syrup. *(The peaches can be refrigerated, covered and immersed in the syrup, for up to 3 days.)*

TO MAKE THE RASPBERRY SAUCE: Puree the berries in a blender or food processor. You can leave the sauce as is, with the seeds, or strain it. Add 1 tablespoon — more if you'd like — of the peach syrup, then cover and chill until needed. *(The sauce can be refrigerated for up to 3 days.)*

When ready to serve, cut the peaches in half and pit them. For each sundae, pour a spoonful of the poaching syrup into the bottom of a parfait glass or wineglass. Top with half of a peach, a scoop of ice cream, and then the other peach half. Spoon over some raspberry sauce and top with lightly whipped cream and, if you'd like, some raspberries and/or toasted almonds. Serve immediately.

olive oil ice cream

CAN REMEMBER EXACTLY WHEN I FIRST had olive oil ice cream — it was in 1997 at the small husband-and-wife Parisian bistro L'Avant-Goût. The whole dessert was winning: a warm individual apple tart made with crisp pastry, a scoop of the ice cream, and a smattering of caramelized black olives. It was startling, memorable, and worth learning to do at home.

The ice cream is made just as you would a custard-based vanilla ice cream, but you replace some of the cream with a fruity olive oil. You want an oil with flavor, but not one with a peppery finish, so taste before you pour.

BE PREPARED: The ice cream must be frozen for at least 2 hours.

2 cups whole milk	Pinch of salt, preferably fleur
1 cup heavy cream	de sel
5 large egg yolks	½ cup fruity extra-virgin olive oil
½ cup sugar	2 teaspoons pure vanilla extract

Have a heatproof bowl with a strainer set over it ready for the cooked custard.

Bring the milk and cream to a boil in a large heavy-bottomed saucepan.

Meanwhile, in a large bowl, whisk the yolks and sugar together until very well blended and just slightly thickened. Whisking without stop, drizzle in about one third of the hot liquid — adding it slowly will temper the eggs and keep them from cooking. Once the eggs are acclimatized to the heat, you can whisk in the remaining liquid a little more quickly. Add the salt and pour the custard back into the pan.

Cook the custard over medium heat, stirring constantly with a wooden spoon or silicone spatula and making sure to get into the edges of the pan, until the custard thickens slightly and coats the back of the spoon; if you run your finger down the bowl of the spoon, the custard should not run into the track. The custard should reach at least 170 degrees F, but no more than 180 degrees F, on an instant-read thermometer.

Immediately remove the pan from the heat and pour the custard through the strainer into the bowl; discard whatever remains in the strainer. Add the olive oil and whisk energetically; stir in the vanilla extract.

The custard needs to chill before you churn it, and while you can put it directly into the fridge, the quickest and easiest way to bring down the temperature is to set the bowl into a larger bowl filled with ice cubes and cold water and stir the custard from time to time as it cools. It's ready to use when it's cold.

Scrape the chilled custard into the bowl of an ice cream maker and churn according to the manufacturer's instructions. Pack the ice cream into a container and freeze for at least 2 hours, or until it is firm enough to scoop.

MAKES ABOUT
1 QUART

SERVING
If the ice cream is very firm, allow it to sit on the counter for a few minutes before scooping. I like to serve it with Crispy, Crackly Apple-Almond Tart (page 458), which is very much in the style of L'Avant-Goût's tart (or see Bonne Idée, page 459, for a version of its tart). The ice cream is also extremely good with Sablé Breton Cookies (see Bonne Idée, page 465) or as part of an old-fashioned American hot fudge sundae (the ice cream is spectacularly good with chocolate). Or follow the lead of trendy chefs in Paris these days and serve it with just a drizzle of olive oil and a few grains of fleur de sel or flaky Maldon sea salt.

STORING
Packed tightly in a covered container, the ice cream will keep in the freezer for about 2 weeks.

fundamentals
and flourishes

BUBBLE-TOP BRIOCHES (PAGE 496)

fundamentals
and flourishes

everyday vinaigrette

MAKES ABOUT
¼ CUP

SERVING
Although vinaigrette with
salad is the classic match,
you can also think of it as
a sauce (and, in fact, the
French refer to a vinaigrette
as a sauce) — a pick-me-
up for warm steamed
vegetables or simply
cooked fish.

STORING
Kept in a tightly closed
jar, the vinaigrette can be
stored in the refrigerator
for at least a week; shake
before serving.

AT ITS CORE, VINAIGRETTE, the basic salad dressing of France and so many other countries, is nothing more than oil and vinegar. But how much of each? And what kind? And should there be a soupçon of mustard as well? These are the questions that used to encourage partisanship and create the great salad divide. But nowadays, in the age of liberated cuisine, vinaigrette is a season-to-taste affair, with each salad maker free to play with the proportions.

Whatever you decide, always use the best-quality oils and vinegars and always match the acidity of the vinaigrette to the type of greens you're dressing. When you've got fragile greens, you might even want to use milder lemon juice in place of the vinegar, or forgo the vinegar completely and just drizzle them with oil, since vinegar is not only a strong flavor but a powerful wilter. And no matter how you prepare the vinaigrette, always toss it with your greens at the very last minute. If you want to get everything together ahead of time, you can prepare the vinaigrette in the salad bowl, top it with the salad, and toss everything together when you get to the table.

Vinaigrettes can be mixed with a fork or a whisk, shaken in a jar (my preferred method), or whirred together in a blender or food processor. If you're mixing by hand, mix the vinegar, salt, and pepper together first (if you're using mustard, it goes in with this combo), so that the vinegar can dissolve the salt, then add the oil little by little, mixing all the while. If you don't add garlic or shallots or fresh herbs to the vinaigrette, you can make a large quantity (it multiplies almost ad infinitum) and keep it tightly covered in the refrigerator for a week or more — just shake before serving.

Unless you add a spot of mustard to a vinaigrette, you're likely to have a vinaigrette that separates — it's that old thing of oil and water, it's only natural, and there are a lot of chefs these days who think a broken vinaigrette is appealing. If it disturbs you, try adding just the teensiest drop of hot water to the vinaigrette to bring it together.

1 tablespoon wine vinegar (red or white)	3 tablespoons extra-virgin olive oil
¼ teaspoon Dijon mustard, or more to taste (optional)	Salt and freshly ground pepper

Put all the ingredients in a small jar, cover, and shake vigorously until blended.

lemon vinaigrette

Omit the vinegar and mustard and use 1½ to 2 tablespoons fresh lemon juice. You can also use other citrus juice — just adjust the quantity of oil as you go.

garlic or shallot vinaigrette

Add a finely minced small garlic clove or a spoonful of rinsed minced shallot to the dressing — you can let the garlic or shallot rest in the vinaigrette for about 1 hour to intensify the flavor, but you shouldn't store this dressing for more than a day in the refrigerator, or the flavor will be too strong and the dressing may taste off. For a milder flavor, steep for about 15 minutes, then strain.

herb vinaigrette

Add finely chopped fresh herbs to the vinaigrette at the last minute or add a pinch of dried herbs — I like herbes de Provence in dressings — and give them a little time to meld with the dressing.

nut oil vinaigrette

Replace 1 to 2 tablespoons of the olive oil with walnut or hazelnut oil, and choose a mild vinegar, such as sherry or Champagne. I think vinaigrettes made with nut oils are nice with a dab of mustard and very good when a rinsed minced shallot is added too.

tapenade vinaigrette

THIS VINAIGRETTE IS GOOD over salad greens, steamed vegetables (particularly cauliflower and potatoes), poached fish, and eggs.

1 tablespoon tapenade, home-made (page 487) or store-bought
1 tablespoon sherry vinegar
Pinch of minced garlic (optional)
Pinch of grated lemon zest
Salt and freshly ground pepper
¼ cup extra-virgin olive oil

MAKES ABOUT ⅓ CUP

STORING
Kept refrigerated, the vinaigrette will hold for about 1 week. Bring it to room temperature and whisk before using.

Whisk together the tapenade, vinegar, garlic (if you're using it), and lemon zest in a bowl. Season sparingly with salt and moderately with pepper, then whisk in the olive oil. This is not the kind of vinaigrette that will blend and hold together, but do whisk it before serving. Alternatively, you can make the vinaigrette in a mini processor or a blender.

anchoiade

MAKES ABOUT
½ CUP

SERVING
Shake the sauce in a covered jar or beat it with a fork before using — it has a tendency to separate. If you're serving the sauce over cooked vegetables or fish, you can warm it very gently in a saucepan over low heat or in a microwave oven.

STORING
Stored in a covered jar, the sauce will keep in the refrigerator for up to 1 week.

ANCHOIADE IS A PROVENÇAL SAUCE made from anchovies, garlic, a splash of vinegar, and olive oil. It's by no means a wallflower sauce, and it almost goes without saying, it's not a sauce for anyone who's on the fence about anchovies. It is, however, a sauce that can sharpen the flavor profile of just about any raw vegetable, many steamed vegetables (it's particularly good with potatoes and cauliflower), just as many mild fish (try it with cod), and every salad green. It's also good with hard-boiled eggs. Use it as a drizzle, the way you would balsamic vinegar, a dressing, or a dip.

If you've got a mortar and pestle, make your anchoiade with it; grinding is a good way to get the best texture from the anchovies.

1 2-ounce tin anchovies packed in olive oil (about 8 fillets), drained
1–2 small garlic cloves, split and germ removed

½ cup olive oil
1 teaspoon red wine vinegar
Salt (yes, even with anchovies) and freshly ground pepper

IF USING A FOOD PROCESSOR OR BLENDER: Chop or mash the anchovies before putting them in the work bowl. Add the garlic and a little of the olive oil and process to blend. Add the wine vinegar, pulse, and then, with the machine running, gradually add the remaining olive oil, processing until the sauce is smooth. Season to taste with salt and pepper.

IF USING A MORTAR AND PESTLE: Put the anchovies in the mortar and grind them to a paste with the pestle, moistening them with a little olive oil if needed to keep things moving. Add the garlic and a little more oil and grind until the garlic is reduced to a paste. Stir in the wine vinegar, then gradually add the remaining olive oil, working it into the anchoiade with the pestle. Season to taste with salt and pepper.

black olive tapenade

MAKES A
GENEROUS
⅓ CUP

FRANCE DOESN'T HAVE A LOCK ON TAPENADE, the chunky olive spread, but it's a staple in many French homes, particularly those in Provence and the Côte d'Azur, where olive trees are abundant and their fruit is a part of so many dishes. I call tapenade a spread, but while it's spreadable, it's probably more correctly dubbed a condiment, since you use it to enliven at least 101 things, from pasta, hard-boiled eggs, tomatoes, and cheese (look at the recipe for tomato tartlets with mozzarella or goat cheese, page 164) to salads (Niçoise, of course, page 125), salmon (you can stuff the salmon with tapenade; see page 299), and chicken — a little tapenade smoothed under the skin provides a lot of pizzazz (page 202).

Since fine-quality tapenade is available all over France — you can find it at the Gallic equivalent of the corner deli — few French cooks ever make it themselves. Fortunately for those of us who love it, it's fast and easy enough to make at home with a food processor or blender. This is a basic recipe, one that can be multiplied if you'd like more and one that can be personalized (see Bonne Idée).

SERVING
Use the tapenade as a spread on crackers to go with cocktails or as a condiment, adding a little spoonful whenever you want to give a dish an interesting — and salty — edge.

STORING
Kept in a well-sealed jar, the tapenade will hold in the refrigerator for at least 1 week.

¼ pound pitted oil-cured black olives (about ½ cup), chopped	Pinch of thyme (fresh or dried)
1 anchovy, drained	Pinch of piment d'Espelette (see Sources) or cayenne, or to taste
Grated zest and juice of ¼ lemon	About 1 tablespoon extra-virgin olive oil
Pinch of rosemary (fresh or dried)	

Put all of the ingredients in a food processor (a mini is good here) or blender and process, scraping down the sides of the bowl as needed, until the olives are pureed. It's up to you how smooth or chunky you want to make the puree. Check the consistency, and if you'd like it a little thinner, add more oil drop by drop. Taste and add more herbs, hot pepper, or lemon juice, if you want them.

BONNE IDÉE
If you'd like the tapenade to be a bit saltier, add some capers — rinse and pat them dry before tossing them into the processor. You can replace the black olives with green, and you can also make a tapenade by replacing half the olives with sun-dried tomatoes. Actually, you can replace all the olives with tomatoes — what you get won't truly be tapenade, but it is good. You can also swap orange zest for the lemon (but not orange juice), or use a combination of orange and lemon zest. If you like tapenade, I'm sure that you can find many ways to make your own house blend.

basil pesto

MAKES ABOUT
1 CUP

SERVING
Pesto can be a pasta sauce (thin it with a splash of the pasta cooking water); it can be served over tomatoes and/or mozzarella cheese (or, if you'd like, you can stir a little into a vinaigrette and then drizzle it over a salad); and it can be flavoring for a soup (for maximum effect, add the pesto at the table so each person can enjoy that first whiff of garlic and basil).

STORING
If you pack the pesto tightly into a jar and pour a thin film of olive oil over the top to keep it from darkening, it can be refrigerated for up to 3 days. Stir before using. You can also freeze it for up to 2 months, though it will blacken. Thaw overnight in the refrigerator and stir before using.

BONNE IDÉE
Herb Coulis. An herb coulis is lighter than a pesto and purer in flavor, so it's nice swirled into pureed soups or drizzled over steamed vegetables or simply cooked chicken, fish, or beef. Figure on 2 cups fresh herb leaves and ½ cup extra-virgin olive oil, and make the coulis as you would pesto. You can use any herb — think cilantro, parsley, arugula (not an herb, but . . .), basil, or dill. Depending on what you'll be serving it with, you might add a little grated lemon or orange zest to the mix at the end.

DEPENDING ON WHERE YOU ARE IN FRANCE, you might see either pesto or *pistou* (very Provençal) on the menu, but no matter the name, the ingredients will be the same: basil, garlic, pine nuts, Parmesan, and olive oil.

As with vinaigrette and other simple sauces, you can have a basic recipe, but what you really need is a willingness to make adjustments so you get the blend you like best.

1–2 garlic cloves (to taste), split, germ removed, and crushed	Salt
	About ½ cup extra-virgin olive oil
2 tablespoons pine nuts	½ cup freshly grated Parmesan
2 cups lightly packed fresh basil leaves	Freshly ground pepper

The best and most authentic way to make pesto is with a mortar and pestle, but you can also make it in a blender or food processor. Start by pounding or whirring the garlic, nuts, and basil leaves with a little salt and a drizzle of oil, just to get things moving. Slowly add up to ½ cup more oil, stirring with the pestle or whirring until it is as thin as you'd like it to be. Stir or pulse in the cheese, taste, and season with salt and pepper.

mango chatini

THINK OF A CHATINI AS A SALSA or a chutney, a zesty little something that's eaten over or alongside something else. Part of the cuisine of the island of Mauritius, which was once French, chatini is spicier than traditional French food and nice to have with curries or over rice. This tropical chatini, a mix of mango, ginger, and onion, is both cool and hot and is particularly good with Cardamom Rice Pilaf (page 382), Olive-Olive Cornish Hens (page 225), or even the already spicy Spice-Crusted Tuna (page 304).

Juice of 1 lime
1   teaspoon grated fresh ginger, or to taste
1   large ripe but firm mango, peeled, pitted, and finely diced
1   spring onion, trimmed, quartered lengthwise, and thinly sliced, or 2–3 scallions, white and light green parts only, thinly sliced

2   teaspoons finely chopped fresh cilantro
    Salt and freshly ground pepper
    Pinch of piment d'Espelette (see Sources) or cayenne (optional)

Stir the lime juice and ginger together in a small serving bowl. Add the mango, onion, and cilantro and season with salt, pepper, and, if you'd like, a pinch of piment d'Espelette or cayenne.

MAKES ABOUT
2 CUPS

SERVING
I treat chatini as a condiment, like mustard, and bring it to the table so my guests can take as much or as little as they want.

STORING
If you don't add the lime juice and cilantro, you can mix the ingredients together, cover the bowl, and either leave it at room temperature or chill it for a couple of hours. When ready to serve, add the lime juice and cilantro — it's always best to add lime juice just before serving, since the acid in the juice will "cook" tender fruits and herbs.

mayonnaise

SERVING
Use your luxurious
homemade mayonnaise
just as you would mayo
from a jar, but put it in a
prettier dish — it deserves
a little special treatment.

STORING
The basic mayonnaise will
keep for a day or two, but
anything made with fresh
garlic is best used the day it
is made.

BONNE IDÉES
Because its flavor is so pure
and basic, mayonnaise
lends itself to variation. You
can add herbs or spices,
capers or cornichons, chile
peppers (I love adding
a bit of canned chipotle
chile and its adobo), or
even ketchup, for a great
Russian dressing. To get
you started, here are a few
French classics.

Aïoli (Garlic Mayonnaise).
Peel, split, and remove
the germ from 1 to 6 garlic
cloves. Crush and very
finely mince the garlic, or
push it through a press.
Add the mashed garlic to
the yolk, and carry on. The
best and most authentic
way to make aïoli, though,
is with a mortar and pestle:
Crush the garlic with some
salt in the mortar, then
add the yolk and continue.
Because aïoli is from the
South of France — it's
most prized in Provence
— olive oil, a staple of
the region, should be
your oil of choice for this
mayonnaise.

I MAY SHOCK YOU WHEN I SAY that bottled mayonnaise is as popular in France as it is here. And while some of my French foodie friends think it's chic to search out Hellmann's mayonnaise at the specialty boutiques in Paris, I'm always looking for the French brands, which seem to be eggier and closer to real mayonnaise. I reach for the bottled stuff all the time, but when the mayonnaise is going to matter — for instance, when you're using it as a dip for shrimp, making a lobster salad, or serving it with cold asparagus — making your own matters. Happily, preparing mayonnaise is easy, quick (about 10 minutes, start to finish), and rewarding: making an emulsion, which is what mayonnaise is, is akin to alchemy.

You can use any kind of oil you'd like. Many cooks suggest a neutral oil, like grapeseed or canola, thinking that olive oil is too flavorful for mayonnaise, but I like to use a combination of olive and peanut. Whatever you choose, you must have some kind of acid, such as lemon juice or vinegar, or a splash of both.

You can make mayonnaise by hand with a whisk or in a blender or food processor, but no matter how you mix it (or mount it, as the French say for sauces that are made by slowly adding oil or butter), you should have your egg yolk at room temperature, ditto your oil, and you should add the oil literally drop by drop until about half of it is in and you can see that you've got a nice emulsion. After that, slow and steady are the bywords.

If you make this recipe with ½ cup oil, you'll have a very thick, flavorful mayonnaise. Taste it and decide what you want to do — you can add up to about ½ cup more oil without compromising the mix.

1 large egg yolk, preferably organic, at room temperature	Salt
About 2 teaspoons fresh lemon juice or wine vinegar, or a combination	½–1 cup oil, mild (such as grapeseed or canola) or more flavorful (such as peanut, corn, or olive), or a combination
¼ teaspoon Dijon mustard, or more to taste	Freshly ground pepper

Put the yolk, 2 teaspoons lemon juice and/or vinegar, and the mustard in a bowl (or a blender or food processor), add some salt, and whisk (or whir) to blend. Drop by drop — really — start adding the oil, whisking (or whirring) all the while. When you've got about ¼ cup oil beaten in and the mix is starting to look like mayonnaise (this usually takes 4 minutes or so), you can add the remaining oil more steadily, but still slowly. Use at least ½ cup oil, and up to about 1 cup, adding as much as you need to get the consistency you want. Taste and add pepper and more salt, if you'd like. If you'd like it a little more piquant, add a smidge more mustard or a few more drops of lemon juice or vinegar.

Roasted Garlic Mayonnaise. Instead of pungent fresh garlic, use a few cloves of soft, sweet roasted garlic.

Rouille. There are many recipes for rouille, some calling for a bit of boiled potato to be beaten into the mayonnaise (this is also sometimes done for aïoli), others calling for roasted red pepper. What is important in a rouille is the garlic flavor and the color, which should be rust, or *rouille*. For a simple, flavorful rouille, make aïoli and whisk in a pinch of saffron threads and, if you'd like, some red pepper flakes or a little minced roasted red pepper.

crème fraîche

C RÈME FRAÎCHE IS LIKE OUR SOUR CREAM, but a bit more versatile, since it can be heated without separating and can also be whipped, like heavy cream. While you can now find crème fraîche in many American markets, it's not always available, so it's nice to know you can make it yourself.

BE PREPARED: You'll need 2 days to turn regular cream into crème fraîche.

MAKES

1 CUP

STORING
You can keep crème fraîche in the refrigerator for about 2 weeks, but know that the longer you keep it, the tangier it becomes.

1 cup heavy cream
1 tablespoon buttermilk or
   plain yogurt

Put the cream and buttermilk or yogurt in a clean jar with a tight-fitting lid, cover the jar, and shake vigorously for a minute or so. Put the jar on the counter and leave it for 12 to 24 hours, or until the cream thickens slightly. How long this will take depends on how warm your room is — the warmer the room, the quicker the thickening.

When the cream is thick, transfer the jar to the refrigerator and let it chill for 1 day before you dip into it.

poached eggs

SERVING

If your eggs are ragged around the edges, you can use scissors to trim them before serving. Poached eggs are excellent over salads, vegetables (they're great with the Warm-Weather Vegetable Pot-au-Feu, page 378), or soups.

STORING

After you've cooled poached eggs in an ice-water bath, you can store them immersed in cold water in the refrigerator for up to 2 days. Reheat in boiling water before serving, as described in the recipe.

POACHED EGGS ARE BOTH ELEGANT AND EASY. And, as much as they seem like something that must be done at the very last minute — how else can the yolks be so lusciously runny? — that's not the case at all: you can poach the eggs up to a couple of days ahead and reheat them right before serving.

Distilled white vinegar
Very fresh large eggs,
 preferably organic

Have a large bowl of cold water and ice cubes near the stove if you won't be serving the eggs immediately or a bowl of hot water if you'll be cooking more than 3 eggs and will need to hold the first round of eggs for a short time while you finish the batch. Also have a perforated skimmer, a flexible fish turner, or a large slotted spatula at hand.

Fill a large skillet with about 2 inches of water and bring to a boil. Add 1 teaspoon vinegar — this helps the whites congeal — and lower the heat so the water barely simmers.

Break an egg into a cup or ramekin. If you'd like perfectly round poached eggs, you can use egg rings or poached-egg spoons (perforated gadgets that hold the eggs in shape), or you can place a pancake ring, the ring of a canning jar, or a tuna can (remove both ends and wash well) in the skillet and tip the egg into the ring. Hold the cup as close to the surface of the water as you can and tip the egg into the skillet. Immediately set the timer for 3 minutes. If you're making more than 1 egg, add the other eggs to the skillet one at a time, but take care not to crowd the pan — I usually make no more than 3 eggs at a time. If you're not using rings, don't be concerned if the whites feather out in all directions — you can trim them later. If the yolks are popping up above the surface of the water, baste them a couple of times.

After 3 minutes, the whites should be set and the yolks only barely firm to the touch. Should you want the eggs slightly more cooked, leave them in the water for another 30 to 60 seconds. Using the skimmer or spatula, carefully lift the eggs out of the skillet in the order you added them. If you're holding the eggs only while you poach some more, drop them into the hot water. When you're ready for them, lift them out with the skimmer or spatula and pat the bottom of the skimmer and the top of the eggs with a paper towel to remove the excess water. If you want to hold the eggs for longer, drop them into the ice-water bath. (The eggs can be stored in cold water in the fridge for up to 2 days.) To reheat the eggs, drain them, fill the bowl with boiling water, and slip in the eggs. Warm the eggs in the water for 1 to 2 minutes, or until heated through. Drain and serve immediately.

ruffly poached eggs

THIS SURPRISING TECHNIQUE FOR POACHING EGGS came to me from Braden Perkins of Hidden Kitchen, a supper club in Paris. This is the simplest way I know to get the kind of eggs you see served over salads; warm asparagus, leeks, or broccoli; pureed vegetables; or mashed potatoes: the kind with whites that are softly set and yolks that are almost firm on the outside and runny at the center. The bonus is that because they are cooked in a bundle of plastic wrap tied at the top with twine, they emerge from their poach with ruffles and pleats around the edges where the plastic was drawn tight. They're beautiful, and their little ridges are just the right conduits for sauce — pour any sauce or vinaigrette over the eggs, and it will drizzle most attractively down the ruffle lines.

With this recipe, you can make 1 egg or many — just make sure to use a large pan so the eggs can bob around freely. Until you get a feel for how quickly the eggs cook, I suggest you make no more than 4 at a time.

Olive oil
Very fresh large eggs,
  preferably organic

Put a large saucepan of water on to boil, and have a teacup and some kitchen string at hand.

For each egg, cut two pieces of plastic wrap, each large enough to wrap generously around the egg, and put one piece on top of the other. Very lightly coat the top piece of plastic with oil, then fit the double layer of wrap into the teacup. Gently crack an egg and tip it into the cup, taking care not to break the yolk. Draw up the edges of the plastic, getting as close as you can to the top of the egg, and twist to tighten the plastic. Tie a piece of string around the neck of the plastic to secure it.

Lower the heat under the saucepan, and when the water is at a very slight simmer, drop in the eggs. Don't worry — the plastic won't melt. Allow the eggs to poach for 5 to 6 minutes, then carefully lift them out of the water with a slotted spoon. If the whites don't look set, poach for a few seconds longer. The easiest way to unpack the eggs is to put them on a flat surface, snip the plastic below the string, and open the plastic. Gently lift each egg from the plastic to a plate, trying not to turn it over. (It's not a problem if it's upside down, it's just that the ruffles are prettier on the top.) Serve immediately.

SERVING
The eggs can be used in the same way you'd use any poached eggs. Fine by themselves with a strip of buttered toast, they really come into their own served over warm vegetables or salads.

STORING
The eggs can be wrapped in the plastic and kept in the refrigerator for a few hours before you poach them, but once poached, they should be served immediately.

brioche dough

MAKES ENOUGH
DOUGH FOR
12 BUBBLE-TOP
BRIOCHES OR
2 BRIOCHE LOAVES

STORING
You can cover the dough
tightly with plastic
wrap and keep it in the
refrigerator for up to 3 days,
or you can wrap it airtight
and freeze it for up to
2 months. Allow the dough
to thaw overnight in the
refrigerator before using it.

I'VE NEVER MET A FRENCH PERSON who's made brioche at home. In fact, my guess is that were I to confront the most enthusiastic French home baker I could find with the question, "Do you make brioche?" the answer would be, "No, why should I?" Why, indeed, when great brioches are available at every boulangerie and passable brioches can be found in the supermarket? The truth is, as much as I love making brioche — I'm over-the-top proud of myself every time I pull a brioche from the oven — I've never made one in France, and if I lived there full-time, my brioche-baking skills would probably get very rusty very fast.

Brioche is an egg bread, like challah, but richer. It has a slightly sweet, definitely buttery flavor, and while it's a soft bread, its crumb's got a little stretch to it — pull a bit of the bread, and it will elongate elegantly. Actually, elegant is probably the best all-around descriptor for brioche, which can be made as individual breads or family-sized loaves.

For those of us in the United States who can't find a great brioche on every corner but love the bread and the dishes that can be made with it (Bubble-Top Brioches, page 496, brioche loaves, page 497, Coupétade, page 419, and French toast, page 418, for starters), there's only one thing to do — take to our ovens.

Nothing's difficult about making brioche if you have a stand mixer, patience, and time. You could make the dough by hand — it's the way it was done for centuries, after all — but it's a workout. What you can't do is rush the rising.

BE PREPARED: Please don't skip the overnight rest — it's what gives the brioche its lovely texture.

¼	cup warm-to-the-touch whole milk	1½	teaspoons salt
¼	cup warm-to-the-touch water	3	large eggs, at room temperature, lightly beaten
3	tablespoons sugar		
4	teaspoons active dry yeast	12	tablespoons (1½ sticks) unsalted butter, at room temperature
2¾	cups all-purpose flour		

Pour the warm milk and water into the bowl of a stand mixer, add a pinch of the sugar, and sprinkle over the yeast. In another bowl, mix the flour and salt together.

When all the yeast has absorbed some liquid, stir with a wooden spoon or spatula until you have a creamy mixture. Fit the mixer with the dough hook, add all of the flour mixture at once, and turn the mixer on and off in a few short pulses to dampen the flour. Set the mixer to medium-low speed and mix for a minute or two, scraping the sides and bottom of the bowl as needed, until you have a shaggy, fairly dry mass. At this point, what you've got won't look like a dough at all — in fact, it will be pretty ugly, but that doesn't matter.

Scrape down the bowl, turn the mixer to low, and add the beaten eggs one third at a time, beating until each addition is incorporated before adding the next. Beat in the remaining sugar, increase the mixer speed to medium, and beat for about 3 minutes, until the dough starts to come together.

Reduce the mixer speed to low and add the butter in 2-tablespoon chunks. I like to squeeze the butter between my fingers to soften it even more just before I toss it into the bowl. Beat for about 30 seconds, or until each piece of butter is on its way to being almost incorporated, before adding the next little chunk of butter. When all the butter is in, you'll have a dough that is very soft, really almost like a batter. Increase the mixer speed to medium-high and beat until the dough pulls away from the sides of the bowl and climbs up the hook, about 10 minutes, or a little longer.

Transfer the dough to a lightly buttered bowl, cover with plastic wrap, and leave it at room temperature until it's nearly doubled in size; it will take at least 1 hour, maybe longer, depending on the warmth of your room.

Deflate the dough by lifting it up around the edges and letting it fall with a slap. Cover the dough with plastic wrap and put it in the refrigerator until it stops rising as energetically, about 2 hours; "slap" it down every 30 minutes.

Press the plastic against the surface of the dough and leave it in the refrigerator to chill overnight. The dough is ready to use after its overnight rest.

bubble-top brioches

MAKES 12
BRIOCHES

SERVING
Brioches are best
eaten warm or at room
temperature, and they
are traditionally eaten at
breakfast. However, the
bread is also the carrier of
choice for smoked salmon
and is often served, cut
into dippers, or soldiers
(mouillettes), with soft-
boiled or coddled eggs.
When I've got brioche in
the house, I find lots of
ways to use it, including
in a starter of Creamy
Mushrooms and Eggs
(page 163). And when it's
stale, there's always pain
perdu, or French toast
(page 418).

STORING
Once baked, the brioches
are really best eaten quickly.
You can store the buns in
a covered container and
slice and toast them the
next day, but you'll lose
some of the texture's lovely
spring and stretch. At that
point, think French toast or
coupétade (page 419).

WHILE THE DOUGH FOR THESE SINGLE-SERVE BRIOCHES is classic, the shape is just a little different from the traditional topknot buns you find in French boulangeries and a lot easier to perfect. I created this almost-Parker-House form one day out of frustration when I'd made perfect brioche dough and what I'd thought were perfect topknot brioches. It looked like I'd done everything right. I glazed the buns and slid them into the oven. But as soon as they began to rise, the topknots tilted to the side like the beret on a cartoon character. The taste was great, and they even looked cute, but cute wasn't what I was after with this rather sophisticated dough, which was why I came up with the bubble brioche: three little balls of dough dropped into a mold or muffin tin. A cinch to do, they rise perfectly and bake into beauties.

If you'd rather have sliceable loaves, see Bonne Idée.

1 recipe Brioche Dough (page 494), chilled	1 large egg, lightly beaten with 1 teaspoon cold water, for glazing

If you're lucky enough to have a dozen individual fluted brioche molds, butter those; if not, butter a 12-cup muffin tin.

Divide the chilled dough into 12 portions. Cut each portion into 3 even pieces, and roll the pieces into balls. The dough is soft and sticky, so here's the easiest way to shape them: Put a little flour on the counter and put some flour on your palms. Put a piece of dough on the counter, cup a hand over it, and roll the dough around under your cupped palm until you've got a nice ball. Using 3 pieces for each brioche, put the balls, prettiest sides up, in the molds or muffin cups.

Place a piece of wax paper on top of the brioches and put the molds or pan in a warm place. Let the brioches rise until they almost fill the cups, 1 to 2 hours, depending on the warmth of the room.

Just before the dough is fully risen, center a rack in the oven and preheat the oven to 400 degrees F.

When the brioches have risen, remove the paper and put the molds or muffin tin on a baking sheet. Brush the bubble tops with the egg glaze — if you've got a feather brush, this is the perfect time to use it. Be gentle, so you don't deflate the dough, and be careful, so you don't dribble glaze between the

BONNE IDÉE
Brioche Loaves. Divide the chilled dough in half. Cut each half into 4 pieces and roll each piece into a log about 3½ inches long. Butter and flour two 7½-x-3½-x-2-inch loaf pans (you can use larger pans, but the loaves won't be as high) and arrange 4 logs crosswise in each pan. Cover the pans lightly and leave them at room temperature until the dough almost fills the pans, 1 to 2 hours. When the loaves are almost risen, preheat the oven to 400 degrees F. Brush each loaf with egg wash (as in the recipe), put the pans on a baking sheet, and bake for 30 to 35 minutes, or until the loaves are nicely risen and beautifully golden. Cool on a rack for 15 minutes, then unmold the loaves and allow them to cool for at least 1 hour before slicing.

dough and the sides of the mold, which would keep the brioches from puffing properly.

Bake the brioches for 20 to 23 minutes, or until they are well risen and deeply golden. If you think they are browning too quickly, you can cover them with a foil tent. Transfer the molds or muffin tin to a cooling rack and let the brioches rest for 5 to 10 minutes before lifting them out of the molds and onto the cooling rack.

tart dough

MAKES ONE 9-
TO 9½-INCH
TART SHELL

STORING
Well wrapped, the
dough can be kept in the
refrigerator for up to 5 days
or frozen for up to 1 month.
Although the fully baked
crust can be wrapped
airtight and frozen for up
to 2 months, I prefer to
freeze the unbaked crust in
the pan and bake it directly
from the freezer — it has
a fresher flavor. Just add
about 5 minutes or so to
the baking time.

WHILE I USE THIS DOUGH FOR SAVORIES, it's really an all-purpose recipe that produces a not-too-rich, slightly crisp crust that is as happy holding pastry cream for a strawberry tart as it is encasing a creamy cheese filling for a quiche. This is a good dough to use anytime you see a recipe calling for *pâte brisée*.

BE PREPARED: The dough should chill for at least 3 hours.

1¼ cups all-purpose flour
1 teaspoon sugar
½ teaspoon salt
6 tablespoons (¾ stick) very
   cold (or frozen) unsalted
   butter, cut into bits

1 large egg
1 teaspoon ice water

TO MAKE THE DOUGH IN A FOOD PROCESSOR: Put the flour, sugar, and salt in the processor and whir a few times to blend. Scatter the bits of butter over the flour and pulse several times, until the butter is coarsely mixed into the flour. Beat the egg with the ice water and pour it into the bowl in 3 small additions, whirring after each one. (Don't overdo it — the dough shouldn't form a ball or ride on the blade.) You'll have a moist, malleable dough that will hold together when pinched. Turn the dough out onto a work surface, gather it into a ball (if the dough doesn't come together easily, push it, a few spoonfuls at a time, under the heel of your hand or knead it lightly), and flatten it into a disk.

TO MAKE THE DOUGH BY HAND: Put the flour, sugar, and salt in a large bowl. Drop in the bits of butter and, using your hands or a pastry blender, work the butter into the flour until it is evenly distributed. You'll have large and small butter bits, and that's fine — uniformity isn't a virtue here. Beat the egg and water together, drizzle over the dough, and, using a fork, toss the dough until it is evenly moistened. Reach into the bowl and, using your fingertips, mix and knead the dough until it comes together. Turn it out onto a work surface, gather it into a ball (if the dough doesn't come together easily, push it, a few spoonfuls at a time, under the heel of your hand or knead it some more), and flatten it into a disk.

Chill the dough for at least 3 hours. (*The dough can be refrigerated for up to 5 days.*)

When you're ready to make the tart shell, butter a 9- to 9½-inch fluted tart pan with a removable bottom (butter it even if it's nonstick).

TO ROLL OUT THE DOUGH: I like to roll out the dough between sheets of wax paper or plastic wrap or in a lightly floured rolling cover, but you can roll it out on a lightly floured work surface. If you're working between sheets of paper or plastic wrap, lift the paper or plastic often so that it doesn't roll into the dough, and turn the dough over frequently. If you're just rolling on the counter, make sure to lift and turn the dough and reflour the counter often. The rolled-out dough should be about ¼ inch thick and at least 12 inches in diameter.

Transfer the dough to the tart pan, easing it into the pan without stretching it. (What you stretch now will shrink in the oven later.) Press the dough against the bottom and up the sides of the pan. If you'd like to reinforce the sides of the crust, you can fold some of the excess dough over, so that you have a double thickness around the sides. Using the back of a table knife, trim the dough even with the top of the pan. Prick the base of the crust in several places with a fork.

Chill — or freeze — the dough for at least 1 hour before baking.

Center a rack in the oven and preheat the oven to 400 degrees F. Press a piece of buttered foil (or use nonstick foil) against the crust's surface. If you'd like, you can fill the covered crust with rice or dried beans (which will be inedible after this but can be used for baking for months to come) to keep the dough flat, but this isn't really necessary if the crust is well chilled. Line a baking sheet with a silicone baking mat or parchment paper and put the tart pan on the sheet.

TO PARTIALLY BAKE THE CRUST: Bake for 20 minutes, then very carefully remove the foil (with the rice or beans). Return the crust to the oven and bake for another 3 to 5 minutes, or until it is lightly golden. Transfer the baking sheet to a cooling rack and allow the crust to cool before you fill it.

TO FULLY BAKE THE CRUST: Bake for an additional 10 minutes, or until it is an even golden brown. Transfer the baking sheet to a cooling rack and allow the crust to cool before you fill it.

sweet tart dough

MAKES ONE 9-
TO 9½-INCH
TART SHELL

STORING
Well wrapped, the
dough can be kept in the
refrigerator for up to 5 days
or frozen for up to 1 month.
While the fully baked crust
can be wrapped airtight
and frozen for up to
2 months, I prefer to freeze
the unbaked crust in the
pan and bake it directly
from the freezer — it has
a fresher flavor. Just add
about 5 minutes or so to
the bake time.

CALLED *PÂTE SABLÉE*, THIS IS ESSENTIALLY a tender, very buttery sablé cookie dough rolled (or pressed) into a tart pan. Although you can fill the unbaked crust and bake both filling and crust together, I always prefer to partially bake the crust and then fill it — it helps prevent the soggy-bottom problem, and I think it accentuates the wonderful flavors of the dough.

1½ cups all-purpose flour	9 tablespoons very cold unsalted
½ cup confectioners' sugar	butter, cut into small pieces
¼ teaspoon salt	1 large egg yolk

Put the flour, confectioners' sugar, and salt in a food processor and pulse a couple of times to combine. Scatter the pieces of butter over the dry ingredients and pulse until the butter is cut in coarsely — you'll have some pieces the size of oatmeal flakes and some the size of peas, and that's just fine. Stir the yolk, just to break it up, and add it a little at a time, pulsing after each addition. When the egg is in, process in long pulses — about 10 seconds each — until the dough, which will look granular soon after the egg is added, forms clumps and curds. Just before you reach this clumpy stage, the sound of the machine working the dough will change — heads up.

Turn the dough out onto a work surface and very lightly knead it just to incorporate any dry ingredients that might have escaped mixing.

If you want to press the dough into a tart pan, now is the time to do it. If you want to roll it out, gather the dough into a ball, flatten it into a disk, wrap it well, and chill it for a couple of hours. *(The dough can be refrigerated for up to 5 days.)*

When you're ready to make the tart shell, butter a 9- to 9½-inch fluted tart pan with a removable bottom (butter the pan even if it's nonstick).

TO MAKE A PRESS-IN CRUST: Press the dough evenly over the bottom and up the sides of the tart pan. You probably won't use all the dough, but it's nice to make a thickish crust so you that you can really enjoy the texture. Press the crust in so that the pieces cling to one another and knit together when baked, but don't use a lot of force — working lightly will preserve the crust's shortbread-ish texture. Prick the crust all over and freeze for at least 30 minutes, preferably longer, before baking.

TO MAKE A ROLLED-OUT CRUST: I like to roll the dough between sheets of wax paper or plastic wrap. Remove the disk from the refrigerator and unwrap it. If it's too hard to roll easily without cracking, give it a few whacks with your rolling pin to get it moving. Roll the dough out evenly, turning it over frequently and lifting the wax paper or plastic often so that it doesn't roll into the dough and form creases. Roll the dough into a circle that's about ¼ inch thick and at least 12 inches in diameter. If the dough is very soft, slide the rolled-out circle onto a baking sheet and into the fridge to rest and firm for about 20 minutes. Fit the dough into the buttered tart pan. Using the back of a knife, trim the excess dough even with the top of the pan. Prick the crust all over and freeze for at least 30 minutes, preferably longer, before baking.

Center a rack in the oven and preheat the oven to 375 degrees F. Butter a piece of aluminum foil (or use nonstick foil) and press the foil snugly against the crust. If the crust is frozen, you can bake it as is; if not, fill it with dried beans or rice (which you can reuse for crusts but won't be able to cook after this).

TO PARTIALLY BAKE THE CRUST: Bake the crust for 25 minutes, then carefully remove the foil (and weights). If the crust has puffed, press it down gently with the back of a spoon. Return the tart to the oven and bake for another 3 to 5 minutes, or until lightly golden. Transfer the baking sheet to a cooling rack and allow the crust to cool before you fill it.

TO FULLY BAKE THE CRUST: Bake the crust for 25 minutes, then carefully remove the foil (and weights). If the crust has puffed, press it down gently with the back of a spoon, and bake the crust for another 8 minutes or so, or until it is firm and golden brown. (I dislike lightly baked crusts, so I often keep the crust in the oven just a little longer. If you do that, just make sure to keep a close eye on the crust's progress — it can go from golden to way-too-dark in a flash.) Transfer the baking sheet to a cooling rack and allow the crust to cool before you fill it.

BONNE IDÉE

Chocolate Shortbread Dough. Like the Sweet Tart Dough, this dough is a cookie dough literally pressed into service as a crust. It can be used anytime a chocolate flavor would be a treat, as in the Double Chocolate and Banana Tart (page 467). Use 1¼ cups all-purpose flour, ¼ cup unsweetened cocoa powder, ¼ cup confectioners' sugar, ¼ teaspoon salt, 9 tablespoons very cold unsalted butter, cut into small pieces, and 1 large egg yolk and follow the recipe directions.

cream puff dough

MAKES ABOUT
24 PUFFS

STORING
The best way to store
cream puffs is to shape
the dough and freeze the
mounds on the baking
sheets, and then, when
they're solid, pack them
airtight in plastic bags.
They can be frozen for up
to 2 months. Bake them
straight from the freezer
— no need to defrost,
just give them a minute
or two more in the oven.
Leftover puffs can be kept
overnight and reheated in a
350-degree-F oven, or they
can be frozen and reheated
before serving.

*P*ÂTE À *CHOUX* IS CREAM PUFF DOUGH or, in direct translation, cabbage dough — so called because someone must have thought that the resulting puffs resembled mini cabbages. Had I been in charge of naming the dough, I'd probably have tried to work the word *magical* into the moniker, because as the dough expands in the oven, it just about triples in size, turns a tempting shade of gold, and hollows, which is as close to magic as most of us get.

Since cream puff dough is truly neither sweet nor salty, it can be used for both sweets, like Profiteroles (see Bonne Idée, page 473), and savories, like Goat-Cheese Mini Puffs (page 7) and my all-time favorite hors d'oeuvre, the French cheese puffs known as Gougères (page 4). The dough can be spooned out small, so you've got bite-sized treats, or big, so that you can fill the puffs with enough salad to call it lunch or enough whipped cream and berries to call it a party.

The dough is the only one I can think of that is cooked and then baked: you make a cooked mixture of milk, butter, and flour before you add the eggs and bake it. It's easy to make the dough by hand and even easier to do it with a mixer; however, once it's made, it must be used immediately. But here's the good news: you can spoon the dough into puffs and then freeze the puffs; when you're ready for them, bake as many as you want straight from the freezer, no defrosting needed.

½ cup whole milk	½ teaspoon salt
½ cup water	1 cup all-purpose flour
8 tablespoons (1 stick) unsalted butter, cut into 4 pieces	4 large eggs, at room temperature
1 tablespoon sugar (if you're using the puffs for some thing sweet)	

Position the racks to divide the oven into thirds and preheat the oven to 425 degrees F. Line two baking sheets with silicone baking mats or parchment paper.

Bring the milk, water, butter, sugar (if you're using it), and salt to a rapid boil in a medium heavy-bottomed saucepan over high heat. Add the flour all at once, lower the heat to medium-low, and immediately start stirring energetically with a wooden spoon or heavy whisk. The dough will come together, and a light crust will form on the bottom of the pan. Keep stirring — with vigor — for another minute or two to dry the dough. The dough should be very smooth.

Turn the dough into the bowl of a stand mixer fitted with the paddle attachment or into a bowl you can use to mix with a hand mixer or a wooden spoon and elbow grease. Let the dough sit for a minute, then add the eggs one by one and beat, beat, beat until the dough is thick and shiny. Make sure that each egg is completely incorporated before you add the next, and don't be concerned if the dough falls apart — by the time the last egg goes in, the dough will come together again. Once the dough is made, it should be used immediately.

TO BAKE THE PUFFS: Using about 1 tablespoon dough for each puff, drop the dough from a spoon onto the lined baking sheets, leaving about 2 inches of puff space between the mounds of dough. *(The puffs can be frozen for up to 2 months.)*

Slide the baking sheets into the oven and immediately turn the oven temperature down to 375 degrees F. Bake for 12 minutes, then rotate the pans from front to back and top to bottom. Continue baking until the puffs are golden, firm, and, of course, puffed, another 12 to 15 minutes or so. Allow the puffs to cool on the baking sheet.

TO FILL THE PUFFS: Using a serrated knife and a gentle sawing motion, you can simply cut off the top quarter or third of each puff, fill the puffs, and top them with the little caps. Or, if you're using a very creamy filling (like pastry cream or the mixture for the goat cheese puffs), you can fill a piping bag fitted with a small plain tip with the filling, then use the tip to poke a hole in the side of each puff and squeeze in the filling.

crème anglaise

MAKES ABOUT
2½ CUPS

STORING
Covered and kept away
from foods with strong
odors, crème anglaise can
be refrigerated for up to
3 days.

CRÈME ANGLAISE, SOMETIMES CALLED POURING CUSTARD, is both a custard sauce (it's the "sea" in Floating Islands, page 427) and the base for French-style ice cream. While you can test the readiness of crème anglaise with your finger, you can measure it more accurately with an instant-read thermometer.

1 cup whole milk

1 cup heavy cream

6 large egg yolks

½ cup sugar

2 teaspoons pure vanilla extract

Fill a large bowl with ice cubes and cold water and have ready a strainer and a heatproof bowl that can hold the finished cream.

Bring the milk and cream to a boil in a medium heavy-bottomed saucepan.

Meanwhile, in a medium bowl, whisk the yolks and sugar together until very well blended and just slightly thickened. Whisking all the while, drizzle in about one quarter of the hot liquid. Once the eggs are acclimatized to the heat, you can whisk in the remaining liquid a little more quickly. Pour the custard into the pan and cook over medium heat, stirring without stop with a wooden spoon or silicone spatula, until the custard thickens slightly and coats the back of the spoon; if you run your finger down the bowl of the spoon, the custard should not run into the track. The custard should reach at least 170 degrees F, but no more than 180 degrees F, on an instant-read thermometer. Immediately remove the pan from the heat and strain the custard into the bowl. Stir in the vanilla extract.

Chill the crème anglaise quickly by putting the bowl into the bowl filled with ice and cold water and stirring the custard occasionally until it is thoroughly chilled, about 20 minutes. Cover tightly and refrigerate. If possible, chill it for 24 hours before using it — the extra chill time will intensify the flavor and allow the cream to thicken a bit more.

vanilla pastry cream

THINK OF PASTRY CREAM AS PUDDING, and you'll have an idea of its thick and velvety texture. The fact that pastry cream is so very thick often surprises people, but its thickness is classic, and it's what makes it perfect for its job: to be a filling for tarts, éclairs, cream puffs, or cakes.

MAKES ABOUT
2 CUPS

STORING
The pastry cream can be kept tightly covered in the refrigerator for up to 3 days.

2 cups whole milk	1½ teaspoons pure vanilla extract
6 large egg yolks	3½ tablespoons unsalted butter,
½ cup sugar	cut into bits, at room
⅓ cup cornstarch, sifted	temperature

Bring the milk to a boil in a small saucepan or in a microwave oven.

Meanwhile, in a medium heavy-bottomed saucepan, whisk the yolks together with the sugar and cornstarch until thick and well blended. Whisking without stop, drizzle in about ¼ cup of the hot milk — this will temper, or warm, the yolks — then, still whisking, add the remainder of the milk in a steady stream. Put the pan over medium heat and, whisking vigorously, constantly, and thoroughly (make sure to get into the edges of the pan), bring the mixture to a boil. Keep at a boil — still whisking — for 1 to 2 minutes, then pull the pan from the heat.

Whisk in the vanilla extract. Let stand for 5 minutes, then whisk in the bits of butter, stirring until the butter is fully incorporated and the pastry cream is smooth and silky. Scrape the cream into a bowl. You can press a piece of plastic wrap against the surface of the custard to create an airtight seal and refrigerate the pastry cream until cold or, if you want to cool the custard quickly — as I always do — put the bowl with the pastry cream into a larger bowl filled with ice cubes and cold water and stir the pastry cream occasionally until it is thoroughly chilled, about 20 minutes.

BONNE IDÉES
Because the recipe is so basic, it lends itself to variation.

Rum-Scented Pastry Cream. When you add the vanilla extract, add 1 to 2 tablespoons dark rum, to taste.

Liqueur-Scented Pastry Cream. You can flavor the pastry cream with various liqueurs, such as amaretto, kirsch, or Grand Marnier. Reduce the vanilla extract to 1 teaspoon, and after you've added it, add 2 teaspoons liqueur. If you want more flavor (and you might), add more liqueur, 1 teaspoon at a time.

Coffee or Espresso Pastry Cream. Make a coffee or espresso extract by dissolving 2 tablespoons instant coffee or espresso in 2 tablespoons boiling water. Add 1 tablespoon of the extract to the pastry cream after you've added the vanilla extract, then, if you want more flavor, add additional extract, 1 teaspoon at a time.

chocolate pastry cream

MAKES ABOUT
2½ CUPS

STORING
The pastry cream can be
kept tightly covered in the
refrigerator for up to 3 days.

L IKE ITS SISTER, VANILLA PASTRY CREAM (page 505), this chocolate cream
can fill tarts, puffs, éclairs, or cakes.

2 cups whole milk	Pinch of salt
4 large egg yolks	7 ounces bittersweet chocolate, melted
6 tablespoons sugar	
3 tablespoons cornstarch, sifted	2½ tablespoons unsalted butter, cut into bits, at room temperature

Bring the milk to a boil in a small saucepan or in a microwave oven.

Meanwhile, in a medium heavy-bottomed saucepan, whisk the yolks together with the sugar, cornstarch, and salt until thick and well blended. Whisking without stop, drizzle in about ¼ cup of the hot milk — this will temper, or warm, the yolks — then, still whisking, add the remainder of the milk in a steady stream. Put the pan over medium heat and, whisking vigorously, constantly, and thoroughly (make sure to get into the edges of the pan), bring the mixture to a boil. Keep at a boil — still whisking — for 1 to 2 minutes, then pull the pan from the heat.

Whisk in the melted chocolate. Let stand for 5 minutes, then whisk in the bits of butter, stirring until the butter is fully incorporated and the custard is smooth and silky. Scrape the cream into a bowl. You can press a piece of plastic wrap against the surface of the custard to create an airtight seal and refrigerate the custard until chilled or, if you want to cool the custard quickly — as I always do — put the bowl with the custard into a larger bowl filled with ice cubes and cold water and stir the custard occasionally until it is thoroughly chilled, about 20 minutes.

lemon curd

THIS RECIPE WAS GIVEN TO ME during a cooking class I took with Jacques Pourcel, who, with his brother Laurent, has a Michelin-starred restaurant in Provence and nineteen other restaurants around the world. At least I thought this was the recipe the chef handed out, but after I made it and was delighted with the results, I realized I'd made a mistake. I was supposed to use just yolks, and instead I made the curd with whole eggs. Made my way, the curd is just a tiny bit lighter and just a little less fussy to cook, since whites can take more heat than yolks.

MAKES A
GENEROUS
2 CUPS

1¼ cups sugar
4 large eggs
1 tablespoon light corn syrup

About ¾ cup fresh lemon juice (from 4–5 lemons)
8 tablespoons (1 stick) unsalted butter, cut into chunks

In a medium heavy-bottomed saucepan, whisk the sugar and eggs together until blended. Whisk in the corn syrup and lemon juice and then drop in the chunks of butter.

Put the saucepan over medium heat and start whisking, taking care to work the whisk into the edges of the pan. If your whisk is too big to clean the edges of the pan, switch to a wooden spoon or a silicone spatula. Keep heating and whisking the mixture without stop. After about 6 to 8 minutes, you'll notice the curd starting to thicken — it won't be very thick, but the change is easily perceptible. When the curd is thickened and, most important, you see a bubble or two burble to the surface and then pop immediately, remove the pan from the heat.

Scrape the curd into a heatproof bowl or a canning jar or two. Press a piece of plastic wrap against the surface to create an airtight seal, and let the curd cool to room temperature. Chill before serving.

SERVING
The curd can be used straight from the jar as a spread or a tart filling. For another great way to use the curd, try it with Sablé Breton Galette with Berries (page 464).

STORING
Packed into an airtight container — I always keep a piece of plastic wrap pressed against the surface — the curd can be refrigerated for at least 3 weeks.

bittersweet chocolate sauce

MAKES ABOUT
1½ CUPS

STORING
Packed into an airtight container, the sauce can be kept in the refrigerator for up to 3 weeks. If you want to use the sauce warm, heat it gently in a microwave oven or in a saucepan over very low heat.

WHEN THIS SAUCE IS WARM, it's ideal for pouring over cakes or around tarts or profiteroles; when it's chilled, it can be spooned over cookies or used to fill them.

½ cup heavy cream
½ cup whole milk
½ cup water

6 tablespoons sugar
¼ pound bittersweet chocolate, finely chopped

Put all of the ingredients in a heavy-bottomed saucepan, put the saucepan over medium-low heat, and bring to a boil, stirring occasionally to blend. Lower the heat and let the sauce simmer for 10 to 15 minutes — don't leave the kitchen, this is a bubble-up brew — or until the sauce is thick enough to coat a metal or wooden spoon. If you run your finger down the bowl of the spoon, the sauce should not run into the track.

If you want to use the sauce in its pourable state, let it cool for about 10 minutes, then pour away. If you want to save it for later, cool it, pack it into an airtight container, and chill it until needed.

hot fudge sauce

Not typically french, but when you've got great ice cream (pages 479, 511, and 513), you want great sauce.

(pages 479, 511, and 513)

4 tablespoons (½ stick) unsalted butter, cut into 8 pieces

6 ounces bittersweet or semisweet chocolate, finely chopped

¾ cup heavy cream

3 tablespoons light corn syrup

2 tablespoons sugar

¼ teaspoon salt

MAKES ABOUT
1¼ CUPS

STORING
Packed into a tightly covered jar, the sauce will keep in the refrigerator for up to 3 weeks. Before serving, warm it gently in a microwave oven or over low heat until it is pourable.

Fit a heatproof bowl over a saucepan of simmering water, making sure the bottom of the bowl is above, not touching, the water. Put the butter in the bowl, top with the chocolate, and heat, stirring once or twice, until the ingredients are melted. Keep the heat very low — you don't want the mixture to get so hot that the butter and chocolate separate. Transfer the bowl to the counter when the mixture is smooth.

In a small heavy-bottomed saucepan, stir together the cream, corn syrup, sugar, and salt and bring to a boil. Boil for 1 minute, then pull the pan from the heat.

Pour about one quarter of the hot cream over the chocolate and, working with a silicone spatula or wooden spoon and starting in the center of the bowl, stir the mixtures together in ever-widening concentric circles. When smooth, add the remainder of the cream in 2 additions, stirring gently until the sauce is shiny and smooth.

Allow the sauce to cool for about 10 minutes before using.

warm caramel sauce

MAKES ABOUT
1 CUP

SERVING
The sauce should be served warm. Use it over cakes or ice cream, as a dipping sauce for cookies, or as a side sauce with waffles.

STORING
Packed into a jar with a piece of plastic wrap pressed against its surface, the sauce will keep in the refrigerator for at least a month. Before serving, reheat it gently either in a microwave oven on low power or over the lowest heat possible.

WITH A JAR OF THIS IN YOUR REFRIGERATOR, you can turn a scoop of ice cream or a slice of the plainest cake into a dinner-party dessert. Because the sauce has a little bit of corn syrup, it is both easy to make and satin-smooth.

1 cup sugar

3 tablespoons water

1 tablespoon light corn syrup

¾ cup heavy cream, warm or at room temperature

1 tablespoon unsalted butter, at room temperature

Pinch of salt

Put the sugar, water, and corn syrup in a medium heavy-bottomed saucepan and cook over medium-high heat, swirling the pan occasionally but not stirring, until the caramel turns a medium amber. If any sugar spatters onto the sides of the pan, wipe it down with a pastry brush dipped in cold water. And if you're not sure of the color — it can be difficult to judge color in a pan — put a drop on a white plate.

Lower the heat and, standing away from the pan to avoid sputters and spats, add the cream, butter, and salt. The mixture will bubble furiously, but the bubbles will die down, and when they do, use a wooden spoon or silicone spatula to stir the sauce until it is smooth. Pour into a bowl or heatproof jar — a canning jar is perfect. Cool until just warm before serving.

vanilla ice cream

THINK OF THIS AS PRIMORDIAL ICE CREAM, the one from which all other ice creams spring. It is a classic recipe built on a base of crème anglaise, and it is this cooked-custard base that defines it as French ice cream. Ice cream that's made without a cooked base is called Philadelphia. Of the two, the richer and creamier one is French — it's the work of those egg yolks.

Don't be afraid of putting a little heat under the custard as you cook it — medium heat is fine — but, most important, don't stop stirring! Also, don't stop cooking until the custard is thick enough for you to run your finger down the bowl of a spoon and have the track stay. While I often use the finger test, I like to take the custard's temperature with an instant-read thermometer.

About the vanilla: You can use either vanilla beans or extract, but no matter what you use, it must be of the best quality. If you use beans, they should be plump, pliable, and very fragrant; split and scrape them and allow them to infuse the hot milk and cream with their flavor — give yourself an extra 30 minutes for this. If you use extract, make sure it's pure and aromatic.

BE PREPARED: You'll need to freeze the ice cream for at least 2 hours before serving.

MAKES ABOUT

1 QUART

SERVING
If the ice cream is very firm, allow it to sit on the counter for a few minutes before scooping.

STORING
Packed tightly in a covered container, the ice cream will keep in the freezer for about 2 weeks.

2 cups whole milk	6 large egg yolks
2 cups heavy cream	¾ cup sugar
2 plump, moist vanilla beans, split and scraped (see box, page 396), or 1 tablespoon pure vanilla extract	

Have a heatproof bowl with a strainer set over it at the ready for the cooked custard.

Bring the milk and cream to a boil in a large heavy-bottomed saucepan. If you're using vanilla beans, toss the seeds and pods into the pan, remove the pan from the heat, cover, and allow the mixture to stand for at least 30 minutes, so that the liquid takes on the vanilla's flavor. At the end of this infusion period, bring the milk and cream back to a boil and remove the vanilla pods (you can use them to make vanilla sugar; see page 396). If you're using extract, you'll add it later.

In a medium bowl, whisk the yolks and sugar together until very well blended and just slightly thickened. Whisking without stop, drizzle in about one third of the hot liquid — adding the hot liquid slowly will temper the eggs and keep them from cooking. Once the eggs are acclimatized to the heat, you can whisk in the remaining liquid a little more quickly. Pour the custard back into the pan and cook over medium heat, stirring constantly with a wooden spoon or silicone spatula and making sure to get into the edges of the pan, until the custard thickens slightly and coats the back of the spoon; if you run your finger down the bowl of the spoon, the custard should not run into the track. The custard should reach at least 170 degrees F, but no more than 180 degrees F, on an instant-read thermometer. Immediately remove the pan from the heat and pour the custard through the strainer into the bowl. Stir in the vanilla extract, if you're using it.

The custard needs to chill before you churn it, and while you can put it directly into the fridge, the quickest and easiest way to bring down the temperature is to set the bowl into a larger bowl filled with ice cubes and cold water; stir the custard from time to time as it cools. It's ready to use when it's cold.

Scrape the chilled custard into the bowl of an ice cream maker and churn according to the manufacturer's instructions. Pack the ice cream into an airtight container and freeze it for at least 2 hours, or until it is firm enough to scoop.

dark chocolate ice cream

I'D SUGGEST THAT YOU CHOOSE a really assertive chocolate for this ice cream, since you're mixing it with cream and eggs, which will tone down the flavor, and everything is milder when chilled. As almost all French ice creams are, this one is custard-based, a guarantee that it will be smooth and rich. And since it starts with a ganache, it will be even smoother.

BE PREPARED: You'll need to freeze the ice cream for at least 2 hours before serving.

MAKES ABOUT
1 QUART

SERVING
If the ice cream is very firm — and ice cream made with good chocolate can be pretty firm — allow it to sit on the counter for a few minutes before scooping.

STORING
Packed tightly in a covered container, the ice cream will keep in the freezer for about 2 weeks.

6 ounces bittersweet or semisweet chocolate, finely chopped	1 cup whole milk
	4 large egg yolks
	⅓ cup sugar
1½ cups heavy cream	Pinch of salt

Put the chocolate in a large heatproof bowl. Bring ¾ cup of the cream to a boil. Pour the cream over the chocolate and let it sit for a minute, then, using a silicone spatula or wooden spoon and starting in the center of the mixture, slowly stir the cream into the chocolate.

Have a heatproof bowl with a strainer set over it at the ready for the cooked custard.

Bring the milk and the remaining ¾ cup cream to a boil in a medium heavy-bottomed saucepan.

Meanwhile, in a bowl, whisk the yolks and sugar together until very well blended and just slightly thickened. Whisking without stop, drizzle in about one third of the hot liquid — adding the hot liquid slowly will temper the eggs and keep them from cooking. Once the eggs are acclimatized to the heat, you can whisk in the remaining liquid a little more quickly. Add the salt and pour the custard back into the pan.

Cook over medium heat, stirring constantly with a wooden spoon or silicone spatula and making sure to get into the edges of the pan, until the custard thickens slightly and coats the back of the spoon; if you run your finger down the bowl of the spoon, the custard should not run into the track. The custard should reach at least 170 degrees F, but no more than 180 degrees F, on an instant-read thermometer. Immediately remove the pan from the heat and pour the custard through the strainer into the bowl. Slowly and gently stir the custard into the ganache.

The custard needs to chill before you churn it, and while you can put it directly into the fridge, the quickest and easiest way to bring down the temperature is to set the bowl into a larger bowl filled with ice cubes and cold water; stir the custard from time to time as it cools. It's ready to use when it's cold.

Scrape the chilled custard into the bowl of an ice cream maker and churn according to the manufacturer's instructions. Pack the ice cream into an airtight container and freeze for at least 2 hours, or until it is firm enough to scoop.

sources

GENERAL COOKWARE AND BAKEWARE

Everything from silicone spatulas, baking mats, mandolines, and graters to Dutch ovens, skillets, and tagines.

> www.amazon.com
> www.broadwaypanhandler.com
> www.surlatable.com
> www.williams-sonoma.com

SPECIALIZED BAKEWARE

You can find brioche, financier, madeleine, and coeur à la crème molds at these sites, as well as instant-read thermometers, piping bags and tips, and other small tools and gadgets.

> www.amazon.com
> www.surlatable.com

SPICES: EVERYDAY AND UNUSUAL, AND PEPPERCORNS TOO

> www.amazon.com (piment d'Espelette)
> www.kalustyans.com
> www.penzeys.com
> www.thespicehouse.com

FLEUR DE SEL AND OTHER SPECIALTY SALTS

> www.amazon.com
> www.atthemeadow.com (salts from around the world)
> www.lepicerie.com

NUT OILS (WALNUT, HAZELNUT, AND PISTACHIO)

> www.amazon.com (Leblanc oils from France)

PRESERVED LEMONS (*CITRONS CONFITS*)

> www.amazon.com
> www.kalustyans.com

FOIE GRAS, DUCK BREASTS, AND CHORIZO

> www.dartagnan.com

TRUFFLES AND TRUFFLE OIL

> shop.plantin.com

CHOCOLATE

These sites carry the full range of high-quality chocolate — white, semisweet, bittersweet, and unsweetened — and cocoa powder too.

> www.amazon.com
> www.kingarthurflour.com
> www.worldwidechocolate.com

ALL-BUTTER PUFF PASTRY (DUFOUR)

> www.wholefoodsmarket.com

EXTRACTS AND SYRUPS

> www.amazon.com (Monin rose syrup)
> www.kalustyans.com (rose syrup)
> www.starkaywhite.com (rose essence)
> www.kingarthurflour.com
> www.sonomasyrup.com (excellent vanilla and almond extracts)

ALMOND, HAZELNUT, AND CHICKPEA FLOURS

> www.amazon.com
> www.bobsredmill.com
> www.kalustyans.com
> www.kingarthurflour.com
> www.wholefoodsmarket.com

index